Lecture Notes in Computer Science

Commenced Publication in 1973
Founding and Former Series Editors:
Gerhard Goos, Juris Hartmanis, and Jan van Leeuwen

Mirosław Kutyłowski
Witold Charatonik   Maciej Gębala (Eds.)

Fundamentals
of Computation Theory

17th International Symposium, FCT 2009
Wrocław, Poland, September 2-4, 2009
Proceedings

 Springer

Volume Editors

Mirosław Kutyłowski
Wrocław University of Technology
Institute of Mathematics and Computer Science
ul. Wybrzeże Wyspiańskiego 27, 50-370 Wrocław, Poland
E-mail: Miroslaw.Kutylowski@pwr.wroc.pl

Witold Charatonik
University of Wrocław, Institute of Computer Science
ul. Joliot-Curie 15, 50-383 Wrocław, Poland
E-mail: Witold.Charatonik@ii.uni.wroc.pl

Maciej Gębala
Wrocław University of Technology
Institute of Mathematics and Computer Science
ul. Wybrzeże Wyspiańskiego 27, 50-370 Wrocław, Poland
E-mail: Maciej.Gebala@pwr.wroc.pl

Library of Congress Control Number: Applied for

CR Subject Classification (1998): F.1, F.2, F.4, G.2

LNCS Sublibrary: SL 1 – Theoretical Computer Science and General Issues

ISSN   0302-9743
ISBN-10   3-642-03408-X Springer Berlin Heidelberg New York
ISBN-13   978-3-642-03408-4 Springer Berlin Heidelberg New York

springer.com

© Springer-Verlag Berlin Heidelberg 2009
Printed in Germany

Typesetting: Camera-ready by author, data conversion by Scientific Publishing Services, Chennai, India
Printed on acid-free paper   SPIN: 12726417   06/3180   5 4 3 2 1 0

Preface

The Symposium on Fundamentals of Computation Theory was established in 1977 for researchers interested in all aspects of theoretical computer science, in particular in algorithms, complexity, and formal and logical methods. It is a biennial conference, which has previously been held in Poznań (1977), Wendisch-Rietz (1979), Szeged (1981), Borgholm (1983), Cottbus (1985), Kazan (1987), Szeged (1989), Gosen-Berlin (1991), Szeged (1993), Dresden (1995), Kraków (1997), Iaşi (1999), Riga (2001), Malmö (2003), Lübeck (2005) and Budapest (2007).

The 17th International Symposium on Fundamentals of Computation Theory (FCT 2009) was held in Wrocław, September 2–4, 2009, and was organized jointly by the Institute of Mathematics and Computer Science of Wrocław University of Technology and the Institute of Computer Science, University of Wrocław. The conference was held at Wrocław University of Technology.

The suggested topics of FCT 2009 included, but were not limited to:

Algorithms: algorithm design and optimization; combinatorics and analysis of algorithms; computational complexity; approximation, randomized, and heuristic methods; parallel and distributed computing; circuits and Boolean functions; online algorithms; machine learning and artificial intelligence; computational geometry; computational algebra

Formal methods: automata and formal languages; computability and nonstandard computing models; algebraic and categorical methods; logics and model checking; principles of programming languages; program analysis and transformation; specification, refinement and verification; type systems; concurrency theory; database theory, semi-structured data and finite model theory; models of reactive, hybrid and stochastic systems

Emerging fields: security and cryptography; ad hoc and mobile systems; quantum computation; computational biology; high-performance computing; algorithmic game theory

The Program Committee invited lectures from Martin Dietzfelbinger (Ilmenau), Thomas A. Henzinger (Lausanne), and Moti Yung (New York) and, from the 67 submissions, selected 29 papers for presentation at the conference and inclusion in the proceedings. This volume contains the texts or the abstracts of the invited lectures and the texts of the accepted papers.

We would like to thank the members of the Program Committee for the evaluation of the submissions and their subreferees for their excellent cooperation in this work. We are grateful to the contributors to the conference, in particular to the invited speakers for their willingness to present interesting new developments.

September 2009

Mirosław Kutyłowski
Witold Charatonik
Maciej Gębala

In Memoriam Prof. Dr. math. Ingo Wegener (1950–2008)

Ingo Wegener passed away on November 26, 2008, at the age of 57. This is a great loss for theoretical computer science in Europe, far beyond the field of complexity theory and efficient algorithms, which was his scientific home.

Ingo Wegener studied mathematics in Bielefeld until 1976, when he received his "Diplom." He earned his PhD in 1978, and obtained his "Habilitation" in 1981. For a while he was an associate professor in Frankfurt, until he was appointed professor at the University of Dortmund in 1987, for the field of "Efficient Algorithms and Complexity." This position he held until his death.

In the course of his career of more than 30 years, Ingo Wegener made substantial contributions to several, rather different, research fields. He started with contributions to search problems, documented in his first book. The second stage can be characterized by "The Complexity of Boolean Functions" (the title of his important monograph of 1987). Ingo Wegener made important contributions to the area of binary decision diagrams, a central method for representing and manipulating Boolean functions, again leading up to a monograph of the subject that made the state of the art in the field easily accessible. Starting in the late 1990s, he initiated the study of metaheuristics like evolutionary algorithms, genetic algorithms, and simulated annealing with the methods of complexity theory and algorithm analysis, leading to a deeper understanding of the behavior of such strategies.

Apart from his own scientific contributions Ingo Wegener also was a gifted and devoted teacher, and an excellent science organizer.

The commemorative talk will pay tribute to Ingo Wegener as a great researcher, a devoted academic teacher, and a dear colleague, who is missed by many.

Martin Dietzfelbinger

Conference Organization

Conference and Program Chairs

Mirosław Kutyłowski (Wrocław, Poland) - Chair
Witold Charatonik (Wrocław, Poland) - Co-chair

Program Committee

Roberto Amadio (Paris, France)
Manuel Bodirsky (Paris, France)
Jacek Cichoń (Wrocław, Poland)
Anuj Dawar (Cambridge, UK)
Giorgio Delzanno (Genova, Italy)
Cunsheng Ding (Hong Kong, China)
Thomas Erlebach (Leicester, UK)
Joachim von zur Gathen (Bonn, Germany)
Andrew D. Gordon (Cambridge, UK)
Thomas Jansen (Dortmund, Germany)
Stasys Jukna (Frankfurt, Germany)
Maciej Koutny (Newcastle, UK)
Antonin Kucera (Prague, Czech Republic)
Stefano Leonardi (Rome, Italy)
Maciej Liśkiewicz (Lubeck, Germany)
Tomasz Łuczak (Poznań, Poland)
Alexander Okhotin (Turku, Finland)
Andreas Podelski (Freiburg, Germany)
Sergio Rajsbaum (Mexico, Mexico)
Jose Rolim (Geneva, Switzerland)
Piotr Sankowski (Warszawa, Poland)
Vladimiro Sassone (Southampton, UK)
Helmut Seidl (Munich, Germany)
Maria José Serna Iglesias (Barcelona, Spain)
Paul Spirakis (Patras, Greece)
Jean-Marc Talbot (Provence, France)
Jerzy Tiuryn (Warszawa, Poland)
Stephan Waack (Gottingen, Germany)
Igor Walukiewicz (Bordeaux, France)
Thomas Zeugmann (Hokkaido, Japan)

Organizing Committee

Maciej Gębala (Chair)
Małgorzata Januszkiewicz

Steering Committee

Bogdan S. Chlebus (Warsaw, Poland and Denver, USA)
Zoltán Ésik (Szeged, Hungary)
Marek Karpiński (Bonn, Germany), Chair
Andrzej Lingas (Lund, Sweden)
Miklos Santha (Paris, France)
Eli Upfal (Providence, RI, USA)
Ingo Wegener (Dortmund, Germany)

Additional Reviewers

Laila El Aimani
Walid Belkhir
Dietmar Berwanger
Przemysław Biecek
Laurent Bienvenu
Manuel Bodirsky
Tomáš Brázdil
Vaclav Brozek
Didier Caucal
Jérémie Chalopin
Hubie Chen
Amin Coja-Oghlan
Peter Damaschke
Carsten Damm
Mike Domaratzki
Laszlo Egri
Michael Elberfeld
David Eppstein
Germain Faure
Eric Fusy
Tommy Färnqvist
Anna Gambin
Leszek Gasieniec

Hermann Gruber
Tobias Gärtner
Martin Haubrock
Emmanuel Haucourt
Andreas Jakoby
Mamadou Kante
Jarkko Kari
Stefan Kiefer
Marcin Kik
Darek Kowalski
Dexter Kozen
Michal Kunc
Martin Kutrib
Markku Laine
Peter Lammich
Pierre Leone
Jerome Leroux
Daniel Loebenberger
Gert Lube
Alexander Malkis
Bodo Manthey
Viviana Mascardi
Robert Mercas

Sotiris Nikoletseas
Michael Nuesken
Timo von Oertzen
Katarzyna Paluch
Sylvain Perifel
Giovanni Pighizzini
Michał Przykucki
Vojtěch Řehák
Gaétan Richard
Yves Roos
Nicole Schweikardt
Uwe Schöning
Geraud Senizergues
Frédéric Servais
Johannes Textor
Tigran Tonoyan
Helene Touzet
Jerzy Tyszkiewicz
Tomasz Waleń
Filip Zagórski
Marcin Zawada
Konstantin Ziegler

Table of Contents

Invited Lectures

Contributions

How to Guard the Guards Themselves

Moti Yung

Google Inc. and Department of Computer Science, Columbia University
moti@cs.columbia.edu

Abstract. The first 20 years of modern cryptography dealt with various cryptosystems, their modeling and their security, while assuming the availability of secure keys. Theses keys were the guards of security and based on their unavailability to the adversary, security was proved. In the last decade or so, however, as cryptography has been employed in practice, the realization that keys (the guards of security) needs to be guarded as well was realized and cryptosystems and algorithms have to be designed to take this into consideration. I will review some major directions in this research area.

Keywords: Public Key cryptography, Cryptographic Keys, Physical Security, Key Evolving Cryptosystems, Threshold cryptosystems, Proactive Cryptosystems, Attacks, Leakage, Countermeasures.

Protecting Keys: Why and How?

As cryptography has been embedded in software or in devices, it has been realized that the keys of cryptosystems cannot always be assumed to be secure. In fact, the state of security of systems and software is much that attacks on the computing environments is more likely than cryptanalysis of the mathematics behind the cryptosystem.

In addition, models such as kleptography and side channel attacks have realized that there are new ways to view attacks on cryptosystems: either active attack by the manufacturer, or attacks by observing physical signals coming from key dependent computations.

These issues has given rise to a revision in cryptosystem design. Designs that attempt to provide the functionality of the system but, in addition, take care of better protecting the keys have been considered.

There are various ways to protect keys. Threshold system distribute the cryptosystem (i.e., the key) among various processor and requires all or a quorum of the processors to be available at the time of performing the cryptographic operation. The adversary in this case needs to break into a large number (threshold) of processors in order to break the system and learn the keys; learning less than the threshold does not break the system. Proactive systems, in turn, add the time dimension to the "space dimension" protection of threshold cryptosystem. An attacker has to break into a large number of processors within a given time interval, after which the system refreshes the distributed key representation and the old key fragments are not anymore of help in recovering the key (unless

M. Kutyłowski, M. Gębala, and W. Charatonik (Eds.): FCT 2009, LNCS 5699, pp. 1–2, 2009.

enough of them (i.e., above the threshold number) have been captured already within a single time interval between refreshing).

The above systems requires redundancy, i.e. additional processors. What if we want a single device cryptosystem and we may assume that the adversary gets to learn the key on the device. The first answer is that in this case there is nothing to do. But, it is not necessarily true. System can have a public key that lasts a long time, but its secret key can evolve over time. An adversary getting a key at one period of time cannot break the system in some other periods. For example in a "forward secure" signature scheme when the adversary gets the secret signing key at one period, it cannot compute prior time keys (since the key is evolving by applying a one-way transformation at the end of each period). Thus, the adversary may have keys for the current period and for the future ones (and can forge signatures coming from these periods), but cannot forge signatures of past periods. Additional notions of key evolving schemes exists ("key insulated" systems and "intrusion-resilient" systems) that protect the device even better (i.e., past and future periods are protected) by allowing it to interact (only when the key evolves) with some other (base) device. This base device is only useful for updates and cannot have any other function.

Another direction in protecting systems against attacks on keys, is to assume that part of the key is learn-able by the adversary and still to protect the system. Such systems can be robust against leakage of some properties of the keys (like as in side-channel physical leaking). The ideas of exposure-resilient (i.e., partial memory leakage) and leakage-resilient (i.e., aganist computation leakage) and formal models to capture leakage in computing architectures, are some of the ideas that have been investigated and are currently considered against memory and computation leakages of computing systems.

Conclusion:
The above mechanisms and techniques developed in designing them, represent various basic an d promising directions, and, in my assessment, demonstrate one important issue which is described by the following situation: *There is a system problem and keys or part of them are leaked or may be revealed; while there are many methods in systems security to deal with it, one has also to look at the design itself (i.e. the cryptographic method) and attempt to revise it, taking into account the new exposure (new adversary).*

More generally: Security is about an adversary which is outside the system and thus is a fundamental problem (it is not going to be solved by adding resources, for example– the adversary is still there outside the control of the system). Thus, it is imperative that any adversary argument against a designed cryptosystem has to also be considered (as a feedback loop) by the designer of the mechanism itself, and this feedback constitutes an "adversary-designer game." This game is fundamental in security research (both defining new adversaries and new solutions), and should always be kept in mind. Thus, an adversary that attacks the core (guards) of a system gives rise to the old question: who will guard the guards themselves? Who, what and how to do it, is indeed very much a relevant question in this context of basic security research.

Alternating Weighted Automata*

Krishnendu Chatterjee[1], Laurent Doyen[2,**], and Thomas A. Henzinger[3]

[1] Institute of Science and Technology, Austria
[2] Université Libre de Bruxelles (ULB), Belgium
[3] École Polytechnique Fédérale de Lausanne (EPFL), Switzerland

Abstract. Weighted automata are finite automata with numerical weights on transitions. Nondeterministic weighted automata define quantitative languages L that assign to each word w a real number $L(w)$ computed as the maximal value of all runs over w, and the value of a run r is a function of the sequence of weights that appear along r. There are several natural functions to consider such as Sup, LimSup, LimInf, limit average, and discounted sum of transition weights.

We introduce alternating weighted automata in which the transitions of the runs are chosen by two players in a turn-based fashion. Each word is assigned the maximal value of a run that the first player can enforce regardless of the choices made by the second player. We survey the results about closure properties, expressiveness, and decision problems for nondeterministic weighted automata, and we extend these results to alternating weighted automata.

For quantitative languages L_1 and L_2, we consider the pointwise operations $max(L_1, L_2)$, $min(L_1, L_2)$, $1 - L_1$, and the sum $L_1 + L_2$. We establish the closure properties of all classes of alternating weighted automata with respect to these four operations.

We next compare the expressive power of the various classes of alternating and nondeterministic weighted automata over infinite words. In particular, for limit average and discounted sum, we show that alternation brings more expressive power than nondeterminism.

Finally, we present decidability results and open questions for the quantitative extension of the classical decision problems in automata theory: emptiness, universality, language inclusion, and language equivalence.

1 Introduction

A classical *language* is a set of infinite words over a finite alphabet Σ, or equivalently a function $L : \Sigma^\omega \to \{0, 1\}$. Either a word w belongs to the language

---

* This research was supported in part by the Swiss National Science Foundation under the Indo-Swiss Joint Research Programme, by the European Network of Excellence on Embedded Systems Design (ArtistDesign), by the European Combest, Quasimodo, and Gasics projects, by the PAI program Moves funded by the Belgian Federal Government, and by the CFV (Federated Center in Verification) funded by the F.R.S.-FNRS.
** Postdoctoral researcher of the F.R.S.-FNRS.

M. Kutyłowski, M. Gębala, and W. Charatonik (Eds.): FCT 2009, LNCS 5699, pp. 3–13, 2009.
© Springer-Verlag Berlin Heidelberg 2009

and then $L(w) = 1$, or w does not belong to the language and then $L(w) = 0$. Languages are natural models of computation for reactive programs: each execution of a program is an infinite sequence of events (or a word), and the set of all executions (or the language) defines the possible behaviors of the program. Finite automata can be used to define languages, and questions about the correctness of programs can be reduced to decision problems on automata, such as emptiness and language inclusion [14,7].

A *quantitative language* is a function $L : \Sigma^\omega \to \mathbb{R}$, generalizing the classical languages (called *boolean languages* in this paper). A natural interpretation of the value $L(w)$ of a word w is the cost incurred by a program to produce the execution w, for example in terms of energy or memory consumption. Values can also be used to quantify the reliability or the quality of executions, rather than simply classifying them as good or bad. Hence, quantitative languages provide a more accurate model of program computation.

To define quantitative languages, we use *weighted automata*, i.e., finite automata with numerical weights on transitions. To compute the value of a word in a weighted automaton, we need to fix a *mode of branching* and a *value function*. In this paper, we consider four modes of branching (alternating, universal, nondeterministic, and deterministic) and five value functions (Sup, LimSup, LimInf, limit average, and discounted sum). In an *alternating* weighted automaton, the value of an input word is determined by two players playing in rounds, starting in the initial state of the automaton. If the current state is q and the next input letter is σ, the first player (called the maximizer) chooses one transition (q, σ, s) where s is a set of states in which the second player (called the minimizer) then chooses a state q'. The next round starts in q' and the game proceeds for infinitely many rounds, constructing an infinite weighted path whose value is computed as the value function of its weights. The value of the input word is the maximal value of such a path that the maximizer can enforce no matter what choices the minimizer makes. When the choices available to the maximizer are trivial (i.e., in every state q and for every input letter σ, there is exactly one transition (q, σ, s)), the weighted automaton is *universal*, and when the choices available to the minimizer are trivial (i.e., for every transition (q, σ, s), the set s is a singleton), the weighted automaton is *nondeterministic*. A *deterministic* weighted automaton is both universal and nondeterministic. Note that for weighted automata with weights in $\{0, 1\}$, these definitions coincide with the classical finite automata theory [2,10], and in particular the LimSup- and LimInf-automata can then be viewed as Büchi and coBüchi automata respectively.

We survey the results about closure properties, expressiveness, and decision problems for nondeterministic weighted automata [3,4], and we extend these results to alternating weighted automata. For closure properties, we consider a natural generalization of the classical operations of union, intersection, and complement of boolean languages. We define the *maximum*, *minimum*, and *sum* of two quantitative languages L_1 and L_2 as the quantitative language that assigns $\max(L_1(w), L_2(w))$, $\min(L_1(w), L_2(w))$, and $L_1(w) + L_2(w)$ to each word w. The numerical *complement* L^c of a quantitative language L is defined by

$L^c(w) = 1 - L(w)$ for all words w.[1] We give the closure properties of all classes of weighted automata with respect to these four quantitative operations, extending the results of [4]. For expressiveness, we compare the sets of quantitative languages definable by the various classes of weighted automata, and we give a complete picture of their relationships. For decision problems, we consider a quantitative generalization of the classical questions of emptiness, universality, language inclusion, and language equivalence. The quantitative *emptiness* and *universality* problems ask, given a weighted automaton A (defining quantitative language L_A) and a rational number ν, if $L_A(w) \geq \nu$ for some (resp., all) words w. The quantitative *language-inclusion* and *language-equivalence* problems ask, given two weighted automata A and B, if $L_A(w) \leq L_B(w)$ (resp., $L_A(w) = L_B(w)$) for all words w. For nondeterministic weighted automata, the quantitative emptiness problem is decidable in polynomial time for every value function, and the quantitative universality, language-inclusion, and language-equivalence problems are PSPACE-complete for all modes of branching of Sup-, LimSup-, and LimInf-automata [3]. We extend these results to alternating weighted automata. The main open question remains the decidability of the universality problem for limit-average and discounted-sum automata.

2 Definitions

While weighted automata have been studied extensively over finite words [12,9], we focus on weighted automata over infinite words.

Value functions. We consider the following value functions $\mathsf{Val} : \mathbb{Q}^\omega \to \mathbb{R}$ to define quantitative languages. Given an infinite sequence $v = v_0 v_1 \dots$ of rational numbers, define

- $\mathsf{Sup}(v) = \sup\{v_n \mid n \geq 0\}$;
- $\mathsf{LimSup}(v) = \limsup_{n \to \infty} v_n = \lim_{n \to \infty} \sup\{v_i \mid i \geq n\}$;
- $\mathsf{LimInf}(v) = \liminf_{n \to \infty} v_n = \lim_{n \to \infty} \inf\{v_i \mid i \geq n\}$;
- $\mathsf{LimAvg}(v) = \liminf_{n \to \infty} \dfrac{1}{n} \cdot \sum_{i=0}^{n-1} v_i$;
- for $0 < \lambda < 1$, $\mathsf{Disc}_\lambda(v) = \sum_{i=0}^{\infty} \lambda^i \cdot v_i$.

Alternating weighted automata. An *alternating weighted automaton* over a finite alphabet Σ is a tuple $A = \langle Q, q_I, \Sigma, \delta, \gamma \rangle$, where

- Q is a finite set of states, and $q_I \in Q$ is the initial state;
- $\delta \subseteq Q \times \Sigma \times (2^Q \setminus \{\varnothing\})$ is a finite set of labeled transitions;
- $\gamma : Q \times \Sigma \times Q \to \mathbb{Q}$ is a weight function.

---

[1] One can define $L^c(w) = k - L(w)$ for any constant k without changing the results of this paper.

We require that A is *total*, that is for all $q \in Q$ and $\sigma \in \Sigma$, there exists $(q, \sigma, s) \in \delta$ for at least one nonempty set $s \subseteq Q$. An automaton A is *universal* if for all $q \in Q$ and $\sigma \in \Sigma$, there exists $(q, \sigma, s) \in \delta$ for exactly one $s \subseteq Q$; it is *nondeterministic* if for all $(q, \sigma, s) \in \delta$, the set s is a singleton; and it is *deterministic* if it is both universal and nondeterministic.

The set of transitions $(q, \sigma, s_i) \in \delta$ from a state q over σ can be described by a boolean formula over Q, namely $\varphi(q, \sigma) = \bigvee_{(q,\sigma,s_i)\in\delta} \bigwedge_{q_j \in s_i} q_j$. For example, the formula $\varphi(q, \sigma) = (q_1 \wedge q_2) \vee (q_3 \wedge q_4)$ corresponds to the transitions $(q, \sigma, \{q_1, q_2\})$ and $(q, \sigma, \{q_3, q_4\})$. In a game interpretation of alternation, two players (the maximizer and the minimizer) are constructing a path in the automaton A while reading the input word. If the current state is q and the next input symbol is σ, then the maximizer (also called the nondeterministic player) chooses a set of states s_i such that $(q, \sigma, s_i) \in \delta$ (i.e., such that the formula $\varphi(q, \sigma)$ is satisfied when true is assigned to every state $q \in s_i$), and the minimizer (also called the universal player) then chooses a state $q' \in s_i$. Thus in the formula $\varphi(q, \sigma)$, disjunctions correspond to nondeterministic choices, and conjunctions correspond to universal choices. The outcome of the game is an infinite weighted path in the automaton, and the value of the input word is the maximal value of such a path that the maximizer can enforce regardless of the choices of the minimizer. We obtain the *dual* of an alternating weighted automaton by exchanging disjunctions and conjunctions in the boolean formulas of the transition relations.

Formally, a *run* of A over an infinite word $w = \sigma_0 \sigma_1 \ldots$ is a weighted Q-labelled tree (T, λ, γ') where $T \subseteq \mathbb{N}^*$ is a nonempty prefix-closed set of nodes (i.e., $x \cdot c \in T$ implies $x \in T$ for all $x \in \mathbb{N}^*$ and $c \in \mathbb{N}$), $\lambda : T \to Q$ and $\gamma' : \{(x, x \cdot c) \mid x \cdot c \in T\} \to \mathbb{Q}$ are labelings of the tree such that: (i) $\lambda(\epsilon) = q_I$ (where ϵ is the empty sequence) and (ii) if $x \in T$ and $\lambda(x) = q$, then there exists a set $s = \{q_1, \ldots, q_k\} \subseteq Q$ such that $(q, \sigma_{|x|}, s) \in \delta$ and for all $1 \le c \le k$, we have $x \cdot c \in T$ and $\lambda(x \cdot c) = q_c$. Moreover, $\gamma'(x, x \cdot c) \doteq \gamma(q, \sigma_{|x|}, q_c)$.

A *path* in a run $\rho = (T, \lambda, \gamma')$ is a set $\pi \subseteq T$ such that $\epsilon \in \pi$ and for all $x \in \pi$, there exists a unique $c \in \mathbb{N}$ such that $x \cdot c \in \pi$. We denote by $\mathsf{Run}^A(w)$ the set of all runs of A over w, and by $\mathsf{Path}(\rho)$ the set of all paths in a run ρ. We define $\gamma_\rho(\pi) = v_0 v_1 \ldots$ such that for all $i \ge 0$, $v_i = \gamma'(x, x')$ where x, x' are the unique nodes of π with $|x'| = |x| + 1 = i + 1$.

Given a value function $\mathsf{Val} : \mathbb{Q}^\omega \to \mathbb{R}$, we say that the alternating Val-automaton A defines the quantitative language $L_A : \Sigma^\omega \to \mathbb{R}$ such that for all $w \in \Sigma^\omega$:

$$L_A(w) = \sup_{\rho \in \mathsf{Run}^A(w)} \quad \inf_{\pi \in \mathsf{Path}(\rho)} \mathsf{Val}(\gamma_\rho(\pi)).$$

The *alternating* $\{0,1\}$-*automata* are the special case of alternating weighted automata where all transition weights are either 0 or 1. In the case of Sup, LimSup, and LimInf, the $\{0,1\}$-automata define *boolean languages* $L : \Sigma^\omega \to \{0,1\}$ that are traditionally viewed as sets of words $\{w \in \Sigma^\omega \mid L(w) = 1\}$. Note that the LimSup- and LimInf- $\{0,1\}$-automata are the classical Büchi and coBüchi automata respectively. A word is in the boolean language of an alternating Büchi (resp. coBüchi) automaton if there exists a run over that word all of whose paths contain infinitely many 1-weighted edges (resp. finitely many 0-weighted edges).

Composition. Given two quantitative languages L and L' over Σ, and a rational number c, we denote by $\max(L, L')$ (resp. $\min(L, L')$, $L+L'$, $c+L$, and cL) the quantitative language that assigns $\max\{L(w), L'(w)\}$ (resp. $\min\{L(w), L'(w)\}$, $L(w)+L'(w)$, $c+L(w)$, and $c \cdot L(w)$) to each word $w \in \Sigma^\omega$. We say that $c+L$ is the *shift by c* of L and that cL is the *scale by c* of L. The language $1-L$ is called the *complement* of L. The max, min and complement operators for quantitative languages are natural generalizations of respectively the union, intersection and complement operators for boolean languages.

Reducibility. A class $\mathcal{C}$ of alternating weighted automata is *reducible* to a class $\mathcal{C}'$ of alternating weighted automata if for every $A \in \mathcal{C}$ there exists $A' \in \mathcal{C}'$ such that $L_A = L_{A'}$, i.e. $L_A(w) = L_{A'}(w)$ for all words $w \in \Sigma^\omega$. In particular, a class of weighted automata *can be determinized* if it is reducible to its deterministic counterpart. Two classes of weighted automata have the same expressiveness if they are reducible to each other.

Decision problems. We present quantitative generalizations of the classical decision problems in automata theory. Given two quantitative languages L_1, L_2, we write $L_1 \sqsubseteq L_2$ if $L_1(w) \leq L_2(w)$ for all words $w \in \Sigma^\omega$.

Given a weighted automaton A and a rational number $\nu \in \mathbb{Q}$, the *quantitative emptiness problem* asks whether there exists a word $w \in \Sigma^\omega$ such that $L_A(w) \geq \nu$, and the *quantitative universality problem* asks whether $L_A(w) \geq \nu$ for all words $w \in \Sigma^\omega$. Given two weighted automata A and B, the *quantitative language-inclusion problem* asks whether $L_A \sqsubseteq L_B$, and the *quantitative language-equivalence problem* asks whether $L_A = L_B$. All results presented in this paper also hold for the decision problems defined above with inequalities replaced by strict inequalities.

Notation. We use acronyms to denote classes of weighted automata. The first letter can be A(lternating), N(ondeterministic), U(niversal), or D(eterministic). For $X \in \{A, N, U\}$ and $Y \in \{D, N, U\}$ (with $X \neq Y$), we use the notation ${}_Y^X$ to denote the classes of automata for which the X and Y versions have the same expressiveness. Note that if the expressiveness of alternating and deterministic automata coincide for some class (i.e., X=A and Y=D), then the expressiveness of the four modes of branching is the same. The second part of the acronyms is one of the following: BW(Büchi), CW(coBüchi), SUP, LSUP(LimSup), LINF(LimInf), LAVG(LimAvg), or DISC.

3   Closure Properties

We present the closure properties of alternating weighted automata with respect to the pointwise operations max, min, complement and sum.

We say that a class $\mathcal{C}$ of weighted automata is *closed* under a binary operator $\text{op}(\cdot, \cdot)$ (resp. a unary operator $\text{op}'(\cdot)$) if for all $A_1, A_2 \in \mathcal{C}$, there exists $A_{12} \in \mathcal{C}$ such that $L_{A_{12}} = \text{op}(L_{A_1}, L_{A_2})$ (resp. $L_{A_{12}} = \text{op}'(L_{A_1})$). All closure properties that presented in this paper are constructive: when $\mathcal{C}$ is closed under an operator, we can always construct the automaton $A_{12} \in \mathcal{C}$ given $A_1, A_2 \in \mathcal{C}$. We say that the *cost* of the closure property of $\mathcal{C}$ under a binary operator op is at most $O(f(n_1, m_1, n_2, m_2))$ if for all automata $A_1, A_2 \in \mathcal{C}$ with n_i states and m_i transitions (for $i = 1, 2$ respectively), we construct an automaton $A_{12} \in \mathcal{C}$ such that $L_{A_{12}} = \text{op}(L_{A_1}, L_{A_2})$ with at most $O(f(n_1, m_1, n_2, m_2))$ states. We define analogously the cost of closure properties under unary operators. For all reductions presented, the size of the largest weight in A_{12} is linear in the size p of the largest weight in A_1, A_2 (however, the time needed to compute the weights is quadratic in p, as we need addition, multiplication, or comparison, which are quadratic operations over the rationals).

Note that every class of weighted automata is closed under shift by c and under scale by $|c|$ for all $c \in \mathbb{Q}$. For discounted-sum automata, we can define the shift by c by making a copy of the initial states and adding c to the weights of all its outgoing transitions. For the other automata, it suffices to add c to all weights of an automaton to obtain the automaton for the shift by c of its language. Analogously, scaling by factor $|c|$ the weights of an automaton gives the scale by $|c|$ of its language. As a consequence, all closure properties also hold if the complement of a quantitative language L was defined as $k - L$ for any constant k.

Theorem 1. *The closure properties of alternating weighted automata are shown in Table 1.*

For example, according to Theorem 1, every class of alternating and nondeterministic weighted automata is closed under max, and every class of alternating and universal weighted automata is closed under min, all with cost $O(n_1 + n_2)$. This follows from the definition of alternating automata since the maximum and minimum of two quantitative languages can be obtained by an initial (either nondeterministic or universal) choice between the corresponding alternating automata.

The closure properties of nondeterministic weighted automata are established in [4]. The results for universal weighted automata are essentially obtained by duality since (i) if we interpret a universal automaton as a nondeterministic one, and if we replace each weight v by $1 - v$, then we obtain the complement of its quantitative language, and (ii) the maximum of two quantitative languages is the complement of the minimum of their complement.

For complementation, the positive closure results for LimSup- and LimInf-automata are obtained as a direct extension of the complementation results for NBW and UCW [10], and for Disc-automata by dualizing the automaton and replacing every weight v by $1 - \lambda - v$ (where λ is the discount factor). The negative results for Sup-, LimSup-, and LimInf-automata follow from a similar result in the case of $\{0, 1\}$-automata. We give the essential argument for showing that alternating LimAvg-automata are not closed under complement.

Table 1. Closure properties. The cost is given for the positive results, and the negative results are marked by ×. For example, given two alternating Sup-automata with n_1 and n_2 states, respectively, there is an alternating Sup-automaton with $O(n_1 + n_2)$ states that defines the max of their quantitative language; and there exist two universal LimAvg-automata such that the max of the their quantitative language cannot be defined by a universal LimAvg-automaton.

		max	min	complement	sum
alternating	ASUP	$O(n_1 + n_2)$	$O(n_1 + n_2)$	×	$O(n_1 \cdot m_1 \cdot n_2 \cdot m_2)$
	ALSUP	$O(n_1 + n_2)$	$O(n_1 + n_2)$	$O(m \cdot n^2)$	$O(n_1 \cdot m_1 \cdot n_2 \cdot m_2)$
	ALINF	$O(n_1 + n_2)$	$O(n_1 + n_2)$	$O(m \cdot n^2)$	$O(n_1 \cdot m_1 \cdot n_2 \cdot m_2)$
	ALAVG	$O(n_1 + n_2)$	$O(n_1 + n_2)$	×	×
	ADISC	$O(n_1 + n_2)$	$O(n_1 + n_2)$	$O(n)$	$O(n_1 \cdot n_2)$
universal	USUP	$O(n_1 \cdot m_1 \cdot n_2 \cdot m_2)$	$O(n_1 + n_2)$	×	$O(n_1 \cdot m_1 \cdot n_2 \cdot m_2)$
	ULSUP	$O(n_1 \cdot n_2)$	$O(n_1 + n_2)$	×	$O(n_1 \cdot n_2 \cdot 2^{m_1 \cdot m_2})$
	ULINF	$O(n_1 \cdot n_2 \cdot (m_1 + m_2))$	$O(n_1 + n_2)$	$O(m \cdot 2^{n \log n})$	$O(n_1 \cdot m_1 \cdot n_2 \cdot m_2)$
	ULAVG	×	$O(n_1 + n_2)$	×	×
	UDISC	×	$O(n_1 + n_2)$	×	$O(n_1 \cdot n_2)$
nondeterm.	NSUP	$O(n_1 + n_2)$	$O(n_1 \cdot m_1 \cdot n_2 \cdot m_2)$	×	$O(n_1 \cdot m_1 \cdot n_2 \cdot m_2)$
	NLSUP	$O(n_1 + n_2)$	$O(n_1 \cdot n_2 \cdot (m_1 + m_2))$	$O(m \cdot 2^{n \log n})$	$O(n_1 \cdot m_1 \cdot n_2 \cdot m_2)$
	NLINF	$O(n_1 + n_2)$	$O(n_1 \cdot n_2)$	×	$O(n_1 \cdot n_2 \cdot 2^{m_1 \cdot m_2})$
	NLAVG	$O(n_1 + n_2)$	×	×	×
	NDISC	$O(n_1 + n_2)$	×	×	$O(n_1 \cdot n_2)$
deterministic	DSUP	$O(n_1 \cdot n_2)$	$O(n_1 \cdot m_1 \cdot n_2 \cdot m_2)$	×	$O(n_1 \cdot m_1 \cdot n_2 \cdot m_2)$
	DLSUP	$O(n_1 \cdot n_2)$	$O(n_1 \cdot n_2)$	×	$O(n_1 \cdot n_2 \cdot 2^{m_1 \cdot m_2})$
	DLINF	$O((m_1 + m_2) \cdot 2^{n_1 + n_2})$	$O((m_1 + m_2) \cdot 2^{n_1 + n_2})$	×	$O(n_1 \cdot n_2 \cdot 2^{m_1 \cdot m_2})$
	DLAVG	×	×	×	×
	DDISC	×	×	$O(n)$	$O(n_1 \cdot n_2)$

Consider the alphabet $\Sigma = \{a, b\}$ and the language L_a that assigns to every word $w \in \Sigma^\omega$ the limit-average number of the a's in w. Formally, for an infinite word w, let w_j be its prefix of length j and let w_j^a and w_j^b denote the number of a's and b's in w_j, respectively. Then for $w \in \Sigma^\omega$ we have

$$L_a(w) = \liminf_{n \to \infty} \frac{1}{n} \cdot w_n^a.$$

Let us denote by $\hat{L}_b$ the language $(1 - L_a)$ and assume towards contradiction that there exists an ALAVG A with set Q of states for the language $\hat{L}_b$. Let β be the maximum absolute value of the weights in A. Since $\hat{L}_b(a^\omega) = 0$ and $\hat{L}_b(b^\omega) = 1$, we must have $L_A(a^\omega) = 0$ and $L_A(b^\omega) = 1$. By memoryless determinacy of perfect-information limit-average games [5], it follows that the following assertions hold: (a) it is possible to fix choices of the minimizer in the automaton on the letter a such that in the resulting non-deterministic automaton the sum of weights of all a-cycles C is at most 0; and (b) it is possible to fix choices of the minimizer in the automaton on the letter b such that in the resulting non-deterministic automaton the sum of weights of all b-cycles C is at most $|C|$. We fix the choices for the minimizer as above and consider a word w that consists of sequences of a's and b's of increasing length such that every sequence of a and b

is of length at least $10 \cdot |Q| \cdot \beta$ and the long-run average number of b's oscillates between 0 and 1, i.e.

$$\liminf_{n \to \infty} \frac{1}{n} \cdot w_n^b = 0; \qquad \limsup_{n \to \infty} \frac{1}{n} \cdot w_n^b = 1.$$

Any run on a sequence of a's consists of a prefix of length at most Q (with sum of weights at most $|Q| \cdot \beta$), and then nested a-cycles where the sum of weights is at most 0. Similarly, any run on a sequence of b's consists of a prefix of length at most Q (with sum of weights at most $|Q| \cdot \beta$), and then nested b-cycles where the sum of weights is at most the length of the nested cycles. It is then easy to show that $L_A(w) \leq \frac{1}{10}$ while $\hat{L}_b(w) = 1$. Hence, we have a contradiction and the result follows.

Finally, every class of alternating weighted automata is closed under sum, except for LimAvg. Below, we give the proof that alternating LimAvg automata are not closed under sum. Consider the languages L_a and L_b over alphabet $\Sigma = \{a, b\}$ that assigns to each word w the long-run average number of a's and b's in w respectively. Let $L_+ = L_a + L_b$. Assume that L_+ is defined by an ALAVG A with set of states Q (we assume w.l.o.g that every state in Q is reachable). From every state $q \in Q$, the value of the words a^ω and b^ω in A is 1 since $L_+(w_q \cdot a^\omega) = L_+(w_q \cdot b^\omega) = 1$ for all finite words $w_q \in \Sigma^*$. Therefore, by memoryless determinacy of perfect-information limit-average games [5], we can fix a memoryless strategy for the maximizer (in the restriction of A to transitions over a's) such that all paths in the resulting graph have value at least 1. Hence, every cycle in this graph has average weight at least 1. The same result holds for the restriction of A to transitions over b's. Now, we can easily construct an input word $w = a^{n_1} b^{m_1} a^{n_2} b^{m_2} \ldots$ such that $L_a(w) = L_b(w) = 0$, but the maximizer has a strategy (essentially to use the memoryless strategies for a^ω and b^ω) such that for all strategies of the minimizer, the outcome path has value arbitrarily close to 1, yielding a contradiction as then $L_A(w) = 1$ while $L_+(w) = 0$.

4   Expressive Power

The expressive power of nondeterministic weighted automata has been studied in detail in [3]. We present these results and extend them to alternating and universal weighted automata. Note that for each value function, the deterministic automata are reducible to the other modes of branching, and all modes of branching are reducible to alternating automata (as a straightforward consequence of the definition).

Theorem 2. *The relative expressive power of alternating weighted automata is as follows: a class C of alternating weighted automata can be reduced to a class C' if and only if there exists a path from C to C' in the directed graph of Figure 1.*

Note that Theorem 2 also holds if transition weights are irrational numbers. For Sup-automata, the alternating and deterministic automata have the same expressive power, thus we denote this class by $\hat{\delta}$SUP. For LimInf- and LimSup-automata,

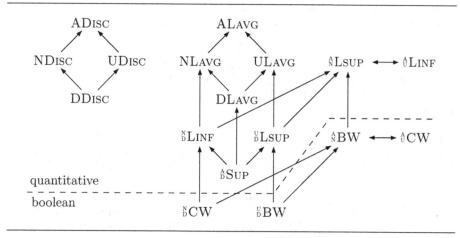

Fig. 1. Reducibility relation. A class $\mathcal{C}$ of automata can be reduced to $\mathcal{C}'$ iff $\mathcal{C} \to^* \mathcal{C}'$.

the relative expressive power is the same as for $\{0, 1\}$-automata, and the proofs are based on generalization of the constructions for the boolean case [10].

For LimAvg- and Disc-automata, the main result is that nondeterministic automata cannot be determinized [3]. From that and the fact that ALAVG and ADISC are closed under max and min while NLAVG and NDISC are not closed under min, and ULAVG and UDISC are not closed under max, it follows that the alternating automata are reducible neither to nondeterministic automata, nor to universal automata.

When comparing different classes of weighted automata, the most surprising result is probably the fact that the class of DBW (which defines a strict subclass of the ω-regular languages) are not reducible to NLAVG, and similarly DCW are not reducible to ULAVG.

Finally, note that Disc-automata are incomparable with the other classes of weighted automata. This follows from the property that the value of a path in a Disc-automaton is essentially determined by a finite prefix, in the sense that the values of two paths can be arbitrarily close if they have sufficiently long common prefixes. In other words, the quantitative language defined by a discounted-sum automaton is a continuous function in the Cantor topology. In contrast, for the other classes of weighted automata, the value of an infinite path depends essentially on its tail and is independent of finite prefixes.

5   Decision Problems

We study the complexity of the quantitative emptiness, universality, language-inclusion, and language-equivalence problems for alternating weighted automata.

Theorem 3. *Table 2 summarizes the known complexity results for the quantitative decision problems of alternating weighted automata.*

Table 2. Complexity results for the quantitative decision problems. The decidability of the problems marked by ? is, to the best of our knowledge, open.

		emptiness	universality	inclusion	equivalence
alternating	ASup	PSPACE-complete	PSPACE-complete	PSPACE-complete	PSPACE-complete
	ALsup	PSPACE-complete	PSPACE-complete	PSPACE-complete	PSPACE-complete
	ALinf	PSPACE-complete	PSPACE-complete	PSPACE-complete	PSPACE-complete
	ALavg	?	?	?	?
	ADisc	co-r.e.	co-r.e.	co-r.e.	co-r.e.
universal	USup	PSPACE-complete	PTIME	PSPACE-complete	PSPACE-complete
	ULsup	PSPACE-complete	PTIME	PSPACE-complete	PSPACE-complete
	ULinf	PSPACE-complete	PTIME	PSPACE-complete	PSPACE-complete
	ULavg	?	PTIME	?	?
	UDisc	co-r.e.	PTIME	co-r.e.	co-r.e.
nondeterm.	NSup	PTIME	PSPACE-complete	PSPACE-complete	PSPACE-complete
	NLsup	PTIME	PSPACE-complete	PSPACE-complete	PSPACE-complete
	NLinf	PTIME	PSPACE-complete	PSPACE-complete	PSPACE-complete
	NLavg	PTIME	?	?	?
	NDisc	PTIME	co-r.e.	co-r.e.	co-r.e.
deterministic	DSup	PTIME	PTIME	PTIME	PTIME
	DLsup	PTIME	PTIME	PTIME	PTIME
	DLinf	PTIME	PTIME	PTIME	PTIME
	DLavg	PTIME	PTIME	PTIME	PTIME
	DDisc	PTIME	PTIME	PTIME	PTIME

The quantitative emptiness problem for nondeterministic weighted automata can be solved by a reduction to the problem of finding the maximal value of an infinite path in a graph. This is decidable because pure memoryless strategies for resolving nondeterminism exist for all quantitative objectives that we consider [6,8,1]. By duality, we get the same results for the quantitative universality problem of universal weighted automata.

The universality problem is known to be PSPACE-complete for finite automata and for NBW [11,13]. This result extends easily to nondeterministic Sup- and LimSup-automata and to the related problems of quantitative language inclusion and equivalence. The results about expressive power and the duality between LimSup and LimInf, and between nondeterministic and universal modes of branching allow to derive the PSPACE-completeness results of Table 2.

The main open question about decision problems remains the decidability of quantitative universality for LimAvg- and Disc-automata. For Disc-automata, a partial answer is known since the quantitative universality problem is co-recursively enumerable [3].

References

1. Andersson, D.: An improved algorithm for discounted payoff games. In: ESSLLI Student Session, pp. 91–98 (2006)
2. Chandra, A.K., Kozen, D., Stockmeyer, L.J.: Alternation. Journal of the ACM 28(1), 114–133 (1981)

3. Chatterjee, K., Doyen, L., Henzinger, T.A.: Quantitative languages. In: Kaminski, M., Martini, S. (eds.) CSL 2008. LNCS, vol. 5213, pp. 385–400. Springer, Heidelberg (2008)
4. Chatterjee, K., Doyen, L., Henzinger, T.A.: Expressiveness and closure properties for quantitative languages. In: Proc. of LICS: Logic in Computer Science. IEEE Comp. Soc. Press, Los Alamitos (2009)
5. Ehrenfeucht, A., Mycielski, J.: Positional strategies for mean payoff games. International Journal of Game Theory 8, 109–113 (1979)
6. Filar, J., Vrieze, K.: Competitive Markov Decision Processes. Springer, Heidelberg (1997)
7. Grädel, E., Thomas, W., Wilke, T. (eds.): Automata, Logics, and Infinite Games. LNCS, vol. 2500. Springer, Heidelberg (2002)
8. Karp, R.M.: A characterization of the minimum cycle mean in a digraph. Discrete Mathematics 23(3), 309–311 (1978)
9. Kuich, W., Salomaa, A.: Semirings, Automata, Languages. Monographs in Theoretical Computer Science. An EATCS Series, vol. 5. Springer, Heidelberg (1986)
10. Kupferman, O., Vardi, M.Y.: Weak alternating automata are not that weak. ACM Trans. Comput. Log. 2(3), 408–429 (2001)
11. Meyer, A.R., Stockmeyer, L.J.: The equivalence problem for regular expressions with squaring requires exponential space. In: Proc. of FOCS: Foundations of Computer Science, pp. 125–129. IEEE, Los Alamitos (1972)
12. Schützenberger, M.P.: On the definition of a family of automata. Information and control 4, 245–270 (1961)
13. Sistla, A.P., Vardi, M.Y., Wolper, P.: The complementation problem for Büchi automata with applications to temporal logic. Theoretical Computer Science 49, 217–237 (1987)
14. Vardi, M.Y., Wolper, P.: An automata-theoretic approach to automatic program verification. In: Proc. of LICS: Logic in Computer Science, pp. 332–344. IEEE, Los Alamitos (1986)

Maintaining Arrays of Contiguous Objects

Michael A. Bender[1], Sándor P. Fekete[2], Tom Kamphans[2,*], and Nils Schweer[2]

[1] Department of Computer Science, State University of New York at Stony Brook
Stony Brook, NY 11794-4400, USA
[2] Braunschweig University of Technology, Department of Computer Science,
Algorithms Group, 38106 Braunschweig, Germany

Abstract. In this paper we consider methods for dynamically storing a set of different objects ("modules") in a physical array. Each module requires one free *contiguous* subinterval in order to be placed. Items are inserted or removed, resulting in a fragmented layout that makes it harder to insert further modules. It is possible to relocate modules, one at a time, to another free subinterval that is contiguous and does not overlap with the current location of the module. These constraints clearly distinguish our problem from classical memory allocation. We present a number of algorithmic results, including a bound of $\Theta(n^2)$ on physical sorting if there is a sufficiently large free space and sum up NP-hardness results for arbitrary initial layouts. For online scenarios in which modules arrive one at a time, we present a method that requires $O(1)$ moves per insertion or deletion and amortized cost $O(m_i \lg \hat{m})$ per insertion or deletion, where m_i is the module's size, $\hat{m}$ is the size of the largest module and costs for moves are linear in the size of a module.

1 Introduction

Maintaining a set of objects is one of the basic problems in computer science. As even a first-year student knows, allocating memory and arranging objects (e.g., sorting or garbage collection) should not be done by moving the objects, but merely by rearranging pointers.

The situation changes when the objects to be sorted or placed cannot be rearranged in a virtual manner, but require actual physical moves; this is the case in a densely packed warehouse, truck or other depots, where items have to be added or removed. Similarly, allocating space in a fragmented array is much harder when one contiguous interval is required for each object: Even when there is sufficient overall free space, placing a single item may require rearranging the other items in order to create sufficient *connected* free space. This scenario occurs for the application that initiated our research: Maintaining modules on a Field Programmable Gate Array (FPGA); reconfigurable chips that consist of a two-dimensional array of processing units. Each unit can perform one basic operation depending on its configuration, which can be changed during runtime. A module is a configuration for a set of processing units wired together to fulfill a certain task. As a lot of FPGAs allow only whole columns to be reconfigured,

---

* Supported by DFG grant FE 407/8-3, project "ReCoNodes".

M. Kutyłowski, M. Gębala, and W. Charatonik (Eds.): FCT 2009, LNCS 5699, pp. 14–25, 2009.
© Springer-Verlag Berlin Heidelberg 2009

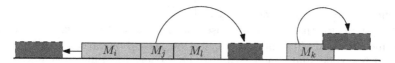

Fig. 1. A module corresponds to a set of columns on an FPGA. Each module occupies a contiguous block of array cells. Module M_i is shifted and module M_j is flipped. The move of module M_k is forbidden, because the current and the target position overlap. If these kind of moves would be allowed connecting the total free space could always be done by shifting all modules to one side.

we allow the modules to occupy only whole columns on the FPGA (and deal with a one-dimensional problem). Moreover, because the layout of the modules (i.e., configurations and interconnections of the processing units) is fixed, we have to allocate *connected* free space for a module on the FPGA. In operation, different modules are loaded onto the FPGA, executed for some time and are removed when their task is fulfilled, causing *fragmentation* on the FPGA. When fragmentation becomes too high (i.e., we cannot place modules, although there is sufficent free space, but no sufficent amount of connected free space), the execution of new task has to be delayed until other tasks are finished and the corresponding modules are removed from the FPGA. To reduce the delay, we may reduce fragmentation by moving modules. Moving a module means to stop its operation, copy the module to an unoccupied space, restart the module in the new place, and declare the formerly occupied space of the module as free space; see Figure 1. Thus, it is important that the current and the target position of the module are *not overlapping* (i.e., they do not share a column). This setting gives rise to two approaches: We may either use simple placing strategies such as first fit and compact the whole FPGA when necessary (as discussed in [1]), or use more elaborated strategies that organize the free space and avoid the need for complete defragmentations.

Related Work. There is a large body of work on storage allocation; e.g., [2] for an overview and [3, 4] for competitive analysis of some algorithms. Many storage allocation algorithms also have analogues in bin packing [5]. The salient feature of most traditional memory-allocation and bin-packing heuristics is that once an item is allocated, it cannot be moved, unlike the model is this paper. There is also a tremendous amount of work on classical sorting (see, e.g., [6]).

Physical allocation, where elements can be placed and then moved, has received less attention. Itai, Konheim, and Rodeh consider maintaining n unit-size objects sorted in an $O(n)$ sized array by appropriately maintaining a linear number of gaps interspersed between the elements at an amortized cost of $O(\lg^2 n)$ per insert, and the problem is deamortized in [7]. The packed memory array Bender, Demaine, and Farach-Colton [8] and Bender and Hu [9] investigate a similar problem in the context of external-memory and cache-oblivious algorithms. Bender, Farach-Colton, and Mosteiro [10] show that probabilistically a modified insertion sort runs in $O(n \lg n)$ by leaving appropriate gaps between elements. In these papers, elements have unit size and there is a fixed order that needs to be maintained dynamically, unlike the problem in this paper.

A different problem is described by [11], who consider densely packed physical storage systems for the U.S. Navy, based on the classical 15-puzzle, where items can be moved to an adjacent empty cell. How should one arrange and maintain the set of free cells, and how can objects be retrieved as quickly as possible?

Finally, if the sequence of modules (i.e., their size, processing time, and arrival time) is fully known, then the problem can be stated as a strip packing problem (without rotation) with release times for rectangles with widths and heights corresponding to the module's size and time, respectively. There is a $(1 + \varepsilon)$-approximation for (classical) offline strip packing [12]. For the case with release times, Augustine et al. [13] give a $O(\lg n)$ approximation and a 3-approximation for heights bounded by one. For approaches from the FPGA community see [1] and the references cited in this paper.

This Paper. Dealing with arrangements of physical objects or data that require contiguous memory allocation and nonoverlapping moves gives rise to a variety of problems that are quite different from virtual storage management:

- Starting configuration vs. full management. We may be forced to start from an arbitrary configuration, or be able to control the placement of objects.
- Physical sorting. Even when we know that it is possible to achieve connected free space, we may not want to get an arbitrary arrangement of objects, but may be asked to achieve one in which the objects are sorted by size.
- Low-cost insertion. We may be interested in requiring only a small number of moves per insertion, either on average, or in the worst case.
- Objective functions. Depending on the application scenario, the important aspects may differ: We may want to minimize the moves for relocating objects, or the total mass that is moved. Alternatively, we may perform only very few moves (or none at all), at the expense of causing waiting time for the objects that cannot be placed; this can be modeled as minimizing the makespan of the corresponding schedule.

Main Results. Our main results are as follows:

- We demonstrate that sorting the modules by size may require $\Omega(n^2)$ moves.
- We show that keeping the modules in sorted order is sufficient to maintain connected free space and to achieve an optimal makespan, requiring $O(n)$ moves per insertion or deletion.
- We give an alternative strategy that guarantees connected free space; in most steps, this requires $O(1)$ moves for insertion, but may be forced to switch to sorted order in $O(n^2)$ moves for high densities.
- We present an online method that needs $O(1)$ moves per insertion or deletion.
- We perform a number of experiments to compare the strategies.
- For the sake of completeness, we briefly cite and sketch that it is strongly NP-hard to find an optimal defragmentation sequence when we are forced to start with an arbitrary initial configuration, that (unless P is equal to NP) it is impossible to approximate the maximal achievable free space within any constant, and prove that achieving connected space is always possible for low module density.

The rest of this paper is organized as follows. In Section 2, we introduce the problem and notation. Section 3 discusses aspects of complexity for a (possibly bad) given starting configuration. Section 4 focuses on sorting. Section 5 introduces two insertion strategies that always guarantee that free space can be made connected. Moreover, we present strategies that achieve low (amortized or worst-case) cost per insertion. Some concluding thoughts are given in Section 6.

2   Preliminaries

Motivated by our FPGA application, we model the problem as follows: Let A be an array (e.g., a memory or FPGA columns) that consists of $|A|$ cells. A module M_i of size m_i occupies a subarray of size m_i in A (i.e., m_i consecutive cells). We call a subarray of maximal size where no module is placed a *free space*. The ith free space (numbered from left to right) is denoted by F_i and its size by f_i.

A module located in a subarray, A_s, can be *moved* to another subarray, A_t, if A_t is of the same size as A_s and all cells in A_t are empty (particularly, both subarrays **do not have a cell in common**). Moves are distinguished into *shifts* and *flips*: If there is at least one module located between A_s and A_t we call the move a flip, otherwise a shift; see Fig. 1. Following the two approaches mentioned in the introduction, we are mainly interested in the following problems.

Offline Defragmentation: We start with a given configuration of modules in an array A and look for a sequence of moves such that there is a free space of maximum size. We state the problem formally:

Given: An array A, and a set of modules, $M_1, M_2, ..., M_n$, placed in A.

Task: Move the modules such that there is a free space of maximum size.

Online Storage Allocation: This problem arises from inserting a sequence of modules, $M_1, M_2, \ldots, M_n$, which arrive in an online fashion, the next module arrives after the previous one has been inserted. After insertion, a module stays for some period of time in the array before it is removed; the duration is not known when placing an object. If an arriving module cannot be placed (because there is no sufficient connected free space), it has to wait until the array is compacted or other modules are removed. The modules in the array can be moved as described above to create free space for further insertions.

Our goals are twofold: On the one hand we want to minimize the *makespan* (i.e., the time until the last module is removed from the array) and, on the other hand, we want to minimize the costs for the moves. Moves are charged using a function, $c(m_i)$, which is linear in m_i. For example, we can simply count the number of moves using $c_1(m_i) := 1$, or we count the moved mass (i.e., we sum up the sizes of the moved modules) with $c_2(m_i) := m_i$. Formally:

Given: An empty array, A, a sequence of modules, $M_1, M_2, ..., M_n$, arriving one after the other.

Task: Place the modules in A such that (1) the makespan and (2) the total costs for all moves performed during the insertions is minimized.

3   Offline Defragmentation

In this section, we assume that we are given an array that already contains n modules. Our task is to compact the array; that is, move the modules such that we end up with one connected free space. Note that a practical motivation in the context of dynamic FPGA reconfiguation as well as some heuristics were already given in our paper [1]. As they lay the basis of some of the ideas in the following sections and for the sake of completeness, we briefly cite and sketch the corresponding complexity results.

Theorem 1. *Rearranging an array with modules $M_1, \ldots, M_n$ and free spaces $F_1, \ldots, F_k$ such that there is a free space of maximum size is strongly NP-complete. Moreover, there is no deterministic polynomial-time approximation algorithm within any polynomial approximation factor (unless P=NP).*

The proof is based on a reduction of 3-PARTITION, see Figure 2. The sizes of the first $3k$ modules correspond to the input of a 3-PARTITION instance, the size of the free spaces, B, is the bound from the 3-PARTITION instance. We can achieve a free space of maximum size, if and only if we can move the first $3k$ modules to the free spaces, which corresponds to a solution for the 3-PARTITION instance. The inapproximability argument uses a chain of immobile modules of increasing size that can be moved once a 3-PARTITION has been found, see [1].

This hardness depends on a number of immobile modules, i.e., on relatively small free space. If we define for an array A of length $|A|$ the density to be $\delta = \frac{1}{|A|} \sum_{i=1}^{n} m_i$, it is not hard to see that if

$$\delta \leq \frac{1}{2} - \frac{1}{2|A|} \cdot \max_{i=1,\ldots,n} \{m_i\} \quad \text{or} \tag{1}$$

$$\max_{i=1,\ldots,n} \{m_i\} \leq \max_{j=1,\ldots,k} \{f_j\}. \tag{2}$$

is fulfilled, the total free space can always be connected with $2n$ steps by Algorithm 1 which shifts all modules to the right in the first loop and all modules to the left in the second loop. Starting at the right and left end, respectively.

Theorem 2. *Algorithm 1 connects the total free space with at most $2n$ moves and uses $O(n)$ computing time.*

In the following, we use the idea of Algorithm 1 for maintenance strategies that can accommodate any module for which there is sufficient total free space.

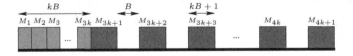

Fig. 2. Reducing 3-Partition to the MDP

> **Input**: An array A with n modules $M_1, \ldots, M_n$ (numbered from left to right) such that Eq. (1) or Eq. (2) is fulfilled.
> **Output**: A placement of $M_1, \ldots, M_n$ such that there is only one free space.
> 1 **for** $i = n$ **to** 1 **do**
> 2   Shift the M_i to the right as far as possible.
> 3 **for** $i = 1$ **to** n **do**
> 4   Shift M_i to the left as far as possible.

Algorithm 1. LeftRightShift

4   Sorting

In the next section, we present some strategies that are based on sorting the set of modules by their size. But more than that, sorting is always an important task. Thus, in this section we focus on the sorting problem for modules solely. Note that we cannot apply classical sorting algorithms such as Quicksort or Selection Sort, because they assume that every object is of the same size. We state an algorithm that is similar to Insertion Sort and show that it can be applied to our setting. It sorts n modules in an array with $O(n^2)$ steps. Moreover we show that this is best possible up to a constant factor. More precisely, we deal with the following problem: Given an array, A, with modules $M_1, \ldots, M_n$ and free spaces $F_1, \ldots, F_k$. Sort the modules according to their size such that there is only one free space in A. It is necessary to be able to move every module. Therefore we assume in this section that Eq. (2) is fulfilled in the initial placement. Note that if Eq. (2) is not fulfilled, there are instances for which it is NP-hard to decide whether it can be sorted or not; this follows from a similar construction as in Section 3.

4.1   Sorting n Modules with $O(n^2)$ Steps

To sort a given configuration, we first apply Algorithm 1, performing $O(n)$ moves.[1] Afterwards, there is only one free space at the right end of A and all modules are lying side by side in A. We number the modules in the resulting position from left to right from 1 to n. The algorithm maintains a list I of unsorted modules. As long as I is not empty, we proceed as follows: We flip the largest unsorted module, M_k, to the right end of the free space and shift all unsorted modules that were placed on the right side of M_k to the left. Note that afterwards there is again only one free space in A.

Theorem 3. *Let A be an array with modules $M_1, \ldots, M_n$, free spaces $F_1, \ldots, F_k$, and let Eq. (2) be satisfied. Then Algorithm 2 sorts the array with $O(n^2)$ steps.*

Proof. The while loop is executed at most n times. In every iteration there is at most one flip and n shifts. This yields an upper bound of n^2 on the total number of moves.

---
[1] A short proof of correctness for this procedure can be found in [1].

Input: An array A such that Eq. (2) is satisfied.
Output: The modules $M_1, \ldots, M_n$ side by side in sorted order and one free
space at the left end of A.

1   Apply Algorithm 1
2   $I := \{1, \ldots, n\}$
3   **while** $I \neq \emptyset$ **do**

4       $k = \text{argmax}_{i \in I}\{m_i\}$
5   flip M_k to the right end of the free space
6       $I = I \setminus \{k\}$
7   **for** $i = k+1, \ldots, n$ **and** $i \in I$ **do**

8   shift M_i to the left as far as possible

Algorithm 2. SortArray

For correctness, we prove the following invariant: At the end of an iteration of
the while loop, all M_j, $j \notin I$, lie side by side at the right end of A in increasing
order (from left to right) and all M_j, $j \in I$, lie side by side at the left end of A.
We call the first sequence of modules sorted and the other one non-sorted.

Now, assume that we are at the beginning of the jth iteration of the while loop.
Let k be the index of the current maximum in I. By the induction hypothesis
and by Eq. (2), the module M_k can be flipped to the only free space. This step
increases the number of sorted elements lying side by side at the right end of
A. Since in every step the module of maximum is chosen, the increasing order
in the sequence of sorted modules is preserved. Furthermore, this step creates
a free space of size m_k that divides the sequence of non-sorted modules into
two (possible empty) subsequences. By the numbering of the modules, the left
subsequence contains only indexes smaller than k. This ensures that in the second
while loop only modules from the right subsequence are shifted. Again, since M_k
is chosen to be of maximum size all shifts are well defined. At the end of the
iteration, the non-sorted modules lie side by side and so do the sorted ones. □

4.2 A Lower Bound of $\Omega(n^2)$

We show that Algorithm 2 needs the minimum number of steps (up to a constant
factor) to sort n modules. In particular, we prove that any algorithm needs $\Omega(n^2)$
steps to sort the following example. The example consists of an even number of
modules, $M_1, \ldots, M_n$, with size $m_i = k$ if i is odd and $m_i = k+1$ if i is even
for a $k \geq 2$. There is only one free space of size $k+1$ in this initial placement at
the left end of A, see Fig. 3.

Lemma 1. *The following holds for any sequence of shifts and flips applied to
the instance shown in Fig. 3:*

(i) There are never two free spaces, each of size greater than or equal to k.
*(ii) There might be more than one free space but there is always exactly one
having either size k or size $k+1$.*

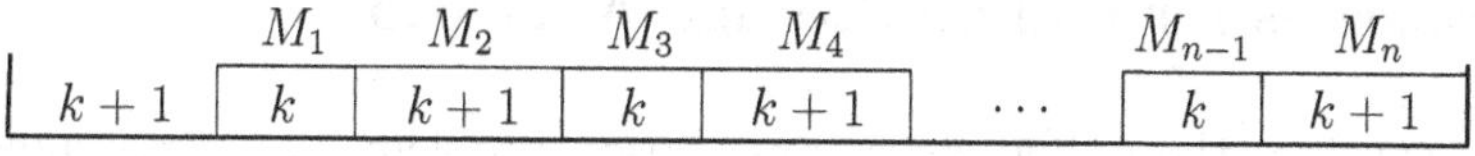

	M_1	M_2	M_3	M_4			M_{n-1}	M_n
$k+1$	k	$k+1$	k	$k+1$	$\cdots$		k	$k+1$

Fig. 3. Sorting an array is in $\Omega(n^2)$

Proof. (i) is obvious because otherwise the sum of the sizes of the free spaces would exceed the total free space. (ii) follows because in the last step either a module of size k or $k+1$ was moved leaving a free of size k or $k+1$, resp.   □

Lemma 2. *Let ALG be an algorithm that uses a minimum number of steps to sort the above instance. Then the following holds:*

(i) There is never more than one free space in A.

(ii) A module of size k will only be shifted (and never be flipped).

Proof. Consider a step that created more than one free space. This is possible only if a module, M_i, of size k was moved (i.e., there is one free space of size k). By Lemma 1, all other free spaces have sizes less than k. Thus, only a module, M_j, of size k can be moved in the next step. Since we care only about the order of the sizes of the modules not about their numbering the same arrangement can be obtained by moving M_j to the current place of M_i and omitting the flip of M_i (i.e., the number of steps in ALG can be decreased); a contradiction.

From (i) we know that there is always one free space of size $k+1$ during the execution of ALG. Flipping a small module to this free space creates at least two free spaces. Hence, a small module will only be shifted.   □

Theorem 4. *Any algorithm that sorts the modules in the example from Fig. 3 needs at least $\Omega(n^2)$ steps.*

Proof. Let ALG be an algorithm that needs the minimum number of steps. W.l.o.g. we assume that at the end the large modules are on the left side of the small ones. We consider the array in its initial configuration and, in particular, a module, M_i, of size k. There are $\frac{i-1}{2}$ small modules, the same number of large modules and one free space of size $k+1$ to the left of M_i. Because small modules are only shifted in ALG the number of small modules on the left side of M_i will not change but the number of large ones will finally increase to $\frac{n}{2}$. Since a shift moves M_i at most a distance of $k+1$ to the right, M_i has to be shifted at least once for every large module that is moved to M_i's left. Taking the free space into account this implies that M_i has to be shifted at least $\frac{n}{2} - (\frac{i-1}{2} + 1)$ times, for any odd i between 1 and n. Hence, for $i = 2j - 1$ we get a lower bound of $\sum_{j=1}^{\frac{n}{2}} \frac{n}{2} - j = \frac{1}{8}n^2 - \frac{1}{4}n$ on the number of shifts in ALG. Additionally, every large module has to be flipped at least once, because it has a small one to its left in the initial configuration. This gives a lower bound of $\frac{1}{8}n^2 - \frac{1}{4}n + \frac{1}{2}n = \frac{1}{8}n^2 + \frac{1}{4}n$ on the total number of steps in ALG and therefore a lower bound on the number of steps for any algorithm.   □

5   Strategies for Online Storage Allocation

Now, we consider the online storage allocation problem, i.e., we assume that we have the opportunity to start with an empty array and are able to control the placement of modules. We consider strategies that handle the insertion and deletion of a sequence of modules. AlwaysSorted achieves an optimal makespan, possibly at the expense of requiring up to $O(n^2)$ moves per insertion; the algorithm ClassSort that is designed to require very few moves, but at the cost of larger makespan. Additionally, we present a simple local heuristic, LocalShift.

AlwaysSorted. This algorithm inserts the modules such that they are sorted according to their size; that is, the module sizes decrease from left to right. Note that the sorted order ensures that if a module, M_i, is removed from the array all modules lying on the right side of M_i (these are at most as large as M_i) can be shifted m_i units to the left. Now the algorithm works as follows: Before a module, M_j, is inserted, we shift all modules to the left as far as possible starting at the left side of the array. Next we search for the position that M_j should have in the array to keep the sorted order. We shift all modules lying on the right side of the position m_j units to the right if possible; after that M_j is inserted.

Theorem 5. *AlwaysSorted achieves the optimal makespan. The algorithm performs $O(n)$ moves per insertion in the worst case.*

Proof. All modules are shifted to the left as far as possible before the next module is inserted. After that, there is only one free space at the right side of A. If this free space is at least as large as the next module, the insertion is performed, meaning that a module has to wait if and only if the total free space is smaller than the module size; no algorithm can do better.   □

DelayedSort. The idea is to reduce the number of moves by delaying the sorting until it is really necessary: We maintain a large free space on the left or the right side (alternatingly). First, we check if we can insert the current module M_i, i.e., if $m_i \leq \sum f_j$. Now, if we can insert M_i maintaining $\max m_i \leq \max f_j$ we insert M_i using First-Fit. Otherwise, we check if M_i can be inserted—maintaining the above condition—after compacting the array using by shifting all modules to the side where we currently keep the large free space, beginning with the module next to the free space. If maintaining the condition is not possible, we sort the array using Alg. 2 and insert the module into the single free space left after sorting. Note that this strategy also achieves the optimal makespan.

ClassSort. For this strategy we assume that the size of the largest module at most half the size of the array. We round the size of a module, M_i, to the next larger power of 2; we denote the rounded size by m_i'.

We organize the array in $a = \lceil \lg \frac{|A|}{2} \rceil$ *classes*, $C_0, C_1, \ldots, C_a$. Class C_i has *level i* and stores modules of rounded size 2^i. In addition, each class reserves 0, 1, or 2 (initially 1) *buffers* for further insertions. A buffer of level i is a free space of size 2^i. We store the classes sorted by their level in decreasing order.

The numbers of buffers in the classes provide a sequence, $S = s_a, \ldots, s_0$, with $s_i \in \{0, 1, 2\}$. We consider this sequence as a redundant binary number; see Brodal [14]. Redundant binary numbers use a third digit to allow additional freedom in the representation of the counter value. More precisely, the binary number $d_\ell d_{\ell-1} \ldots d_0$ with $d_i \in \{0, 1, 2\}$ represents the value $\sum_{i=0}^{\ell} d_i 2^i$. Thus, for example, 4_{10} can be represented as 100_2, 012_2, or 020_2. A redundant binary number is *regular*, if and only if between two 2's there is one 0, and between two 0's there is one 2. The advantage of regular redundant binary numbers is that we can add or subtract values of 2^k taking care of only $O(1)$ carries, while usual binary numbers with ℓ digits and $11 \ldots 1_2 + 1_2 = 100 \ldots 0_2$ cause ℓ carries.

Inserting and deleting modules benefits from this advantage: The reorganization of the array on insertions and deletions corresponds to subtracting or adding, respectively, an appropriate value 2^k to the regular redundant binary numbers that represents the sequence S. In details: If a module, M_j, with $m'_j = 2^i$ arrives, we store the module in a buffer of the corresponding class C_i.[2] If there is no buffer available in C_i, we have a carry in the counter value; that is, we split one buffer of level $i + 1$ to two buffers of level i; corresponding, for example, to a transition of $\ldots 20 \ldots$ to $\ldots 12 \ldots$ in the counter. Then, we subtract 2^i and get $\ldots 11 \ldots$. Now, the counter may be irregular; thus, we have to change another digit. The regularity guarantees that we change only $O(1)$ digits [14]. Similarly, deleting a module with $m'_j = 2^i$ corresponds to adding 2^i to S.

Theorem 6. *ClassSort performs $O(1)$ moves per insertion or deletion in the worst case. Let $\hat{m}$ be the size of the largest module in the array, c a linear function and $c(m_i)$ the cost of moving a module of size m_i. Then the amortized cost for inserting or deleting a module of size m_i is $O(m_i \lg \hat{m})$.*

Proof. The number of moves is clear. Now, observe a class, C_i. A module of size 2^i is moved, if the counter of the next smaller class, C_{i-1}, switches from 0 to 2 (for the insertion case). Because of the regular structure of the counter, we have to insert at least modules with a total weight of 2^{i-1} before we have to move a module of size 2^i again. We charge the cost for this move to theses modules. On the other hand, we charge every module at most once for every class. As we have $\lg \hat{m})$ classes, the stated bound follows. The same argument holds for the case of deletion. Note that we move modules only, if the free space inside a class is not located on the right side of the class (for insertion) or on the left side (for deletion). Thus, alternatingly inserting and deleting a module of the same size does not result in a large number of moves, because we just imaginarily split and merge free spaces.   □

LocalShift. We define the distance between two blocks (modules or free spaces) as the number of blocks that lie between these two blocks. For a free space F_i we call the set of blocks that are at most at a distance $k \in \mathbb{N}$ from F_i the k-neighborhood of F_i. The algorithm LocalShift works as follows: If possible

---

[2] Initially, the array is empty. Thus, we create the classes $C_1, \ldots, C_i$ if they do not already exist, reserving one free space of size 2^k for every class C_k.

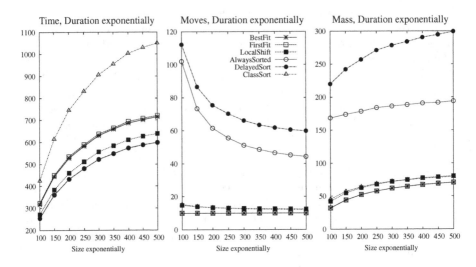

Fig. 4. Experiments with exponential distribution for size and duration

we use BestFit to insert the next module M_j. Otherwise, we look at the k-neighborhood of any free space (from left to right). If shifting the modules from the k-neighborhood, lying on the left side of F_i, to the left as far as possible (starting a the left side) and the modules lying on the right side to the right as far as possible (starting at the right side) would create a free space that is at least as large as M_j we actually perform these shifts and insert M_j. If no such free space can be created, M_j has to wait until at least one modules is removed from the array. This algorithm performs at most $2k$ moves per insertion.

6   Comparison and Conclusion

To test our strategies, we generated a number of random input sequences and analyzed the performance of our strategies as well as the simple FirstFit and Best-Fit approaches in an array of size 2^{10}. A sequence consists of 100,000 modules, each module has a randomly chosen size and duration time. For each sequence, size and time are shuffled using several probability distributions. We analyzed three objectives: the time to complete the whole sequence (the makespan), the number of moved modules ($c(m_i) = 1$) and the moved mass ($c(m_i) = m_i$). Our experiments (see Fig. 4 for an example) showed that LocalShift performs very well, as it constitutes a compromise between a moderate number moves and a low makespan. Both makespan and moves turn out to be nearly optimal.

The more complex strategy ClassSort performed only slightly worse than LocalShift concerning moves, but disappoints in its resulting makespan. In contrast, both types of sorting-related strategies have—of course—a good makespan, but need a lot of moves. Unsurprisingly, FirstFit and BestFit need the fewest moves (as they perform moves only on inserting a module, but never move a previously placed module). Their makespan turned out to be clearly better than ClassSort, but worse than LocalShift and the sorting strategies.

A comparison of the sorting strategies, AlwaysSorted and DelayedSort, showed that delaying the sorting of the array until it is really necessary pays off for the number of moves, but not if we count the moved mass, this is because the shift from maintaining one large free space to sorting (caused by not enough free space to accompany the largest item) results in a sequence with several moves of the heaviest items, which is not the case for AlwaysSorted.

We have introduced the systematic study of dynamic storage allocation for contiguous objects. There are still a number of open questions, such as the worst-case number of moves required to achieve connected free space or cheaper certificates for guaranteeing that connected free space can be achieved.

References

[1] Fekete, S.P., Kamphans, T., Schweer, N., Tessars, C., van der Veen, J.C., Angermeier, J., Koch, D., Teich, J.: No-break dynamic defragmentation of reconfigurable devices. In: Proc. Internat. Conf. Field Program. Logic Appl. (FPL 2008) (2008)

[2] Knuth, D.E.: The Art of Computer Programming: Fundamental Algorithms, 3rd edn., vol. 1. Addison-Wesley, Reading (1997)

[3] Luby, M.G., Naor, J., Orda, A.: Tight bounds for dynamic storage allocation. SIAM Journal on Discrete Math. 9, 155–166 (1996)

[4] Naor, J., Orda, A., Petruschka, Y.: Dynamic storage allocation with known durations. Discrete Applied Mathematics 3, 203–213 (2000)

[5] Coffman, E.G., Garey, M.R., Johnson, D.S.: Approximation algorithms for bin packing: A survey. In: Hochbaum, D.S. (ed.) Approximation Algorithms for NP-Hard Problems, pp. 46–93. PWS Publishing Company, Boston (1996)

[6] Knuth, D.E.: The Art of Computer Programming: Sorting and Searching, 3rd edn., vol. 3. Addison-Wesley, Reading (1997)

[7] Willard, D.E.: A density control algorithm for doing insertions and deletions in a sequentially ordered file in good worst-case time. Information and Computation 97, 150–204 (1992)

[8] Bender, M.A., Demaine, E.D., Farach-Colton, M.: Cache-oblivious B-trees. SIAM J. Comput. 35, 341–358 (2005)

[9] Bender, M.A., Hu, H.: An adaptive packed-memory array. Transactions on Database Systems 32 (2007); Special Issue on PODS 2006

[10] Bender, M.A., Farach-Colton, M., Mosteiro, M.A.: Insertion sort is O(n log n). Theory of Computing Systems 39, 391–397 (2006); Special Issue on FUN 2004

[11] Gue, K.R., Kim, B.S.: Puzzle-based storage systems. TR, Auburn University (2006)

[12] Kenyon, C., Remila, E.: Approximate strip packing. In: Proc. 37th Annu. IEEE Sympos. Found. Comput. Sci., pp. 31–36 (1996)

[13] Augustine, J., Banerjee, S., Irani, S.: Strip packing with precedence constraints and strip packing with release times. In: Proc. 18th Annu. ACM Sympos. Parallel Algor. Architect., pp. 180–189 (2006)

[14] Brodal, G.S.: Worst-case efficient priority queues. In: Proceedings of the Seventh Annual ACM-SIAM Symposium on Discrete Algorithms (SODA 1996), Atlanta, Georgia, pp. 52–58 (1996)

The k-Anonymity Problem Is Hard

Paola Bonizzoni[1,*], Gianluca Della Vedova[2,*], and Riccardo Dondi[3,**]

[1] DISCo, Università degli Studi di Milano-Bicocca, Milano, Italy
[2] Dipartimento di Statistica, Università degli Studi di Milano-Bicocca Milano, Italy
[3] Dipartimento di Scienze dei Linguaggi, della Comunicazione e degli Studi Culturali,
Università degli Studi di Bergamo, Bergamo, Italy
bonizzoni@disco.unimib.it, gianluca.dellavedova@unimib.it,
riccardo.dondi@unibg.it

Abstract. The problem of publishing personal data without giving up privacy is becoming increasingly important. An interesting formalization recently proposed is the k-anonymity. This approach requires that the rows in a table are clustered in sets of size at least k and that all the rows in a cluster are related to the same tuple, after the suppression of some records. The problem has been shown to be NP-hard when the values are over a ternary alphabet, $k = 3$ and the rows length is unbounded. In this paper we give a lower bound on the approximation of two restrictions of the problem, when the records values are over a binary alphabet and $k = 3$, and when the records have length at most 8 and $k = 4$, showing that these restrictions of the problem are APX-hard.

1 Introduction

In many research fields, for example in epidemic analysis, the analysis of large amounts of personal data is essential. However, a relevant issue in the management of such data is the protection of individual privacy. One approach to deal with such problem is the k-anonymity model, introduced in [7,8,6]. The input of the k-anonymity approach is a table, where the rows of the table represent records belonging to different individuals. Then some of the entries in the table are suppressed so that for each record r in the resulting table, there exist at least $k - 1$ other records identical to r. It follows that the resulting data is not sufficient to identify each individual. A different version of the problem employs the generalization of entry value [1]. However, in this paper we will focus only on the suppression model.

A simple parsimonious principle leads to the optimization problem where the number of entries in the table to be suppressed and generalized has to be minimized. The k-anonymity problem is known to be NP-hard for rows of unbounded length with values over ternary alphabet and $k = 3$ [1]. Moreover, a polynomial-time $O(k)$-approximation algorithm on arbitrary input alphabet,

---

* Partially supported by FAR 2008 grant "Computational models for phylogenetic analysis of gene variations".
** Partially supported by FAR 2009 grant "Algoritmi per il trattamento di sequenze".

as well as some other approximation algorithms for some restricted cases, are known [1]. Recently, approximation algorithms with factor $O(\log k)$ have been proposed [5], even for generalized versions of the problem [4].

In this paper, we further investigate the approximation and computational complexity of the k-anonymity problem, settling the APX-hardness for two interesting restrictions of the problem: (i) when the matrix entries are over a *binary* alphabet and $k = 3$, or (ii) when the matrix has 8 columns and $k = 4$. We notice that these are the first inapproximability results for the k-anonymity problem. More precisely, in this paper we first design an L-reduction [3] from the Minimum Vertex Cover problem to 3-anonymity problem over binary alphabet. Then, we design a second L-reduction from the Minimum Vertex Cover problem to 4-anonymity problem when the rows are of length 8. Those two restrictions are of particular interests as some data can be inherently binary (e.g. gender) and publicly revealed data tend to have only a few columns, therefore solving such restriction could help for most practical cases.

The rest of the paper is organized as follows. In Section 2 we introduce some preliminary definitions, in Section 3 we show that the 3-anonymity is APX-hard, even when the matrix is restricted to binary data, while in Section 4 we show that the 4-anonymity problem is APX-hard, even when the rows have length bounded by 8.

2   Preliminary Definitions

In this section we introduce preliminary definitions that will be used in the rest of the paper. A graph $\mathcal{G} = (V, E)$ is cubic when each vertex in V has degree three. Given an alphabet Σ, a row r is a vector of elements taken from the set Σ, and the j-th element of r is denoted by $r[j]$. Let r_1, r_2 be two equal-length rows. Then $H(r_1, r_2)$ is the Hamming distance of r_1 and r_2, i.e. $|\{i : r_1[i] \neq r_2[i]\}|$. Let R be a set of l rows, then a *clustering* of R is a partition $P = (P_1, \ldots, P_t)$ of R.

Given a clustering $P = (P_1, \ldots, P_t)$ of R, we define the cost of a set P_i, denoted by $c(P_i)$, as $|P_i||\{j : \exists r_1, r_2 \in P_i, \ r_1[j] \neq r_2[j]\}|$, that is the number of entries of the rows in P_i that must be deleted in order to make all such rows identical. The cost of P, denoted by $c(P)$, is defined as $\sum_{P_i \in P} c(P_i)$.

We are now able to formally define the k-Anonymity Problem (k-AP) as follows: given set R of rows over an alphabet Σ, compute a clustering $P = (P_1, \ldots, P_t)$ of R, with $|P_i| \geq k$ for each set P_i, so that $c(P)$ is minimum.

Notice that, given a clustering $P = (P_1, \ldots, P_t)$ of R, $|P_i| \max_{r_1, r_2 \in P_i}\{H(r_1, r_2)\}$ is a lower bound for $c(P_i)$, since all the positions for which r_1 and r_2 differ will be deleted in each row of P_i. We will study two restrictions of the k-anonymity problem. In the first restriction, denoted by 3-ABP, the rows are over a binary alphabet $\Sigma = \{0_b, 1_b\}$ and $k = 3$. In the second restriction, denoted by 4-AP(8), $k = 4$ and the rows are over an arbitrary alphabet and have length 8.

In the rest of the paper we present two different reductions from the Minimum Vertex Cover on Cubic Graphs (MVCC) problem, which is known to be APX-hard [2]. Consider a cubic graph $\mathcal{G} = (V, E)$, where $|V| = n$ and $|E| = m$, the

MVCC problem asks for a subset $V' \subseteq V$ of minimum cardinality, such that for each edge $(v_i, v_j) \in E$, at least one of v_i or v_j belongs to V'.

3   APX-Hardness of 3-ABP

In this section we will show that 3-ABP is APX-hard via an L-reduction from Minimum Vertex Cover on Cubic Graphs (MVCC). Let $\mathcal{G} = (V, E)$ be an instance of MVCC, the reduction builds an instance R of 3-ABP associating with each vertex $v_i \in V$ a set of rows R_i and with each $e = (v_i, v_j) \in E$ a row $r_{i,j}$. Actually, starting from the cubic graph $\mathcal{G}$, the reduction builds an intermediate multigraph, denoted as *gadget graph* $\mathcal{VG}$, – an example of a gadget graph obtainable through our reduction is represented in Fig. 1. The reduction associates with each vertex v_i of $\mathcal{G}$ a vertex gadget VG_i containing a *core* vertex gadget CVG_i and some other vertices and edges called respectively jolly vertices and jolly edges. More precisely, the vertex-set of a core vertex gadget CVG_i consists of the seven vertices $c_{i,1}, c_{i,2}, c_{i,3}, c_{i,4}, c_{i,5}, c_{i,6}, c_{i,7}$. The vertices $c_{i,1}$, $c_{i,2}$ and $c_{i,3}$ of CVG_i are called *docking vertices*. The edge-set of CVG_i consists of nine edges between vertices of CVG_i (see Fig. 1). Such a set of edges is defined as the set of *core edges* of VG_i. The vertex-set of a vertex gadget consists of the seven vertices of CVG_i and of three more vertices $J_{i,1}, J_{i,2}, J_{i,3}$, called *jolly vertices* of VG_i. The edge-set of VG_i consists of the edge-set of CVG_i and of three set of four parallel edges (see Fig. 1). More precisely, for each docking vertex $c_{i,z}$ adjacent to a jolly vertex $J_{i,z}$, we define a set $E_{i,z}^J$ of four parallel edges between $c_{i,z}$ and $J_{i,z}$. The set of edges $E_i^J = \bigcup_{z \in \{1,2,3\}} E_{i,z}^J$ is called the set of *jolly edges* of VG_i.

Each edge (v_i, v_j) of $\mathcal{G}$ is encoded by an edge gadget EG_{ij} consisting of a single edge that connects a docking vertex of VG_i with one of VG_j, so that in the resulting graph each docking vertex is an endpoint of exactly one edge gadget (this can be achieved trivially as the original graph is cubic.) The resulting graph, denoted by $\mathcal{VG}$, is called *gadget graph*. An edge gadget is said to be *incident* on a vertex gadget VG_i if it is incident on a docking vertex of VG_i. In our reduction we will associate a row with each edge of the graph gadget. Therefore 3-ABP is equivalent to partitioning the edge set of the gadget graph into sets of at

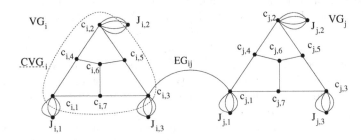

Fig. 1. Gadgets for v_i, v_j, (v_i, v_j)

least three edges. Hence in what follows we may use edges of $\mathcal{VG}$ to denote the corresponding rows. Before giving some details, we present an overview of the reduction.

First, the input set R of rows is defined, so that each row corresponds to an edge of the gadget graph. Then, it is shown that, starting from a general solution, we can restrict ourselves to a canonical solution, where there exist two possible partitions of the rows of a vertex gadget (and possibly some rows of an edge gadget). Such partitions are denoted as *type a* and *type b* solution. Finally, the rows of a vertex gadget that belongs to a *type b* (*type a* resp.) solution are related to vertices in the cover (not in the cover, respectively) of the graph $\mathcal{G}$.

We are now able to introduce our reduction. All the rows in R are the juxtaposition of $n + 2$ blocks, where the i-th block, for $1 \leq i \leq n$, is associated with vertex $v_i \in V$, the $(n+1)$-th block is called *jolly block*, and the $(n+2)$-th block is called *edge block*. The first n blocks are called *vertex blocks*, and each vertex block has size 21. The jolly block has size $6n$, and the edge block has size $3n$.

The rows associated with edges of the gadget graph $\mathcal{VG}$ are obtained by introducing the following notions.

Let $c_{i,j}$ be a vertex of CVG_i, $1 \leq i \leq n$, $1 \leq j \leq 7$, and let r be a row, the *vertex encoding v-enc$_{i,j}$* of $c_{i,j}$ applied to r is defined as follows:

- v-$enc_{i,j}(r)$ assigns value 1_b to the positions $3j - 2$, $3j - 1$ and $3j$ of the i-th block of row r.

Let VG_i be a vertex gadget, $1 \leq i \leq n$, and let r be a row, the *gadget encoding g-enc$_i$* of VG_i applied to r is defined as follows:

- g-$enc_i(r)$ assigns value 1_b to the positions $3i - 2$, $3i - 1$ and $3i$ of the edge block of row r.

Finally, let $J_{i,x}$ be a jolly vertex of VG_i, $1 \leq i \leq n$, $1 \leq x \leq 3$, and let r be a row, the *jolly encoding j-enc$_{i,x}$* of $J_{i,x}$ applied to r is defined as follows:

- j-$enc_{i,x}(r)$ assigns value 1_b to the positions $6(i - 1) + x$, $6(i - 1) + x + 1$ of the jolly block of row r.

We define the rows associated with the edges of $\mathcal{VG}$ according to the types of those edges. Let $c_{i,x}, c_{i,y} \in CVG_i$ and let $(c_{i,x}, c_{i,y})$ be a *core edge*, then the row $r_{i,x,y}$ associated with $(c_{i,x}, c_{i,y})$ is obtained as follows:

$$r_{i,x,y} = g\text{-}enc_i \left(v\text{-}enc_{i,y} \left(v\text{-}enc_{i,x} \left(0^{30n} \right) \right) \right).$$

Consider a docking vertex $c_{i,x} \in CVG_i$ and a jolly vertex $J_{i,x}$ of CVG_i adjacent to $c_{i,x}$. Each row associated with a jolly edge $(c_{i,x}, J_{i,x})$ is called *jolly row* and the set of the 4 jolly rows incident to vertex $c_{i,x}$ is called jolly row set of $c_{i,x}$. Assume that $c_{i,x}$ is adjacent to vertices $c_{i,y}$, $c_{i,z}$ of CVG_i, then each jolly row $r_{i,x,y,z}$ associated with $(c_{i,x}, J_{i,x})$ is obtained as follows:

$$r_{i,x,y,z} = j\text{-}enc_{i,x} \left(g\text{-}enc_i \left(v\text{-}enc_{i,z} \left(v\text{-}enc_{i,y} \left(v\text{-}enc_{i,x} \left(0^{30n} \right) \right) \right) \right) \right).$$

Let E_{ij} be an *edge gadget* connecting VG_i and VG_j in docking vertices $c_{i,x}$ and $c_{j,y}$ respectively. The row $r_{i,j,x,y}$ associated with E_{ij} is obtained as follows:

$$r_{i,j,x,y} = g\text{-}enc_j \left(g\text{-}enc_i \left(v\text{-}enc_{j,y} \left(v\text{-}enc_{i,x} \left(0^{30n}\right)\right)\right)\right).$$

For example consider the row $r_{i,1,4}$ associated with the core edge $(c_{i,1}, c_{i,4})$. Observe that $v\text{-}enc_{i,1}$ sets to 1 the first three positions of the i-th block of $r_{i,1,4}$, while $v\text{-}enc_{i,4}$ sets to 1 the positions 10, 11, 12 of the i-th block of $r_{i,1,4}$. Finally, $g\text{-}enc_i$ sets to 1 the positions $3i-2$, $3i-1$ and $3i$ of the edge block of $r_{i,1,4}$. Edge $(c_{i,1}, c_{i,4})$ is associated with the following row $r_{i,1,4}$:

$$\underbrace{000\ldots000}_{block\ 0}\ldots\underbrace{111\ 000\ 000\ 111\ 000}_{block\ i}\ldots\ldots\underbrace{000\ldots000}_{jolly\ block}\underbrace{000\ldots111\ldots000}_{edge\ block}.$$

Observe that by construction only jolly rows may have a 1_b in a position of the jolly block. It is immediate to notice that clustering together three or more jolly rows associated with parallel edges has cost 0.

We recall that in what follows we may use edges of $\mathcal{VG}$ to denote the corresponding rows.

The cost of a solution S is specified by introducing the notion of virtual cost of a single row r of R. Let S be a solution of 3-ABP, and let C be the cluster of S to which r belongs. Let r be a non-jolly row, we define the *virtual cost* of r in the solution S, denoted as $virt_S(r)$, as the cost of C divided by the number of non-jolly rows in C. Otherwise, if r is a jolly row, then $virt_S(r) = 0$. Given the above notion, observe that the cost $c(C)$ of set C is equal to $\sum_{r \in C} virt_S(r)$ and that for a solution S, the cost $c(S)$ of set S is equal to $\sum_{r \in R} virt_S(r)$.

In the following we will consider only *canonical solutions* of 3-ABP, that is solutions where the rows for each vertex gadget VG_i and edge gadgets eventually incident on VG_i are clustered into *type a* and *type b* solutions constructed as follows.

The *type a* solution defines the partition of the rows for vertex gadget VG_i and consists of six clusters: three clusters of rows of CVG_i, each one is made of the three edges incident on vertex v, where v is one of the three vertices $c_{i,4}$, $c_{i,5}$ and $c_{i,7}$, and three more clusters, each one consisting of the jolly rows associated with one of the three docking vertices of VG_i.

The *type b* solution defines the partition of the rows for a vertex gadget VG_i and some edge gadgets incident on VG_i. It consists of four clusters containing rows of CVG_i. One of them consists of the three edges incident on $c_{i,6}$. The remaining three clusters are associated with the three docking vertices of VG_i. For each docking vertex $c_{i,x}$, the cluster associated with $c_{i,x}$ consists of the two core edges of CVG_i that are incident on $c_{i,x}$, together with either the edge gadget incident on $c_{i,x}$ or one jolly edge incident in $c_{i,x}$. Finally, there are three more clusters, each one consisting of all remaining jolly edges associated with parallel edges incident on one of the three docking vertices of VG_i. Notice that in a *type b* solution each cluster associated with a docking vertex may contain an edge gadget or not, the only requirement is that at least one of the clusters contains an edge gadget.

Proposition 1. *Let S be a canonical solution, and let VG_i, VG_j be two vertex gadgets such that the rows of VG_i are clustered in type a solution in S and rows of VG_j are clustered in a type b solution in S. Then each edge gadget has a virtual cost of 12 in S, the rows of VG_i have a total virtual cost of 81, while the rows of VG_j have a total cost of 99.*

In the following we state two basic results that will be used to show the L-reduction from MVCC to 3-ABP:

1. each solution S of 3-ABP can be modified in polynomial time into a canonical solution S' whose cost is at most that of S (Lemma 10);
2. the graph $\mathcal{G}$ has a vertex cover of size p iff the 3-ABP problem has a canonical solution of cost $99 \cdot p + 81 \cdot (n - p) + 12m$, where 81 is the total virtual cost of the rows of a *type a* solution, while 99 is the total virtual cost of the rows of a vertex gadget in a *type b* solution (Theorem 12).

First, we introduce a basic property of the 3-ABP problem.

Proposition 2. *Given a solution S of 3-ABP, we can compute in polynomial time a solution S', such that $c(S') \leq c(S)$ and each cluster of S' has size at most 5.*

Due to Proposition 2, in what follows we assume that a solution S contains clusters of size at least 3 and at most 5. We will first introduce some basic Lemmas that will help in excluding some possible solutions.

Lemma 3. *Let S be a solution of 3-ABP and let C be a cluster of S consisting of rows of CVG_i. Then $virt_S(r) \geq 9$ for each row r of C, and $virt_S(r) \geq 12$ if the rows in C are not all incident on a common vertex of CVG_i.*

Lemma 4. *Let S be a solution of 3-ABP and let C be a cluster of S consisting of rows of VG_i, such that C contains at least one jolly row of VG_i and at least one row of CVG_i, then the virtual cost of each non-jolly row in C is at least 12.*

Lemma 5. *Let S be a solution of 3-ABP with a cluster C containing a row of VG_i. Then the virtual cost of each non-jolly row of C is at least 9.*

Proof. Notice that if C contains a jolly row, by construction, by Lemma 3 and by Lemma 4, the lemma holds. Hence assume that C contains no jolly row. If a cluster C of S does not consist of three non-jolly rows of VG_i incident on a common vertex, by construction of VG_i, each non-jolly row of C has a virtual cost of at least 12. Hence, in any arbitrary solution each non-jolly row of C has a virtual cost of at least 9. □

An immediate consequence of Lemma 5 and of the construction of VG_i, is that a *type a* solution is the optimal solution for the rows associated with edges of VG_i.

Lemma 6. *Let S be a solution of 3-ABP with a cluster C containing more than one edge gadget. Then*

1. *if exactly two edge gadgets EG_1 and EG_2 are in C, then $virt_S(EG_1)$, $virt_S(EG_2) \geq 21$; if the edge gadgets are not incident on a common vertex gadget, then $virt_S(EG_1)$, $virt_S(EG_2) \geq 27$, and if C contains a row r of a vertex gadget, such that that r is not adjacent to both EG_1 and EG_2, then $virt_S(EG_1)$, $virt_S(EG_2)$, $virt_S(r) \geq 30$;*
2. *if exactly three edge gadgets EG_1, EG_2, EG_3 are in C, then $virt_S(EG_1)$, $virt_S(EG_2)$, $virt_S(EG_3) \geq 27$, and if there is no pair of edge gadgets in $\{EG_1, EG_2, EG_3\}$ incident on a common vertex gadget, then $virt_S(EG_1)$, $virt_S(EG_2)$, $virt_S(EG_3) \geq 36$;*
3. *if more than three edge gadgets are in C, then the virtual cost of each edge gadget in S is at least 36.*

Lemma 7. *Let S be a solution of 3-ABP with a cluster C containing an edge gadget EG_{ij} incident on vertex gadgets VG_i and VG_j, two rows r_x, r_y adjacent to EG_{ij}, where r_x belongs to VG_i and r_y belongs to VG_j. Then $c(C) \geq 18|C|$.*

Lemma 8. *Let S be a solution of 3-ABP with a cluster C containing an edge gadget EG_{ij} and a jolly row j_i. Then $virt_S(EG_{ij}) \geq 18$.*

Proof. Observe that by by construction $H(EG_{ij}, j_i) \geq 14$. Defining the virtual cost of the rows in C, the virtual cost of j_i is split among the set $s(j)$ rows of C which are not jolly rows. Moreover, by Prop. 2, we can assume that $|s(j)| \leq 4$. If $|s(j)| = 4$, then there is at least one row r in $s(j)$ such that there exist at least 3 positions where EG_{ij} and j_i have the same value, while r has a different value. Hence, before it is redefined, the virtual cost is at least 17 for each row in C. Since the virtual cost of j_i is split among 4 rows and $\frac{17}{4} > 4$, the lemma follows. If $|s(j)| \leq 3$, then a virtual cost of at least $\frac{14}{3}$ is added to the rows of $s(j)$ and the lemma holds.   □

By construction of the gadget graph $\mathcal{VG}$, it follows Lemma 9.

Lemma 9. *Let S be a solution containing a cluster C with at least an edge gadget EG_{ij}. Then $virt_S(E_{ij}) \geq 12$.*

Now, we will show our key transformation of a generic solution into a canonical solution without increasing its cost.

Lemma 10. *Let S be a solution, then we can compute in polynomial time a canonical solution S_c such that $c(S_c) \leq c(S)$.*

The proof of the stated result is based on the fact that, whenever a solution S is not a canonical one, it can be transformed into a canonical one by applying Alg. 1. In the following we only sketch the correctness proof of Alg. 1 that is largely based on the previous Lemmas. Let us denote by S_1 and S_2 respectively, the solution before and after applying Alg. 1. Observe that by construction all the edge gadgets in the solution S_2 computed by Alg. 1 are clustered in a *type b* solution.

Iteratively, Alg. 1 first examines a sequence $C_1, \cdots, C_l$ of clusters of S_1 containing some unmarked edge gadgets. Given a cluster C examined at step i, the

---

Algorithm 1. ComputeCanonical(S)

    Data: a solution S_1 consisting of the set $\{C_1, \cdots, C_k\}$ of clusters
1 **foreach** *set C_i* **do**
2   Let $E(C_i)$ be the set of edge gadgets in C_i;
3   unmark all edge gadgets in $E(C_i)$;
4 Define solution $S_2 = \emptyset$;
5 **while** *there is a cluster C in $\{C_1, \cdots, C_k\}$ with an unmarked edge gadget* **do**
6   Let $V(C)$ be the smallest possible set of vertex gadgets such that each
        unmarked edge gadget in C has at least one endpoint in $V(C)$;
        `/* |C| ≤ 5, hence we can compute V(C) in polynomial time. We`
        `assume that if a cluster C contains only an edge gadget EGi,j`
        `and rows of vertex gadget VGi, then V(C) = {VGi} .          */`
7   Add to solution S_2 a *type b* solution for all vertex gadgets in $V(C)$ and all
        unmarked edge gadgets E' incident on such vertices;
        `// E' ⊇ Eu(C), with Eu(C) the set of unmarked edge gadgets of`
        `E(C)`
8   Mark the edge gadgets in E';
9 Add to S_2 a *type a* solution for each vertex gadget that has not been assigned a
   type b solution in the iteration (line $6 - 10$);
10 **return** S_2

---

algorithm imposes a *type b* solution on a set $V(C)$ (built at line 7 of Alg. 1) of
vertex gadgets and on a set E' of edge gadgets so that $E^u(C) \subseteq E'$ (see line 7
of Alg. 1) that have not been previously *marked* as assigned to a *type b* solution.
This fact implies that the virtual cost of rows associated with vertex gadgets in
$V(C)$ (actually, only with the core vertex gadgets in $V(C)$) and edge gadgets in
E' is modified in solution S_2 w.r.t. the virtual cost in solution S_1. Notice that
by Lemma 9, each edge gadget EG_{ij} in $E' - E^u(C_i)$, has virtual cost of at least
12 in solution S_1, and virtual cost 12 in solution S_2. Hence the virtual cost of
each EG_{ij} in $E' - E^u(C_i)$ is optimal in S_2. Now, we consider the rows associated
with core vertex gadgets in $V(C)$ and edge gadgets in $E^u(C)$. For simplicity's
sake, let us denote by $virt_S(V(C))$ the sum of the virtual cost of the set of rows
associated with core vertex gadgets in $V(C)$ in a solution S and similarly, let us
denote by $virt_S(E^u(C))$ the sum of the virtual cost of the set of rows associated
with unmarked edge gadgets in $E^u(C)$.

    Observe that, by construction, $E^u(C_1), \ldots, E^u(C_k)$ produced at lines $5 - 8$
of Alg. 1 are pairwise disjoint. Moreover, notice that for a row r added at line
9 of Alg. 1, $virt_{S_2}(r) \leq virt_{S_1}(r)$, since a *type a* solution is always optimal for
a vertex gadgets, while only the rows clustered in a *type b* solution of S_2 can
be suboptimal. Consequently, it is immediate to conclude that the correctness
of the Alg. 1 relies on proving that at an arbitrary step i the following Claim
holds. Moreover, let us recall that the cost of a solution is the sum of the virtual
cost of rows in the solution.

Claim 11. *Let C_i be a cluster of solution S_1, then $virt_{S_2}(V(C_i)) - virt_{S_1}(V(C_i))$
$\leq virt_{S_1}(E^u(C_i)) - virt_{S_2}(E^u(C_i))$.*

(*Sketch of the proof*). Recall that we can assume that $|C_i| \leq 5$. First, notice that, by Proposition 1, $virt_{S_2}(V(C_i)) - virt_{S_1}(V(C_i)) \leq 18|V(C_i)|$ and that the cost of each edge gadget in a canonical solution is equal to 12.

We distinguish several cases depending on the size of $E^u(C_i)$ and the size of the set $V(C_i)$ defined at line 6 of Alg. 1.

First, we have to consider the case when $E^u(C_i) > 1$. This case is considered in Lemma 6, where lower bounds on the virtual costs of the edge gadgets of $E^u(C_i)$ in S_1 are presented. Similarly, the case when $E^u(C_i) = 1$, is considered in Lemma 7 and in Lemma 8.   □

Theorem 12. *Let $\mathcal{G} = (V, E)$ be an instance of MVCC. Then $\mathcal{G}$ has a cover of size p if and only if the corresponding instance R of 3-ABP has a (canonical) solution S of cost $99p + 81(n - p) + 12m$.*

Proof. Let us show that if $\mathcal{G}$ has a vertex cover V' of size p, then R has a solution S of cost $99p + 81(n - p) + 12m$. Since V' is a vertex cover then it is possible to construct a canonical solution S for R consisting of a *type b* solution for all vertex gadgets associated with vertices in V' and a *type a* solution for all other vertex gadgets. Indeed each edge gadget can be clustered in a *type b* solution of a vertex gadget to which the edge is incident, choosing arbitrarily whenever there is more than one possibility. Finally, for each docking vertex, its jolly rows that are not used in some *type b* solution are clustered together. The cost derives immediately by previous observations.

Let us consider now a solution S of 3-ABP over instance R with cost $99p + 81(n - p) + 12m$. By Lemma 10 we can assume that S is canonical solution, therefore R has a set C' of p vertex gadgets that are associated with a *type b* solution. By construction, each edge gadget must be in a *type b* solution, for otherwise S is a not canonical solution. Hence the set of vertices of $\mathcal{G}$ associated with vertex gadgets in C' is a vertex cover of $\mathcal{G}$ of size p.   □

Since the cost of a canonical solution of 3-ABP and the size of a vertex cover of the graph $\mathcal{G}$ are linearly related, it follows that the reduction is an L-reduction, thus completing the proof of APX-hardness.

4   APX-Hardness of 4-AP(8)

In this section we prove that 4-AP(8) is APX-hard via an L-reduction from Minimum Vertex Cover on Cubic Graphs (MVCC). Given a cubic graph $\mathcal{G} = (V, E)$, with $V = \{v_1, \ldots, v_n\}$ and $E = \{e_1, \ldots, e_m\}$, we will construct an instance R of 4-AP(8) consisting of a set R_i of 5 rows for each vertex $v_i \in V$, an *edge row* $r(i, j)$ for each edge $e = (v_i, v_j) \in E$ and a set F of 4 rows. The 8 columns are divided in 4 blocks of two columns each. For each vertex v_i, all the rows in R_i have associated a block called edge block, denoted as $b(R_i)$, so that $b(R_i) \neq b(R_j)$ for each v_j adjacent to v_i in $\mathcal{G}$. The latter property can be easily enforced in polynomial time as the graph is cubic.

The entires of the rows in $R_i = \{r_{i,1}, \ldots, r_{i,5}\}$, are over the alphabet $\Sigma(R_i) = \{a_{i,1}, \ldots, a_{i,5}, a_i\}$. The entries of the columns corresponding to the edge block

$b(R_i)$, as well as to the odd columns are set to a_i for all the rows in R_i. The entries of the even columns not in $b(R_i)$ of each row $r_{i,h}$ are set to $a_{i,h}$.

For each edge $e = (v_i, v_j)$, we define a row $r(i, j)$ (called *edge row*) of R. Row $r(i, j)$ has value a_i (equal to the values of the rows in R_i) in the two columns corresponding to the edge block $b(R_i)$, value a_j (equal to the values of the rows in R_j) in the two columns corresponding to the edge block $b(R_j)$, and value $t_{i,j}$ in all other columns. Given a set of rows R_i, we denote by $E(R_i)$ the set of rows $r(i, j)$, $r(i, l)$, $r(i, h)$, associated with edges of $\mathcal{G}$ incident in v_i. Finally, we introduce in the instance R of 4-AP(8) a set of 4 rows $F = \{f_1, f_2, f_3, f_4\}$, over alphabet $\Sigma(F) = \{u_1 \ldots, u_4\}$. Each row f_i is called a *free row* and all its entries have value u_i.

W.l.o.g. we can assume that there exists only one cluster F_c, called the *filler cluster*, whose cost is equal to $8|F_c|$. The free rows must belong to F_c, as each free row has Hamming distance 8 with all other rows of R; at the same time if there exists two clusters F_c, F'_c exist, whose cost is equal to $8|F_c|$ and $8|F'_c|$ respectively, then we can merge them without increasing the cost of the solution. Notice that, by construction, $\Sigma(R_i) \cap \Sigma(R_j) = \emptyset$, hence two rows have Hamming distance smaller than 8 only if they both belong to $R_i \cup E(R_i)$ for some i. This observation immediately imply the following proposition.

Proposition 13. *Let S be a solution of 4-AP(8), and let C be a cluster of S, where each row in C has cost strictly less than 8. Then $C \subseteq R_i \cup E(R_i)$.*

Since in $R_i \cup E(R_i)$ there are 8 rows, there can be at most two sets having rows in $R_i \cup E(R_i)$ and satisfying the statement of Proposition 13. Consider a solution S and a set of rows R_i. We will say that S is a *black* solution for R_i if in S there is a cluster containing 4 rows of R_i and a cluster containing one row of R_i and the three rows of $E(R_i)$. We will say that S is a *red* solution for R_i if in S there is a cluster consisting of all 5 elements of R_i. By an abuse of language we will say respectively that R_i is black (resp. red) in S. Given an instance R of 4-AP(8), a solution where each set R_i is either black or red is called a *normal solution*. Notice that a normal solution consists of a filler cluster and a red or black solution for each R_i. The main technical step in our reduction consists of proving Lemma 17, that is that starting from a solution S, it is possible to compute in polynomial time a normal solution S' with cost not larger than that of S.

Next we show that moving the rows of R_i that are in the filler cluster to another existing cluster that contains some rows of R_i (if possible) or to a new cluster, does not increase the cost of the solution.

Lemma 14. *In each feasible solution S of 4-AP(8), at least three even positions not in the edge block are deleted from a row of R_i.*

Lemma 15. *Let S be a solution of 4-AP(8). Then we can compute in polynomial time a solution S' with cost not larger than that of S and such that in S' there exist at most two sets containing rows of R_i.*

Hence, in what follows we assume that in any solution there are at most two sets containing rows of a set R_i.

Lemma 16. *Let S be a solution S of 4-AP(8). Then it is possible to compute in polynomial time a solution S', whose cost is not larger than that of S, such that the filler cluster F_c of S' contains all free rows and some (possibly zero) edge rows. Moreover in S' there are at most two clusters containing rows of R_i.*

Now we are ready to prove Lemma 17.

Lemma 17. *Let S be a solution S of 4-AP(8). Then it is possible to compute in polynomial time a normal solution S' with cost not larger than that of S.*

Proof. Consider a generic set of rows R_i. By Lemma 16 all rows of R_i are not in the filler cluster. This fact implies that, if R_i is neither red or black in S, the rows of R_i can be partitioned in S in the following two ways: (i) a cluster C_1 contains three rows of R_i and a row of $E(R_i)$, while C_2 contains two rows of R_i and two rows of $E(R_i)$, or (ii) a cluster C of S contains all rows of R_i and some rows of $E(R_i)$.

In the first case, replace C_1 and C_2 with two clusters C'_1, C'_2 where C'_1 consists of 4 rows of R_i and C'_2 consists of a row of R_i and all rows of $E(R_i)$ (it is immediate to notice that C'_1, C'_2 have cost 12 and 24 respectively, while C_1 and C_2 have both cost 24). In the second case move all rows in $C \cap E(R_i)$ to the filler cluster. Let x be $|C \cap E(R_i)|$, then the cost of C in S is $6 \cdot (5 + x)$, while the cost of those rows in the new solution is equal to $3 \cdot 5 + 8 \cdot x$. Since $x \leq 3$, the cost of the new solution is strictly smaller than that of S. □

Notice that, given a normal solution S, each set R_i red in S has a cost of 15, each set R_i black in S has a cost of 36 (distribuited as a cost of 12 to the rows of R_i and a cost of 24 to the 3 edge rows in the black solution of R_i), and the filler cluster F_c has cost $8|F_c|$. Now, it is easy to see that Lemma 18 holds.

Lemma 18. *Let S be a normal solution with k red sets R_i. Then S has cost $12(|V| - k) + 15k + 8|E| + 32$.*

Now, we can show that the sets of rows R_i that are red in a normal solution S corresponds to a cover of the graph $\mathcal{G}$.

Lemma 19. *Let S be a normal solution of 4-AP(8) of cost $12(|V| - k) + 15k + 8|E| + 32$. Then it can be computed in polynomial time a vertex cover of $\mathcal{G}$ of size k.*

Proof. Since S is a normal solution of 4-AP(8) of cost $12(|V| - k) + 15k + 8|E|$, then all the sets R_i must be associated with either a red or a black solution. Furthermore, since all the edge rows have a cost of 8 in S, then, it follows that there must exist k sets R_i associated with a red solution, and $|V| - k$ associated with a black solution.

Notice that, given two black sets R_i and R_j, there cannot be an edge between two vertices v_i and v_j of $\mathcal{G}$ associated with R_i and R_j, by definition of black solution. Hence, vertices associated with black sets of S form an independent set of $\mathcal{G}$, which in turn implies that the vertices associated with red sets are a vertex cover of $\mathcal{G}$. □

Theorem 20. *The 4-AP(8) problem is APX-hard.*

Proof. Let C be a vertex cover of graph $\mathcal{G}$. Then, it is easy to see that a normal solution of cost at most $12|V| + 3|C| + 8|E| + 32$ can be computed in polynomial time by defining a black solution for each set R_i associated with a vertex $v_i \in V \setminus C$, a red solution for each set R_i associated with a vertex $v_i \in C$, and assigning all the remaining rows to the filler cluster F_c.

On the other side, by Lemma 19, starting from a normal solution of 4-AP(8) having size $12(|V| - k) + 15k + 8|E| + 32$, we can compute in polynomial time a cover of size k for $\mathcal{G}$.

Since the cost of a canonical solution of 4-AP(8) and the size of a vertex cover of the graph $\mathcal{G}$ are linearly related, the reduction is an L-reduction, thus completing the proof of APX-hardness. □

References

1. Aggarwal, G., Feder, T., Kenthapadi, K., Motwani, R., Panigrahy, R., Thomas, D., Zhu, A.: Anonymizing Tables. In: Eiter, T., Libkin, L. (eds.) ICDT 2005. LNCS, vol. 3363, pp. 246–258. Springer, Heidelberg (2004)
2. Alimonti, P., Kann, V.: Some APX-Completeness Results for Cubic Graphs. Theoretical Computer Science 237(1-2), 123–134 (2000)
3. Ausiello, G., Crescenzi, P., Gambosi, G., Kann, V., Marchetti-Spaccamela, A., Protasi, M.: Complexity and Approximation: Combinatorial Optimization Problems and Their Approximability Properties. Springer, Heidelberg (1999)
4. Gionis, A., Tassa, T.: k-Anonymization with Minimal Loss of Information. IEEE Trans. Knowl. Data Eng. 21(2), 206–219 (2009)
5. Park, H., Shim, K.: Approximate algorithms for k-Anonymity. In: Chan, C.Y., Ooi, B.C., Zhou, A. (eds.) ACM SIGMOD International Conference on Management of Data, pp. 67–78. ACM Press, New York (2007)
6. Samarati, P.: Protecting Respondents' Identities in Microdata Release. IEEE Trans. Knowl. Data Eng. 13(6), 1010–1027 (2001)
7. Samarati, P., Sweeney, L.: Generalizing Data to Provide Anonymity When Disclosing Information (Abstract). In: Seventeenth ACM SIGACT-SIGMOD-SIGART Symposium on Principles of Database Systems, p. 188. ACM Press, New York (1998)
8. Sweeney, L.: k-Anonymity: a Model for Protecting Privacy. International Journal on Uncertainty, Fuzziness and Knowledge-based Systems 10(5), 557–570 (2002)

Independence Results for
n-Ary Recursion Theorems[*]

John Case and Samuel E. Moelius III

Department of Computer & Information Sciences,
University of Delaware,
101 Smith Hall,
Newark, DE 19716
{case,moelius}@cis.udel.edu

Abstract. The *n-ary first* and *second recursion theorems* formalize two distinct, yet similar, notions of *self-reference*. Roughly, the n-ary first recursion theorem says that, for any n algorithmic tasks (of an appropriate type), there exist n *partial computable functions* that use their own *graphs* in the manner prescribed by those tasks; the n-ary second recursion theorem says that, for any n algorithmic tasks (of an appropriate type), there exist n *programs* that use their own *source code* in the manner prescribed by those tasks.

Results include the following. The constructive 1-ary form of the first recursion theorem is *independent* of either 1-ary form of the second recursion theorem. The constructive 1-ary form of the first recursion theorem does *not* imply the constructive 2-ary form; *however*, the constructive 2-ary form *does* imply the constructive n-ary form, for each $n \geq 1$. For each $n \geq 1$, the *not-necessarily-constructive* n-ary form of the second recursion theorem does *not* imply the presence of the $(n + 1)$-ary form.

1 Introduction

The *n-ary first* and *second recursion theorems* [1, Ch. 11][1] formalize two distinct, yet similar, notions of *self-reference*. (Henceforth, we shall refer to these simply as the *first* and *second recursion theorems*.) In a sense, the first recursion theorem asserts the existence of *partial computable functions* that refer to their own *graphs*; the second recursion theorem asserts the existence of *programs* that refer to their own *source code*. Formally, each theorem asserts the existence of solutions to systems of a certain type of equation. We discuss each theorem in detail in the sections that follow.

---

[*] This paper received some support from NSF Grant CCR-0208616.
[1] In [1], what is called the second recursion theorem in Chapter 11 proper (i.e., Theorem IV) is a *strictly weaker* pseudo-fixpoint variant of Kleene's original formulation [2, Theorems 5.1 and 5.3]. The correct formulation can be found in [1, page 214, problem 11-4] and in Section 1.3 herein.

M. Kutyłowski, M. Gębala, and W. Charatonik (Eds.): FCT 2009, LNCS 5699, pp. 38–49, 2009.

(a)
```
let rec fib0 = function 0 -> 0 | x -> fib1(x-1)
    and fib1 = function 0 -> 1 | x -> fib0(x-1) + fib1(x-1)
```

(b)
$$\Theta_0(\alpha_0, \alpha_1)(x) = \begin{cases} 0, & \text{if } x = 0; \\ \alpha_1(x-1), & \text{otherwise.} \end{cases}$$

$$\Theta_1(\alpha_0, \alpha_1)(x) = \begin{cases} 1, & \text{if } x = 0; \\ \alpha_0(x-1) + \alpha_1(x-1), & \text{otherwise.} \end{cases}$$

Fig. 1. (a) A system of recursive equations in Ocaml. The functions assigned to `fib0` and `fib1` are the minimal fixpoint of (Θ_0, Θ_1), where the computable operators $\Theta_0, \Theta_1 : \mathcal{P}^2 \to \mathcal{P}$ are as in (b).

1.1 The First Recursion Theorem

Many programming languages allow one to define functions using *recursive equations*, or systems thereof. Each programming language has its own syntactic nuances; however, a system of n such equations typically has the following form. The left-hand-side of each equation contains one of n function variables; the right-hand-side of each equation contains an expression involving some subset of those n variables. For the programming language Ocaml [3], an example is given in Figure 1(a).

The functions *defined* by such a system of equations constitute *some* solution of that system. Depending upon the semantics of the programming language, however, there may exist systems of equations for which there are *no* solutions, and there may exist systems of equations for which there are *multiple* solutions.

The first recursion theorem asserts that, for a very natural class of equations, there will always exist a solution to a system of equations drawn from that class; in fact, there will exist a solution that is, in some sense, *simplest* among all possible solutions. The first recursion theorem applies to those systems of equations that can be expressed using *computable operators*; the *simplest* solutions of such systems are called *minimal fixpoints*. We discuss each of these topics below.

Let $\mathbb{N}$ be the set of natural numbers, $\{0, 1, 2, ...\}$. Let lowercase Roman letters, with or without decorations (e.g., a, b_0, c'), range over elements of $\mathbb{N}$, unless stated otherwise. Let $\mathcal{P}$ be the set of all partial functions mapping $\mathbb{N}$ to $\mathbb{N}$. Let lowercase Greek letters, with or without decorations (e.g., α, β_0, γ'), range over elements of $\mathcal{P}$, unless stated otherwise. Let $(F_i)_{i \in \mathbb{N}}$ be any canonical enumeration of the finite functions [1,4]. For each n, each $\alpha_0, ..., \alpha_{n-1}$, and each $\beta_0, ..., \beta_{n-1}$, $(\alpha_0, ..., \alpha_{n-1}) \subseteq (\beta_0, ..., \beta_{n-1}) \stackrel{\text{def}}{\iff} [\alpha_0 \subseteq \beta_0 \wedge \cdots \wedge \alpha_{n-1} \subseteq \beta_{n-1}]$.

Intuitively, a *computable operator* is a mapping $\Theta : \mathcal{P}^n \to \mathcal{P}$ ($n \geq 1$) for which there exists an algorithm for listing the graph of the partial function $\Theta(\alpha_0, ..., \alpha_{n-1})$ from listings of the graphs of the partial functions $\alpha_0, ..., \alpha_{n-1}$; moreover, the content of the resulting graph does *not* depend upon the enumeration order chosen for each of $\alpha_0, ..., \alpha_{n-1}$ [1, §9.8].[2] Uppercase Greek letters,

---

[2] Rogers [1] calls the computable operators, *recursive operators*.

with or without decorations (e.g., Θ, Ψ_0, Ω'), range over computable operators, unless stated otherwise.

Computable operators have the following *monotonicity* and *continuity* properties [1, page 147]. For each n, and each $\Theta : \mathcal{P}^n \to \mathcal{P}$, (a) and (b) below.

(a) *Monotonicity*: For each $\alpha_0, ..., \alpha_{n-1}$ and $\beta_0, ..., \beta_{n-1}$, if $(\alpha_0, ..., \alpha_{n-1}) \subseteq (\beta_0, ..., \beta_{n-1})$, then $\Theta(\alpha_0, ..., \alpha_{n-1}) \subseteq \Theta(\beta_0, ..., \beta_{n-1})$.
(b) *Continuity*: For each $\alpha_0, ..., \alpha_{n-1}$, and each $(x, y) \in \Theta(\alpha_0, ..., \alpha_{n-1})$, there exist $i_0, ..., i_{n-1}$ such that $(F_{i_0}, ..., F_{i_{n-1}}) \subseteq (\alpha_0, ..., \alpha_{n-1})$ and $(x, y) \in \Theta(F_{i_0}, ..., F_{i_{n-1}})$.

For each n, each $\alpha_0, ..., \alpha_{n-1}$, and each $\Theta_0, ..., \Theta_{n-1} : \mathcal{P}^n \to \mathcal{P}$, $(\alpha_0, ..., \alpha_{n-1})$ is a *fixpoint* of $(\Theta_0, ..., \Theta_{n-1}) \overset{\text{def}}{\Leftrightarrow}$

$$
\begin{aligned}
\alpha_0 &= \Theta_0(\alpha_0, ..., \alpha_{n-1}); \\
&\vdots \\
\alpha_{n-1} &= \Theta_{n-1}(\alpha_0, ..., \alpha_{n-1}).
\end{aligned}
\tag{1}
$$

Intuitively, an $\alpha_0, ..., \alpha_{n-1}$ as in (1) can be thought of as a collection of functions that *refer to themselves*. What each α_i *does* with the information obtained from this self/other-reference is determined by Θ_i.

For each n, each $\alpha_0, ..., \alpha_{n-1}$, and each $\Theta_0, ..., \Theta_{n-1} : \mathcal{P}^n \to \mathcal{P}$, $(\alpha_0, ..., \alpha_{n-1})$ is the *minimal* fixpoint of $(\Theta_0, ..., \Theta_{n-1}) \overset{\text{def}}{\Leftrightarrow}$ (a) and (b) below.[3]

(a) $(\alpha_0, ..., \alpha_{n-1})$ is a fixpoint of $(\Theta_0, ..., \Theta_{n-1})$.
(b) For each $\beta_0, ..., \beta_{n-1}$, if $(\beta_0, ..., \beta_{n-1})$ is a fixpoint of $(\Theta_0, ..., \Theta_{n-1})$, then $(\alpha_0, ..., \alpha_{n-1}) \subseteq (\beta_0, ..., \beta_{n-1})$.

Condition (b) gives the sense in which a minimal fixpoint represents the *simplest* possible solution to a system of recursive equations: any other solution is *more complicated* in that there are *more pairs* in the graphs of its functions.

For each n, the n-ary form of the first recursion theorem says that, for each $\Theta_0, ..., \Theta_{n-1} : \mathcal{P}^n \to \mathcal{P}$, $(\Theta_0, ..., \Theta_{n-1})$ *has* a minimal fixpoint $(\alpha_0, ..., \alpha_{n-1})$, and, moreover, each of $\alpha_0, ..., \alpha_{n-1}$ is partial computable. Thus, if a system of equations can be written in the form of (1), for some $\Theta_0, ..., \Theta_{n-1}$, then that system has a simplest possible solution, namely, the minimal fixpoint of $(\Theta_0, ..., \Theta_{n-1})$. The example given in Figure 1(a) can be written in this way, using the computable operators Θ_0 and Θ_1 of Figure 1(b).

For obvious reasons, the first recursion theorem is also called the *minimal fixpoint theorem*.

1.2   The First Recursion Theorem in Programming Systems

From a programming languages standpoint, one should care, not only that a minimal fixpoint solution exists for any given system of equations, but also that

---

[3] It is straightforward to show that such a fixpoint must be *unique*; hence, we are justified in calling it *the* minimal fixpoint.

there exist *programs witnessing* that minimal fixpoint. This idea is formalized
in the following paragraphs.

Let $\mathcal{PC}$ be the set of all partial *computable* functions mapping $\mathbb{N}$ to $\mathbb{N}$. An
effective programming system (eps) [1,4] is an onto numbering $(\psi_q)_{q\in\mathbb{N}}$ of $\mathcal{PC}$
such that $\lambda q, x.\psi_q(x)$ is partial computable. An eps may be thought of as an
abstraction of the notion of *programming language*, in the following sense. If one
were to take the programs in some programming language for $\mathcal{PC}$, and number
those programs, e.g., length-lexicographically, then the function which sends q
to the semantics of the qth program would be an eps.

For each $n \geq 1$, we say that the *not-necessarily-constructive n-ary form of the
minimal fixpoint theorem* (n-mfp) *holds in* eps $(\psi_q)_{q\in\mathbb{N}}$ $\overset{\text{def}}{\Leftrightarrow}$ for each $\Theta_0, ..., \Theta_{n-1}$:
$\mathcal{P}^n \to \mathcal{P}$, there exist $e_0, ..., e_{n-1}$ such that

$$(\psi_{e_0}, ..., \psi_{e_{n-1}}) \text{ is the minimal fixpoint of } (\Theta_0, ..., \Theta_{n-1}). \tag{2}$$

Thus, $e_0, ..., e_{n-1}$ *witness* the minimal fixpoint of $(\Theta_0, ..., \Theta_{n-1})$ in $(\psi_q)_{q\in\mathbb{N}}$.

Intuitively, $e_0, ..., e_{n-1}$ is a collection of *programs* that have *limited* knowledge
of one another. More specifically, each e_i can refer to *only* the *extensional* (synonym: *denotational*) characteristics of $e_0, ..., e_{n-1}$, i.e., their I/O behavior [5].

As it turns out, n-mfp is ubiquitous.

Proposition 1. For each $n \geq 1$, and each eps $(\psi_q)_{q\in\mathbb{N}}$, n-mfp holds in $(\psi_q)_{q\in\mathbb{N}}$.

Proof of Proposition. Let n and $(\psi_q)_{q\in\mathbb{N}}$ be as stated. Let $\Theta_0, ..., \Theta_{n-1} : \mathcal{P}^n \to \mathcal{P}$
be fixed. By the first recursion theorem, $(\Theta_0, ..., \Theta_{n-1})$ has a minimal fixpoint
$(\alpha_0, ..., \alpha_{n-1})$, and each of $\alpha_0, ..., \alpha_{n-1}$ is partial computable. Thus, since $(\psi_q)_{q\in\mathbb{N}}$
is an *onto* map of $\mathcal{PC}$, there exist $e_0, ..., e_{n-1}$ such that $\psi_{e_0} = \alpha_0 \wedge \cdots \wedge \psi_{e_{n-1}} = \alpha_{n-1}$. $\square$ (**Proposition 1**)

One problem with n-mfp is that it lacks *constructivity*. That is, n-mfp merely
requires that the witnessing programs, $e_0, ..., e_{n-1}$, *exist*. However, it would
seem reasonable to expect that one could *construct* $e_0, ..., e_{n-1}$ from (codes for)
$\Theta_0, ..., \Theta_{n-1}$.

For each n, let a numbering $(\Omega_j)_{j\in\mathbb{N}}$ of the computable operators of type
$\mathcal{P}^n \to \mathcal{P}$ be *effective* $\overset{\text{def}}{\Leftrightarrow}$ the predicate $\lambda i, j, i_0, ..., i_{n-1}.[F_i \subseteq \Omega_j(F_{i_0}, ..., F_{i_{n-1}})]$ is
partial computable.[4] Let $\langle \cdot, \cdot \rangle$ be any fixed pairing function.[5] For each x, $\langle x \rangle \overset{\text{def}}{=} x$,
and, for each $x_0, ..., x_{n-1}$, where $n > 2$, $\langle x_0, ..., x_{n-1} \rangle \overset{\text{def}}{=} \langle x_0, \langle x_1, ..., x_{n-1} \rangle \rangle$.

For each $n \geq 1$, we say that the *constructive n-ary form of the minimal fix-
point theorem* (n-MFP) *holds in* eps $(\psi_q)_{q\in\mathbb{N}}$ $\overset{\text{def}}{\Leftrightarrow}$ there exist computable functions
$\mu_0, ..., \mu_{n-1} : \mathbb{N}^n \to \mathbb{N}$, and an effective numbering $(\Omega_j)_{j\in\mathbb{N}}$ of the computable
operators of type $\mathcal{P}^n \to \mathcal{P}$ such that, for each $\jmath = (j_0, ..., j_{n-1})$, (2) holds with
$e_i = \mu_i(\jmath)$ and $\Theta_i = \Omega_{j_i}$, for each $i < n$, i.e.,

$$(\psi_{\mu_0(\jmath)}, ..., \psi_{\mu_{n-1}(\jmath)}) \text{ is the minimal fixpoint of } (\Omega_{j_0}, ..., \Omega_{j_{n-1}}). \tag{3}$$

---

[4] Rogers' proof of the fundamental operator theorem [1, Theorem 9-XXIII] shows that
such numberings exist.

[5] A *pairing function* is computable, 1-1, onto, and of type $\mathbb{N}^2 \to \mathbb{N}$ [1, page 64].

(Note that capital letters are used to distinguish the constructive forms of the first recursion theorem, e.g., n-MFP, from the not-necessarily-constructive forms, e.g., n-mfp.) Intuitively, each $\jmath = (\jmath_0, ..., \jmath_{n-1})$ names a system of equations, i.e.,

$$
\begin{aligned}
\alpha_0 &= \quad \Omega_{\jmath_0}(\alpha_0, ..., \alpha_{n-1}); \\
&\vdots \\
\alpha_{n-1} &= \Omega_{\jmath_{n-1}}(\alpha_0, ..., \alpha_{n-1}).
\end{aligned}
\tag{4}
$$

The functions $\mu_0, ..., \mu_{n-1}$ find the simplest possible solution of that system, in the sense of (3).

Unlike n-mfp, there *do* exist epses in which n-MFP does *not* hold, for each $n \geq 1$. (See Theorem 10 below, for example.) This leads one to ask: what can be said of those epses in which n-MFP holds? What can be said of those epses in which n-MFP does *not* hold? We revisit these questions in Section 2.

1.3 The Second Recursion Theorem

While the first recursion theorem is about *partial computable functions* that refer to their own *graphs*, the second recursion theorem is about *programs* that refer to their own *source code*. Formally: for each $n \geq 1$, the n-ary form of the second recursion theorem (n-krt)[6] holds in eps $(\psi_q)_{q \in \mathbb{N}} \overset{\text{def}}{\Leftrightarrow}$ for each $\alpha_0, ..., \alpha_{n-1} \in \mathcal{PC}$, there exist $e_0, ..., e_{n-1}$ such that

$$
\begin{aligned}
\psi_{e_0} &= \quad \alpha_0(\langle e_0, ..., e_{n-1}, \cdot \rangle); \\
&\vdots \\
\psi_{e_{n-1}} &= \alpha_{n-1}(\langle e_0, ..., e_{n-1}, \cdot \rangle).
\end{aligned}
\tag{5}
$$

The above can be interpreted as follows. Each e_i constructs *copies* of $e_0, ..., e_{n-1}$ — including e_i, itself. Then, e_i performs its associated task, α_i, using these self/other-copies.

These self/other-copies provide e_i *complete, low-level* knowledge of $e_0, ..., e_{n-1}$. As such, e_i is able to reflect upon the *intensional* (synonym: *conno-tational*) characteristics of $e_0, ..., e_{n-1}$, e.g., their sizes, runtimes, memory usage, etc. Of course, by simulating $e_0, ..., e_{n-1}$, it is possible for e_i to reflect upon their *extensional* characteristics as well [5].

The proof of Theorem 5 in [8] (Theorem 2 below) features a nice application of 2-krt. We give some highlights of the proof below. Let $(\varphi_p)_{p \in \mathbb{N}}$ be any standard numbering of $\mathcal{PC}$.[7] For each $p \in \mathbb{N}$, let W_p be the domain of φ_p. Thus, $(W_p)_{p \in \mathbb{N}}$ is a (standard) numbering of the computably enumerable (ce) sets [1].

---

[6] The 'k' in n-krt is for "Kleene". The 1-ary forms of the two recursion theorems are due to him. The generalized n-ary first recursion theorem is due to Manna, *et al.* [6, pages 30 and 31]. The 2-ary form of the second recursion theorem follows essentially from Smullyan's [7, page 75, Theorem 5]. The generalized n-ary second recursion theorem appears to be a folk theorem.

[7] Any standard numbering is *acceptable*. As such, n-krt holds in such a numbering, for each $n \geq 1$. (See the discussion surrounding Theorem 5 below.)

Theorem 2 (Case [8, Theorem 5]). There is *no* algorithm to extend a computable partial order to ce total order, in the following sense. There is *no* computable function $f : \mathbb{N} \to \mathbb{N}$ such that, for each x and y, if

- φ_x is a characteristic function for a finite set A,[8]
- φ_y is a characteristic function for a set $R \subseteq A \times A$, *and*
- the transitive closure of R is a partial order on A,

then $W_{f(x,y)}$ is a *total* order on A which includes the transitive closure of R.[9]

The proof of Theorem 2 begins by supposing that such an f exists. Two programs, e_0 and e_1, are then obtained via an application of 2-krt. Intuitively, e_0 plays the role of x in Theorem 2, while e_1 plays the role of y. Each program: (1) constructs copies of both *itself* and the *other*, (2) computes $f(e_0, e_1)$ using these self/other-copies, and then (3) begins listing $W_{f(e_0,e_1)}$. By reacting to the pairs so listed, e_0 and e_1 are able to cause f to *fail* to meet its specification, thereby obtaining a contradiction.

Another interesting application of 2-krt appears in the proof of [10, Theorem 3].

Like n-mfp (Section 1.2), there is no constructivity in the definition of n-krt. Unlike n-mfp, however, there *do* exist epses in which n-krt does *not* hold, for each $n \geq 1$.[10]

Nearly every mainstream programming language supports recursive equations of the form of (1). In this sense, the first recursion theorem is explicitly *built-in* to such programming languages. No mainstream programming language seems to have the *second* recursion theorem so *explicitly* built-in, however. We recommend that such programming languages *be* developed since they would have applications, e.g., for self-modeling in artificial intelligence, as suggested by [14,15,16,17].[11]

1.4 *Constructive* Forms of the Second Recursion Theorem

The second recursion theorem has constructive forms similar to those presented for the first recursion theorem in Section 1.2 (i.e., n-MFP). For each $n \geq 1$, the *n-ary form of the relatively constructive second recursion theorem* (n-RelKRT) *holds in* eps $(\psi_q)_{q \in \mathbb{N}} \overset{\text{def}}{\Leftrightarrow}$ there exist computable functions $r_0, ..., r_{n-1} : \mathbb{N}^n \to \mathbb{N}$, and an eps $(\xi_p)_{p \in \mathbb{N}}$ such that, for each $\boldsymbol{p} = (p_0, ..., p_{n-1})$, (5) holds with $e_i = r_i(\boldsymbol{p})$ and $\alpha_i = \xi_{p_i}$, for each $i < n$, i.e.,

---

[8] A *characteristic function for a set A* is a (total) function $g : \mathbb{N} \to \{0, 1\}$ such that $(\forall x)[g(x) = 1 \Leftrightarrow x \in A]$.

[9] The action of f in Theorem 2 can be seen as a form of *topological sort* [9].

[10] This follows from Riccardi's [2, Theorem 3.9] (also [11, Theorem 2.9]) and the existence of Friedberg numberings [12,13], for example.

[11] We would also like to understand *mathematically* the usefulness and possible profundity of perfect n-ary self/other-modeling and self/other-knowledge; hence, a future project is to *insightfully* characterize, for each $n \geq 1$, the epses in which n-krt holds.

$$\psi_{r_0(\boldsymbol{p})} = \quad \xi_{p_0}\big(\langle r_0(\boldsymbol{p}), ..., r_{n-1}(\boldsymbol{p}), \cdot\rangle\big);$$
$$\vdots \tag{6}$$
$$\psi_{r_{n-1}(\boldsymbol{p})} = \xi_{p_{n-1}}\big(\langle r_0(\boldsymbol{p}), ..., r_{n-1}(\boldsymbol{p}), \cdot\rangle\big).$$

In (6), $(\psi_q)_{q\in\mathbb{N}}$ is an eps for representing *self-referential programs* (e.g., $r_0(\boldsymbol{p})$, ..., $r_{n-1}(\boldsymbol{p})$), while $(\xi_p)_{p\in\mathbb{N}}$ is an eps for representing programs for *tasks* (e.g., $p_0, ..., p_{n-1}$).

The 1-ary form of RelKRT was introduced in [18]. Therein, it was shown that 1-krt and 1-RelKRT are *equivalent*, in the following sense.

Theorem 3 (Case, Moelius [18, Theorem 2]). For each eps $(\psi_q)_{q\in\mathbb{N}}$, 1-krt holds in $(\psi_q)_{q\in\mathbb{N}} \Leftrightarrow$ 1-RelKRT holds in $(\psi_q)_{q\in\mathbb{N}}$.

Thus, for any eps containing self-referential programs, there exists *some* effective numbering of all algorithmic tasks from which those self-referential programs can be found constructively.

A special case of RelKRT that has been considered frequently in the literature (e.g., in [2,11,5]) is the following. For each $n \geq 1$, the *constructive n-ary form of the second recursion theorem* (*n*-KRT) *holds in* eps $(\psi_q)_{q\in\mathbb{N}} \overset{\text{def}}{\Leftrightarrow}$ there exist computable functions $r_0, ..., r_{n-1} : \mathbb{N}^n \to \mathbb{N}$ such that, for each $\boldsymbol{q} = (q_0, ..., q_{n-1})$, (6) holds with $(\psi_q)_{q\in\mathbb{N}} = (\xi_p)_{p\in\mathbb{N}}$, i.e.,

$$\psi_{r_0(\boldsymbol{q})} = \quad \psi_{q_0}\big(\langle r_0(\boldsymbol{q}), ..., r_{n-1}(\boldsymbol{q}), \cdot\rangle\big);$$
$$\vdots \tag{7}$$
$$\psi_{r_{n-1}(\boldsymbol{q})} = \psi_{q_{n-1}}\big(\langle r_0(\boldsymbol{q}), ..., r_{n-1}(\boldsymbol{q}), \cdot\rangle\big).$$

KRT is a special case of RelKRT in that the eps for representing self-referential programs (i.e., $(\psi_q)_{q\in\mathbb{N}}$), and the eps for representing programs for tasks (i.e., $(\xi_p)_{p\in\mathbb{N}}$), are the same.

In his thesis, Riccardi showed the following.

Theorem 4 (Riccardi [2, Theorem 3.15], [11, Theorem 2.13]). There exists an eps $(\psi_q)_{q\in\mathbb{N}}$ such that $(\forall n \geq 1)[n\text{-krt holds in } (\psi_q)_{q\in\mathbb{N}}]$, but 1-KRT does *not* hold in $(\psi_q)_{q\in\mathbb{N}}$.

In addition to the above, Riccardi's thesis featured another remarkable result. An eps $(\psi_q)_{q\in\mathbb{N}}$ is *acceptable* $\overset{\text{def}}{\Leftrightarrow}$ every other eps can be compiled into $(\psi_q)_{q\in\mathbb{N}}$, i.e., $(\forall \text{ eps } (\xi_p)_{p\in\mathbb{N}})(\exists \text{ computable } t : \mathbb{N} \to \mathbb{N})(\forall p)[\psi_{t(p)} = \xi_p]$ [1,4,2,11,5].

Theorem 5 (Riccardi [2, Theorem 3.6], [11, Theorem 2.6]). For each eps $(\psi_q)_{q\in\mathbb{N}}$, $(\psi_q)_{q\in\mathbb{N}}$ is acceptable $\Leftrightarrow$ 2-KRT holds in $(\psi_q)_{q\in\mathbb{N}}$.

It can be shown that, if $(\psi_q)_{q\in\mathbb{N}}$ is an acceptable eps, then $(\psi_q)_{q\in\mathbb{N}}$ has the following desirable properties.

(a) $(\psi_q)_{q\in\mathbb{N}}$ has an implementation of every *control structure*.[12]
(b) For each $n \geq 1$, n-MFP holds in $(\psi_q)_{q\in\mathbb{N}}$.

---

[12] See [2,11] for an explanation of this result.

(c) For each $n \geq 1$, n-KRT holds in $(\psi_q)_{q \in \mathbb{N}}$.
(d) For each $n \geq 1$, n-RelKRT holds in $(\psi_q)_{q \in \mathbb{N}}$.[13]

These observations and Riccardi's Theorem 5 above imply the following.

Corollary 6 (of Theorem 5). For each eps $(\psi_q)_{q \in \mathbb{N}}$, 2-KRT holds in $(\psi_q)_{q \in \mathbb{N}}$ $\Leftrightarrow (\forall n \geq 1)[n$-KRT holds in $(\psi_q)_{q \in \mathbb{N}}]$.

Thus, having the ability to find just *two* self-referential programs constructively for any *two* programs for tasks implies having the ability to find n self-referential programs constructively for any n programs for tasks, *provided* that the two varieties of program reside in the same eps.

What if one were allowed to program the tasks in some *other* eps? That is, if one were to replace 2-KRT by 2-RelKRT in Theorem 5, would the result still hold? We answer this question in the *affirmative* in Section 2.

1.5 Organization

In Sections 2 and 3, we explore the relationships among the forms of the recursion theorems mentioned above. In Section 2, we focus, primarily, on the constructive forms of the two recursion theorems; in Section 3 we focus on the second recursion theorem. Due to space constraints, nearly all proofs are omitted. Complete proofs of all theorems can be found in [19].

For the remainder, we focus exclusively on effective numberings of $\mathcal{PC}$ (i.e., epses). However, it is worth mentioning that the two recursion theorems also have applications to effective numberings of subsets of the *computable* functions. See, for example, [20,21,22].

2 Constructive Forms of the Recursion Theorems

In this section, we explore the relationships among the constructive forms of the two recursion theorems (i.e., MFP, RelKRT, and KRT). Our main results of this section (summarized in Figure 2) are:

- 2-MFP entails acceptability (Theorem 7).
- 2-RelKRT entails acceptability (Theorem 9).
- 1-KRT does *not* entail 1-MFP (Theorem 10).
- 1-MFP entails *neither* 1-krt (Theorem 11) *nor* 2-MFP (Corollary 12).

Theorem 7 and its corollary are our first main results.

---

[13] In fact, (d) follows from (c).

Since acceptability yields all of the properties considered herein, we must restrict attention to *non*-acceptable epses in order to understand the interrelatedness of these properties. epses corresponding to standard, general purpose programming languages (e.g., Lisp, C++, or Ocaml) are acceptable. However, independence proofs (e.g., in set theory and herein) often require the construction of pathological models.

$$2\text{-MFP} \longrightarrow 1\text{-MFP}$$
$$\updownarrow$$
$$2\text{-KRT} \longrightarrow 1\text{-KRT} \longrightarrow 1\text{-krt}$$
$$\updownarrow \qquad\qquad \updownarrow$$
$$2\text{-RelKRT} \longrightarrow 1\text{-RelKRT}$$

Fig. 2. A summary of the main results of Section 2. Arrows indicate entailment relationships. The reflexive-transitive closure of the above diagram represents *all* of the entailment relationships that hold among the forms of the recursion theorem appearing therein.

Theorem 7. For each eps $(\psi_q)_{q\in\mathbb{N}}$, if 2-MFP holds in $(\psi_q)_{q\in\mathbb{N}}$, then $(\psi_q)_{q\in\mathbb{N}}$ is acceptable.

Corollary 8 (of Theorem 7). For each eps $(\psi_q)_{q\in\mathbb{N}}$, 2-MFP holds in $(\psi_q)_{q\in\mathbb{N}}$ $\Leftrightarrow (\forall n \geq 1)[n\text{-MFP holds in } (\psi_q)_{q\in\mathbb{N}}]$.

Thus, having the ability to find a minimal fixpoint solution constructively for *any two* recursive equations implies having the ability to find a minimal fixpoint solution constructively for *any number of* recursive equations.

Proof of Theorem 7. Let $(\psi_q)_{q\in\mathbb{N}}$ be as stated. Let $\mu_0, \mu_1 : \mathbb{N}^2 \to \mathbb{N}$ and $(\Omega_j)_{j\in\mathbb{N}}$ witness 2-MFP in $(\psi_q)_{q\in\mathbb{N}}$. Let $(\varphi_p)_{p\in\mathbb{N}}$ be any acceptable eps. Let j_0 be such that, for each α_0 and α_1,

$$\Omega_{j_0}(\alpha_0, \alpha_1) = \begin{cases} \varphi_{\alpha_1(0)}, & \text{if } \alpha_1(0) \text{ converges;} \\ \emptyset, & \text{otherwise.} \end{cases} \tag{8}$$

Let $t : \mathbb{N} \to \mathbb{N}$ be such that, for each p,

$$t(p) = \mu_0(j_0, j_1), \text{ where } j_1 \text{ is } \textit{first found} \text{ such that } \Omega_{j_1}(\emptyset, \emptyset)(0) = p. \tag{9}$$

Clearly, t is computable. To complete the proof, it then suffices to show that, for each p, $\psi_{t(p)} = \varphi_p$. Let p be fixed. Let j_1 be that which is selected in the computation of $t(p)$. Thus, $\Omega_{j_1}(\emptyset, \emptyset)(0) = p$. Let (α_0, α_1) be the minimal fixpoint of $(\Omega_{j_0}, \Omega_{j_1})$. Note that

$$\begin{aligned} (0, p) \in \Omega_{j_1}(\emptyset, \emptyset) \quad &\{\text{by the choice of } j_1\} \\ \subseteq \Omega_{j_1}(\alpha_0, \alpha_1) \quad &\{\text{by the monotonicity of } \Omega_{j_1}\} \\ = \alpha_1 \quad &\{\text{because } (\alpha_0, \alpha_1) \text{ is a fixpoint of } (\Omega_{j_0}, \Omega_{j_1})\}. \end{aligned} \tag{10}$$

Thus,

$$\begin{aligned} \psi_{t(p)} = \psi_{\mu_0(j_0, j_1)} \quad &\{\text{by (9) and the choice of } j_1\} \\ = \alpha_0 \quad &\{\text{by the choices of } \mu \text{ and } \alpha_0\} \\ = \Omega_{j_0}(\alpha_0, \alpha_1) \quad &\{\text{because } (\alpha_0, \alpha_1) \text{ is a fixpoint of } (\Omega_{j_0}, \Omega_{j_1})\} \\ = \varphi_p \quad &\{\text{by (8) and (10)}\}. \end{aligned}$$

$\square$ **(Theorem 7)**

Theorem 9 just below says that 2-RelKRT entails acceptability. Recall that Riccardi's Theorem 5 above said: having the ability to find just *two* self-referential programs constructively for any *two* programs for tasks implies having the ability to find n self-referential programs constructively for any n programs for tasks, *provided* that the two varieties of program reside in the same eps. Theorem 9 says that Riccardi's result still holds even if the two varieties of program are allowed to reside in *distinct* epses. The proof of Theorem 9 is similar to Riccardi's proof of Theorem 5 (see [2, Theorem 3.6] or [11, Theorem 2.6]).

Theorem 9. For each eps $(\psi_q)_{q \in \mathbb{N}}$, if 2-RelKRT holds in $(\psi_q)_{q \in \mathbb{N}}$, then $(\psi_q)_{q \in \mathbb{N}}$ is acceptable.

Theorem 10 just below says that 1-KRT does *not* entail 1-MFP. This result was a surprise to us. MFP provides its witnessing programs access to *only* their extensional characteristics. krt, on the other hand, provides its witnessing programs access to *both* their intensional *and* extensional characteristics. (See the discussions following (2) in Section 1.2, and (5) in Section 1.3). Thus, we had expected an entailment relationship to hold between n-krt and n-MFP, and, thus, between n-KRT and n-MFP. As Theorem 10 asserts, however, this is not the case. Understanding *why* is the subject of future research.[14] The proof of Theorem 10 is a *finite-injury priority argument* [1, page 166].

Theorem 10. There exists an eps $(\psi_q)_{q \in \mathbb{N}}$ such that 1-KRT holds in $(\psi_q)_{q \in \mathbb{N}}$, but 1-MFP does *not* hold in $(\psi_q)_{q \in \mathbb{N}}$.

Theorem 11 just below says that 1-MFP does *not* entail 1-krt.

Theorem 11. There exists an eps $(\psi_q)_{q \in \mathbb{N}}$ such that 1-MFP holds in $(\psi_q)_{q \in \mathbb{N}}$, but 1-krt does *not* hold in $(\psi_q)_{q \in \mathbb{N}}$.

Corollary 12 just below says that 1-MFP does *not* entail 2-MFP. Recall that Corollary 8 above said: 2-MFP entails n-MFP, for each $n \geq 1$. Corollary 12 says, essentially, that this collapse which occurs *upward* of $n = 2$ does *not* extend *below* $n = 2$.

Corollary 12 (of Theorems 7 and 11). There exists an eps $(\psi_q)_{q \in \mathbb{N}}$ such that 1-MFP holds in $(\psi_q)_{q \in \mathbb{N}}$, but 2-MFP does *not* hold in $(\psi_q)_{q \in \mathbb{N}}$.

We have not investigated whether n-krt entails 1-MFP, for $n \geq 2$. However, we conjecture: there exists an eps $(\psi_q)_{q \in \mathbb{N}}$ such that $(\forall n \geq 1)[n$-krt holds in $(\psi_q)_{q \in \mathbb{N}}]$, but 1-MFP does *not* hold in $(\psi_q)_{q \in \mathbb{N}}$. We also think it would be interesting to explore properties complementary to 1-MFP, in the spirit of [23].

3   The Second Recursion Theorem

In this section, we explore the relationships among various forms of the second recursion theorem (i.e., KRT and krt). Our main results of this section (summarized in Figure 3) are:

---

[14] Perhaps this has something to do with minimal versus *non*-minimal fixpoints.

$$1\text{-KRT} \longrightarrow 1\text{-krt} \longleftarrow 2\text{-krt} \longleftarrow 3\text{-krt} \longleftarrow \cdots$$

Fig. 3. A summary of the main results of Section 3. Arrows indicate entailment relationships. The reflexive-transitive closure of the above diagram represents *all* of the entailment relationships that hold among the forms of the recursion theorem appearing therein.

– For each $n \geq 1$, n-krt does *not* entail $(n + 1)$-krt (Theorem 13).
– 1-KRT does *not* entail 2-krt (Theorem 14).

Theorem 13 just below says that, for each $n \geq 1$, n-krt does *not* entail $(n + 1)$-krt. Thus, the existence of self-referential programs for any n algorithmic tasks does *not* imply the existence of self-referential programs for any $n+1$ algorithmic tasks. The proof of Theorem 13 is a finite-injury priority argument.

Theorem 13. For each $n \geq 1$, there exists an eps $(\psi_q)_{q \in \mathbb{N}}$ such that n-krt holds in $(\psi_q)_{q \in \mathbb{N}}$, but $(n + 1)$-krt does *not* hold in $(\psi_q)_{q \in \mathbb{N}}$.

Theorem 14 just below says that 1-KRT does *not* entail 2-krt. Thus, having the ability to find *one* self-referential program *constructively* for any *one* algorithmic task does *not* imply having the ability to find *two* self-referential programs — *constructively* or *otherwise* — for any *two* algorithmic tasks. The proof of Theorem 14 is a finite-injury priority argument.

Theorem 14. There exists an eps $(\psi_q)_{q \in \mathbb{N}}$ such that 1-KRT holds in $(\psi_q)_{q \in \mathbb{N}}$, but 2-krt does *not* hold in $(\psi_q)_{q \in \mathbb{N}}$.

References

1. Rogers, H.: Theory of Recursive Functions and Effective Computability. McGraw Hill, New York (1967); Reprinted. MIT Press (1987)
2. Riccardi, G.: The Independence of Control Structures in Abstract Programming Systems. PhD thesis, SUNY Buffalo (1980)
3. INRIA: Objective Caml, http://caml.inria.fr/ocaml/index.en.html
4. Machtey, M., Young, P.: An Introduction to the General Theory of Algorithms. North-Holland, Amsterdam (1978)
5. Royer, J.S.: A Connotational Theory of Program Structure. LNCS, vol. 273. Springer, Heidelberg (1987)
6. Manna, Z., Ness, S., Vuillemin, J.: Inductive methods for proving properties of programs. In: Proc. of ACM Conference on Proving Assertions about Programs, pp. 27–50 (1972)
7. Smullyan, R.: Theory of Formal Systems. Annals of Mathematics Studies, vol. 47. Princeton University Press, Princeton (1961)
8. Case, J.: Sortability and extensibility of the graphs of r.e. partial and total orders. Zeitschrift für Mathematische Logik und Grundlagen der Mathematik 22(1), 1–18 (1976)

9. Knuth, D.: The Art of Computer Programming, 2nd edn. Fundamental Algorithms, vol. I. Addison-Wesley, Reading (1973)

10. Wiehagen, R., Zeugmann, T.: Learning and consistency. In: Lange, S., Jantke, K.P. (eds.) GOSLER 1994. LNCS (LNAI), vol. 961, pp. 1–24. Springer, Heidelberg (1995)

11. Riccardi, G.: The independence of control structures in abstract programming systems. Journal of Computer and System Sciences 22(2), 107–143 (1981)

12. Friedberg, R.M.: Three theorems on recursive enumeration. I. Decomposition. II. Maximal set. III. Enumeration without duplication. Journal of Symbolic Logic 23(3), 309–316 (1958)

13. Kummer, M.: An easy priority-free proof of a theorem of Friedberg. Theoretical Computer Science 74(2), 249–251 (1990)

14. Adami, C.: What do robots dream of? Science 314(5802), 1093–1094 (2006)

15. Bongard, J., Zykov, V., Lipson, H.: Resilient machines through continuous self-modeling. Science 314(5802), 1118–1121 (2006)

16. Conduit, R.: To sleep, perchance to dream. Science 315(5816), 1219–1220 (2007); A letter, including responses from Adami, C., Lipson, H., et al.

17. Schmidhuber, J.: Prototype resilient, self-modeling robots. Science 316(5825), 688 (2007); A letter, including responses from Lipson, H., et al.

18. Case, J., Moelius, S.: Characterizing Programming Systems Allowing Program Self-reference. In: Cooper, S.B., Löwe, B., Sorbi, A. (eds.) CiE 2007. LNCS, vol. 4497, pp. 125–134. Springer, Heidelberg (2007)

19. Case, J., Moelius, S.: Independence Results for n-Ary Recursion Theorems (Expanded Version) (2009), http://www.cis.udel.edu/~moelius/publications

20. Kozen, D.: Indexings of subrecursive classes. Theoretical Computer Science 11(3), 277–301 (1980)

21. Royer, J., Case, J.: Subrecursive Programming Systems: Complexity and Succinctness. Birkhäuser, Boston (1994)

22. Bertot, Y., Komendantsky, V.: Fixed point semantics and partial recursion in Coq. In: PPDP 2008: Proc. of 10th Intl. ACM SIGPLAN Conference on Principles and Practice of Declarative Programming, pp. 89–96 (2008)

23. Case, J., Moelius, S.: Properties Complementary to Program Self-Reference. In: Kučera, L., Kučera, A. (eds.) MFCS 2007. LNCS, vol. 4708, pp. 253–263. Springer, Heidelberg (2007)

Depletable Channels: Dynamics and Behaviour

Pietro Cenciarelli, Daniele Gorla, and Ivano Salvo

University of Rome, "La Sapienza", Dpt. of Computer Science
{cenciarelli,gorla,salvo}@di.uniroma1.it

Abstract. A simple model of multi-hop communication in ad-hoc networks is considered. Similar models are often adopted for studying energy efficiency and load balancing of different routing protocols. We address an orthogonal question never considered by the networking community: whether, regardless of specific protocols, two networks may be considered as equivalent from the viewpoint of the communication service they provide. In particular, we consider equivalent two networks with identical maximum and minimum inhibiting flow, and prove that this notion of equivalence coincides with a standard trace-based notion of equivalence borrowed from the theory of concurrency. We finally study the computational complexity of the proposed equivalence and discuss possible alternatives.

1 Introduction

In recent years, much attention has been devoted to research in the area of ad hoc networking. Many complex theoretical problems are at stake and a variety of efficient routing protocols have been studied for exchanging information across a network without using centralized control [25,24,6].

Ad hoc networks are typically wireless, and *multi-hop* communication is adopted because of limited wireless transmission range. Moreover, they usually exhibit *dynamic* behaviour in that their topology may vary over time as a result of mobility or resource consumption. In particular, a crucial kind of resource in most sensor network applications is *energy* [3,4].

In this paper we study the dynamics of ad hoc communication in a rather simple, and yet significant network model. Dynamics is meant in the sense of *change of state* and is induced by energy consumption. Similar models have been adopted for studying energy efficiency and load balancing of different routing protocols [10,18]. Here we address an orthogonal question which has not received attention in the literature on computer networks as yet: whether, regardless of specific protocols, two networks may be considered as *equivalent* from the viewpoint of the communication service they provide.

In our framework, a network is a (possibly cyclic) oriented graph equipped with a function associating with each node a non-negative integer representing *depletable charge*. We are interested in networks as channels for transmitting information. Thus, we consider *communication channels*, i.e. networks with a chosen pair of nodes called *source* and *target*. At a given time a number of

M. Kutyłowski, M. Gębala, and W. Charatonik (Eds.): FCT 2009, LNCS 5699, pp. 50–61, 2009.

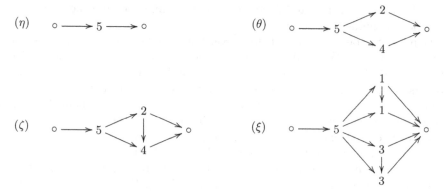

Fig. 1. Four channels

atomic items are fed to the source and instantly flow to the target. Charges may change as result of information passing through the net. Each item passing through a node consumes one unit of the node's charge, thus leaving the channel in a state of lower energy.

In drawing channels, we let n stand for a node of charge n. Circles (∘) are used to denote nodes whose charge is large enough to be irrelevant. Source and target are drawn respectively as the leftmost and rightmost node in the picture. Four channels are depicted in Figure 1. When three items are transmitted along channel θ, node charges may change as shown below.

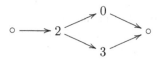

In particular, this result is obtained by routing two items along the northern path, ∘ 5 2 ∘, and one along the southern, ∘ 5 4 ∘. In this new state the channel is still capable of transmitting two more items, after which the channel is *dead*, i.e. any transmission from source to target is inhibited by some exhausted node. Different routings of three items are also possible in θ: for example, letting them all pass south. On the other hand, not all of them may choose the northern path, as its capacity is limited to 2 by the upper node. For the same reason θ can only transmit up to five items, which is the value of its minimum cut. Indeed, all four channels in the picture support a maximum flow of 5; but are they all *equivalent*?

In our model, where fault tolerance is not at stake, we may intuitively agree that η and θ are indistinguishable in the source-to-target communication service they provide. For example, we could view η as the *specification* of a communication service and θ as a possible implementation. However, would ζ implement η correctly? We argue that the two channels may *behave* differently: while η and θ are always alive after *any* transmission of four items, not so for ζ, where the 4-valued flow sending two items along the path ∘ 5 2 4 ∘ and two along ∘ 5 4 ∘ yields a dead channel. Similarly, channel ξ may be killed by a flow of just four items. Then again: can ζ and ξ be considered as different implementations of the same communication service?

The present paper moves a first step towards a formal study of energy-sensitive network behaviour. We study a natural notion of network equivalence which equates η with θ of Figure 1, but not with ζ and ξ. In particular, we shall equate two nets with identical maximum flow and minimum inhibiting flow (i.e., the minimum number of items whose transmission leads to a dead channel). Such an equivalence has a well known corresponding notion in the theory of concurrency, i.e. it corresponds to *(complete) trace equivalence* [1] built up over the labeled transition system arising from all the possible transmissions a channel can be engaged in. More refined notions of behavioural equivalence are studied in concurrency; most notably *bisimulation* [19,16]. We show that, in spite of its simplicity, our model exhibits a variety of natural notions of behavioural equivalences, whose richness is comparable with that of process calculi. In particular, we shall reveal in Section 5 that, although trace equivalent, ζ and ξ in Figure 1 do exhibit different behaviour and can in fact be distinguished in terms of bisimulation.

We believe that a theory of behavioural equivalence relating different network topologies and charge distributions may provide guidance in solving optimization problems and a better understanding of protocol properties, such as invariance with respect to sameness of behaviour.

The paper is structured as follows. First, we present our model of energy-sensitive network channels in Section 2, by describing a simple graph-based model and the associated dynamic behaviours expressed in terms of labeled transitions from a channel to another one. Then, in Section 3, we define a notion of channel equivalence by means of *intrinsic* features of channels; we then relate such an equivalence to a standard trace-based equivalence built up over the transitions previously defined. This is the main result of the paper. Section 4 tackles complexity issues and shows that trace equivalence is a computationally hard problem, even when restricting to acyclic networks. Section 5 relates trace equivalence with bisimulation. Section 6 discusses related work and draws conclusions. Because of limited space, proofs do not include full details; full proofs can be found in the on-line technical report available at http://www.dsi.uniroma1.it/~gorla/papers/CGS-nets-full.pdf

2   The Model

An *oriented graph* (V, E) consists of a set V of *vertices* (or *nodes*) and a set $E \subseteq V \times V$ of ordered pairs of vertices, called *edges*. A *walk* is a sequence $u_1 \ldots u_n$ of nodes such that (u_i, u_{i+1}) is an edge, for all $i < n$. We call *network* a finite oriented graph equipped with a function η associating with each node a non-negative integer representing *depletable charge*. We write just η to denote a network (V, E, η) when its underlying graph, called *topology*, is understood.

We study networks as means to transmit information. Once fixed a *source* node, written s, and a *target* node, written t, we call the network a *communication channel* (*channel* for short). A *path* in a channel is a (possibly cyclic) directed walk from s to t. The set of paths of a channel η is denoted by $P(\eta)$.

Paths are often defined in the literature as *acyclic* walks, and path-oriented definitions of *flow* associate numerical values separately to paths *and* cycles [2, Section 3.5]. In our framework, this would amount to allowing *spontaneous* flow, not originating in the source and depleting the network by cycling in it without ever reaching the target. Since we are interested in modeling information traveling the net as result of a communication act by s, we restrict our attention to flows *from s to t*. Formally: let r_{vp} denote the number of times in which a node v is repeated in a path p (zero if $v \notin p$); A *flow* for η is a function $\phi : P(\eta) \to \mathbb{N}$ such that $\phi(v) \leq \eta(v)$, for every $v \in V$, where $\phi(v)$ denotes the amount of v's charge consumed by ϕ, that is $\phi(v) = \sum_{p \in P(\eta)} r_{vp} \cdot \phi(p)$. The *value* of ϕ is $\sum_{p \in P(\eta)} \phi(p)$. We denote by max_η the value of the maximum flow for η. We call η a *dead* channel if $max_\eta = 0$.

To capture the notion of channel dynamics, we introduce a labeled *transition* relation $\xrightarrow{}$ over channels of identical topology, where $(V, E, \eta) \xrightarrow{n} (V, E, \theta)$ is defined to hold when there exists a flow ϕ of value n in η such that $\theta(v) = \eta(v) - \phi(v)$ for all nodes v. The flow ϕ is said to *witness* the transition. A transition $\eta \xrightarrow{n} \theta$, and likewise any witness of it, is said to *inhibit* η if θ is dead. We denote by min_η the smallest value of an inhibiting flow in η.

To conclude, we now give two simple properties of the labeled transition system just defined, namely *composition* and *decomposition* of transitions.

Proposition 1. *If $\eta \xrightarrow{n} \theta \xrightarrow{m} \zeta$ are transitions, so is also $\eta \xrightarrow{n+m} \zeta$.*

Proof. Let ϕ and ψ witness the two transitions above. It is easy to check that the function assigning $\phi(p) + \psi(p)$ to each path p of η is indeed a flow of value $n + m$. □

Proposition 2. *If $\eta \xrightarrow{n+m} \zeta$ is a transition, so are $\eta \xrightarrow{n} \theta \xrightarrow{m} \zeta$, for some θ.*

Proof. It is sufficient to show it for $m = 1$; the general result follows from Proposition 1. Let ϕ witness the $n + 1$ transition and let p be a path with $\phi(p) \geq 1$. The function assigning $\phi(q)$ to all paths $q \neq p$ and $\phi(p) - 1$ to p is clearly a flow witnessing a transition $\eta \xrightarrow{n} \theta$, while $\theta \xrightarrow{1} \zeta$ is obtained by the flow assigning 1 to p and 0 to all other paths. □

3   Behavioural Equivalence

Two channels may be indistinguishable in the service they provide; such are η and θ of Figure 1. This statement can be made precise by equipping our model with a notion of channel *behaviour*, so that channels exhibiting identical behaviour may be considered as different implementations of the same communication service. To that effect, we first identify the *observations* an external user is allowed to make on a channel. This establishes the level of abstraction at which channels may be distinguished.

The very first attempt one can do in this direction is to equate all channels with the same maximum flow. In this way, we would equate two channels by only considering an intrinsic (or structural) property of the equated channels, without looking at their dynamic behaviour that arises from the transitions defined for our model. However, it is possible to bridge the structural view put forward by the maximum flow and the dynamic behaviour arising from the transitions. Indeed, as a first theoretical result of this paper, we prove that this structural property of the channel has a well-known counterpart in concurrency theory: it corresponds to what is usually called *general trace equivalence* for labeled transition systems [1]. By straightforwardly adapting the standard definitions to our framework, a *general trace* for a channel η is a sequence $\langle n_1 \ldots n_k \rangle$ such that there exist transitions $\eta_0 \xrightarrow{n_1} \eta_1 \ldots \xrightarrow{n_k} \eta_k$ where $\eta_0 = \eta$.

Lemma 1. *For every η and $n \leq max_\eta$, there exists η' such that $\eta \xrightarrow{n} \eta'$.*

Theorem 1. *Two channels have identical maximum flow if and only if they have identical sets of general traces.*

Proof. (If) By contradiction: assume, e.g., that $max_\eta < max_\zeta = n$. Then, there exists ζ' such that $\zeta \xrightarrow{n} \zeta'$. However, there exists no η' such that $\eta \xrightarrow{n} \eta'$; contradiction.

(Only if) Let $max_\eta = max_\zeta$ and let $\langle n_1 \ldots n_k \rangle$ be a general trace of η. By Proposition 1, $\eta \xrightarrow{n} \eta'$, for some η' and $n = n_1 + \ldots + n_k$. Since $n \leq max_\eta = max_\zeta$, by Lemma 1 $\zeta \xrightarrow{n} \zeta'$, for some ζ'. By Proposition 2, we conclude that $\langle n_1 \ldots n_k \rangle$ is a general trace of ζ. □

In this way, we would equate all the channels in Figure 1: they all have a maximum flow of value 5. In particular, every net η with $n = max_\eta$ is equivalent to the net

$$\circ \to n \to \circ$$

However, as noticed in the introduction, ζ and ξ can be distinguished from η and θ by observing death. Since users *do* notice when channels are dead, we seek a more refined notion of equivalence capable of distinguishing ζ and ξ from η and θ.

To this aim, we can also consider the smallest value of an inhibiting flow, viz. min_η. We can now equate two channels that have the same maximum and minimum inhibiting flow value. In this way, channels η and θ of Figure 1 would be equated (since $max_\eta = max_\theta = min_\eta = min_\theta = 5$), channels ζ and ξ would be equated (since $max_\zeta = max_\xi = 5$ and $min_\zeta = min_\xi = 4$), but the last two ones would not be equivalent to the first two ones, as desired.

Also in this case, this refined notion of equivalence has a well-known counterpart in concurrency theory: it corresponds to what is usually called *(complete) trace equivalence* [1]. A *complete trace* (or, simply, a *trace*) for a channel η is a sequence $\langle n_1 \ldots n_k \rangle$ such that there exist transitions $\eta_0 \xrightarrow{n_1} \eta_1 \ldots \xrightarrow{n_k} \eta_k$ where $\eta_0 = \eta$ and η_k is dead. We denote by $tr(\eta)$ the set of complete traces of a channel η. Two channels are *complete trace equivalent* (or, simply, *trace equivalent*) if they have identical sets of complete traces.

To prove this characterization (that is the main theoretical result of our paper), we use some classical definitions and results from the theory of network flows (e.g., residual net and augmenting path); we refer the reader to [2,8] or to our on-line full version of this paper for all the details. A *cut* of a channel is a subset S of the vertices such that $s \in S$ and $t \notin S$. We denote by $S^\rightarrow$ the set of edges (u, v) such that $u \in S$ and $v \notin S$. We write $u \overset{p}{\rightsquigarrow} v$ to specify that the first and last nodes of a walk p are u and v respectively; $u \rightsquigarrow v$ denotes such a walk when the name p is not relevant. If p is a walk of the form $u \rightsquigarrow v \rightsquigarrow v' \rightsquigarrow w$, we denote by $v \overset{p}{\rightsquigarrow} v'$ the portion of p from v to v'. Given a node u and a set K of edges, we write $u \triangleleft K$ to mean that every path $u \rightsquigarrow t$ includes at least one edge of K.

Lemma 2. *Let η be a channel and ϕ an inhibiting flow of value $n < max_\eta$; then, there exists an inhibiting flow of value $n + 1$.*

Proof. To prove this result, we find it useful to work in a framework where values are associated with edges and flows are expressed by assigning a flow to every edge (and not to every path). Graphs where vertices are weighted can be easily transformed in graphs where edges are weighted by applying a well-known *node splitting* technique [2, Section 2.4]. Moreover, the edge-oriented presentation of flows is less abstract than the path-oriented one, in that there may be more path-oriented flows corresponding to one edge-oriented [2, Theorem 3.5].

Since ϕ inhibits η, we have that ϕ saturates at least one cut of η, i.e. $\phi(e) = \eta(e)$, for every $e \in S^\rightarrow$; let us consider all such cuts and let S be a maximal cut (w.r.t. to '$\subseteq$'). Since the value of ϕ is smaller than max_η, by standard results [2] there exists an augmenting path for η after ϕ.

We now prove that there exists an augmenting path p' that crosses S exactly once, where an augmenting path *crosses* a cut if it includes at least one edge (u, v) such that, within η, it holds that $u \triangleleft S^\rightarrow$ and $v \ntriangleleft S^\rightarrow$. It is easy to show that every augmenting path crosses S at least once. Let us fix one of them, say p, and let (u, v) be the first edge in p that crosses S. There must be a path $v \overset{q}{\rightsquigarrow} t$ in η after ϕ, otherwise S would not be maximal. Indeed, we can prove the following

Technical lemma: Let η be a channel and ϕ a flow that saturates one of its cuts S. Assume that there exists a $v \notin S$ and a non-empty $K \subseteq E$ such that $v \triangleleft K$ and all the edges in K are saturated by ϕ. Then, there exists a cut of η greater than S still saturated by ϕ.

Hence, we have that $p' \triangleq s \overset{p}{\rightsquigarrow} u, v \overset{q}{\rightsquigarrow} t$ is an augmenting path with exactly one edge crossing S, viz. (u, v).

Let ϕ' be the flow obtained by updating ϕ with p' as follows:

$$\phi'(u, v) \triangleq \begin{cases} \phi(u, v) + 1 & \text{if } (u, v) \in p' \\ \phi(u, v) - 1 & \text{if } (v, u) \in p' \\ \phi(u, v) & \text{otherwise} \end{cases}$$

It can be proved [8] that ϕ' is a flow for η of value $n + 1$; if we prove that ϕ' inhibits the channel, we have done. To this aim, it suffices to prove that it saturates S. If it was not the case, p' would include (v, u), for some $(u, v) \in S^{\rightarrow}$. Since $u \in S$, $u \vartriangleleft S^{\rightarrow}$; hence, (v, u) cannot be the edge of p' that crosses S. Then, it can either be $v \vartriangleleft S^{\rightarrow}$ or $v \not\vartriangleleft S^{\rightarrow}$; however, both these possibilities lead to a contradiction:

$v \not\vartriangleleft S^{\rightarrow}$: since $s \vartriangleleft S^{\rightarrow}$, $v \not\vartriangleleft S^{\rightarrow}$ implies that there must be an edge crossing S *before* (v, u) in p'; since $t \not\vartriangleleft S^{\rightarrow}$, $u \vartriangleleft S^{\rightarrow}$ implies that there must be an edge crossing S *after* (v, u) in p'; since p' has only one edge crossing S, this case is not possible.

$v \vartriangleleft S^{\rightarrow}$: in this case, by the technical lemma, we could exhibit a cut saturated by ϕ greater than S.   □

Theorem 2. *Two channels are trace equivalent if and only if they have identical maximum and minimum inhibiting flow.*

Proof. (If) Let $\langle n_1 \ldots n_k \rangle \in tr(\eta)$; because of Proposition 1, there exists an inhibiting transition for η with value $n = n_1 + \ldots + n_k$. If $n \in \{min_\eta, max_\eta\}$, by hypothesis we have that there exists an inhibiting transition for θ with value n; otherwise, we can start from a minimum inhibiting flow and use Lemma 2 for $n - min_\eta$ times to obtain an inhibiting flow for θ with value n. In both cases, by Proposition 2 we have that $\langle n_1 \ldots n_k \rangle \in tr(\theta)$, as desired.

(Only if) Let us consider the traces $\langle min_\eta \rangle$ and $\langle max_\eta \rangle$, both belonging to $tr(\eta)$; by hypothesis, they also belong to $tr(\theta)$. If by contradiction were $max_\theta > max_\eta$ (it cannot be '<' because $\langle max_\eta \rangle \in tr(\theta)$), we would have that $\langle max_\theta \rangle \in tr(\theta)$ but $\langle max_\theta \rangle \notin tr(\eta)$, in contradiction with $tr(\eta) = tr(\theta)$. If $min_\theta < min_\eta$, the proof is similar. Thus, $max_\theta = max_\eta$ and $min_\theta = min_\eta$, as desired.   □

Notice that every channel is trace equivalent to a channel, that we call *canonical*, with a very simple topology (in particular, it has no cycles). Let us define the channel $\gamma_{m,n}$ as:

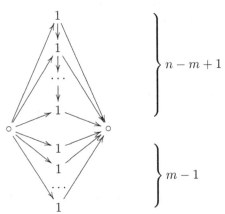

It is easy to check that $min_{\gamma_{m,n}} = m$ and $max_{\gamma_{m,n}} = n$. Thus, $\gamma_{m,n}$ can be considered the standard representative of the trace-equivalence class of all the nets with minimum inhibiting flow m and maximum flow n.

4   Complexity Issues

Theorem 2 characterizes trace equivalence in terms of maximum flow and minimum inhibiting flow. It is well-known that there exist polynomial time algorithms for finding the maximum flow in a net. We are left with studying the complexity of the following problem, that we call *minimum inhibiting flow* (MIF, for short):

> **MIF:** Given a network η, find the value of the minimum inhibiting flow for η.

MIF can be turned into a decisional problem:

> **DMIF:** Given a network η and an integer k, is there an inhibiting flow for η with value at most k?

Theorem 3. *MIF is NP-complete.*

Proof. Clearly, DMIF is in NP; by standard techniques, we can exploit this fact to also prove that MIF is in NP.

To show that MIF is NP-hard, we reduce the problem of finding a maximal matching of a given cardinality in a bipartite graph to DMIF. We recall that a maximal matching in a graph (V, E) is a set of edges $F \subseteq E$ such that:

- $\forall e, e' \in F$ it holds that $e \cap e' = \varnothing$;
- $\forall e \in E \exists e' \in F$ such that $e \cap e' \neq \varnothing$.

Let $G = (V_1, V_2, E)$ be a bipartite undirected graph. We consider the channel (V', E', η), where

- $V' = V_1 \cup V_2 \cup \{s, t\}$, for $\{s, t\} \cap (V_1 \cup V_2) = \varnothing$;
- $E' = \{(u, v) : \{u, v\} \in E \wedge u \in V_1 \wedge v \in V_2\} \cup \bigcup_{u \in V_1} \{(s, u)\} \cup \bigcup_{u \in V_2} \{(u, t)\}$;
- $\eta(v) = 1$ for every $v \in V_1 \cup V_2$.

It is easy to show that G has a maximal matching of cardinality k if and only if η has an inhibiting flow of value k.   □

We observe that, in the reduction just shown, we need to consider acyclic unitary networks only, i.e. networks in which depletable charge of each node is 1. This implies that MIF is an intractable problem even in this restricted case.

It is now worth noting that in concurrency theory complexity measures are usually expressed in terms of the size of the labeled transition system (LTS, for short) resulting from all the labeled transitions of a given process (in our case, a channel). This is because the definitions and characterizations of process equivalences are usually given on the LTSs of the equated processes, and not on the processes themselves. Even for simple models like CCS, trace equivalence is exponential in the size of the LTS [23], while other equivalences (like, e.g., *bisimilarity* [19,16]) are polynomial [12]. However, if expressed in terms of the size of the process, all these equivalences become (at least) exponential, since the number of states of a LTS is exponential in the size of its originating process.

Thanks to Theorem 2, we could have directly checked equivalences on the LTSs resulting from the equated channels. However, also in our case we would have an exponential blow up of the number of states. For example, consider the channel:

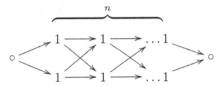

It has $2n + 2$ vertices and it produces a LTS with 2^n states: there are 2^n paths along which a unitary flow can be sent.

We have instead defined our behavioural equivalence by relying on properties of the equated channels, and not of their LTSs. Nevertheless, as we have just shown, trace equivalence seems not verifiable in polynomial time (w.r.t. the size of the equated channels); this should not be surprising. On one hand, this agrees with the usual hardness of trace equivalence in concurrency theory mentioned above; on the other hand, this stimulates future work on more efficiently verifiable, but still properly discriminating, equivalences.

5   Beyond Trace Equivalence

To conclude our presentation of trace equivalence, let us pinpoint some of its limitations; such issues are standard in concurrency theory and scales to our model too. The main issue is that trace equivalence is not preserved by transitions. Indeed, consider the nets η and the canonical net $\gamma_{2,2n}$, for any $n > 1$:

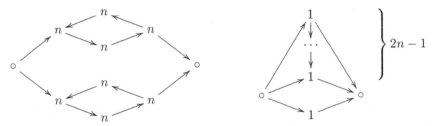

Clearly, they are trace equivalent. Then, consider the unitary transition of η that inhibits its norther cycle by taking n times such a cycle; it turns η into the channel η' having 0 on every node of its northern cycle. There is no unitary transition of $\gamma_{2,2n}$ that leads to a channel that is trace equivalent to η'. Indeed, if the unitary flow passes through the bottom vertex, the resulting channel has a maximum flow of $2n - 1$ (whereas $max_{\eta'} = n$); if the flow passes through (some of) the top $2n - 1$ vertices, the resulting channel has a minimum inhibiting flow greater than 1 (whereas $min_{\eta'} = 1$).

In concurrency theory, a classical notion of equivalence that is more finely grained than those based on traces relies on the notion of *bisimulation*. In our framework, this a symmetric relation $\Re$ on channels such that $\eta \Re \theta$ and $\eta \xrightarrow{n} \eta'$

imply $\theta \xrightarrow{n} \theta'$, for some θ' such that $\eta' \, \Re \, \theta'$. Two channels η and θ are called *bisimulation equivalent* if they are related by a bisimulation. In view of Theorem 2, it follows immediately from the definition that bisimulation equivalence is included in trace equivalence. Moreover, by what we have just said, the inclusion is strict: the channels η and $\gamma_{2,2n}$ depicted above are *not* bisimulation equivalent. Another example is given by channels ζ and ξ of Figure 1: after sending two items along $\circ\,5\,2\,4\,\circ$ in ζ we have a net with maximum flow at 2; on the contrary, every 2-valued flow in ξ yields a channel with maximum flow greater than 2.

A challenging issue for future work is finding a characterization of bisimulation equivalence in terms of structural properties of channels, in the same spirit as the characterizations we have provided for trace equivalence in this paper.

6   Conclusions and Related Work

We presented a simple model of communication networks, called channels. The communication infrastructure is modeled by a graph connecting a sender s with a receiver t. Nodes have a depletable charge. Labeled transitions are used to describe the dynamics of channels, where states of the LTS are channels of identical topology and labels are the number of information units transmitted in a communication from s to t via a legal network flow. We equated channels by means of intrinsic channel properties (that is, their maximum flow and minimum inhibiting flow) and studied their complexity. Finally, we showed that such equivalence coincides with a natural notion of equivalence borrowed from concurrency theory.

There are several research lines that can be pursued to develop the framework presented in this paper. First of all, we assume that source and target are *fixed* during a channel evolution. More realistic models include scenarios where only the target is fixed (e.g., sensor networks) or where both source and target can be any node of the net. Moreover, our model assumes that the network topology does never change during the computation. This is clearly a simplifying assumption and makes our model unsuited for MANETs. It would be challenging to introduce in the model such advanced features and study the resulting equivalences.

Related work. In the last years, network scenarios have been modeled and studied by means of process algebraic techniques. In such papers, the authors usually first give a syntax for writing nets, featuring some distinguishing issues of the modeled applications; then, they give an operational semantics and a behavioural equivalence to reason over nets; finally, the theory is used in some concrete application, e.g. to verify the correctness of some network protocol or to equate different networks with the same behaviour. According to the kind of network modeled, we mention: [11,13,22], where mobile ad hoc networks are considered; [15,17,14], where wireless systems are considered; [5], where peer-to-peer overlay networks are considered. Our approach clearly follows this research line. However, we do not have a process syntax and just write networks via their physical topology, assuming that some suitable software is hardcoded into every node of the net to properly implement some routing strategy. A somehow similar approach has been followed by some of the authors in a previous paper [7], where the framework was based on (hyper)graph rewriting. There, apart from functional equivalence, other network measures (e.g., robustness) were related to bisimulation in the model.

It is worth saying that our MIF problem somehow resembles the Network Inhibition Problem (NIP) [20]. There, every edge of a flow net is equipped with a destruction cost; the problem is to find a flow that leaves the net in the worst possible condition (i.e., with the minimum max flow) and whose cost is smaller than a given quantity. In *loc. cit.*, it is proved that NIP is NP-complete for several class of graphs, but polynomially approximable for most of them (e.g., planar or grid).

A related paper is [21], where a network model (somehow similar to ours) is used to study the complexity of finding optimal flow subnetworks. A challenging issue for future research is the understanding of how the two approaches relate to each other.

To conclude, we have proposed a usage of formal models different from those usually exploited in the network community. There, formal models are often used [9] for model checking and simulations to study, e.g., correctness of network protocols, optimal schedulings, network measures or power consumption.

Acknowledgements. Thanks to Flavio Chierichetti for his valuable support in the proof of Theorem 3.

References

1. Aceto, L., Fokkink, W., Verhoef, C.: Structural operational semantics. In: Bergstra, J., Ponse, A., Smolka, S. (eds.) Handobook of Process Algebra, pp. 197–292. North-Holland, Amsterdam (2001)
2. Ahuja, R., Magnanti, T., Orlin, J.: Network Flows, theory, algorithms, and applications. Prentice-Hall, New Jersey (1993)
3. Akkaya, K., Younis, M.F.: A survey on routing protocols for wireless sensor networks. Ad Hoc Networks 3(3), 325–349 (2005)
4. Akyildiz, I., Su, W., Sankarasubramaniam, Y., Cayirci, E.: A survey on sensor networks. IEEE Communications Magazine 40(8), 102–116 (2002)
5. Borgström, J., Nestmann, U., Alima, L.O., Gurov, D.: Verifying a structured peer-to-peer overlay network: The static case. In: Priami, C., Quaglia, P. (eds.) GC 2004. LNCS, vol. 3267, pp. 250–265. Springer, Heidelberg (2005)
6. Boukerche, A. (ed.): Algorithms and Protocols for Wireless Sensor Networks. Wiley-IEEE press (2008)
7. Cenciarelli, P., Gorla, D., Tuosto, E.: Network applications of graph bisimulation. In: Ehrig, H., Heckel, R., Rozenberg, G., Taentzer, G. (eds.) ICGT 2008. LNCS, vol. 5214, pp. 131–146. Springer, Heidelberg (2008)
8. Cormen, T.H., Leiserson, C.E., Rivest, R.L.: Introduction to Algorithms. MIT Press, Cambridge (1990)

9. Fehnker, A., McIver, A.: Formal techniques for the analysis of wireless networks. In: 2nd International Symposium on Leveraging of Formal Maethods, Verification and Validation (IEEE-ISOLA), pp. 263–270. IEEE Press, New York (2006)
10. Ganjali, Y., Keshavarzian, A.: Load balancing in ad hoc networks: single-path routing vs. multi-path routing. In: INFOCOM 2004. Twenty-third Annual Joint Conference of the IEEE Computer and Communications Societies, vol. 2, pp. 1120–1125. IEEE press, New York (2004)
11. Godskesen, J.C.: A calculus for mobile ad hoc networks. In: Murphy, A.L., Vitek, J. (eds.) COORDINATION 2007. LNCS, vol. 4467, pp. 132–150. Springer, Heidelberg (2007)
12. Kanellakis, P., Smolka, S.: CCS Expressions, Finite State Processes and Three Problems of Equivalence. Information and Conputation 86(1), 43–68 (1990)
13. Merro, M.: An observational theory for mobile ad hoc networks. In: Proc. of MFPS, ENTCS, vol. 173, pp. 275–293 (2007)
14. Merro, M., Sibilio, E.: A timed calculus for wireless networks. In: Proc. of FSEN (to appear, 2009)
15. Mezzetti, N., Sangiorgi, D.: Towards a calculus for wireless systems. In: Proc. of MFPS, ENTCS, vol. 158, pp. 331–353 (2006)
16. Milner, R.: Communication and Concurrency. Prentice Hall, New Jersey (1989)
17. Nanz, S., Hankin, C.: A framework for security analysis of mobile wireless networks. Theoretical Computer Science 367(1-2), 203–227 (2006)
18. Nehra, N., Patel, R.B., Bhat, V.K.: Routing with load balancing in ad hoc network: A mobile agent approach. In: 6th IEEE/ACIS International Conference on Computer and Information Science, pp. 489–495 (2007)
19. Park, D.: Concurrency and automata on infinite sequences. In: Deussen, P. (ed.) GI-TCS 1981. LNCS, vol. 104, pp. 167–183. Springer, Heidelberg (1981)
20. Phillips, C.A.: The network inhibition problem. In: Proc. of STOC, pp. 776–785. ACM Press, New York (1993)
21. Roughgarden, T.: On the severity of braess's paradox: Designing networks for selfish users is hard. Journal of Computer and System Science 72(5), 922–953 (2006)
22. Singh, A., Ramakrishnan, C., Smolka, S.A.: A process calculus for mobile ad hoc networks. In: Lea, D., Zavattaro, G. (eds.) COORDINATION 2008. LNCS, vol. 5052, pp. 296–314. Springer, Heidelberg (2008)
23. Stockmeyer, L., Meyer, A.: Word Problems Requiring Exponential Time. In: Proc. of 5th Symp. on Theory of Computing (STOC), pp. 1–9. ACM Press, New York (1973)
24. Toh, C.: Ad Hoc Mobile Wireless Networks: Protocols and Systems. Prentice Hall, New Jersey (2002)
25. Tonguz, O.K., Ferrari, G.: Ad Hoc Wireless Networks: A Communication-Theoretic Perspective. John Wiley & Sons, Chichester (2006)

Noise-Resilient Group Testing: Limitations and Constructions

Mahdi Cheraghchi[*]

School of Computer and Communication Sciences
EPFL, 1015 Lausanne, Switzerland
mahdi.cheraghchi@epfl.ch

Abstract. We study combinatorial group testing schemes for learning d-sparse boolean vectors using highly unreliable disjunctive measurements. We consider an adversarial noise model that only limits the number of false observations, and show that any noise-resilient scheme in this model can only approximately reconstruct the sparse vector. On the positive side, we give a general framework for construction of highly noise-resilient group testing schemes using randomness condensers. Simple randomized instantiations of this construction give non-adaptive measurement schemes, with $m = O(d \log n)$ measurements, that allow efficient reconstruction of d-sparse vectors up to $O(d)$ false positives even in the presence of δm false positives and $\Omega(m/d)$ false negatives within the measurement outcomes, for *any* constant $\delta < 1$. None of these parameters can be substantially improved without dramatically affecting the others. Furthermore, we obtain several explicit (and incomparable) constructions, in particular one matching the randomized trade-off but using $m = O(d^{1+o(1)} \log n)$ measurements. We also obtain explicit constructions that allow fast reconstruction in time $\mathsf{poly}(m)$, which would be sublinear in n for sufficiently sparse vectors.

1 Introduction

Group testing is an area in applied combinatorics that deals with the following problem: Suppose that in a large population of individuals, it is suspected that a small number possess a condition or property that can only be certified by carrying out a particular test. Moreover suppose that a *pooling strategy* is permissible, namely, that it is possible to perform a test on a chosen group of individuals in parallel, in which case the outcome of the test would be positive if at least one of the individuals in the group possesses the condition. The trivial strategy would be to test each individual separately, which takes as many tests as the population size. The basic question in group testing is: how can we do better? The idea of group testing is believed to be emerged during the screening process of draftees in World War II. Since then, a vast amount of tools and

---

[*] Research supported by Swiss NSF grant 200020-115983/1.

M. Kutyłowski, M. Gębala, and W. Charatonik (Eds.): FCT 2009, LNCS 5699, pp. 62–73, 2009.

techniques have been developed in this area, and the problem has found a large number of applications apart from its original aim (from testing for defective items, e.g., defective light bulbs or resistors, as a part of industrial quality assurance to DNA sequencing and DNA library screening in molecular biology, and less obvious applications such as multiaccess communication, data compression, pattern matching, streaming algorithms, software testing, and compressed sensing, to name a few). We refer the reader to the books by Du and Hwang [1,2] for a detailed account of the major developments in this area.

More formally, the goal in group testing is to reconstruct a d-sparse[1] boolean vector[2] $x \in \mathbb{F}_2^n$, for a known integer parameter $d > 0$, from as few observations as possible. Each observation is the outcome of a measurement that outputs the bitwise OR of a prescribed subset of the coordinates in x. Hence, a measurement can be seen as a binary vector in $\mathbb{F}_2^n$ which is the characteristic vector of the subset of the coordinates being combined together. More generally, a set of m measurements can be seen as an $m \times n$ binary matrix (that we call the *measurement matrix*) whose rows define the individual measurements.

In this work we study group testing in presence of highly unreliable measurements that can produce false outcomes. We will mainly focus on situations where up to a constant fraction of the measurement outcomes can be incorrect. Moreover, we will mainly restrict our attention to *non-adaptive* measurements; the case in which the measurement matrix is fully determined before the observation outcomes are known. Nonadaptive measurements are particularly important for applications as they allow the tests to be performed independently and in parallel, which saves significant time and cost.

On the negative side, we show that when the measurements are allowed to be highly noisy, the original vector x cannot be uniquely reconstructed. Thus in this case it would be inevitable to resort to approximate reconstructions, i.e., producing a sparse vector $\hat{x}$ that is close to the original vector in Hamming distance. In particular, our result shows that if a constant fraction of the measurements can go wrong, the reconstruction might be different from the original vector in $\Omega(d)$ positions, irrespective of the number of measurements. For most applications this might be an unsatisfactory situation, as even a close estimate of the set of positives might not reveal whether any particular individual is defective or not, and in certain scenarios (such as an epidemic disease or industrial quality assurance) it is unacceptable to miss any affected individuals. This motivates us to focus on approximate reconstructions with *one-sided* error. Namely, we will require that the support of $\hat{x}$ contains the support of x and be possibly larger by up to $O(d)$ positions. It can be argued that, for most applications, such a scheme is as good as exact reconstruction, as it allows one to significantly narrow-down the set of defectives to up to $O(d)$ *candidate positives*. In particular, as observed in [3], one can use a *second stage* if necessary and individually test the resulting set of candidates to identify the exact set of positives, hence resulting in a so-called *trivial two-stage* group testing algorithm. Next, we will show that in

---

[1] We define a d-sparse vector as a vector with at most d nonzero coefficients.
[2] We use the notation $\mathbb{F}_q$ for a field (or at times, an alphabet) of size q.

any scheme that produces no or little false negative in the reconstruction, only up to $O(1/d)$ fraction of false negatives (i.e., observation of a 0 instead of 1) in the measurements can be tolerated, while there is no such restriction on the amount of tolerable false positives. Thus, one-sided approximate reconstruction breaks down the symmetry between false positives and false negatives in our error model.

On the positive side, we give a general construction for noise-resilient measurement matrices that guarantees approximate reconstructions up to $O(d)$ false positives. Our main result is a general reduction from the noise-resilient group testing problem to construction of well-studied combinatorial objects known as *randomness condensers* that play an important role in theoretical computer science. Different qualities of the underlying condenser correspond to different qualities of the resulting group testing scheme, as we describe later. Using the state of the art in derandomization theory, we obtain different instantiations of our framework with incomparable properties summarized in Table 1. In particular, the resulting randomized constructions (obtained from optimal lossless condensers and extractors) can be set to tolerate (with overwhelming probability) *any* constant fraction (< 1) of false positives, an $\Omega(1/d)$ fraction of false negatives, and produce an accurate reconstruction up to $O(d)$ false positives (where the positive constant behind $O(\cdot)$ can be made arbitrarily small), which is the best trade-off one can hope for, all using only $O(d \log n)$ measurements. This almost matches the information-theoretic lower bound $\Omega(d \log(n/d))$ shown by simple counting. We will also show explicit (deterministic) constructions that can approach the optimal trade-off, and finally, those that are equipped with fully efficient reconstruction algorithms with running time polynomial in the number of measurements.

Related Work. There is a large body of work in the group testing literature that is related to the present work; in this short presentation, we are only able

Table 1. A summary of constructions in this paper. The parameters $\alpha \in [0, 1)$ and $\delta \in (0, 1]$ are arbitrary constants, m is the number of measurements, e_0 (resp., e_1) the number of tolerable false positives (resp., negatives) in the measurements, and e'_0 is the number of false positives in the reconstruction. The fifth column shows whether the construction is deterministic (Det) or randomized (Rnd), and the last column shows the running time of the reconstruction algorithm.

m	e_0	e_1	e'_0	Det/ Rnd	Rec. Time
$O(d \log n)$	αm	$\Omega(m/d)$	$O(d)$	Rnd	$O(mn)$
$O(d \log n)$	$\Omega(m)$	$\Omega(m/d)$	δd	Rnd	$O(mn)$
$O(d^{1+o(1)} \log n)$	αm	$\Omega(m/d)$	$O(d)$	Det	$O(mn)$
$d \cdot \mathsf{quasipoly}(\log n)$	$\Omega(m)$	$\Omega(m/d)$	δd	Det	$O(mn)$
$d \cdot \mathsf{quasipoly}(\log n)$	αm	$\Omega(m/d)$	$O(d)$	Det	$\mathsf{poly}(m)$
$\mathsf{poly}(d)\mathsf{poly}(\log n)$	$\mathsf{poly}(d)\mathsf{poly}(\log n)$	$\Omega(e_0/d)$	δd	Det	$\mathsf{poly}(m)$

to discuss a few with the highest relevance. The exact group testing problem in the noiseless scenario is handled by what is known as *superimposed coding* (see [4,5]) or the closely related concepts of *cover-free families* or *disjunct matrices*[3]. It is known that, even for the noiseless case, exact reconstruction of d-sparse signals (when d is not too large) requires at least $\Omega(d^2 \log n / \log d)$ measurements (several proofs of this fact are known, e.g., [6,7,8]). An important class of superimposed codes is constructed from combinatorial designs, among which we mention the construction based on MDS codes given by Kautz and Singleton [9], which, in the group testing notation, achieves $O(d^2 \log^2 n)$ measurements.

Approximate reconstruction of sparse vectors up to a small number of false positives (that is one focus of this work) has been studied as a major ingredient of trivial two-stage schemes [3,10,11,12,13,14]. In particular, a generalization of superimposed codes, known as *selectors*, was introduced in [12] which, roughly speaking, allows for identification of the sparse vector up to a prescribed number of false positives. They gave a non-constructive result showing that there are such (non-adaptive) schemes that keep the number of false positives at $O(d)$ using $O(d \log(n/d))$ measurements, matching the optimal "counting bound". A probabilistic construction of asymptotically optimal selectors (resp., a related notion of *resolvable matrices*) is given in [14] (resp., [13]), and [15,16] give slightly sub-optimal "explicit" constructions based on certain expander graphs obtained from dispersers.

To give a concise comparison of the present work with those listed above, we mention some of the qualities of the group testing schemes that we will aim to attain: (1) low number of measurements; (2) arbitrarily good degree of approximation; (3) maximum possible noise tolerance; (4) efficient, deterministic construction: As typically the sparsity d is very small compared to n, a measurement matrix must be ideally *fully explicitly constructible* in the sense that each entry of the matrix should be computable in deterministic time $\mathsf{poly}(d, \log n)$; (5) fully efficient reconstruction algorithm: For a similar reason, the length of the observation vector is typically far smaller than n; thus, it is desirable to have a reconstruction algorithm that identifies the support of the sparse vector in time polynomial in the number of measurements (which might be exponentially smaller than n). While the works that we mentioned focus on few of the criteria listed above, our approach can potentially attain *all* at the same time. As we will see later, using the best known constructions of condensers we will have to settle to sub-optimal results in one or more of the aspects above. Nevertheless, the fact that any improvement in the construction of condensers would readily translate to improved group testing schemes (and also the rapid growth of derandomization theory) justifies the significance of the construction given in this work.

---

[3] A d-superimposed code is a collection of binary vectors with the property that from the bitwise OR of up to d words in the family one can uniquely identify the comprising vectors. A d-cover-free family is a collection of subsets of a universe, none of which is contained in any union of up to d of the other subsets.

2   Preliminaries

For non-negative integers e_0 and e_1, we say that an ordered pair of binary vectors (x, y), each in $\mathbb{F}_2^n$, are (e_0, e_1)-close (or x is (e_0, e_1)-close to y) if y can be obtained from x by flipping at most e_0 bits from 0 to 1 and at most e_1 bits from 1 to 0. Hence, such x and y will be $(e_0 + e_1)$-close in Hamming-distance. Further, (x, y) are called (e_0, e_1)-far if they are not (e_0, e_1)-close. Note that if x and y are seen as characteristic vectors of subsets X and Y of $[n]$, respectively[4], they are $(|Y \setminus X|, |X \setminus Y|)$-close. Furthermore, (x, y) are (e_0, e_1)-close iff (y, x) are (e_1, e_0)-close. A group of m non-adaptive measurements for binary vectors of length n can be seen as an $m \times n$ matrix (that we call the *measurement matrix*) whose (i, j)th entry is 1 iff the jth coordinate of the vector is present in the disjunction defining the ith measurement. For a measurement matrix A, we denote by $A[x]$ the outcome of the measurements defined by A on a binary vector x, that is, the bitwise OR of those columns of A chosen by the support of x. As motivated by our negative results, for the specific setting of the group testing problem that we are considering in this work, it is necessary to give an *asymmetric* treatment that distinguishes between inaccuracies due to false positives and false negatives. Thus, we will work with a notion of error-tolerating measurement matrices that directly and conveniently captures this requirement, as given below:

Definition 1. Let $m, n, d, e_0, e_1, e_0', e_1'$ be integers. An $m \times n$ measurement matrix A is called (e_0, e_1, e_0', e_1')-correcting for d-sparse vectors if, for every $y \in \mathbb{F}_2^m$ there exists $z \in \mathbb{F}_2^n$ (called a *valid decoding of y*) such that for every $x \in \mathbb{F}_2^n$, whenever (x, z) are (e_0', e_1')-far, $(A[x], y)$ are (e_0, e_1)-far. The matrix A is called *fully explicit* if each entry of the matrix can be computed in time $\mathrm{poly}(\log n)$.

Intuitively, the definition states that two measurements are allowed to be confused only if they are produced from close vectors. In particular, an (e_0, e_1, e_0', e_1')-correcting matrix gives a group testing scheme that reconstructs the sparse vector up to e_0' false positives and e_1' false negatives even in the presence of e_0 false positives and e_1 false negatives in the measurement outcome. Under this notation, unique (exact) decoding would be possible using an $(e_0, e_1, 0, 0)$-correcting matrix if the amount of measurement errors is bounded by at most e_0 false positives and e_1 false negatives. However, when $e_0' + e_1'$ is positive, decoding may require a bounded amount of ambiguity, namely, up to e_0' false positives and e_1' false negatives in the decoded sequence. In the combinatorics literature, the special case of $(0, 0, 0, 0)$-correcting matrices is known as *d-superimposed codes* or *d-separable matrices* and is closely related to the notions of *d-cover-free families* and *d-disjunct* matrices (cf. [1] for precise definitions). Also, $(0, 0, e_0', 0)$-correcting matrices are related to the notion of *selectors* in [12] and *resolvable matrices* in [13].

The *min-entropy* of a distribution $\mathcal{X}$ with finite support S is given by $H_\infty(\mathcal{X}) := \min_{x \in S}\{-\log \mathrm{Pr}_{\mathcal{X}}(x)\}$, where $\mathrm{Pr}_{\mathcal{X}}(x)$ is the probability that $\mathcal{X}$ assigns to x. The *statistical distance* of two distributions $\mathcal{X}$ and $\mathcal{Y}$ defined on the same finite

---

[4] We use the shorthand $[n]$ for the set $\{1, 2, \ldots, n\}$.

space S is given by $\frac{1}{2}\sum_{s\in S}|\Pr_{\mathcal{X}}(s) - \Pr_{\mathcal{Y}}(s)|$, which is half the ℓ_1 distance of the two distributions when regarded as vectors of probabilities over S. Two distributions $\mathcal{X}$ and $\mathcal{Y}$ are said to be ϵ-close if their statistical distance is at most ϵ. We will use the shorthand $\mathcal{U}_n$ for the uniform distribution on $\mathbb{F}_2^n$, and $X \sim \mathcal{X}$ for a random variable X drawn from a distribution $\mathcal{X}$. A function $C \colon \mathbb{F}_2^n \times \mathbb{F}_2^t \to \mathbb{F}_2^\ell$ is a *strong* $k \to_\epsilon k'$ *condenser* if for every distribution $\mathcal{X}$ on $\mathbb{F}_2^n$ with min-entropy at least k, random variable $X \sim \mathcal{X}$ and a *seed* $Y \sim \mathcal{U}_t$, the distribution of $(Y, C(X, Y))$ is ϵ-close to some distribution $(\mathcal{U}_t, \mathcal{Z})$ with min-entropy at least $t + k'$. The parameters ϵ, $k - k'$, and $\ell - k'$ are called the *error*, the *entropy loss* and the *overhead* of the condenser, respectively. A condenser with zero entropy loss is called *lossless*, and a condenser with zero overhead is called a *strong* (k, ϵ)-*extractor*. A condenser is *explicit* if it is polynomial-time computable.

3 Negative Results

In coding theory, it is possible to construct codes that can tolerate up to a constant fraction of adversarially chosen errors and still guarantee unique decoding. Hence it is natural to wonder whether a similar possibility exists in group testing, namely, whether there is a measurement matrix that is robust against a constant fraction of adversarial errors and still recovers the measured vector exactly. The result below shows that this is not possible[5]:

Lemma 2. *Suppose that an* $m \times n$ *measurement matrix* A *is* (e_0, e_1, e_0', e_1')-*correcting for d-sparse vectors. Then* $(\max\{e_0, e_1\} + 1)/(e_0' + e_1' + 1) \leq m/d$. □

The above lemma[6] gives a trade-off between the tolerable error in the measurements versus the reconstruction error. In particular, for unique decoding to be possible one can only guarantee resiliency against up to $O(1/d)$ fraction of errors in the measurement. On the other hand, tolerance against a constant fraction of errors would make an ambiguity of order $\Omega(d)$ in the decoding inevitable. Another trade-off is given by the following lemma:

Lemma 3. *Suppose that an* $m \times n$ *measurement matrix* A *is* (e_0, e_1, e_0', e_1')-*correcting for d-sparse vectors. Then for every* $\epsilon > 0$, *either* $e_1 < (e_1' + 1)m/(\epsilon d)$ *or* $e_0' \geq (1 - \epsilon)(n - d + 1)/(e_1' + 1)^2$. □

As mentioned in the introduction, it is an important matter for applications to bring down the amount of false negatives in the reconstruction as much as possible, and ideally to zero. The lemma above shows that if one is willing to keep the number e_1' of false negatives in the reconstruction at the zero level (or bounded by a constant), only an up to $O(1/d)$ fraction of false negatives in the measurements can be tolerated (regardless of the number of measurements),

---

[5] We remark that the negative results in this section hold for both adaptive and non-adaptive measurements.

[6] The omitted proofs can be found in the full version of this paper.

unless the number e'_0 of false positives in the reconstruction grows to an enormous amount (namely, $\Omega(n)$ when $n - d = \Omega(n)$) which is certainly undesirable.

As shown in [6], exact reconstruction of d-sparse vectors of length n, even in a noise-free setting, requires at least $\Omega(d^2 \log n / \log d)$ non-adaptive measurements. However, it turns out that there is no such restriction when an approximate reconstruction is sought for, except for the following bound which can be shown using simple counting and holds for adaptive noiseless schemes as well:

Lemma 4. *Let A be an $m \times n$ measurement matrix that is $(0, 0, e'_0, e'_1)$-correcting for d-sparse vectors. Then $m \geq d \log(n/d) - d - e'_0 - O(e'_1 \log((n - d - e'_0)/e'_1))$, where the last term is defined to be zero for $e'_1 = 0$.* □

This is similar in spirit to the lower bound obtained in [12] for the size of selectors. According to the lemma, even in the noiseless scenario, any reconstruction method that returns an approximation of the sparse vector up to $e'_0 = O(d)$ false positives and without false negatives will require $\Omega(d \log(n/d))$ measurements. As we will show in the next section, an upper bound of $O(d \log n)$ is in fact attainable even in a highly noisy setting using only non-adaptive measurements. This in particular implies an asymptotically optimal trivial two-stage group testing scheme.

4   A Noise-Resilient Construction

In this section we introduce our general construction and design measurement matrices for testing D-sparse vectors[7] in $\mathbb{F}_2^N$. The matrices can be seen as adjacency matrices of certain unbalanced bipartite graphs constructed from good randomness condensers or extractors. The main technique that we use to show the desired properties is the *list-decoding view* of randomness condensers, extractors, and expanders, developed over the recent years starting from the work of Ta-Shma and Zuckerman on *extractor codes* [17]. We start by introducing the terms that we will use in this construction and the analysis.

Definition 5. (mixtures, agreement, and agreement list) Let Σ be a finite set. A *mixture* over Σ^n is an n-tuple $S := (S_1, \ldots, S_n)$ such that every S_i, $i \in [n]$, is a nonempty subset of Σ. The *agreement* of $w := (w_1, \ldots w_n) \in \Sigma^n$ with S, denoted by $\mathsf{Agr}(w, S)$, is the quantity $\frac{1}{n}|\{i \in [n]\colon w_i \in S_i\}|$. Moreover, we define the quantity $\mathsf{wgt}(S) := \sum_{i \in [n]} |S_i|$ and $\rho(S) := \mathsf{wgt}(S)/(n|\Sigma|)$, where the latter is the expected agreement of a random vector with S. For a code $\mathcal{C} \subseteq \Sigma^n$ and $\alpha \in (0, 1]$, the α-*agreement list* of $\mathcal{C}$ with respect to S, denoted by $\mathsf{LIST}_\mathcal{C}(S, \alpha)$, is the set[8] $\mathsf{LIST}_\mathcal{C}(S, \alpha) := \{c \in \mathcal{C}\colon \mathsf{Agr}(c, S) > \alpha\}$.

Definition 6. (induced code) Let $f\colon \Gamma \times \Omega \to \Sigma$ be a function mapping a finite set $\Gamma \times \Omega$ to a finite set Σ. For $x \in \Gamma$, we use the shorthand $f(x)$ to denote

---

[7] In this section we find it more convenient to use capital letters $D, N, \ldots$ instead of $d, n, \ldots$ that we have so far used and keep the small letters for their base-2 logarithms.

[8] When $\alpha = 1$, we consider codewords with full agreement with the mixture.

the vector $y := (y_i)_{i \in \Omega}$, $y_i := f(x, i)$, whose coordinates are indexed by the elements of Ω in a fixed order. The *code induced by* f, denoted by $\mathcal{C}(f)$ is the set $\{f(x) : x \in \Gamma\}$. The induced code has a natural encoding function given by $x \mapsto f(x)$.

Definition 7. (codeword graph) Let $\mathcal{C} \subseteq \Sigma^n$, $|\Sigma| = q$, be a q-ary code. The *codeword graph* of $\mathcal{C}$ is a bipartite graph with left vertex set $\mathcal{C}$ and right vertex set $n \times \Sigma$, such that for every $x = (x_1, \ldots, x_n) \in \mathcal{C}$, there is an edge between x on the left and $(1, x_1), \ldots, (n, x_n)$ on the right. The *adjacency matrix* of the codeword graph is an $n|\Sigma| \times |\mathcal{C}|$ binary matrix whose (i, j)th entry is 1 iff there is an edge between the ith right vertex and the jth left vertex.

The following is a straightforward generalization of the result in [17] that is also shown in [18]:

Theorem 8. *Let* $f : \mathbb{F}_2^n \times \mathbb{F}_2^t \to \mathbb{F}_2^\ell$ *be a strong* $k \to_\epsilon k'$ *condenser, and* $\mathcal{C} \subseteq \Sigma^{2^t}$ *be its induced code, where* $\Sigma := \mathbb{F}_2^\ell$. *Then for any mixture* S *over* Σ^{2^t} *we have* $|\mathsf{LIST}_\mathcal{C}(S, \rho(S)2^{\ell-k'} + \epsilon)| < 2^k$. $\qquad\qquad \square$

Now using the above tools, we are ready to describe our construction of error-tolerant measurement matrices. We first state a general result without specifying the parameters of the condenser, and then instantiate the construction with various choices of the condenser, resulting in matrices with different properties.

Theorem 9. *Let* $f : \mathbb{F}_2^n \times \mathbb{F}_2^t \to \mathbb{F}_2^\ell$ *be a strong* $k \to_\epsilon k'$ *condenser, and* $\mathcal{C}$ *be its induced code, and define the capital shorthands* $K := 2^k$, $K' := 2^{k'}$, $L := 2^\ell$, $N := 2^n$, $T := 2^t$. *Suppose that the parameters* $p, \nu, \gamma > 0$ *are chosen such that* $(p + \gamma)L/K' + \nu/\gamma < 1 - \epsilon$, *and* $D := \gamma L$. *Then the adjacency matrix of the codeword graph of* $\mathcal{C}$ *(which has* $M := TL$ *rows and* N *columns) is a* $(pM, (\nu/D)M, K - D, 0)$-*correcting measurement matrix for* D-*sparse vectors. Moreover, it allows for a reconstruction algorithm with running time* $O(MN)$.

Proof. Let $\mathcal{M}$ be the adjacency matrix of the codeword graph of $\mathcal{C}$. It immediately follows from the construction that the number of rows of $\mathcal{M}$ (denoted by M) is equal to TL. Moreover, notice that the Hamming weight of each column of $\mathcal{M}$ is exactly T. Let $x \in \mathbb{F}_2^N$ and denote by $y \in \mathbb{F}_2^M$ its encoding, i.e., $y := \mathcal{M}[x]$, and by $\hat{y} \in \mathbb{F}_2^M$ a *received word*, or a *noisy* version of y. The encoding of x can be schematically viewed as follows: The coefficients of x are assigned to the left vertices of the codeword graph and the encoded bit on each right vertex is the bitwise OR of the values of its neighbors. The coordinates of x can be seen in one-to-one correspondence with the codewords of $\mathcal{C}$. Let $X \subseteq \mathcal{C}$ be the set of codewords corresponding to the support of x. The coordinates of the noisy encoding $\hat{y}$ are indexed by the elements of $[T] \times [L]$ and thus, $\hat{y}$ naturally defines a mixture $S = (S_1, \ldots, S_T)$ over $[L]^T$, where S_i contains j iff $\hat{y}$ at position (i, j) is 1. Observe that $\rho(S)$ is the relative Hamming weight (denoted below by $\delta(\cdot)$) of $\hat{y}$; thus, we have $\rho(S) = \delta(\hat{y}) \le \delta(y) + p \le D/L + p = \gamma + p$, where the last inequality comes from the fact that the relative weight of each column of $\mathcal{M}$ is exactly $1/L$ and that x is D-sparse. Furthermore, from the assumption we know that the number of false negatives in the measurement is at most $\nu T L/D = \nu T/\gamma$. Therefore, any codeword in X must have agreement at least $1 - \nu/\gamma$ with S. This is because S is indeed constructed from a mixture of the elements in X, modulo false positives (that do not decrease the agreement) and at most $\nu T/\gamma$ false negatives each of which can reduce the agreement by at most $1/T$. Accordingly, we consider a decoder which simply outputs a binary vector $\hat{x}$ supported on the coordinates corresponding to those codewords of $\mathcal{C}$ that have agreement larger than $1 - \nu/\gamma$ with S. Clearly, the running time of the decoder is linear in the size of the measurement matrix. By the discussion above, $\hat{x}$ must include the support of x. Moreover, Theorem 8 applies for our choice of parameters, implying that $\hat{x}$ must have weight less than K.   □

Instantiations

Now we instantiate the general result given by Theorem 9 with various choices of the underlying condenser and compare the obtained parameters.

Applying Optimal Extractors. Radhakrishan and Ta-Shma showed that nonconstructively, for every k, n, ϵ, there is a strong (k, ϵ)-extractor with seed length $t = \log(n - k) + 2\log(1/\epsilon) + O(1)$ and output length $\ell = k - 2\log(1/\epsilon) - O(1)$, which is the best one can hope for [19]. In particular, they show that a random function achieves these parameters with probability $1 - o(1)$. Plugging this result in Theorem 9, we obtain a non-explicit measurement matrix from a simple, randomized construction that achieves the desired trade-off with high probability:

Corollary 10. *For every choice of constants $p \in [0, 1)$ and $\nu \in [0, \nu_0)$, $\nu_0 := (\sqrt{5 - 4p} - 1)^3/8$, and positive integers D and $N \geq D$, there is an $M \times N$ measurement matrix, where $M = O(D \log N)$, that is $(pM, (\nu/D)M, O(D), 0)$-correcting for D-sparse vectors of length N and allows for a reconstruction algorithm with running time $O(MN)$.*   □

This instantiation, in particular, reproduces a result on randomized construction of approximate group testing schemes with optimal number of measurements in [14], but with stringent conditions on the noise tolerance of the scheme.

Applying Optimal Lossless Condensers. The probabilistic construction of Radhakrishan and Ta-Shma can be extended to the case of lossless condensers and one can show that a random function is with high probability a strong $k \rightarrow_\epsilon k$ condenser with seed length $t = \log n + \log(1/\epsilon) + O(1)$ and output length $\ell = k + \log(1/\epsilon) + O(1)$ [20]. This combined with Theorem 9 gives the following corollary:

Corollary 11. *For positive integers $N \geq D$ and every constant $\delta > 0$ there is an $M \times N$ measurement matrix, where $M = O(D \log N)$, that is $(\Omega(M), \Omega(1/D)M, \delta D, 0)$-correcting for D-sparse vectors of length N and allows for a reconstruction algorithm with running time $O(MN)$.*   □

Both results obtained in Corollaries 10 and 11 almost match the lower bound of Lemma 4 for the number of measurements. However, we note the following distinction between the two results: Instantiating the general construction of Theorem 9 with an extractor gives us a sharp control over the fraction of tolerable errors, and in particular, we can obtain a measurement matrix that is robust against *any* constant fraction (bounded from 1) of false positives. However, the number of false positives in the reconstruction will be bounded by some constant fraction of the sparsity of the vector that cannot be made arbitrarily close to zero. On the other hand, a lossless condenser enables us to bring down the number of false positives in the reconstruction to an arbitrarily small fraction of D (which is, in light of Lemma 2, the best we can hope for), but on the other hand, does not give as good a control on the fraction of tolerable errors as in the extractor case, though we still obtain resilience against the same order of errors.

Applying the Guruswami-Umans-Vadhan's Extractor. While Corollaries 10 and 11 give probabilistic constructions of noise-resilient measurement matrices, certain applications require a fully explicit matrix that is guaranteed to work. To that end, we need to instantiate Theorem 9 with an explicit condenser. First, we use a nearly-optimal explicit extractor due to Guruswami, Umans and Vadhan, summarized in the following theorem:

Theorem 12. *[18] For all positive integers $n \geq k$ and all $\epsilon > 0$, there is an explicit strong (k, ϵ)-extractor* $\mathsf{Ext} \colon \mathbb{F}_2^n \times \mathbb{F}_2^t \to \mathbb{F}_2^\ell$ *with $\ell = k - 2\log(1/\epsilon) - O(1)$ and $t = \log n + O(\log k \cdot \log(k/\epsilon))$.* □

Applying this result in Theorem 9 we obtain a similar trade-off as in Corollary 10, except for a higher number of measurements which would be bounded by $O(2^{O(\log^2 \log D)} D \log N) = O(D^{1+o(1)} \log N)$.

Applying the Zig-Zag Lossless Condenser. In [20] an explicit lossless condenser with optimal output length is constructed. In particular they show the following:

Theorem 13. *[20] For every $k \leq n \in \mathbb{N}$, $\epsilon > 0$ there is an explicit $k \to_\epsilon k$ condenser[9] with seed length $O(\log^3(n/\epsilon))$ and output length $k + \log(1/\epsilon) + O(1)$.*

Combined with Theorem 9, we obtain a similar result as in Corollary 11, except for a higher number of measurements, namely, $M = D2^{\log^3(\log N)} = D \cdot$ quasipoly$(\log N)$.

Measurements Allowing Sublinear Time Reconstruction. The naive reconstruction algorithm of Theorem 9 works efficiently in linear time in the size of the measurement matrix. However, as mentioned in the introduction, for very sparse vectors (i.e., $D \ll N$) it might be of practical importance to have a reconstruction algorithm that runs in *sublinear* time in N, the length of the

---

[9] Though not explicitly mentioned in [20], these condensers can be considered to be strong.

vector, and ideally, polynomial in the number of measurements, which is merely poly$(\log N, D)$ if the number of measurements is optimal.

Observe that the main computational task done by the reconstruction algorithm in Theorem 9 is in fact computation of a suitable agreement list for the induced code of the underlying condenser. Several explicit constructions of condensers are equipped with efficient algorithms for computation of agreement lists that substantially outperform exhaustive search. Namely, for such constructions the set $\mathsf{LIST}_C(S, \rho(S)+\epsilon)$ can be computed in time poly$(2^t, 2^\ell, 2^k, 1/\epsilon)$, which can be much smaller than 2^n. Here we consider two such constructions that achieve the most favorable parameters for our application: Trevisan's extractor[10] [21] and a lossless condenser due to Guruswami et al. [18]. We use the following improvement of Trevisan's extractor due to Raz et al.:

Theorem 14. *[22] For every* $n, k, \ell \in \mathbb{N}$, $(\ell \leq k \leq n)$ *and* $\epsilon > 0$, *there is an explicit strong* (k, ϵ)-*extractor* $\mathsf{Tre} \colon \mathbb{F}_2^n \times \mathbb{F}_2^t \to \mathbb{F}_2^\ell$ *with* $t = O(\log^2(n/\epsilon) \cdot \log(1/\alpha))$, *where* $\alpha := k/(\ell - 1) - 1$ *must be less than* $1/2$. $\square$

Using this result in Theorem 9, we obtain a measurement matrix for which the reconstruction is possible in polynomial time in the number of measurements. Specifically, we obtain the same parameters as in Corollary 10 using Trevisan's extractor except for the number of measurements, $M = O(D2^{\log^3 \log N}) = D \cdot$ quasipoly$(\log N)$.

In the world of lossless condensers, Guruswami et al. [18] show the following:

Theorem 15. *[18] For all constants* $\alpha \in (0,1)$ *and every* $k \leq n \in \mathbb{N}$, $\epsilon > 0$ *there is an explicit strong* $k \to_\epsilon k$ *condenser with seed length* $t = (1+1/\alpha)\log(nk/\epsilon) + O(1)$ *and output length* $\ell = d + (1 + \alpha)k$. *Moreover, the condenser has efficient list recovery.* $\square$

As before, we use this construction in Theorem 9 and obtain the following:

Corollary 16. *For positive integers* $N \geq D$ *and any constants* $\delta, \alpha > 0$ *there is an* $M \times N$ *measurement matrix, where* $M = O(D^{3+\alpha+2/\alpha}(\log N)^{2+2/\alpha})$, *that is* $(\Omega(e), \Omega(e/D), \delta D, 0)$-*correcting for* D-*sparse vectors of length* N, *where* $e := (\log N)^{1+1/\alpha} D^{2+1/\alpha}$. *Moreover, the matrix allows for a reconstruction algorithm with running time* poly(M). $\square$

Acknowledgment

The author is thankful to Amin Shokrollahi for introducing him to the group testing problem and his comments on an earlier draft of this paper, and to Venkatesan Guruswami for several illuminating discussions that led to considerable improvement of the results presented in this work.

---

[10] Trevisan's extractor belongs to a class of extractors obtained from *black-box pseudorandom generators*. Ta-Shma and Zuckerman [17] show that for any such construction the agreement list is efficiently computable.

References

1. Du, D.Z., Hwang, F.: Combinatorial Group Testing and its Applications, 2nd edn. World Scientific, Singapore (2000)
2. Du, D.-Z., Hwang, F.K.: Pooling Designs and Nonadaptive Group Testing. World Scientific, Singapore (2006)
3. Knill, E.: Lower bounds for identifying subset members with subset queries. In: Proceedings of SODA, pp. 369–377 (1995)
4. Dyachkov, A., Rykov, V.: A survey of superimposed code theory. Problems of Control and Information Theory 12(4), 229–242 (1983)
5. Knill, E., Bruno, W.J., Torney, D.C.: Non-adaptive group testing in the presence of errors. Discrete Appl. Math. 88(1–3), 261–290 (1998)
6. D'yachkov, A.G., Rykov, V.: Bounds of the length of disjunct codes. Problems of Control and Information Theory 11, 7–13 (1982)
7. Ruszinkó: On the upper bound of the size of the r-cover-free families. J. Comb. Theory., Series A 66, 302–310 (1994)
8. Füredi, Z.: On r-cover-free families. J. Comb. Theory, Series A 73, 172–173 (1996)
9. Kautz, W., Singleton, R.: Nonrandom binary superimposed codes. IEEE Transactions on Information Theory 10, 363–377 (1964)
10. Macula, A.: Probabilistic nonadaptive and two-stage group testing with relatively small pools and DNA library screening. J. Comb. Optim. 2, 385–397 (1999)
11. Berger, T., Mandell, J., Subrahmanya, P.: Maximally efficient two-stage group testing. Biometrics 56, 833–840 (2000)
12. De Bonis, A., Gasieniec, L., Vaccaro, U.: Optimal two-stage algorithms for group testing problems. SIAM Journal on Computing 34(5), 1253–1270 (2005)
13. Eppstein, D., Goodrich, M., Hirschberg, D.: Improved combinatorial group testing algorithms for real-world problem sizes. SIAM J. Comp. 36(5), 1360–1375 (2007)
14. Cheng, Y., Du, D.Z.: New constructions of one- and two-stage pooling designs. Journal of Computational Biology 15(2), 195–205 (2008)
15. Indyk, P.: Explicit constructions of selectors with applications. In: Proceedings of SODA (2002)
16. Chlebus, B., Kowalski, D.: Almost optimal explicit selectors. In: Liśkiewicz, M., Reischuk, R. (eds.) FCT 2005. LNCS, vol. 3623, pp. 270–280. Springer, Heidelberg (2005)
17. Ta-Shma, A., Zuckerman, D.: Extractor codes. IEEE Transactions on Information Theory 50(12), 3015–3025 (2004)
18. Guruswami, V., Umans, C., Vadhan, S.: Unbalanced expanders and randomness extractors from Parvaresh-Vardy codes. In: Proc. of the 22nd IEEE CCC (2007)
19. Radhakrishnan, J., Ta-Shma, A.: Tight bounds for depth-two superconcentrators. In: Proceedings of the 38th FOCS, pp. 585–594 (1997)
20. Capalbo, M., Reingold, O., Vadhan, S., Wigderson, A.: Randomness conductors and constant-degree expansion beyond the degree/2 barrier. In: Proceedings of the 34th STOC, pp. 659–668 (2002)
21. Trevisan, L.: Extractors and pseudorandom generators. Journal of the ACM 48(4), 860–879 (2001)
22. Raz, R., Reingold, O., Vadhan, S.: Extracting all the randomness and reducing the error in Trevisan's extractor. JCSS 65(1), 97–128 (2002)

Martingales on Trees and the Empire Chromatic Number of Random Trees

Colin Cooper[1], Andrew R.A. McGrae[2], and Michele Zito[2]

[1] Department of Computer Science, Kings' College, London WC2R 2LS, UK
colin.cooper@kcl.ac.uk
[2] Department of Computer Science, University of Liverpool, Liverpool, L69 3BX, UK
{A.R.A.McGrae,M.Zito}@liverpool.ac.uk

Abstract. We study the empire colouring problem (as defined by Percy Heawood in 1890) for maps whose dual planar graph is a tree, with empires formed by exactly r countries. We prove that, for each fixed $r > 1$, with probability approaching one as the size of the graph grows to infinity, the minimum number of colours for which a feasible solution exists takes one of seven possible values.

1   Introduction

Assume that the n vertices of a graph G can be partitioned into blocks $B_1, B_2, \ldots$ of size $r > 1$, so that B_i contains vertices labelled $(i-1)r+1, (i-1)r+2, \ldots, ir$. The *r-empire chromatic number* of G is the minimum number of colours $\chi_r(G)$ needed to colour the vertices of G in such a way that all vertices in a same block receive the same colour, but pairs of blocks connected by at least one edge of G are coloured differently. Let $\mathcal{T}_n$ denote a random n-vertex labelled tree (as defined, say, in [3]). Building on previous work by two of us [11], in this paper we prove that with probability approaching one as n tends to infinity (or *asymptotically almost surely* (a.a.s.) as we will say from now on) $\chi_r(\mathcal{T}_n)$ takes one of seven possible values, for fixed $r > 1$. This significantly improves the results in [11], where it was proved that there exists a positive integer $s_r = O(r/\log r)$ such that

$$s_r < \chi_r(\mathcal{T}_n) \le 2r \qquad a.a.s.$$

The proof of our results relies on a martingale argument and on tight estimates on the first two moments of a random variable counting the number of r-empire colourings of $\mathcal{T}_n$ using at most s colours. The key ingredient in the argument is a new martingale construction on the set of n-vertex labelled trees which may be of independent interest.

The reader at this point may question the reasons for studying this type of colourings. Our interest in the problem comes from its relationship with other important colouring problems. First of all its decision version reduces easily to the classical vertex colouring problem, but it is not clear to what extent the two are equivalent. Secondly, if G is planar, the blocks represent groups of countries belonging to the same "empire" and a colouring in the sense described above

M. Kutyłowski, M. Gębala, and W. Charatonik (Eds.): FCT 2009, LNCS 5699, pp. 74–83, 2009.
© Springer-Verlag Berlin Heidelberg 2009

corresponds to a map colouring that gives all countries in the same empire the same colour and different colours to adjacent empires. This *r-empire colouring problem* was defined by Heawood [4] in the same paper in which he refuted a previous "proof" of the famous Four Colour Theorem (note that the 1-empire colouring problem is just planar graph colouring). It has been proved that $6r$ colours are always sufficient, and in some cases necessary to solve this problem [6], however not much is known about the distribution of the values of $\chi_r(G)$ over the set of all planar graphs on n vertices. Our work is a first step in this direction, and it indicates that, at least for trees, the worst-case predictions are very pessimistic: $2r$ colours are necessary and sufficient to colour all trees [11, Theorem 1], but, in fact, $\chi_r(\mathcal{T}_n) = O(r/\log r)$ a.a.s. Finally, the empire colouring problem is also related to the problem of colouring graphs of given *thickness* [5] (a graph has thickness t if t is the minimum integer such that its edges can be partitioned into at least t planar graphs). The problem is unsolved even in the worst-case sense. It is known that the chromatic number of any graph of thickness two must be between eight and twelve but the exact solution of this problem is not known.

The rest of the paper is organized as follows. In Section 2 we outline our results and proof strategy. In Section 3 we list a number of key properties of $\mathcal{T}_n$ and its r-empire colourings. Section 4 is devoted to the definition of a martingale on the set of n-vertex labelled trees. In Section 5 we prove that $\chi_r(\mathcal{T}_n)$ is concentrated in an interval of size six a.a.s. Finally, in Section 6 we give tight estimates on the actual location of this interval.

2   Results and Proof Methods

Let Z be a random variable defined on some combinatorial structure $\mathcal{G}$. If $\mathcal{G}$ can be defined in some "orderly" way (formalised by the notion of filter discussed in Section 4) the difference $Z - \mathrm{E}Z$ can be estimated by associating a sequence of random variables $X_0, X_1, \ldots X_t$ called a Doob martingale (see Section 4) to Z in such a way that $X_0 = \mathrm{E}Z$ and $X_t = Z$ and no X_i is "too far" from X_0. More specifically, if the martingale differences $X_i - X_{i-1}$ are small one can get upper bounds on the probability that Z is far from $\mathrm{E}Z$ which become smaller and smaller as the size of the structures considered becomes large. In this way (deterministic) information about $\mathrm{E}Z$ can be used to make a.a.s. statements about Z.

This approach has been applied successfully to various problems including the occupancy [7], the analysis of quicksort [10], and, in a less direct way, the vertex colouring of the random graph $\mathcal{G}_{n,p}$ [15]. We briefly outline the proof strategy used in the last paper as it is particularly relevant to our problem. To obtain information about the range of variability of $\chi(\mathcal{G}_{n,p})$ the authors proved that (a) any subgraph of $\mathcal{G}_{n,p}$ with less than some $z = z(n,p)$ vertices is relatively sparse and, therefore, easy to colour with just three colours and that (b) if k is such that a large enough proportion of the graphs considered is k-colourable then the set of vertices that fail to be coloured is small (in particular it's $o(z)$). We will adopt a similar approach here. We will start by proving that any subgraph induced by a small collection of blocks in $\mathcal{T}_n$ (and any subgraph obtained from it by removing any number of blocks) has small minimum degree (this is Lemma 2 in Section 3). Then we will provide an orderly definition of the class of labelled n-vertex trees and, using a suitably defined Doob martingale on such structures, prove that at least $n - 3r\sqrt{(n-1)\log\omega(n)}$ of the vertices of $\mathcal{T}_n$ can be coloured with $s_r + 1$ colours with probability at least $1 - 1/\omega(n)$ (see Lemma 4 in Section 5). These two results are sufficient to prove the following theorem.

Theorem 1. *For fixed $r > 1$ the r-empire chromatic number of $\mathcal{T}_n$ is a.a.s. concentrated over six consecutive integers.*

One problem with the martingale approach outlined above is that it does not give precise information on the location of these concentration intervals. To get that, one often needs to rely on additional results. Using asymptotic information about the first two moments of the number of r-empire colourings with s colour classes obtained in [11] (see Section 3) we will be able to prove the following result.

Theorem 2. *For every fixed integer $r > 1$, $\chi_r(\mathcal{T}_n)$ satisfies*

$$s_r \leq \chi_r(\mathcal{T}_n) \leq s_r + 6.$$

Furthermore if $r > \frac{2(s_r-1)^2}{2s_r-3}\log s_r$ then $s_r + 1 \leq \chi_r(\mathcal{T}_n) \leq s_r + 6$.

Table 1 gives the range for $\chi_r(\mathcal{T}_n)$ for the first few values of r. Note that by [11, Theorem 1] $\chi_r(\mathcal{T}_n) \leq 2r$ for every fixed positive r. Thus Theorem 2 improves the results in [11] for $r \geq 6$. Also, we found that $r = 43$ is the smallest value of r for which the concentration range has length seven: $\chi_{43}(\mathcal{T}_n) \in \{16, 17, 18, 19, 20, 21, 22\}$.

Table 1. The concentration intervals of $\chi_r(\mathcal{T}_n)$ for $r \leq 12$

r	2	3,4	5,6,7	8,9	10,11,12
$\chi_r(\mathcal{T}_n)$	3,4,5,6,7,8	4,5,6,7,8,9	5,6,7,8,9,10	6,7,8,9,10,11	7,8,9,10,11,12

The observant reader will have noticed that, although Theorem 1 and Theorem 2 prove that $\chi_r(\mathcal{T}_n)$ a.a.s. belongs to a set of values of small fixed size, they are weaker than analogous statements [1,2,9] proved in the past for other models of random graphs. We speculate that this may be due to the particular features of the problem at hand. The precise information on the moments of the relevant random variables helps arguing that six consecutive values suffice most of the times. However the main weakness seems to be in the fact that the martingale defined in Section 4, in a sense, builds the tree one edge at a time, whereas the r-empire colourings put joint constraints on blocks of vertices.

3   Relevant Properties of Random Trees

To make our concentration argument go through we need asymptotic information about the number of r-empire colourings of $\mathcal{T}_n$ using a specific number of colours and we need to prove that certain "small" induced subgraphs of $\mathcal{T}_n$ are sparse. Results in [11] address the first issue. A colouring is *balanced* if its colour classes have the same size. Let $W_{r,s}(\mathcal{T}_n)$ be the number of balanced r-empire colourings of $\mathcal{T}_n$ using s colours. For each integer $r \geq 2$, and $s \geq 2$ let $c_{s,r} = s^{\frac{1}{r}-1}(s-1)$ and $a_n = n^{-\frac{s-1}{2}}(c_{s,r})^n$. The following result was proved in [11].

Theorem 3. *For each integer $r \geq 2$, $s \geq 2$, and $k \geq 1$, there exists a positive real number $C_{s,r,k}$, independent of n, such that*

$$\mathrm{E}W_{r,s}(\mathcal{T}_n)^k \sim C_{s,r,k} \times (a_n)^k.$$

The next two results, also from [11], follow from Theorem 3 and, respectively, Markov's and Chebyshev's inequalities.

Theorem 4. *For each fixed $r > 1$ there exists a positive integer s_r such that $W_{r,s}(\mathcal{T}_n) = 0$ a.a.s. for $s \leq s_r$.*

Theorem 5. *For each fixed $r > 1$, $W_{r,s}(\mathcal{T}_n) > 0$ with probability at least $b_{r,s}(n) > 0$ for $s > s_r$. Furthermore there exist positive constants $b_{r,s}$ such that $b_{r,s}(n) \to b_{r,s}$ as n tends to infinity.*

We move now to the density properties of small subgraphs of $\mathcal{T}_n$. In what follows a set of vertices U in a tree T spans an edge e of T if $e \subseteq U$. We start by arguing that the vertices of $\mathcal{T}_n$ belonging to any given small collection H of blocks in $\mathcal{T}_n$ don't span too many edges.

Lemma 1. *For any $\delta > 0$, let integers h and m be such that $h < n^{3/5-\delta}$ and $m < rh$. The probability that the vertices in a given collection of h blocks in $\mathcal{T}_n$ spans m specific edges is at most*

$$\left(1 + \frac{2}{n}\right)^{rh-1-m} \left(\frac{e}{n}\right)^m.$$

Remark. Note that the result does not exclude the possibility that other edges may belong to the graph induced by the vertices in the given blocks. In the proof we will use $f \in E(H)$ to signify that the vertices in the collection H spans edge f (and possibly others). On the other hand $E(H) = \{f\}$ will denote the fact that f is *the only* edge spanned by the vertices in (the blocks of) H.

Proof. The probability of interest can be estimated by counting the number of labelled trees on n vertices for which a particular collection H of h blocks spans m particular edges. Using inclusion-exclusion we have

$$\Pr[f_1, \ldots, f_m \in E(H)] = \sum_{k=0}^{rh-1-m} \binom{rh-1-m}{k}$$
$$\times (-1)^k \Pr[|H| = h \wedge E(H) = \{f_1, \ldots, f_m, g_1, \ldots, g_k\}]. \qquad (1)$$

We next argue that, in fact, the right-hand side of (1) is asymptotic to $\Pr[E(H) = \{f_1, \ldots, f_m\}]$ as the addition of more edges makes the event less and less likely. First note that we have

$$\Pr[f_1, \ldots, f_m \in E(H)] \leq$$

$$\leq \sum_{k=0}^{rh-1-m} \binom{rh-1-m}{k} \Pr[E(H) = \{f_1, \ldots, f_m, g_1, \ldots, g_k\}].$$

From now on call $T(k)$ the kth term in the sum above. By an old result of Moon [12, Theorem 2] we have that

$$\Pr[E(H) = \{f_1, \ldots, f_m, g_1, \ldots, g_k\}] = n^{-m-k} \prod_{i=1}^{rh-m-k} |C_i|$$

(where $C_1, \ldots, C_{rh-m-k}$ are the components formed on the vertices of H by the edges $f_1, \ldots, f_m, g_1, \ldots, g_k$). We claim that, for each integer $k \in \{0, \ldots, rh-2-m\}$, assuming w.l.o.g. that edge g_{k+1} connects components C_{j_1} and C_{j_2}, we have

$$T(k+1) = \frac{rh-1-m-k}{(k+1)n} \left(\frac{|C_{j_1}| + |C_{j_2}|}{|C_{j_1}| \cdot |C_{j_2}|} \right) T(k). \tag{2}$$

To believe this claim note that the addition of g_{k+1} reduces the number of components by one because two components (possibly two isolated vertices) of the forest on $m + k$ edges spanning H, say C_{j_1} and C_{j_2}, get connected.

Since $1 \leq |C_i| \leq rh$ and $|C_{j_1}| + |C_{j_2}| \leq rh$, implies

$$\frac{|C_{j_1}| + |C_{j_2}|}{|C_{j_1}| \cdot |C_{j_2}|} \leq 2,$$

equation (2) leads to a recurrence providing an upper bound on $T(k+1)$ in terms of $T(k)$. Solving it with initial condition $T(0) = n^{-m} \prod_{i=1}^{rh-m} |C_i|$ gives

$$T(k) \leq \left(\frac{2}{n} \right)^k \binom{rh-1-m}{k} n^{-m} \prod_{i=1}^{rh-m} |C_i|.$$

Thus, by the binomial theorem,

$$\Pr[f_1, \ldots, f_m \in E(H)] \leq \left(1 + \frac{2}{n} \right)^{rh-1-m} n^{-m} \prod_{i=1}^{rh-m} |C_i|.$$

The result follows from the inequality

$$\prod_{i=1}^{rh-m} x_i \leq \left(\frac{rh}{rh-m} \right)^{rh-m},$$

which is true of any set of positive integers $x_1, \ldots, x_{rh-m}$ adding to rh. $\qquad \square$

The following is the relatively simple consequence of Lemma 1 that will be used in the proof of Theorem 1.

Lemma 2. *For any $\delta > 0$, any collection of less than $n^{3/5-\delta}$ blocks in $\mathcal{T}_n$ has average degree less than five a.a.s.*

Proof. In this proof H denotes a collection of blocks in $V(\mathcal{T}_n)$ and $|H|$ the number of blocks in H. We will prove that the probability of

$$\text{BAD} \equiv \exists H \; |H| < n^{\frac{3}{5}-\delta} \wedge |E(H)| \geq \frac{5}{2}|H|$$

tends to zero as n tends to infinity. Let $M = \binom{rh}{2}$. By a simple union bound,

$$\Pr[\text{BAD}] \leq \sum_{h=2}^{\lfloor n^{\frac{3}{5}-\delta}\rfloor} \binom{n/r}{h} \sum_{m=\lceil 5h/2\rceil}^{rh-1} \binom{M}{m} \Pr[f_1, \ldots, f_m \in E(H)]$$

(here f_j are edges connecting two vertices belonging to some blocks of H). By Lemma 1

$$\Pr[f_1, \ldots, f_m \in E(H)] \leq (1+o(1))\left(\frac{e}{n}\right)^m.$$

Hence

$$\Pr[\text{BAD}] \leq (1+o(1)) \sum_{h=2}^{\lfloor n^{3/5-\delta}\rfloor} \binom{n/r}{h} \sum_{m=\lceil 5h/2\rceil}^{rh-1} \binom{M}{m}\left(\frac{e}{n}\right)^m$$

$$\leq (1+o(1)) \sum_{h=2}^{\lfloor n^{3/5-\delta}\rfloor} \left(\frac{ne}{rh}\right)^h \sum_{m=\lceil 5h/2\rceil}^{rh-1} \left(\frac{Me^2}{mn}\right)^m$$

$$\leq (1+o(1)) \sum_{h=2}^{\lfloor n^{3/5-\delta}\rfloor} \left(\frac{ne}{rh}\right)^h \sum_{m=\lceil 5h/2\rceil}^{rh-1} \left(\frac{r^2he^2}{5n}\right)^m$$

where the last inequality holds because $M \leq (rh)^2/2$ and $m > 5h/2$. Now, the argument of the inner sum is less than one for sufficiently large n. Therefore

$$\Pr[\text{BAD}] \leq (1+o(1)) \sum_{h=2}^{\lfloor n^{3/5-\delta}\rfloor} \left(\frac{ne}{rh}\right)^h rh \left(\frac{r^2he^2}{5n}\right)^{\frac{5h}{2}}$$

$$= (1+o(1)) \sum_{h=2}^{\lfloor n^{3/5-\delta}\rfloor} rh \left[\left(\frac{r^4e^6}{5^{5/2}}\right)\left(\frac{h}{n}\right)^{3/2}\right]^h$$

$$\leq (1+o(1)) \sum_{h=2}^{\lfloor n^{3/5-\delta}\rfloor} rh \left[\left(\frac{r^4e^6}{5^{5/2}}\right)\left(\frac{1}{n}\right)^{\frac{3}{5}+\frac{3\delta}{2}}\right]^h.$$

Thus, there exists $C > 0$ (depending on r and δ but independent of n) such that

$$\Pr[\text{BAD}] \leq (1+o(1))rn^{\frac{6}{5}-2\delta}\left[\left(\frac{r^4e^6}{5^{5/2}}\right)\left(\frac{1}{n}\right)^{\frac{3}{5}+\frac{3\delta}{2}}\right]^2 \leq Cn^{-\delta}. \qquad \square$$

4   Martingales

In this section we describe our martingale construction over the set of all labelled trees on n vertices. We start by recalling few relevant definitions and results (the interested reader may consult [8, Section 6.7] or [14, Chapter 4] for a more extensive treatment of the topic). A σ-field $(\Omega, \mathcal{F})$ is a set Ω, along with a family $\mathcal{F}$ of subsets that contains the empty set and is closed under complementation and countable unions.

Definition 1. *Given the σ-field $(\Omega, 2^\Omega)$, a filter is a sequence $\mathcal{F}_0 \subseteq \mathcal{F}_1 \subseteq \ldots \subseteq \mathcal{F}_{n-1} \subseteq \mathcal{F}_n = 2^\Omega$ such that*

1. *$\mathcal{F}_0 = \{\emptyset, \Omega\}$,*
2. *$(\Omega, \mathcal{F}_i)$ is a σ-field.*

One way to define a filter is to form each $\mathcal{F}_i$ by means of a partition $(P^i_j)_{j \in J_i}$ of Ω: $\mathcal{F}_i$ is then the collection of all sets that may be defined as unions of blocks in the partition. Note that the partition defining $\mathcal{F}_{i+1}$ is a refinement of the one defining $\mathcal{F}_i$. Filters are used in the definition of martingale which we state for completeness.

Definition 2. *Let $(\Omega, \mathcal{F}, \Pr)$ be a probability space with a filter $(\mathcal{F}_i)_{i \geq 0}$. Suppose that $X_0, X_1, \ldots$ are random variables such that, for each $i \geq 0$, X_i is $\mathcal{F}_i$-measurable. The sequence $X_0, \ldots, X_n$ is a martingale provided that, for all $i \geq 0$,*

$$\mathrm{E}(X_{i+1} \mid \mathcal{F}_i) = X_i.$$

Doob martingales (see for instance [8]) give a simple way to construct a martingale from any given random variable Z. The following result, known as Azuma's inequality (see, for instance, [14, Theorem 4.16]), gives bounds on the probability that $|Z - \mathrm{E}Z|$ is large using a Doob martingale.

Theorem 6. *Let $(\Omega, \mathcal{F})$ be a σ-field and $\mathcal{F}_0 \subseteq \mathcal{F}_1 \subseteq \ldots \subseteq \mathcal{F}_n$ a filter. Let the random variable Z be $\mathcal{F}_n$-measurable, and let $X_0, X_1, \ldots, X_n$ be the martingale obtained by setting $X_i = \mathrm{E}(Z \mid \mathcal{F}_i)$. Suppose that for each $i = 1, \ldots, n$ there is a constant c_i such that*

$$|X_i - X_{i-1}| \leq c_i. \tag{3}$$

Then, for any $t > 0$,

$$\Pr[Z - \mathrm{E}Z < -t] \leq \exp\left\{-2t^2 / \sum_{i=1}^{n} (c_i)^2\right\},$$

$$\Pr[Z - \mathrm{E}Z > t] \leq \exp\left\{-2t^2 / \sum_{i=1}^{n} (c_i)^2\right\}.$$

Martingales on random trees. It is well-known (see for instance [13]) that a bijection maps each n-vertex tree T labelled over the set $\{1,\ldots,n\}$ to a unique sequence of $n-2$ numbers in the same set, referred to as its *Prüfer code*. Given a sequences $(c_1,\ldots,c_{n-2})$, the first $n-2$ edges of the corresponding tree are the sets $\{c_i,\ell_i\}$, where ℓ_i is the smallest element of $\{1,\ldots,n\} \setminus \{\ell_1,\ldots,\ell_{i-1}\}$ that does not occur in $(c_i,\ldots,c_{n-2})$. The last edge of T will always connect vertex labelled n with the single element of $\{1,\ldots,n-1\} \setminus \{\ell_1,\ldots,\ell_{n-2}\}$. Conversely the code of T can be retrieved by peeling off the vertices of T picking the leaf with the smallest label each time and setting c_i as the parent of the leaf removed at step i in this process. We denote by $C(T)$ the Prüfer code of T (in fact it is handy to work with sequences of the form $(c_1,\ldots,c_{n-2},n)$). Prüfer codes are very handy because they define a very simple encoding of random trees into sequences of positive integers. For our purposes, however, we also need to define another, related sequence. Let $L(T) = (u_1,\ldots,u_{n-1})$ be the permutation of the set $\{1,\ldots,n-1\}$ corresponding to the order in which leaves are peeled off T to get $C(T)$. Note that the pairs (u_i,c_i), for $i \in \{1,\ldots,n-1\}$ define the edges of T. Thus if $n=8$ and $C(T) = (3,1,2,6,6,1,8)$ then $L(T) = (4,3,5,2,7,6,1)$.

Given $L(T)$, denote by S_L the set of Prüfer codes whose corresponding trees share the same sequence $L = L(T) = (u_1,\ldots,u_{n-1})$, and define a filter on $(S_L, 2^{S_L})$ by generating S_i, for $i \in \{0,\ldots,n-1\}$, from a partition $(P_j^i)_{j \in J_i}$ of S_L such that P_j^i contains all Prüfer codes in S_L sharing the same prefix $(c_1^j, c_2^j, \ldots, c_i^j)$ (here we assume that codes are ordered lexicographically). If $Z = Z(T_n)$ is a random variable defined on the random tree T_n, we may bound the difference $Z - EZ$ using the Doob martingale associated with the filter $(S_i)_{i \geq 0}$ defined over $S_{L(T_n)}$, provided we have some means of estimating the martingale differences in (3). This is possible because of the following result which translates small differences in Z on rather similar trees to small differences between consecutive elements of the martingale sequence.

Lemma 3. *Let Z be a random variable defined on T_n and let $X_0, X_1, \ldots$ be the Doob martingale defined on Z. Then, for each $i > 0$*

$$|X_i - X_{i-1}| \leq |Z(T) - Z(T')|$$

where T and T' are two labelled trees on n vertices such that $C(T) \in S_{L(T')}$ and the Prüfer codes $C(T)$ a $C(T')$ only differ at position i.

Proof (Sketch). The proof is similar to that of [15, Theorem 5]. The relevant measure-preserving mapping in this case relates a (tree with) Prüfer code starting with the prefix $(c_1, c_2, \ldots, c_{i-1}, c_i)$ to one starting with $(c_1, c_2, \ldots, c_{i-1}, c_i')$ provided the codes coincide at positions $i+1, i+2, \ldots$. Also notice that, given a sequence $(c_1, c_2, \ldots, c_i)$ of numbers in $\{1,\ldots,n\}$, all trees T with $C(T) \in S_{L(T')}$ and such that all Prüfer codes share the same prefix $(c_1, c_2, \ldots, c_i)$ are assigned the same probability n^{n-2-i}.   □

5   Concentration

To be able to prove Theorem 1 we still need to argue that most vertices of $\mathcal{T}_n$ can be coloured with $s_r + 1$ colours.

In the following result we use the fact, which follows directly from Theorem 5, that $s_r + 1$ is in fact the smallest integer s^* for which $\Pr[\chi_r(\mathcal{T}_n) \leq s^*] \geq 1/\omega(n)$ for any function tending to infinity arbitrarily slowly. Note that s^* cannot be less than $s_r + 1$ as $\Pr[\chi_r(\mathcal{T}_n) \leq s_r]$ is exponentially small by Theorem 4.

Lemma 4. *Let n be a positive integer and $\omega(n)$ a function of n which tends to infinity as n grows. With probability greater than $1 - 1/\omega(n)$ all but at most $3r\sqrt{(n-1)\log\omega(n)}$ of the vertices of $\mathcal{T}_n$ can be coloured using $s_r + 1$ colours.*

Proof. Let $Y_{s_r+1}(\mathcal{T}_n)$ be the minimal size of a set of vertices U in $\mathcal{T}_n$ such that $\mathcal{T}_n \setminus U$ is $s_r + 1$ colourable. Let T and T' be two instances of $\mathcal{T}_n$ belonging to the same S_L whose Prüfer codes differ in one position. Then

$$|Y_{s_r+1}(T) - Y_{s_r+1}(T')| \leq 3r$$

(as the symmetric difference of $E(T)$ and $E(T')$ spans $3r$ vertices). Thus by Theorem 6,

$$\Pr[Y_{s_r+1} - EY_{s_r+1} \geq \alpha\sqrt{n-1}] \leq \exp\left\{-2\alpha^2/9r^2\right\}, \tag{4}$$

$$\Pr[Y_{s_r+1} - EY_{s_r+1} \leq -\alpha\sqrt{n-1}] \leq \exp\left\{-2\alpha^2/9r^2\right\}. \tag{5}$$

Now, choose $\alpha = 3r\sqrt{\log\omega(n)}$ so that $\exp\left\{-2\alpha^2/9r^2\right\} = 1/\omega(n)$. It follows from (4) that $EY_{s_r+1} < \alpha\sqrt{n-1}$. Thus, using (5), we have

$$\Pr[Y_{s_r+1} \geq 2\alpha\sqrt{n-1}] < 1/\omega(n). \qquad \square$$

Proof of Theorem 1. By Lemma 4 a.a.s. all vertices of $\mathcal{T}_n$ outside some set U, $|U| < 3r\sqrt{(n-1)\log\omega(n)}$, can be coloured with $s_r + 1$ colours. Note that any empire of $\mathcal{T}_n$ is either in U or its intersection with U is empty. We will prove that $\chi_r(\mathcal{T}_n) \leq s_r + 6$ a.a.s. To see this note that the set of blocks spanned by U has size less than $n^{3/5-\delta}$, for any $\delta < 1/10$. Hence, by Lemma 2, it is 5-colourable. The colouring of $\mathcal{T}_n$ can be completed using at most $s_r + 1$ new colours. $\qquad \square$

6   Location, Location, Location

The results so far are interesting in that they improve (at least for $r > 6$) the results in [11]. However they have one significant weakness. They do not provide any information on the actual location of the concentration interval. Theorem 2 addresses this issue. It can be derived using the concentration result proved in the last section, and using information about the first two moments of $W_{r,s}(\mathcal{T}_n)$.

Proof of Theorem 2. Let

$$u_s = \frac{2(s-1)^2}{2s-3}\log s \qquad c_s = \frac{6s^3}{6s^2 - 3s + 2}\log(s+1).$$

Theorem 3 implies that, for each integer $s > 1$, $\chi_r(\mathcal{T}_n) > s$ a.a.s. if $r > u_s$, and $\chi_r(\mathcal{T}_n) \leq s$ with some positive probability for $r < c_{s-1}$. Note that for $c_{s-1} < u_s < c_s$, for all positive integers s. Thus if s is the smallest integer such that $r < c_s$ two possibilities arise:

1. $u_s < r < c_s$, or
2. $c_{s-1} \leq r \leq u_s$.

In the first case we know by Theorem 4 that $\chi_r(\mathcal{T}_n) > s_r$ a.a.s. and, by Theorem 1, $\chi_r(\mathcal{T}_n) \leq s_r + 6$ a.a.s. In the second one we cannot exclude the possibility that $\chi_r(\mathcal{T}_n) = s_r$.   □

References

1. Achlioptas, D., Moore, C.: The chromatic number of random regular graphs. In: Jansen, K., Khanna, S., Rolim, J.D.P., Ron, D. (eds.) RANDOM 2004 and AP-PROX 2004. LNCS, vol. 3122, pp. 219–228. Springer, Heidelberg (2004)
2. Achlioptas, D., Naor, A.: The two possible values of the chromatic number of a random graph. Annals of Mathematics 162, 1335–1351 (2005)
3. Drmota, M.: Random Trees. Springer, Wien (2009)
4. Heawood, P.J.: Map colour theorem. Quarterly Journal of Pure and Applied Mathematics 24, 332–338 (1890)
5. Hutchinson, J.P.: Coloring ordinary maps, maps of empires, and maps of the moon. Mathematics Magazine 66, 211–226 (1993)
6. Jackson, B., Ringel, G.: Solution of Heawood's empire problem in the plane. Journal für die Reine und Angewandte Mathematik 347, 146–153 (1984)
7. Kamath, A., Motwani, R., Palem, K., Spirakis, P.: Tail bounds for occupancy and the satisfiability threshold conjecture. Random Structures and Algorithms 7, 59–80 (1995)
8. Karlin, S., Taylor, H.M.: A First Course in Stochastic Processes. Academic Press, New York (1975)
9. Łuczak, T.: A note on the sharp concentration of the chromatic number of random graphs. Combinatorica 11, 295–297 (1991)
10. McDiarmid, C., Hayward, R.: Strong concentration for quicksort. In: SODA 1992: Proceedings of the third annual ACM-SIAM symposium on Discrete algorithms, pp. 414–421. Society for Industrial and Applied Mathematics, Philadelphia (1992)
11. McGrae, A.R., Zito, M.: Colouring random empire trees. In: Ochmański, E., Tyszkiewicz, J. (eds.) MFCS 2008. LNCS, vol. 5162, pp. 515–526. Springer, Heidelberg (2008)
12. Moon, J.W.: Enumerating labelled trees. In: Harary, F. (ed.) Graph Theory and Theoretical Physics, pp. 261–272. Academic Press, New York (1967)
13. Moon, J.W.: Counting Labelled Trees. Canadian Mathematical Congress, Montreal (1970)
14. Motwani, R., Raghavan, P.: Randomized Algorithms. Cambridge University Press, Cambridge (1995)
15. Shamir, E., Spencer, J.: Sharp concentration of the chromatic number on random graphs $G_{n,p}$. Combinatorica 7, 121–129 (1987)

Competitive Group Testing and Learning Hidden Vertex Covers with Minimum Adaptivity

Peter Damaschke and Azam Sheikh Muhammad

Department of Computer Science and Engineering,
Chalmers University, 41296 Göteborg, Sweden
{ptr,azams}@chalmers.se

Abstract. Suppose that we are given a set of n elements d of which are "defective". A group test can check for any subset, called a pool, whether it contains a defective. It is well known that d defectives can be found by using $O(d \log n)$ pools. This nearly optimal number of pools can be achieved in 2 stages, where tests within a stage are done in parallel. But then d must be known in advance. Here we explore group testing strategies that use a nearly optimal number of pools and a few stages although d is not known to the searcher. One easily sees that $O(\log d)$ stages are sufficient for a strategy with $O(d \log n)$ pools. Here we prove a lower bound of $\Omega(\log d / \log \log d)$ stages and a more general pools vs. stages tradeoff. As opposed to this, we devise a randomized strategy that finds d defectives using $O(d \log(n/d))$ pools in 3 stages, with any desired probability $1 - \epsilon$. Open questions concern the optimal constant factors and practical implications. A related problem motivated by, e.g., biological network analysis is to learn hidden vertex covers of a small size k in unknown graphs by edge group tests. (Does a given subset of vertices contain an edge?) We give a 1-stage strategy using $O(k^3 \log n)$ pools, with any FPT algorithm for vertex cover enumeration as a decoder.

1   Background and Contributions

The *group testing* problem is to find d elements called *positive* (or synonymously, *defective*) elements in a set X of size n by queries of the following type. The searcher can choose arbitrary subsets $Q \subset X$ called *pools*, and ask whether Q contains at least one defective. Group testing has several applications, most notably in biological and chemical testing.

Throughout this paper, log means $\log_2$ if no other base is mentioned. Nondefective elements are called *negative*. A *positive pool* is a pool containing some defective, thus responding Yes to a group test. A *negative pool* is a pool without defectives, thus responding No to a group test.

By the information-theoretic lower bound, at least $\log \binom{n}{d} \approx d \log(n/d)$ pools are needed to find d defectives even if the number d is known in advance, and it is an easy exercise to devise an *adaptive* query strategy using $O(d \log(n/d))$ pools. Here, a strategy is called *adaptive* if queries are asked sequentially, that is, every pool can be prepared based on the outcomes of all earlier queries. For

M. Kutyłowski, M. Gębala, and W. Charatonik (Eds.): FCT 2009, LNCS 5699, pp. 84–95, 2009.

many applications however, the time consumption of adaptive strategies is hardly acceptable, and strategies that work in a few *stages* are strongly preferred: The pools for every stage must be prepared in advance, depending on the outcomes of earlier stages, and then they are queried in parallel.

It is well known that 1-stage strategies need $\Omega(d^2 \log n / \log d)$ pools, and $O(d^2 \log n)$ pools are sufficient. The currently best factor is 4.28; see [7] and the references there. The first 2-stage strategy using a number of pools within a constant factor of optimum, more precisely $7.54 \, d \log(n/d)$, was developed in [10] and later improved to essentially $4 \, d \log(n/d)$ [13] and finally $1.9 \, d \log(n/d)$, or even $1.44 \, d \log(n/d)$ for large enough d [7]. These strategies use stage 1 to find $O(d)$ candidate elements including all defectives, which are then tested individually in stage 2.

The 2-stage strategies still require the knowledge of an upper bound d on the number of defectives, and they guarantee an almost optimal query complexity only relative to this d which can be much larger than the true number of defectives in the particular case. As opposed to this, adaptive strategies with $O(d \log(n/d))$ pools do not need any prior knowledge of d. Beginning with [3,11,12], substantial work has been done to minimize the constant factor in $O(d \log(n/d))$, called the *competitive ratio*. The currently best results are in [16]. Our problem with unknown d was also raised in [14], and several batching strategies have been proposed and studied experimentally. To our best knowledge, the present paper is the first to establish rigorous results for this question:

Can we take the best of two worlds and perform group testing without prior knowledge of d in a few stages, using a number of pools close to the information-theoretic lower bound? This question is not only of theoretical interest. If the number d of defectives varies a lot between the problem instances, then the conservative policy of assuming some "large enough" d systematically requires unnecessarily many tests, while a strategy with underestimated d even fails to find all defectives.

It is fairly obvious that a 1-stage strategy cannot do better than n individual tests. On the bright side, $O(\log d)$ stages are sufficient to accommodate a strategy with $O(d \log(n/d))$ pools: Simply double the assumed d in every other stage, and apply the best 2-stage strategy repeatedly, including a check if all defectives have been found. In this paper we prove that any deterministic strategy that insists on $O(d \log n)$ pools needs $s = \Omega(\log d / \log \log d)$ stages in the worst case. This clearly separates the complexity of the cases with known and unknown d. By the same proof technique we show tradeoff lower bounds for pools and stages. In particular, the number of pools in deterministic strategies with constantly many stages cannot be limited to any function $f(d) \log n$. Whereas the proof idea is a standard "version space" argument counting the number of consistent hypotheses, the details of the adversary strategy and counting process are not obvious. We explore a hypergraph representation of the query results. There remains a $\log \log d$ gap between our current bounds. We conjecture that our proof can be refined to give a matching $\Omega(\log d)$ lower bound.

The next result shows the power of randomization: We propose a Las Vegas strategy that uses $O(d \log n)$ pools in only 3 stages and succeeds with any prescribed constant probability, arbitrarily close to 1. Obviously, the only thing we need is a good upper bound on d, because then we can apply any known 2-stage strategy with $O(d \log n)$ pools, using our bound instead of the unknown actual d. And such an estimate for d is obtained by $O(\log n)$ *randomized* pools in stage 1. Once more, the principal idea is simple (we use pools of exponentially growing size and guess d based on the query outcomes), but the practical challenge is to achieve low constant factors in the total query number $O(d \log n)$. Similarly, by using $O(d^2 \log n)$ pools we need only 2 stages, with arbitrarily high constant probability. Note that we can always recognize in the last stage whether all defectives have been found (and d was not underestimated), by one extra query to the complement of the candidate set. In the unlikely negative case we can simply repeat the strategy with a somewhat larger bound d, hence we eventually find all defectives in a constant expected number of stages and within the same asymptotic query complexity. An open question is whether $O(d \log n)$ randomized pools in 2 stages are sufficient.

Related to this discussion, one may wonder if determining the *exact* number of defectives by group tests is perhaps easier than actually identifying the defectives. Note that in applications like environmental testing we may only be interested in the amount of contamination of samples, rather than in individual items. However, our lower-bound proof yields as a byproduct that the complexity is the same.

In related work [8] we studied query strategies and the computational complexity of learning Boolean functions depending on only a few unknown relevant variables. Group testing is the special case where the Boolean function is already known to be the disjunction of the relevant variables.

One modern application of group testing is the reconstruction of biological networks, e.g., protein interaction networks, by experiments that signal the presence of at least one interaction in a "pool" of proteins. If a group test is available that signals interaction of one fixed protein called a *bait*, with a pool of other proteins, the problem of finding all interaction partners of a bait is just the group testing problem. Since the degrees d of vertices in interaction networks are very different and tests are time-consuming, we arrive at exactly the problem setting considered in this paper.

Instead of learning a whole graph, i.e., the neighbors of every vertex, we may want to learn only a small set of vertices that is incident to all edges, that is, a small *vertex cover*. In interaction networks they can be expected to play a major role, as a small vertex cover represents, e.g., a small group of proteins involved in all interactions [15]. Suppose that an *edge group test* is available that tells, for a pool Q of vertices, whether some vertices in Q are joined by an edge. This assumption is also known as the complex model of group testing. Then we encounter the problem of *learning a hidden vertex cover*: Given a graph with a known vertex set but an unknown edge set, and a number k, identify a vertex cover of size at most k (or all of them), by using a possibly small number of edge group tests. Learning hidden structures in graphs has been intensively studied for many structures and query models, we refer to [1,2,4] for recent results and a survey. Learning a hidden star [1] is a related but quite different problem.

Note that the vertex cover problem is NP-complete already for "known" graphs, on the other hand, it is a classical example of a fixed-parameter tractable (FPT) problem: It can be solved in $O(b^k p(n))$ time, with some constant base b and some fixed polynomial p. In a sense we extend the classical FPT result and show that *hidden* vertex covers can be learned efficiently and nonadaptively if k is small.

Organization of the paper: In Section 2 we derive a lower bound tradeoff for stages vs. pools in deterministic group testing strategies when d is not given to the searcher. Section 3 presents a randomized strategy for estimating the number of defectives, leading to, e.g., a randomized competitive 3-stage group testing strategy. In Section 4 we give our FPT-style result for learning hidden vertex covers. Section 5 discusses potentially interesting questions for further research. In order to emphasize the main ideas and also due to space limitations we have omitted technicalities in several proofs, but in principle the proofs are complete.

2 A Lower Bound for Adaptivity in Competitive Deterministic Group Testing

In this section we give an adversarial answer strategy that forces a certain minimum number stages upon a searcher who wants to keep the number of pools restricted. Consider a set X of elements, containing an unknown subset of defectives.

Definition 1. *Given a set P of pools, the* response vector t *assigns every positive (negative) pool the value 1 (0). Let P^+ and P^- be the set of positive and negative pools, respectively. The* response hypergraph $RH(P,t)$ *has the vertex set $V := X \setminus \bigcup_{Q \in P^-} Q$, and every $Q \in P^+$ is turned into a hyperedge $Q \cap V$ of $RH(P,t)$.*

Intuitively that means: The response vector just describes the outcome of a group testing experiment on the set P of pools. The vertices of $RH(P,t)$ are all elements that appear in no negative pool. The hyperedges of $RH(P,t)$ are the positive pools restricted to these vertices, that is, all elements recognized as negative are removed.

A *hitting set* of a hypergraph is a set of vertices that intersects every hyperedge. Note that a superset of a hitting set is a hitting set, too. From the definitions it follows immediately:

Lemma 1. *Given a response vector t, the family of possible sets of defectives, i.e. those consistent with t, is exactly the family of hitting sets of $RH(P,t)$.* □

Before we state our adversary strategy in detail, we outline its structure. Consider any deterministic group testing strategy that works in stages. The main idea of our adversary strategy is to answer the queries in every stage in such a way that $RH(P, t)$ has some hitting set that is much smaller than the vertex set. This leaves the searcher uncertain about the status (positive or negative) of all the other vertices in $RH(P, t)$. Note that an adversary working against a *deterministic* searcher can hide defectives after having seen the pools. The second idea is a standard technical trick used in many lower-bound proofs to simplify the analysis: The adversary may cautiously reveal some extra information. Specifically, our adversary tells the searcher a subset of defectives that forms already a hitting set of $RH(P, t)$. The effect is that all hyperedges of $RH(P, t)$ are now "explained" by the revealed defectives, thus $RH(P, t)$ does not contain any further useful information for the searcher. Hence the searcher can even totally forget the hypergraph, and the searcher's knowledge is represented by two sets: the already known defectives, and the elements whose status is yet unknown; each of the latter elements can be (independently!) positive or negative. We will play with the cardinalities of these two sets and make the searcher's life as hard as possible. Specifically:

Let f be any monotone increasing function and d the true number of defectives. Suppose that the searcher is aiming for at most $f(d) \log n$ queries in total. Let us consider the moment prior to any stage. Suppose that k defectives are already known and u elements are yet undecided. As we might have $d = k$, the searcher can prepare a set P of at most $f(k) \log n$ pools for the next stage. (Actually, the number of pools already used up in earlier stages must be subtracted, which makes the limit even lower, but our analysis does not take advantage of this fact.) These queries in P can generate at most $2^{f(k) \log n} = n^{f(k)}$ different response vectors. The adversary chooses some number $h \le u$ and announces that h or more further elements are also defective. In particular, there exist $\binom{u}{h}$ possible sets of exactly h further defectives. By the pigeonhole principle, some family T of at least $\binom{u}{h}/n^{f(k)}$ of these candidate sets generate the same (consistent) response vector t. Now the adversary answers with just this response vector t. Let Y denote the union of all sets in T.

Lemma 2. *Y is entirely in the vertex set of $RH(P, t)$.*

Proof. Assume that some $q \in Y$ is in some pool Q which is negative in t, that means, $t(Q) = 0$. By the definition of Y, element q also belongs to some $Z \subseteq Y$ such that response vector t is generated if Z is the actual set of defectives. This contradicts $Q \cap Z = \emptyset$. $\qquad\square$

Define $y = |Y|$. Finally, the adversary actually names a set H of h new defectives in Y, in compliance with t. By Lemma 1, H is a hitting set in $RH(P, t)$. Since arbitrary supersets of H are hitting sets, too, and Y is included in $RH(P, t)$ by Lemma 2, it follows that H plus any of the $y - h$ elements of $Y \setminus H$ build a hitting set of $RH(P, t)$. Using Lemma 1 again, we conclude that the $y - h$ elements of $Y \setminus H$ may still be defective or not, independently of each other.

Since Y must contain at least $\binom{u}{h}/n^{f(k)}$ different subsets of size h, we get the following chain of inequalities:

$$\frac{y^h}{h!} > \binom{y}{h} \geq \frac{\binom{u}{h}}{n^{f(k)}} > \frac{(u-h)^h}{h!n^{f(k)}}.$$

Multiplication with $h!$ and taking the h-th root yields $y > (u-h)/n^{f(k)/h}$.

In summary, after the stage the searcher knows $k+h$ defectives, and at least $y - h > (u-h)/n^{f(k)/h} - h$ elements are undecided. Thus we update k, u by $k := k + h$ and $u := y - h$. This concludes the discussion of any one stage.

In the following, s denotes the number of stages the adversary wants to enforce, k_i and u_i indicates the value of k and u, respectively, before stage i, and h_i is the value of h in stage i. The adversary will choose the h_i in such a way that u is still positive after s stages. Her choice of numbers $h_i > f(k_i)$ is solely based on $f(k_i)$.

Remember that the function f is fixed; this allows us to neglect some minor terms in the expression for the updated u, without affecting the asymptotics: For each d and $\delta > 0$ there exists N such that, for $n > N$, at least $(1-\delta)u/n^{f(k)/h}$ elements are undecided after the considered stage. This can be seen as follows: Since $k \leq d$ holds at any time, the largest possible $f(k)$ depends on d only. Furthermore, since our adversary will always choose values $h > f(k)$ depending on the $f(k)$ only, the ratios h/u become arbitrarily small when we start at large enough n. Since δ can be made arbitrarily small, we will suppress it for simplicity, and assume that at least $u/n^{f(k)/h}$ elements are undecided after the considered stage.

Let $k_1 = 1$, that is, one defective is revealed in the beginning. We let our adversary choose the h_i such that $\sum_i f(k_i)/h_i \leq 1$. Since $u_1 = n - 1$ and $u_{i+1} \geq u_i/n^{f(k_i)/h_i}$, we have that after any number i of stages, u_i is still positive, as desired.

Specifically, let $h_i := sf(k_i)$ in stage $i = 1, \ldots, s$, that is, $f(k_i)/h_i = 1/s$ and $k_{i+1} = k_i + h_i = k_i + sf(k_i)$. Now we can formulate a somewhat technical but general result:

Theorem 1. *Let f be any monotone increasing function with $f(d) \geq d$ for all d. Any deterministic group testing strategy that uses, for arbitrary combinations d, n, at most $f(d) \log n$ pools for finding a previously unknown number d of defectives out of n elements, needs at least s stages in the worst case, where s is defined as the minimum number with the following property: If the operator $k := k + sf(k)$ is iterated s times starting from $k = 1$, then $k \geq d$ is reached.* $\square$

We illustrate the use of Theorem 1 for the most important cases. Due to the information-theoretic lower bound, the smallest meaningful function f to look at is $f(d) = d$.

Corollary 1. *Any deterministic group testing strategy that uses, for arbitrary combinations d, n, only $O(d \log n)$ pools for finding a previously unknown number d of defectives out of n elements needs $\Omega(\log d / \log \log d)$ stages in the worst case.*

Proof. With the previous denotations, $f(k) = k$ yields $k_{i+1} = (s+1)k_i$, hence $d = k_{s+1} = (s+1)^s$, and $s > \log d / \log \log d$. □

We remark that raising the number of pools by a constant factor a does not help very much: Since $f(k) = ak$, our adversary chooses $k := (as+1)k$ and still achieves $s = \Theta(\log d / \log \log d)$, although with a smaller constant factor. Next, for comparison with the setting where d is known, it is interesting to consider $f(d) = d^2$, because this number of pools would allow a 1-stage strategy if d were known beforehand (see Section 1). However, our adversary strategy for unknown d essentially squares k in every iteration, leading to $s = \Omega(\log \log d)$. Finally, consider an arbitrary but fixed function f that may be rapidly growing.

Corollary 2. *Let f be any monotone increasing function. No deterministic group testing strategy that uses at most $f(d) \log n$ pools for finding a previously unknown number d of defectives out of n elements can succeed in constantly many stages.*

Proof. It suffices to notice in Theorem 1 that the number s of iterations needed to reach $k \geq d$ depends on d. □

This contrasts sharply to our result in the next section where we give randomized strategies with constantly many stages, based on a randomized estimate of d. A simple but interesting observation in this context is that finding the exact number of defectives is not easier than solving the whole group testing problem:

Theorem 2. *Any group testing strategy that exactly determines the previously unknown number of defectives must also identify the set of defectives.*

Proof. Assume that a searcher has applied any group testing strategy to some set of elements containing d defectives, and after that the searcher knows d. Let P be the set of pools ever used, and t the response vector. By Lemma 1, the possible sets of defectives are exactly the hitting sets of $RH(P, t)$. Hence, by assumption, all hitting sets of $RH(P, t)$ have the same cardinality. This is possible only if $RH(P, t)$ has only the trivial hitting set consisting of all vertices. Using Lemma 1 again, it follows that the searcher knows the defectives. □

3   Randomized Competitive Group Testing in Only Three Stages

In this section we show that the number d of defectives in a set of n elements can be "conservatively" estimated by $O(\log n)$ randomized nonadaptive group tests, i.e., the estimate is smaller than d with an arbitrarily small prescribed failure probability, but d is overestimated only by a constant expected factor. Thus, the estimate can be further used in any group testing strategy that needs an upper bound on d.

Let $b > 1$ be a fixed positive real number. We prepare a sequence of pools indexed by integers i as follows. We put every element independently with probability $1 - (1 - 1/n)^{b^i}$ in the ith pool. The ith pool is negative with probability

$q_i := (1 - 1/n)^{db^i}$, since this is the probability that all d defectives are outside the pool. The test outcomes of all pools are independent, as we have chosen the elements of the pools independently. Also note that, regardless of the unknown value of d, our sequence q_i is doubly exponential: Every number is the bth power of the previous number and the bth root of the next number. This is a nice invariant that enables a "uniform" analysis for all possible values of d.

Let e denote Euler's number and $k := \lfloor \log_b n \rfloor$. We have $q_0 = (1-1/n)^n \approx 1/e$ if $d = n$, and $q_k \approx (1 - 1/n)^n \approx 1/e$ if $d = 1$. That means, q_0 is "away from" 0 even if $d = n$, and q_k is "away from" 1 even if $d = 1$. Now let i range from some constant negative index to k plus some positive constant. Then group testing on this sequence of pools yields, with high probability, some negative pools in the beginning even if $d = n$, and some positive pools in the end even if $d = 1$. Notice that we prepare roughly $\log_b n = \log n / \log b$ pools.

In the following, a "hat" on a variable symbol means an estimate of the value (obtained by any proposed algorithm). We want $\hat{d} \geq d$ subject to a small acceptable failure probability, but also a small ratio $\hat{d}/d > 1$. An estimate $\hat{d} < d$ would make the subsequent stages of a group testing strategy fail, while a generous $\hat{d}$ would cause unnecessarily many group tests.

We propose a simple algorithm to estimate d from the test outcomes. It uses another positive integer parameter s that we discuss later. The subsequent lemmas are meant with respect to this algorithm. Here it is:

Let i be the largest index of a negative pool; we will refer to i as the *main index*. Then let $\hat{q}_{i-s} := 1/2$ and estimate d accordingly, by $\hat{d} := -1/(b^{i-s} \log(1 - 1/n))$.

Remember that $b > 1$ is some fixed base. We choose s large enough to make $1/2^{b^s}$ "small", see the details below. With these presumptions we get:

Lemma 3. *The probability of $\hat{d} < d$ is $O(1/2^{b^s} \log b)$.*

Proof. The event $\hat{d} < d$ is equivalent to the event that the algorithm returns a main index i with $q_{i-s} < 1/2$. In this case, i is one of the indices with $q_i < 1/2^{b^{s+j}}$, $j \geq 0$. Hence the probability of this failure is bounded by $\sum_{j \geq 0} 1/2^{b^{s+j}}$. Since $1/2^{b^s}$ is already small due to the choice of s, and every term is the bth power of the previous one, the sequence then decreases rapidly: After every $\log_b 2 = 1/\log b$ indices it is reduced to the square. Thus we get a failure probability as claimed, with a small hidden constant. □

In order to express the expected competitive ratio we define a function F with argument $b > 1$ by:

$$F(b) := \max_{0 \leq \theta < 1} \sum_{i=-\infty}^{\infty} \frac{b^{-i+\theta}}{2^{b^{i-\theta}}} \prod_{k=1}^{\infty} \left(1 - \frac{1}{2^{b^{i-\theta+k}}}\right).$$

Although the expression for $F(b)$ looks complicated, it is not hard to prove that $F(b)$ is monotone in b, and to get good simple bounds for $F(b)$. However, here we do not further analyze F, as this affects only the constant factors in our final result below. Some numerical values may illustrate the behaviour of F:

#pools	$1 \log n$	$2 \log n$	$4 \log n$	$8 \log n$	$16 \log n$	$32 \log n$
b	2.000	1.414	1.190	1.091	1.045	1.022
$F(b)$	1.466	0.830	0.549	0.397	0.307	0.247

Lemma 4. *The expectation of $\hat{d}/d$ is at most $F(b) \cdot b^s$.*

Proof. We (arbitrarily) shift indices such that $1/2^{b^{-1}} > q_0 \geq 1/2^{b^0}$ and define θ such that $0 \leq \theta < 1$ and $q_0 = 1/2^{b^{-\theta}}$. If the main index is i, the algorithm yields $\hat{q}_{i-s} = 1/2$ whereas $q_{i-s} := 1/2^{b^{i-s-\theta}}$, hence $\hat{d}/d = b^{-i+\theta} \cdot b^s$. From $q_i = 1/2^{b^{i-\theta}}$ and the definition of main index, the assertion follows. □

Altogether we have shown the following result:

Theorem 3. *For any $b > 1$ and any positive integer s, there is a randomized 1-stage group testing strategy with about $\log n / \log b$ pools that provides an estimate $\hat{d}$ for the number d of defectives in a set of n elements, such that $\hat{d} < d$ holds only with probability $O(1/2^{b^s} \log b)$, and $\hat{d}/d < F(b) \cdot b^s$ in expectation.* □

Corollary 3. *Let us be given a set of n elements d of which are defective, where the number d is not known in advance.*

(i) For any $\epsilon > 0$, there is a randomized group testing strategy that finds all defectives in 2 stages using an expected number of $O(d^2 \log n)$ pools, and succeeds with probability at least $1 - \epsilon$.
(ii) For any $\epsilon > 0$, there is a randomized group testing strategy that finds all defectives in 3 stages using an expected number of $O(d \log(n/d))$ pools, and succeeds with probability at least $1 - \epsilon$.

Proof. By Theorem 3 we get in stage 1 some $\hat{d}$ that exceeds d with the desired proability $1 - \epsilon$, keeping the expected $\hat{d}/d$ constant at the same time. Then we apply one of the established 2-stage group testing stategies for a maximum number $\hat{d}$ of defectives and obtain (ii). For (i) we show similarly that the expected $(\hat{d}/d)^2$ remains constant, and apply a 1-stage group testing stategy for at most $\hat{d}$ defectives. □

Since the probability of $\hat{d}$ decreases rapidly as the value grows, large deviations from the expected number of pools are very unlikely. On the other hand, note that $\hat{d}/d$ is not necessarily close to 1. The best choice of the method parameters b, s that minimize, e.g., the hidden factor in $O(d \log(n/d))$ depends on ϵ and the largest relevant d. This needs to be further explored. We did some numerical experiments adopting the $1.44\, d \log(n/d)$ bound for 2-stage group testing [7]. With bases $1.2 < b < 1.5$ we get factors from $3 + 1/d \log b$ to $6 + 1/d \log b$, for ϵ from 0.1 down to 0.02.

4   Learning Hidden Vertex Covers by Edge Group Tests

In this section we consider the problem of learning all minimal vertex covers of size at most k from edge group tests. Note that, in general, this does not uniquely determine the graph, because there may exist minimal vertex covers with more than k vertices.

Definition 2. *A set of pools is $(2, k)$-disjunct if, for any $k+2$ vertices $w_1, \ldots, w_k$ and u, v, there exists a pool that includes u, v and excludes $w_1, \ldots, w_k$.*

There exist $(2, k)$-disjunct matrices with $O(k^3 \log n)$ pools. The simplest randomized construction is to put every vertex in a pool independently with probability $2/k$. Bounds on the size of a more general type of disjunct matrices can be found in [5].

Let $VC(n, k)$ denote the time for enumerating the minimal vertex covers of size at most k in a (known!) graph of n vertices. The time depends on the state-of-the-art of FPT vertex cover algorithms, which is beyond the scope of this work. However, we have $VC(n, k) = O(b^k p(n))$ where $b < 2$ is some fixed base and p some fixed polynomial, see [9] for more details. If only one vertex cover is sought, one can apply faster algorithms such as [6].

Theorem 4. *We can learn all (minimal) vertex covers of size at most k in one stage using $O(k^3 \log n)$ edge group tests and $O(VC(n, k))$ time for auxiliary computations.*

Proof. We take a set of pools that forms a $(2, k)$-disjunct matrix. Consider any pair of vertices $\{u, v\}$. Clearly, if $\{u, v\}$ belongs to some negative pool then uv is a non-edge. The other case is that $\{u, v\}$ belongs to positive pools only. Assume that $u, v \notin C$ for some vertex cover C with $|C| \leq k$. Due to $(2, k)$-disjunctness, some pool includes u, v and excludes C. This pool must be positive, as it contains u, v. But the pool must be negative, as every edge intersects C. This contradiction shows that every vertex cover C with $|C| \leq k$ contains u or v. Hence, for the purpose of learning these small vertex covers, we may simply assume that uv is an edge if $\{u, v\}$ appears in positive pools only. This might be wrong in the unknown graph, but the family of vertex covers of size at most k is preserved.

This reasoning also yields the following parameterized decoding algorithm that actually generates the family of vertex covers of size at most k from the test outcomes: Construct an auxiliary graph where uv is an edge if and only if $\{u, v\}$ belongs to positive pools only. This can be done in $O(k^3 n^2 \log n)$ time, which is dominated by the time for the final step: Compute the minimal vertex covers of size at most k in this graph.   □

On the other hand, the trivial information-theoretic lower bound gives:

Proposition 1. *Any strategy (which may even be adaptive) for learning hidden vertex covers of size at most k needs $\Theta(k \log(n/k))$ edge group tests.*   □

An obvious question is what is the best exponent of k in the query number $O(k^{O(1)} \log n)$, depending on the number of stages. In Theorem 4 we did not use prior knowledge of the size of a smallest vertex cover. If our k is too small, we just obtain an empty result which is correct. However, if we want *some* vertex cover, we have to determine the minimum size k of a vertex cover first. Here, an $O(\log k)$-stage deterministic strategy or a randomized 1-stage method similar to Section 3 should work. Note that the complements of vertex covers in a graph are exactly the independent sets, which in turn corresponds to negative pools. Hence we could again use a randomized sequence of pools of exponentially growing size and estimate k based on the largest negative pool. Working out the details is left for further research.

5   Discussion

More research is needed on the practical side: Our current lower bounds do not say too much about realistic problem sizes, but we conjecture that they can be further raised. An obvious weakness in the analysis in Section 2 is that the searcher is allowed to use the maximum number of pools in every new stage, not counting the pools used up earlier. Asymptotically this is negligible, but for moderate d our adversary gives away some power by this simplification. One may also think of more sophisticated adversary strategies that exploit more structure of the response hypergraphs.

In Section 3 we have, for the sake of simplicity, estimated d based on the largest negative pool only. Combining the responses of all pools around the main index by some averaging rule may yield even better and more robust estimates. One idea is to use the sth largest negative pool for the estimation, rather than the index of the largest negative pool minus s. In fact, extensive simulations done in Matlab suggest that this improves the competitive ratio for any given failure probability consistetly by about 20%. An obvious plan is to analyze and understand this rule also in theory and to figure out the hidden constants we can achieve in Corollary 3. Moreover, a 2-stage estimator where stage 1 roughly determines the magnitude of d such that stage 2 can focus on the range of the most likely d may save many pools. Yet another idea comes up: We studied the problem of estimating the unknown $d \leq n$ independently, and then we just applied the result to competitive group testing. For this purpose however, we may restrict d straightaway to $O(n/\log n)$ (since otherwise trivial individual testing is anyhow better), and thus further reduce the total number of pools in Corollary 3.

Similar questions arise for learning hidden vertex covers. Finally, an ambitious application is the use of such strategies for unravelling biological interaction networks by edge group tests in a massively parallel way. Efficiency on realistic graphs may be tested by simulations on public interaction databases.

Acknowledgments

This work was inspired by the first author's participation in the wonderful Dagstuhl Seminar 08301 "Group Testing in the Life Sciences" (2008) and supported by the Swedish Research Council (Vetenskapsrådet), grant no. 2007-6437, "Combinatorial inference algorithms – parameterization and clustering".

References

1. Alon, N., Asodi, V.: Learning a Hidden Subgraph. SIAM J. Discr. Math. 18, 697–712 (2005)
2. Angluin, D., Chen, J.: Learning a Hidden Graph Using $O(\log n)$ Queries per Edge. J. Computer and System Sci. 74, 546–556 (2008)
3. Bar-Noy, A., Hwang, F.K., Kessler, H., Kutten, S.: A New Competitive Algorithm for Group Testing. Discr. Appl. Math. 52, 29–38 (1994)
4. Bouvel, M., Grebinski, V., Kucherov, G.: Combinatorial Search on Graphs Motivated by Bioinformatics Applications. In: Kratsch, D. (ed.) WG 2005. LNCS, vol. 3787, pp. 16–27. Springer, Heidelberg (2005)
5. Chen, H.B., Fu, H.L., Hwang, F.K.: An Upper Bound on the Number of Tests in Pooling Designs for the Error-Tolerant Complex Model. Optim. Letters 2, 425–431 (2008)
6. Chen, J., Kanj, I.A., Xia, G.: Simplicity is Beauty: Improved Upper Bounds for Vertex Cover. Technical report (2008)
7. Cheng, Y., Du, D.Z.: New Constructions of One- and Two-Stage Pooling Designs. J. Comp. Biol. 15, 195–205 (2008)
8. Damaschke, P.: On Parallel Attribute-Efficient Learning. J. Computer and System Sci. 67, 46–62 (2003)
9. Damaschke, P.: Parameterized Enumeration, Transversals, and Imperfect Phylogeny Reconstruction. Theor. Computer Sci. 351, 337–350 (2006)
10. De Bonis, A., Gasieniec, L., Vaccaro, U.: Optimal Two-Stage Algorithms for Group Testing Problems. SIAM J. Comp. 34, 1253–1270 (2005)
11. Du, D.Z., Park, H.: On Competitive Group Testing. SIAM J. Comp. 23, 1019–1025 (1994)
12. Du, D.Z., Xue, G., Sun, S.Z., Cheng, S.W.: Modifications of Competitive Group Testing. SIAM J. Comp. 23, 82–96 (1994)
13. Eppstein, D., Goodrich, M.T., Hirschberg, D.S.: Improved Combinatorial Group Testing Algorithms for Real-World Problem Sizes. SIAM J. Comp. 36, 1360–1375 (2007)
14. Kahng, A.B., Reda, S.: New and Improved BIST Diagnosis Methods from Combinatorial Group Testing Theory. IEEE Trans. CAD of Integr. Circuits and Systems 25, 533–543 (2006)
15. Lappe, M., Holm, L.: Unraveling Protein Interaction Networks with Near-Optimal Efficiency. Nature Biotech. 22, 98–103 (2003)
16. Schlaghoff, J., Triesch, E.: Improved Results for Competitive Group Testing. Comb., Prob. and Comp. 14, 191–202 (2005)

Combinatorial Queries and Updates
on Partial Words

Adrian Diaconu, Florin Manea*, and Cătălin Tiseanu

Faculty of Mathematics and Computer Science, University of Bucharest
Str. Academiei 14, 010014, Bucharest, Romania
{adr.diaconu,flmanea,ctiseanu}@gmail.com

Abstract. In this paper we define four combinatorial queries on partial words, asking if a factor of a partial word is a k-repetition, k-free, overlap-free, and primitive, respectively. We show how a given partial word can be preprocessed efficiently in order to answer each of these queries in constant time. Also, we define an update operation for partial words: add a new symbol at the rightmost end of a given partial word; further, we show that the data structures obtained during the preprocessing mentioned above can be updated efficiently in order to still be able to answer all the combinatorial queries, for the updated word, in constant time.

1 Introduction

Partial words, a canonical extension of the classical words, are sequences that, besides regular symbols, may have a number of unknown symbols, called holes or wild cards. The study of the combinatorial properties of partial words was initiated by Berstel and Boasson in their paper [1], having as motivation an intriguing practical problem, namely gene comparison, related to the central topics of Combinatorics on Words. Until now, several such combinatorial properties of the partial words have been investigated: periodicity, conjugacy, freeness and primitivity (see [3,4,5,6,7,13,14,16,17]). Part of these studies consisted in finding efficient algorithms for testing if a word verifies or not a given combinatorial property ([6,8,16]). We refer to [2] for an extensive survey on partial words.

Motivated by the fact that, usually, we are not interested only in the properties of a given word, but also in the properties of its factors, we consider the following problem: given a partial word as input, construct data structures (using efficient algorithms) that enable us to answer in constant time combinatorial queries regarding the factors of that word (is a given factor a repetition?, is a given factor primitive?, etc.). Further, we move our attention to infinite partial words, or, from the computational point of view, arbitrarily long words. Such words were defined and studied in recent papers ([7,13,14,16]). The most natural way to construct such words is, in our opinion, to add symbols to previously

---

* Florin Manea acknowledges partial support from the Romanian Ministry of Education and Research (PN-II Program, Projects *GlobalComp* and *SEFIN*).

M. Kutyłowski, M. Gębala, and W. Charatonik (Eds.): FCT 2009, LNCS 5699, pp. 96–108, 2009.

constructed words. Thus, we define an update operation for partial words: add a new symbol at a word's rightmost end. After such an operation is performed, we investigate how the data structures constructed during the preprocessing phase can be brought up to date, in order to still be able to answer in constant time the previously defined queries.

We emphasize from the beginning the main difference between the problems approached in this paper and the algorithmic problems on partial words, studied so far ([2,6,8,16]): here we are interested in how can we construct data structures that allow us to answer, in constant time, various combinatorial queries regarding every factor of a partial word, and, also, that can be easily updated when the word is updated; on the other hand, the problems approached so far in this line of research consisted in testing combinatorial properties of the entire input word. Also, in a sense, the problems discussed here are dynamic versions of some algorithmic problems approached in the literature, since in this setting there exists an interaction (modeled by queries and updates) between the data structures constructed by the algorithms and the environment.

The structure of the paper is the following: first we provide some basic definitions for partial words; then, we define the data structures used throughout the paper, and propose several algorithms for their manipulation. Further, we define the combinatorial queries for partial words and show how we can perform the desired preprocessing in order to answer these queries. Finally, we define the update operation and show how the data structures defined in the previous section can be enhanced, such that the answer to any query can still be given constant time.

2   Basic Definitions

A *partial word* of length n over the alphabet A is a partial function $u: \{1, \ldots, n\} \overset{\circ}{\to} A$. For $i \in \{1, \ldots, n\}$, if $u(i)$ is defined we say that i *belongs to the domain of u* (denoted by $i \in D(u)$), otherwise we say that i *belongs to the set of holes of u* (denoted by $i \in H(u)$). For convenience, finite partial words are seen as words over the extended alphabet $A \cup \{\diamond\}$: a partial word u of length n is depicted as $u = a_1 \ldots a_n$, where $a_i = u(i)$, for $i \in D(u)$, and $a_i = \diamond$, otherwise. In this way, one can easily define the catenation, respectively the equality, of partial words, as the catenation, respectively the equality, of the corresponding words over $A \cup \{\diamond\}$ (see [2] for details); we denote by λ the empty partial word (i.e., the partial word of length 0). If u and v are two partial words of equal length, then u *is said to be contained in v*, $u \subset v$, if all the elements of $D(u)$ are contained in $D(v)$ and $u(i) = v(i)$ for all $i \in D(u)$. Two partial words u *and v are compatible*, $u \uparrow v$, if there exists a partial word w such that $u \subset w$ and $v \subset w$. We say that *the partial word u is a factor of the partial word w* if there exist partial words x and y such that $w = xuy$. If $w = a_1 \ldots a_n$, we denote by $w[i..j]$ the factor $a_i \ldots a_j$ of w, and by $w[i]$ the symbol a_i.

Let $w \in (A \cup \{\diamond\})^*$ be a partial word. w *is said to be a k-repetition* if $w = x_1 \ldots x_k$ and there exists a non-empty partial word u such that $x_i \subset u$ for all

$i \in \{1, \ldots, k\}$. w is said to be *primitive* if it is not a k-repetition, for any $k > 1$. w is said to be *k-free* if it does not contain a k-repetition. A word of the form $x_1 y_1 x_2 y_2 x_3$ for which there exist two partial words x and y, with $|x| > 0$, such that $x_i \subset x$, for $i \in \{1, 2, 3\}$, and $y_j \subset y$, for $j \in \{1, 2\}$, is called *overlap*; w is said to be *overlap-free* if it does not contain an overlap. The reader interested in more definitions and results on partial words is referred to [2].

3 Data Structures

From the very beginning, note that the time bounds we prove in the following hold on the unit-cost RAM model. In this paper we will deal extensively with the following (static) data structures problem:

Problem 1. Given an array T with n elements (labeled $T[1], \ldots, T[n]$) from a totally ordered set (with order relation $\leq$), and a natural constant L, preprocess this array in order to answer queries "find $\mathrm{minpos}_T(i, i + L - 1)$", where $\mathrm{minpos}_T(i, i + L - 1) = \mathrm{argmin}_{k \in \{i, \ldots, i+L-1\}} T[k]$ (i.e. $\mathrm{minpos}_T(i, i + L - 1)$ returns the position of the smallest value in the interval of T starting on position i and having length L: $T[i], T[i+1], \ldots, T[i+L-1]$); in case of multiple possible answers, we assume that minpos returns the rightmost (greatest) position where the smallest value in the interval is found.

For this problem, we search solutions that have a time efficient preprocessing phase (i.e., construction of data structures which help us answer queries), and require only constant time to answer every possible query. We propose here two such solutions, and show that they have similar time complexity. However, we present both of them since they can be extended to solve differently a dynamic version of Problem 1 (Problem 3, which we approach later): we show that the extension of the first solution performs well in the worst case, while the extension of the second one has a better performance in terms of amortized time complexity (see [9] for a basic discussion on this type of complexity measure).

The first solution is based on the Range Minimum Query problem [10,11,12]:

Problem 2. (Range Minimum Query, RMQ) Given an array T with n elements from a totally ordered set (with order relation $\leq$), preprocess this array in order to be able to answer queries "find $\mathrm{minpos}_T(i, j)$", where $\mathrm{minpos}_T(i, j) = \mathrm{argmin}_{k \in \{i, \ldots, j\}} T[k]$; in case of multiple possible answers, we assume that minpos returns the rightmost position where the smallest value in the interval is found.

It is not hard to see that this problem is a generalization of Problem 1; several solutions of this problem are presented in [10]. The most efficient of them ([12]) requires $\mathcal{O}(n)$ preprocessing time, $\mathcal{O}(n)$ space to store the data structures constructed, and $\mathcal{O}(1)$ time to answer each query. We can apply this solution of Problem 2 directly to obtain a solution for Problem 1 (with the same time and space complexity bounds).

The second solution that we propose for Problem 1 makes use of the linear data structure called *deque (double ended queue)*, described in [15]. The deque is a linear list where both the insertion (push) and deletion (pop) operation can be executed at any of the list's ends (called in the following *back* and *front*).

The main idea in this approach (called *the deque-based approach* in the following) is to insert one by one, in increasing order, the numbers $\{1, 2, \ldots, n\}$ in the back end of a deque D_T, using the following algorithm:

– At the insertion of the number i in the back end of the deque D_T, we pop from the back end of the deque all the numbers k that verify $T[k] \geq T[i]$; also, we pop from the front of the deque all the numbers k such that $k \leq i - L$.

It is not hard to verify the following properties of the deque constructed above. First, if the first value of D_T is less or equal to $i - L$ then, when i is inserted in the deque, we will pop this value from the front end of the deque; in this way, D_T contains only numbers in the interval $[i - L + 1..i]$. Also, if i and k are elements of D_T, such that k is closer to the front of the deque than i, then $k < i$ and $T[k] < T[i]$; this ensures that the element k placed at the front end of the deque verifies $T[k] < T[j]$, for all other elements j of D_T. Finally, after i was inserted D_T contains all the elements k from the interval $[i - L + 1..i]$ that verify $T[k] < T[i]$. To conclude, after i was inserted, the element in front of the deque is $\text{minpos}_T(i - L + 1, i)$.

We briefly analyze the execution of the procedure described above. First we insert the numbers $1, \ldots, L$ in the deque, doing the necessary pop operations, as described above. At this point the element situated in the front end of the deque is $\text{minpos}_T(1, L)$. Further, we continue to insert the numbers from $L + 1$ to n, and, at each step, we make the necessary pops. It is not hard to see that using this algorithm one can compute and store in an array A, of length $n - L + 1$, the values $A[i] = \text{minpos}_T(i, i + L - 1)$; basically $A[i]$ is the element situated in the front of the deque D_T after the number $i + L - 1$ was inserted in the deque.

Once the array A is computed, we can answer a query $\text{minpos}_T(i, i + L - 1)$ in $\mathcal{O}(1)$ time by returning the value $A[i]$. Also, note that every i, $1 \leq i \leq n$, is inserted once in the deque and popped at most once, thus the overall complexity of the preprocessing of the array T is $\mathcal{O}(n)$. But this is, also, the total time needed to perform n insertions in the deque, therefore the amortized complexity of an insertion operation is $\mathcal{O}(1)$ (although a single insertion may require, in the worst case, L pops from the deque, thus an execution time linear in L).

In the following, we are interested in a dynamic version of Problem 1:

Problem 3. We consider the following update operation for an array T: insert a number M at the end of the array T. Preprocess T and define an algorithmic method to update the data structures constructed during the preprocessing (if necessary, construct additional data structures), such that we can still answer minpos queries, defined in Problem 1, for an array obtained from T after an arbitrary sequence of update operations was applied to it.

Again, we propose two solutions for this problem, based on the two solutions proposed for Problem 1, respectively.

The first approach is inspired by one of the solutions of Problem 2 presented in [10]. We describe how the first update is performed, as any other update can be performed similarly. First, we preprocess the array T as in the RMQ-based solution of Problem 1, discussed previously. At the beginning of this update we memorize in a variable Nr the length n of the array before any update operation was performed. Further, the algorithm works as described below:

– We define the array M_{n+1} with $\log_2(L)$ elements:
$M_{n+1}[k] = \mathrm{minpos}_T(n + 1 - 2^k + 1, n + 1)$, for all k such that $1 \leq k \leq \log_2(L)$.
These values are computed, in $\mathcal{O}(\log_2 L)$ time, using the formula:

$$M_{n+1}[k] = \begin{cases} \mathrm{minpos}_T(n - 2^k + 2, n), & \text{if } T[\mathrm{minpos}_T(n - 2^k + 2, n)] < T[n + 1], \\ n + 1, & \text{otherwise.} \end{cases}$$

– We also set: $M_{n+1}[0] = n + 1$.

It is clear that this update algorithm is performed in $\mathcal{O}(\log_2 L)$ time plus the time needed to add a new element to the array T and the time needed to store the array M_{n+1}. Once the new elements of M are computed we can answer queries $\mathrm{minpos}_T(i, j)$ in constant time for all i and j, such that $i \leq j$ and $j - i \leq L$, using the following strategy: if $i = j$ we return j; if $i < j$ and $j \leq Nr$ we obtain the value $\mathrm{minpos}_T(i, j)$ using the data structures constructed in the solution for the not-updated array T; if $i < j$ and $j > Nr$ we set $k = \lfloor \log_2(j - i + 1) \rfloor$ and:

$$\mathrm{minpos}_T(i, j) = \begin{cases} \mathrm{minpos}_T(i, i + 2^k - 1), & \text{if } T[M_{i+2^k-1}[k]] < T[M_j[k]], \\ M_j[k], & \text{if } T[M_{i+2^k-1}[k]] \geq T[M_j[k]] \end{cases}$$

In this relation we obtain $\mathrm{minpos}_T(i, i + 2^k - 1)$ from the data structures constructed during the preprocessing of T, before the update was performed.

Further updates can be made similarly, because after the completion of the t-th update we have stored data structures (the ones produced by the preprocessing of the initial array T, and the arrays M_k constructed, and stored, at each update) that allow us to return in constant time the answer to queries $\mathrm{minpos}_T(j - 2^k + 1, j)$, for all $j \leq n + t$. We only have to know where to look for the result: either in the data structures produced initially, or in the data structures produced during the updates; but this can be easily clarified: when we need to answer a query $\mathrm{minpos}_T(i, j)$ we check if $j \leq Nr$, and in this case search for the answer in the data structures produced during the initial preprocessing phase, or, otherwise, we search the answer in the newly constructed arrays. As a final remark, we store the arrays M_{Nr+t}, for $t \geq 1$, as the rows of a matrix, and each time we compute a new array, we add it, as a new row, to this matrix.

It is not hard to see that this approach works in a more general setting, derived from Problem 2. Namely, we can apply a similar strategy to update an array T in order to be able to answer at minpos queries for intervals of any length, not only for all the intervals of length less or equal to L.

The second approach, more efficient in terms of amortized complexity, relays on the deque-based solution of Problem 1. The basic idea is that an update of the array T leads to the insertion of a new element in the deque constructed for this array during the initial preprocessing. This insertion is handled in the same way as in the preprocessing phase, since, basically, the algorithm presented for Problem 1 treats every element of the array T as an element that was newly inserted in that array, and updates the deque according to the value of this element. As explained before, the amortized cost of an insertion in the deque is $\mathcal{O}(1)$, thus an update requires $\mathcal{O}(1)$ amortized time (but up to $\mathcal{O}(L)$ time in the worst case) plus the time needed to add a new element in the array T and a new element, $A[n + 2 - L]$, in the array A (recall that $A[i] = \text{minpos}_T(i, i + L - 1)$). After this update was done, we can still answer queries $\text{minpos}_T(i, i + L - 1)$ in constant time, for all $i \in \{1, \ldots, n + 2 - L\}$.

In the following we address the problem of adding a new element to an array: it is clear that this operation can be done in linear time, in the worst case, by creating a new array which contains the elements stored in the initial array and the value to be added; however, such an insertion can be done in constant amortized time (see [9] for details). In the case of adding columns to matrices, things are just a little bit more complicated. Assume that we have a matrix B with n rows and m columns, and we want to perform the following update: add a new column to this matrix. We will store the elements of B using $1+m$ arrays: Col and B^i, with $i \in \{1, \ldots, m\}$. B^i stores the elements of the i-th column of the matrix, while $Col[i]$ stores the memory address where the array B^i is placed; when adding the column B^{m+1} we simply have to add its address in the Col array, and the time complexity of this operation is $\mathcal{O}(1)$ amortized and $\mathcal{O}(m)$ in the worst case. Accessing an element of the matrix $B[i][j]$ can still be done in $\mathcal{O}(1)$ time: we select the array B^j, using the array Col, and return $B^j[i]$. Note also that a similar method can be applied when we want to add rows to a matrix. When we deal with upper (lower) triangular matrices we only need to store the columns (respectively, rows) of that matrix, thus we can apply the same strategy to store and update such matrices.

Finally, we consider another type of update: we add both a new row and a new column to a matrix B, with r rows and c columns. Such matrices will be stored using $2 + c + r$ arrays (Col, Row, B_i, for $i \in \{1, \ldots, r\}$, and B^j, for $j \in \{1, \ldots, c\}$) and two values, C and R. The value C stores the number of columns and R the number of rows of B, before any update was performed on this matrix. These values remain unaffected by the updates. Initially, B_i stores the elements $B[i][1], B[i][2], \ldots, B[i][c]$, for $i \in \{1, \ldots, r\}$, while B^j is empty, for $j \in \{1, \ldots, c\}$; $Row[i]$ stores the address of B_i and $Col[j]$ stores the memory address of B^j. We assume that t, $t \geq 0$, updates were applied to B, and this matrix has, now, $n = R + t$ rows and $m = C + t$ columns. If we update again B, and add a new row and a new column, we proceed as follows: we create the arrays B_{n+1} (consisting of the elements $B[n + 1][1], B[n + 1][2], \ldots, B[n + 1][m + 1]$) and B^{m+1} (consisting in the elements $B[1][m + 1], \ldots, B[n][m + 1]$), add the address of B_{n+1} in the array Row and the address of B^{m+1} in the array Col; these operations require, clearly, $\mathcal{O}(n + m)$ time. Accessing an element of the matrix $B[i][j]$ can still be done in $\mathcal{O}(1)$ time: if $j \leq C + \max(i - R, 0)$ we select the array B_i, using the array Row, and return $B_i[j]$; otherwise we select the array B^j, using the array Col, and return $B^j[i]$.

We stress that the methods to store matrices, proposed here, do not change, conceptually, the way we work with the elements of a matrix at all: we just memorize them in a manner that allows us fast updating, as well as fast access.

Therefore, for simplicity, we will see the i-th row/column of a matrix with n columns/rows as an array with n elements, although these elements are not stored on consecutive memory locations.

4   Queries

We address the following problem regarding partial words:

Problem 4. Given a partial word w, with n symbols (labeled $w[1], \ldots, w[n]$), over the alphabet V, preprocess this partial word in order to answer the queries:

– "is w[i..j] a k-repetition?", denoted $\mathbf{rep}(i, j, k)$, where $i, j, k \in \{1, \ldots, n\}, i < j$.
– "is w[i..j] k-free?", denoted $\mathbf{free}(i, j, k)$, where $i, j, k \in \{1, \ldots, n\}, i < j$.
– "is w[i..j] overlap-free?", denoted $\mathbf{o\text{-}free}(i, j)$, where $i, j \in \{1, \ldots, n\}, i < j$.
– "is w[i..j] primitive?", denoted $\mathbf{prim}(i, j)$, where $i, j \in \{1, \ldots, n\}, i < j$.

In the following we propose a solution of this problem which has a time efficient preprocessing phase and requires constant time to answer every possible query.

First we will compute two matrices A and T, which are useful in order to be able to answer efficiently the four types of queries listed above. The matrix A, with n rows and $\lfloor n/2 \rfloor$ columns, is defined as follows (for $i \in \{1, \ldots, n\}$, and $l \in \{1, \ldots, \lfloor n/2 \rfloor\}$):

$$A[i][l] = \begin{cases} \max\{k \mid k \leq i, i - k \text{ is divisible by } l, \text{ and } w[k] \neq \diamond\}, \\ \quad \text{if there exists } k \leq i \text{ such that } i - k \text{ is divisible by } l, w[k] \neq \diamond; \\ i - \lfloor (i-1)/l \rfloor l, \text{ otherwise.} \end{cases}$$

Basically, $A[i][l]$ equals k, if all the symbols $w[k + l], \ldots, w[i]$ are equal to $\diamond$ and $w[k] \neq \diamond$, or, if such a value k does not exist, $A[i][l]$ equals the leftmost position t of the word where a symbol $\diamond$ is found and $i - t$ is divisible by l. This matrix can be computed by dynamic programming, in time $\mathcal{O}(n^2)$:

$$A[i][l] = \begin{cases} i, \text{ if } w[i] \neq \diamond \text{ or } i \leq l \\ A[i - l][l], \text{ otherwise} \end{cases}$$

The matrix T, with n rows and $\lfloor n/2 \rfloor$ columns, is defined by:

$$T[i][l] = \max\{m \mid m \leq \lfloor i/l \rfloor + 1, \text{ for which there exists } a \in V \text{ such that } \\ w[i - jl] \sqsubset a, \forall j \in \{0, \ldots, m - 1\}\},$$

The elements of this matrix can be computed by dynamic programming, in time $\mathcal{O}(n^2)$, using the relation:

$$T[i][l] = \begin{cases} 1, \text{ if } i \leq l, \\ T[i - l][l] + 1, \text{ if } i > l \text{ and } w[i] \uparrow w[A[i - l][l]], \\ (i - A[i - l][l])/l, \text{ otherwise.} \end{cases}$$

In the following, we denote by $T[][l]$ the array consisting of the l-th column of T.

Remark 1. For some i, j and k, such that $1 \leq i \leq j \leq n$ and $l = j-i+1 \leq \lfloor n/2 \rfloor$, we have $k \leq T[\text{minpos}_{T[][l]}(i,j)][l]$ if and only if the factor $w[i - (k-1)l..j]$ of w is a k-repetition. Indeed, we have $T[x][l] \geq k$, for all $x \in \{i, i+1, \ldots, j\}$, if and only if there exists $a_x \in V$ such that $w[x - tl] \subset a_x$, for all $t \in \{0, \ldots, k\}$ and $x \in \{i, i+1, \ldots, j\}$. This is equivalent to the fact that all the words $w[i - tl..j - tl]$, for all $t \in \{0, \ldots, k\}$, are contained in the word $a_i a_{i+1} \ldots a_j$, therefore $w[i - (k-1)l..j]$ is a k-repetition.

Remark 1 gives a hint on how we can preprocess the partial word w in order to be able to answer efficiently queries "is $w[i..j]$ a k-repetition?", for all $i, j, k \in \{1, \ldots, n\}, i < j$:

Algorithm REP

1. Construct the matrix T for the word w, as described above.
2. Solve Problem 1 for each of the arrays $T[][l]$ and intervals of length l, with $l \in \{1, \ldots, \lfloor n/2 \rfloor\}$.
q. The answer to a query $\mathbf{rep}(i, j, k)$ is obtained as follows: if $j-i+1$ is divisible by k, we compute $l = (j-i+1)/k$; if $T[\text{minpos}_{T[][l]}(j-l+1, j)][l] \geq k$ then the answer to the given query is **yes**; otherwise the answer is **no**.

Both step 1 and step 2 of the above algorithm take $\mathcal{O}(n^2)$ time, since each array $T[][l]$ can be preprocessed in time $\mathcal{O}(n)$ (to be able to answer minpos queries for this array in constant time), and there are $\lfloor n/2 \rfloor$ such arrays. Thus the total preprocessing time is $\mathcal{O}(n^2)$, and this enables us to answer **rep** queries (as described in step q) in constant time.

We now focus on how we can preprocess w in order to answer efficiently **free** queries.

For that, we define the matrix H, with n rows and columns, as follows:

$$H[i][j] = \begin{cases} k, \text{ where } k \text{ is the greatest natural number such that } w[i..j] \\ \quad \text{contains a } k\text{-repetition, given that } i < j. \\ 1, \text{ if } i = j \\ 0, \text{ if } i > j \end{cases}$$

We compute the elements of H by dynamic programming:

$$H[i][j] = \begin{cases} \max(H[i][j-1], H[i+1][j]), \text{ if } i < j \text{ and} \\ \quad \text{if } w[i..j] \text{ is not a } (\max(H[i][j-1], H[i+1][j]) + 1)\text{-repetition.} \\ \max(H[i][j-1], H[i+1][j]) + 1, \text{ if } i < j \text{ and} \\ \quad \text{if } w[i..j] \text{ is a } (\max(H[i][j-1], H[i+1][j]) + 1)\text{-repetition.} \\ 1, \text{ if } i = j. \\ 0, \text{ if } i > j. \end{cases}$$

Note that H can be computed in time $\mathcal{O}(n^2)$, if we already performed the preprocessing steps 1 and 2 of Algorithm **REP**, and we are able to answer in constant time **rep** queries.

Now we can describe the preprocessing that permits us to answer efficiently queries "is $w[i..j]$ k-free?", for $i, j, k \in \{1, \ldots, n\}, i < j$:

Algorithm FREE
1. Preprocess the partial word w as described in **Algorithm REP**.
2. Construct the matrix H for the partial word w, as described above.
q. The answer to a query **free**(i, j, k) is obtained as follows: if $H[i][j] \geq k$ then the answer is **no**, otherwise the answer is **yes**.

The total time needed for the preprocessing done in the first two steps of this algorithm is $\mathcal{O}(n^2)$, as we explained above. We can answer **free** queries in $\mathcal{O}(1)$ time, as described in step q.

Further, we approach the **o-free** queries. We compute the matrix O with n rows and n columns, defined by: $O[i][j] = 1$ if $w[i..j]$ contains an overlap, and $O[i][j] = 0$ otherwise. The values stored in this matrix are computed in time $\mathcal{O}(n^2)$, by dynamic programming:

$O[i][j] = 1$ if and only if $O[i][j-1] = 1$ or $O[i+1][j] = 1$ or (**rep**$(i, j-1, 2)$ =yes and $w[\lfloor (j-i)/2 \rfloor] \uparrow w[j]$ and $w[i] \uparrow w[j]$), for $i, j \in \{1, \ldots, n\}$ with $j - i \geq 2$

The preprocessing we use to answer efficiently queries "is w$[i..j]$ overlap-free?", for $i, j \in \{1, \ldots, n\}, i < j$, is described in the following:

Algorithm O-FREE
1. Preprocess the partial word w as described in **Algorithm REP**.
2. Construct the matrix O for the partial word w, as described above.
q. The answer to a query **o-free**(i, j) is obtained as follows: if $O[i][j] = 0$ then the answer is **yes**, otherwise the answer is **no**.

The overall time needed for the preprocessing done in the first two steps of this algorithm is $\mathcal{O}(n^2)$; also, we will be able to answer **o-free** queries in $\mathcal{O}(1)$ time, as described in step q.

The last type of queries we discuss in this paper are the primitivity queries **prim**. In this case we will use the matrix Pr with n rows and columns, where:

$$Pr[i][j] = \begin{cases} 1, & \text{if } w[i..j] \text{ is primitive} \\ 0, & \text{otherwise} \end{cases}$$

To compute the value $Pr[i][j]$ we go through all the positive divisors d of $(j - i + 1)$ and check if $w[i..j]$ is a d-repetition using **rep** queries. If there exists at least one number d such that $w[i..j]$ is a d-repetition we set $Pr[i][j] = 0$; otherwise, we set $Pr[i][j] = 1$. A brute force implementation of this algorithm achieves a time complexity of $\mathcal{O}(n^2\sqrt{n})$. However, the number of divisors we need to analyze in order to compute all the values of Pr is $(\sum_{i=1}^{n} \sigma(i))$, where $\sigma(i)$ is the number of positive divisors of i. But $\sum_{i=1}^{n} \sigma(i) = \sum_{i=1}^{n} \lfloor n/i \rfloor \leq \sum_{i=1}^{n} n/i$, since we can count for every i how many numbers it divides (that is $\lfloor n/i \rfloor$). This means that $\sum_{i=1}^{n} \sigma(i) \in \mathcal{O}(n \log_2 n)$, because $((\sum_{i=1}^{n} \frac{1}{i})/(\log_2 n))$ converges to a positive constant.

Therefore, the first step in the computation of the elements of the matrix Pr is to keep, in an array, the lists of divisors for every $l \in \{1, \ldots, n\}$. This data structure will take $\mathcal{O}(n \log_2 n)$ space and can be computed in $\mathcal{O}(n \log_2 n)$ using a sieve method: we go through all the numbers i from 1 to n and add i to the lists of divisors of the numbers $i, 2i, \ldots, \lfloor n/i \rfloor i$. Then, we act as we described above, but searching the divisors of the length of a given factor in the newly computed array, and obtain the overall complexity $\mathcal{O}(n^2 \log_2 n)$ for the computation of the elements of the matrix Pr.

The preprocessing algorithm that enables us to answer in constant time queries "is w[i..j] primitive?", for $i, j \in \{1, \ldots, n\}, i < j$, is the following:

Algorithm PRIMITIVE

1. Preprocess the partial word w as described in **Algorithm REP**.
2. Construct the matrix Pr, as described above.
q. The answer to a query **prim**(i, j) is obtained as follows: if $Pr[i][j] = 0$ then the answer is **no**, otherwise the answer is **yes**.

The overall time needed for the preprocessing done in the first two steps of this algorithm is $\mathcal{O}(n^2 \log_2 n)$ and the time needed to answer a query is, clearly, $\mathcal{O}(1)$.

5   Updates

In this section we propose a solution for the dynamic version of Problem 4:

Problem 5. Consider the following update operation for a partial word w: add a symbol $a \in V \cup \{\diamond\}$ at the rightmost end of w, to obtain wa. Preprocess w and define a method to update the data structures constructed during the preprocessing in order to answer in constant time **rep, free, o-free** and **prim** queries, for a word obtained after several update operations were applied to w.

We describe how to solve Problem 5 when exactly one update is applied to a given partial word. If the word is updated more than once we simply iterate this method. Assume that we are given the partial word w, of length n, for which we compute the matrices A, T, H, O and Pr, as described in Section 4. Also, we memorize the value $Nr = n$, which remains unchanged by further updates.

Now, assume that we add to the partial word w the symbol $a \in V \cup \{\diamond\}$ and obtain the word $w' = wa$; we have $w'[n+1] = a$. First we update the matrices A and T, by adding to each of them a new column and a new row, defined by:

$-$For the matrix A and $0 < l \leq \lfloor n/2 \rfloor$:

$$A[n+1][l] = \begin{cases} n+1, & \text{if } w'[n+1] \neq \diamond \\ A[n+1-l][l], & \text{otherwise.} \end{cases}$$

$-$For the matrix T and $0 < l \leq \lfloor n/2 \rfloor$:

$$T[n+1][l] = \begin{cases} T[n+1-l][l]+1, & \text{if } w'[n+1] \uparrow w[A[n+1-l][l]], \\ (n+1-A[n+1-l][l])/l, & \text{otherwise.} \end{cases}$$

$T[i][\lfloor (n+1)/2 \rfloor]$ and $A[i][\lfloor (n+1)/2 \rfloor]$, for $i \leq n$, are computed using the recurrence relations defined in the previous section.

As we have explained in Section 3, we can add the new rows and columns to the matrices T and A in time $\mathcal{O}(n)$, and the computation of the newly inserted elements requires also $\mathcal{O}(n)$ time. Now we only have to construct additional data structures in order to still be able to answer in constant time queries $\text{minpos}_{T[][l]}(i,j)$, for the new matrix T and $i,j \in \{1,\ldots,n+1\}$, $l \in \{1,\ldots,\lfloor(n+1)/2\rfloor\}$ and $j - i + 1 = l$. But the update of T consisted in adding to each of the arrays $T[][l]$ a new element and, if n is odd, a new column $T[][\lfloor(n+1)/2\rfloor]$; for the columns $T[][l]$ we can apply the solution RMQ-based of Problem 3, with update time $\mathcal{O}(\log_2 l)$ and query time $\mathcal{O}(1)$, and for the column $T[][\lfloor(n+1)/2\rfloor]$ we run one of the efficient algorithms solving Problem 1. Thus, we can still answer in constant time any $\text{minpos}_{T[][l]}$ query for all the columns $T[][l]$, $l \in \{1,\ldots,\lfloor(n+1)/2\rfloor\}$. Alternatively, as described in Section 3 this update can be done in amortized time $\mathcal{O}(1)$ for each column, using the deque data structure, and still need only a constant time to answer queries. To conclude, the time needed to update the structures T and A, and to compute some additional structures for answering in constant time minpos queries, is either $\mathcal{O}(n\log_2 n)$ time, in the RMQ-based approach, or $\mathcal{O}(n)$ amortized time, in the deque-based approach. The time needed to complete an update, in the second approach, is upper bounded by $\mathcal{O}(n^2)$, by the general considerations made in Section 3. However, a more careful analysis (which we do not present here due to space constraints), taking into account the particular definition of the matrix T, shows that a more exact upper bound of the time needed to complete such an update is, as in the first approach, $\mathcal{O}(n\log_2 n)$.

Any further update is performed in the same manner, with the same time complexity: we compute and add new rows and columns to A and T, and we process the new T in order to answer in constant time minpos queries.

When updating the matrices H and O we use the same relations as in the previous sections to compute and add to each of them a new column: $H[i][n+1]$, for $i \leq n + 1$, and, respectively, $O[i][n + 1]$, for $i \leq n + 1$ (we do not need to actually compute a new row for any of these matrices, since the elements $H[i][j]$ and $O[i][j]$, with $i > j$, are all null). Note that we update H and O only after A, T, and the structures required to answer minpos queries for T were updated; thus the time needed to update O and H is $\mathcal{O}(n\log_2 n)$, or $\mathcal{O}(n)$ amortized time.

Finally, we describe how the first update of the matrix Pr is done. First, we update the list of all the divisors of the numbers $1,\ldots,n$ by adding $n + 1$ and its divisors to that list (this can be done in $O(\sqrt{n})$ time). The total number of divisors in this list is now $\mathcal{O}((n+1)\log_2(n+1)) = \mathcal{O}(n\log_2 n)$. Adding a new symbol a to w creates $n + 1$ new factors: $w' = w'[1..n+1] = wa$, $w'[2..n+1]$, $\ldots w'[n+1..n+1]$; we apply the same method as in the former section to verify which of these words are primitive, and store the results as a new column of Pr: $Pr[i][n + 1]$, with $i \in \{1,\ldots,n+1\}$. The overall complexity of this update is, by the same arguments presented in the previous Section, $\mathcal{O}(n\log_2 n)$; again, we update Pr only after A, T, and the structures required to answer minpos queries for T were updated.

Once all the structures are updated, we can answer queries exactly as we described in the previous section, at the step q of each of the algorithms discussed.

6 Conclusions and Future Work

We have proved the following theorem:

Theorem 1. *A given partial word w, of length n, can be processed in time $\mathcal{O}(n^2)$, respectively $\mathcal{O}(n^2 \log_2 n)$, in order to be able to answer* **rep**, **free**, **o-free** *and, respectively,* **prim** *queries, in time $\mathcal{O}(1)$. If update operations, in which a new symbol is added to the rightmost end of w, are applied, the data structures constructed in the processing above can be updated in at most $\mathcal{O}(n \log_2 n)$ time (or $\mathcal{O}(n)$ amortized time), respectively at most $\mathcal{O}(n \log_2 n)$ time, per update, and still answer* **rep**, **free**, **o-free** *and, respectively,* **prim** *queries, in time $\mathcal{O}(1)$.*

We stress out that the time bounds obtained here are not trivial: a preprocessing phase consisting in the direct application of algorithms which test the discussed combinatorial properties (such as those presented in [6,16]) for each factor of the initial word, in order to be able to answer the combinatorial queries we defined, would be, clearly, less efficient. This result may become useful in solving other problems on partial words. For example, it can be directly applied to identify and count efficiently all the k-repetitions/ k-free/ overlap-free/ primitive factors of a given word. It seems an interesting problem to count efficiently all the distinct k-repetitions/ k-free/ overlap-free/ primitive factors in a partial word (i.e., all the distinct full words compatible with such factors of the partial word), and we think that the algorithms we proposed here can be applied as initial steps in solving these problems efficiently.

Of course, the algorithms we presented may be directly applied to solve the same problems for full words; however, we believe that in the case of full words more efficient algorithms can be developed, using specific data structures (such as suffix trees or suffix arrays). Nevertheless, we are interested in lowering the time bounds showed for the preprocessing phases here, while keeping the condition that each query should be answered in constant time. Another way to continue our work is to see how the complexity of the preprocessing time decreases in the case of algorithms which answer queries in non-constant (yet small, for example logarithmic) time. Finally, we are interested in analyzing new update operations (for example, replacing, in a partial word, a given hole of that word with a specific symbol), and new types of queries.

References

1. Berstel, J., Boasson, L.: Partial words and a theorem of Fine and Wilf. Theor. Comput. Sci. 218(1), 135–141 (1999)
2. Blanchet-Sadri, F.: Algorithmic Combinatorics on Partial Words. Chapman & Hall/CRC Press (2007)

3. Blanchet-Sadri, F., Hegstrom, R.A.: Partial words and a theorem of Fine and Wilf revisited. Theor. Comput. Sci. 270(1-2), 401–419 (2002)
4. Blanchet-Sadri, F., Duncan, S.: Partial words and the critical factorization theorem. J. Comb. Theory Ser. A 109(2), 221–245 (2005)
5. Blanchet-Sadri, F.: Primitive partial words. Discr. Appl. Math. 148(3), 195–213 (2005)
6. Blanchet-Sadri, F., Anavekar, A.R.: Testing primitivity on partial words. Discr. Appl. Math. 155, 279–287 (2007)
7. Blanchet-Sadri, F., Mercaş, R., Scott, G.: A generalization of Thue freeness for partial words. Theoret. Comput. Sci. 410, 793–800 (2009)
8. Blanchet-Sadri, F., Mercaş, R., Rashin, A., Willett, E.: An Answer to a Conjecture on Overlaps in Partial Words Using Periodicity Algorithms. In: Dediu, A.H., Ionescu, A.M., Martiń-Vide, C. (eds.) LATA 2009. LNCS, vol. 5457, pp. 188–199. Springer, Heidelberg (2009)
9. Cormen, T.H., Leiserson, C.E., Rivest, R.R.: Introduction to Algorithms. MIT Press, Cambridge (1990)
10. Demaine, E., Weimann, O.: Advanced Data Structures, Lecture Notes from MIT, Lecture 15 (2007), http://courses.csail.mit.edu/6.851/spring07/lec.html
11. Gabow, H.N., Bentley, J.L., Tarjan, R.E.: Scaling and related techniques for geometry problems. In: Proc. 16th ACM STOC, pp. 135–143 (1984)
12. Harel, D., Tarjan, R.E.: Fast algorithms for finding nearest common ancestors. SIAM J. Comput. 13, 338–355 (1984)
13. Halava, V., Harju, T., Kärki, T.: Square free partial words. Inf. Proc. Letters 108, 115–118 (2008)
14. Halava, V., Harju, T., Kärki, T., Séébold, P.: Overlap-freeness in infinite partial words. Theoret. Comput. Sci. 410, 943–948 (2009)
15. Knuth, D.E.: The Art of Computer Programming, 3rd edn. Fundamental Algorithms, vol. 1. Addison-Wesley, Reading (1997)
16. Manea, F., Mercas, R.: Freeness of Partial Words. Theor. Comput. Sci. 389(1-2), 265–277 (2007)
17. Shur, A.M., Konovalova, Y.V.: On the periods of partial words. In: Sgall, J., Pultr, A., Kolman, P. (eds.) MFCS 2001. LNCS, vol. 2136, pp. 657–665. Springer, Heidelberg (2001)

The Longest Haplotype Reconstruction Problem Revisited

Riccardo Dondi*

Dipartimento di Scienze dei Linguaggi, della Comunicazione e degli Studi Culturali
Università degli Studi di Bergamo, Via Donizetti 3, 24129 Bergamo, Italy
riccardo.dondi@unibg.it

Abstract. The *Longest Haplotype Reconstruction* (LHR) problem has been introduced in Computational Biology for the reconstruction of the haplotypes of an individual, starting from a matrix of incomplete haplotype fragments. In this paper, we reconsider the LHR problem, proving that it is **NP**-hard even in the restricted case when the input matrix is error-free. Then, we investigate the approximation complexity of the problem, showing that it cannot be approximated within factor $2^{\log^{\delta} nm}$ for any constant $\delta < 1$, unless $\textbf{NP} \subseteq DTIME[2^{poly \log nm}]$. Finally, we give a fixed-parameter algorithm, where the parameter is the size of the reconstructed haplotypes.

1 Introduction

The human genome is usually considered as a string or a vector over alphabet $\{A, C, G, T\}$. It has been observed that a large part of the human genome (more than 99%) is identical in any two individuals, and variability is observed in few sites, called *Single Nucleotide Polymorphisms* (SNPs). The SNPs of an individual constitute the *haplotype* of that individual. It is particularly relevant to study the haplotype of an individual, as it distinguishes each individual among the population and can be used for drug-design and medical applications.

A SNPs is formally defined as a position of the genome where a variation of a single nucleotide is observed in at least 5% of the population. Each variant is called an *allele*. Usually, it is observed the presence of two possible alleles, denoted as 0 and 1, for each position of the genome. Furthermore, diploid organisms like humans have two copies of each chromosome, hence, in a given interval, the genome is associated with two haplotypes, usually described as strings or vectors over alphabet $\{0, 1\}$.

The reconstruction of haplotypes has been deeply studied in Computational Biology and several versions of the problem have been proposed [4]. The general problem, starting from the draft version of the SNPs produced by sequencing techniques, aims to reconstruct the two haplotypes of each individual.

Here we focus on a combinatorial problem which is a variant of the *Single Individual Haplotyping Problem* (SIH). The SIH problem aims to reconstruct the

* Partly supported by FAR 2009 grant "Algoritmi per il trattamento di sequenze".

M. Kutyłowski, M. Gębala, and W. Charatonik (Eds.): FCT 2009, LNCS 5699, pp. 109–120, 2009.

haplotypes of an individual, starting from small pieces (a few hundreds of bases long), called *fragments*, of the genome. The fragments come from both copies of the chromosome, but current technologies are not able to tell which copy of the chromosome the fragments belong to. Furthermore, the presence of errors and missing data in the fragments makes harder the problem of reconstructing the haplotypes from the given set of fragments.

In [11,7], several versions of the SIH problem were introduced. In the formulations proposed, a fragment of SNPs sites is described as a vector over alphabet $\{0, 1, -\}$, where $0, 1$ denote the two distinct alleles of an SNP site, and $-$ represents a missing value. The instance of different versions of the problem consists of an $n \times m$ matrix M, where each entry $M[i, j] \in \{0, 1, -\}$. The i-th row of M corresponds to the i-th *fragment*, while the j-th column of M corresponds to the j-th SNP. A position where $M[i, j] = -$ is called a *hole*. A *conflict* occurs at a given SNP site (column) j iff there exists two fragments (rows) i_1, i_2 in M, so that $M[i_1, j] \neq M[i_2, j]$ and both $M[i_1, j], M[i_2, j]$ are different from $-$. A *gap* in a row j of M is a maximal run of holes delimited on both sides by non-hole entries.

In this paper, we consider a version of the SIH problem introduced in [11], the *Longest Haplotype Reconstruction Problem* (LHR). Starting from a matrix M of fragments, the goal is to reconstruct two haplotypes, so that the sum of the lengths of the two resulting haplotypes is maximized. The LHR problem admits a polynomial time algorithm when the input matrix M is gapless [11,5], while it is **APX**-hard when each fragment contains at most one gap [5]. We investigate several aspects of the LHR problem, introducing a slightly different formulation of the problem. First, in Section 3 we show that the problem is **NP**-hard even when the input matrix is error-free. This case is particularly interesting, since all the other versions of the SIH problem introduced in [11,7] are trivially in **P** when the input matrix is error-free. The result implies that the original version of the LHR problem is not in **NPO**. Furthermore, we investigate both the parameterized complexity and the approximation complexity of the problem. In Section 4 we investigate the approximation complexity of the problem, by showing that the problem cannot be approximated within factor $2^{\log^\delta nm}$ for any constant $\delta < 1$, unless $\mathbf{NP} \subseteq DTIME[2^{poly \log nm}]$. Then, we give a fixed-parameter algorithm where the parameter is the size of the solution, that is the sum of the lengths of the resulting haplotypes. Due to space constraints, some of the proofs are omitted.

2   Preliminary Definitions

A fragment is a vector over alphabet $\{0, 1, -\}$. The aligned fragments are represented as a matrix M, consisting of n rows (the fragments) and m columns (the SNPs). We denote by $M[i, j]$ the value at row i, column j of matrix M. Given a matrix M we denote by M_i the submatrix of M composed by the first i rows of M, with $1 \leq i \leq n$. Two rows (fragments) i_1, i_2 of M are *compatible* iff $M[i_1, j] \neq M[i_2, j]$ implies $M[i_1, j] = -$ or $M[i_2, j] = -$, otherwise i_1, i_2 *conflict*.

A matrix M is *compatible* iff all the rows of M are compatible. A matrix M is *error-free* iff there exists a partition of the rows of M in two sets R_1 and R_2, such that each of R_1,R_2 does not contain conflicting rows.

Given a set of compatible rows R of M, we define the haplotype h_R *induced* by R as the haplotype obtained by defining position j equal to α, with $\alpha \in \{0,1\}$, if there exists at least one row i of R so that $M[i,j] = \alpha$, and value - otherwise. Notice that, since R is compatible, for each column j of M, $M[i_1,j] \neq$ - and $M[i_2,j] \neq$ - imply $M[i_1,j] = M[i_2,j]$, for $i_1, i_2 \in R$.

If $M[i,j] \neq$ -, then we say that the i-th row of M *covers* the j-th column, otherwise it does not cover the j-th column. Similarly, given a set R of compatible rows of M, the induced haplotype h_R covers the j-th column if its j-th position (column) is different from -. The *size* of row i, denoted as $s(i)$, is the number of columns covered by i; similarly, the *length* or the *size* of haplotype h_R, denoted as $s(h_R)$ is the number of columns covered by $h_{M'}$. Given a set R of compatible rows of M, then R covers the j-th column if the corresponding haplotype h_R covers the j-th column. Given a set R of compatible rows of M, we denote by $c(R)$ the length $s(h_R)$ of the haplotype induced by R.

We are now ready to give the formal definition of the LHR problem.

Problem 1 (LHR). *(Longest Haplotype Reconstruction)*
Input: *a matrix M of fragments;*
Output: *two compatible subsets of rows R_1, R_2 of M, with $R_1 \cap R_2 = \emptyset$, so that $c(R_1) + c(R_2)$ is maximized.*

It is easy to see that Problem 1 is in **NPO**, as h_{R_i}, $i \in \{1,2\}$, can be reconstructed from R_i in polynomial time. Notice that the definition of the LHR problem introduced in [11], denoted as LHR-1, is slightly different. The output of the LHR-1 problem consists of an error-free matrix M' obtained by removing rows from M, so that the rows of M' can be partitioned in compatible sets R_1, R_2 and $c(R_1) + c(R_2)$ is maximized. In Section 3, we will show that the LHR problem is **NP**-hard even when the input matrix is error-free. This implies that the LHR-1 problem is not in **NPO**, as, given an error-free matrix M', it is **NP**-hard to partition M' into compatible sets R_1, R_2, so that $c(R_1) + c(R_2)$ is maximized.

3   Error-Free Matrices

In this section we consider the case when input matrix M is error-free. This restriction of the LHR problem is denoted by LHR-EF. In what follows, we will show that the LHR-EF problem is instead **NP**-hard. We prove the result by reducing the Maximum Not-All-Equal 3-Satisfiability problem (MaxNAES), which is known to be **NP**-hard [13], to LHR-EF.

Problem 2 (MaxNAES). *(Maximum Not-All-Equal 3-Satisfiability)*
Input: *a set U of variables, a collection C of clauses of at most three literals, where a literal is a variable or a negated variable in U;*

Output: *a truth assignment for U such that each clause in a largest cardinality subset $C' \subseteq C$ contains at least one true literal and at least one false literal.*

Let $I = (U, C)$ be an instance of MaxNAES, with $p = |U|$ and $q = |C|$. An assignment A not *equally satisfies* a clause $c \in C$, iff A assigns value true to a literal of c and value false to a literal of c. We build a matrix M, instance of LHR-EF, as follows. Matrix M consists of $2p$ rows and $p + q$ columns. Row $2i - 1$ is associated with the literal x_i, while row $2i$ is associated with literal $\bar{x}_i$, $1 \leq i \leq p$.

Assume that literal x_i appears in clauses $c_{i,1}, \ldots, c_{i,y}$ and that literal $\bar{x}_i$ appears in clauses $c_{j,1}, \ldots, c_{j,z}$. Row $2i - 1$ of M is defined as follows: (1) $M[2i - 1, i] = 1$; (2) $M[2i - 1, p + h] = 1$, for each $h \in \{i_1, \ldots, i_y\}$; (3) in any other column l, $M[2i - 1, l] = $ -. Row $2i$ of M is defined as follows: (1) $M[2i, i] = 0$; (2) $M[2i, p + h] = 1$, for each $h \in \{j_1, \ldots, j_z\}$; (3) in any other column l, $M[2i, l] = $ -. It is easy to see that the following lemma holds.

Lemma 1. *Matrix M is error-free.*

Theorem 1. *LHR-EF problem is **NP**-hard.*

Proof. First, we show that, given a solution of size at least k for the MaxNAES problem over instance I, we can compute in polynomial time a solution of size at least $2p + q + k$ for the LHR-EF problem over the corresponding instance M. Consider an assignment A that not equally satisfies a set of clauses $C' \subseteq C$, we compute in polynomial time a corresponding solution S of LHR-EF as follows. S consists of two compatible sets of rows R_1 and R_2. For each variable x_i set to true in A, we assign the corresponding row $2i - 1$ to the set R_1, and for each variable x_i set to false in A we assign the corresponding row $2i$ to the set R_1. The remaining rows are assigned to the set R_2. By the property of assignment A and by construction, exactly one of the rows $2i - 1$, $2i$, with $1 \leq i \leq p$, is assigned to the set R_j, $j \in \{1, 2\}$. Hence both R_1 and R_2 are compatible sets of rows. By construction each column h, with $1 \leq h \leq p$, of M is covered by a row of R_1 and by a row of R_2. Now, consider a column j of M and the corresponding c_j, with $p + 1 \leq j \leq p + q$. By construction, at least one of the sets R_1 or R_2 covers column j, as the corresponding clause c_j contains a true literal (in this case column j is covered by R_1) or a false literal (in this case column j is covered by R_2). Furthermore, each clause c_j not equally satisfied in C' contains both a true and a false literal, hence column j is covered by both R_1 and R_2. Hence there exist at least $2p + q + k$ columns covered by R_1 and R_2.

Now we show that, given a solution S of size at least $2p + q + k$ for the LHR-EF problem over instance M, we can compute in polynomial time a solution of size k for the MaxNAES problem over the corresponding instance I. Assume that S consists of two compatible sets R_1, R_2 of rows of M, with $R_1 \cap R_2 = \emptyset$. For each i, $1 \leq i \leq p$, exactly one of the rows $2i - 1$ and $2i$, belongs to the set R_j, with $j \in \{1, 2\}$. Indeed, by construction row $2i - 1$ conflicts with exactly one row of M (row $2i$) and row $2i$ conflicts with exactly one row of M (row $2i - 1$). Now, consider the set R_1 and define the assignment A as follows: if row $2i - 1$ belongs to R_1, assign value true to variable x_i, otherwise assign value false to variable x_i. We claim that if column $p + j$ is covered by both R_1 and R_2, then clause c_j is not equally satisfied. Indeed, if the $p + j$-th column is covered by a row i of R_1 and a row l of R_2, then by construction in c_j there exists a true literal x_i that corresponds to row i and there exists a false literal x_l that corresponds to row l. Since both R_1 and R_2 cover the first p columns of M, and as the h-th column, with $p + 1 \leq h \leq p + q$, is covered by at least one of R_1 and R_2, it follows that A not equal satisfies at least k clauses. $\square$

4   Hardness of Approximation

In this section we show that the LHR problem cannot be approximated within factor $2^{\log^\delta nm}$ for any constant $\delta < 1$, unless $\mathbf{NP} \subseteq DTIME[2^{poly \log nm}]$, where n and m are the number of rows and columns of M respectively. First, we prove the inapproximability result for the Single LHR problem (S-LHR), a variant of the LHR problem introduced in [5]. Then, the inapproximability result for the S-LHR problem is extended to the LHR problem, via an L-reduction from S-LHR to LHR. For details on the L-reduction, see [3].

The S-LHR problem is defined as follows: given a matrix M, the goal is to find a subset R of compatible rows of M, so that the number of columns covered by R is maximized. The S-LHR problem is known to be **APX**-hard [5]. Here, we consider a restricted version of the S-LHR problem, called *Dense Single Longest Haplotype Reconstruction* problem (DS-LHR). An instance of DS-LHR consists of a matrix M, where for each pair of rows i_1, i_2 of M, there exists a column j in M, so that $M[i_1, j], M[i_2, j] \neq$ -. In what follows, we prove the inapproximability results of the DS-LHR problem by applying the self improvement technique [8,9,10]. As DS-LHR is a restricted case of S-LHR, the inapproximability result holds also for S-LHR. Via an L-reduction from Maximum Independent Set on cubic graphs, which is known to be **APX**-hard [2], we can show the following result.

Lemma 2. *The DS-LHR problem is* **APX**-*hard.*

Now, let M_1 and M_2 be two instances of the DS-LHR problem. In what follows, we define the product $M_1 \times M_2$ between M_1 and M_2. The product $M_1 \times M_2$ is a matrix, denoted by $M_{1,2}$, consisting of $|M_1||M_2|$ rows and $2|M_1||M_2|$ columns.

First, we describe the structure of the matrix $M_{1,2}$ (see Fig.1), then we define the values of the entries of $M_{1,2}$. The rows of $M_{1,2}$ are first grouped in $|M_1|$ groups each of size $|M_2|$, where the i-th group, denoted as $S(i)$, is associated with the i-th row of M_1, $1 \leq i \leq |M_1|$. The j-th row of group $S(i)$, $1 \leq i \leq |M_1|$, $1 \leq j \leq |M_2|$, is associated with the j-th row of M_2. It follows that a row r of $M_{1,2}$ is associated with a pair of coordinates, (r_a, r_b), with $1 \leq r_a \leq |M_1|$ and $1 \leq r_b \leq |M_2|$. Row $r = (r_a, r_b)$ is the r_b-th row of group $S(r_a)$.

The rows of $M_{1,2}$ have length $2|M_1||M_2|$. The submatrix induced by the first $|M_1||M_2|$ columns of $M_{1,2}$ is denoted as the M_1-*submatrix* of $M_{1,2}$, or simply the M_1-submatrix, the submatrix induced by the last $|M_1||M_2|$ columns of $M_{1,2}$ is denoted as the M_2-*submatrix* of $M_{1,2}$, or simply the M_2-submatrix. In the M_1-submatrix, the columns are grouped in $|M_2|$ blocks each of size $|M_1|$, where the i-th block is denoted as $G_1(i)$. Conversely, in the M_2-submatrix, the columns are grouped in $|M_1|$ blocks each of size $|M_2|$, where the i-th block is denoted as $G_2(i)$. As for the case of rows, a column c of $M_{1,2}$ is associated with a pair of coordinates (c_a, c_b). A column $c = (c_a, c_b)$, with $1 \le c_a \le |M_2|$ and $1 \le c_b \le |M_1|$, of the M_1-submatrix is the c_b-th column of block $G_1(c_a)$. A column $c = (c_a, c_b)$ of the M_2-submatrix, with $1 \le c_a \le |M_1|$ and $1 \le c_b \le |M_2|$, is the c_b-th column of block $G_2(c_a)$.

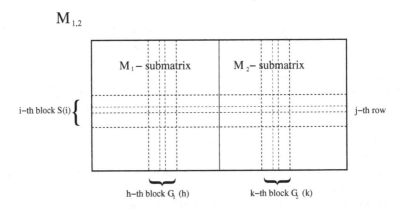

Fig. 1. The structure of matrix $M_{1,2}$

Now, we can define the values of the entries of matrix $M_{1,2}$. Let i be a row of matrix $M_{1,2}$, with $i = h|M_2| + p$, $0 \le h < |M_1|$ and $1 \le p \le |M_2|$ (that is i is the p-th row of group $S(h+1)$ in $M_{1,2}$).

Consider the entry $M_{1,2}[i,j]$ of the M_1-submatrix, with $j = k|M_2| + q$, $0 \le k < |M_2|$ and $1 \le q \le |M_1|$, (that is j is the q-th columns of block $G_1(k+1)$ in $M_{1,2}$):

- $M_{1,2}[i,j] = M_1[h+1, q]$, if position $M_2[p, k+1] \ne$ -;
- else (that is $M_2[p, k+1] =$ -), $M_{1,2}[i,j] =$ -.

Consider the entry $M_{1,2}[i,j]$ of the M_2-submatrix, with $j = |M_1||M_2| + k|M_2| + q$, $0 \le k < |M_1|$ and $1 \le q \le |M_2|$, (that is j is the q-th columns of block $G_2(k+1)$ in $M_{1,2}$):

- $M_{1,2}[i,j] = M_2[p, q]$, if $M_1[h+1, k+1] \ne$ -;
- else (that is position $M_1[h+1, k+1] =$ -), $M_{1,2}[i,j] =$ -.

Given a row l of $M_{1,2}$, let h be a block (either a block $G_1(h)$ or a block $G_2(h)$) of matrix $M_{1,2}$, we denote by $M_{1,2}[l]^{|h}$ the restriction of row l to the columns of block h.

Property 1. Let l be a row of $M_{1,2}$ having coordinates (i, j), let h be a block of the M_1-submatrix, let k be a block of the M_2-submatrix:

- either $M_{1,2}[l]^{|h} = (-)^{|M_1|}$ (when $M_2[j, h] = -$) or $M_{1,2}[l]^{|h}$ is equal to row i of M_1 (when $M_2[j, h] \neq -$);
- either $M_{1,2}[l]^{|k} = (-)^{|M_2|}$ (when $M_1[i, k] = -$) or $M_{1,2}[l]^{|k}$ is equal to row j of M_2 (when $M_1[i, k] \neq -$).

The result in Lemma 3 are fundamental to show that $M_{1,2}$ is an instance of DS-LHR.

Lemma 3. *Let M_1 and M_2 be two instances of DS-LHR and let $i = (r_{a,i}, r_{b,i})$ and $j = (r_{a,j}, r_{b,j})$ be two rows of $M_{1,2}$. Then:*

1. *there exists a column l of M_1 where $M_1[r_{a,i}, l] = \alpha_i$ and $M_1[r_{a,j}, l] = \alpha_j$, with $\alpha_i, \alpha_j \neq -$, iff there exists a column l' of the M_1-submatrix of $M_{1,2}$ where $M_{1,2}[i, l'] = \alpha_i$ and $M_{1,2}[j, l'] = \alpha_j$;*
2. *there exists a column l of M_2 where $M_2[r_{b,i}, l] = \beta_i$ and $M_2[r_{b,j}, l] = \beta_j$, with $\beta_i, \beta_j \neq -$, iff there exists a column l' of the M_2-submatrix of $M_{1,2}$ where $M_{1,2}[i, l'] = \beta_i$ and $M_{1,2}[j, l'] = \beta_j$.*

Proof. We will show that the result holds for the M_1-submatrix. The result for the M_2-submatrix follows similarly. Since M_2 is an instance of the DS-LHR problem, it follows that there exists a column l of M_2 where rows $M_2[r_{b,i}, l]$, $M_2[r_{b,j}, l] \neq -$. By Property 1, the restrictions $M_{1,2}[i]^{|l}$, $M_{1,2}[j]^{|l}$ are equal to rows $r_{a,i}$ and $r_{a,j}$ of M_1 respectively. Since M_1 is an instance of the DS-LHR problem, it follows that there exists a column h of matrix M_1, so that $M_1[r_{a,i}, h] = \alpha_i$, $M_1[r_{a,j}, h] = \alpha_j$, with $\alpha_i, \alpha_j \neq -$. Hence, let l' be the h-th column of block $G_1(l)$ of the M_1-submatrix, then $M_{1,2}[i, l'] = \alpha_i$, $M_{1,2}[j, l'] = \alpha_j$.

Let $i = (r_{a,i}, r_{b,i})$, $j = (r_{a,j}, r_{b,j})$ be two rows of $M_{1,2}$, so that $M_{1,2}[i, l'] = \alpha_i$, $M_{1,2}[j, l'] = \alpha_j$, where $\alpha_i, \alpha_j \neq -$ and l' is the l-th column of the block $G_1(h)$ of the M_1-submatrix. Since rows i and j have a value different from $-$ in the l-th column of the block $G_1(h)$, it follows by construction that $M_2[r_{b,i}, h]$, $M_2[r_{b,j}, h] \neq -$. But then, by Property 1, $M_{1,2}[i]^{|h}$, $M_{1,2}[j]^{|h}$ are equal to rows $r_{a,i}$, $r_{a,j}$ of M_1 respectively. Hence, $M_1[r_{a,i}, l] = \alpha_i$, $M_1[r_{a,j}, l] = \alpha_j$. □

From Lemma 3 and from the properties of DS-LHR problem, follow Lemma 4 and Lemma 5.

Lemma 4. *Let M_1 and M_2 be two instances of DS-LHR, then $M_1 \times M_2 = M_{1,2}$ is an instance of DS-LHR.*

Lemma 5. *Let M_1 and M_2 be two instances of DS-LHR. Rows $i = (r_{a,i}, r_{b,i})$ and $j = (r_{a,j}, r_{b,j})$ of $M_{1,2}$ are compatible if and only if rows $r_{a,i}$ and $r_{a,j}$ of M_1 are compatible and rows $r_{b,i}$ and $r_{b,j}$ of M_2 are compatible.*

Now, we investigate the relation between solutions of the DS-LHR problem over instances M_1 and M_2, and a solution of the DS-LHR problem over instance $M_{1,2}$.

Lemma 6. *Let M_1 and M_2 be two instances of DS-LHR and $M_1 \times M_2 = M_{1,2}$. Let S_1, S_2 be solutions of DS-LHR over instances M_1 and M_2 respectively, we can compute in polynomial time a solution S' of DS-LHR over instance $M_{1,2}$ so that $c(S') = 2c(S_1)c(S_2)$.*

Lemma 7. *Let M_1 and M_2 be two instances of DS-LHR and $M_1 \times M_2 = M_{1,2}$. Let S' be a solution of DS-LHR over instance $M_{1,2}$, we can compute in polynomial time solutions S_1, S_2 of DS-LHR over instances M_1, M_2 respectively, so that $c(S') \leq 2c(S_1)c(S_2)$.*

Proof. Let S' be a solution of the DS-LHR problem over instance $M_{1,2}$. Two rows $r_i = (r_{a,i}, r_{b,i})$, $r_j = (r_{a,j}, r_{b,j})$ of S' must be compatible. By Lemma 5, it follows that the rows $r_{a,i}$, $r_{a,j}$ of M_1 are compatible and that the rows $r_{b,i}$, $r_{b,j}$ of M_2 are compatible.

Given solution S', define $S_1 = \{r_{a,i} : (r_{a,i}, r_{b,j}) \in S'\}$, $S_2 = \{r_{b,j} : (r_{a,i}, r_{b,j}) \in S'\}$. By construction two rows $r_{a,i}, r_{a,j}$, with $r_{a,i}, r_{a,j} \in S_1$, are compatible, and two rows $r_{b,w}, r_{b,v}$ with $r_{b,w}, r_{b,v} \in S_2$ are compatible.

In what follows we will show that $c(S') \leq 2c(S_1)c(S_2)$. First, consider the columns of the M_1-submatrix of $M_{1,2}$. Define H as a subset of blocks of the M_1-submatrix, where $h \in H$ iff S' covers at least one column of h. By Proposition 1, for each row $i = (r_{a,i}, r_{b,i})$ of $M_{1,2}$ and for each $h \in H$, $M_{1,2}[i]^{|h}$ is either equal to row $r_{a,i}$ of M_1 or to $(-)^{|M_1|}$. Denote by $c(S', h)$ the number of columns of block h covered by S'. Let h_{max} be a block of H, so that $c(S', h_{max}) \geq c(S', h)$, for each $h \in H$. By Property 1 the rows of S' restricted to block h_{max} are a subset of the rows in S_1. It follows that S' covers at most $|H|c(S', h_{max})$ columns of the M_1-submatrix, and that $|H|c(S', h_{max}) \leq |H|c(S_1)$.

Now, consider the columns of the M_2-submatrix. Define H' as the set of blocks of the M_2-submatrix, where $h' \in H'$ iff S' covers at least one column of h'. Let h'_{max} be a block of H, so that $c(S', h'_{max}) \geq c(S', h)$, for each $h \in H'$. It follows that S' covers at most $|H'|c(S', h'_{max})$ columns of the M_2-submatrix, and that $|H'|c(S', h'_{max}) \leq |H'|c(S_2)$.

Now, it holds $c(S') \leq |H|c(S', h_{max}) + |H'|c(S', h'_{max})$. By construction, for each block $h \in H$, there exists a row $i = (r_{a,i}, r_{b,i}) \in S'$ having a value different from $-$ in block h. Hence, by construction, $M_2[r_{b,i}, h] \neq -$, and since $r_{b,i} \in S_2$, it follows that $c(S_2) \geq |H|$. Similarly $c(S_1) \geq |H'|$. It follows that $c(S') \leq |H|c(S', h_{max}) + |H'|c(S', h'_{max}) \leq |H|c(S_1) + |H'|c(S_2) \leq 2c(S_1)c(S_2)$.   □

Next, given an instance M of DS-LHR inductively define the instance M^k of DS-LHR as follows: $M^1 = M$ and $M^k = M \times M^{k-1}$. We can prove by induction that M^k is an instance of DS-LHR. Indeed, obviously M^1 is an instance of DS-LHR. Assume that M^{k-1} is an instance of DS-LHR. By Lemma 4 it follows that also $M^k = M \times M^{k-1}$ is an instance of DS-LHR. As a consequence of Lemma 6 and Lemma 7, the following results hold.

Lemma 8. *Let M, M^k, with $k \geq 1$, be instances of DS-LHR. Let $Opt(M)$ be the optimum of the DS-LHR problem over instance M and let $Opt(M^k)$ be the* *optimum of the DS-LHR problem over instance* M^k, *then it holds* $Opt(M^k) = 2^{k-1}Opt(M)^k$.

Lemma 9. *Let* M, M^k *be an instance of DS-LHR. Given a solution* S *over instance* M^k *of the DS-LHR problem, we can compute in polynomial time a solution* S' *of the DS-LHR problem over instance* M *so that* $c(S') \leq 2^{k-1}c(S)^k$.

Now, we are ready to state the main result of this section. Recall that n and m denote the number of columns and rows respectively of the input matrix M.

Theorem 2. *For any constant* $\delta < 1$, *DS-LHR cannot approximated within factor* $2^{\log^\delta nm}$, *unless* **NP** $\subseteq DTIME[2^{poly \log nm}]$.

Proof. Suppose that the DS-LHR problem can be approximated within factor $2^{\log^\delta nm}$, for some constant δ, in polynomial time. For any fixed value ε, define

$$k = \left(\frac{\log^\delta(nm)}{\log(1+\varepsilon)} \right)^{1/(1-\delta)}.$$

Let M be an instance of DS-LHR, we can compute in polynomial time an instance M^k having n^k rows and $2^{k-1}m^k$ columns. We have assumed that DS-LHR can be approximated within factor $2^{\log^\delta nm}$ in time $O(|M^k|)^d$, for some constant d, where $O(|M^k|)^d = O(n^k 2^{k-1}m^k)^d$. It follows that $O(n^k 2^{k-1}m^k)^d = O((2nm)^{kd}) = O(2^{kd \log 2nm}) = O(2^{poly \log nm})$. By Lemma 9, we can compute in polynomial time an approximate solution of DS-LHR over instance M with approximation factor $(2^{\log^\delta(mn)^k})^{1/k} \leq 1+\varepsilon$, which implies we have designed a PTAS for the DS-LHR problem. □

We have proved that DS-LHR, and hence S-LHR, is not approximable within factor $2^{\log^\delta nm}$ for any constant $\delta < 1$, unless **NP** $\subseteq DTIME[2^{poly \log nm}]$. We use the L-reduction from S-LHR to LHR presented in [5] to extend the inapproximability result to the LHR problem. The L-reduction considers an input matrix M of the S-LHR problem, so that M does not contain duplicated rows. Then the L-reduction builds a matrix M', instance of the LHR problem, duplicating each row of M. It is easy to see that there exists a solution of S-LHR of size h iff there exists a solution of LHR of size $2h$. Hence we have described an L-reduction with constant $\alpha = 2$ and $\beta = \frac{1}{2}$, and the inapproximability result for the S-LHR problem can be extended to LHR.

Theorem 3. *For any constant* $\delta < 1$, *LHR cannot approximated within factor* $2^{\log^\delta nm}$, *unless* **NP** $\subseteq DTIME[2^{poly \log nm}]$.

5 A Fixed-Parameter Algorithm

In this section we present a fixed-parameter algorithm for the LHR problem, where the parameter is the size of the solution, that is the number of columns covered by two haplotypes h_{R_1}, h_{R_2} induced by the disjoint subsets R_1, R_2 of rows of matrix M. The size of the solution is denoted in the sequel by k. For an introduction to parametrized complexity, see [6,12].

First, let l be a row of M that covers the maximum number of SNPs (columns). We can assume that $s(l) < k$, otherwise we can return l as a solution to the LHR problem. Hence, we can assume that $s(i) < k$, for each row i, $1 \le i \le n$.

The algorithm is based on the color-coding technique [1]. First, we recall the basic definition of perfect hash functions.

Definition 1. *Let S be a set, a family F of functions from S to $\{1, \ldots, k\}$ is perfect if for any subset $S' \subseteq S$ consisting of k elements, there exists an injective function $f \in F$ from S' to $\{1, \ldots, k\}$.*

Consider a family F_c of perfect hash functions, $F_c : \{1, \ldots, m\} \to \{1, \ldots, k\}$, that associates a label in $\{1, \ldots, k\}$ with each column of the matrix M. Since F_c is perfect, there exists an injective function $f \in F_c$ that assigns to each column covered by h_{R_1} and h_{R_2} a distinct label in $\{1 \ldots, k\}$.

Fix a function $f \in F_c$. Given a column j, we denote by $\lambda(j)$ the label in $\{1, \ldots, k\}$ associated by f with j. Given a row i of M, we denote by $l(i)$ the set of labels associated with the columns covered by i. The haplotype h_{R_1} consists of k_1 covered positions and the haplotype h_{R_2} consists of k_2 covered positions, with $k_1, k_2 \le k$, $k_1 + k_2 = k$. Notice that the set of columns covered by h_{R_1} and h_{R_2} are not necessarily disjoint. Define $L_i \subseteq \{1, \ldots, k\}$, with $i \in \{1, 2\}$, as the set of labels associated by function f with the k_i columns of M covered by haplotype h_{R_i}. Observe that there exist at most 2^k possible subsets L_i, with $i \in \{1, 2\}$, hence there are at most 2^{2k} pairs of subsets (L_1, L_2).

Fix a pair of sets of labels L_1 and L_2. For each set of labels L_i, with $i \in \{1, 2\}$, define the *agreement* vector b_i of L_i, as a binary vector of size k_i, so that the j-th component of b_i, denoted as $b_i[j]$, represents the value of the column labeled by $j \in L_i$ in the haplotype h_{R_i}, $i \in \{1, 2\}$. Since each agreement vector b_i has size $k_i \le k$, it follows that there exist at most 2^k possible vectors b_i, with $i \in \{1, 2\}$, which implies that there exist at most 2^{2k} pairs of agreement vectors (b_1, b_2).

Given a pair of agreement vectors (b_1, b_2), we say that a row r of M agrees with the agreement vector b_j, $j \in \{1, 2\}$, iff $M[r, h] = b_j[\lambda(h)]$, for each column h in $s(r)$. It is easy to see that the following lemma holds.

Lemma 10. *Let r_a and r_b be two rows of M that agree with the same agreement vector b_i, $i \in \{1, 2\}$, then r_a and r_b are compatible.*

Fix a pair of vectors (b_1, b_2), define $LH_{b_1, b_2, L_1, L_2}[j; L_1', L_2']$, where $1 \le j \le n$, $L_i' \subseteq L_i$, $i \in \{1, 2\}$, as follows: $LH_{b_1, b_2, L_1, L_2}[j; L_1', L_2']$ is equal to 1, iff there exists a solution for the matrix M_j (that is the submatrix of M consisting of the first j rows), where the haplotype h_{R_i} covers a set of columns labeled by the set L_i', $i \in \{1, 2\}$, else is equal to 0.

Now, we define the recurrence to compute $LH_{b_1, b_2, L_1, L_2}[j; L_1', L_2']$, for fixed sets of labels L_1, L_2 and fixed agreement vectors b_1, b_2.

$$LH_{b_1,b_2,L_1,L_2}[j; L_1', L_2'] = \max \begin{cases} LH_{b_1,b_2,L_1,L_2}[j-1; L_1', L_2'] \\ LH_{b_1,b_2,L_1,L_2}[j-1; L_1' - P_j, L_2'] \\ \quad \text{if } P_j \subseteq L_1', P_j \subseteq l(j), \text{ and } j \text{ agrees with } b_1 \\ LH_{b_1,b_2,L_1,L_2}[j-1; L_1', L_2' - P_j] \\ \quad \text{if } P_j \subseteq L_2', P_j \subseteq l(j), \text{ and } j \text{ agrees with } b_2 \end{cases}$$

$$(1)$$

Notice that the following conditions holds:

- $LH_{b_1,b_2,L_1,L_2}[j; \emptyset, \emptyset] = 1$, for each $1 \leq j \leq n$;
- $LH_{b_1,b_2,L_1,L_2}[1; L_1', L_2'] = 0$, for each $L_1' \subseteq L_1$, $L_2' \subseteq L_2$, with $L_1', L_2' \neq \emptyset$;
- $LH_{b_1,b_2,L_1,L_2}[1; L_1', \emptyset] = 1$ for each $L_1' \subseteq L_1$ such that $L_1' \subseteq l(1)$ and $l(1)$ agrees with b_1, else $LH_{b_1,b_2,L_1,L_2}[1; L_1', \emptyset] = 0$;
- $LH_{b_1,b_2,L_1,L_2}[1; \emptyset, L_2'] = 1$ for each $L_2' \subseteq L_2$ such that $L_2' \subseteq l(1)$ and $l(1)$ agrees with b_2, else $LH_{b_1,b_2,L_1,L_2}[1; \emptyset, L_2',] = 0$.

First, we show the correctness of Recurrence 1 in Lemma 11 and Lemma 12, then we discuss the time complexity of the algorithm.

Lemma 11. *Let M_j be a submatrix of M and let R_1, R_2 be two disjoint compatible sets of rows of M_j, such that R_i, $i \in \{1, 2\}$, covers columns labeled by set L_i', $i \in \{1, 2\}$. Then, $LH_{b_1,b_2,L_1,L_2}[j; L_1', L_2'] = 1$.*

Proof. Let h_{R_1} and h_{R_2} be the haplotypes induced by the sets R_1 and R_2 respectively. First notice that, by hypothesis, a row l that belongs to R_x, with $x \in \{1, 2\}$, must agree with vector b_x. Assume that we have already computed the values $LH_{b_1,b_2,L_1,L_2}[j-1; L_1'', L_2'']$, for each $L_1'' \subseteq L_1$ and $L_2'' \subseteq L_2'$. By induction hypothesis, if there exist two disjoint sets R_1', R_2' of rows of M_{j-1} that cover the sets of columns labeled by L_1'' and L_2'' respectively, then $LH_{b_1,b_2,L_1,L_2}[j-1; L_1'', L_2''] = 1$. Assume that row j covers a set of columns labeled by P_j and assume w.l.o.g. that $j \in R_1$. It follows that the disjoint subsets $R_1 \setminus \{j\}$, R_2 of rows of M_{j-1}, cover columns labeled by sets L_1'', L_2' respectively, with $L_1'' = L_1' \setminus \{P_j\}$. Then, by induction hypothesis, $LH_{b_1,b_2,L_1,L_2}[j-1; L_1'', L_2'] = 1$, and since row j and the rows in $R_1 \setminus \{j\}$ agrees with b_1, $LH_{b_1,b_2,L_1,L_2}[j; L_1', L_2'] = 1$ by the second case of Recurrence 1. The case when $j \in R_2$ is similar. If $j \notin R_1, R_2$, then R_1 and R_2 are both compatible sets of rows of M_{j-1}, with $R_1 \cap R_2 = \emptyset$, hence by induction $LH_{b_1,b_2,L_1,L_2}[j-1; L_1', L_2'] = 1$. $\square$

Lemma 12. *Let M_j be a submatrix of M and let $L_1' \subseteq L_1$, $L_2' \subseteq L_2$ be two subsets of labels so that $LH_{b_1,b_2,L_1,L_2}[j; L_1', L_2'] = 1$. Then, there exist two disjoint compatible sets R_1 and R_2 of rows of M_j that cover columns labeled by sets L_1' and L_2' respectively.*

Lemma 13. *Given a labeling function $f : M \rightarrow \{1, \ldots, k\}$, two sets $L_1 \subseteq \{1, \ldots, k\}$, $L_2 \subseteq \{1, \ldots, k\}$ of labels, and two binary agreement vectors b_1, b_2 associated with L_1, L_2 respectively, Recurrence 1 computes $LH_{b_1,b_2,L_1,L_2}[j; L_1', L_2']$, for each $L_1' \subseteq L_1$ and $L_2' \subseteq L_2$, in time $O(n2^{3k})$.*

Proof. Consider Recurrence (1) and assume that we have already computed value $LH_{b_1,b_2,L_1,L_2}[i; L_1'', L_2'']$, for each $i < j$, $L_1'' \subseteq L_1'$ and $L_2'' \subseteq L_2'$. In order to compute value $LH_{b_1,b_2,L_1,L_2}[j; L'_1, L'_2]$, for each choice of set $P_j \subseteq l(j)$, we must look for a constant number of values. Since each fragment covers at most $k-1$ columns and $l(j) \subseteq \{1, \ldots, k\}$, there exist at most 2^k possible subsets $P_j \subseteq l(j)$, hence we have to consider at most $O(2^k)$ cases for each row j. As the number of entries in $LH_{b_1,b_2,L_1,L_2}[i; L''_1, L''_2]$ is $n2^{2k}$, the time complexity to compute value $LH_{b_1,b_2,L_1,L_2}[j; L'_1, L'_2]$ is $O(n2^{3k})$. $\qquad\square$

The number of possible sets L_x, with $x \in \{1, 2\}$, is $O(2^k)$, hence there exist at most $O(2^{2k})$ pairs of sets (L_1, L_2). There exist at most $O(2^k)$ binary agreement vectors b_x associated with set L_x, with $x \in \{1, 2\}$, hence there exist at most $O(2^{2k})$ pairs of agreement vectors (b_1, b_2). Since a perfect family of hash functions of size $O(\log n2^{O(k)})$ can be constructed in $O(2^{O(k)} n \log n)$ time [1], the overall time complexity of the algorithm is $O(n \log n2^{O(k)})$.

References

1. Alon, N., Yuster, R., Zwick, U.: Color-Coding. Journal of the ACM 42(4), 844–856 (1995)
2. Alimonti, P., Kann, V.: Some APX-Completeness Results for Cubic Graphs. Theoretical Computer Science 237(1-2), 123–134 (2000)
3. Ausiello, G., Crescenzi, P., Gambosi, G., Kann, V., Marchetti-Spaccamela, A., Protasi, M.: Complexity and Approximation: Combinatorial Optimization Problems and Their Approximability Properties. Springer, Heidelberg (1999)
4. Bonizzoni, P., Della Vedova, G., Dondi, R., Li, J.: The Haplotyping Problem: an Overview of Computational Models and Solutions. Journal of Computer and Science Technology 18, 675–688 (2003)
5. Cilibrasi, R., van Iersel, L., Kelk, S., Tromp, J.: The Complexity of the Single Individual SNP Haplotyping Problem. Algorithmica 49(1), 13–36 (2007)
6. Downey, R., Fellows, M.: Parameterized Complexity. Springer, Heidelberg (1999)
7. Greenberg, H.J., Hart, W.E., Lancia, G.: Opportunities for Combinatorial Optimization in Computational Biology. INFORMS Journal on Computing 16(3), 211–231 (2004)
8. Hein, J., Jiang, T., Wang, L., Zhang, K.: On the complexity of Comparing Evolutionary Trees. Discrete Applied Mathematics 71, 153–169 (1996)
9. Jiang, T., Li, M.: On the Approximation of Shortest Common Supersequences and Longest Common Subsequences. SIAM J. Comput. 24, 1122–1139 (1995)
10. Karger, D., Motwani, R., Ramkumar, G.D.S.: On Approximating the Longest Path in a Graph. SIAM J. Comput. 24, 1122–1139 (1995)
11. Lancia, G., Bafna, V., Istrail, S., Lippert, R., Schwartz, R.: SNPs Problems, Complexity and Algorithms. In: Meyer auf der Heide, F. (ed.) ESA 2001. LNCS, vol. 2161, pp. 182–193. Springer, Heidelberg (2001)
12. Niedermeier, R.: Invitation to Fixed-Parameter Algorithms. Oxford University Press, Oxford (2006)
13. Schaefer, T.J.: The Complexity of Satisfiability Problems. In: Tenth Annual ACM Symposium on Theory of Computing (STOC), pp. 216–226. ACM Press, New York (1978)

Earliest Query Answering
for Deterministic Nested Word Automata

Olivier Gauwin[1,2,3], Joachim Niehren[1,3], and Sophie Tison[2,3]

[1] INRIA, Lille
[2] University of Lille 1
[3] Mostrare project, INRIA & LIFL (CNRS UMR8022)

Abstract. Earliest query answering (EQA) is an objective of streaming algorithms for XML query answering, that aim for close to optimal memory management. In this paper, we show that EQA is infeasible even for a small fragment of XPath unless P=NP. We then present an EQA algorithm for queries and schemas defined by deterministic nested word automata (DNWAs) and distinguish a large class of DNWAs for which streaming query answering is feasible in polynomial space and time.

1 Introduction

Streaming algorithms process input streams in an incremental manner, and write their output to some external output collection. The data content on the input stream may be huge, so that only fragments of bounded size can be memorized in main memory at every time point. Furthermore, the input stream is usually restricted to a single reading pass (see [1,2] for more general models).

Streaming algorithms for XML input data streams that contain XML documents, *i.e.*, linearizations of unranked trees or equivalently nested words. In this paper, we are mainly interested in streaming query answering for node selection queries in XML documents, which return collections of tuples of nodes. Such queries may be defined in the W3C standard language XPath 2.0, whose core has the same expressiveness as first-order logic for unranked trees, or by tree automata. The domain of queries can be restricted by schemas defined by the W3C standard XML Schema or again by tree automata.

For illustration, let us simplify XML documents into words with alphabet $\{a, b\}$, and consider the monadic query Q_0 that selects all b positions succeeded by aa in words of $\{a, b\}^*$. This query can be defined by the first-order formula $lab_b(x) \wedge lab_a(x+1) \wedge lab_a(x+2)$ with one free variable x. Its answer set on word $t_0 = abbaabaaba$ is $Q_0(t_0) = \{3, 6\}$. A streaming algorithm for query Q_0 reads some word $t \in \{a, b\}^*$ from the input stream and computes $Q_0(t)$ incrementally. The first answer candidate encountered is letter b at position 2. Whether it will be selected or not depends on the continuation of the stream, and thus position 2 must be stored by all streaming algorithms. We call such answer candidates *alive*. The next event is letter b at position 3. Good streaming algorithms reject candidate 2 now and discard it from memory. In turn, position 3 becomes alive and must be stored. It can be safely selected from position 5 on, written to the external output collection, and discarded from internal memory.

M. Kutyłowski, M. Gębala, and W. Charatonik (Eds.): FCT 2009, LNCS 5699, pp. 121–132, 2009.

We need a notion of streamability that accounts for both space and time. We call a class E of query definitions *streamable*, if there exists a polynomial p and an algorithm mapping query definitions $e \in E$ to streaming algorithms A_e in time $p(|e|)$, such that A_e computes the answer set of query Q_e for all trees t on the input stream, with space and time per step bounded by $p(|e|)$ independently of t. Bar-Yossef et al. [3] showed for a class of XPath queries, that the maximal number of simultaneous alive answer candidates (for all positions of the input stream) is indeed a lower space bound for every streaming query answering algorithm. This number is called the *concurrency* $concur_Q(t)$ of a query Q for an unranked tree t. Classes of queries with unbounded concurrency are thus not streamable. Few positive streamability results exist. Boolean queries (returning true or false) defined by tree automata with languages of trees of bounded depth are streamable [4,5]. Simply compute all runs in parallel on the fly with a stack of bounded depth. Benedikt et. al. [6] showed P-time streamability for the fragment of Boolean Core XPath 1.0 queries in shallow trees, that never look forwards. Heuristics are proposed to approximate earliest rejection. Streamability results for monadic queries are lacking so far.

Earliest query answering (EQA) is the objective of many recent approaches that hint for streaming algorithms with polynomial time and space [3,7,8,9,10]. The strategy is to memorize alive answer candidates only, in order to reach close to optimal memory management. EQA trades space for time: all EQA algorithms need to decide at every step, whether the current answer candidates are safe for selection or rejection (otherwise they are alive). We call these two decision problems SUFFICIENCY for selection resp. rejection. Benedikt et al [6] noticed (Theorem 1) that REJECTION SUFFICIENCY for Boolean XPath queries that never look forwards is PSPACE-hard.

As a first contribution, we present hardness results for SELECTION SUFFICIENCY. For arbitrary classes of query definitions, we show how to reduce SELECTION SUFFICIENCY to a language INCLUSION problem. As a corollary, we obtain coNP-hardness of SELECTION SUFFICIENCY for a small fragment of Forward XPath filters with only child and descendant axis (without schemas) by reduction to UNIVERSALITY of Boolean queries [11]. Thus, the P-time streaming algorithms in [7,12] cannot be earliest, except if P=NP. This result shows that [7] does not fully reach its progressiveness objective, and furthermore it contradicts Theorem 3 of [12] on optimal memory management (without proof). As a counter example, consider the Forward XPath expression //a[not[child::c] and [child::b]], which queries for a-nodes without c-children but with a b-child. Both algorithms will keep a-nodes in memory even when encountering a c-child (and remove them only after closing the last child).

As a second contribution, we provide an EQA algorithm for n-ary queries defined by deterministic nested word automata (dNWAs) [13,14]. Our result relies on new automata constructions deciding selection and rejection SUFFICIENCY in an incremental manner. Without determinism, we show that SELECTION SUFFICIENCY for Boolean NWAs is EXPTIME-complete by reduction to UNIVERSALITY of tree automata [15]. Let Q_e be queries with fixed arity $n \geq 0$ that are defined by a pair of dNWAs $e = (A, B)$ which recognizes the canonical language and the domain (aka schema) of the query respectively, and let $t \in L(B)$ be a tree satisfying the schema on the input stream. Our EQA algorithm for e computes $Q_e(t)$ with the following costs, where $d = depth(t)$ is the depth of the tree and $c = concur_{Q_e}(t)$ the concurrency of the query on the tree:

- polynomial precomputation time in $O(|A|^3 \cdot |B|^3)$;
- polynomial space for all steps in $O(c \cdot d \cdot |A| \cdot |B|)$;
- polynomial time for all steps in $O(c \cdot |A|^2 \cdot |B|^2)$.

As a corollary, a subclass E of queries defined by dNWAs is streamable, if depth and concurrency are bounded by some polynomial p such that $d = depth(t) \leq p(|B|)$ and $c = concur_{Q_e}(t) \leq p(|A| \cdot |B|)$ for all $e = (A, B) \in E$ and $t \in L(B)$.

Related work. Preliminary versions of this paper were presented at the workshops Plan-X'08 and AutoMathA'09. Independently, we showed in [16] how to decide bounded concurrency for queries defined by dNWAs in P-time, by reduction to bounded valuedness of recognizable tree relations.

Schemas defined by dNWAs subsume extended deterministic DTDs with restrained competition [17] modulo a P-time transformation. Kumar, Madhusudan and Viswanathan [10] investigate EQA by dNWAs, but for a restricted class of monadic queries which always allow for immediate node selection at opening time. Similarly, Benedikt and Jeffrey [9] consider immediate node selection at opening and closing time, for XPath filters on depth-bounded documents. Madhusudan and Viswanathan [18] propose a streaming algorithm for monadic queries defined by NWAs. They impose a serious restriction on their automata so that the SUFFICIENCY becomes trivially decidable in P-time.

NWAs are equivalent modulo P-time to pushdown forest automata [19,8,20]. Berlea's [8] P-time EQA algorithm for queries defined by a variant of pushdown forest automata is very different to ours in that no determinism is assumed. This works out, since he assumes infinite signatures so that UNIVERSALITY and SUFFICIENCY become trivially decidable, in contrast to a finite signature, where SUFFICIENCY becomes EXPTIME-hard. With infinite signature, however, schemas can no more be expressed, closure under complement fails, and MSO is no more captured (in contrast to what is stated in Section 3.1 of [8]). Thus, while EQA becomes much simpler, it looses much of its interest.

Bar-Yossef et. al. [3] proposed a streaming algorithm with optimal memory management for monadic queries in shallow trees defined in a fragment of Forward XPath queries. Unfortunately, this algorithm is incorrect since it doesn't try to decide REJECTION SUFFICIENCY. Whether this problem might be solvable by adding further restrictions is open.

Outline. In Sec. 2, we show how to define queries for unranked trees. In Sec. 3 we recall nested word automata. In Sec. 4, we present hardness results for SUFFICIENCY problems. In Sec. 5, we show how to decide SUFFICIENCY for queries defined by dNWAs incrementally, in order to obtain an EQA algorithm in Sec. 6.

All proofs can be found online in the extended version.

2   Queries and Schemas in Unranked Trees

The set T_Σ of *unranked trees* over a finite set Σ is the least set that contains all pairs $a(t_1, \ldots, t_m)$ consisting of a letter $a \in \Sigma$ and an *hedge* $(t_1, \ldots, t_m) \in T_\Sigma^m$ were $m \geq 0$. Nodes of trees and hedges are words over natural numbers defined by $nod(a(t_1, \ldots, t_m)) = \{\epsilon\} \cup nod((t_1, \ldots, t_m))$ and $nod((t_1, \ldots, t_m)) = \cup_{i=1}^m \{i \cdot \pi \mid \pi \in nod(t_i)\}$. We denote the label of node $\pi \in nod(t)$ by $lab^t(\pi) \in \Sigma$. The empty word ϵ is the root of all trees (but of no hedge). The word $\pi \cdot i \in nod(t)$ is the ith child of π. Let $child^t \subseteq nod(t)^2$ be the father-child relation and $lab_a^t = \{\pi \mid lab^t(\pi) = a\}$ the labeling relation for $a \in \Sigma$.

Linearizations of unranked trees in preorder are called *nested words* in [14,13]. We write $nw(t)$ for the nested word of t. For instance, if $t = a(b, c(d), f)$ then $nw(t) = (\mathtt{op}, a) \cdot (\mathtt{op}, b) \cdot (\mathtt{cl}, b) \cdot (\mathtt{op}, c) \cdot (\mathtt{op}, d) \cdot (\mathtt{cl}, d) \cdot (\mathtt{cl}, c) \cdot (\mathtt{op}, f) \cdot (\mathtt{cl}, f) \cdot (\mathtt{cl}, a)$. In XML syntax, an opening tag $(\mathtt{op}, a)$ is written as $<a>$ and a closing tag $(\mathtt{cl}, a)$ is written as $</a>$. We ignore data values throughout this paper. We consider streaming algorithms receiving nested words $nw(t)$ on the input stream. The positions of $nw(t)$ can be identified with the following set of events:

$$eve(t) = \{\mathtt{start}\} \cup (\{\mathtt{op}, \mathtt{cl}\} \times nod(t))$$

If $lab^t(\pi) = a$ then event $(\mathtt{op}, \pi)$ specifies an occurrence of opening tag $<a>$ in an XML stream, and event $(\mathtt{cl}, \pi)$ the corresponding occurence of closing tag $</a>$. Fig. 1(c) illustrates a nested word with edges of relating corresponding events, established by some parser in parallel preprocessing. Let $\prec^t$ be the total order on $eve(t)$, *i.e.*, the order of the tags in the XML stream, and for every e except $\mathtt{start}$ let $pr(e)$ be the immediate predecessor of e in that order. For hedges, events are defined by: $eve(h) = \{\mathtt{start}\} \cup (\{\mathtt{op}, \mathtt{cl}\} \times nod(h))$.

A *schema* is a tree language $S \subseteq T_\Sigma$. An n-ary query is a function Q with schema S is a function Q with domain $dom(Q) = S$ that selects a set of n-tuples of nodes $Q(t) \subseteq nod(t)^n$ for every tree $t \in S$. Boolean queries are queries of arity $n = 0$. The canonical language of an n-ary query Q is a set of annotated trees $L_Q \subseteq T_{\Sigma \times \mathbb{B}^n}$, where $\mathbb{B} = \{0, 1\}$ are the Booleans. For all trees $t \in dom(Q)$ and tuples $\nu \in nod(t)^n$, we define an annotated tree $t' = t * \nu$ in $T_{\Sigma \times \mathbb{B}^n}$ that has the same structure as t, *i.e.*, $nod(t') = nod(t)$, while annotating the node labels of t by bit vectors, such that $lab^{t'}(\pi) = (lab^t(\pi), \beta)$ for all nodes $\pi \in nod(t)$, where $\beta = (b_1, \ldots, b_n)$, $\nu = (\pi_1, \ldots, \pi_n)$ and $b_i = 1 \Leftrightarrow \pi = \pi_i$ for all $1 \leq i \leq n$. The canonical language of an n-ary query Q is the set of all annotated trees for Q, *i.e.*: $L_Q = \{t * \nu \mid \nu \in q(t)\}$. For Boolean queries, $L_Q \subseteq dom(Q)$.

Queries $Q_{(A,B)}$ in unranked trees can be defined by a pair (A, B) of automata with languages $L(A) = L_Q$ and $L(B) = dom(Q_{(A,B)})$. If $L(B) = T_\Sigma$ then we write Q_A for $Q_{(A,B)}$.

3   Nested Word Automata

In the present paper, we consider NWAs [13] as automata operating directly on unranked trees (as proposed in [20] and similarly to pushdown forest automata

[19,8]) whereas they usually operate on linearizations of unranked trees $nw(t)$ or slightly more general nested words.

An NWA $A = (\Sigma, \Gamma, stat, init, fin, rul)$ consists of a finite signature Σ of node labels, a finite set $stat$ with subsets $init, fin \subseteq stat$ of initial and final states, a finite set Γ of stack symbols, and a set $rul \subseteq \{op, cl\} \times \Sigma \times \Gamma \times stat^2$ of rules. We denote rules as:

$$p_0 \xrightarrow{\alpha\ a:\gamma} p_1$$

where $\alpha \in \{op, cl\}$, $p_0, p_1 \in stat$, $a \in \Sigma$, $\gamma \in \Gamma$. Whenever necessary, we will upper index components of A, as for instance, writing rul^A instead of rul.

An NWA traverses the sequence of events of a given tree t, while annotating all events of t by states and all nodes of t by stack symbols. Let p_0 be the state of the previous event processed, and (α, π) be the current event. The automaton chooses some rule with action α and label $a = lab^t(\pi)$ whose left hand side is p_0. If $\alpha = op$ then it annotates node π with stack symbol γ. If $\alpha = cl$ then the rule matches only, if the stack symbol annotated at opening time to π is equal to the stack symbol γ of the rule. For matching rules, the automaton annotates state p_1 on the right hand side to the current event.

More formally, a run of an NWA on a tree t is a function r with two types $r : eve(t) \to stat$ and $r : nod(t) \to \Gamma$ which maps events to states and nodes to stack symbols, such that $r(\text{start}) \in init$ and the following rule belongs to rul for all $\pi \in nod(t)$ with $a = lab^t(\pi)$, and actions $\alpha \in \{op, cl\}$.

$$r(pr(\alpha, \pi)) \xrightarrow{\alpha\ a:r(\pi)} r((\alpha, \pi))$$

An example of a run of an NWA on the tree $a(a, a(a, a(b), b)))$ is given in Fig. 1. It tests whether this tree satisfies the Boolean XPath query $[//a[child::b]]$, or equivalently the first-order formula $\exists x(lab_a(x) \wedge \exists y(child(x, y) \wedge lab_b(y)))$. When opening an a-node in its initial state 0, this NWA guesses whether it matches the a-position of the XPath expression (state 1) or not (state 0). From state 1, it waits while traversing a sequence of states $(2^*1)^*$, until some b-child is opened, before concluding success in state 3. The information of being a child of the a-node opened in state 1 is annotated by stack symbol y, and passed over from the left to the right.

A run r of A on a tree t is successful if $r((cl, \epsilon)) \in fin^A$. The set of all possible runs of the NWA A on the tree t is denoted $runs^A(t)$ and the subset of all successful runs by $runs\_succ^A(t)$. The recognized language $L(A)$ is the set of all trees $t \in T_\Sigma$ that permit a successful run by A, i.e., $L(A) = \{t \in T_\Sigma \mid runs\_succ^A(t) \neq \emptyset\}$. For a hedge $(t_1, \ldots, t_k)$, a run is successful if $r(\text{start}) \in init^A$ and $r((cl, k)) \in fin^A$.

An NWA is *deterministic* or a *dNWA*, if it has a single initial state, no two op rules for the same letter use the same state on the left, and no two cl rules for the same letter use the same stack symbol and the same state on the left. The unique run of a dNWA A on a tree t can be computed in a streaming manner, if it exists. The input is the nested word $nw(t)$ of some t that is enriched by the nesting relation by parallel preprocessing with a SAX parser, and the output is

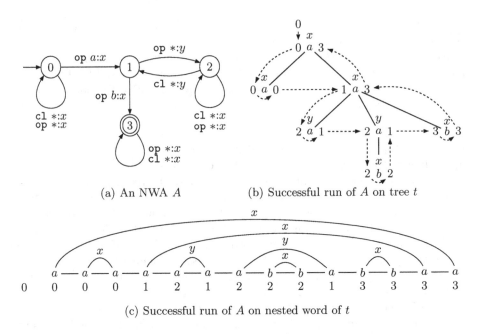

(a) An NWA A

(b) Successful run of A on tree t

(c) Successful run of A on nested word of t

Fig. 1. An NWA checking the Boolean XPath filter $[//a[child::b]]$ by successful runs

the sequence of states that A assigns to the events of t. In order to do so, A has to be stored, and at every time point the current state and the stack of symbols that are annotated to the nodes on the path from the root to the current node. The maximal memory needed at any time point is $O(|A| + depth(t) + 1)$.

4   Complexity of Earliest Query Answering

We present the decision problems of EQA algorithms for n-ary node selection queries and establish lower complexity bounds.

We have to define sufficient events for tuple selection. For every $\eta \in eve(t) - \{\texttt{start}\}$, let the tree prefix $t^{\preceq\eta}$ be the fragment of t which contains all nodes of t opened before or at event η. Note that $t^{\preceq(\texttt{cl},\pi)}$ contains all proper descendants of π in t, while $t^{\preceq(\texttt{op},\pi)}$ does not. For two trees $t, t' \in T_\Sigma$ and $\eta \in eve(t)$ we define $equal_\eta(t, t')$ by $\eta \in eve(t) \cap eve(t')$ and $t^{\preceq\eta} = t'^{\preceq\eta}$, i.e., t and t' have the same prefix until η.

Definition 1. *(Sufficient events for selection) Let Q be an n-ary query over Σ and $t \in dom(Q)$ a tree. We relate tuples $\nu \in nod(t)^n$ to events $\eta \in eve(t)$ that are sufficient for their selection:*

$$(\nu, \eta) \in sel_Q(t) \iff (\nu \in nod(t^{\preceq\eta})^n \wedge \forall t' \in dom(Q). \; equal_\eta(t, t') \Rightarrow \nu \in Q(t'))$$

Note that $(\nu, \eta) \in sel_Q(t)$ implies $\nu \in Q(t)$. Furthermore, successors of sufficient events are sufficient. Consider for instance the monadic query Q_1 with schema

$T_{\{a,b,c\}}$ defined by the XPath expression $//a[child::c]/child::b$, or equivalently by the first-order formula $lab_b(x) \wedge \exists y\, (lab_a(y) \wedge child(y,x) \wedge \exists z\, (child(y,z) \wedge lab_c(z)))$ with one free variable x. On tree $t = b(a, a(a, b, c))$, the earliest time point to select node $2 \cdot 2$ is event $(\mathsf{op}, 2 \cdot 3)$ when the c-child is opened, $i.e.$, $((2 \cdot 2), (\mathsf{op}, 2 \cdot 3)) \in sel_{Q_1}(t)$. For query Q_2 defined by the same XPath expression, but with a more restrictive schema, requiring that all inner a-nodes have at least one c-child, we can select node $2 \cdot 2$ at opening time, $i.e.$, $((2 \cdot 2), (\mathsf{op}, 2 \cdot 2)) \in sel_{Q_2}(t)$.

For optimal memory management, it is equally important to discard *rejected* answer candidates in an earliest manner, $i.e.$, candidates that will never be selected in any possible future. Going one step further, one might also want to remove rejected *partial* candidates, for which no completion will ever be selected in any future. Partial candidates ν are elements of $nod_\oslash(t^{\preceq \eta})^n = (nod(t^{\preceq \eta}) \uplus \{\oslash\})^n$, the symbol $\oslash$ denoting components where no selection occurred so far. Completions $compl(\nu, t, \eta)$ are complete candidates obtained by replacing $\oslash$-components of ν by nodes of t opened after η.

Definition 2. *(Sufficient events for rejection) We call a candidate ν rejected at event η, or equivalently η sufficient for failing ν, if no completion of ν can be selected in the future:*

$$(\nu, \eta) \in rej_Q(t) \Leftrightarrow \begin{cases} \nu \in nod_\oslash(t^{\preceq \eta})^n \;\wedge\; \forall t' \in dom(Q). \\ equal_\eta(t, t') \Rightarrow \forall \nu' \in compl(\nu, t', \eta).\; \nu' \notin Q(t') \end{cases}$$

We call a candidate ν *alive* at event η, if η is not sufficient for selection or rejection of ν, $i.e.$, $(\nu, \eta) \notin sel_Q(t) \cup rej_Q(t)$. EQA algorithms store only alive candidates. The maximal number of alive candidates at a same event, except for $\oslash^n$, is called *concurrency* [3], and written $concur_Q(t)$. For sake of clarity, we treat REJECTION SUFFICIENCY only in the extended version of the paper.

SUFFICIENCY has to be decided for all candidates by all EQA algorithms at every event. SELECTION SUFFICIENCY for a class of query definitions E is the problem that receives as input a definition $e \in E$ of a query Q_e with arity n, a tree $t \in T_\Sigma$, an event $\eta \in eve(t)$, and a tuple $\nu \in nod(t)^n$, and sends as output the truth value of $(\nu, \eta) \in sel_Q(t)$. We provide hardness results SELECTION SUFFICIENCY for some query classes E.

First, we consider Boolean queries defined by XPath filters F in the following fragment. All trees satisfy the label constraint $*$, while only trees $a(\ldots)$ satisfy the label constraint a. A filter $[child::\ell\, F]$ is satisfied by all trees with a subtree at a child position of the root that satisfies ℓ and F. A filter $[//\ell\, F]$ is satisfied by trees having a subtree satisfying ℓ and F. We freely omit filter $[true]$ in examples.

$$F ::= [child::\ell\, F] \mid [//\ell\, F] \mid [F_1\ and\ F_2] \mid [not\, F] \mid [true] \quad \text{for } \ell \in \Sigma \cup \{*\}$$

Proposition 1. SUFFICIENCY *for Boolean queries defined in the above fragment of XPath is coNP-hard, even without schema assumptions.*

As a consequence, every EQA algorithm for a larger fragment of XPATH cannot be in polynomial time, except if P=NP.

Second, we study this problem for queries defined by automata. For nondeterministic ones, SUFFICIENCY remains hard, even with Boolean queries.

Proposition 2. SUFFICIENCY *for Boolean* NWA *queries is* EXPTIME-*hard.*

However, when restricted to deterministic NWAs, the problem becomes tractable.

Theorem 1. SUFFICIENCY *for n-ary dNWA queries is in polynomial time.*

This justifies the use of dNWAs in the following, and shows that SUFFICIENCY is EXPTIME-complete for NWAs (by using NWA determinization).

5   Inferring Safe States

For dNWA queries, we propose a method for deciding SUFFICIENCY at each event of a tree. Our solution is based on a new dNWA construction. Given a dNWA A for the query, we build a dNWA $E(A)$ that accepts the same language, and contains enough information in its states to decide for selection sufficiency at each event immediately. For clarity, sufficiency for rejection is presented in the full version of the paper, and schemas are discussed at the end of Section 6.

We define a partial run r of an NWA A on a tree t like a run, except that it operates only on a prefix $t^{\leq \eta}$ for some event $\eta \in eve(t)$. We write $p\_runs^A(t)$ for the set of all partial runs of A on t. Let A be a dNWA over $\Sigma \times \mathbb{B}^n$ defining a query Q_A, $t \in T_\Sigma$, $\eta \in eve(t)$, and $\nu \in nod(t)^n$. We call a state $p \in stat^A$ safe for selection of ν at event η if the existence of a partial run r of A on t that maps η to p implies $(\nu, \eta) \in sel_{Q_A}(t)$. In other terms, these are the states that ensure sufficiency for selection when they are reached.

$$safe\_sel^A_{(\nu, \eta)}(t) = \{p \mid (\exists r \in p\_runs^A(t * \nu) \wedge r(\eta) = p) \Rightarrow (\nu, \eta) \in sel_{Q_A}(t)\}$$

The remainder of this section describes how these states can be computed by a new dNWA $E(A)$, which permits to decide sufficiency. Here we need some auxiliary definitions. Let $runs^A_{p_0 \to p_1}(h)$ be the set of runs of an NWA A on a hedge h that start in state p_0 and end in state p_1. The operator $ev\_cl^A(h, p_0, a, \gamma)$ evaluates hedge h from state p_0 and subsequently applies a closing rule with label a and state γ:

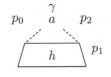

$$ev\_cl^A(h, p_0, a, \gamma) = \{p_2 \mid \exists r \in runs^A_{p_0 \to p_1}(h). \; p_1 \xrightarrow{\text{cl } a:\gamma} p_2 \in rul^A\}$$

We consider continuations through hedges in $H_{sel} = T^*_{\Sigma \times \{0\}^n}$. The operator $univ\_sel^A(a, \gamma, P)$ computes all states, from where all hedges in H_{sel} can be evaluated and closed wrt a and γ into a state of $P \subseteq stat^A$:

$$univ\_sel^A(a, \gamma, P) = \{p_0 \mid \forall h \in H_{sel}. \; ev\_cl^A(h, p_0, a, \gamma) \cap P \neq \emptyset\}$$

Given A, t, and ν, we can compute inductively the safe states $S_{sel}(\eta) = safe\_sel^A_{(\nu, \eta)}(t)$ for all events $\eta \in eve(t)$. First, for the closing event of the root, the set of safe states for selection are the final states: $S_{sel}((cl, \epsilon)) = fin^A$. Second, at each node π, the safe states for opening events can be computed from those of the corresponding closing event:

$$S_{sel}((op, \pi)) = univ\_sel^A(a, \gamma, S_{sel}((cl, \pi)))$$

$$\frac{p_0 \xrightarrow{\text{op } a:\gamma_1} p_1 \in rul^A \qquad S_1 = univ\_sel^A(a, \gamma_1, S_0)}{(p_0, S_0) \xrightarrow{\text{op } a:(\gamma_1, S_0)} (p_1, S_1) \in rul^{E(A)}} \qquad \frac{p_0 \xrightarrow{\text{cl } a:\gamma_0} p_1 \in rul^A \qquad S_0, S_1 \subseteq stat^A}{(p_0, S_0) \xrightarrow{\text{cl } a:(\gamma_0, S_1)} (p_1, S_1) \in rul^{E(A)}}$$

$$init^{E(A)} = (init^A, fin^A) \qquad fin^{E(A)} = \{(p, fin^A) \mid p \in fin^A\}$$

Fig. 2. Construction of $E(A)$ from A

where $a = lab^t(\pi)$ and $\gamma = r^A(\pi)$. Third, the safe states for the opening event of π are equal to those for the closing events of children of π, *i.e.*, $S_{sel}((\text{op}, \pi)) = S_{sel}((\text{cl}, \pi \cdot i))$.

These propagation rules allow to infer $safe\_sel^A_{(\nu, \eta)}(t)$ for all events η. This can be done by running the NWA $E(A)$ defined in Fig. 2, which adds safe states to each state of A. The signature of $E(A)$ is $\Sigma \times \mathbb{B}^n$ as for A. The state sets may be exponentially large, since $stat^{E(A)} = stat^A \times 2^{stat^A}$ and $\Gamma^{E(A)} = \Gamma^A \times 2^{stat^A}$. Stack symbols are used to pass safe states from parents to all their children.

Proposition 3. *Let A be a dNWA on $\Sigma \times \mathbb{B}^n$ that defines a query, and $t * \nu \in T_{\Sigma \times \mathbb{B}^n}$. Then $E(A)$ is a dNWA that accepts the same language as A. Furthermore, if r^A (resp. $r^{E(A)}$) is the unique run of A (resp. $E(A)$) on $t * \nu$ then $r^{E(A)}(\eta) = (r^A(\eta), safe\_sel^A_{(\nu, \eta)}(t))$ for all $\eta \in eve(\eta) - \{\text{start}\}$.*

A detailed proof is in the long version of the paper.[1] Running automaton $E(A)$ for a candidate permits to test sufficiency for selection at the event when it happens. At most one run has to be processed per candidate, thanks to determinism.

6   EQA Algorithm for dNWAs

We present an EQA algorithm for queries defined by dNWAs A which runs in polynomial time per step. The idea is to run the earliest automaton $E(A)$ of Section 5 on the input stream in order to decide SELECTION SUFFICIENCY for all answer candidates at all time points, without constructing $E(A)$ explicitly, since it may be of exponential size compared to A. Recall that deciding REJECTION SUFFICIENCY is needed for all EQA algorithms too, even though not discussed in this extended abstract.

Running E(A) on the Fly. Given a dNWA A over $\Sigma \times \mathbb{B}^n$ and a tree $t * \nu$ over the same signature, we want to compute a run of $E(A)$ on $t * \nu$ in polynomial time in the size of A. The application of closing rules of $E(A)$ is easy, since it only has to look for a rule of A. Applying opening rules of $E(A)$ is a little more tedious, since we have to compute the set $univ\_sel(a, \gamma, P)$ while given $a \in \Sigma$, $\gamma \in \Gamma^A$, and $P \subseteq stat^A$.

---

[1] Note that for sake of clarity, this construction does not hold for earliest selection of () at the **start** event, for Boolean queries. However, this case can be processed easily by considering every possible label of the root.

$$\frac{a \in \Sigma \times \{0\}^n \qquad p_1 \xrightarrow{\text{op } a:\gamma} p_3 \in rul^A \qquad p_4 \xrightarrow{\text{cl } a:\gamma} p_2 \in rul^A}{acc_{H_{sel}}(p_1, p_2) \;\text{:-}\; acc_{H_{sel}}(p_3, p_4).}$$

$$\frac{p \in stat^A}{acc_{H_{sel}}(p, p).} \qquad \frac{p_1, p_2, p_3 \in stat^A}{acc_{H_{sel}}(p_1, p_2) \;\text{:-}\; acc_{H_{sel}}(p_1, p_3), acc_{H_{sel}}(p_3, p_2).}$$

Fig. 3. Inference rules for the definition of $acc_{H_{sel}}^A$

When assuming the completeness of A beside of determinism (which can be ensured in polynomial time), these sets can be computed by reduction to information on accessibility through hedges for A. Given a set $H \subseteq T_{\Sigma \times \mathbb{B}^n}^*$ of hedges, and states $p_1, p_2 \in stat^A$, we define the following accessibility predicate:

$$acc_H^A(p_1, p_2) \quad \Leftrightarrow \quad \exists h \in H.\; runs_{p_1 \to p_2}^A(h) \neq \emptyset$$

We compute it for $H_{sel} = T_{\Sigma \times \{0\}^n}^*$, with the Datalog program in Fig. 3.

Proposition 4. *The collection of values $acc_{H_{sel}}^A(p_1, p_2)$ can be computed in time $O(|\Sigma| \cdot |A|^3)$ for every dNWA A.*

To explain the computation of $univ\_sel^A$, we introduce $befClose^A(a, \gamma, P)$, the set of states that lead to a state of P after closing a with γ:

$$befClose^A(a, \gamma, P) \;=\; \{p_0 \mid \exists p_1 \in P.\; p_0 \xrightarrow{\text{cl } a:\gamma} p_1 \in rul^A\}$$

Lemma 1. *For complete dNWAs A, the safe states $univ\_sel^A(a, \gamma, P)$ are:*

$$\{p \mid acc_{H_{sel}}^A(p, p_0) \Rightarrow p_0 \in befClose^A(a, \gamma, P)\}$$

Generic Algorithm. Our algorithm will be obtained by instantiating the skeleton in Fig. 4 of a generic EQA algorithm, which is parametrized by a class E of query definitions. The static input of the algorithm is a query definition $e \in E$, and its dynamic input on the stream is a nested word $nw(t)$. We assume that the nested word is parsed by some parallel preprocessor. Our algorithm can thus process the stream of events of t while knowning their matching relation. It then adds the tuples of $Q(t)$ to the external output collection incrementally at the earliest possible event. The main idea is to generate all candidate tuples, test their aliveness repeatedly, output selected candidates and remove rejected candidates.

Instantiation for dNWAs. Now suppose that the query is defined by a dNWA A. For every candidate ν we maintain its current state $(p, S) \in stat^{E(A)}$ and a sequence $\Upsilon \in (\Gamma^{E(A)})^*$ that we call stack, whose length is the depth of the current node of t. Sufficiency for selection $(\nu, \eta) \in sel_Q(t)$ holds iff $p \in S$.

Updating the current set of candidates at event η means to apply a rule of $E(A)$ to the current state $(p, S) \in E(A)$, and for opening events to create all new candidates, where the current node is used. More precisely, for generating

```
fun  answer(e,t)  %  e ∈ E,  t ∈ dom(Q_e)
    let  Q = Q_e
    let  candidates  =  set.new(∅)
in
    for  η  in  eve(t)  in  streaming−order  do
        candidates.update(η)
        for  ν  in  candidates  do
            if  (ν,η) ∈ sel_Q(t)
                then  add−output(ν)
                      candidates.remove(ν)
            elseif  (ν,η) ∈ rej_Q(t)
                then  candidates.remove(ν)
```

Fig. 4. Generic EQA algorithm for a class E of query definitions

these candidates, we can restrict to the ones generated by continuations of the runs of old candidates. Thus, the number of candidates to process at an event is bounded by $c + i$, where $c = concur_Q(t)$ is the concurrency of the query Q, and $i = immediate_Q(t)$ is the number of new candidates that immediately get safe for selection or rejection. We have seen already how to apply rules of $E(A)$ in polynomial time in the size of A. The node state of the rule is pushed to stack Υ for opening events, and popped from Υ for closing events.

Theorem 2. *For every dNWA A recognizing a canonical language over $\Sigma \times \mathbb{B}^n$, and tree $t \in T_\Sigma$, the time needed to process one event is in $O((c+i) \cdot |\Sigma| \cdot |A|^2)$ and the space in $O(c \cdot d \cdot |A|)$, where $d = depth(t)$ is the depth of t, $c = concur_{Q_A}(t)$ and $i = immediate_{Q_A}(t)$.*

Adding Schemas. With respect to sufficiency checking, we can integrate the schema into the query. Validation of the document with respect to the schema is an independent task, that we run in parallel. Given an n-ary query Q and a schema S, define a query Q_{sel}^S with domain T_Σ:

$$Q_{sel}^S(t) = Q(t) \text{ if } t \in S, \text{ and } nod(t)^n \text{ otherwise}$$

It is easy to check that $sel_Q = sel_{Q_{sel}^S}$ so that we can test sufficiency for selection as before. The overall costs of the resulting EQA algorithm with schemas have already been reported in the introduction.

Conclusion. We distinguished a large class of streamable query-schema definitions defined by dNWAs. This class was obtained by designing an EQA algorithm in a first step and bounding the concurrency of the query and the depth of trees in a second. We have shown that EQA is infeasible for nondeterministic NWAs if $n \geq 1$, as well as for Forward XPath with child and descendant axis. In subsequent work [21], we have shown that these classes are indeed not streamable, and distinguished schema restricted fragments of Forward XPath, that can be proven to be streamable by P-time compilation into dNWAs. This proves that the notion of determinism of dNWAs is essential for streamability. An open question is whether we can extend our EQA algorithm to deterministic pushdown automata.

Acknowledgments. This work was partially supported by the Enumeration project ANR-07-blanc and the project CODEX of ANR-08-Defis.

References

1. Grohe, M., Koch, C., Schweikardt, N.: Tight lower bounds for query processing on streaming and external memory data. TCS 380, 199–217 (2007)
2. Schweikardt, N.: Machine models and lower bounds for query processing. In: ACM PODS, pp. 41–52 (2007)
3. Bar-Yossef, Z., Fontoura, M., Josifovski, V.: Buffering in query evaluation over XML streams. In: ACM PODS, pp. 216–227 (2005)
4. Segoufin, L., Vianu, V.: Validating streaming XML documents. In: ACM PODS, pp. 53–64 (2002)
5. Segoufin, L., Sirangelo, C.: Constant-memory validation of streaming XML documents against DTDs. In: Schwentick, T., Suciu, D. (eds.) ICDT 2007. LNCS, vol. 4353, pp. 299–313. Springer, Heidelberg (2006)
6. Benedikt, M., Jeffrey, A., Ley-Wild, R.: Stream firewalling of XML constraints. In: ACM SIGMOD, pp. 487–498 (2008)
7. Olteanu, D.: SPEX: Streamed and progressive evaluation of XPath. IEEE Trans. on Know. Data Eng. 19, 934–949 (2007)
8. Berlea, A.: Online evaluation of regular tree queries. Nordic Journal of Computing 13, 1–26 (2006)
9. Benedikt, M., Jeffrey, A.: Efficient and expressive tree filters. In: Arvind, V., Prasad, S. (eds.) FSTTCS 2007. LNCS, vol. 4855, pp. 461–472. Springer, Heidelberg (2007)
10. Kumar, V., Madhusudan, P., Viswanathan, M.: Visibly pushdown automata for streaming XML. In: WWW, pp. 1053–1062 (2007)
11. Miklau, G., Suciu, D.: Containment and equivalence for a fragment of XPath. Journal of the ACM 51, 2–45 (2004)
12. Gou, G., Chirkova, R.: Efficient algorithms for evaluating XPath over streams. In: ACM SIGMOD, pp. 269–280 (2007)
13. Alur, R., Madhusudan, P.: Adding nesting structure to words. Journal of the ACM 56, 1–43 (2009)
14. Alur, R., Madhusudan, P.: Visibly pushdown languages. In: 36th ACM Symposium on Theory of Computing, pp. 202–211 (2004)
15. Seidl, H.: Haskell overloading is DEXPTIME-complete. Information Processing Letters 52, 57–60 (1994)
16. Gauwin, O., Niehren, J., Tison, S.: Bounded delay and concurrency for earliest query answering. In: Dediu, A.H., Ionescu, A.M., Martiń-Vide, C. (eds.) LATA 2009. LNCS, vol. 5457, pp. 350–361. Springer, Heidelberg (2009)
17. Martens, W., Neven, F., Schwentick, T.: Which XML schemas admit 1-pass pre-order typing? In: Eiter, T., Libkin, L. (eds.) ICDT 2005. LNCS, vol. 3363, pp. 68–82. Springer, Heidelberg (2004)
18. Madhusudan, P., Viswanathan, M.: Query automata for nested words (2009)
19. Neumann, A., Seidl, H.: Locating matches of tree patterns in forests. In: Arvind, V., Sarukkai, S. (eds.) FST TCS 1998. LNCS, vol. 1530, pp. 134–146. Springer, Heidelberg (1998)
20. Gauwin, O., Niehren, J., Roos, Y.: Streaming tree automata. Information Processing Letters 109, 13–17 (2008)
21. Gauwin, O., Niehren, J.: Streamable fragments of Forward XPath (2009)

Multiway In-Place Merging*

Viliam Geffert and Jozef Gajdoš

Department of Computer Science, P. J. Šafárik University
Jesenná 5, 04154 Košice, Slovakia
viliam.geffert@upjs.sk, jozef.gajdos@upjs.sk

Abstract. We present an algorithm for asymptotically efficient k-way merging. Given an array A containing sorted subsequences $A_1, \ldots, A_k$ of respective lengths $n_1, \ldots, n_k$, where $\sum_{i=1}^{k} n_i = n$, our algorithm merges $A_1, \ldots, A_k$ in-place, into a single sorted sequence, performing $\lceil \lg k \rceil \cdot n + o(n)$ element comparisons and $3 \cdot n + o(n)$ element moves. That is, our algorithm runs in linear time, with the number of moves independent of k, the number of input sequences.

Keywords: In-place algorithms, merging, sorting.

1 Introduction

We study the computational complexity of the *multiway in-place merging*. Given an array A consisting of k sorted subsequences $A_1, \ldots, A_k$ of respective lengths $n_1, \ldots, n_k$, where $\sum_{i=1}^{k} n_i = n$, the multiway in-place merging problem is to rearrange the elements of A to a single sorted sequence. Here k denotes a fixed constant parameter. We assume that only one extra storage location (in addition to the array A) is available for storing elements aside. To store array indices, counters, etc., only $O(1)$ integer variables, of $O(\lg n)$ bits each, are available.[1]

So far, the problem has been studied for $k = 2$ only [3]. In the worst case, this algorithm uses $n + o(n)$ comparisons, $3n + o(n)$ element moves and $O(1)$ auxiliary locations. Thus, by repeated application of this algorithm, we could carry out multiway merging in linear time, for arbitrary $k \geq 2$. However, implemented this way, the k-way merging would perform $\lceil \lg k \rceil \cdot n + o(n)$ element comparisons and $3 \cdot \lceil \lg k \rceil \cdot n + o(n)$ element moves. We show that the number of moves *does not depend on k*. Namely, using the algorithm of [3] as our starting point, we show that multiway in-place merging is possible with $\lceil \lg k \rceil \cdot n + O((n \cdot \lg n)^{2/3}) \leq \lceil \lg k \rceil \cdot n + o(n)$ comparisons and $3 \cdot n + O((n \cdot \lg n)^{2/3}) \leq 3 \cdot n + o(n)$ moves. Thus, the number of moves does not grow in k, the number of merged sequences. This should be compared with the respective lower bounds: Any comparison based k-way in-place merging algorithm must perform at least $\lg k \cdot n - k \cdot \lg n - O(1)$ comparisons and $\lfloor 3/2 \cdot n \rfloor$ moves.

---

* This work was supported by the Slovak Grant Agency for Science (VEGA) under contract 1/0035/09.
[1] Throughout the paper, $\lg x$ denotes the binary logarithm of x.

M. Kutyłowski, M. Gębala, and W. Charatonik (Eds.): FCT 2009, LNCS 5699, pp. 133–144, 2009.

2   Comparisons in a Simple Multiway Merging

To explain how elements are compared, we first solve a simpler task. Assume that we are given an array A, consisting of k sorted subsequences $A_1, \ldots, A_k$ that are to be merged into a single sorted sequence. The lengths of these subsequences are $n_1, \ldots, n_k$, respectively, with $\sum_{i=1}^{k} n_i = n$. Assume also that we are given an extra array B of the same size n, which will be used as an output zone.

During the computation, we use auxiliary index variables $i_1, \ldots, i_k$ and o_c, where i_j points to the smallest element of A_j not yet processed. This element will be called the *current input element of the j-th sequence*, or simply the *j-th input element*. The index o_c points to the leftmost empty position in the array B.

Then the straightforward implementation of the merge routine proceeds as follows. Find the smallest element not yet processed, among elements at the positions $i_1, \ldots, i_k$, and move this element to the output zone in B. After that, update the necessary index variables and repeat the process until all the elements have been merged. Implemented this way, we would use $(k-1) \cdot n$ comparisons and n element moves in total.

The number of comparisons can be reduced by implementing a selection tree of depth $\lceil \lg k \rceil$ above the k current input elements. Initially, to build a selection tree, $k-1$ comparisons are required. Then the smallest element can be moved to the output. After this, the following element in the same subsequence is inserted in the tree and the selection tree is updated, with only $\lceil \lg k \rceil$ comparisons. To avoid element moves, only pointers to elements are stored in the selection tree. (For more details concerning this data structure, see [4,5].) Now we have $k-1$ comparisons for the first element, but only $\lceil \lg k \rceil$ comparisons per each other element. This gives $(k-1) + \lceil \lg k \rceil \cdot (n-1) \leq \lceil \lg k \rceil \cdot n + O(1)$ comparisons.

3   Comparisons in a Blockwise Merging

Here we describe one of the cardinal tricks used in our algorithm. As an additional assumption, now $A_1, \ldots, A_k$ are divided into blocks of equal size s (this value will be determined later) and, before the merging starts, these blocks are mixed up quite arbitrarily. Because of this permutation, we no longer know the original membership of blocks in the sequences $A_1, \ldots, A_k$. Still, the relative order of elements inside individual blocks is preserved. Moreover, we assume that $n_1, \ldots, n_k$, the respective lengths of input sequences, are positive integer multiples of s, and hence, before mixing the blocks up, there was always a block boundary between the last element of A_i and the first element of A_{i+1}, for each i.

Before passing further, we define the following relative order of blocks in the array A. Let X be a block with the leftmost and the rightmost elements denoted by x_L and x_R, respectively, which will be represented in the form $X = \langle x_\mathrm{L}, x_\mathrm{R} \rangle$. Similarly, let $Y = \langle y_\mathrm{L}, y_\mathrm{R} \rangle$ be an another block. We say that the block X is smaller than or equal to Y, if $x_\mathrm{L} < y_\mathrm{L}$, or $x_\mathrm{L} = y_\mathrm{L}$ and $x_\mathrm{R} \leq y_\mathrm{R}$.

Now the modified algorithm proceeds as follows. First, using the above block ordering, find the smallest k blocks in A. These blocks become the k *current input blocks*, their leftmost elements the k *current input elements*. The j-th current input block is denoted by X_j, and the j-th current input element by x_j. Positions of $x_1, \ldots, x_k$ are kept in index variables $i_1, \ldots, i_k$. Above these elements, we build a selection tree. All remaining blocks are called *common blocks*.

After that, the merging process proceeds in the same way as described in Sect. 2: Using the selection tree, determine i_j, the position of the smallest input element not yet processed, and move this element to the output zone in the array B. Then the element on the right of x_j, within the same block X_j, becomes a new j-th current input element and the selection tree is updated. This can be repeated until one of the current input blocks becomes empty.

When this happens, i.e., each time the element x_j, just moved to the output zone, was the rightmost element in the corresponding input block X_j, the block X_j is "discarded" and the smallest (according to our relative block ordering) common block not yet processed becomes the new j-th current input block. The leftmost element in this block becomes the new j-th current input element. Since the blocks are mixed in the array A, we need to scan sequentially all blocks (not yet processed only) to determine which one of them is the smallest. This consumes $O((n/s)^2)$ additional comparisons: there are at most n/s blocks and such search is activated only if one of the input blocks has been discarded as empty, i.e., at most n/s times.

Despite the fact that, before merging, the blocks are mixed up and their origin in the sequences $A_1, \ldots, A_k$ is ignored, it can be shown that the elements are transported to the output zone in sorted order. The number of element comparisons is bounded by $\lceil \lg k \rceil \cdot n + O((n/s)^2)$, under assumption that we can distinguish discarded blocks from those not yet processed, at no extra cost.

4   In-Place Merging, Simplified Case

Now we shall convert the above merging algorithm into a procedure working "almost" in-place: The subsequences $A_1, \ldots, A_k$ are again of respective lengths $n_1, \ldots, n_k$ that are positive integer multiples of s, but we no longer have a separate array B of size n. Instead, we have some extra $k \cdot s$ elements positioned at the very end of the array A. These elements are greater than any of the elements in $A_1, \ldots, A_k$. During the computation, they can be mixed with other elements, but their original contents cannot be destroyed. We shall call them *buffer elements*. We also have one extra location to put a single element aside.

The sorted output is formed within the same array A, in the locations occupied by $A_1, \ldots, A_k$. Therefore, the moves are performed in a different way, based on the idea of internal buffering [7,3]. Nevertheless, the comparisons are performed in the same way as described in Sect. 3.

4.1   Initialization

Divide the array A into blocks of equal size s. Since the lengths of all sequences $A_1, \ldots, A_k$ are integer multiples of s, there is always a block boundary between the last element of A_i and the first element of A_{i+1}, for each i. Similarly, the buffer elements, positioned at the very end, form the last k blocks.

Initially, the last k blocks become *free blocks*, their starting positions are stored in a *free block stack* of height k. After that, the position of one free block is picked out of the stack and this block is used as a so-called *escape block*. We also maintain a *current escape position* e_c, which is initially the position of the leftmost element in the escape block. We create a hole here by putting the buffer element at this position aside.

Now, find the smallest k blocks (not necessarily equal to leftmost blocks in $A_1, \ldots, A_k$) in the area occupied by $A_1, \ldots, A_k$, according to the relative block ordering of Sect. 3. This is done with $O(k^2) \leq O(1)$ comparisons, by the use of some k cursors (index variables) moving along in A, since the sequences $A_1, \ldots, A_k$ are sorted. These blocks will initially become the k *current input blocks* $X_1, \ldots, X_k$. For each j, the first element x_j in X_j becomes a j-th *current input element*, its position is kept in the index variable i_j. Above the k input elements, we build a selection tree of depth $\lceil \lg k \rceil$, using $k-1 \leq O(1)$ comparisons.

The leftmost block of the array A becomes an *output block* and a position $o_c = 1$ pointing there becomes a *current output position*. The initial output position may coincide with a position of some current input element. Observe that $e_c \bmod s = o_c \bmod s$, which is an invariant we shall keep in the course of the entire computation. All other blocks are called *common blocks*.

In general, the algorithm maintains current positions of the following blocks: free blocks, the number of which ranges between 0 and k, their leftmost positions are stored in the free block stack; exactly k input blocks, the current input positions inside these blocks are stored in $i_1, \ldots, i_k$; one output block with the current output position o_c inside this block; and one escape block with the current escape position e_c inside. The values o_c and e_c are synchronized modulo s. Usually, all these blocks are disjoint and the merging proceeds as described in Sect. 4.2. However, after the initiation, the output block may overlay one of the input blocks, if the leftmost block in A_1 has been selected as an input block. If this happens, we start in a special mode of Sect. 4.8.

4.2   Standard Situation

During the computation, the $k \cdot s$ buffer elements can be found at the following locations: to the left of the j-th input element x_j in the j-th input block X_j, for $j \in \{1, \ldots, k\}$, to the right of e_c in the escape block, with the hole at the position e_c, and also in free blocks, consisting of buffer elements only.

The elements merged already, from all the input blocks, form a contiguous output zone at the very beginning of A, ending at the position $o_c - 1$. Hence, the next element to be output will go to the position o_c in the output block.

All elements not merged yet are scattered in blocks between the output zone and the end of the array A. The permutation of these blocks is allowed. Thus, the origin of the blocks in the subsequences $A_1, \ldots, A_k$ cannot be recovered. However, the elements keep their relative positions within each block. So optional free blocks, input blocks, escape block, and common blocks can reside anywhere in this area. The output block spans across the current output position o_c, so its left part belongs to the output zone. As the output grows to the right, the elements lying to the right of o_c are moved from the output block to the corresponding positions in the escape block, to the right of e_c. Since $o_c \bmod s = e_c \bmod s$, the relative positions of escaping elements are preserved within the blocks.

Now we are ready for merging. Using the selection tree, we determine x_j, the smallest element among the k current input elements in the blocks $X_1, \ldots, X_k$, and move this element to the output zone as follows:

Step A. The element at the position o_c in the output block escapes to the hole at the position e_c.
Step B. The smallest input element x_j not yet processed is moved from the position i_j to its final position at o_c.
Step C. A new hole is created at the position $e_c + 1$ by moving its buffer element to the place released by the smallest input element just moved. After that, all necessary index variables are incremented and the selection tree is updated.

This gives 3 moves and $\lceil \lg k \rceil$ comparisons per each element transported to its final location. Now there are various special cases to consider.

4.3 Escape Block Becomes Full

If the rightmost element of the output block is moved to the last position of the escape block, the new hole cannot be created at the position $e_c + 1$ in Step C. Instead, one free block at the top of the stack becomes the new escape block and a new hole is created at the beginning of this block. This is accomplished by removing its starting position from the free block stack and assigning it to e_c.

The subsequent move of the buffer element from the new position of e_c to the place released by the smallest input element does not increase the number of moves; it replaces the move in Step C. It should be pointed out that, at this moment, there must exist at least one free block.

4.4 Current Input Block Becomes Empty

We check next whether the smallest element x_j, just moved to the output zone, was the last element in the input block X_j. If so, we have an entire block consisting of buffer elements, with hole at the end after Step B. This hole is filled in the standard way, described in Step C, but the old input block X_j becomes a free block and its position is saved in the stack.

Next, we find a new j-th input block X_j, and assign a new value to i_j. Since the blocks are mixed, we scan sequentially the remaining common blocks and determine the smallest one, according to the block ordering introduced in Sect. 3. This block should become the new j-th input block. Even though this smallest block is not necessarily picked from the j-th input sequence A_j, the elements are still transported to the output zone in sorted order. (Due to a size limit, the argument is omitted.)

Free blocks, as well as all remaining current input blocks, are ignored in this scanning. Moreover, the elements to the left of e_c in the escape block (if not empty) together with the elements to the right of o_c in the output block are viewed as a single logical block. If this logical block should be processed next, the program control jumps to the mode described in Sect. 4.5. If the escape block is empty, both e_c and o_c point to the beginning of their respective blocks. Then the escape block is skipped and the output block is handled as a common block, so we may even find out that the new input block is located at the same position as the output block. This special mode is explained in Sect. 4.8.

The search for new input blocks costs $O((n/s)^2)$ additional comparisons: there are $O(n/s)$ blocks in total and such search is activated only if one of the input blocks is exhausted, i.e., at most $O(n/s)$ times.

4.5 One of the Input Blocks Overlays the Escape Block

If the common block that should be processed next is the logical block composed of the left part of the escape block and the right part of the output block, then both the new current input block X_j and the escape block are located within the same physical block. Here x_j is always positioned to the left of e_c and the buffer elements are both to the left of x_j and to the right of e_c.

Once the position of x_j is initiated, all actions are performed in the standard way described in Sect. 4.2. This special case returns automatically to the standard mode as soon as e_c reaches a block boundary.

4.6 Output Block Overlays the Escape Block or a Free Block

Next we check whether the output zone, crossing a block boundary, does not bump into any "special" block. This may happen only if e_c points to the beginning of the escape block that is empty, since the positions of o_c and e_c are synchronized. Let us first consider that the output block overlays the escape block, i.e., they are both located within the same physical block. The element movement corresponds now to a more efficient scheme, without Step A:

Step B'. The smallest input element x_j not yet processed is moved to the hole at the position $o_c = e_c$.
Step C'. A new hole is created at the position $o_c+1 = e_c+1$ by moving its buffer element to the place released by x_j. Then all necessary index variables are incremented and the selection tree is updated.

This mode is terminated as soon as o_c and e_c reach a block boundary. We also need a slightly modified version of the routine described in Sect. 4.4. If one of the input blocks becomes empty, it becomes free as usual, but the combined output/escape block is skipped in the search for the next input block.

If the output zone crosses a block boundary and o_c is equal to some f_ℓ, the leftmost position of a block stored in the free block stack, the new output block and the corresponding free block are overlaid. Since e_c points to the beginning of an empty escape block, we can swap the free block with the escape block by swapping the pointers stored in f_ℓ and e_c. Second, one move suffices to transport the hole from one block to another. This element move is for free, because the next s transports will require only $2s$ moves, instead of $3s$. The program control is switched to the mode in which the output and escape blocks are overlaid.

4.7   Output Block Overlays a Current Input Block

If o_c points to some X_j after crossing a block boundary, the output block overlays the j-th input block X_j. Again, this can happen only if e_c points to the beginning of an empty escape block. There are now two cases to consider.

First, if the j-th current input element x_j is the leftmost element of X_j, the program control is switched to the mode to be described in Sect. 4.8.

Second, if x_j is not the leftmost element of X_j, we dispose of the empty escape block as free, create a hole at o_c by moving a single buffer element from the position o_c to e_c, and overlay the output block by a new escape block, by assigning the value of o_c to e_c. The additional transportation of the hole is for free, because we can charge it as (nonexistent) Step A for the next element that will be transported to the output. In this special mode, *three blocks* are overlaid, namely, the output, escape, and the current input block X_j. The buffer elements are between the hole at $e_c = o_c$ and the current input element x_j. The elements are moved according to Step B' and Step C' of Sect. 4.6. However:

(1) If the rightmost input element of this combined block has been transported to the output, the input block X_j separates from the output/escape block, since we search for the next input block. But here, unlike in Sect. 4.4, no block is disposed as free. The program control switches to the mode of Sect. 4.6.

(2) If this block becomes full, i.e., for some $h \neq j$, an element x_h from another input block X_h is moved to the output and, after Step B', the position o_c "bumps" into x_j, we change one free block into a new escape block. That is, we take f_ℓ, a starting position of one block from the stack, set $e_c := f_\ell + (o_c \bmod s)$, and move one buffer element from the position e_c to i_h in X_h. This replaces Step C' for the element x_h. Then we follow the instructions of Sect. 4.8.

4.8   Output Zone Bumps into a Current Input Element

The program jumps to this mode from Sects. 4.1, 4.4, and 4.7. In any case, we have an empty escape block, with $e_c \bmod s = o_c \bmod s$. Moreover, the output block and some input block X_j are overlaid, with o_c pointing to x_j. As long as the elements to be output are selected in X_j, we need no actual transportation, just the positions of o_c and i_j are moved to the right. To keep e_c synchronized with o_c, we move the hole along the escape block in parallel.

(1) If o_c and i_j reach the block boundary, we search for the next input block to be processed. Thus, unless something "exceptional" happens, the program returns to the standard mode. (The possible exceptions are those discussed in Sects. 4.6, 4.7, and 4.9.) The single move placing the hole back to the beginning of the escape block substitutes Step C for the last element merged.

(2) If the element to be transported to the output zone is an element x_h from another input block X_h, for some $h \neq j$, some rearrangements are necessary. First, move x_j from the position o_c to e_c. Second, transport x_h to o_c. Finally, create a new hole at e_c+1 by moving its buffer element to the place released by x_h. The result is that the current input block X_j, overlaid by the output block, jumps and overlays the escape block. This transported one element to the output, with three moves. The control is switched to the mode of Sect. 4.5.

4.9   Common Blocks Are Exhausted

If one of the current input blocks becomes empty, but there is no common block to become a new input block, the above procedure is stopped. At this point, the output zone is followed by a residual zone of size n', starting at the position o_c and consisting of the right part of the output block, $k-1$ unmerged input blocks, at most k free blocks, and one escape block. Thus, $n' \leq (2k+1) \cdot s$.

The residual zone can be sorted, e.g., by the use of Heapsort, performing $O(k \cdot s \cdot \lg(k \cdot s)) \leq O(s \cdot \lg s)$ comparisons and moves. Since the buffer elements are greater than any other element, we are done, the entire array A is sorted.

4.10   Summary

Summing up the costs paid for maintaining the selection tree, transporting the elements to the output zone, searching for smallest input blocks, and for sorting the residual zone, it is easy to see that the above algorithm uses $\lceil \lg k \rceil \cdot n + O((n/s)^2) + O(s \cdot \lg s)$ element comparisons and $3 \cdot n + O(s \cdot \lg s)$ moves.

5   In-Place Merging

Now we are ready for the general case. Namely, the lengths of $A_1, \ldots, A_k$ are not necessarily multiples of s. Moreover, there are no $k \cdot s$ buffer elements available. Recall that these two assumptions were used in our simplified version described in Sect. 4. Our task is to prepare conditions so that our simplified algorithm can be used as a subroutine to carry out the merging process. (See also Fig. 1.)

5.1   Initial Calculations

First, we partition A into blocks of equal size s, the last block having a size $s' \in \{0, \ldots, s-1\}$. A block will be called a *guarded block*, if a boundary between some sequences A_i and A_{i+1} is located inside, or if a sequence boundary coincides with the left or the right boundary of this block. The first and the last blocks of A are also guarded. Initially, a guarded block may contain some largest elements in A_i, called *tail elements*, together with some smallest elements in A_{i+1}, called *head elements*. If an entire short sequence falls within a single block, all elements of that sequence are head elements. Clearly, the initial number of guarded blocks is at most $2 \cdot k$. The leftmost positions of all guarded blocks are easily computable in $O(1)$ time from the values of $n_1, \ldots, n_k$ and s.

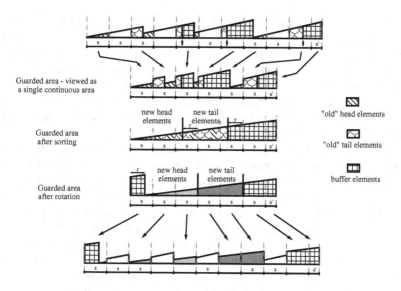

Fig. 1. Rearranging elements in the guarded area

5.2   Allocation of Buffer Elements

To allocate *buffer elements*, we use a procedure similar to the one described in Sect. 2. This time the selection tree is built above last elements of $A_1, \ldots, A_k$. Using this tree, we can determine the largest element, which becomes a new buffer element. However, this buffer element is not moved, only the corresponding index variable, pointing to it, is decremented so that the next element to the left becomes a part of the selection tree and the tree is updated. This process is repeated until we allocate sufficiently many buffer elements and, moreover, the number of remaining tail elements is divisible by s.

Let TOT be the total number of all elements in guarded blocks, H the total number of head elements, T the total number of tail elements, and B the total number of buffer elements. Initially, $B = 0$. We also use a constant number of indexes per each sequence A_i to keep track of the boundaries between the head, common, tail, and buffer elements in A_i. Each time a new buffer element is allocated by the use of the selection tree, there are the following possibilities:

Case 1. If the new buffer element was a tail element, we set $B := B + 1$ and $T := T - 1$. Clearly, $B + H = (B_o + H_o) + 1$, and hence also $(B + H) \bmod s = ((B_o + H_o) + 1) \bmod s$, where B_o, T_o, and H_o denote the "old" number of buffer, tail, and head elements, before the selection of the new buffer element.

Case 2. If we cross the left block boundary of the guarded block, the next block to the left becomes another new guarded block and all its elements become tail elements. The situation changes as follows: $\text{TOT} := \text{TOT} + s$, $B := B + 1$, and $T := T + s - 1$. Note that also here $(B + H) \bmod s = ((B_o + H_o) + 1) \bmod s$.

Case 3. If the zone of buffer elements growing at the end of some sequence A_i bumps into the head elements at the beginning of A_i, the rightmost head element of A_i can be selected as a new buffer element. That is, $\text{B} := \text{B}+1$ and $\text{H} := \text{H}-1$. (This also happens if some sequence A_i falls entirely within a single guarded block.) This gives $(\text{B} + \text{H}) \bmod s = (\text{B}_o + \text{H}_o) \bmod s$. However, this can happen at most $k \cdot s$ times, because the initial number of head elements is $\text{H} \leq k \cdot s$ and this number never increases. If all elements of an entire sequence A_i have become buffer elements, we simply attach these elements to buffer elements of A_{i-1}.

First, we repeat this process $k \cdot s + s'$ times, so there are enough buffer elements (namely, $k \cdot s + s'$) for the merging process.

Second, to ensure that the sequence boundaries match the block boundaries, we keep on allocating new buffer elements in the same way as described above, until $(\text{B} + \text{H}) \bmod s = s'$. This can be accomplished by using at most $k \cdot s + (s-1)$ additional iterations: Normally, in each iteration, the value $\text{B} + \text{H}$ is incremented by 1. The only exception is Case 3, which can happen at most $k \cdot s$ times. Therefore, the total number of allocated buffer elements is bounded by $2 \cdot k \cdot s + 2 \cdot (s-1)$, using $(k-1) + \lceil \lg k \rceil \cdot (2 \cdot k \cdot s + 2 \cdot (s-1) - 1) \leq O(k \cdot s \cdot \lg k)$ comparisons.

Recall that we started with at most $2 \cdot k$ guarded blocks, thus containing $\text{TOT} \leq 2 \cdot k \cdot s$ elements. After $2 \cdot k \cdot s + 2 \cdot (s-1)$ iterations, needed to satisfy the two conditions mentioned above, the value of TOT can increase by at most $2 \cdot k \cdot s + 2 \cdot (s-1)$: the number of elements in guarded blocks increases in Case 2 only. If, in a given step, we add a new guarded block, the next $s-1$ elements selected from the same sequence are tail elements (Case 1), in which case TOT does not change. The final number of all elements in guarded blocks is therefore bounded by $4 \cdot k \cdot s + 2 \cdot (s-1)$, and hence the number of guarded blocks by $4 \cdot k + 2$.

Thus, with a constant number of index variables, we can keep pointers to the starting positions of all guarded blocks. This allows us to view all guarded blocks as if they formed a single continuous "guarded area" containing $\text{TOT} = \text{H}+\text{T}+\text{B}$ elements. All blocks forming the guarded area are of size s, except for the block of size $s' < s$ placed at the very end of the array A. Therefore $\text{TOT} \bmod s = s'$, which together with $(\text{B} + \text{H}) \bmod s = s'$ implies that $\text{T} \bmod s = 0$. (In other words, the final number of tail elements is an integer multiple of s.)

5.3   Rearranging the Guarded Area

Now we sort the guarded area in-place, using, e.g., Heapsort, performing $O(\text{TOT} \cdot \lg(\text{TOT})) \leq O(k \cdot s \cdot \lg(k \cdot s)) \leq O(s \cdot \lg s)$ comparisons and moves. After sorting, the order of elements in the guarded area is: $\text{H} + \text{T}$ head and tail elements (possibly mixed) followed by B buffer elements (the largest elements of A). Since the head and tail elements might be mixed, the status of some of them can change. From this point forward, the first H elements of the guarded area will become the (new) head elements, and the next T elements the (new) tail elements. The boundaries between the new head, new tail, and buffer elements within the guarded area are easily determined from H, T, and B. (From now on, we will refer to the new head and new tail elements simply as the head and tail elements.) It should be pointed out that these manipulations in the guarded area do not increase k, the number of input sequences to be merged.

After sorting, we perform a cyclic shift $r = (s - \text{H}) \bmod s$ positions to the right of all elements within the guarded area, so that the boundary between the head and tail elements matches a block boundary. The boundary between the tail and buffer elements will match a block boundary automatically, because T is an integer multiple of s. Observe that the first guarded block now starts with r buffer elements followed by the smallest $s - r$ sorted head elements. This rotation does not require any element comparisons, only $O(k \cdot s)$ moves.

5.4   Finishing Touch

We are ready for merging. The very last block of size $s' < s$, containing buffer elements only, becomes a *dead block*. This block is excluded from the subsequent merging. The very first block, containing r buffer and $s - r$ head elements, becomes the first input block and its leftmost head element becomes its current input element. The guarded blocks containing buffer elements only become free blocks, their starting positions are stored in the free block stack. (See Sect. 4.1.) All remaining blocks in A (the guarded area included) become common blocks. In addition to the first input block (just obtained), we now determine the remaining $k - 1$ input blocks, using a sequential scanning of common blocks described in Sect. 4.4. This consumes $O(k \cdot n/s)$ additional comparisons.

At this point, we can use the simpler version of our algorithm, described in Sect. 4, to merge elements of the array A. This requires $\lceil \lg k \rceil \cdot n + O((n/s)^2) + O(s \cdot \lg s)$ element comparisons and $3 \cdot n + O(s \cdot \lg s)$ moves. (However, the height of the free block stack is $2k+2$, instead of k used in Sect. 4.) After this merging, the array A is in sorted order with the exception of a continuous area of buffer elements at the end (including the dead block). Since the buffer elements are the largest elements of A, we can complete the task by sorting the buffer elements in-place using, e.g., Heapsort. This consumes $O(k \cdot s \cdot \lg(k \cdot s)) \leq O(s \cdot \lg s)$ comparisons and moves [6,8,9]. Alternatively, we could also use an algorithm sorting in-place with $O(s \cdot \lg s)$ comparisons but only $O(s)$ moves [2].

5.5   Summary

By fixing the block size to $s = \lceil n^{2/3} / \lg^{1/3} n \rceil$, and by summing up the costs paid for the selection of the buffer elements, sorting and rotating the guarded area, sequential scanning for the initial input blocks, merging the elements using the simpler version of Sect. 4, and the final sorting of the buffer elements, we get that the total number of comparisons and moves is bounded, respectively, by

$$
\begin{aligned}
C_k(n) \leq\ & O(k \cdot s \cdot \lg k) + O(k \cdot s \cdot \lg(k \cdot s)) + O(k \cdot n/s) + \\
& \left[\lceil \lg k \rceil \cdot n + O((n/s)^2) + O(s \cdot \lg s) \right] + O(k \cdot s \cdot \lg(k \cdot s)) \\
\leq\ & \lceil \lg k \rceil \cdot n + O((n \cdot \lg n)^{2/3}) \leq \lceil \lg k \rceil \cdot n + o(n)\,, \\
M_k(n) \leq\ & O(k \cdot s \cdot \lg(k \cdot s)) + O(k \cdot s) + [3 \cdot n + O(s \cdot \lg s)] + O(k \cdot s \cdot \lg(k \cdot s)) \\
\leq\ & 3 \cdot n + O((n \cdot \lg n)^{2/3}) \leq 3 \cdot n + o(n)\,.
\end{aligned}
$$

Theorem 1. *An array A consisting of k sorted subsequences $A_1, \ldots, A_k$ of respective lengths $n_1, \ldots, n_k$, where $\sum_{i=1}^{k} n_i = n$, can be merged in-place performing $\lceil \lg k \rceil \cdot n + o(n)$ element comparisons and $3 \cdot n + o(n)$ element moves.*

6   Conclusion

In this paper we have shown that multiway in-place merging can be accomplished with an almost optimal number of element comparisons and moves. The presented algorithm performs $\lceil \lg k \rceil \cdot n + o(n)$ element comparisons and $3 \cdot n + o(n)$ element moves. That is, the number of moves is independent of k, the number of input sequences to be merged. The corresponding lower bounds are $\lg k \cdot n - k \cdot \lg n - O(1)$ for the number of comparisons and $\lfloor 3/2 \cdot n \rfloor$ for the number of moves carried out by any in-place comparison based merging algorithm. Thus, if k is a power of 2, the best possible number of comparisons is $\lg k \cdot n \pm o(n)$. For arbitrary k (not necessarily a power of 2), the existence of an in-place algorithm matching the lower bound is an open problem.

Note that our algorithm does not merge stably. First, the buffer elements can be mixed up and the original order of equal buffer elements cannot be recovered. Second, several blocks can contain equal elements. Since common blocks can also be mixed up arbitrarily, the original order of such homogeneous blocks is forgotten. Whether there exists an asymptotically optimal stable multiway in-place merging algorithm, with the number of moves independent of the number of input sequences, is left as another open problem.

So far, the problem of stable merging has not been sufficiently resolved even for $k = 2$. The best known 2-way stable in-place merging algorithms were published in [3,1]: Both of them use $n_1 \cdot (t+1) + n_2/2^t + o(n) \le n + o(n)$ comparisons, where $n_1 \le n_2$ and $t = \lfloor \lg(n_2/n_1) \rfloor$, which is asymptotically optimal. However, in [3], the number of moves is $12n_1 + 5n_2 + o(n)$, while in [1] it is $7n_1 + 6n_2 + o(n)$. We are convinced that the number of moves can be significantly improved.

References

1. Chen, J.: Optimizing Stable In-Place Merging. Theoret. Comput. Sci. 302, 191–210 (2003)
2. Franceschini, G., Geffert, V.: An In-Place Sorting with $O(n \cdot \lg n)$ Comparisons and $O(n)$ Moves. J. Assoc. Comput. Mach. 52, 515–537 (2005)
3. Geffert, V., Katajainen, J., Pasanen, T.: Asymptotically Efficient In-Place Merging. Theoret. Comput. Sci. 237, 159–181 (2000)
4. Katajainen, J., Pasanen, T.: In-Place Sorting with Fewer Moves. Inform. Process. Lett. 70, 31–37 (1999)
5. Katajainen, J., Pasanen, T., Teuhola, J.: Practical In-Place Mergesort. Nordic J. Comput. 3, 27–40 (1996)
6. Knuth, D.E.: The Art of Computer Programming, 2nd edn. Sorting and Searching, vol. 3. Addison-Wesley, Reading (1998)
7. Mannila, H., Ukkonen, E.: A Simple Linear-Time Algorithm for In Situ Merging. Inform. Process. Lett. 18, 203–208 (1984)
8. Wegener, I.: Bottom-Up-Heapsort, a New Variant of Heapsort Beating, on an Average, Quicksort (If n Is Not Very Small). Theoret. Comput. Sci. 118, 81–98 (1993)
9. Williams, J.W.J.: Heapsort (Algorithm 232). Comm. Assoc. Comput. Mach. 7, 347–348 (1964)

On Convex Greedy Embedding Conjecture for 3-Connected Planar Graphs

Subhas Kumar Ghosh and Koushik Sinha

Honeywell Technology Solutions,
151/1, Doraisanipalya, Bannerghatta Road,
Bangalore, INDIA-560076
subhas.kumar@honeywell.com, koushik.sinha@honeywell.com

Abstract. In the context of geographic routing, Papadimitriou and Ratajczak conjectured that every 3-connected planar graph has a greedy embedding (possibly planar and convex) in the Euclidean plane. Recently, greedy embedding conjecture has been resolved, though the construction do not result in a drawing that is planar and convex. In this work we consider the planar convex greedy embedding conjecture and make some progress. We show that in planar convex greedy embedding of a graph, weight of the maximum weight spanning tree (T) and weight of the minimum weight spanning tree (MST) satisfies $\mathsf{wt}(T)/\mathsf{wt}(\mathsf{MST}) \le (|V| - 1)^{1-\delta}$, for some $0 < \delta \le 1$. In order to present this result we define a notion of weak greedy embedding. For $\beta \ge 1$ a β–weak greedy embedding of a graph is a planar embedding such that local optima is bounded by β. We also show that any three connected planar graph has a β–weak greedy planar convex embedding in the Euclidean plane with $\beta \in [1, 2\sqrt{2} \cdot d(G)]$, where $d(G)$ is the ratio of maximum and minimum distance between pair of vertices in the embedding of G, and this bound is tight.

1 Introduction

1.1 Greedy Embedding Conjecture

An *embedding* of an undirected graph $G = (V, E)$ in a metric space (X, d) is a mapping $x : V(G) \to X$. In this work we will be concerned with a special case when X is the plane ($\mathbb{R}^2$) endowed with the Euclidean (i.e. l_2) metric. The function x then maps each edge of the graph G to the line-segments joining the images of its end points. We say that embedding is *planar* when no two such line-segments (edges) intersect at any point other than their end points. Let $d(u, v)$ denote the Euclidean distance between two points u and v.

Definition 1. Greedy embedding ([1]): *A greedy embedding x of a graph $G = (V, E)$ into a metric space (X, d) is a function $x : V(G) \to X$ with the following property: for every pair of non-adjacent vertices $s, t \in V(G)$ there exists a vertex $u \in V(G)$ adjacent to s such that $d(x(u), x(t)) < d(x(s), x(t))$.*

M. Kutyłowski, M. Gębala, and W. Charatonik (Eds.): FCT 2009, LNCS 5699, pp. 145–156, 2009.

This notion of greedy embedding was defined by Papadimitriou and Ratajczak in [1]. They have presented graphs which do not admit a greedy embedding in the Euclidean plane, and conjectured following:

Conjecture 1 (Greedy embedding conjecture). Every 3-connected planar graph has a greedy embedding in the Euclidean plane.

A *convex embedding* of a planar graph is a "planar embedding" with a property that all faces, including the external faces are "convex". Additionally, Papadimitriou and Ratajczak stated the following stronger form of the conjecture:

Conjecture 2 (Convex greedy embedding conjecture). Every 3-connected planar graph has a greedy convex embedding in the Euclidean plane.

Note that every 3-connected planar graph has a convex embedding in the Euclidean plane (using Tutte's rubber band algorithm [2,3]). In [1] it was shown that $K_{r,5r+1}$ admits no greedy embedding for $r > 0$. Which imply that both hypotheses of the conjecture are necessary: there exist graphs that are planar but not 3-connected ($K_{2,11}$), or 3-connected but not planar ($K_{3,16}$), that does not admits any greedy embedding. Also, they show that high connectivity alone does not guarantee a greedy embedding. Papadimitriou and Ratajczak in [1] also provided examples of graphs which have a greedy embedding (e.g., Hamiltonian graphs). Note that if $H \subseteq G$ is a spanning subgraph of G, i.e. $V(H) = V(G)$ then every greedy embedding of H is also a greedy embedding of G. Hence, the conjecture extends to any graph having a 3-connected planar spanning subgraph.

1.2 Known Results

Recently, greedy embedding conjecture (conjecture-1) has been proved in [4]. In [4] authors construct a greedy embedding into the Euclidean plane for all circuit graphs – which is a generalization of 3-connected planar graphs. Similar result was independently discovered by Angelini, Frati and Grilli [5].

Theorem 1 ([4]). *Any 3-connected graph G without having a $K_{3,3}$ minor admits a greedy embedding into the Euclidean plane.*

Convex greedy embedding conjecture (conjecture-2) has been proved for the case of all planar triangulations [6] (existentially, using probabilistic methods). Note that the Delaunay triangulation of any set of points in the plane is known to be greedy [7], and a variant of greedy algorithm (greedy-compass algorithm) of [8] works for all planar triangulations.

Surely convex greedy embedding conjecture implies conjecture-1, however not otherwise. The greedy embedding algorithm presented in [4,5] does not necessarily produce a convex greedy embedding, and in fact the embedding may not even be a planar one [9]. In this work we consider the convex greedy embedding conjecture (conjecture-2).

An alternative way to view the greedy embedding is to consider following path finding algorithm on a graph $G = (V, E)$ given embedding x. The algorithm in every step recursively selects a vertex that is closer to destination than current vertex. To simplify notation we write $d(s, t)$ in place of $d(x(s), x(t))$, when embedding x is given. Clearly, if x is a greedy embedding of G then for any choice of $s, t \in V$, we have a *distance decreasing path* $s = v_0, v_1, \ldots, v_m = t$, such that for $i = 1, \ldots, m$, $d(x(v_i), x(v_m)) < d(x(v_{i-1}), x(v_m))$. Thus given G and x, a greedy path finding algorithm succeeds for every pair of vertices in G iff x is a greedy embedding of G.

This simple greedy path finding strategy has many useful applications in practice. Ad hoc networks and sensor nets has no universally known system of addresses like IP addresses, and due to resource limitations it is prohibitive to store and maintain large forwarding tables at each node in such networks. To overcome these limitations, *geometric routing* uses geographic coordinates of the nodes as addresses for routing purposes [10]. Simplest of such strategy can be greedy forwarding strategy as described above. However, this simple strategy sometimes fails to deliver a packet because of the phenomenon of "voids" (nodes with no neighbor closer to the destination). In other words the embedding of network graph, provided by the assigned coordinates is not a greedy embedding in such cases. To address these concerns, Rao et al. [11] proposed a scheme to assign coordinates using a distributed variant of Tutte embedding [2]. On the basis of extensive experimentation they showed that this approach makes greedy routing much more reliable.

1.3   Our Contribution

In this work we show that given a 3-connected planar graph $G = (V, E)$, an embedding $x : V \to \mathbb{R}^2$ of G is a planar convex greedy embedding if and only if, in the embedding x, weight of the maximum weight spanning tree ($\mathsf{wt}(T)$) and weight of the minimum weight spanning tree ($\mathsf{wt}(\mathsf{MST})$) satisfies $\mathsf{wt}(T)/\mathsf{wt}(\mathsf{MST}) \leq (|V| - 1)^{1-\delta}$, for some $0 < \delta \leq 1$.

In order to obtain this result we consider a weaker notion of greedy embedding. *Weak[1] greedy embedding* allows path finding algorithm to proceed as long as local optima is bounded by a factor. Formally,

Definition 2 (Weak greedy embedding). *Let $\beta \geq 1$. A β–weak greedy embedding x of a graph $G = (V, E)$ is a planar embedding of G with the following property: for every pair of non-adjacent vertices $s, t \in V(G)$ there exists a vertex $u \in V(G)$ adjacent to s such that $d(x(u), x(t)) < \beta \cdot d(x(s), x(t))$.*

Surely if G admits a 1-weak greedy embedding then it is greedily embeddable. We show that every 3-connected planar graph has a β-weak greedy convex embedding in $\mathbb{R}^2$ with $\beta \in [1, 2\sqrt{2} \cdot d(G)]$, where $d(G)$ is the ratio of maximum and minimum distance between pair of vertices in the embedding of G.

Rest of the paper is organized as follows. In section-2 we define β-weak greedy convex embedding and provide a brief outline of the results. Subsequently, in section-3 we derive various results on the β-weak greedy convex embedding and

---

[1] Not to be confused with the weaker version of the conjecture. Here weakness is w.r.t. greedy criteria, and not convexity of embedding.

show that every 3-connected planar graph has a β-weak greedy convex embedding in $\mathbb{R}^2$ with $\beta \in [1, 2\sqrt{2} \cdot d(G)]$. Finally, in section-4 we derive the new condition on the weight of the minimum weight spanning tree and maximum weight spanning tree that must be satisfied in the greedy convex embedding for every 3-connected planar graphs. Section-5 contains some concluding remarks. We will use standard graph theoretic terminology from [12].

2   Weak Greedy Embedding of 3-Connected Planar Graphs

In this section we define β-weak greedy convex embedding, and provide an outline of the proof. In rest of the section $x : V(G) \rightarrow \mathbb{R}^2$ be a planar convex embedding of $G = (V, E)$ which produces a one-to-one mapping from V to $\mathbb{R}^2$. We shall specifically consider Tutte embedding ([2,3]). Since x is fixed, given a graph G, we will not differentiate between $v \in V(G)$ and its planar convex embedding under x viz. $x(v)$.

First let us consider following recursive procedure for β–weak greedy path finding given in Algorithm-1. If β is chosen as the minimum value such that $\forall t \in V - \{s\}$ at least one branch of this recursive procedure returns success then we will call that value of $\beta = \beta_s$ optimal for vertex s. Given (s, β_s) for a vertex $t \in V - \{s\}$ there can be more than one β_s–weak greedy path from s to t. Let $H(s, \beta_s) \subseteq G$ be a subgraph of G induced by all vertices and edges of β_s–weak greedy st–paths for all possible terminal vertex $t \in V - \{s\}$. Let $T(s, \beta_s)$ be any spanning tree of $H(s, \beta_s)$. Surely, $T(s, \beta_s)$ has unique β_s–weak greedy st–paths for all possible terminal vertex $t \in V - \{s\}$ from s. We will call $T_s = T(s, \beta_s)$ optimal weak greedy tree w.r.t vertex s. Define $\beta_{\max} = \max_{s \in V}\{\beta_s\}$. We note that procedure WEAK $-$ GREEDY $(s, t, \beta_{\max})$ with parameter $\beta_{\max}$ succeeds to find at least one $\beta_{\max}$–weak greedy st–paths for all possible vertex pairs $s, t \in V$. In following our objective will be to obtain a bound on $\beta_{\max}$ for any 3-connected planar graph G under embedding x. To obtain this bound we will use the properties of weak greedy trees.

Algorithm WEAK $-$ GREEDY (s, t, β)
if $s = t$ **then**
  | return success.
else
  | $B \stackrel{\triangle}{=} \{v : (s, v) \in E \text{ and } d(v, t) < \beta \cdot d(s, t)\}$.
  | **if** $B = \emptyset$ **then**
  | | return failure.
  | **else**
  | | $\forall v \in B$: WEAK $-$ GREEDY (v, t, β).
  | **end**
end

Algorithm 1. β–weak greedy path finding

What follows is a brief description of how we obtain the stated results. In the planar convex embedding of G, let weight of an edge $e = uv$ be its length i.e. $\mathsf{wt}(e) = d(u,v)$. Define $\mathsf{wt}(T(s,\beta_s)) = \sum_{e \in E(T(s,\beta_s))} \mathsf{wt}(e)$. We obtain a lower and upper bound on the weight of $T(s,\beta_s)$. On the other hand we also obtain a upper bound on the weight of any spanning tree T of G in its embedding $\mathsf{wt}(T)$, and a lower bound on the weight of any minimum spanning tree MST of G, $\mathsf{wt}(\mathsf{MST})$. Surely $\mathsf{wt}(\mathsf{MST}) \leq \mathsf{wt}(T_s) \leq \mathsf{wt}(T)$, and from this we derive an upper and a lower bound on $\beta_{\max}$. Let $d_{\max}(G) = \max_{u,v \in V} d(u,v)$ be the diameter of G, and let minimum edge length in embedding of G be $d_{\min}(G)$. In following (in Section-3.1) we derive that, $\mathsf{wt}(T) \leq \sqrt{2} \cdot (|V| - 1) \cdot d_{\max}(G)$. Subsequently (in Section-3.2), we show that, $d_{\max}(G) \leq \mathsf{wt}(\mathsf{MST}) \leq 2.5 \cdot d_{\max}^2(G)$. Finally (in Section-3.3), we derive upper and lower bounds on the the weight of $T(s,\beta_s)$ as:

$$d_{\min}(G) \cdot (\beta_{\max} - 1) \cdot (|V| - 1) \leq \mathsf{wt}(T_s) \leq 2 \cdot d_{\max}(G) \cdot \left(\frac{\beta_{max}^{|V|-1} - 1}{\beta_{max} - 1} \right)$$

Using the fact that $\mathsf{wt}(\mathsf{MST}) \leq \mathsf{wt}(T_s) \leq \mathsf{wt}(T)$, we than show using the bounds described above - that any three connected planar graph has a β-weak greedy convex embedding in $\mathbb{R}^2$ with $\beta \in [1, 2\sqrt{2} \cdot d(G)]$, where $d(G) = d_{\max}(G)/d_{\min}(G)$. Our main result states that given a 3-connected planar graph $G = (V, E)$, an embedding $x : V \to \mathbb{R}^2$ of G is a planar convex greedy embedding if and only if, in the embedding x, weight of the maximum weight spanning tree $(\mathsf{wt}(T))$ and weight of the minimum weight spanning tree $(\mathsf{wt}(\mathsf{MST}))$ satisfies $\mathsf{wt}(T)/\mathsf{wt}(\mathsf{MST}) \leq (|V| - 1)^{1-\delta}$, for some $0 < \delta \leq 1$. To establish one side of this implication we use the bounds on the weight of $T(s,\beta_s)$ and the upper bound on the weight of the MST.

3   Bounding the Weight of Trees

In following we first describe upper bound on the weight of any spanning tree T of G in its planar convex embedding. In order to obtain this bound we use some ideas from [13].

3.1   Upper Bound on the Weight of Spanning Tree

Given a graph $G = (V, E)$ and its planar convex embedding, let $d_{\max}(G) = \max_{u,v \in V} d(u,v)$ be the diameter of G and let T be any spanning tree of G. For $i = 1, \ldots, |V| - 1$ let e_i be ith edge of T (for a fixed indexing of edges). Let D_i be the open disk with center c_i such that c_i is the mid point of $e_i = uv$, and D_i having diameter $d(u,v)$. We will call D_i a diametral circle of e_i. Let $\bar{D}_i$ be the smallest disk (closed) that contains D_i. Define $D = \cup_{e_i \in E(T)} \bar{D}_i$. Following can be found in [14]:

Lemma 1 (Lemma-3 from [14]). *D is contained into a closed disk D' having its center coinciding with D and having diameter at most $\sqrt{2} \cdot d_{\max}(G)$.*

Using Lemma-1 we can now obtain a bound on $\mathsf{wt}(T)$. Let $\mathsf{Circ}(D_i)$ denote the circumference of circle D_i, i.e. $\mathsf{Circ}(D_i) = \pi \cdot \mathsf{wt}(e_i)$.

Lemma 2. $\mathsf{wt}(T) \le \sqrt{2} \cdot (|V| - 1) \cdot d_{\max}(G)$

Proof. Clearly, $\mathsf{wt}(T) = \sum_{e_i \in E(T)} \mathsf{wt}(e_i) = 1/\pi \cdot \sum_{e_i \in E(T)} \mathsf{Circ}(D_i)$. Let D' be a closed disk in which $D = \cup_{e_i \in E(T)} \bar{D}_i$ is contained, where $\bar{D}_i$ is the smallest disk (closed) that contains D_i. Using Lemma-1, and noting spanning tree T has $(|V| - 1)$ edges, $\mathsf{wt}(T) \le 1/\pi \cdot (|V| - 1) \cdot \mathsf{Circ}(D') \le 1/\pi \cdot (|V| - 1) \cdot \left(\pi\sqrt{2} \cdot d_{\max}(G)\right) \le \sqrt{2} \cdot (|V| - 1) \cdot d_{\max}(G)$. □

3.2   Bound on the Weight of Minimum Weight Spanning Tree

In the planar convex embedding of G let MST be a minimum weight spanning tree of G and let $\mathsf{wt}(\mathsf{MST})$ be its weight. In this section we obtain an upper and a lower bound on $\mathsf{wt}(\mathsf{MST})$. Let $V \subset \mathbb{R}^2$ be the point set given (as images of vertex set) by the embedding. Let $\mathcal{E}$ be the set of all line-segments uv corresponding to the all distinct pair of end-points $u, v \in V$. Also, let EMST be a spanning tree of V whose edges are subset of $\mathcal{E}$ such that weight $\mathsf{wt}(\mathsf{EMST})$ is minimum (EMST is a Euclidean minimum spanning tree of the point set V). Surely, $\mathsf{wt}(\mathsf{EMST}) \le \mathsf{wt}(\mathsf{MST})$: convex embedding produces a straight-line embedding of G, and hence the line segments corresponding to the edges of G in embedding are also subset of $\mathcal{E}$. Let u and v be vertices having distance $d_{\max}(G)$. Any EMST would connect u and v. Hence we have:

Lemma 3. $\mathsf{wt}(\mathsf{MST}) \ge \mathsf{wt}(\mathsf{EMST}) \ge d_{\max}(G)$.

We will also require upper bound on the weight of minimum spanning tree for which we have:

Lemma 4. *In planar convex embedding of G,* $\mathsf{wt}(\mathsf{MST}) \le 5/2 \cdot d_{\max}^2(G)$.

Proof. Recall, using Lemma-1 we have that D is contained into a closed disk D' having its center coinciding with D and having diameter at most $\sqrt{2} \cdot d_{\max}(G)$. Let $\mathsf{Area}(D)$ denote the area of circle D, i.e. $\mathsf{Area}(D) = \pi \cdot (d/2)^2$, where D is a circle having diameter d. Now, $\mathsf{wt}(\mathsf{MST}) = \sum_{e_i \in E(\mathsf{MST})} \mathsf{wt}(e_i) = 1/\pi \cdot \sum_{e_i \in E(\mathsf{MST})} \mathsf{Circ}(D_i)$. Now by Lemma-1, all the points that we would like to count in $\sum_{e_i \in E(\mathsf{MST})} \mathsf{Circ}(D_i)$ are contained in $\mathsf{Area}(D')$. Except that some of the points that appear on the circumference of more than one circles, must be counted multiple times. In order to bound that we shall use following result from [14].

Lemma 5 (Lemma-2 from [14]). *For any point $p \in \mathbb{R}^2$, p is contained in at most five diametral circles drawn on the edges of the MST of a point set $V \subset \mathbb{R}^2$.*

Using Lemma-1, and using the Lemma-5, we have:

$$\mathsf{wt}(\mathsf{MST}) \le \frac{1}{\pi} \cdot 5 \cdot \mathsf{Area}(D') \le \frac{1}{\pi} \cdot 5 \cdot \pi \left(\frac{\sqrt{2} \cdot d_{\max}(G)}{2}\right)^2 = \frac{5}{2} \cdot d_{\max}^2(G). \quad \square$$

3.3   Bound on the Weight of Weak Greedy Trees

Given a graph $G = (V, E)$ and its planar convex embedding, let $T_s = T(s, \beta_s)$ be an optimal weak greedy tree w.r.t a vertex $s \in V$. Let t be any leaf vertex of T_s, and consider the β_s–weak greedy st–path.

Definition 3 (Increasing and decreasing sequence). *For a β_s–weak greedy st–path $P_{st} = \{s = u_0, u_1, \ldots, u_k = t\}$, an ordered vertex sequence $\{u_{i_0}, \ldots, u_{i_r}\}$ of P_{st} is an increasing sequence of length r if $d(u_{i_0}, t) \leq \ldots \leq d(u_{i_r}, t)$ holds. Similarly, an ordered sequence of vertices $\{u_{i_0}, \ldots, u_{i_r}\}$ of P_{st} is a decreasing sequence of length r if $d(u_{i_0}, t) \geq \ldots \geq d(u_{i_r}, t)$ holds. Usually, we will refer any maximal (by property of monotonically non-decreasing or non-increasing) sequence of vertices as increasing or decreasing sequence.*

It is straightforward to observe that if an st–path is β_s–weak greedy for $\beta_s > 1$, then it has a monotonically non-decreasing sequence of vertices. However, every st–path must have a trailing monotonically decreasing sequence that reaches t. We will call an increasing sequence $\{u_{i_0}, \ldots, u_{i_r}\}$ of P_{st} a β-increasing sequence of length r if it is maximal and for $j = 1, \ldots, r, d(u_{i_j}, t) \leq \beta d(u_{i_{j-1}}, t)$ holds (with equality for at least one j). We will denote it as $\mathsf{inc}(r, d, \beta)$, where d indicates $d(u_{i_0}, t)$. Proof of following lemmas (Lemma-6, Lemma-7, and Lemma-8) has been omitted due to space limitation, and detailed proof can be found in [15].

Lemma 6. *Let $\mathsf{inc}(k, d, \beta) = \{u_{i_0}, \ldots, u_{i_k}\}$ be a β-increasing sequence of length k from a β_s–weak greedy st–path such that $d(u_{i_0}, t) = d$. Then $d(\beta^k - 1) \leq \mathsf{wt}(\mathsf{inc}(k, d, \beta)) \leq d(\beta^k - 1)(\beta + 1/\beta - 1)$. Where $\mathsf{wt}(\mathsf{inc}(k, d, \beta))$ is the sum of the weight of the edges of $\mathsf{inc}(k, d, \beta)$.*

Like $\mathsf{inc}(r, d, \beta)$, for $\gamma > 1$ by $\mathsf{dec}(r, d, \gamma)$ we will denote a decreasing sequence $\{u_{i_0}, \ldots, u_{i_r}\}$ of P_{st} as a γ-decreasing sequence of length r if it is maximal and for $j = 1, \ldots, r, d(u_{i_{j-1}}, t) \leq \gamma d(u_{i_j}, t)$ holds (with equality for at least one j), where d indicates $d(u_{i_0}, t) = d$.

Lemma 7. *Let $\mathsf{dec}(k, d, \gamma) = \{u_{i_0}, \ldots, u_{i_k}\}$ be a γ-decreasing sequence of length k such that $d(u_{i_0}, t) = d$. Then $d(1 - 1/\gamma) \leq \mathsf{wt}(\mathsf{dec}(k, d, \gamma)) \leq dk(1 + 1/\gamma)$.*

Now, for a path P_{st} such that t is a leaf vertex of the tree T_s, P_{st} can be written as $\mathsf{inc}(r_0, d_0, \beta) \circ \mathsf{dec}(r_1, d_1, \gamma) \circ \ldots \circ \mathsf{inc}(r_{l-1}, d_{l-1}, \beta) \circ \mathsf{dec}(r_l, d_l, \gamma)$ (where $\circ$ denotes sequential composition), such that $d_0 = d(s, t)$, $r_l \neq 0$, and for each $i = 1, \ldots, l$ we have $d_i \leq \beta^{r_{i-1}} d_{i-1}$ when i is odd and $d_i \geq d_{i-1}/\gamma^{r_{i-1}}$ when i is even. In other words, P_{st} is a combination of increasing and decreasing sequences with at least one increasing sequence and a trailing decreasing sequence. Also every sequence starts at a distance from t, where the immediate previous sequence ends.

Lemma 8. *Let $P(k, \beta)$ be a k length β–weak greedy st–path such that t is a leaf vertex of the tree T_s. Then*

$$d_{\min}(G) \cdot k \cdot (\beta - 1) \leq \mathsf{wt}(P(k, \beta)) \leq 2 \cdot d_{\max}(G) \cdot \left(\frac{\beta^k - 1}{\beta - 1} \right)$$

Finally we bound the weight of β-weak greedy spanning tree T_s.

Lemma 9

$$d_{\min}(G) \cdot (\beta_{\max} - 1) \cdot (|V| - 1) \leq \mathsf{wt}(T_s) \leq 2 \cdot d_{\max}(G) \cdot \left(\frac{\beta_{max}^{|V|-1} - 1}{\beta_{max} - 1} \right)$$

Proof. Assume that T_s has l many leaf nodes. Then weight of the tree is $\mathsf{wt}(T_s) = \sum_{i=1}^{l} \mathsf{wt}(P(k_i, \beta))$. Where $\sum_{i=1}^{l} k_i = |V| - 1$. In order to obtain the upper bound we observe that $\mathsf{wt}(P(k_i, \beta))$ is maximized with any one of $k_i = |V| - 1$. Hence using upper bound on $\mathsf{wt}(P(k, \beta))$ from Lemma-8 we have: $\mathsf{wt}(T_s) \leq 2 \cdot d_{\max}(G) \cdot (\beta_{max}^{|V|-1} - 1)/(\beta_{max} - 1)$. On the other hand, for the lower bound we have $l = |V| - 1$ and $1 \leq i \leq |V| - 1 : k_i = 1$. Using lower bound on $\mathsf{wt}(P(k, \beta))$ from Lemma-8 we have: $\mathsf{wt}(T_s) \geq d_{\min}(G) \cdot (\beta_{\max} - 1) \cdot (|V| - 1)$ □

3.4   Bound on $\beta_{\max}$

As stated in the beginning of this section, we now compare the bound on the weight of any spanning tree T of G with that of T_s as derived in Lemma-2, Lemma-3 and Lemma-9 to obtain an upper and lower bound on $\beta_{\max}$.

Theorem 2. *Let $G = (V, E)$ be any three connected planar graph. Then G has a β-weak greedy convex embedding in $\mathbb{R}^2$ with $\beta \in [1, 2\sqrt{2} \cdot d(G)]$. Also, this bound is achieved by Tutte embedding.*

Proof. Let T_s be any β-weak greedy spanning tree of G with respect to vertex $s \in V$. Let T be any spanning tree of G, and let MST be any minimum weight spanning tree of G. Then using $\mathsf{wt}(T_s) \geq \mathsf{wt}(\mathsf{MST})$, Lemma-3, and upper bound on the $\mathsf{wt}(T_s)$ from Lemma-9 we obtain:

$$2 \cdot d_{\max}(G) \cdot \left(\frac{\beta_{max}^{|V|-1} - 1}{\beta_{max} - 1} \right) \geq \mathsf{wt}(T_s) \geq \mathsf{wt}(\mathsf{MST}) \geq \mathsf{wt}(\mathsf{EMST}) \geq d_{\max}(G)$$

Which implies:

$$\left(\frac{\beta_{max}^{|V|-1} - 1}{\beta_{max} - 1} \right) \geq \frac{1}{2} \tag{1}$$

And this holds for any $\beta_{max} > 1$ when $|V| \geq 3$. On the other hand using $\mathsf{wt}(T_s) \leq \mathsf{wt}(T)$, Lemma-2, and lower bound on the $\mathsf{wt}(T_s)$ from Lemma-9:

$$d_{\min}(G) \cdot (\beta_{\max} - 1) \cdot (|V| - 1) \leq \mathsf{wt}(T_s) \leq \mathsf{wt}(T) \leq \sqrt{2} \cdot (|V| - 1) \cdot d_{\max}(G)$$

Now using $d(G) = d_{\max}(G)/d_{\min}(G)$ we have:

$$\beta_{max} \leq \sqrt{2} \cdot \frac{d_{\max}(G)}{d_{\min}(G)} + 1 \leq \sqrt{2} \cdot d(G) + 1 \leq 2\sqrt{2} \cdot d(G) \tag{2}$$

Finally, to show that this bound is tight consider Tutte embedding of a cube (see figure-1(a)) with all edges assigned with same weights. It can be seen that in this embedding $\beta \leq 1$. On the other hand, when we reduce the weight on the edges BF and DH (see figure-1(b)) we obtain an embedding in which there is no greedy path between pair B and D, while there is a β-weak greedy path with β approaching $d(G)/2$.

$\square$

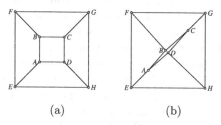

(a)   (b)

Fig. 1. Illustration of Tutte embedding of a cube: (a) Equal edge weights, (b) Unequal edge weights

If we consider Tutte embedding of a 3–connected planar graph G with arbitrary weights on the edges, then it is not difficult to see that above bound on β depends entirely on the choice of the edge weights in the Tutte embedding.

4   Characterizing Convex Greedy Embedding

Theorem 3. *For sufficiently large $|V|$ for a 3-connected planar graph $G = (V, E)$ if embedding $x : V \to \mathbb{R}^2$ of G is such that the maximum weight spanning tree (T) and minimum weight spanning tree (MST) satisfies,* $\mathsf{wt}(T)/\mathsf{wt}(\mathsf{MST}) \leq (|V| - 1)^{1-\delta}$, *for some $0 < \delta \leq 1$, then embedding x is a convex greedy embedding of G.*

Proof. Observe that we have following relations, $\mathsf{wt}(\mathsf{MST}) \leq \mathsf{wt}(T_s) \leq \mathsf{wt}(T)$. Since $\mathsf{wt}(\mathsf{MST}) > 0$, using lower bound on $\mathsf{wt}(T_s)$ from Lemma-9 and using upper bound on $\mathsf{wt}(\mathsf{MST})$ from Lemma-4 we obtain:

$$\frac{2 \cdot d_{\min}(G) \cdot (\beta_{\max} - 1) \cdot (|V| - 1)}{5 \cdot d_{\max}^2(G)} \leq \frac{\mathsf{wt}(T)}{\mathsf{wt}(\mathsf{MST})}$$

And hence, $\beta_{\max} \leq \left(\dfrac{5 \cdot d_{\max}(G) \cdot d(G)}{2 \cdot (|V| - 1)} \right) \cdot \left(\dfrac{\mathsf{wt}(T)}{\mathsf{wt}(\mathsf{MST})} \right) + 1$

Now if weight of the maximum and minimum spanning tree in the planar convex embedding of G is such that $\mathsf{wt}(T)/\mathsf{wt}(\mathsf{MST}) \leq (|V| - 1)^{1-\delta}$ for some $0 < \delta \leq 1$, then for sufficiently large $|V|$, $\beta_{\max} \to 1$ from above (note that $\beta_{\max} > 1$ by Equation-1).

$\square$

In following we show the more interesting direction:

Theorem 4. *Given a 3-connected planar graph* $G = (V, E)$, *if embedding* $x :$ $V \to \mathbb{R}^2$ *of* G *is a convex greedy embedding then in embedding* x *the maximum weight spanning tree* (T) *and minimum weight spanning tree* (MST) *satisfies:* $\mathsf{wt}(T)/\mathsf{wt}(MST) \leq (|V| - 1)^{1-\delta}$, *for some* $0 < \delta \leq 1$.

Proof. For a 3-connected planar graph $G = (V, E)$, let an embedding $x : V \to \mathbb{R}^2$ of G be a convex greedy embedding. Let us also assume that $\mathsf{wt}(T)/\mathsf{wt}(MST) \geq (|V| - 1)$. W.l.o.g. let $\mathsf{wt}(MST) = 1$. Since T is a spanning tree it has $(|V| - 1)$ edges, and hence has at least one edge $e \in T$ of weight $\mathsf{wt}(e) \geq 1$. Given that x is a convex planar embedding of a 3-connected planar graph G, we have that each edge belongs to exactly two faces of the graph (in fact a graph is 3-connected and planar if and only if each edge is in exactly two non-separating induced cycles [16]). So we consider two cases: (Case - 1) e is on two internal faces F and F', and (Case - 2) e is on the boundary face. We need few definitions [17]. For a graph G, a *thread* is a path P of G such that any degree 2 vertex x of G is not an end vertex of P. A sequence $S = (G_0, \{x_i P_i y_i : i = 1, \ldots, k\})$ is an *ear-decomposition* of G if:

1. G_0 is a subdivision of K_4,
2. $x_i P_i y_i$ is a path with end-vertices x_i and y_i such that $G_i = G_{i-1} \cup P_i$ is a subgraph of G, and $G_{i-1} \cap P_i = \{x_i, y_i\}$, but x_i, y_i do not belong to a common thread of G_{i-1} for $i = 1, \ldots, k$, and
3. $G_k = G$.

We will need following result from [17]:

Lemma 10 ([17]). *Let* G *be a 3–connected graph,* $e = uv \in E(G)$. *Let* C_1 *and* C_2 *be non-separating cycles of* G *such that* $C_1 \cap C_2 = uev$. *Then there exists an ear-decomposition of* G *such that* $C_1 \cup C_2 \subset G_0$.

Case - 1: In this case $e = uv$ is on two internal faces F_1 and F_2. Consider a vertex u' from face F_1 and another vertex v' from face F_2. First consider K_4, which has four faces, and exactly one planar convex embedding. However, vertices u, v, u', v' must be spanned by the MST using exactly 3 edges. If e is chosen in the MST then other edges are of length 0, as $\mathsf{wt}(e) \geq 1$ and $\mathsf{wt}(MST) = 1$. If e is not selected in MST - then it can be easily seen that either $\mathsf{wt}(MST) > 1$, or the drawing is not planar - a contradiction. In specific this can be seen as follows (see Figure-2): consider that $uu', u'v$ and $u'v'$ is selected in MST - then we have $uu' + u'v \geq uv$ (where, uv is an edge in the external face uvu') and this implies either $uu' + u'v + u'v' > uv \geq 1$, or $u'v' = 0$. Now, let G be a 3-connected planar graph that is distinct from K_4. Then there exists an ear-decomposition of G such that $e = uv$ and faces F_1 and F_2 are such that $F_1 \cup F_2 \subset G_0$, where G_0 is a subdivision of K_4, by Lemma-10. We can contract edges of $F_1 \cup F_2$ while keeping edge e to obtain a K_4. In this process we never increase the weight of the MST, and hence obtain the contradiction as above.

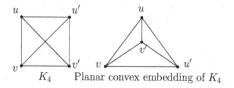

K_4 Planar convex embedding of K_4

Fig. 2. Illustration to the proof of Case - 1 for K_4

Case - 2: In this case $e = uv$ is on the boundary face. Since minimal external face must be a triangle there exists another vertex u' on the external face. Consider another internal vertex v'. Again vertices u, v, u', v' must be spanned by the MST using at least 3 edges. If e is chosen in the MST then other edges are of length 0, as $\mathsf{wt}(e) \geq 1$ and $\mathsf{wt}(\mathsf{MST}) = 1$. On the other hand if e is not selected in MST - then $\mathsf{wt}(\mathsf{MST}) > 1$ if embedding is convex, a contradiction.   □

5   Concluding Remarks

With Theorem-3 and Theorem-4, and the example presented above (Figure-1) we can ask following question: For every 3–connected planar graph G, is it possible to choose edge weights in the Tutte embedding such that we obtain a greedy convex embedding? We believe that answer to this question will help in making progress towards resolving original convex greedy embedding conjecture of Papadimitriou and Ratajczak [1].

We would like to clarify that though the β–weak greedy path finding algorithm presented above is stateless, it is not a practical routing algorithm - as number of messages will be large even for constant values of β, when $\beta > 1$, and the routing procedure also forms cycles. The purpose of defining β–weak greedy path finding procedure was to derive the main results of this paper.

References

1. Papadimitriou, C.H., Ratajczak, D.: On a conjecture related to geometric routing. Theor. Comput. Sci. 344(1), 3–14 (2005)
2. Tutte, W.T.: Convex Representations of Graphs. Proc. London Math. Soc. s3-10(1), 304–320 (1960)
3. Thomassen, C.: Tutte's spring theorem. J. Graph Theory 45(4), 275–280 (2004)
4. Leighton, T., Moitra, A.: Some results on greedy embeddings in metric spaces. In: FOCS 2008: Proceedings of the 49th Annual IEEE Symposium on Foundations of Computer Science (FOCS 2008), Washington, DC, USA. IEEE Computer Society Press, Los Alamitos (2008)
5. Angelini, P., Frati, F., Grilli, L.: An algorithm to construct greedy drawings of triangulations. In: Tollis, I.G., Patrignani, M. (eds.) GD 2008. LNCS, vol. 5417. Springer, Heidelberg (2009)
6. Dhandapani, R.: Greedy drawings of triangulations. In: SODA 2008: Proceedings of the nineteenth annual ACM-SIAM symposium on Discrete algorithms, Philadelphia, PA, USA, pp. 102–111. Society for Industrial and Applied Mathematics (2008)

7. Bose, P., Morin, P.: Online routing in triangulations. In: Aggarwal, A.K., Pandu Rangan, C. (eds.) ISAAC 1999. LNCS, vol. 1741, pp. 113–122. Springer, Heidelberg (1999)
8. Bose, P., Morin, P., Brodnik, A., Carlsson, S., Demaine, E.D., Fleischer, R., Munro, J.I., López-Ortiz, A.: Online routing in convex subdivisions. In: Lee, D.T., Teng, S.-H. (eds.) ISAAC 2000. LNCS, vol. 1969, pp. 47–59. Springer, Heidelberg (2000)
9. Frati, F.: Private communication (2009)
10. Kuhn, F., Wattenhofer, R., Zhang, Y., Zollinger, A.: Geometric ad-hoc routing: of theory and practice. In: PODC 2003: Proceedings of the twenty-second annual symposium on Principles of distributed computing, pp. 63–72. ACM, New York (2003)
11. Rao, A., Papadimitriou, C., Shenker, S., Stoica, I.: Geographic routing without location information. In: MobiCom 2003: Proceedings of the 9th annual international conference on Mobile computing and networking, pp. 96–108. ACM Press, New York (2003)
12. Bondy, J.A., Murty, U.S.R.: Graph Theory. Graduate Texts in Mathematics, vol. 244. Springer, Heidelberg (2008)
13. Monma, C., Suri, S.: Transitions in geometric minimum spanning trees. Discrete Comput. Geom. 8(3), 265–293 (1992)
14. Clementi, A.E.F., Crescenzi, P., Penna, P., Rossi, G., Vocca, P.: On the complexity of computing minimum energy consumption broadcast subgraphs. In: Ferreira, A., Reichel, H. (eds.) STACS 2001. LNCS, vol. 2010, pp. 121–131. Springer, Heidelberg (2001)
15. Ghosh, S.K., Sinha, K.: Some results on convex greedy embedding conjecture for 3-connected planar graphs. CoRR abs/0905.3812v1 (2009)
16. Kelmans, A.: The concept of a vertex in a matroid, the non-separating cycles, and a new criterion for graph planarity. In: Algebraic Methods in Graph Theory, Colloq. Math. Soc. Janos Bolyai, Szeged, Hungary, vol. 1, pp. 345–388. North-Holland, Amsterdam (1978)
17. Kelmans, A.: On convex embeddings of planar 3-connected graphs. J. Graph Theory 33(2), 120–124 (2000)

On Random Betweenness Constraints

Andreas Goerdt

Technische Universität Chemnitz, Fakultät für Informatik
Straße der Nationen 62, 09107 Chemnitz, Germany
goerdt@informatik.tu-chemnitz.de
http://www.tu-chemnitz.de/informatik/TI/

Abstract. Ordering constraints are analogous to instances of the satisfiability problem in conjunctive normalform, but instead of a boolean assignment we consider a linear ordering of the variables in question. A clause becomes true given a linear ordering iff the relative ordering of its variables obeys the constraint considered.

The naturally arising satisfiability problems are **NP**-complete for many types of constraints. We look at random ordering constraints. Previous work of the author shows that there is a sharp unsatisfiability threshold for certain types of constraints. The value of the threshold however is essentially undetermined. We pursue the problem to approximate the precise value of the threshold. We show that random instances of the betweenness constraint (definition see Subsection 1.1) are satisfiable with high probability iff the number of randomly picked clauses is $< 0.9 \cdot n$, where n is the number of variables considered. This improves the previous bound which is $< 0.82 \cdot n$ random clauses.

Keywords: Algorithms, logic, random structures, probabilistic analysis.

1 Introduction

1.1 Result

Let V always be a set of n variables. A 3-clause over V is an *ordered* 3-tuple (x, y, z) consisting of three different variables. Thus we have $n(n-1)(n-2) = (n)_3$ clauses altogether. A formula, also called ordering constraint is a set of clauses. Given a linear ordering of all n variables a clause evaluates to true if its variables satisfy a given constraint with respect to the ordering. A formula becomes true when all its clauses are true. This is the satisfiability problem the present paper deals with.

The clause (x, y, z) interpreted as a *betweenness* constraint is true iff y is between x and z, that is we have $x < y < z$ or $z < y < x$ with respect to the ordering considered. The corresponding satisfiability problem is **NP**-complete [20].

We consider random ordering constraints interpreted as betweenness constraints. The random instance $F(V, m)$ or the corresponding probability space is obtained by picking a sequence (or set) of exactly m clauses without repetition

M. Kutyłowski, M. Gębala, and W. Charatonik (Eds.): FCT 2009, LNCS 5699, pp. 157–168, 2009.
© Springer-Verlag Berlin Heidelberg 2009

with uniform probability. Thus $F(V, m)$ is analogous to the well known random graph $G(n, m)$. More closely related to $F(V, m)$ are random 3-SAT formulas, see for example [4] [3] [10] [19]. The present paper is a successor to [14].

As common in the theory of random structures this paper deals with properties holding with high probability, that is $1 - o(1)$ when n becomes large and $m = m(n)$ is a given function. An additional piece of notation: A sequence of events E_n in some probability spaces holds with *uniformly positive probability* (abbreviated as *wupp*) if there is a constant $\varepsilon > 0$ such that $\text{Prob}[E_n] > \varepsilon$ for all sufficiently large n.

The probability space $F(V, p)$ is obtained by picking each clause independently with probability p. We call it the binomial space. For $p = a/n^2$ the expected number of clauses is an. Moreover, the number of clauses is asymptotically equal to an with high probability. Techniques as detailed on pages 34/35 of [5] show that the spaces $F(n, m)$ and $F(n, p)$ with $pn^3 = m = O(n)$ are for most questions of interest equivalent. This applies in particular to the satisfiability problems treated here as they are monotone problems. Following common usage we omit the technical details to show this each time.

The initial inspiration for the paper [14] came from some experiments (performed only for $n \leq 300$ for running time reasons.) These experiments show that the random betweenness constraint becomes unsatisfiable for an random clauses when a is between 1.5 and 1.6. Results obtained in the cited paper collects

Fact 1. *For the random betweenness instance $F(V, m)$ with $m = an$ the following events have high probability:*

(a) For $a \leq C$ the instance is satisfiable where $C < 0.82$.
(b) For $a > 4 \cdot \ln 2 \approx 2.77$ the instance is unsatisfiable.
(c) There exist numbers $C = C(n)$, $0.8 \leq C \leq 2.77$, such that for each constant $\varepsilon > 0$ we have unsatisfiability for $a \geq (C + \varepsilon)$ and satisfiability for $a \leq (C - \varepsilon)$.

Fact 1 (c) means that we have a sharp threshold for unsatisfiability, but we do not know the threshold value precisely. This is typical when the techniques form [12] are used. Given Fact 1 (a) it seems to be non-trivial to show that $F(V, m)$ is satisfiable with high probability for any m substantially larger than $0.82n$. We make some progress and prove

Theorem 2. *For $m = rn$ with constant $r \leq 0.9$ the random betweenness instance $F(V, m)$ is satisfiable wupp.*

Theorem 2 together with Fact 1 (c) implies a high probability result.

Corollary 3. *The random betweenness constraint with $m = rn$ and $r < 0.9$ is satisfiable with high probability.*

There are two different techniques to show that random structures are solvable (for example colourable in case of graphs or satisfiable in case of k-SAT instances:) On the one hand it has been successful to analyze heuristic algorithms and show that they find a solution to a random instance. On the other hand,

and more recently non-constructive methods have been shown to be successful. In [2] it is shown that random k-SAT instances are satisfiable based on the second moment of the number of solutions and general probability estimates. Our proof consists of a first non-constructive part based on the second moment and a second constructive part. It may be the first time that a combination of these techniques is used to show the existence of a solution. See also [1] for the relationship of constructive and non-constructive proofs.

1.2 More Remarks the Literature

Ordering constraints differ from traditional constraints like k-SAT or more general kinds of constraints in that the underlying assignment must be an *ordering* of all variables. This means on the one hand that each variable can receive one out of n values, its position in the ordering. On the other hand each of the n values can only be used once. Altogether we have $n! >> 2^n$ many assignments as opposed to only 2^n in the case of satisfiability.

Beyond random k-SAT there is a considerable body of work on random constraints with finite domain from which the values for each variable are taken. Only a small selection of the literature, in part due to Michael Molloy is [17], [18], [16]. The paper [17] points out that the investigation of thresholds is not only of structural interest, but has also algorithmic relevance: Random instances at thresholds often have some algorithmic hardness which makes them attractive as test cases for algorithms.

As far as we know systematic experimental studies of random ordering constraints have not been made. Our preliminary experiments indicate that instances closer to the threshold become harder. This shows that our study is relevant from the algorithmic point of view. Results – of a different flavour however – on the relationship between thresholds (phase transitions) and algorithmic hardness can be found in the recent [1].

Ordering constraints tend to occur in knowledge representation formalisms. In [15] for example the cyclic ordering constraint occurs. In [8] a weighted version of an extended betweenness constraint is used to describe some biological situation. From the point of view of worst case complexity ordering constraints are investigated in [13]. A recent breakthrough is [6]. We find [7] and [9] considering optimization versions of ordering constraints.

2 Outline of the Proof of Theorem 2

We need 2-clauses. A 2-clause simply is a pair of distinct variables $x < y$, and we have $n(n-1) = (n)_2$ 2-clauses altogether. Given an ordering of the variables the 2-clause is satisfied iff x is smaller than y. A boolean assignment of the set of variables V is an assignment $a : V \rightarrow \{0, 1\}$ such that $n/2$ variables receive the value 1 and $n/2$ the value 0. Thus, in our case boolean assignments are *balanced*. A clause (x, y, z) is satisfied in the *boolean sense* by a iff it does *not* evaluate to $(0, 1, 0)$ or to $(1, 0, 1)$. Thus we have six out of 8 different possibilities to satisfy a clause in the boolean sense. A formula is satisfied in the boolean sense by a iff each clause is satisfied by a. A boolean assignment is equivalent to a partition of V into two sets V_0 and V_1 each with $n/2$ variables: V_0 the set of variables set to 0 and V_1 the set of variables set to 1. Let $A = y_1 < y_2 < y_3 < \ldots < y_n$. It induces the partition $V_l = \{y_1, \ldots, y_{n/2}\}$ and V_u is the upper half of the ordering. These notations directly imply

Proposition 4. *If the betweenness constraint F is satisfied by the ordering A then F is satisfied by the boolean assignment equivalent to the partition V_l and V_u.*

The following reduction allows to shrink a given betweenness constraint.

Definition 5. Let F be a betweenness constraint and let V_0, V_1 be a partition of V into two disjoint sets of $n/2$ variables each. If F is satisfied by the boolean assignment equivalent to V_0 and V_1 we say that the constraints $F_0 = F_{V_0}$ over V_0 and $F_1 = F_{V_1}$ over V_1 are defined. Their definition is as follows.

Let (x, y, z) be a clause from F with at least two variables from V_0. It induces clauses as follows in F_0 :

- $(x, y, z) \in (V_0, V_0, V_0) (= V_0 \times V_0 \times V_0)$ implies $(x, y, z) \in F_0$
- $(x, y, z) \in (V_0, V_0, V_1)$ implies $x < y \in F_0$
- $(x, y, z) \in (V_1, V_0, V_0)$ implies $y > z \in F_0$.

Let (x, y, z) be a clause from F with at least two variables from V_1. It induces clauses as follows in F_1 : $(x, y, z) \in (V_1, V_1, V_1)$ implies $(x, y, z) \in F_1$, $(x, y, z) \in (V_1, V_1, V_0)$ implies $x > y \in F_1$, and $(x, y, z) \in (V_0, V_1, V_1)$ implies $y < z \in F_1$.

F in the preceding definition has no clauses from (V_0, V_1, V_0) and (V_1, V_0, V_1) as it is satisfied by the boolean assignment associated to V_0 and V_1. The simple relationship between F and F_0 and F_1 is made clear by

Proposition 6. *Let F, V_0, and V_1 be such that F_0 and F_1 are defined. F is satisfied by a linear ordering with $V_0 < V_1$ iff F_0 and F_1 are both satisfiable.*

We consider the random instance $F = F(V, m)$. Given a boolean assignment a we define indicator random variables X_a and Y_a : $X_a(F) = 1$ if F is satisfied in the boolean sense by a. $X = \sum_a X_a$ is the number of satisfying boolean assignments. $Y_a(F) = 1$ iff F is satisfied by an ordering A which induces the *same partition* as a. (That is $V_l = V_0$ and $V_u = V_1$.) We let $Y = \sum_a Y_a$. The following remark follows from Proposition 4.

Remark 7
(a) $Y_a \leq X_a$.
(b) $Prob[F$ is satisf. as betweenness constraint $] = Prob[Y \geq 1] \leq Prob[X \geq 1]$

We have $n!$ orderings as possible solutions for a given betweenness constraint F. It is natural to consider the random variable which gives the number of satisfying orderings. However, in part due to the large number of $n! >> 2^n$ solution candidates this random variable seems not easy to deal with. The random variable

Y seems to be useful because it counts orderings associated to the same boolean assignment only once. It thus has to do only with 2^n candidates. The proof of the next proposition uses analytical techniques introduced in [2]. It is presented in the Appendix.

Proposition 8. *For the random instance $F(V, m)$ with $m = rn, r \leq 1$ we have:*
(a) $E[X] \geq (3/2)^{n(1-\varepsilon)}$ for any constant $\varepsilon > 0$.
(b) $E[X^2] \leq C \cdot (E[X])^2$ for an appropriate constant C.

As X is a random variable which is ≥ 0 and has finite variance we can use the Paley-Zygmund inequality: For any $0 \leq \Theta \leq 1$

$$\text{Prob}[X \geq \Theta E[X]] \geq (1 - \Theta)^2 (E[X])^2 / E[X^2]. \qquad (1)$$

With Proposition 8 as $E[X] \geq 1$ we directly get (but do not really need)

Corollary 9. *The event $X \geq 1$ holds wupp.*

Given a boolean assignment a, we consider the random instance $F_a(V, m)$ which is $F(V, m)$ conditioned on the event $X_a = 1$. Thus $F_a(V, m)$ consists of m clauses each satisfying the boolean assignment a. We have $(3/4)(n)_3$ clauses satisfying a. The probability of a given instance of m such clauses is $1/((3/4)(n)_3)_m$ (in case of sequences of clauses without repetition – a mere formality.) In the next section we prove the main

Lemma 10. *Let a be an arbitrary boolean assignment. We consider the random instance $F_a(V, m)$ with $m = rn, r \leq 0.9$. Then the event $Y_a = 1$ holds wupp.*

While Proposition 8 holds for $r > 0.9$, at present we cannot prove Lemma 10 much beyond $r = 0.9$. At this point the reader may wonder why we cannot derive Theorem 2 directly with Corollary 9 and the preceding Lemma. This however is not clear. The underlying probability spaces are not as closely related as it seems. In particular an instance from $F(V, m)$ with $X \geq 1$ may not be very random any more. It thus may not have much to do with a random instance $F_a(V, m)$ to which the Lemma refers. Instead we only use the second moment of X in the

Proof of Theorem 2. For a suitable constant $\varepsilon > 0$ and any boolean assignment a we have with Lemma 10

$$E[Y_a] = \text{Prob}[X_a = 1] \cdot \text{Prob}\,[Y_a = 1 | X_a = 1] \geq \text{Prob}[X_a = 1] \cdot \varepsilon. \qquad (2)$$

The second estimate above is Lemma 10. The first equation follows from the formula of total probability as $\text{Prob}\,[Y_a = 1 \,|\, X_a = 0] = 0$ (Remark 7 (a).) Then we get $EY \geq \varepsilon \cdot EX \to \infty$ (with Prop. 8 (a).)

Furthermore we have

$$E[Y^2] \leq \sum_{(a,b)} \text{Prob}[X_a = 1 \text{ and } X_b = 1] = E[X^2] \leq C(EX)^2 \leq (C/\varepsilon^2)(EY)^2$$

using Remark 7 (a) for the first estimate and Proposition 8 (b) to bound $E[X^2]$. Now, Theorem 2 follows with Equation (1). $\qquad \square$

3   Proof of Lemma 10

For $F = F_a(V, m)$, we have $Y_a(F) = 1$ iff both formulas F_0 and F_1 as in Definition 5 are satisfiable (Proposition 6, $V_0 = a^{-1}(0)$ and $V_1 = a^{-1}(1)$). In F the number of clauses from each of the 6 admissable possibilities among (V_i, V_k, V_j) with $i, j, k = 0, 1$ is concentrated at its expectation, that is asymptotically $(1/6)m$ with high probability. With high probability 2 clauses which overlap in 2 variables do not occur as m is linear in n. Therefore F_0 and F_1 have $(1/6)m$ many 3-clauses and $(2/6)m$ many 2-clauses each over $n/2$ variables. Moreover, F_0 and F_1 are stochastically independent (given their respective number of clauses which is concentrated). Thus F_0 and F_1 are two independent random formulas with asymptotically $(1/3)rn$ 3-clauses and $(2/3)rn$ 2-clauses over n variables (scaling to n variables instead of $n/2$.)

We switch to the binomial space because the subsequent probability calculations appear slightly easier. The random instance $F = F(n, p, q)$ is obtained by throwing each 3-clause randomly with p and each 2-clause with q. Following the remark in the Introduction instead of F_0 and F_1 we consider the random instance $F(n, c/n^2, d/n)$ with

$$c = (1/3) \cdot r \text{ and } d = (2/3) \cdot r, \text{ and } r = 0.9$$

which are fixed for the rest of this section. We show that $F(n, c/n^2, d/n)$ is satisfiable wupp and Lemma 10 follows from the independence of F_0 and F_1 and Proposition 6.

Definition 11. The directed (multi-)graph G_F associated to F has as vertices the variables of F. Its edges are given by: The clause $C = (x, y, z) \in F$ induces the edges $(x, y), (y, z)$ and (x, z) each marked with C. The clause $x < y \in F$ induces the edge (x, y).

Clearly, if G_F is cycle free then F is satisfiable (by any topological ordering of G_F.) To reduce a formula F we apply

Algorithm 12. Input: A formula F.
$V_1 :=$ the set of those variables which occur exactly once in a 3-clause of F and nowhere else.
$V_2 :=$ those variables x which occur *only* at the position $x < -$. This means that all 2-clauses with x are of the form $x < y$ and we have no 3-clauses with x. Here the case that x does not occur at all is included.
$V_3 :=$ the variables x which occur *only* and at least once as $- < x$
The result F' of the algorithm is obtained by deleting all variables from $V_1 \cup V_2 \cup V_3$ and clauses containing them from F.

The algorithm is correct in the sense of

Lemma 13. *If F' is satisfiable then F is satisfiable.*

We iterate Algorithm 12 and therefore need

Definition 14. (a) For a given formula F we let $F_k :=$ the formula obtained after k iterations of Algorithm 12.

(b) The $w_{2,k}$ and $w_{3,k}$ for $k \geq 0$ are defined inductively by

$$w_{2,0} = w_{3,0} = 0,$$
$$w_{2,k+1} = \exp\left(-d(1 - w_{2,k})\right) \cdot \exp\left(-3c(1 - w_{3,k})^2\right),$$
$$w_{3,k+1} = \exp\left(-d(1 - w_{2,k})\right) \cdot w_{2,k+1}.$$

In $F(n, c/n^2, d/n)$ we have that the variable x, conditioned on the event that the 2-clause $x < y$ is present, is deleted with probability $(1 - d/n)^n \cdot (1 - c/n^2)^{3(n-1)(n-2)}$ by Algorithm 12. This is $w_{2,1}$, asymptotically. Conditioned on the 3-clause (x, y, z) we have $(1 - d/n)^{2n} \cdot (1 - c/n^2)^{3(n-1)(n-2)-1}$ which is $w_{3,1}(1 + o(1))$. We will see that $w_{i,k} \leq$ the deletion probability of x after the k'th iteration conditioned on the event that x is in a i-clause before the k'th interation $(i = 2, 3.)$

A Maple calculation shows that the $w_{i,k}$ both seem to go firmly to 1 when k gets large. For our proof we stay in the finite realm and observe that for $r = 0.9$

$$w_{2,1} = 0.2313..., \quad w_{3,1} = 0.1224... \text{ and we need } w_{2,50}, w_{3,50} > 0.9. \tag{3}$$

For the notation G_{F_k} in the subsequent Lemma recall Definition 11 and Definition 14 (a).

Lemma 15. *Let* $k = 50$, $S = 3 \cdot \ln n$, *and* $F = F(n, c/n^2, d/n)$, *and* $w := 1 - w_{3,50} < 0.1$.

(a) The expected number of simple paths of length $= S$ in G_{F_k} is $o(1)$.
(b) The expected number of cycles of length $2 \leq s \leq S$ in G_{F_k} is

$$< \left(\sum_{s=2}^{S} \frac{1}{s} \cdot (3cw + d)^s\right) + o(1) < \sum_{s=2}^{S} \left(\frac{0.7}{s}\right)^s + o(1)$$

Proof of Lemma 10. The probability to have a cycle of length $\geq S$ is $o(1)$ by (a) of Lemma 15. The probability to have a cycle of length $\leq S$ in G_{F_k} is bounded above by the expectation, which is

$$< \sum_{s=2}^{S} \frac{(0.7)^s}{s} + o(1) < (0.7)^2/2 \cdot \sum_{s \geq 0} (0.7)^s + o(1).$$

The geometric series shows that this is asymptotically bounded above by a constant < 1. Applying the remark after Definition 11 for the induction basis and Lemma 13 inductively we see that $F(n, c/n^2, d/n)$ is satisfiable wupp. Then Lemma 10 follows with the remark at the end of the second paragraph of this section.   □

Proof of Lemma 15 (a). Consider a possible simple path of length S, $(x_0, x_1, x_2, \ldots x_{S-1}, x_S)$ with t edges induced by 3-clauses, that is labelled with their respective 3-clause. W.l.o.g. we can restrict attention to paths which do not use 2 edges induced by one clause because in this case we have the clause (x, y, z) and the piece $(\ldots, x, y, z, \ldots)$ in the path. We substitute it with $(\ldots, x, z, \ldots)$. Let $y_1, \ldots y_t$ be the additional variables of the 3-clauses inducing edges of the path. The number of such paths altogether is $< n^{S+1} \cdot (3n)^t$. The probability for this path to be present in the random F is $(3c/n^2)^t (d/n)^{S-t}$. The Binomial Theorem shows that the expected number of paths of length S is $< n(3c + d)^S = n(0.9 + 0.6)^S = n(1.5)^S$. We analyze the effect of $k = 50$ iterations of Algorithm 12 based on the well-known fact that sparse random structures are locally (hyper-)tree-like. The technique is in principle presented in [19].

For definiteness consider the variable $y = y_1$. Except of those clauses present because the path is in F – on which we condition – the distribution of the number of 2-clauses $y <$ – and $y >$ – follows the binomial distribution with parameters n or $n - 1$ and d/n. For 3-clauses with y we have parameters approximately $3n^2 - 1$ and c/n^2. The probability that we get $> \log n$ variables neighbouring y is very small, $O(1/n^{\Omega(\log \log n)})$. The probability that one of the random neighbours of y is already present in the path is $O(\log n/n)$. Therefore the probability that there *exists* a neighbour of y already present in the path is $O((\log n)^2/n)$. In case a neighbour of a variable is already present in the part seen, that is generated, we speak of an *overlap*.

We consider the next generation of neighbours of y – conditional on the event that the preceding two exceptions do *not* occur for the first generation. For each neighbour of the first generation the number of new neighbours can be approximated very well by the binomial distributions as before. We explore the random formula for up to distance k from y in this way. The probability that an overlap occurs at some point is $O((\log n)^{2(k+1)}/n)$ given that the number of neighbours each time is $\leq \log n$. We condition on the high probability event that no overlap occurs *and* that we have always only $\leq \log n$ neighbours in the neighbourhood of y up to distance k. In this case the neighbourhood is a (hyper-)tree whose neighbour distributions are very well approximated by the binomial distributions above. (We omit a further formalization, in particular the precise conditionings at this point.)

We analyze what Algorithm 12 does to such a random (hyper-)tree. The probability that a variable in depth $k - 1$ is deleted in the first iteration is asymptotically $w_{2,1}$ if it is reached by a 2-clause from the previous generation. If it is a 3-clause we get $w_{3,1}$. For variables in depth $k - 2$ and the second iteration we get at least $w_{2,2}$ and $w_{3,2}$. Finally for y itself we get at least $w_{3,k} > 0.9$ That is the 3-clause with y of the path is present in F_k only with probability $w < 0.1$.

As the path is of length $S = O(\log n)$ we get that *all* neighbourhoods of the y's are disjoint trees with (approximately) the same binomial neighbour distribution as before – unless we have an overlap which happens with probability $O(\mathrm{poly}(\log n)/n)$.

Case 1. No overlap at all. Assuming that the y_i are all distinct and the neighbourhoods of the y_i are disjoint we get for the expectation

$$n \cdot \sum_{t=0}^{S} \binom{S}{t} (3cw)^t d^{S-t} = n(3cw + d)^S.$$

This can be bounded as $\leq n(0.1 + 0.6)^S$. As $\ln(0.7) < -(1/3)$ and $S = 3 \ln n$ we get a bound of $1/n^\varepsilon$.

Case 2. One overlap. One overlap causes one or two neighbourhoods not to be disjoint trees. We assume conservatively that the respective variables y_i are not deleted. For the expectation in this case we get

$$n \sum_{t=1}^{S} \binom{S}{t} (3c)^2 (3cw)^{t-2} d^{S-t} \cdot \frac{\text{poly}(\log n)}{n}.$$

This can be bounded by $\text{poly}(\log n)(1/w)^2(3cw + d)^S = o(1)$.

Case 3. Two overlaps. This case is treated similarly.

Case 4. Three or more overlaps. In this case we assume conservatively that no deletion occurs. We get for the expectation, recall $3c + d = 1.5$,

$$n \cdot \sum_{t=3}^{S} \binom{S}{t} (3c)^t \cdot d^{S-t} \cdot \frac{\text{poly}(\log n)}{n^3} \leq n \cdot (1.5)^S \cdot \frac{\text{poly}(\log n)}{n^3}.$$

As $\ln(1.5) \cdot 3 < 1.3$ we get $o(1)$ in this case, too.

We also need to consider the possibility that the y's themselves are not distinct. We can analyze this as the overlaps above. Similarly for overlaps among the y's themselves and the neighbourhoods of the y's. □

Proof of Lemma 15 (b). For cycles of length $2 \leq s \leq S$ without any overlap among the y's (notation as above) or their neighbourhoods we get with the Binomial Theorem an expectation of at most (see [21] , [11] or [14] for similar calculations) $1 / s \cdot (3cw + d)^s$. With exactly one overlap anywhere we get a bound of $(1/w)^2(3cw + d)^s \cdot (\text{poly}(\log n) / n) = O(1/n^{1-\varepsilon})$. For two or more overlaps we get $\text{poly}(\log n) / n^2 \cdot (3c + d)^S = O(1/n^{0.7})$. As $S = O(\log n)$ the $O-$terms remain $o(1)$ even after the sum over s is computed and the proof ends. □

4   Conclusion

Concerning our constant $r = 0.9$: The contribution is that the bound of $r < 0.82$ from [14] can be beaten – by more advanced techniques. Our proof does not work for $r \geq 0.95$: The $w_{i,k}$ remain too small. An analytical proof that the $w_{i,k} \to 1$ for large k would improve our proof.

Acknowledgement. Special thanks to Anja Lau for help with the calculus.

References

1. Achlioptas, D., Coja-Oghlan, A.: Algorithmic Hardness from Phase Transitions. In: Proceedings 49th IEEE Symposium on Foundations of Computer Science, pp. 793–802. IEEE Press, Los Alamitos (2008)
2. Achlioptas, D., Moore, Ch.: Random k-SAT: Two Moments Suffice to Cross a Sharp Threshold. SIAM Journal on Computing 36(3), 740–762 (2006)
3. Beame, P., Karp, R., Pitassi, T., Saks, M.: The Efficiency of Resolution and Davis-Putnam Procedures. SIAM Journal on Computing 31(4), 1048–1075 (2002)
4. Broder, A., Frieze, A., Upfal, E.: On the Satisfiability and Maximum Satisfiability of Random 3-CNF Formulas. In: Proceedings 4th ACM-SIAM Symposium on Discrete Algorithms, pp. 322–330. ACM/ SIAM (1993)
5. Bollobas, B.: Random Graphs. Academic Press, London (1985)
6. Bodirsky, M., Kára, J.: The Complexity of Temporal Constraint Satisfaction Problems. In: Proceedings 40th ACM Symposium on Theory of Computing, pp. 29–38. ACM Press, New York (2008)
7. Ailon, N., Alon, N.: Hardness of Fully Dense Problems. Information and Computation 205(8), 1117–1129 (2007)
8. Christof, Th., Jünger, M., Kececioglu, J., Mutzel, P., Reinelt, G.: A Branch-and-Cut Approach to Physical Mapping with End-Probes. In: Proceedings of the 1st Annual International Conference on Computational Molecular Biology (RECOMB), pp. 84–92 (1997)
9. Chor, B., Sudan, M.: A Geometric Approach to Betweenness. SIAM Journal on Disctete Mathematics 11(4), 511–523 (1998)
10. Dubois, O., Boufkhad, Y., Mandler, J.: Typical Random 3-SAT Formulae and the Satisfiability Threshold. In: Proceedings 11th ACM-SIAM Symposium on Discrete Algorithms, pp. 126–127. ACM/ SIAM (2000)
11. Erdös, P., Renyi, A.: On the Evolution of Random Graphs. Publications of the Mathematical Institute of the Hungarian Academy of Science 5, 17–61 (1960)
12. Friedgut, E.: Hunting for Sharp Thresholds. Random Structures and Algorithms 26(1-2), 37–51 (2005)
13. Guttmann, W., Maucher, M.: Variations on an Ordering Theme with Constraints. In: Proceedings Fourth IFIP International Conference on Theoretical Computer Science (TCS). IFIP International Federation for Information Processing, vol. 209, pp. 77–90. Springer, Heidelberg (2006)
14. Goerdt, A.: On Random Ordering Constraints. In: Proceedings Computer Science in Russia (CSR). LNCS. Springer, Heidelberg (to appear 2009)
15. Isli, A., Cohen, A.G.: An Algebra for Cyclic Ordering of 2D Orientation. In: Proceedings 15th American Conference on Artificial Intelligence (AAAI), pp. 643–649. AAAI/MIT Press (1998)
16. Hatami, H., Molloy, M.: Sharp Thresholds for Constraint Satisfaction Problems and Homomorphisms. Random Structures and Algorithms 33(3), 310–332 (2008)
17. Molloy, M.: Models and Thresholds for Random Constraint Satisfaction Problems. In: Proceedings 34th ACM Symposium on Theory of Computing, pp. 209–217. ACM Press, New York (2002)
18. Molloy, M.: When does the Giant Component Bring Unsatisfiability? Combinatorica 28, 693–734 (2008)
19. Molloy, M.: Cores in Random Hypergraphs and Boolean Formulas. Random Structures and Algorithms 27, 124–135 (2005)

20. Opatrny, J.: Total Ordering Problem. SIAM Journal on Computing 8(1), 111–114 (1979)
21. Palasti, I.: On the Threshold Distribution Function of Cycles in a Directed Random Graph. Studia Scientiarum Mathematicarum Hungarica 6, 67–73 (1971)

A Appendix, Proof of Proposition 8

Proof of (a). Stirling: $EX = \sqrt{2/(\pi n)} \left(2 \cdot (3/4)^r\right)^n > (3/2)^{n(1-\varepsilon)}$ (as $r \leq 1$). $\square$

Proof of (b). Given 2 assignments a, b with overlap $2l = \alpha n$, that is we have $2l$ variables which have the same truth value under both a and b, the probability that a random clause is satisfied by both a and b is $= (3/4) \cdot (1 - \alpha \cdot (1 - \alpha))$. This can be seen by elementary consideration and implies that

$$E\left[X^2\right] = \sum_{(a,b)} \text{Prob}[X_a = 1 \text{ and } X_b = 1] =$$

$$= \binom{n}{n/2} \cdot \sum_{l=0}^{n/2} \binom{n/2}{l}^2 \cdot \left(\frac{3}{4} \cdot \left(1 - \frac{l}{n/2} \cdot \left(1 - \frac{l}{n/2}\right)\right)\right)^m. \tag{4}$$

With $\phi(\alpha) := (3/4 \cdot (1 - \alpha \cdot (1 - \alpha)))^r$ we get for the sum of (4) as $m = rn$

$$S_n := \sum_{l=0}^{n/2} \binom{n/2}{l}^2 \cdot \left(\phi\left(\frac{l}{n/2}\right)\right)^n. \tag{5}$$

We apply the next Lemma with $q := 2$, $t := n/2$, $z := l$ to S_n.

Lemma 16 (Laplace Lemma [2]). *Let $\phi(\alpha)$ be a positive, twice-differentiable function on $[0, 1]$ and let $q \geq 1$ be a fixed integer. Let $t = n/q$ and let*

$$S_n := \sum_{z=0}^{t} \binom{t}{z}^q \phi(z/t)^n \quad and \quad g(\alpha) := \frac{\phi(\alpha)}{\alpha^\alpha (1 - \alpha)^{1-\alpha}}$$

where $g(\alpha)$ is defined on $[0, 1]$ and $0^0 := 1$.

If there exists $\alpha_{\max} \in (0, 1)$ such that $g(\alpha_{\max}) =: g_{\max} > g(\alpha)$ for all $\alpha \neq \alpha_{\max}$ and $g''(\alpha_{\max}) < 0$, then there is a constant $C = C(q, g_{\max}, g''(\alpha_{\max}), \alpha_{\max}) > 0$ such that for all sufficiently large n we have $S_n < C \cdot n^{-(q-1)/2} \cdot (g_{\max})^n$.

We get from (5) and the Laplace Lemma that $S_n \leq C \cdot (1/\sqrt{n}) \cdot (g_{\max})^n$. From Stirling's formula and (4) we get

$$E[X^2] \leq 2^n \cdot \sqrt{\frac{2}{\pi n}} \cdot C \cdot \frac{1}{\sqrt{n}} \cdot (g_{\max})^n = D \cdot \frac{1}{n} \cdot (2 \cdot g_{\max})^n.$$

Below we show that $g_{\max} = 2 \cdot (3/4)^{2r}$ (see Equation (6)) and the claim holds because $EX = \sqrt{2/(\pi n)} \cdot 2^n \cdot (3/4)^{rn}$ (cf. proof of (a).)

We check that the Laplace Lemma is applicable. For the function $\phi(\alpha)$ (definition before Equation (5)) we have for $\alpha \in [0, 1]$ that $\phi(\alpha) \geq 0$. And $\phi(\alpha)$ is twice differentiable and symmetric around $\alpha = 1/2$. For $\alpha = 1/2$ we have its minimum on $[0, 1]$ which is $\phi(1/2) = (3/4)^{2r}$. (Elementary calculus for the proof.)

We come to

$$g(\alpha) = \frac{\phi(\alpha)}{\alpha^\alpha (1-\alpha)^{1-\alpha}} = \frac{(3/4 \cdot (1 - \alpha \cdot (1 - \alpha)))^r}{\alpha^\alpha (1-\alpha)^{1-\alpha}}.$$

It turns out that $g(\alpha)$ is maximized at

$$g_{\max} = g(1/2) = 2 \cdot (3/4)^{2r}. \tag{6}$$

First, $g'(\alpha) =$

$$\left(\frac{3}{4}\right)^r \underbrace{\underbrace{(1 - \alpha + \alpha^2)^{r-1}}_{=((\alpha-1)^2+\alpha)^{r-1}>0} \underbrace{\frac{1}{\alpha^\alpha (1-\alpha)^{1-\alpha}}}_{>0}}_{>0} \cdot \underbrace{\left[r(2\alpha - 1) - (1 - \alpha + \alpha^2) \ln\left(\frac{\alpha}{1-\alpha}\right)\right]}_{=:h(\alpha)}$$

and $g'(1/2) = 0$, as $h(1/2) = 0$. Moreover,

$$g''(1/2) = 1/3 \cdot 9^r \left(2^{-4r+4}r - 24 \cdot 16^{-r}\right)$$

which is easily seen to be < 0 even for $r < 3/2$.

We consider $\alpha \in (0, 1/2), r \in (0, 3/2)$. We have

$$h'(\alpha) = \underbrace{2r - \underbrace{(2\alpha - 1)}_{<0} \cdot \underbrace{\ln\left(\frac{\alpha}{1-\alpha}\right)}_{<0}}_{<2r<3} - (1 - \alpha + \alpha^2) \cdot \underbrace{\left(\frac{1}{\alpha} + \frac{1}{1-\alpha}\right)}_{=:k(\alpha)}.$$

We can rewrite $k(\alpha) = 1/\alpha + 1/(1 - \alpha) - 1$ and

$$k'(\alpha) = -\frac{1}{\alpha^2} + \frac{1}{(1-\alpha)^2} = \frac{2\alpha - 1}{\alpha^2 \cdot (1-\alpha)^2} < 0$$

$\Rightarrow k(\alpha)$ strictly monotonously decreasing in $(0, 1/2)$.

$k(1/2) = 3 \Rightarrow k(\alpha) > 3, \forall \alpha \in (0, 1/2)$

$\Rightarrow h'(\alpha) < 0, \forall \alpha \in (0, 1/2), 0 < r < 3/2$

$\Rightarrow h(\alpha)$ is strictly monotonously decreasing in $(0, 1/2)$.

$h(1/2) = 0 \Rightarrow h(\alpha) > 0, \forall \alpha \in (0, 1/2)$

$\Rightarrow g'(\alpha) > 0, \forall \alpha \in (0, 1/2)$

$\Rightarrow g(\alpha)$ strictly monotonously increasing in $(0, 1/2)$. $\square$

Directed Graphs of Entanglement Two

Erich Grädel, Łukasz Kaiser, and Roman Rabinovich

Mathematische Grundlagen der Informatik, RWTH Aachen University
{graedel,kaiser,rabinovich}@logic.rwth-aachen.de

Abstract. Entanglement is a complexity measure for directed graphs that was used to show that the variable hierarchy of the propositional modal μ-calculus is strict. While graphs of entanglement zero and one are indeed very simple, some graphs of entanglement two already contain interesting nesting of cycles. This motivates our study of the class of graphs of entanglement two, as these are both simple in a sense and already complex enough for modelling certain structured systems.

Undirected graphs of entanglement two were already studied by Belkhir and Santocanale and a structural decomposition for such graphs was given. We study the general case of directed graphs of entanglement two and prove that they can be decomposed as well, in a way similar to the known decompositions for tree-width, DAG-width and Kelly-width. Moreover, we show that all graphs of entanglement two have both DAG-width and Kelly-width three. Since there exist both graphs with DAG-width three and graphs with Kelly-width three, but with arbitrary high entanglement, this confirms that graphs of entanglement two are a very basic class of graphs with cycles intertwined in an interesting way.

1 Introduction

In recent years, several parameters have been proposed to measure the structural complexity of directed graphs in a similar way as *tree-width* measures the complexity of undirected ones. While tree-width indicates how closely a graph resembles a tree, the intuition behind complexity measures for directed graphs is that acyclic graphs are simple, and that we can measure the complexity of a graph by the extent to which its cycles are intertwined, or entangled. It has turned out that there are several different ways to make this intuition precise, and several methods to obtain such complexity measures. The two main methodologies are appropriate *decompositions* of the graph, similar to tree decompositions, and *graph searching games*, also called robber-and-cops games, where a number of cops try to catch a fugitive on the graph. The movements of the fugitive are restricted by the edges of the graph, and the number of cops that are necessary to catch the fugitive determine the complexity of the graph.

DAG-width, introduced in [1,2] is defined by DAG-decompositions. A DAG-decomposition of width k of a graph $\mathcal{G}$ is given by a directed acyclic graph (DAG) $\mathcal{D}$ and a map that associates with every node of the DAG a set of at most k vertices of $\mathcal{G}$, covering the entire graph $\mathcal{G}$ in such a way that for

M. Kutyłowski, M. Gębala, and W. Charatonik (Eds.): FCT 2009, LNCS 5699, pp. 169–180, 2009.

every $d \in \mathcal{D}$, the edges of $\mathcal{G}$ leaving a node strictly below d are guarded by vertices in d. DAG-width can also be characterised by a variant of a graph searching game (the directed cops and visible robber game), but with the somewhat unsatisfactory restriction that the cops are only allowed to use robber-monotone strategies, i.e. a move of the cops must never enlarge the portion of the graph in which the robber can move. It has recently been proved [3] that this restriction is necessary. Indeed, there exist families of graphs on which the difference between the DAG-width and the number of cops that can catch the robber with a non-monotone strategy is unbounded.

Kelly-width, see [4], is a similar measure that can either be defined by a some-what refined notion of decomposition, called Kelly-decompositions, or by a graph searching game in which the robber is invisible for the cops, and inert, i.e. he can move only when a cop is about to land on his current position. Again, the correspondence between decompositions and games only holds with the restriction to monotone strategies [3].

Entanglement, introduced in [5], has been motivated by applications concern-ing the modal μ-calculus and parity games. It is defined by the entanglement game, in which the movements of both cops and robber are more restricted than in other graph searching games. In each move the cops either stay where they are or place one of them on the current position of the robber. The rob-ber then moves, along an edge, to a new vertex that must not be occupied by a cop. If no such vertex exists, the robber is caught. Here, strategies need not be monotone.

Entanglement is in a sense more delicate than tree-width, DAG-width, or Kelly-width [4]. There exist graphs with tree-width two and arbitrary large en-tanglement, as well as graphs with DAG-width two and unbounded entangle-ment. There exist a number of other measures for directed graphs, including directed tree-width [6], pathwidth, cycle rank [7], D-width [8]. For surveys over different measures, we refer to [9,10].

The strengths of the entanglement measure are the close connection with modal logics and bisimulation invariant properties, and the natural game-theo-retic characterisation. Entanglement has been a crucial ingredient in the proof that the variable hierarchy of the modal μ-calculus is strict [11]. Further, it has been proved that parity games can be efficiently solved on game graphs with bounded entanglement[1]. The entanglement does not increase when we take bisimulation quotients, and as a consequence of this observation it has been proved that winning regions of parity games are definable in least fixed point logic on graphs of bounded entanglement [12].

The main weakness of the entanglement measure (at the current state of the art) is that it does not come with a natural notion of decomposition, such as the ones for tree-width, DAG-width, or Kelly-width. Decompositions are crucial for algorithmic applications, since they allow to break the structure into smaller parts and process these in a systematic way. A structural characterisation of

---

[1] An analogous result also holds for bounded DAG-width and bounded Kelly-width.

entanglement has been given in [11] in terms of the minimal feedback of the finite unravellings of the graph to a tree with back-edges. However, while this produces a game-free definition of entanglement, it does not give a decomposition.

In this paper we study graphs of entanglement two. While graphs of entanglement zero and one are indeed very simple, graphs of entanglement two may already have an arbitrary nesting of cycles, and they are rich enough to model interesting classes of structured systems. We provide structural characterisations of this class, and find appropriate decompositions, similar to the ones for tree-width, DAG-width, and Kelly-width. Moreover, we show that all graphs of entanglement two have both DAG-width and Kelly-width three. Since there exist both graphs with DAG-width three and graphs with Kelly-width three, but with arbitrary high entanglement, this confirms that graphs of entanglement two are a very basic class of graphs with cycles intertwined in an interesting way.

For lack of space, this conference paper does not contain proofs of all results. For the full version, see [13].

2   Entanglement

In this paper, a graph is always meant to be finite and directed. To deal with undirected graphs, we view undirected edges $\{u, v\}$ as pairs (u, v) and (v, u) of directed edges, so undirected graphs are directed graphs with a symmetric edge relation. For a graph $\mathcal{G} = (V, E)$ and $V' \subseteq V$, we write $\mathcal{G}[V']$ to denote the subgraph of $\mathcal{G}$ induced by the vertex set V'. For a vertex $a \in V$, we write $\mathcal{G} \setminus a$ for $\mathcal{G}[V \setminus \{a\}]$. Further, let $vE = \{w \in V : (v, w) \in E\}$.

Entanglement is defined by way of the *entanglement game* $\mathrm{EG}_k(\mathcal{G})$, played by a robber against k cops on a directed graph $\mathcal{G}$. Initially, all cops are outside the graph and the robber selects an arbitrary starting vertex v_0 of $\mathcal{G}$. The players move in turn. In each move the cops either stay where they are, or place one of them on the current position of the robber. The robber must then move from her current position v, along an edge, to a successor $w \in vE$ that is not occupied by a cop. If no such position exists, the robber is caught, and the cops have won. Notice that the robber has to leave her current position no matter whether or not a cop has occupied that position. The robber wins if she is never caught, i.e. if the play lasts forever.

Definition 1. *The* entanglement *$\mathrm{ent}(\mathcal{G})$ of a graph $\mathcal{G}$ is the minimal number k such that k cops have a winning strategy in the entanglement game $\mathrm{EG}_k(\mathcal{G})$.*

The entanglement game is, in essence, a reachability game: the cops try to reach a state of the game at which the robber is captured. It is well known that such games are determined via memoryless strategies, i.e. one of the two players has a winning strategy that depends only on the current position, not on the history of the play. We can thus restrict our attention to memoryless strategies.

For a formal definition of strategies in an entanglement game $\mathrm{EG}_k(\mathcal{G})$ on a graph $\mathcal{G} = (V, E)$, we describe a play by a sequence $\pi \in S^{\leq \omega}$, where $S = V \times \mathcal{P}_{\leq k}(V)$. Here $\mathcal{P}_{\leq k}(V)$ is the set of subsets of V of size at most k, and $(v, P) \in S$

denotes a position where the robber is on v and the cops occupy the vertices
in P. For brevity, we suppress the information about whose turn to move it is.
A (memoryless) strategy of the robber in $\mathrm{EG}_k(\mathcal{G})$ can be described by a partial
function $\rho : S \cup \{\epsilon\} \to V$ with the property that $\rho(v, P) \in vE \setminus P$. Here $\rho(\epsilon)$
describes the choice of the initial vertex by the robber. Similarly, a (memoryless)
strategy of the cops is described by a partial function $\sigma : S \to V \cup \{\square, \bot\}$
describing which cop moves to the current vertex occupied by the robber:

- if $\sigma(v, P) = \bot$ then the cops stay where they are, and the next position is
  (v, P) (but now it is the robber's turn);
- if $\sigma(v, P) = \square$ then it must be the case that $|P| < k$ and the next position
  is $(v, P \cup \{v\})$ (a cop from outside comes to vertex v);
- otherwise $\sigma(v, P) = u \in P$ (the cop from vertex u goes to v), and the next
  position is $(v, (P \setminus \{u\}) \cup \{v\})$.

A strategy ρ of the robber and a strategy σ of the cops define a unique
play $\pi = (v_0, P_0)(v_1, P_1)(v_2, P_2)\ldots$ that is consistent with ρ and σ. It starts in
position $(v_0, P_0) = (\epsilon, \emptyset)$ meaning that the cops and the robber are outside of the
graph. After the initial move of the robber the position is $(v_1, P_1) = (\rho(\epsilon), \emptyset)$.
For every $n > 0$ the vertex v_{2n+1} occupied by the robber after her $(n + 1)$-st
move is determined by $\rho(v_{2n}, P_{2n})$, and the set P_{2n} occupied by the cops after
their nth move is determined by $\sigma(v_{2n-1}, P_{2n-1})$. Finally, we have $P_{2n+1} = P_{2n}$
and $v_{2n} = v_{2n-1}$. A play ends, and is won by the cops, if, for some n, there is
no position $w \in v_{2n}E \setminus P_{2n}$. Infinite plays are won by the robber.

A strategy of the robber (or the cops) is *winning* if the robber (cops) wins
every play consistent with it. As reachability games are determined in memoryless strategies, there is either a winning strategy for the robber or for the cops
in every entanglement game.

It is easy to characterise the graphs of entanglement zero and one [5].

Proposition 2. *Let $\mathcal{G}$ be any finite directed graph.*

(1) $\mathrm{ent}(\mathcal{G}) = 0$ if, and only if, $\mathcal{G}$ is acyclic.
(2) $\mathrm{ent}(\mathcal{G}) = 1$ if, and only if, $\mathcal{G}$ is not acyclic, and in every strongly connected
*   component there is a node whose removal makes the component acyclic.*

As a consequence, for $k = 0$ and $k = 1$, the problem whether a given graph has
entanglement k is NLOGSPACE-complete.

However, already the graphs of entanglement two provide a quite rich and
challenging class. For the case of *undirected graphs*, a characterisation of entanglement two has been given by Belkhir and Santocanale [14]. It says that every
undirected graph $\mathcal{G} = (V, E)$ of entanglement at most two can be obtained from
a forest $\mathcal{T}$ by adding, for every edge $\{a, b\}$ of the forest, new vertices $v_1^{a,b}, \ldots, v_m^{a,b}$
with edges $\{a, v_i^{a,b}\}$ and $\{b, v_i^{a,b}\}$ for every i, and possibly deleting the edge $\{a, b\}$.

However, the real interest of entanglement is about directed graphs rather
than undirected ones. We generalise the result of Belkhir and Santocanale to
directed graphs of entanglement two, and we present two structural characterisations and a kind of a tree decomposition of members of this class.

3   Graphs of Entanglement Two

To motivate and give intuition for the class of graphs of entanglement two, we introduce a class $\mathcal{F}$ of graphs (V, E, F) where $F \subseteq V$ is a set of marked vertices. The class $\mathcal{F}$ is defined inductively, as follows:

(1) The graph consisting of one marked vertex and without edges is in $\mathcal{F}$.
(2) $\mathcal{F}$ is closed under removing edges, i.e. if $(V, E, F) \in \mathcal{F}$ and $E' \subseteq E$ then $(V, E', F) \in \mathcal{F}$.
(3) For $\mathcal{G}_1, \mathcal{G}_2 \in \mathcal{F}$ with marked vertices F_1 and F_2, the disjoint union of $\mathcal{G}_1$ and $\mathcal{G}_2$ with marked $F_1 \cup F_2$ is in $\mathcal{F}$.
(4) For $\mathcal{G}_1 = (V_1, E_1, F_1), \mathcal{G}_2 = (V_2, E_2, F_2) \in \mathcal{F}$, their marked sequential composition $\mathcal{G}$ is in $\mathcal{F}$, where $\mathcal{G} = (V_1 \cup V_2, E_1 \cup E_2 \cup F_1 \times V_2, F_1 \cup F_2)$.
(5) For $\mathcal{G} = (V, E, F) \in \mathcal{F}$, the graph $\mathcal{G}'$ with added marked loop is in $\mathcal{F}$, where for a new vertex v,

$$\mathcal{G}' = (V \cup \{v\}, E \cup (F \times \{v\}) \cup (\{v\} \times V), \{v\}).$$

Notice that the rules (2)–(4) add no cycles and do not increase the entanglement. New cycles are created only in item (5), but only between the marked vertices and a new node, which is the only one marked afterwards.

All graphs in the class $\mathcal{F}$ have entanglement two. Before we explain the meaning of the marked vertices F (in Section 4), let us describe a few sub-classes of $\mathcal{F}$ and possible uses for graphs of entanglement two.

A sub-class of $\mathcal{F}$ are trees with edges directed to the root and, additionally, any set of back-edges going downwards. More formally, such trees can be described as structures $\mathcal{T} = (T, E_T \cup E_{back})$ where (T, E_T) is a tree with edges directed to the root and for any back-edge $(w, v) \in E_{back}$ it must be the case that w is reachable from v in (T, E_T). Such graphs have entanglement at most two. A winning strategy for the cops is to chase the robber with one cop until she goes along a back-edge (w, v). Then she is blocked by this cop in the subtree rooted at w. Now the second cop chases the robber until she takes another back-edge, and so on, until she is caught at a leaf.

Another class of graphs included in $\mathcal{F}$ are control-flow graphs for structured programs (that do not use `goto`). Control flow of such programs can be modelled by using sequential and parallel composition (corresponding to items (3) and (4) in the definition of $\mathcal{F}$), and loops with single entry and exit point, which are a special case of item (5) in the definition of $\mathcal{F}$.

Consider for example the graph presented in Figure 1. Removing v_0 from this graph leaves only two non-trivial strongly connected components, namely the v_1-loop and the v_2-loop, and one trivial component consisting of a single vertex.[2] The loops can be decomposed as well by removing v_1 and v_2, respectively, and finally the v_3-loop and the v_4-loop can be decomposed. This decomposition induces a strategy for the cops, who first place one of them on v_0 and then chase

---

[2] We consider only non-trivial strongly connected components, i.e. not single vertices *without self-loops*.

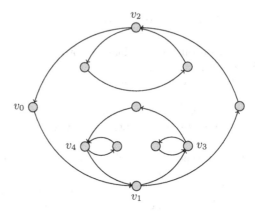

Fig. 1. Example graph of entanglement two

the robber on v_1 with the other cop. If the robber enters the v_1-loop, the cop from v_0 is used to chase him on v_3 and v_4 and so the robber is caught. If the robber does not enter the v_1-loop, the cop from v_1 chases him on v_2 and catches.

As one of our main results, we show in Theorem 11 that a decomposition, generalising the above example, can be found for each graph of entanglement two. As a consequence, we prove in Theorem 12 that graphs of entanglement two can be characterised in a way similar to the above definition of the class $\mathcal{F}$. More precisely, a graph has entanglement at most two if, and only if, each of its strongly connected components belongs to a class $\mathcal{F}'$, which is defined similarly to the class $\mathcal{F}$, but with item (5) changed as follows.

(5') For $\mathcal{G} = (V, E, F) \in \mathcal{F}'$, the graph $\mathcal{G}'$ with added loop is in $\mathcal{F}'$, where

$$\mathcal{G}' = (V \cup \{v\}, E \cup (F \times \{v\}) \cup (\{v\} \times V), \{v\} \cup F'),$$

and F' is any subset of the previously marked vertices F such that $\mathcal{G}[F']$ is acyclic and no vertices in F' are reachable from $V \setminus F'$.

A consequence of our proofs, stated in Proposition 13, is that graphs of entanglement two have both DAG-width and Kelly-width at most 3. This confirms that graphs of entanglement two are simple according to all known graph measures, and strengthens our motivation to study them as the most basic class of graphs where cycles are already nested in interesting ways.

4   Entanglement of Graphs with Exit Vertices

In this section, we introduce a technical notion: the entanglement of a graph with exit vertices, which is crucial for subsequent proofs. To provide intuition for this notion, consider the graph in Figure 1 with the vertex v_0 removed. This graph contains two non-trivial strongly connected components: the v_1-loop and the v_2-loop. The v_2-loop has entanglement one, so it is clearly simpler than the entire graph. On the other hand, the v_1-loop has entanglement two. Nevertheless, we claim that also the v_1-loop is in a sense simpler than the entire graph, despite having the same entanglement. Indeed, observe that not only can two cops catch the robber on the v_1-loop, but they can do it in such a way that the only vertex through which the robber can exit this loop, v_1, remains blocked during the whole play after the robber visits it. This leads to the notion we study here.

In the rest of this section, we focus on strongly connected subgraphs of a graph. Let $\mathcal{G}$ be a graph and $\mathcal{G}'$ a strongly connected subgraph of $\mathcal{G}$. The set $\mathrm{Ex}(\mathcal{G}, \mathcal{G}')$ of *exit vertices* of $\mathcal{G}'$ in $\mathcal{G}$ is the set of all $v \in \mathcal{G}'$ for which there is a vertex $u \in \mathcal{G} \setminus \mathcal{G}'$ with $(v, u) \in E$ (we write $v \in \mathcal{G}$ if $\mathcal{G} = (V, E)$ and $v \in V$).

To study subgraphs that contain exit vertices in a way that is independent of the bigger graph in the context, we say that $\mathcal{G}^*$ is a *graph with exit vertices* when $\mathcal{G}^* = (V, E, F)$, where (V, E) is a graph and F is any subset of V representing the exits. The following notion is used while decomposing a graph $\mathcal{G}$.

Definition 3. *Let $\mathcal{G}$ be a graph and let $v \in \mathcal{G}$. A v-component of $\mathcal{G}$ is a graph $\mathcal{C} = (C, E, F)$ with exit vertices such that (C, E) is a strongly connected component of $\mathcal{G} \setminus v$ and $F = \mathrm{Ex}(\mathcal{G}, \mathcal{C})$.*

In a strongly connected graph $\mathcal{G}$, for a vertex v, let $\leq_v$ be the topological order on the set of strongly connected components of $\mathcal{G} \setminus v$, i.e.

$$\mathcal{C} \leq_v \mathcal{C}' \iff \text{there is a path from } \mathcal{C} \text{ to } \mathcal{C}' \text{ in } \mathcal{G} \setminus v.$$

The *entanglement game with exit vertices* $\mathrm{EG}_k^*(\mathcal{G})$ is played on a graph $\mathcal{G} = (V, E, F)$ with exit vertices in the same way as the entanglement game, but with an additional winning condition for the robber: she wins a play when she succeeds in reaching an exit vertex after the last cop has entered $\mathcal{G}$ from outside. More formally, the robber wins a play if it reaches a position (v, P) such that $v \in F$ and $|P| = k$. (This includes the case when the robber already sits on an exit vertex at the time when the last cop comes to that vertex.) In the context of subgraphs inside a larger graph this new winning condition means that the robber can leave the subgraph and get back to the bigger graph.

We define a variant of the entanglement game to mark the vertex from which a play starts. For $v \in \mathcal{G}$, the game $\mathrm{EG}_k^*(\mathcal{G}, v)$ is played in the same way as $\mathrm{EG}_k^*(\mathcal{G})$, except that the robber does not choose a vertex to start on, but starts on v.

Definition 4. *A graph with exit vertices $\mathcal{G}$ is k-complex if the robber has a winning strategy (which we call a robber $\mathcal{G}$-strategy) in the entanglement game with exit vertices $\mathrm{EG}_{k+1}^*(\mathcal{G})$. If the cops have a winning strategy in $\mathrm{EG}_{k+1}^*(\mathcal{G})$ (called a cops $\mathcal{G}$-strategy), then $\mathcal{G}$ is k-simple.*

First, let us show that existence of a vertex v with only k-simple components gives a bound on entanglement. The strategy for the cops is to place a cop on v and to play in each v-component $\mathcal{C}$ according to their $\mathcal{C}$-strategy.

Proposition 5. *If there is a vertex v in a graph $\mathcal{G}$ such that all v-components are k-simple, then $\mathrm{ent}(\mathcal{G}) \leq k + 1$.*

In the rest of this section, we prove that the converse holds for the case $k = 1$. This will lead to Theorem 7 and form the basis of a structural characterisation of graphs of entanglement two in Section 5. First, we need that for strongly connected components the choice of the starting vertex is irrelevant.

Lemma 6. *Let $\mathcal{G}$ be a strongly connected k-complex graph with exit vertices. Then the robber wins $\mathrm{EG}^*_{k+1}(\mathcal{G}, v)$ for all $v \in \mathcal{G}$.*

To prove the converse of Proposition 5, we need to consider various configurations of complex components. We will show that the existence of certain combinations of 1-complex components implies that the graph has entanglement greater than two. This will be used to show that every graph of entanglement two contains a vertex so that after its removal all components are 1-simple.

Theorem 7. *On a strongly connected graph $\mathcal{G} = (V, E)$, two cops have a winning strategy in the game $\mathrm{EG}_2(\mathcal{G})$ if and only if there exists a vertex $a \in \mathcal{G}$ such that every a-component is 1-simple.*

Proof idea. Proposition 5 shows one direction. For the other one, assume that for every $v \in V$ there is a 1-complex v-component, but the cops can win $\mathrm{EG}_2(\mathcal{G})$. We construct a sequence of vertices a_i and corresponding 1-complex a_i-components C_i that are maximal with respect to $\leq_{a_i}$ such that the intersection of all components is not empty. Every new vertex a_i is taken from the intersection of already constructed components. If, at a stage of construction, the components do not intersect, we have to consider various cases how the components are combined with each other:

- two components that are incomparable with respect to $\leq_v$,
- complex components that do not intersect and contain their respective defining vertices,
- disjoint complex components, one of which is maximal,
- two intersecting components, one of which contains the defining vertex of the other,
- and finally multiple pairwise non-intersecting components.

Every such case leads to a winning strategy of the robber in $\mathrm{EG}_2(\mathcal{G})$, which contradicts the assumption. Because we always take new vertices a_i from the intersection of the already constructed components and $a_i \notin C_i$, the intersection becomes smaller in every construction step and the construction finitely stops. Then we get a case when the robber has a winning strategy, which again contradicts the assumption.

It is clear that the entanglement of a graph is bounded by the entanglement of its strongly connected components, so we have the following corollary.

Corollary 8. *Let $\mathcal{G}$ be a graph. In $\mathrm{EG}_2(\mathcal{G})$, the cops have a winning strategy if and only if in every strongly connected component C of $\mathcal{G}$, there exists a vertex $a \in C$, such that every a-component of C is 1-simple.*

The above fails for graphs of entanglement three or greater.

Theorem 9. *For every $k > 2$ there is a graph $\mathcal{G}_k$ of entanglement k in that, for every vertex a, there is a $(k-1)$-complex a-component.*

5 Decompositions for Entanglement Two

The proof of Theorem 7 shows the structure of a strongly connected graph $\mathcal{G}$ of entanglement two. It has a vertex a_0 such that the graph $\mathcal{G} \setminus a_0$ can be decomposed into 1-simple a_0-components. We can divide them into two classes: *leaf* components, from which one cop expels the robber, and *inner* components, where one cop does not win, but blocks all exit vertices making the other cop free from guarding the simple component. It turns out that every inner component C_0 again has a vertex a_1 such that C_0 decomposes in 1-simple a_1-components and so on. We shall show that a_1 is the vertex where the second cop stays (blocking all exit vertices of C_0) when the first cop leaves a_0. Let us define the decomposition for graphs of entanglement two.

Definition 10. *An* entanglement two decomposition *of a strongly connected graph $\mathcal{G} = (V_G, E_G)$ is a triple $(\mathcal{T}, F, g)$, where $\mathcal{T}$ is a nontrivial directed tree $\mathcal{T} = (T, E)$ with root r and edges directed away from the root, and F and g are functions $F : T \to 2^{V_G}$ and $g : T \to V_G$ with the following properties:*

(1) $F(r) = V_G$,
(2) $g(v) \in F(v)$ for all $v \in T$,
(3) if $(v, w_1) \in E$ and $(v, w_2) \in E$, then $F(w_1) \cap F(w_2) = \emptyset$, for $w_1 \neq w_2$,
(4) for $(v, w) \in E$, $\mathcal{G}[F(w)]$ is a strongly connected component of $\mathcal{G}[F(v)] \setminus g(v)$,
(5) the subgraph of $\mathcal{G}$ induced by the vertex set $\left(F(v) \setminus g(v) \right) \setminus \left(\bigcup_{w \in vE} F(w) \right)$
    is acyclic for all $v \in T$,
(6) no vertex in $\mathrm{Ex}(\mathcal{G}, \mathcal{G}[F(v)])$ is reachable from $\mathcal{G}[\bigcup_{w \in vE} F(w)]$ in $\mathcal{G} \setminus g(v)$,
    for all $v \in T$.

We shall call tree vertices and (abusing the notation) their F-images bags *and g-images* decomposition points.

From the above definition follows that if $(v, w) \in E$ then $F(w) \subsetneq F(v)$ and that if $v \in T$ is a leaf in $\mathcal{T}$ then $\mathcal{G}[F(v)] \setminus g(v)$ is acyclic. Observe further that successors $vE = \{w_1, \ldots, w_m\}$ of each bag v are partially ordered in the following sense: $\{w_1, \ldots, w_m\}$ form a DAG $\mathcal{D}$ such that, for all $w_i, w_j \in vE$, w_j is reachable from w_i in $\mathcal{D}$ if and only if $F(w_j)$ is reachable from $F(w_i)$ in $\mathcal{G}[F(v)] \setminus g(v)$.

Look again at the class of trees with back-edges defined in Section 3. The decomposition of a tree with back-edges $\mathcal{T} = (T, E_T, E_{back})$ can be given as $(T', E'_T, F, \mathrm{id}_{T'})$ where T' is T without leaves, $E'_T = \{(v, w) \mid (w, v) \in E_T$ and v is not a leaf in $\mathcal{T}\}$, and if $v \in T'$ then $F(v)$ is the subtree rooted at v and $g(v) = v$. One can verify that $(T', E'_T, F, \mathrm{id}_{T'})$ is indeed a decomposition of $\mathcal{T}$.

Having defined the decomposition for entanglement two, we are ready to state our two main results characterising directed graphs of entanglement two. An entanglement two decomposition of a graph $\mathcal{G}$ gives raise to a winning strategy for the cops in $\mathrm{EG}_2(\mathcal{G})$. Conversely, if two cops win $\mathrm{EG}_2(\mathcal{G})$ then we can use the characterisation from Theorem 7 to give an entanglement two decomposition.

Theorem 11. *A strongly connected graph $\mathcal{G} = (V, E)$ has entanglement at most two if and only if $\mathcal{G}$ has an entanglement two decomposition.*

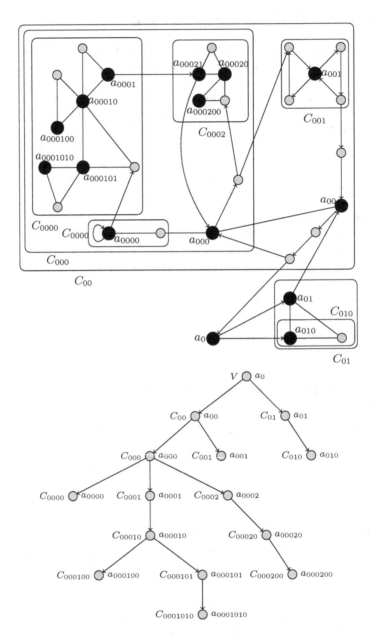

Fig. 2. A typical graph of entanglement two and its entanglement two decomposition. Lines without arrows denote edges in both directions. On the upper picture, the components (images of function F) are shown as squares (only up to level 4), blocking vertices (images of function g) are shown as filled circles. On the picture below, the decomposition tree of the graph is given. The bags are labelled with images from functions F and g.

This theorem allows us to complete the characterisation of directed graphs of entanglement two given in Section 3. But first observe, that there is a connection between the entanglement two decomposition and the characterisations of undirected graphs of entanglement two given by Belkhir and Santocanale [14].

For an entanglement two decomposition of an undirected graph $\mathcal{G} = (V, E)$, consider a connected component, which is an undirected tree $\mathcal{T} = (V_T, E_T)$ with additional vertices (as described in Section 2). Choose an arbitrary leaf $v \in V_T$ as a root. We get a decomposition tree after orienting all edges from E_T (if an edge was deleted, restore it before orienting) away from the root and deleting all leaves other than v. We define the functions F and g as follows: $F(v)$ is V_T and $g(v)$ is v. In general, if, for a bag w, the functions F and g on w are already defined, let $\mathcal{C}$ be a strongly connected component of $\mathcal{G}[F(w)] \setminus g(w)$. Choose a vertex u in $\mathcal{C}$ with an edge between w and u and set $F(u) = \mathcal{C}$ and $g(u) = u$.

Recall the definition of the class $\mathcal{F}'$ in Section 3 for the following theorem.

Theorem 12. *A strongly connected directed graph $\mathcal{G}$ has entanglement at most two if and only if $\mathcal{G} \in \mathcal{F}'$.*

From Theorem 11 it follows that, in time $O(n^3)$ where n is the size of the input graph $\mathcal{G}$, one can not only decide whether $\mathcal{G}$ has entanglement at most two, but also compute an entanglement two decomposition of $\mathcal{G}$. The algorithm proceeds by first looking for a vertex a_0 such that all a_0-components are 1-simple by linear search. The existence of a_0 is guaranteed by Theorem 7. Then the a_0-components are computed. In every component the algorithm finds a vertex a_1 that blocks all blocking vertices of that component. If there is no such a_1, the algorithm returns "robber wins". Otherwise the procedure continues with the vertex a_1 instead of a_0 until there is no a_i-component for some i (i.e. the a_{i-1}-component is of entanglement one). In this case the algorithm returns "Cops win" and the computed decomposition.

6 DAG-Width and Kelly-Width for Entanglement Two

Entanglement two decomposition of a graph leads to winning strategies for three cops in games that correspond to DAG Game and Kelly Game. The DAG Game, described in [1,2], differs from the entanglement game only in these ways:

(1) The robber is infinitely fast (i.e. she can make moves along cop free paths rather than only along edges).
(2) The cops are not restricted to go to the vertex where the robber is.
(3) The robber can stay idle if no cop comes on the vertex she occupies.

DAG-width is the least number of cops needed to capture the robber in a monotone way, i.e. the set of vertices reachable for the robber must be monotonically decreasing.

The Kelly Game is played as the DAG Game, but the robber is invisible, i.e. the cops do not know where the robber is, and inert, i.e. the robber can move only if a cop is about to occupy the vertex where she is. *Kelly-width* is the least number of cops needed to capture the robber in a monotone way.

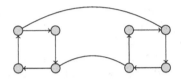

Fig. 3. A graph of entanglement 2 and both DAG-width and Kelly-width 3

Proposition 13. *For any graph* $\mathcal{G}$, *if* $\mathrm{ent}(\mathcal{G}) \leq 2$, *then both the DAG-width and the Kelly-width of* $\mathcal{G}$ *are at most* 3.

Proposition 13 gives the best possible upper bound for the number of cops needed to capture the robber in the same graph in the DAG Game and Kelly Game. Note that the third cop in the DAG Game and the Kelly Game is used to force the robber to move. Figure 3 shows a graph of entanglement two and both DAG-width and Kelly-width three, which is easy to verify.

References

1. Berwanger, D., Dawar, A., Hunter, P., Kreutzer, S.: Dag-width and parity games. In: Durand, B., Thomas, W. (eds.) STACS 2006. LNCS, vol. 3884, pp. 524–536. Springer, Heidelberg (2006)
2. Obdržálek, J.: Dag-width: connectivity measure for directed graphs. In: Proc. of SODA 2006, pp. 814–821. ACM Press, New York (2006)
3. Kreutzer, S., Ordyniak, S.: Digraph decompositions and monotonicity in digraph searching. CoRR abs/0802.2228 (2008)
4. Hunter, P., Kreutzer, S.: Digraph measures: Kelly decompositions, games, and orderings. In: Proc. of SODA 2007, pp. 637–644. SIAM, Philadelphia (2007)
5. Berwanger, D., Grädel, E.: Entanglement — a measure for the complexity of directed graphs with applications to logic and games. In: Baader, F., Voronkov, A. (eds.) LPAR 2004. LNCS, vol. 3452, pp. 209–223. Springer, Heidelberg (2005)
6. Johnson, T., Robertson, N., Seymour, P.D., Thomas, R.: Directed tree-width. J. Comb. Theory, Ser. B 82(1), 138–154 (2001)
7. Eggan, L.C.: Transition graphs and the star-height of regular events. Michigan Math. J. 10, 385–397 (1963)
8. Safari, M.A.: D-width, metric embedding, and their connections. PhD thesis, Vancouver, BC, Canada (2007)
9. Hunter, P.: Complexity and Infinite Games on Finite Graphs. PhD thesis, Computer Laboratory, University of Cambridge (2007)
10. Rabinovich, R.: Complexity measures of directed graphs. Diploma thesis, RWTH-Aachen (2008)
11. Berwanger, D., Grädel, E., Lenzi, G.: The variable hierarchy of the μ-calculus is strict. Theory of Computing Systems 40, 437–466 (2007)
12. Dawar, A., Grädel, E.: The descriptive complexity of parity games. In: Kaminski, M., Martini, S. (eds.) CSL 2008. LNCS, vol. 5213, pp. 354–368. Springer, Heidelberg (2008)
13. Grädel, E., Kaiser, L., Rabinovich, R.: Directed graphs of entanglement two (Full version) (2009), www.logic.rwth-aachen.de/Publications
14. Belkhir, W., Santocanale, L.: Undirected graphs of entanglement 2. In: Arvind, V., Prasad, S. (eds.) FSTTCS 2007. LNCS, vol. 4855, pp. 508–519. Springer, Heidelberg (2007)

Parametrized Regular Infinite Games and Higher-Order Pushdown Strategies

Paul Hänsch, Michaela Slaats*, and Wolfgang Thomas

Lehrstuhl Informatik 7, RWTH Aachen University, Aachen, Germany
paul.haensch@rwth-aachen.de,
slaats@automata.rwth-aachen.de,
thomas@informatik.rwth-aachen.de

Abstract. Given a set P of natural numbers, we consider infinite games where the winning condition is a regular ω-language parametrized by P. In this context, an ω-word, representing a play, has letters consisting of three components: The first is a bit indicating membership of the current position in P, and the other two components are the letters contributed by the two players. Extending recent work of Rabinovich we study here predicates P where the structure $(\mathbb{N}, +1, P)$ belongs to the pushdown hierarchy (or "Caucal hierarchy"). For such a predicate P where $(\mathbb{N}, +1, P)$ occurs in the k-th level of the hierarchy, we provide an effective determinacy result and show that winning strategies can be implemented by deterministic level-k pushdown automata.

1 Introduction

The starting point of this work is the Theorem of Büchi and Landweber [1]. This theorem gives a positive solution to "Church's Problem" on "regular" infinite games. In the simplest setting, we are dealing with a game where two players 1 and 2 choose bits in alternation, first player 1, then player 2, at each moment $i \in \mathbb{N}$. We call $X(i)$ the i-th bit chosen by player 1 and $Y(i)$ the i-th bit of player 2. A sequence $X(0), Y(0), X(1), Y(1), \ldots$ is a play of the game, and it defines (via the concept of characteristic function) two sets $X, Y \subseteq \mathbb{N}$. The winning condition of the game is a regular ω-language, presented in this paper by a monadic second-order formula $\varphi(X, Y)$ over the structure $(\mathbb{N}, +1)$. When a play (X, Y) satisfies this formula over the structure $(\mathbb{N}, +1)$ then player 2 wins the play, otherwise player 1 wins. In a standard way one now introduces the notion of strategy and winning strategy for the two players.

The Büchi-Landweber Theorem states that given a monadic second-order formula $\varphi(X, Y)$ as winning condition, the game associated with φ is determined (i.e., one of the two players has a winning strategy), one can decide who is the winner, and one can construct from φ a corresponding finite-state winning strategy (i.e., a strategy executable by a finite automaton with output).

* Research supported by DFG Research Training Group AlgoSyn ("Algorithmic Synthesis of Reactive and Discrete-Continuous Systems").

M. Kutyłowski, M. Gębala, and W. Charatonik (Eds.): FCT 2009, LNCS 5699, pp. 181–192, 2009.

In the present paper we study a generalized setting in which a fixed set $P \subseteq \mathbb{N}$ is added as a "parameter". So one works in monadic second-order logic over a structure $(\mathbb{N}, +1, P)$ rather than $(\mathbb{N}, +1)$.

There are (at least) two motivations for this model: First, the resulting game can be viewed as an interaction between three agents. In addition to a standard scenario where a "controller" plays against a possibly hostile "environment" which is completely free in its choices, the predicate P represents now a "game context" that has dynamic behavior over time but is fixed and predictable. So one may call the games studied here *two-person games with context*. Secondly, the adjunction of a predicate P to the setting of the Büchi-Landweber Theorem gives a very natural step beyond the regular games, where new phenomena arise.

In [12,13], Rabinovich showed that for recursive P, an analogue of the Büchi-Landweber Theorem holds *if the monadic second-order theory of $(\mathbb{N}, +1, P)$ is decidable*. In this case, determinacy holds again, the winner can be computed, and a recursive winning strategy (rather than a finite-state winning strategy) can be constructed from the winning condition.

The first aim of this paper is to develop a new presentation of Rabinovich's result which rests more on automata theoretic concepts than [12,13]. While in that paper other sources are invoked for central details, we give a self-contained outline, using only standard facts.

Then we refine the claim on recursiveness of strategies in parametrized games, by providing – for a large class of sets P – a tight connection between the "complexity" of P and the complexity of winning strategies. Here we refer to those sets P such that the structure $(\mathbb{N}, +1, P)$ belongs to the "Caucal hierarchy" (of [6]). It is known that in this case the monadic second-order theory of $(\mathbb{N}, +1, P)$ is indeed decidable. A large class of interesting sets P is covered by the hierarchy, among them the powers k^n of a fixed number k, the powers n^k for fixed exponent k, and the set of factorial numbers $n!$. We show, using recent work of Carayol and Slaats [4], that for a set P such that $(\mathbb{N}, +1, P)$ belongs to the k-level of the hierarchy (short: "P is of level k"), a winning strategy (for the respective winner) can be guaranteed that also belongs to the k-th level. More precisely, we use the characterization of the levels of the Caucal hierarchy in terms of higher-order pushdown automata and show that for sets P of level k, winning strategies exist that are executable by deterministic level-k pushdown automata. This gives a substantial improvement over the general property of a strategy to be recursive (computable).

The last section offers a discussion and some open questions; e.g. on those predicates P where $(\mathbb{N}, +1, P)$ does not belong to the Caucal hierarchy but nevertheless the monadic second-order theory of this structure is decidable (for the latter class see e.g. [5,14]).

2 Parametrized Regular Games and Their Solution

We use standard terminology as introduced, e.g., in [9]. By a regular game we mean an infinite two-player game in the sense of Gale and Stewart [8] where the winning condition is given by a regular ω-language. Both players, called 1 and 2, pick in each move an element from a finite alphabet; for notational simplicity we assume here that the alphabet is $\{0,1\}$ for each of the players. (All definitions and results of this paper extend in a straightforward way to the case of arbitrary finite alphabets.) A play is a sequence $X(0), Y(0), X(1), Y(1), \ldots$ where $X(i)$ is supplied by player 1 and $Y(i)$ by player 2. As formalism to express winning conditions we use formulas $\varphi(X,Y)$ of monadic second-order logic (MSO-logic) over $(\mathbb{N}, +1)$; it is known that MSO-logic allows to define precisely the regular ω-languages. So we speak of a regular game. (We use here freely the correspondence between a set P of natural numbers and its characteristic bit sequence χ_P.) When a set P (and a corresponding constant again denoted P) is added, we refer to the structure $(\mathbb{N}, +1, P)$, denote the winning condition sometimes as $\varphi(P, X, Y)$, and speak of a *regular P-game*. A play of this game may be viewed as an ω word over the alphabet $\{0,1\}^3$:

$$
\begin{array}{llcccccc}
\text{Predicate} & 0 & 1 & 1 & 0 & 1 & \ldots & = P \\
\text{Player 1} & 0 & 1 & 0 & 1 & 1 & \ldots & = X \\
\text{Player 2} & 1 & 0 & 1 & 0 & 1 & \ldots & = Y
\end{array}
$$

The aim of this section is a new shape of proof for the following result of Rabinovich [12,13].

Theorem 1. *Regular P-games are determined, and if the MSO-theory of the structure $(\mathbb{N}, +1, P)$ is decidable then the winner can be computed and a recursive winning strategy can be constructed from the winning condition.*

For the proof we use three fundamental results summarized in the following proposition (for details and definitions see [9]):

Proposition 1. (Known Facts)

(a) *Each MSO-formula can be transformed into an equivalent (deterministic) parity automaton.*

(b) *The MSO theory of $(\mathbb{N}, +1, P)$ is decidable iff the following decision problem Aut_P is decidable.*

   Aut_P: *Given a parity (or Büchi) automaton $\mathcal{A}$, does $\mathcal{A}$ accept χ_P?*

(c) *Parity games (even over infinite game arenas) are determined, and the winner has a positional winning strategy.*

Proof (of Theorem 1). We present here a detailed sketch (a full account appears in [10]).

Step 1. Given $\varphi(P, X, Y)$ with fixed interpretation of P, we start with a parity automaton $\mathcal{A}_\varphi$, say with state set Q and $n = |Q|$, that is equivalent to $\varphi(Z, X, Y)$ (i.e. it has arbitrary ω-words over $\{0,1\}^3$ as inputs). First we transform $\mathcal{A}_\varphi$ into a game arena. This just means to split a transition from state p via a triple (b, c, d) of bits into a state q into two transitions: The first takes the "context bit" b and the choice c of player 1 into account and leads from state p to an intermediate state (p, b, c). In this state the bit d supplied by player 2 is processed, and state q is reached. In the states p, Player 1 moves (first in the role of the "context player", then by his own bit) and in the states (p, b, c) player 2 moves. We obtain a finite game arena G_φ. The parity acceptance condition of the automaton is turned into a winning condition over G_φ; the coloring of vertices is inherited from the coloring of the states of the automaton.

Step 2. In a second step we transform G_φ into an infinite game arena which takes into account the fixed choice of the set P. For this we parametrize the vertices p and (p, b, c) by natural numbers, calling the new vertices $(p)_i$, respectively $(p, b, c)_i$. The initial vertex is now $(q_0)_0$. From $(p)_i$ we have an edge to $(p, b, c)_i$ iff in G_φ there is an edge from p to (p, b, c) *and* the bit b indicates correctly whether $i \in P$ or not (being 1 in the first and 0 in the second case). From $(p, b, c)_i$ we have an edge to $(q)_{i+1}$ iff in G_φ there is an edge from (p, b, c) to q. The color of $(p)_i$ is that of p, similarly for $(p, b, c)_i$. Call the resulting game graph G'_φ. Now we have:

> Player 2 wins the regular P-game defined by φ iff Player 2 wins the parity game over G'_φ from its initial vertex.

Note that the game graph G'_φ is acyclic and structured into slices $S_0, S_1, \ldots$, each of which contains only a bounded number of vertices. For $k = 2i$, the slice S_k contains up to $n \ (= |Q|)$ vertices $(p)_i$, and for $k = 2i+1$, the slice S_k contains up to $2n$ vertices $(p, b, c)_i$ (note that b is fixed for given i). In order to have the same time scale in the characteristic sequence χ_P and the sequence of slices, we group the slices into a sequence of pairs $(S_0, S_1), (S_2, S_3), \ldots$ and code this sequence – and hence G'_φ – by an ω-word over an appropriate alphabet Σ. Let us denote by α_φ the ω-word coding G'_φ.

Finally, we note that the transformation of this step can be implemented by a finite automaton, uniformly in P:

Lemma 1. *Given a finite game arena G_φ, there is a finite-state transducer (in the format of a Mealy automaton) which transforms the characteristic sequence of a set P into the corresponding sequence α_φ.*

Step 3. By the memoryless determinacy of parity games, one of the two players has a memoryless winning strategy in G'_φ. From this we obtain the determinacy claim of the Theorem. We now deal with the effectiveness claims and by symmetry focus on player 2 alone. A memoryless strategy for player 2 is a function that maps each vertex $(p, b, c)_i$ to some state $(q)_{i+1}$, i.e. for each i we apply a map from a set with at most $2n$ elements to a set with at most n elements. Let Γ be the finite set of these maps. A memoryless strategy of player 2 is thus coded by an ω-word $\gamma = \gamma(0)\gamma(1) \ldots$ over Γ where $\gamma(i)$ is the map applied at moment i by player 2. It is a straightforward exercise to set up a deterministic parity automaton $\mathcal{T}_\varphi$ that runs on input words over $\Sigma \times \Gamma$ and checks for an ω-word $\alpha_\varphi \circ \gamma := (\alpha_\varphi(0), \gamma(0)), (\alpha_\varphi(1), \gamma(1)), \ldots$ whether γ represents a winning strategy in the parity game coded by α_φ.

Step 4. Invoking the transducer of Lemma 1 of Step 2, we can transform $\mathcal{T}_\varphi$ into an automaton $\mathcal{T}'_\varphi$ that runs over the input alphabet $\{0, 1\} \times \Gamma$ rather than $\Sigma \times \Gamma$. On an input $\chi_P \circ \gamma$, $\mathcal{T}'_\varphi$ computes, using the transducer, the sequence α_φ from χ_P and on $\alpha_\varphi \circ \gamma$ simultaneously simulates $\mathcal{T}_\varphi$. We call $\mathcal{T}'_\varphi$ a "winning strategy *tester*" for φ. Now we have: $\mathcal{T}'_\varphi$ accepts $\chi_P \circ \gamma$ iff γ represents a winning strategy of player 2 in the P-game with winning condition φ.

Step 5. The strategy tester of Step 4 will now be transformed into a nondeterministic "winning strategy *guesser*" $\mathcal{S}_\varphi$ that runs over the input alphabet $\{0,1\}$ only. On the input word χ_P, this automaton guesses a sequence $\gamma \in \Gamma^\omega$ and on $\chi_P \circ \gamma$ works like $\mathcal{T}'_\varphi$. It is obtained in the format of a nondeterministic parity automaton. For convenience we assume it converted into a nondeterministic Büchi automaton $\mathcal{B}_\varphi$.

Proposition 2. *The Büchi automaton $\mathcal{B}_\varphi$ accepts the characteristic sequence of a set P iff player 2 has a winning strategy in the regular P-game with winning condition φ.*

This shows the first effectiveness claim of the Theorem: If the MSO-theory of $(\mathbb{N}, +1, P)$ is decidable, one can decide whether player 2 wins the regular P-game with winning condition φ. It just suffices to apply item (b) of Proposition 1 (of known facts) above.

Step 6. Finally, given that player 2 wins the regular P-game with winning condition φ, we have to construct a recursive strategy for him. In view of Step 5 it suffices to construct effectively an accepting run of $\mathcal{B}_\varphi$ from the assumption that such a run exists. (We use here the fact that the strategy can be extracted from an accepting run of the Büchi automaton.) In terms of MSO-logic, this amounts to the proof of a Selection Lemma: *Assume that the MSO-theory of $(\mathbb{N}, +1, P)$ is decidable. If $(\mathbb{N}, +1) \models \exists Z \psi(P, Z)$ then a satisfying recursive set Z can be constructed (i.e. a procedure that decides for each i whether $i \in Z$).*

We give a proof, following an argument of Siefkes [16], in automata theoretic terminology. It involves the well-known merging relation that was already used by McNaughton [11] in his proof of determinization of Büchi automata.

Let $\mathcal{B}$ be a Büchi automaton with state set S. We call two words $\mathcal{B}$-equivalent (short $u \sim_\mathcal{B} v$) if for each pair s, s' of states, $\mathcal{B}$ can reach s' from s via u iff this is the case for v.

Denote by $P[i, j]$ the segment $\chi_P(i) \ldots \chi_P(j)$ of the characteristic sequence of P. Call two positions i, j *mergable* if there is a $k > i, j$ such that $P[i, k] \sim_\mathcal{B} P[j, k]$. This is an equivalence relation over $\mathbb{N}$ of finite index. We can compute a representative for each merge-equivalence class. For this, one uses the MSO-theory of $(\mathbb{N}, +1, P)$ repeatedly as "oracle", also in order to determine that enough representatives, say $n_1, \ldots, n_m$, have been computed. (Just observe that i and j merge iff $(\mathbb{N}, +1, P)$ satisfies the sentence expressing $\exists z P[i, z] \sim_\mathcal{B} P[j, z]$. We know that all representatives occur up to position k by checking truth of the sentence expressing "$\forall x > k \exists y \leq k : x, y$ merge".)

Again using the MSO-theory of $(\mathbb{N}, +1, P)$ as oracle, we pick a representative n from $n_1, \ldots, n_m$ with the following property: There is a $\mathcal{B}$-run ρ_{acc} on χ_P that visits a certain fixed final state q_f at infinitely many times k that merge with n. (It is clear how to express this property of n.) Note that such q_f and n can be found by a finite search process, due to the finite index of the merging relation and the assumption that an accepting run exists.

Using q_f and n, we construct effectively a run ρ of $\mathcal{B}$ on χ_P visiting q_f infinitely often, thus accepting χ_P. We start out by looking for a position p_0 which merges with n *and* such that q_f is reachable from the initial state q_0 of $\mathcal{B}$ via $P[0, p_0 - 1]$ using a finite run ρ_0. Such p_0 exists by assumption on n. The run ρ_0 will be an initial segment of the desired accepting run ρ. For some $k_0 > n, p_0$ we know $P[n, k_0] \sim_{\mathcal{B}} P[p_0, k_0]$. Hence ρ_0 can be extended such that at position k_0 the same state as that of ρ_{acc} is reached. We can now pick $p_1 > k_0$ such that p_1 merges again with n *and* such that q_f is reachable from q_0 via $P[0, p_1 - 1]$, by a finite run which is an extension of ρ_0. Call this finite run ρ_1. Continuing in this way by successive finite extensions each of which is computable and ends by a final state, we construct the accepting run ρ as desired. By the choice of $n_1, \ldots, n_m$, the number $n \in \{n_1, \ldots, n_m\}$, and the state q_f, we can check for the merge equivalence between n and candidate numbers c by an effective procedure; note that for sufficiently high k we always find that $P[c, k] \sim_{\mathcal{B}} P[n_i, k]$ for some i. So the sequence of numbers $p_0, p_1, \ldots$ is computable if P is recursive. For arbitrary P the sequence is recursive in P.

On the other hand, it is to be noted that the *construction* of this strategy (which is recursive in P) involves an unbounded number of queries to the MSO- theory of $(\mathbb{N}, +1, P)$. These queries are needed for the computation of the above-mentioned paramaters $n_1, \ldots, n_m, n, q_f$. For the original specification φ let p_φ be the corresponding tuple $(n_1, \ldots, n_m, n, q_f)$ of parameters. The function $F : \varphi \mapsto p_\varphi$ captures the complexity of the synthesis problem for the set P; this function (or rather its graph considered as a set S) is Turing-reducible to the MSO-theory of $(\mathbb{N}, +1, P)$. We do not know whether this reducibility relation can be sharpened to tt-reducibility (truth-table reducibility; see [15]). It is known that in general the MSO-theory of $(\mathbb{N}, +1, P)$ is tt-reducible (but not btt-reducible) to the second jump P'' of P ([17]). So for the set S coding the construction of winning strategies we have

$$S \leq_{\mathrm{T}} \text{MSO-theory of } (\mathbb{N}, +1, P) \leq_{\mathrm{tt}} P''.$$

3   Background on Higher-Order Pushdown Automata

In the next two sections we consider sets P such that the structure $(\mathbb{N}, +1, P)$ belongs to the Caucal hierarchy. Caucal introduced in [6] a large class of infinite graphs which can be generated starting from finite trees and graphs applying MSO-interpretations and unfoldings in alternation. The resulting hierarchy is a very rich collection of models each of them having a decidable MSO-theory. In [3] Carayol and Wöhrle showed that the graphs of the Caucal hierarchy coincide with the transition graphs of higher-order pushdown automata. We will develop here a representation of the parameter sets P by higher-order pushdown automata. For this we define a new type of deterministic higher-order pushdown automaton that produces an infinite 0-1-sequence (and hence a set P) as output.

We start with some background definitions, in three stages: We introduce higher-order pushdown systems, higher-order pushdown generators (of sets P), and higher-order pushdown games.

A level-1 stack over a finite alphabet Γ can be seen as a word of Γ^*; the empty stack (written $[\ ]_1$) corresponds just to ε. A *level-$(k+1)$ stack* for $k \geq 1$ is a non-empty sequence of level-k stacks. The empty stack of level $k + 1$ is the level-$(k+1)$ stack containing only the empty stack of level k and is written $[\ ]_{k+1}$. The set of all stacks of some level is written $Stacks_1(\Gamma) := \Gamma^*$ for level 1 and $Stacks_{k+1}(\Gamma) := (Stacks_k(\Gamma))^+$ for level $k \geq 1$.

We define the following partial functions on higher-order stacks called *operations*. On level 1 we have as operations for each symbol $x \in \Gamma$ the operations $push_x$ and pop_x. They are respectively defined on level-1 stacks by $push_x([s_0, \ldots, s_n]_1) = [s_0, \ldots, s_n, x]_1)$ and $pop_x([s_0, \ldots, s_n, x]_1) = [s_0, \ldots, s_n]_1$.

For each level $k+1 \geq 2$, we consider the level-$(k+1)$ operation $copy_k$ which adds a copy of the top-most level-k stack on top of the existing level-k-stacks. We also allow the symmetric operation $\overline{copy}_k$ which removes the top-most level-k stack if it is equal to its predecessor level-k-stack. Formally, these operations are defined on level-$(k+1)$ stacks by $copy_k([s_0, \ldots, s_n]_{k+1}) = [s_0, \ldots, s_n, s_n]_{k+1}$ and $\overline{copy}_k([s_0, \ldots, s_n, s_n]_{k+1}) = [s_0, \ldots, s_n]_{k+1}$. In addition, for each level k, we define a level-k operation written $T_{[\ ]_k}$ allowing to test emptiness at level k. Formally $T_{[\ ]_k}(s)$ is equal to s if $s = [\ ]_k$ and is undefined otherwise.

An operation ψ of level k is extended to stacks of level $\ell > k$ using the definition $\psi([s_0, \ldots, s_n]_\ell) = [s_0, \ldots, \psi(s_n)]_\ell$. We now define inductively $Ops_1 = \{push_x, pop_x \mid x \in \Gamma\} \cup \{T_{[\ ]_1}\}$ and $Ops_{k+1} = Ops_k \cup \{copy_k, \overline{copy}_k, T_{[\ ]_{k+1}}\}$. Moreover, we denote by Ops_k^* the monoid for the compositions of partial functions generated by Ops_k.

Definition 1. *A higher-order pushdown system $\mathcal{A}$ of level k (k-HOPDS for short) is defined as a tuple $(Q, \Sigma, \Gamma, \Delta)$ where Q is the finite set of states, Σ is the input alphabet, Γ is the stack symbol alphabet and $\Delta \subseteq Q \times \Sigma \times Ops_k \times Q$ is the transition relation.*

A configuration is a pair $(p, s) \in Q \times Stacks_k(\Gamma)$. We write $(p, s) \xrightarrow{\alpha} (q, s')$ if there exists a transition $(p, \alpha, \rho, q) \in \Delta$ such that $s' = \rho(s)$.

Now we introduce a notion of regularity for sets of higher-order pushdown stacks which relies on the construction of the stacks by operations. We need "regular" sets of stacks for a new type of tests in deterministic higher-order pushdown automata. This format will be appropriate for the generation of 0-1-sequences (i.e., predicates $P \subseteq \mathbb{N}$).

The notion of *regularity* for (symmetric) operations was introduced independently in [2] and [7]. Observe that from a given level-k-stack a word from Ops_k^* yields a new stack, and a language $O \subseteq Ops_k^*$ a set of stacks. A set of level-k stacks is *regular* if it can be obtained by applying a regular subset of Ops_k^* to the empty level-k stack $[\ ]_k$. We write $OReg_k(\Gamma)$ for the regular sets of stacks of level k.

In the subsequent definition of pushdown automata that produce a 0-1-sequence as output, we refer to a finite family $\mathcal{R}$ of regular sets of stacks. The output alphabet is $\Sigma = \{0, 1, \varepsilon\}$; ε serves as a formal output token for the transitions that do not produce either 0 or 1. By τ we shall denote the identity function on Ops_k, i.e. $\tau(s) = s$ for all $s \in Stacks_k(\Gamma)$.

Definition 2. *A higher-order pushdown sequence generator of level k (short: k-HOPDSG) is a deterministic higher-order pushdown automaton $\mathcal{A}$ of level k with tests in a finite set $\mathcal{R}$ of subsets of $Stacks_k(\Gamma)$ which is given by the tuple $(Q, \Sigma, \Gamma, q_0, \Delta)$ where Q is a finite set of states, $\Sigma = \{0, 1, \varepsilon\}$ is the output alphabet, Γ is the stack alphabet, $q_0 \in Q$ is the initial state, and $\Delta \subseteq Q \times \Sigma \times Ops_k \times \mathcal{R} \times Q$ is the transition relation. The set of tests is defined by $\mathcal{R} = \{T_1, \ldots, T_n\}$ with $T_i \in OReg_k(\Gamma)$ for all $i \in [1, n]$.*

A configuration of $\mathcal{A}$ is again a tuple in $Q \times Stacks_k(\Gamma)$ and the initial configuration is $(q_0, [\ ]_k)$. We write $(p, s) \xrightarrow{\alpha} (q, s')$ if there exists a transition $(p, \alpha, \gamma, T, q) \in \Delta$, such that $s' = \gamma(s)$ and $s \in T$.

The automaton is *deterministic* if for every configuration (q, s) there is at most one transition $(q, \alpha, \gamma, T, p)$ in Δ which can be applied.

An ω-word $\alpha \in \{0, 1\}^{\omega}$ is *defined* by the automaton $\mathcal{A}$ if there exists an infinite run $(q_0, [\ ]_k) \xrightarrow{a_0} (q_1, s_1) \xrightarrow{\alpha_1} (q_2, s_2) \xrightarrow{\alpha_2} (q_3, s_3) \xrightarrow{\alpha_3} \ldots$ such that α is obtained from $\alpha_0 \alpha_1 \alpha_2 \alpha_3 \ldots$ by deleting all occurrences of ε. (Of course, an automaton may produce just a finite word. We focus on the infinite words generated by HOPDSG's.)

The "regular tests" in our level k-HOPDSG's are introduced to obtain a model of computation that is deterministic and generates precisely the sets P such that $(\mathbb{N}, +1, P)$ is in the Caucal hierarchy. Determinism is needed for our game-theoretic context. The automata in the literature have less powerful tests but are non-deterministic. In our model we can restrict to apply a "test" which checks if the operations that follow the current transition can indeed be applied to the current stack. We shall use the tests only in transitions with output ε and then speak of *restricted tests*.

Definition 3. *A set $P \subseteq \mathbb{N}$ is level-k-definable if there is a higher-order pushdown sequence generator $\mathcal{A}$ of level k with restriced tests that defines P.*

Theorem 2. *A structure $(\mathbb{N}, +1, P)$ is in the k-th level of the Caucal hierarchy iff P is level-k-definable.*

As an example for the application of sequence generators, let us describe the idea for a level-2 higher-order pushdown sequence generator defining the set $P = \{2^i \mid i \in \mathbb{N}\}$ of the powers of 2. Note that after output 1 at position 2^i, the next output 1 occurs 2^i steps later at position 2^{i+1}. The idea for the automaton is to remember in its first level 1 stack the current i by the stack content 0^i. Above this bottom-line the automaton can build a tower of i stacks with the contents $0^{i-1}, 0^{i-2}, \ldots, 0$. We can now allow the top symbols of these i stacks to be 0 or 1; so the sequence of $b_1 \ldots b_i$ of top symbols is a binary number (the leading bit corresponds to the bottom stack) which we use to "count" in binary up to 1^i, where of course many steps are needed to proceed from one binary number to the next. When such a new binary number is reached the automaton outputs a 0 (otherwise ε). More precisely, the automaton deletes the stacks with top symbol 1 until it reaches a stack with top symbol 0; it turns it into 1 and goes up again building towers of 0 of decreasing length as at the start:

$$\begin{bmatrix} \mathbf{0} \\ 0\ 1 \\ 0\ 0\ 1 \\ 0\ 0\ 0\ \mathbf{0} \end{bmatrix} \Rightarrow \begin{bmatrix} \mathbf{1} \\ 0\ 1 \\ 0\ 0\ 1 \\ 0\ 0\ 0\ \mathbf{0} \end{bmatrix} \Rightarrow \begin{bmatrix} \\ \\ \\ 0\ 0\ 0\ 1 \end{bmatrix} \Rightarrow \begin{bmatrix} \mathbf{0} \\ 0\ 0 \\ 0\ 0\ 0 \\ 0\ 0\ 0\ 1 \end{bmatrix}$$

Let us continue the example and discuss a regular P-game for $P = \{2^i \mid i \in \mathbb{N}\}$. The winning condition requires that player 2 copies the bits played by player 1 except for the moments $i - 1$ where $i \in P$; in these moments the converse bit is required. An example play won by player 2 could be:

Set P 0 1 1 0 1 0 0 0 1 0 . . .
Player 1   0 1 0 0 1 0 0 1 1 1 . . .
Player 2   1 0 0 1 1 0 0 0 1 1 . . .

It is easy to see that a finite-state winning strategy does not suffice for player 2 to win this game; no finite memory suffices to determine the moments $i - 1$ with $i \in P$. On the other hand, if player 2 has the computational means of a HOPDSG that defines P, he can detect the critical moments without using a look-ahead.

We return to the preparations of main result. In the following we introduce parity games played on the configuration graph of a higher-order pushdown system and a result we need for our main theorem.

Definition 4. *A higher-order pushdown parity game $\mathcal{G}$ of level k (k-HOPDPG) is given by a k-HOPDS $P = (Q, \Sigma, \Gamma, \Delta)$, a partition of the states $Q_0 \uplus Q_1$ and a coloring mapping $\Omega_P : Q \to \mathbb{N}$. The induced game arena is (V_0, V_1, E, Ω) where: $V_0 = Q_0 \times \mathrm{Stacks}_k(\Gamma)$, $V_1 = Q_1 \times \mathrm{Stacks}_k(\Gamma)$, E is the Σ-labeled transition relation of P and Ω is defined for $(p, s) \in Q \times \mathrm{Stacks}_k(\Gamma)$ by $\Omega(p, s) := \Omega_P(p)$.*

Theorem 3 ([4]). *Given a pushdown parity game of level k, we can construct in k-EXPTIME reduced level-k automata[1] describing the winning region, respectively a global positional winning strategy for each of the two players.*

4   Regular P-Games with P in the Pushdown Hierarchy

We now want to show that a regular P-game where P is defined by a higher-order pushdown sequence generator of level k with restricted tests can be solved in k-EXPTIME, and that the winner has a winning strategy which is executable by a level-k pushdown automaton.

Theorem 4. *Let $P \subseteq \mathbb{N}$ be defined by a higher-order pushdown sequence generator $\mathcal{P}$ of level k with restricted tests. The regular P-game where the winning condition is given by a deterministic parity word automaton $\mathcal{C}$ over $\{0, 1\}^3$ is (determined and) solvable: It can be decided who wins the game and for the winner one can construct a level-k HOPDA that computes a winning strategy.*

---

[1] The reduced level-k automata are finite automata running over Ops_k and accepting regular sets of stacks, i.e. sets in $OReg_k(\Gamma)$. See [4] for more details.

In the proof, we first treat solvability and the format of the winning strategy; the statement on complexity is shown afterwards.

Proof. Let $\mathcal{P} = (Q_\mathcal{P}, \Sigma_\mathcal{P}, \Gamma_\mathcal{P}, q_0^\mathcal{P}, \Delta_\mathcal{P})$ be a k-HOPDSG with restricted tests defining P, and let $\mathcal{C} = (Q_\mathcal{C}, \Sigma_\mathcal{C}, q_0^\mathcal{C}, \delta_\mathcal{C}, \Omega_\mathcal{C})$ be a parity word automaton over the alphabet $\Sigma_\mathcal{C} = \{0,1\}^3$ defining the winning condition.

We construct a higher-order pushdown parity game (HOPDPG) $\mathcal{G}_P$, defined by the HOPDS $\mathcal{P}_\mathcal{G} = (Q, \Sigma_\mathcal{P}, \Gamma_\mathcal{P}, q_0, \Delta)$, the state partition Q_1, Q_2 and the coloring Ω, simulating the game between player 1 and player 2 with the external parameter P. The idea is that in $\mathcal{G}_P$ we compute with the help of $\mathcal{P}$, i.e. the level-k stack, the next bit of the sequence χ_P, then let first player 1 choose a bit then player 2. These three bits we store in the state of the current vertex and then compute by $\mathcal{C}$ the color of its vertex. (For this we give $\mathcal{C}$ those three bits as input.) The parity game $\mathcal{G}_P$ is then won by player 2 iff the given regular P-game is won by player 2. Using this allows us to invoke Theorem 3 to solve the game $\mathcal{G}_P$ and compute a winning strategy.

The HOPDS $\mathcal{P}_\mathcal{G}$ works repeatedly in four phases, indicated by the symbols of the alphabet $\Phi := \{\Phi_P, \Phi_1, \Phi_2, \Phi_C\}$. The symbol Φ_P indicates that the next bit of χ_P is computed by $\mathcal{P}$, the symbol Φ_i that player i chooses a bit, and the symbol Φ_C that the next state of $\mathcal{C}$ is computed by evaluating the chosen bits.

The HOPDS $\mathcal{P}_\mathcal{G}$ has the state set $Q = Q_\mathcal{P} \times Q_\mathcal{C} \times \Phi \times \{0,1\}^3$ where for a state $(q_\mathcal{P}, q_\mathcal{C}, x, (b_0, b_1, b_2)) \in Q$ we have that $q_\mathcal{P}$ resp. $q_\mathcal{C}$ is the current state in $\mathcal{P}$ resp. $\mathcal{C}$. Furthermore by the third component we know in which phase of a move we are, and by (b_0, b_1, b_2) we memorize the current bits of χ_P and the last bits chosen by player 1 and player 2. The start state is $q_0 = (q_0^\mathcal{P}, q_0^\mathcal{C}, \Phi_P, (0,0,0))$. The transitions Δ are the following. (Note that the bits b_0', b_1', b_2' are the current choices for χ_P, player 1, respectively player 2.)

- for $(q_\mathcal{P}, \varepsilon, \gamma, T, q_\mathcal{P}') \in \Delta_\mathcal{P}$:
  $((q_\mathcal{P}, q_\mathcal{C}, \Phi_P, (b_0, b_1, b_2)), \varepsilon, \gamma, (q_\mathcal{P}', q_\mathcal{C}, \Phi_P, (b_0, b_1, b_2)))$
- for $b_0' \in \{0,1\}$, $(q_\mathcal{P}, b_0', \gamma, T, q_\mathcal{P}') \in \Delta_\mathcal{P}$:
  $((q_\mathcal{P}, q_\mathcal{C}, \Phi_P, (b_0, b_1, b_2)), b_0', \gamma, (q_\mathcal{P}', q_\mathcal{C}, \Phi_1, (b_0', b_1, b_2)))$
- for $b_1' \in \{0,1\}$: $((q_\mathcal{P}, q_\mathcal{C}, \Phi_1, (b_0, b_1, b_2)), b_1', T, (q_\mathcal{P}, q_\mathcal{C}, \Phi_2, (b_0, b_1', b_2)))$
- for $b_2' \in \{0,1\}$: $((q_\mathcal{P}, q_\mathcal{C}, \Phi_2, (b_0, b_1, b_2)), b_2', T, (q_\mathcal{P}, q_\mathcal{C}, \Phi_C, (b_0, b_1, b_2')))$
- for $\delta_\mathcal{C}(q_\mathcal{C}, (b_0, b_1, b_2)) = q_\mathcal{C}'$:
  $((q_\mathcal{P}, q_\mathcal{C}, \Phi_C, (b_0, b_1, b_2)), \varepsilon, T, (q_\mathcal{P}, q_\mathcal{C}', \Phi_P, (b_0, b_1, b_2)))$

The coloring is given by $\Omega((q_\mathcal{P}, q_\mathcal{C}, x, (b_0, b_1, b_2))) = \Omega_\mathcal{C}(q_\mathcal{C})$ for $x \in \{\Phi_C, \Phi_1, \Phi_2\}$ and $\Omega((q_\mathcal{P}, q_\mathcal{C}, \Phi_P, (b_0, b_1, b_2))) = (2 \cdot n)$ where n is the maximal color in $\Omega_\mathcal{C}$.

The state partitioning is defined by $Q_1 = Q_\mathcal{P} \times Q_\mathcal{C} \times \{\Phi_1, \Phi_P, \Phi_C\} \times \{0,1\}^3$ and $Q_2 = Q_\mathcal{P} \times Q_\mathcal{C} \times \{\Phi_2\} \times \{0,1\}^3$.

The restricted tests which are used in the computation of χ_P, i.e. in the transitions of $\mathcal{P}$ to make the HOPDSG deterministic, are omitted in the game. This can be done because of their special form. Note that in the game $\mathcal{G}_P$ the computation of P is not completely deterministic because we attribute to player 1 the choice of bits for the sequence χ_P. If player 1 chooses such a bit incorrectly, however, then either the current stack operation or one of the subsequent ones will be undefined or he would get stuck in the computation of a later χ_P-bit (here we use the resticted tests). In the case that in a Φ_1-state some operation is not defined on the current stack, player 1 loses immediately; in the second case he will lose because the only color which is seen infinitely often in the game will be even; note that we colored the Φ_P-vertices by an even number that cannot be surpassed; so player 2 wins in this case.

The idea for the construction of the strategy automaton for the player winning the game is similar as above. Assume player 2 wins the game $\mathcal{G}_P$. Then by Theorem 3 we get two regular sets of level-k stacks, say S_0 and S_1 where S_0 contains all configurations[2] where player 2 should take 0 as output and S_1 those where output 1 should be taken.

The strategy automaton is constructed similarly as the automaton $\mathcal{P}_\mathcal{G}$ except that in the transitions with Φ_2 we add as tests once S_0 and and once S_1, which ensure that player 2 takes the right transition. These tests are also used for the output function which outputs the corresponding bit for player 2. — If player 1 wins the game the construction is analogous.

Proposition 3. *The computation of the winner and the winning strategy in Theorem 4 is done in k-exponential time.*

Proof. By Theorem 3 we have a k-ExpTime procedure to compute the winner of the game $\mathcal{G}_P$ and the positional winning strategy for the player winning $\mathcal{G}_P$. As the construction of $\mathcal{G}_P$ is polynomial in the size of the automata $\mathcal{P}$ and $\mathcal{C}$ we have altogether again an algorithm running in k-exponential time to compute the winner of the regular P-game as well as the desired winning strategy automaton.

5 Conclusion

The purpose of the present paper was twofold: First we developed a streamlined proof of a result of Rabinovich [12,13] on regular P-games, using automata theoretic concepts and ideas that go back to Siefkes [16]. The result says that for recursive P, regular P-games can be solved effectively when the MSO-theory of $(\mathbb{N}, +1, P)$ is decidable, and that in this case also a recursive winning strategy for the winner can be constructed.

In the second part of the paper, we considered predicates that can be generated by higher-order pushdown automata (covering a large class of interesting examples) and showed that for such predicates P, regular P-games can be solved with strategies that are again computable by such automata. In this context, we mention some questions.

In natural examples, mentioned e.g. at the end of Section 3, the reference to P in the winning condition involves just a bounded look-ahead on P. In our approach a look-ahead is made superfluous by a corresponding computation from the past, which involves a big overhead. Strategies (maybe even finite-state

---

[2] The state of the configuration (p, s) is stored in the set by pushing it onto the topmost stack, i.e. we have $push_p(s) \in S_0$.

strategies) with bounded look-ahead on P seem to be a natural class, and the range of their applicability should be investigated.

A related question is to decide when a regular P-game where $(\mathbb{N}, +1, P)$ is in the Caucal hierarchy can be solved with finite-state winning strategies.

Finally, one can aim at finding more general frameworks than the Caucal hierarchy as considered here, and develop corresponding more general types of winning strategies (that are more restricted than the recursive strategies).

References

1. Büchi, R., Landweber, L.: Solving sequential conditions by finite state strategies. Transactions of the AMS 138(27), 295–311 (1969)
2. Carayol, A.: Regular sets of higher-order pushdown stacks. In: Jedrzejowicz, J., Szepietowski, A. (eds.) MFCS 2005. LNCS, vol. 3618, pp. 168–179. Springer, Heidelberg (2005)
3. Carayol, A., Wöhrle, S.: The Caucal hierarchy of infinite graphs in terms of logic and higher-order pushdown automata. In: Pandya, P.K., Radhakrishnan, J. (eds.) FSTTCS 2003. LNCS, vol. 2914, pp. 112–123. Springer, Heidelberg (2003)
4. Carayol, A., Slaats, M.: Positional strategies for higher-order pushdown parity games. In: Ochmański, E., Tyszkiewicz, J. (eds.) MFCS 2008. LNCS, vol. 5162, pp. 217–228. Springer, Heidelberg (2008)
5. Carton, O., Thomas, W.: The monadic theory of morphic infinite words and generalizations. Inf. Comput. 176(1), 51–65 (2002)
6. Caucal, D.: On infinite graphs having a decidable monadic theory. In: Diks, K., Rytter, W. (eds.) MFCS 2002. LNCS, vol. 2420, pp. 165–176. Springer, Heidelberg (2002)
7. Fratani, S.: Automates á piles depiles ... de piles. PhD thesis, Université Bordeaux 1 (2005)
8. Gale, D., Stewart, F.M.: Infinite games with perfect information. In: Contributions to the Theory of Games. Princeton University Press, Princeton (1953)
9. Grädel, E., Thomas, W., Wilke, T. (eds.): Automata, Logics, and Infinite Games. LNCS, vol. 2500. Springer, Heidelberg (2002)
10. Hänsch, P.: Infinite games with parameters. Master's thesis, Lehrstuhl für Informatik 7, RWTH Aachen, Aachen, Germany (2009)
11. McNaughton, R.: Testing and generating infinite sequences by a finite automaton. Inform. Contr. 9, 521–530 (1966)
12. Rabinovich, A.: Church synthesis problem with parameters. In: Ésik, Z. (ed.) CSL 2006. LNCS, vol. 4207, pp. 546–561. Springer, Heidelberg (2006)
13. Rabinovich, A.: Church synthesis problem with parameters. Logical Methods in Computer Science 3(4:9), 1–24 (2007)
14. Rabinovich, A., Thomas, W.: Decidable theories of the ordering of natural number with unary predicates. In: Ésik, Z. (ed.) CSL 2006. LNCS, vol. 4207, pp. 562–574. Springer, Heidelberg (2006)
15. Rogers, H.: Theory of Recursive Functions and Effective Computability. McGraw-Hill, New York (1967)
16. Siefkes, D.: The recursive sets in certain monadic second order fragments of arithmetic. Archiv math. Logik 17, 71–80 (1975)
17. Thomas, W.: The theory of successor with an extra predicate. Math. Ann. 237, 121–132 (1978)

Computing Role Assignments of Chordal Graphs*

Pim van 't Hof[1], Daniël Paulusma[1], and Johan M.M. van Rooij[2]

[1] Department of Computer Science, University of Durham,
Science Laboratories, South Road, Durham DH1 3LE, England
{pim.vanthof,daniel.paulusma}@durham.ac.uk
[2] Department of Information and Computing Sciences, Universiteit Utrecht,
PO Box 80.089, 3508TB Utrecht, The Netherlands
jmmrooij@cs.uu.nl

Abstract. In social network theory, a simple graph G is called k-role assignable if there is a surjective mapping that assigns a number from $\{1, \ldots, k\}$ called a role to each vertex of G such that any two vertices with the same role have the same sets of roles assigned to their neighbors. The decision problem whether such a mapping exists is called the k-ROLE ASSIGNMENT problem. This problem is known to be NP-complete for any fixed $k \geq 2$. In this paper we classify the computational complexity of the k-ROLE ASSIGNMENT problem for the class of chordal graphs. We show that for this class the problem becomes polynomially solvable for $k = 2$, but remains NP-complete for any $k \geq 3$. This generalizes results of Sheng and answers his open problem.

1 Introduction

Given two graphs, say G on vertices $u_1, \ldots, u_n$ and R on vertices $1, \ldots, k$ called *roles*, an *R-role assignment* of G is a vertex mapping $r : V_G \to V_R$ such that the neighborhood relation is maintained, i.e., all neighbors of a vertex u's role $r(u)$ in R appear as roles of vertices in the neighborhood of u in G. Such a condition can be formally expressed as

$$\text{for all } u \in V_G : r(N_G(u)) = N_R(r(u)),$$

where $N_G(u)$ denotes the set of neighbors of u in the graph G. An R-role assignment r of G is called a *k-role assignment* of G if $|r(V_G)| = |V_R| = k$. Here, we use the shorthand notation $r(S) = \{r(u) \mid u \in S\}$ for $S \subseteq V_G$. An equivalent definition states that r is a k-role assignment of G if r maps each vertex of G into a positive integer such that $|r(V_G)| = k$ and $r(N_G(u)) = r(N_G(u'))$ for any two vertices u and u' with $r(u) = r(u')$.

Role assignments are introduced by Everett and Borgatti [8], who call them role colorings. They originate in the theory of social behavior. The *role graph* R models roles and their relationships, and for a given society (e.g., a hospital

---

* This work has been supported by EPSRC (EP/D053633/1).

with doctors, nurses and patients) we can ask if its individuals can be assigned roles such that relationships are preserved: each person playing a particular role has exactly the roles prescribed by the model among its neighbors. This way one investigates whether large networks of individuals can be compressed into smaller ones that still give some description of the large network. Because persons of the same social role may be related to each other, the smaller network can contain loops. In other words, given a *simple* instance graph G of n vertices does there exist a *possibly nonsimple* role graph R of $k < n$ vertices in such a way that G has an R-role assignment? From the computational complexity point of view it is interesting to know whether the existence of such assignment can be decided quickly (in polynomial time). This leads to the following two decision problems.

R-ROLE ASSIGNMENT
Input: a simple graph G.
Question: does G have an R-role assignment?

k-ROLE ASSIGNMENT
Input: a simple graph G.
Question: does G have an k-role assignment?

Known results and related work. A *graph homomorphism* from a graph G to a graph R is a vertex mapping $r : V_G \to V_R$ satisfying the property that $r(u)r(v)$ belongs to E_R whenever the edge uv belongs to E_G. If for every $u \in V_G$ the restriction of r to the neighborhood of u, i.e. the mapping $r_u : N_G(u) \to N_R(f(u))$, is bijective, we say that r is *locally bijective* [1,16]. If for every $u \in V_G$ the mapping r_u is injective, we say that r is *locally injective* [9,10]. If for every $u \in V_G$ the mapping r_u is surjective, r is an R-role assignment of G. In this context, r is also called a *locally surjective* homomorphism from G to R.

Locally bijective homomorphisms have applications in distributed computing [2,3,5] and in constructing highly transitive regular graphs [4]. Locally injective homomorphisms, also called partial graph coverings, have applications in models of telecommunication [10] and frequency assignment [11]. Besides social network theory [8,17,19], locally surjective homomorphisms also have applications in distributed computing [6].

The main computational question is whether for every graph R the problem of deciding if an input graph G has a homomorphism of given local constraint to the fixed graph R can be classified as either NP-complete or polynomially solvable. For the locally bijective and injective homomorphisms there are many partial results, see e.g. [10,16] for both NP-complete and polynomially solvable cases, but even conjecturing a classification for these two locally constrained homomorphisms is problematic. This is not the case for the locally surjective constraint and its corresponding decision problem R-ROLE ASSIGNMENT.

First of all, Roberts and Sheng [19] show that the k-ROLE ASSIGNMENT problem is already NP-complete for $k = 2$. The authors of [12] show that the k-ROLE ASSIGNMENT problem is also NP-complete for any fixed $k \geq 3$ and classify the computational complexity of the R-ROLE ASSIGNMENT problem. Let R be a fixed role graph without multiple edges but possibly with self-loops. Then the

R-ROLE ASSIGNMENT problem is solvable in polynomial time if and only if one of the following three cases holds: either R has no edge, or one of its components consists of a single vertex incident with a loop, or R is simple and bipartite and has at least one component isomorphic to an edge. In all other cases the R-ROLE ASSIGNMENT problem is NP-complete, even for the class of bipartite graphs [12]. If the instance graphs are trees, then the R-ROLE ASSIGNMENT problem becomes polynomially solvable for any fixed role graph R [13].

A graph is *chordal* if it does not contain an induced cycle of length at least four. Chordal graphs are also called *triangulated* graphs. This class contains various subclasses such as trees, split graphs and indifference graphs (graphs whose vertices can be assigned some function value such that two vertices are adjacent if and only if their function values are sufficiently close). Due to their nice properties, chordal graphs form an intensively studied graph class both within structural graph theory and within algorithmic graph theory. Sheng [20] presents an elegant greedy algorithm that solves the 2-ROLE ASSIGNMENT problem in polynomial time for chordal graphs with at most one vertex of degree one. He also characterizes all indifference graphs that have a 2-role assignment.

Our results. We provide a polynomial time algorithm for the 2-ROLE ASSIGNMENT problem on chordal graphs. This settles an open problem of Sheng [20]. Contrary to the greedy algorithm of [20], which uses a perfect elimination scheme of a chordal graph with at most one pendant vertex, our algorithm works for an arbitrary chordal graph G by using a dynamic programming procedure on a clique tree decomposition of G. Our second result states that, for any fixed $k \geq 3$, the k-ROLE ASSIGNMENT problem remains NP-complete on chordal graphs.

Paper organization. In Section 2 we explain our notations and terminology. In Section 3 we present a polynomial-time algorithm for solving the 2-ROLE ASSIGNMENT problem for chordal graphs. In Section 4 we show that the k-ROLE ASSIGNMENT problem for chordal graphs stays NP-complete for any fixed $k \geq 3$. Section 5 contains the conclusions and mentions some open problems.

2   Preliminaries

All graphs considered in this paper are undirected, finite and simple, i.e., without loops or multiple edges, unless stated otherwise. For terminology not defined below, we refer to [7].

Let $G = (V, E)$ be a chordal graph. A *clique tree* of G is a tree $T = (\mathcal{K}, \mathcal{E})$ such that $\mathcal{K}$ is the set of maximal cliques of G, and for each vertex $v \in V$ the set $\mathcal{K}_v$ of maximal cliques of G containing v induces a connected subtree in T. It is well-known that a graph is chordal if and only if it has a clique tree, and that a clique tree of a chordal graph can be constructed in linear time (cf. [14]). We refer to a set $K \in \mathcal{K}$ as a *bag* of T. We define the notions *root bag, parent bag, child bag* and *leaf bag* of a clique tree similar to the notions root, parent, child and leaf of a 'normal' tree. If the bag $K_r \in \mathcal{K}$ is the root bag of the clique tree T of G, then we say that T is *rooted at* K_r. Every bag $K \neq K_r$ of the clique tree T has exactly one parent bag K'. We say that a vertex $v \in K$ is *given to* *the parent bag K' if $v \in K \cap K'$, i.e., if v is both in the child bag K and in the parent bag K'. We say that vertex $v \in K$ stays behind if $v \in K \setminus K'$, i.e., if v is in the child bag K but not in the parent bag K'.*

A *hypergraph* H is a pair $(Q, \mathcal{S})$ consisting of a set $Q = \{q_1, \ldots, q_m\}$, called the *vertices* of H, and a set $\mathcal{S} = \{S_1, \ldots, S_n\}$ of nonempty subsets of Q, called the *hyperedges* of H. With a hypergraph $H = (Q, \mathcal{S})$ we associate its *incidence graph* I, which is a bipartite graph with partition classes Q and $\mathcal{S}$, where for any $q \in Q, S \in \mathcal{S}$ we have $qS \in E(I)$ if and only if $q \in S$. A *2-coloring* of a hypergraph $H = (Q, \mathcal{S})$ is a partition (Q_1, Q_2) of Q such that $Q_1 \cap S_j \neq \emptyset$ and $Q_2 \cap S_j \neq \emptyset$ for $1 \leq j \leq n$. A hypergraph H is called *nontrivial* if Q contains at least three vertices. The HYPERGRAPH 2-COLORABILITY problem asks whether a given (nontrivial) hypergraph has a 2-coloring. This problem, also known as SET SPLITTING, is NP-complete (cf. [15]).

3   The Polynomial Algorithm for 2-Role Assignments

In this section, we prove the following result.

Theorem 1. *The* 2-ROLE ASSIGNMENT *problem is solvable in polynomial time for the class of chordal graphs.*

We will start by discussing the different 2-role assignments. Let G be a chordal graph. Following the notation of Sheng [20], the six different role graphs on two vertices are $R_1 = (\{1, 2\}, \emptyset)$, $R_2 = (\{1, 2\}, \{22\})$, $R_3 = (\{1, 2\}, \{11, 22\})$, $R_4 = (\{1, 2\}, \{12\})$, $R_5 = (\{1, 2\}, \{12, 22\})$ and $R_6 = (\{1, 2\}, \{11, 12, 22\})$.

If G contains at most one vertex, then G has no 2-role assignment. Suppose $|V_G| \geq 2$. If G only contains isolated vertices, then G has an R_1-role assignment. If G contains at least one isolated vertex and at least one component with at least two vertices, then G has an R_2-role assignment. If G is disconnected but does not have isolated vertices, then G has an R_3-role assignment.

Now, assume that G is connected and has at least two vertices. If G is bipartite, then G has an R_4-role assignment. If G is non-bipartite, then G has a 2-role assignment if and only if G has an R_5-role assignment or an R_6-role assignment.

We claim that we only have to check whether G has an R_5-role assignment. This is immediately clear if G has a vertex of degree 1, as such a vertex must be mapped to a role of degree 1 and R_6 does not have such a role. If G does not have any degree 1 vertices, we use the following result by Sheng [20].

Theorem 2 ([20]). *Let G be a chordal graph with at most one vertex of degree 1 and no isolated vertices. Then G has an R_5-role assignment.*

We now present a polynomial-time algorithm that solves the R_5-ROLE ASSIGNMENT problem for chordal graphs. From the above, it is clear that this suffices to prove Theorem 1. We start by giving an outline of the algorithm.

Our algorithm takes as input a clique tree $T = (\mathcal{K}, \mathcal{E})$ of a chordal graph $G = (V, E)$. The algorithm outputs an R_5-role assignment of G, or outputs NO if such a role assignment does not exist. The algorithm consists of two phases.

Phase 1. Decide whether or not G has an R_5-role assignment.

In Phase 1, the algorithm processes the maximal cliques of G in a "bottom-up" manner, starting with the leaf bags of T, and processing a bag only after all its child bags have been processed. When processing a bag K with parent K', labels are assigned to the vertices in $K \cap K'$ maintaining the following invariant.

Invariant 1. *Let V' be the set of vertices of G minus those in K and its descendants. If G is R_5-role assignable, then a partial solution on $G[V']$ can be extended to a solution on G if and only if it satisfies the constraints given by the labels of the vertices on $K \cap K'$.*

Each label $L(v)$ contains information about the possible roles that v can get in any R_5-role assignment of G as well as information about the possible roles of the neighbors of v. The possible labels for a vertex v in a bag K are:

$L(v) = 0 \quad$: initial label for every vertex

$L(v) = 1^* \quad$: exactly one vertex with label 1^* in this bag must get role 1, all others must get role 2,

$L(v) = 1 \quad$: v must get role 1, no role restrictions for its neighbors

$L(v) = 2 \quad$: v must get role 2, no role restrictions for its neighbors

$L(v) = 2_1 \quad$: v must get role 2, and at least one neighbor must get role 1

$L(v) = 2_2 \quad$: v must get role 2, and at least one neighbor must get role 2

$L(v) = 1|2 \quad$: v can get either role 1 or 2 without restrictions

$L(v) = 1|2_1$: v can get role 1, or v can get role 2 in which case at least one neighbor must get role 1

$L(v) = 1|2_2$: v can get role 1, or v can get role 2 in which case at least one neighbor must get role 2

Initially, $L(v) = 0$ for every $v \in V$. The label of a vertex can change several times: the arrows in Figure 1 represent all possible transitions between two labels. This figure will be clarified in detail later on. For now, we only note that there no arrows point downwards in Figure 1. This corresponds to the fact that labels in a higher level contain more information than labels in a lower level. For example, if a vertex v in bag K has a label $L(v) = 2_2$ and one of its neighbors in K gets label 2, then we change the label of v into $L(v) = 2$ before processing the parent bag of K. After all, label 2 contains more information than label 2_2, as label 2 contains the information that at least one neighbor of v will get role 2 in Phase 2. Labels changes such as these can also be applied to vertices not in $K \cap K'$, these serve to simplify the algorithm.

The algorithm outputs No if conflicting labels are assigned to vertices in K. The easiest example of this is when K has two vertices with label 1 from different child bags; 1 has no self loop in R_5. Once the algorithm has successfully processed all maximal cliques and no conflicting labels have been created, it concludes that G has an R_5-role assignment and produces such a role assignment in Phase 2.

Phase 2. Produce an R_5-role assignment of G.

An R_5-role assignment of G is constructed in a greedy way satisfying the constraints imposed by the labels. Since Invariant 1 holds, we eventually obtain an R_5-role assignment on G.

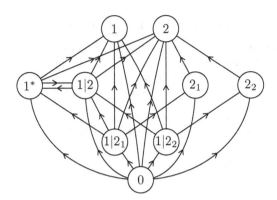

Fig. 1. All possible labels and all possible transitions between them

Before we present the algorithm in detail, we make a useful observation.

Observation 1. *Let $T = (\mathcal{K}, \mathcal{E})$ be a clique tree of a connected chordal graph G, rooted at K_r. For any bag $K \neq K_r$ of T and its parent bag K', we have $K \cap K' \neq \emptyset$ and $K \setminus K' \neq \emptyset$. Moreover, for all K: $|K| \geq 2$.*

Theorem 3. *The R_5-ROLE ASSIGNMENT problem is polynomial time solvable for the class of chordal graphs.*

Proof. Let G be a connected chordal graph, and let $T = (\mathcal{K}, \mathcal{E})$ be a clique tree of G rooted at K_r which we obtain in linear time (cf. [14]). We set $L(u) = 0$ for all $u \in V$ and start with Phase 1. Let K be the bag that is currently being processed. Recall that all child bags of K have already been processed. First assume $K \neq K_r$. So K has a parent bag K'. By Observation 1, at least one vertex in K stays behind, and at least one vertex is given to K'. We shall see that when our algorithm moves to K' then each vertex $u \in K \cap K'$ has $L(u) \neq 0$.

Suppose K is a leaf bag of T. Let v be a vertex that stays behind. If $|K| = 2$, then its other vertex x is given to K'. Because v has degree 1 in G, we must set $L(v) = 1$ and $L(x) = 2_2$, as v must get role 1, x must get role 2, and at least one other neighbor of x must get role 2. Suppose $|K| \geq 3$. We assign label $1|2$ to every vertex in K. We may do so because we can say that v *gives us the freedom to complete any assignment on K*. In other words, if in Phase 2 all vertices in $K \cap K'$ receive role 2, then we assign role 1 to v and role 2 to all remaining vertices of K. If one of the vertices in $K \cap K'$ receives role 1, then we assign role 2 to v and all remaining vertices of K.

We continue with *non-leaf bags* and consider several cases; each dealt with in polynomial time.

Case 1: K contains a v with $L(v) = 1$.
In any R_5-role assignment r of G with $r(v) = 1$, all vertices of $K \setminus \{v\}$ have role 2. Thus, if two vertices (coming from different child bags) in K have label 1, or other vertices in K have label 1^*, we have conflicting labels and output NO.

If $|K| \geq 3$, then we may assign label 2 to every vertex in $K \setminus \{v\}$; as at least two vertices get role 2, all vertices in $K \setminus \{v\}$ will have both a neighbor with role

1 (namely v) and a neighbor with role 2. If $|K| = 2$, then for the only vertex $x \in K \setminus \{v\}$ set $L(x) := 2$ if x had a label in $\{1|2, 1|2_1, 2, 2_1\}$ and set $L(x) := 2_2$ if x had a label in $\{0, 1|2_2, 2_2\}$.

Case 2: K contains a v with $L(v) = 1^*$ and $L(K) = \{0, 1^*, 1|2, 1|2_1, 1|2_2, 2, 2_1, 2_2\}$.
If multiple sets of vertices with label 1^* originate from different child bags, we have conflicting labels and output No. Let $V^* := \{x \in K \mid L(x) = 1^*\}$. We assume that $|V^*| \geq 2$; otherwise replace label 1^* with label 1 and return to Case 1. Because of the vertices with label 1^*, K contains a vertex with role 1 and at least one vertex with role 2. Therefore, we may set $L(x) := 2$ for every $x \in K \setminus V^*$. If $V^* \subseteq (K \cap K')$, then we are done. Otherwise, at least one vertex $v \in V^*$ is left behind. This vertex gives us the freedom to complete any assignment to the vertices in $V^* \cap K'$. Hence, we relabel them to $1|2$. This is so, since if a vertex $x \in V^* \cap K'$ receives role 1, then all neighbors of x (including v) must receive role 2. If all vertices in $V^* \cap K'$ receive role 2, then we can give role 1 to v.

Case 3: K contains a v with $L(v) = 2_2$ and $L(K) = \{0, 1|2, 1|2_1, 1|2_2, 2, 2_1, 2_2\}$.
If K contains any other vertex with label 2, 2_1 or 2_2, then v has its required neighbor and we replace the label 2_2 by 2. Furthermore, if $|K| \geq 3$, then at least one vertex in K will get role 2 and we can also replace the label 2_2 by 2. In both cases, we arrive at another case in this proof which we discuss later on.

The case where $|K| = 2$ remains; let x be the other vertex in K. If $L(x) = 1|2_2$, then we can replace it by $L(x) = 1|2$ since neighbor v will receive role 2. We conclude that by this argument and previous cases $L(x) \in \{0, 1|2, 1|2_1\}$. Now, either x stays behind, or x is given to K'.

If x stays behind, then v is given to K'. The label of x can only be influenced by v. If $L(x) = 1|2$, then x can function as the neighbor with role 2 that v needs, so we may set $L(v) = 2$. If $L(x) \in \{0, 1|2_1\}$, then the fact that none of the neighbors of x will receive role 1 (otherwise x would not have label 0 or $1|2_1$) means we must give x role 1 and leave $L(v) = 2_2$ unaltered. If x is given to K', then v stays behind while it still needs a neighbor with role 2, which can only be x. Hence, we apply the following relabelling to x that forces x to get role 2: $0 \to 2_1, 1|2 \to 2, 1|2_1 \to 2_1$.

Case 4: K contains a v with $L(v) = 2_1$ and $L(K) = \{0, 1|2, 1|2_1, 1|2_2, 2, 2_1\}$.
Similar to the previous case, we can replace any label $1|2_2$ in K by $1|2$. Hence, by the above cases, we may assume that $L(x) \in \{0, 1|2, 1|2_1, 2, 2_1\}$ for every $x \in K$.

Suppose there exists a vertex $x \in K \setminus \{v\}$ with $L(x) \in \{0, 1|2, 1|2_1\}$ that stays behind. This vertex gives us the freedom to change the labels of every vertex $v' \in K \cap K'$ as follows: if $L(v') \in \{0, 1|2, 1|2_1\}$ then we set $L(v') := 1|2$, if $L(v') \in \{2, 2_1\}$ then we set $L(v') := 2$. This is so, since if none of the vertices in $K \cap K'$ receives role 1 in Phase 2, then Phase 2 assigns role 1 to x; otherwise x gets role 2. The latter is fine since v will also receive role 2.

Suppose $L(x) = 2$ for every vertex x that stays behind. For every vertex $v' \in K \cap K'$ with $L(v') = 0$, we set $L(v) = 1|2_1$. We may do this because v' either gets role 1, or gets role 2 in which case it needs at least one neighbor to get role 1. We leave all other labels unaltered.

In the remaining case, at least one vertex with label 2_1 stays behind; w.l.o.g. let this be v. If $K \cap K'$ does not contain a vertex x with $L(x) \in \{0, 1|2, 1|2_1\}$, then we obtain a contradiction (x will never have a neighbor with role 1) and the algorithm outputs No. If $K \cap K'$ contains exactly one vertex x with $L(x) \in \{0, 1|2, 1|2_1\}$, this is the only vertex that can be the role 1 neighbor of v, hence we set $L(x) := 1$. If $K \cap K'$ contains multiple vertices with a label from $\{0, 1|2, 1|2_1\}$, then we set them all to 1^* by the same reasoning. Furthermore, since there will now be a vertex with role 1, we replace any 2_1 by 2 and any $1|2_1$ by $1|2$.

Case 5: K contains a v with $L(v) = 2$ and $L(K) = \{0, 1|2, 1|2_1, 1|2_2, 2\}$.
Since v will receive role 2 and every vertex in K is a neighbor of v, we may change the label of every vertex $x \in K$ with $L(x) = 1|2_2$ or $L(x) = 0$ into $L(x) = 1|2$ or $L(x) = 1|2_1$, respectively. Because of this and the previous cases, we may assume that $L(x) \in \{1|2, 1|2_1, 2\}$ for every vertex $x \in K$. Suppose x is a vertex of K that stays behind with $L(x) \in \{1|2, 1|2_1\}$. Then, just as before, x gives us the freedom to change any label $1|2_1$ in $K \cap K'$ to label $1|2$; x will be the neighbor with role 1 if necessary. Otherwise, if $L(x) = 2$ for all $x \in K \setminus K'$, then we leave all labels in K unaltered; all vertices in $K \setminus K'$ have the required neighbors and add nothing useful to K'.

Case 6: $L(v) \in \{0, 1|2, 1|2_1, 1|2_2\}$ for every $v \in K$.

Case 6a: there exists an $x \in K$ with $L(x) = 1|2$ that is left behind.
If $|K| \geq 3$, then x gives us the freedom to complete any assignment on $K \cap K'$ and we set $L(v) = 1|2$ for all $v \in K$. This is true, because each vertex will get a neighbor with role 2 anyway ($|K| \geq 3$), and if no vertex of $K \cap K'$ gets role 1 in Phase 2, we give role 1 to x. Otherwise, $|K| = 2$; let $K = \{x, y\}$ where y is given to K'. If y will get role 1 in Phase 2, then x will get role 2. If y gets role 2, then it already has a neighbor in K' ($K \setminus K' \neq \emptyset$) with some role and we set x to have the other. Hence, we may set $L(y) := 1|2$.

Case 6b: there exists an $x \in K$ with $L(x) = 1|2_1$ that is left behind.
Suppose $|K| \geq 3$. Using the same arguments as in Case 6a, we can show that we may assign label $1|2$ to every vertex in $K \cap K'$. Otherwise $|K| = 2$. Let $K = \{x, y\}$ where y is given to K'. Notice that if we give y role 1, then we can complete the role assignment by giving role 2 to x. If we want to give role 2 to y, then x will get role 1, since otherwise it has no role 1 neighbor. In this case, the requirements on y depend on the current label of y. As a result, we apply the following replacements for the label of y: $0 \rightarrow 1|2_2$, $1|2 \rightarrow 1|2$, $1|2_1 \rightarrow 1|2$, $1|2_2 \rightarrow 1|2_2$.

Case 6c: there exists an x with $L(x) = 1|2_2$ that is left behind.
If $|K| \geq 3$, then at least one vertex in K gets role 2. Hence we may change the label of x into $1|2$ and return to Case 6a. Thus $|K| = 2$; let $K = \{x, y\}$ where y is given to K'. In this case, y can not get role 1 because then x must get role 2. This is not possible, as then x does not have a neighbor with role 2. We maintain Invariant 1 as follows. If $L(y) \in \{1|2, 1|2_1\}$, then we set $L(y) := 2$. Then x can get role 1. If $L(y) = 1|2_2$, then set $L(y) := 2$ and x will receive role 2. If $L(y) = 0$,

we also set $L(y) := 2$. In that case y needs two neighbors with different roles: in Phase 2 a neighbor of y in K' gets some role. Then we give x the other role.

Case 6d: there exists an x with $L(x) = 0$ that is left behind.
If $|K| \geq 3$ then at least one vertex in K gets role 2. Hence we may change $L(x)$ into $1|2_1$ and return to Case 6b. Thus $|K| = 2$; let $K = \{x, y\}$ where y is given to K'. As x has label 0 and is left behind, x must have degree one in G. Then it must get role 1 while y must get role 2. This leads to the following replacement rules for the label of y: $1|2 \rightarrow 2$, $1|2_1 \rightarrow 2$, $1|2_2 \rightarrow 2_2$. Note that $L(y) \neq 0$, because then we are in a leaf bag.

At some moment we arrive at root bag K_r. Note that we can check in polynomial time if K_r allows an assignment of roles 1 and 2 such that (i) no two vertices in K_r get role 1 and (ii) the labels of the vertices in K_r are satisfied. If we find such an assignment, then we are done by Invariant 1 (which has been maintained during Phase 1). We now start with Phase 2 of the algorithm which follows the reasoning used in Phase 1 in reverse order.   □

Remark. In our polynomial-time algorithm that solves the 2-ROLE ASSIGNMENT problem for chordal graphs we do not have to check if the input graph has an R_6-role assignment (cf. Theorem 2). This is very "fortunate" as the R_6-ROLE ASSIGNMENT problem remains NP-complete when restricted to chordal graphs. This can be seen as follows. Let $(Q, \mathcal{S})$ be a nontrivial hypergraph. In its incidence graph I we add an edge between every pair of vertices in Q. This results in a chordal graph G. It is easy to see that $(Q, \mathcal{S})$ has a 2-coloring if and only if G has an R_6-ROLE ASSIGNMENT.

4   Complexity of the Role Assignment Problem for $k \geq 3$

It is known that the k-ROLE ASSIGNMENT problem is NP-complete for any fixed $k \geq 2$ [12]. Theorem 1 states the 2-ROLE ASSIGNMENT becomes polynomially solvable when the instance graph is chordal. In this section, we show that the problem for chordal graphs gets NP-complete again when k jumps to 3. Our NP-completeness construction is more involved than the one for general graphs in [12] as the latter is not chordal.

Theorem 4. *For $k \geq 3$, the k-ROLE ASSIGNMENT problem is NP-complete for the class of chordal graphs.*

Proof. Let $k \geq 3$. We use a reduction from HYPERGRAPH 2-COLORING. Let $(Q, \mathcal{S})$ be a nontrivial hypergraph with incidence graph I.

We modify I as follows. Firstly, we add an edge between any two vertices in Q; so Q becomes a clique. Secondly, for each $S \in \mathcal{S}$ we take a path $P^S = p_1^S \cdots p_{k-2}^S$ and connect it to S by the edge $p_{k-2}^S S$; so these new paths P^S are pendant paths in the resulting graph. Thirdly, we add a copy H^q of a new graph H for each $q \in Q$. Before we explain how to do this, we first define H. Start with a path $u_1 u_2 \cdots u_{2k-4}$. Then take a complete graph on four vertices a, b, c, d, and a complete graph on four vertices w, x, y, z. Add the edges $cu_1, du_1, u_{2k-4}w, u_{2k-4}x$.

We then take three paths $S = s_1 \cdots s_{k-2}$, $T = t_1 \cdots t_{k-2}$ and $T' = t'_1 \cdots t'_{k-2}$, and we add the edges $s_{k-2}w, ct_{k-2}, dt'_{k-2}$. This finishes the construction of H. We connect a copy H^q to q via the edge qu_1^q, where u_1^q is the copy of the vertex u_1. We call the resulting graph G; notice that this is a connected chordal graph. See Figure 2 for an example.

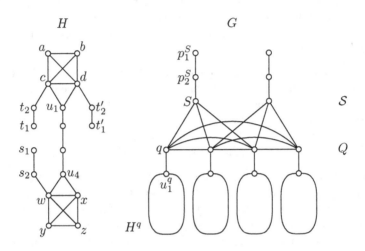

Fig. 2. The graph H (left side) and the graph G (right side) when $k = 4$

We first show that if G has a k-role assignment r, then it has an R^*-role assignment, where R^* denotes the path $r_1 \cdots r_k$ on k vertices with a self-loop in vertices r_{k-1} and r_k. To see this, consider a copy H^q of H in G; we show that we can assign roles to the vertices of H^q in only one way. For convenience, we denote the vertices of H^q without the superscript q.

Note that r must map an induced path of length smaller than k in G to an induced path of the same length in R. Otherwise, r is not a k-role assignment. Hence, we may write $r(t_i) = i$ for $i = 1, \ldots, k-2$ and $r(c) = k-1$. This implies that a vertex with role 1 only has vertices with role 2 in its neighborhood and a vertex with role i for $2 \le i \le k-2$ only has vertices with role $i-1$ and role $i+1$ as neighbors. Then a vertex with role k can only be adjacent to vertices with role $k-1$ or role k. Hence c must have a neighbor with role k.

Suppose $r(d) = k$. Then $r(t'_{k-2}) \in \{k-1, k\}$ and this eventually leads to $r(t'_1) \ge 2$ without a neighbor of role $r(t'_1) - 1$ for t'_1. This is not possible. Hence $r(d) \ne k$. This means that $k \in r(\{a, b, u_1\})$. Since a, b, u_1 are neighbors of d as well and a vertex with role k can only have neighbors with role $k-1$ and k, we then find that d has role $k-1$.

The above implies that a and b have their role in $\{k-2, k-1, k\}$. Suppose $k = 3$. If $r(a) = 1$, then $r(b) = 2$ implying that r is a 2-role assignment (as $r(c) = r(d) = 2$). Suppose $r(a) = 2$. Then a needs a neighbor with role 1. Hence $r(b) = 1$, but then r is a 2-role assignment. Suppose $r(a) = 3$. Then $r(b) \ne 2$, as otherwise b needs a neighbor with role 1. Hence $r(b) = 3$. This means that r is an R^*-role assignment. Suppose $k \geq 4$. If $r(a) = k - 2$, then a needs a neighbor with role $k - 3$. So, $r(b) = k - 3$. However, this is not possible since vertex b with role $k - 3$ is adjacent to vertex c with role $k - 1$. If $r(a) = k - 1$, then $r(b) = k - 2$. This is not possible either. Hence $r(a) = k$ and for the same reasons $r(b) = k$. Then r is an R^*-role assignment.

We claim that $(Q, \mathcal{S})$ has a 2-coloring if and only if G has a k-role assignment.

Suppose $(Q, \mathcal{S})$ has a 2-coloring (Q_1, Q_2). We show that G has an R^*-role assignment, which is a k-role assignment. We assign role i to each p_i^S for $i = 1, \ldots, k - 2$ and role $k - 1$ to each $S \in \mathcal{S}$. As $(Q, \mathcal{S})$ is nontrivial, either Q_1 or Q_2, say Q_2, has size at least two. Then we assign role $k - 1$ to each $q \in Q_1$ and role $k - 2$ to neighbor u_1^q. We assign role k to each $q \in Q_2$ and $k - 1$ to neighbor u_1^q. As $|Q_2| \geq 2$, every vertex in Q has a neighbor with role k. Hence, we can finish off the role assignment by assigning roles to the remaining vertices of each copy H^q of H as follows. For convenience, we remove the superscript q. We map each path S, T, T' to the path $1 \cdots k - 2$, where $r(s_i) = r(t_i) = r(t_i') = i$ for $i = 1, \ldots, k - 2$. If u_1 received role $k - 2$ we assign u_i role $k - 1 - i$ for $i = 2, \ldots, k - 2$ and we assign u_{k-2+i} role $i + 1$ for $i = 1, \ldots, k - 2$. Furthermore, we assign role $k - 1$ to c, d, w, and role k to a, b, x, y, z. If u_1 received role $k - 1$, it already has a neighbor with role k (namely its neighbor in Q). Then we assign u_i role $k - i$ for $i = 2, \ldots, k - 1$ and we assign u_{k-1+i} role $i + 1$ for $i = 1, \ldots, k - 3$. Furthermore, we assign role $k - 1$ to c, d, w, x, and role k to a, b, y, z.

To prove the reverse statement, suppose G has a k-role assignment r. As we have shown above, by construction, G must have an R^*-role assignment. Then each p_i^S must have role i for $i = 1, \ldots, k - 2$. Then $r(S) = k - 1$ for each $S \in \mathcal{S}$, and each S must have a neighbor in Q with role $k - 1$ and a neighbor in Q with role k. We define $Q_1 = \{q \in Q \mid r(q) = k - 1\}$ and $Q_2 = Q \backslash Q_1$. Then we find that (Q_1, Q_2) is a 2-coloring of $(Q, \mathcal{S})$. This completes the proof of Theorem 4. $\square$

5   Conclusions

We have settled an open problem of Sheng [20] by showing that it can be decided in polynomial time if a chordal graph has a k-role assignment when $k = 2$. We also showed that for any fixed $k \geq 3$ the problem stays NP-complete when restricted to chordal graphs.

Role assignments are also studied in topological graph theory. There, a graph G is called an *emulator* of a graph R if G has an R-role assignment. Then the question is which graphs allow planar emulators, see e.g. the recent manuscript [18] for nice developments in this area. An interesting question is the computational complexity of the k-ROLE ASSIGNMENT problem for planar graphs. The answer to this question is already unknown for $k = 2$.

Acknowledgements. The second author thanks Jiří Fiala for fruitful discussions on the subject.

References

1. Abello, J., Fellows, M.R., Stillwell, J.C.: On the complexity and combinatorics of covering finite complexes. Australian Journal of Combinatorics 4, 103–112 (1991)
2. Angluin, D.: Local and global properties in networks of processors. In: 12th ACM Symposium on Theory of Computing, pp. 82–93 (1980)
3. Angluin, D., Gardiner, A.: Finite common coverings of pairs of regular graphs. Journal of Combinatorial Theory B 30, 184–187 (1981)
4. Biggs, N.: Constructing 5-arc transitive cubic graphs. Journal of London Mathematical Society II 26, 193–200 (1982)
5. Bodlaender, H.L.: The classification of coverings of processor networks. Journal of Parallel Distributed Computing 6, 166–182 (1989)
6. Chalopin, J., Métivier, Y., Zielonka, W.: Local computations in graphs: the case of cellular edge local computations. Fundamenta Informaticae 74, 85–114 (2006)
7. Diestel, R.: Graph Theory, 3rd edn. Springer, Heidelberg (2005)
8. Everett, M.G., Borgatti, S.: Role colouring a graph. Mathematical Social Sciences 21, 183–188 (1991)
9. Fiala, J., Kratochvíl, J.: Complexity of partial covers of graphs. In: Eades, P., Takaoka, T. (eds.) ISAAC 2001. LNCS, vol. 2223, pp. 537–549. Springer, Heidelberg (2001)
10. Fiala, J., Kratochvíl, J.: Partial covers of graphs. Discussiones Mathematicae Graph Theory 22, 89–99 (2002)
11. Fiala, J., Kratochvíl, J., Kloks, T.: Fixed-parameter complexity of λ-labelings. Discrete Applied Mathematics 113, 59–72 (2001)
12. Fiala, J., Paulusma, D.: A complete complexity classification of the role assignment problem. Theoretical Computer Science 349, 67–81 (2005)
13. Fiala, J., Paulusma, D.: Comparing universal covers in polynomial time. Theory of Computing Systems (to appear)
14. Galinier, P., Habib, M., Paul, C.: Chordal graphs and their clique graphs. In: Nagl, M. (ed.) WG 1995. LNCS, vol. 1017, pp. 358–371. Springer, Heidelberg (1995)
15. Garey, M.R., Johnson, D.S.: Computers and Intractability. W.H. Freeman and Co., New York (1979)
16. Kratochvíl, J., Proskurowski, A., Telle, J.A.: Covering regular graphs. Journal of Combinatorial Theory B 71, 1–16 (1997)
17. Pekeč, A., Roberts, F.S.: The role assignment model nearly fits most social networks. Mathematical Social Sciences 41, 275–293 (2001)
18. Rieck, Y., Yamashita, Y.: Finite planar emulators for $K_{4,5} - 4K_2$ and Fellows' conjecture. Manuscript (2009), arXiv:0812.3700v2
19. Roberts, F.S., Sheng, L.: How hard is it to determine if a graph has a 2-role assignment? Networks 37, 67–73 (2001)
20. Sheng, L.: 2-Role assignments on triangulated graphs. Theoretical Computer Science 304, 201–214 (2003)

Three-Valued Abstractions of Markov Chains: Completeness for a Sizeable Fragment of PCTL

Michael Huth, Nir Piterman, and Daniel Wagner

Department of Computing
Imperial College London
London, SW7 2AZ, United Kingdom
{m.huth,nir.piterman,dwagner}@doc.ic.ac.uk

Abstract. Three-valued Markov chains and their PCTL semantics abstract – via probabilistic simulations – labeled Markov chains and their usual PCTL semantics. This abstraction framework is *complete* for a PCTL formula if all labeled Markov chains that satisfy said formula have a finite-state abstraction that satisfies it in its abstract semantics. We show that not all PCTL formulae are complete for this abstraction framework. But PCTL formulae whose path modalities occur in a suitable combination of negation polarity and threshold type are proved to be complete, where abstractions are bounded, 3-valued unfoldings of their concrete labeled Markov chains. This set of complete PCTL formulae subsumes widely used PCTL patterns.

1 Introduction

Markov chains are an important modeling formalism for systems that contain stochastic uncertainty and for which the assumption of the "Markov property" (that the transition probability at a state depends only on that state and not on the execution history of the system) is feasible. Markov chains are used in a wide range of applications, e.g., biological sequence analysis, statistical software testing, and formal verification of communication protocols.

In formal verification, we want to validate a system model (and so hopefully the system, too) by proving that it satisfies critical properties. In the context of Markov chains as models, probabilistic computation tree logic [1] has emerged as the defacto standard for expressing such properties. The semantics of that probabilistic logic over Markov chains also renders algorithms for automatically deciding the truth of formulae over *finite-state* Markov chains, leading to the now mature and established methodology of *probabilistic model checking* [2].

But the initial models of systems often have infinitely many states. A system state, e.g., may implicitly encode the value of a continuous-time clock. Since we ultimately want to validate critical properties on systems and not on models, this begs the question of whether truth of some property on an infinite-state system or model can, in principal, be witnessed as truth of that same property on a suitable finite-state model. Suitability here means that the obtained model

M. Kutyłowski, M. Gębala, and W. Charatonik (Eds.): FCT 2009, LNCS 5699, pp. 205–216, 2009.

abstracts certain features of the system but still contains sufficient state and behavior of the system it intends to model.

We therefore study the feasibility of this approach in a formal setting, where systems are identified with infinite-state Markov chains and abstractions are finite-state Markov chains with 3-valued atomic observables such that abstraction is based on probabilistic simulation [3,4]. In this setting, we show negative and positive existence results for finite-state witnesses of truth that depend on the interplay between path modalities (e.g., "true at all reachable states") and threshold types (e.g., "true with probability at least .999"). As we will demonstrate, these results suggest that – from a *practical* perspective – finite-state abstractions for probabilistic computation tree logic and Markov chains more often than not exist. But there may not be an algorithm for computing them.

Related work. In [5], Markov chains and their PCTL semantics are soundly abstracted into 3-valued models, and a model checking algorithm is given for their 3-valued abstract semantics of PCTL. This gives a foundation for counter-example guided abstraction refinement where abstractions have intervals (not real numbers) as probability transitions.

In [6], game-theoretic foundations for truth of PCTL formulae ϕ over Markov chains M are developed. A Hintikka game for ϕ and M, with Büchi type acceptance conditions for infinite plays, is designed so that a "Verifier" player has a winning strategy if M satisfies ϕ. Dually, a "Refuter" player has a winning strategy if M doesn't satisfy ϕ. In loc. cit. it is also observed that a winning strategy could be chosen so that it forces always finite plays for certain path modalities. This insight provides the seed for the results reported here. But proving these results doesn't require any appeal to the games and results of loc. cit.

In [7], stochastic 2-player games are used as abstractions of Markov decision processes (MDPs) and a game simulation is developed and shown to be sound for PCTL. Interestingly, they also show incompleteness in the sense of our paper (for finite games) for the PCTL formula $[\text{tt}Uq]_{>0}$, which *is* expressible in our complete fragment. This contradiction is only apparent since the incompleteness of that formula results solely from the non-determinism in MDPs whereas our work considers Markov chains, which are deterministic.

Outline of paper. In Section 2, we provide the background – notably our abstraction framework – needed for our technical development. The key concept of "completeness" for our abstraction framework and our incompleteness results are presented in Section 3. Completeness results for a fragment of PCTL are presented in Section 4. In Section 5, we put negative and positive results into context and conclude the paper.

2   Background

We define the models of systems considered here.

Definition 1 (Markov chains). *A 3-valued, labeled Markov chain M over a countable set* AP *of atomic propositions is a tuple* $(S, \mathbf{P}, L)$, *where*

1. S *is a countable set of* states,
2. $\mathbf{P}$ *is a* stochastic matrix $\mathbf{P}: S \times S \longrightarrow [0,1]$ *such that the countable sum* $\sum_{s' \in S} \mathbf{P}(s, s')$ *exists and equals 1 for all* $s \in S$,
3. *and* L *is a labeling function* $L: S \times \mathsf{AP} \longrightarrow \{\mathsf{tt}, \mathsf{?}, \mathsf{ff}\}$.

M *is* finitely branching *if* $\{s' \mid \mathbf{P}(s, s') > 0\}$ *is finite for all* $s \in S$. *We write* (M, s_0) *to denote that* M *has a designated initial state* s_0.

Throughout we refer to 3-valued, labeled Markov chains as *models*. Such models can be seen as (possibly infinite) labeled graphs where the outgoing transitions of state s to states s' are decorated with the positive transition probabilities $\mathbf{P}(s, s')$ of the corresponding distribution $\mathbf{P}(s, \cdot)$, and vertices $s \in S$ are labeled with atomic propositions as follows: label $\mathsf{q}?$ marks the states s with $L(s, \mathsf{q}) = \mathsf{?}$, label q at s indicates $L(s, \mathsf{q}) = \mathsf{tt}$, and absence of any q or $\mathsf{q}?$ label at state s implicitly marks $L(s, \mathsf{q}) = \mathsf{ff}$. When all labels for M have value tt or ff, we call model M a *Markov chain, concrete* or *2-valued*. Thus $\mathsf{?}$ abstracts both tt and ff in the familiar information ordering [9].

A widely used notion of probabilistic (bi-)simulation was defined by Larsen and Skou in [3] for probabilistic processes with actions. We define *probabilistic simulation* for our 3-valued models, based on probabilistic simulation for *probabilistic specification systems* with propositional labels in [4].

Definition 2 (Probabilistic simulation). *Let* $M = (S, \mathbf{P}, L)$ *be a model over* AP. *Relation* $H \subseteq S \times S$ *is a* probabilistic simulation *if whenever* $(t, s) \in H$ *then*

1. $L(t, \mathsf{q}) \neq \mathsf{?}$ *implies* $L(t, \mathsf{q}) = L(s, \mathsf{q})$ *for all* $\mathsf{q} \in \mathsf{AP}$.
2. *there is a weight function* $\rho_s: S \times S \longrightarrow [0,1]$ *such that*
   (a) $\sum_{s' \in S} (\mathbf{P}(s, s') \cdot \rho_s(s', t')) = \mathbf{P}(t, t')$ *for all* $t' \in S$;
   (b) $(t', s') \in H$ *whenever* $\rho_s(s', t') > 0$.

We often write tHs *for* $(t, s) \in H$, *and say that* t simulates s, *written* $t \preceq s$, *if there is a probabilistic simulation* H *such that* tHs. *Model* A simulates *model* M, *written* $A \preceq M$, *if this is true of their respective initial states in the model* $A + M$ *that is the disjoint sum of the models* A *and* M.

Definition 3 (PCTL syntax). *The syntax of PCTL is as follows:*

$$\phi ::= \mathsf{q} \mid \neg\phi \mid \phi \wedge \phi \mid \phi \vee \phi \mid [\alpha]_{\bowtie p} \quad \text{(state formulae)}$$
$$\alpha ::= \mathsf{X}\phi \mid \phi \mathsf{U}^{\leq k}\phi \mid \phi \mathsf{W}^{\leq k}\phi \quad \text{(path formulae)}$$

where $\mathsf{q} \in \mathsf{AP}$, $p \in [0,1]$, $\bowtie \in \{<, \leq, \geq, >\}$ *and* $k \in \mathbb{N} \cup \{\infty\}$. *Let PCTL be the set of* state formulae ϕ *generated in this manner. We write* tt *and* ff *for any PCTL formulae* $[\alpha]_{\geq 0}$ *and* $[\alpha]_{>1}$, *respectively.*

Intuitively, $[\alpha]_{\bowtie p}$ specifies the property that the probability of all paths (infinite sequences of states $s_0 s_1 \ldots$ with positive transition probabilities $\mathbf{P}(s_i, s_{i+1})$) that begin at state s and satisfy path formula α is $\bowtie p$. The path modalities X, U, and W stand for Next, Strong Until, and Weak Until (respectively). The value

- $\pi \vDash^m \mathsf{X}\phi$ iff $s_1 \in [\![\phi]\!]_M^m$
- $\pi \vDash^m \phi U^{\leq k}\psi$ iff there is an $l \in \mathbb{N}$ such that $l \leq k$, $s_l \in [\![\psi]\!]_M^m$ and for all $0 \leq j < l$ we have $s_j \in [\![\phi]\!]_M^m$
- $\pi \vDash^m \phi \mathsf{W}^{\leq k}\psi$ iff for all $l \in \mathbb{N}$ such that $0 \leq l \leq k$ we have either $s_l \in [\![\phi]\!]_M^m$ or there is $0 \leq j \leq l$ with $s_j \in [\![\psi]\!]_M^m$

Fig. 1. Path-formula semantics on paths $\pi = s_0 s_1 \ldots$ in interpretation $m \in \{\mathsf{o}, \mathsf{p}\}$

$k = \infty$ is used to express unbounded Untils, whereas $k \in \mathbb{N}$ expresses a proper step bound on Untils. We write $\phi U \phi$ as a shorthand for $\phi U^{\leq \infty}\phi$, and $\phi \mathsf{W} \phi$ as shorthand for $\phi \mathsf{W}^{\leq \infty} \phi$. For example, $\mathsf{X}\mathsf{q}$ holds in paths whose second (next) state satisfies q, whereas $\mathsf{q}U\mathsf{r}$ holds in paths that have a finite prefix of states satisfying q followed by a state satisfying r, and $\mathsf{q}\mathsf{W}\mathsf{r}$ holds in paths that either satisfy $\mathsf{q}U\mathsf{r}$ or where all states satisfy q.

We define semantics for PCTL formulae based on an optimistic and a pessimistic interpretation of labels [10,11]. Optimistically, we interpret a proposition as true if it isn't false, i.e. $[\![\mathsf{q}]\!]_M^{\mathsf{o}} = \{s \in S \mid L(s,\mathsf{q}) \neq \mathsf{ff}\}$; pessimistically, q is true only if the labeling says so, i.e. $[\![\mathsf{q}]\!]_M^{\mathsf{p}} = \{s \in S \mid L(s,\mathsf{q}) = \mathsf{tt}\}$.

Definition 4 (PCTL semantics). *Let $m \in \{\mathsf{o}, \mathsf{p}\}$ be two modes of interpretation, $\neg \mathsf{o} = \mathsf{p}$, and $\neg \mathsf{p} = \mathsf{o}$. For ϕ in PCTL, we define $[\![\phi]\!]_M^m$:*

$$[\![\phi \wedge \psi]\!]_M^m = [\![\phi]\!]_M^m \cap [\![\psi]\!]_M^m \qquad\qquad [\![\phi \vee \psi]\!]_M^m = [\![\phi]\!]_M^m \cup [\![\psi]\!]_M^m$$

$$[\![\neg\phi]\!]_M^m = S \setminus [\![\phi]\!]_M^{\neg m} \qquad\qquad [\![[\alpha]_{\bowtie p}]\!]_M^m = \{s \in S \mid \mathsf{Prob}_M^m(s,\alpha) \bowtie p\}$$

where $\mathsf{Prob}_M^m(s,\alpha)$ is the probability of the measurable set $\mathsf{Path}^m(s,\alpha)$ of paths $\pi = s_0 s_1 \ldots$ in M that begin in $s_0 = s$ and satisfy $\pi \vDash^m \alpha$, defined in Figure 1.

We often write $M^s \vDash^m \phi$ for $s \in [\![\phi]\!]_M^m$ and use $M \vDash^m \phi$ as abbreviation of $M^{s_0} \vDash^m \phi$ for initial state s_0. For 2-valued Markov chains $\vDash^{\mathsf{o}}$ equals $\vDash^{\mathsf{p}}$ and coincides with the familiar and standard PCTL semantics $\vDash$ over Markov chains.

The interpretation m is sound in that verifications of ϕ by $\vDash^{\mathsf{p}}$ on A ($A \vDash^{\mathsf{p}} \phi$) and refutations of ϕ by $\vDash^{\mathsf{o}}$ on A ($A \nvDash^{\mathsf{o}} \phi$) are verifications, respectively refutations, in any concrete M with $A \preceq M$. This soundness requires that PCTL formulae are presented in a particular normalform in which negations occur only on atomic propositions and where probability thresholds are either $\geq$ or $>$:

Definition 5 (Greater-than negation normal form). *The following subset of PCTL constitutes the* Greater-than negation normal form *(GTNNF):*

$$\phi ::= \mathsf{q} \mid \neg\mathsf{q} \mid \phi \wedge \phi \mid \phi \vee \phi \mid [\alpha]_{\bowtie p}$$

$$\alpha ::= \mathsf{X}\phi \mid \phi U^{\leq k}\phi \mid \phi \mathsf{W}^{\leq k}\phi$$

where $\mathsf{q} \in \mathsf{AP}$, $p \in [0,1]$, $\bowtie \in \{\geq, >\}$ and $k \in \mathbb{N} \cup \{\infty\}$.

Every formula ϕ of PCTL that is not in GTNNF can be transformed to a formula in GTNNF, equivalent in the two-valued semantics $\vDash$ over Markov chains, by (1) replacing each sub-formula of the form $[\alpha]_{<p}$ and $[\alpha]_{\leq p}$ by $\neg[\alpha]_{\geq 1-p}$ and $\neg[\alpha]_{>1-p}$ respectively, and then (2) pushing negations inwards. The second step, i. e. pushing negations inwards, is possible without breaking the syntactical restrictions of PCTL, only because the used definition includes both the Weak and the Strong Until. With an intermediate step into PCTL* [13] one gets:

$$\neg[X\,\phi]_{>p} \equiv [\neg X\,\phi]_{\geq 1-p} \equiv [X\,\neg\phi]_{\geq 1-p}$$

$$\neg[\phi U^{\leq k}\psi]_{>p} \equiv [\neg(\phi U^{\leq k}\psi)]_{\geq 1-p} \equiv [(\neg\psi)\,W^{\leq k}(\neg\phi \wedge \neg\psi)]_{\geq 1-p}$$

$$\neg[\phi\,W^{\leq k}\,\psi]_{>p} \equiv [\neg(\phi\,W^{\leq k}\,\psi)]_{\geq 1-p} \equiv [(\neg\psi)U^{\leq k}(\neg\phi \wedge \neg\psi)]_{\geq 1-p}$$

Swapping the roles of $\geq$ and $>$ in the above equivalences yields the dualities for the remaining combinations of temporal operators and threshold types. The negations $\neg\phi$ and $\neg\psi$ above are then processed in the same manner, recursively.

We can now secure the desired soundness result:

Lemma 1. *Let M and A be models and $A \preceq M$. Then for all formulae ϕ in GTNNF we have the implications $A \vDash^p \phi \Rightarrow M \vDash^p \phi$ and $M \vDash^\circ \phi \Rightarrow A \vDash^\circ \phi$.*

This lemma is proved by structural induction on ϕ, using standard fixed-point and duality arguments for Weak and Strong Until formulae. As our paper focuses on completeness not on soundness, we don't feature this proof here.

3   Completeness for PCTL Formulae

The notion of completeness we now define is relative to our class of models, their abstract PCTL semantics, and its abstraction via probabilistic simulation. We refer to this triad as "our abstraction framework" subsequently.

Definition 6 (Finitary completeness). *A PCTL formula ϕ is complete (for our abstraction framework) iff for all Markov chains M that satisfy ϕ there is a finite-state model A such that $A \preceq M$ and $A \vDash^p \phi$. A set of PCTL formulae Γ is complete iff every $\phi \in \Gamma$ is complete.*

Completeness for ϕ thus means that all Markov chains that satisfy ϕ ($M \vDash \phi$) have a finite-state abstraction that also satisfies ϕ in the $\vDash^p$ semantics. We chose $\vDash^p$ for this definition since it, unlike $\vDash^\circ$, is sound for verification.

Example 1. The infinite-state Markov chain M depicted in Figure 2(a) satisfies $\varphi = [qUr]_{>0.7}$. It is simulated by the finite-state model $M_{3,3}^{so}$ in Figure 2(b) and $M_{3,3}^{so} \vDash^p \varphi$. In Section 4, we will see that φ is complete.

Incompleteness of PCTL. We show that full PCTL is incomplete by giving several counterexamples which consist of a concrete Markov chain M and a PCTL formula φ such that no finite-state model A can exist, which simulates M and for which $A \vDash^p \varphi$. These examples are strongly inspired by Dams and Namjoshi's work on completeness for Kripke structures and the modal mu-calculus [12].

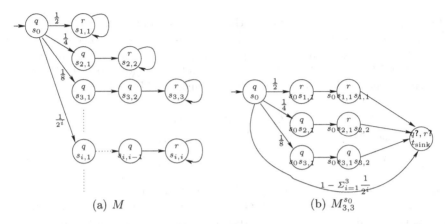

(a) M

(b) $M_{3,3}^{s_0}$

Fig. 2. A model M satisfying $[qUr]_{\geq 1}$ and $[q\,W\,r]_{\geq 1}$, and its unfolding $M_{3,3}^{s_0}$

Lemma 2. *Not all formulae of the form $[\phi U \psi]_{\geq p}$ and $[\phi\,W\,\psi]_{\geq p}$ are complete.*

Proof. We consider $[qUr]_{\geq 1}$ and $[q\,W\,r]_{\geq 1}$. Let M be the Markov chain illustrated in Figure 2(a): The initial state s_0 is labeled q and is infinitely branching with $\mathbf{P}(s_0, s_{i,1}) > 0$ for all $i \geq 1$; its i-th successor $s_{i,1}$ has probability $1/2^i$, all other transition probabilities are 1; the i-th path $s_0 s_{i,1} \ldots s_{i,i}$ consists of $i - 1$ states labeled q and ends in an absorbing state $s_{i,i}$ labeled r. The Markov chain M obviously satisfies any $\varphi \in \{[qUr]_{\geq 1}, [q\,W\,r]_{\geq 1}\}$.

Now assume there is a finite-state model A with $n > 0$ states and initial state a_0, such that $A \models^p \varphi$ and $A \preceq M$. Since A is finite-state there exists a state a_1 in A (a successor of a_0) which simulates infinitely many successors $s_{i_j,1}$ $(j > 0)$ of s_0 in M. Of these states $s_{i_j,1}$ there must be a state $s_{n_0,1}$ which is starting point of a path $s_{n_0,1} \ldots s_{n_0,n_0}$ with $n_0 > n+1$ states labeled q before reaching its absorbing r state. By the definition of simulation this path must be matched by a path $a_1 \ldots a_{n_0}$ in A such that $a_j \preceq s_{n_0,j}$ for all $1 \leq j \leq n_0$. Since A is of finite size n there must be a state $a_{j'}$ re-occurring along this path, and thus there is a loop in A. As the states $s_{n_0,1} \ldots s_{n_0,n_0-1}$ are labeled q, all states of the path $a_1 \ldots a_{n_0}$, and on the loop in this path, must be labeled q or $q?$. Similarly, as the states $s_{n_0,1} \ldots s_{n_0,n_0-1}$ are not labeled r, for all states a_j of the loop we get $L(a_i, r) = \text{ff}$ or $L(a_i, r) = ?$. Now, since $A \models^p \varphi$ by assumption, the states a_j must actually be labeled with q. Otherwise, let $\alpha \in \{qUr, q\,W\,r\}$. If one state a_{i_0} in the loop were labeled $q?$, and so $A^{a_{i_0}} \not\models^p q$, there would be a finite prefix $a_0 a_1 \ldots a_{i_0}$, and thus a measurable cylinder path set with positive probability for which no path pessimistically satisfies α. Thus $\mathsf{Prob}_M^p(a_0, \alpha) < 1$, contradicting $A \models^p \varphi$.

But now we have an overall contradiction: no model that contains a loop of states labeled q can simulate M because this would imply that M contains an infinite path of states labeled q, which the given M clearly does not. Hence there cannot be a finite-state model A such that $A \models^p \varphi$ and $A \preceq M$. □

We can use the same concrete Markov chain M from Figure 2(a) and a similar proof structure to show the incompleteness of $[X \phi]_{\geq p}$.

Lemma 3. *Not all formulae of form $[X \phi]_{\geq p}$ are complete.*

Proof. We consider $\varphi = [X [qUr]_{>0}]_{\geq 1}$ and the Markov chain M from Figure 2(a) which satisfies φ. Again, assume there is a finite-state model A with n states and initial state a_0, such that $A \vDash^p \varphi$ and $A \preceq M$.

Since A is finite-state there exists a state a_1 in A (a successor of a_0) which simulates infinitely many successors $s_{i,1}$ of s_0 in M. Since $A \vDash \varphi$ the state a_1 needs to satisfy $[qUr]_{>0}$. Hence there must be a path $\pi = a_1 \ldots a_k$ where the states $a_1, \ldots, a_{k-1}$ are labeled q and a_k is labeled r. If this path were loop-free, then each of the infinitely many states $s_{i,1}$ would be starting point of a path which reaches an r state after at most k steps. This is a contradiction to the definition of M. Thus π must contain a loop of states labeled q. But this would force M to contain an infinite path $s_{i,1} \ldots$ where all states are labeled q. Again we have a contradiction because M does not contain such a path. $\square$

Sub-formula $[qUr]_{>0}$ in and of itself does not imply incompleteness. In Section 4, we will actually show that formulae of this form are complete.

Incompleteness of formulae of form $[X [\phi U \psi]_{>p}]_{\geq p'}$ requires infinite branching, as in the Markov chain in Figure 2(a). For finitely branching Markov chains this form is complete, as then only a finite number of successor states needs to be considered, on each of which sub-formula $[\phi U \psi]_{>p}$ can be finitely verified (as we show in the next section). Forms $[\phi U \psi]_{\geq 1}$ and $[\phi W \psi]_{\geq 1}$ are also incomplete for finitely branching models (for slightly different Until formulae). We summarize:

Corollary 1. *Full PCTL is incomplete.*

Our incompleteness proofs above work for any simulation notion $\preceq$ satisfying

1. $L(t, q) \neq ?$ implies $L(t, q) = L(s, q)$ for all $q \in AP$
2. $\mathbf{P}(s, s') > 0$ implies $\mathbf{P}(t, t') > 0$ for some t' with $t' \preceq s'$
3. $\mathbf{P}(t, t') > 0$ implies $\mathbf{P}(s, s') > 0$ for some s' with $t' \preceq s'$

whenever $t \preceq s$. In their bi-directionality, these three conditions are reminiscent of Larsen and Skou's probabilistic 2/3-bisimulation [3] and of Dams and Namjoshi's notion of (mixed) reverse simulation for labeled transition systems [12]: conditions (1) and (2) together constrain the abstract model in terms of the concrete model (and are necessary but not sufficient for sound abstraction à la Lemma 1); conditions (1) and (3) constrain the concrete model in terms of the abstract one (and are necessary for securing our incompleteness results).

4   Complete Fragment of PCTL

We now present a complete fragment of PCTL: those PCTL formulae whose path modalities occur in a suitable combination of negation polarity and threshold type. The technical details of this definition, and its alternative characterization via a normal form will be formalized below. In fact, we will show that for this fragment the desired finite abstractions can be obtained by unfolding the infinite model up to a bounded height and width. We first formalize full unfoldings.

Definition 7 (Unfolding). *Let $M = (S, \mathbf{P}, L)$ be a model. The full unfolding of M at s_0 is the model $M_{\text{full}}^{s_0} = (S_{\text{full}}, \mathbf{P}', L')$ where S_{full} is the set of nonempty sequences π over S, transition probability $\mathbf{P}'(s_1 \ldots s_n, s_1 \ldots s_n s_{n+1})$ is $\mathbf{P}(s_n, s_{n+1})$, and $L'(\pi \cdot s) = L(s)$. We restrict the set S_{full} to the set of sequences reachable from s_0 with positive probability.*

If M is a concrete Markov chain, so is $M_{\text{full}}^{s_0}$. Also, M and $M_{\text{full}}^{s_0}$ simulate each other, and so are equivalent. We now formalize finite unfoldings.

Definition 8 (Finite Unfolding)

1. *For $i \in \mathbb{N}$ and $s_0 \in S$, the finite unfolding $M_i^{s_0} = (S_i, \mathbf{P}_i, L_i)$ is the model where S_i is the set of nonempty sequences over S of length at most i, plus a designated sink state t_{sink}. As above $\mathbf{P}_i(s_1 \ldots s_n, s_1 \ldots s_n s_{n+1}) = \mathbf{P}(s_n, s_{n+1})$, $\mathbf{P}_i(s_0 \ldots s_{i-1}, t_{\text{sink}}) = 1$ for each sequence of length i, and $\mathbf{P}_i(t_{\text{sink}}, t_{\text{sink}}) = 1$. Again, $L_i(\pi \cdot s) = L(s)$, and $L(t_{\text{sink}}, \mathsf{q}) = ?$ for all $\mathsf{q} \in \text{AP}$. We restrict S_i to sequences reachable from s_0 with positive probability.*

2. *For $j \in \mathbb{N}$, this model is further restricted to maximal branching degree j as follows. Let $M_{i,j}^{s_0} = (S_{i,j}, \mathbf{P}_{i,j}, L_{i,j})$, where the components of $M_{i,j}^{s_0}$ are as follows. For each $s \in S_i$, let $t_1, t_2, \ldots$ be an enumeration of $\{t_k \in S_i \mid \mathbf{P}_i(s, t_k) > 0\}$ such that $\mathbf{P}_i(s, t_k) \geq \mathbf{P}_i(s, t_{k+1})$ for all $k \in \mathbb{N}$. We then define $\mathbf{P}_{i,j}$ by setting $\mathbf{P}_{i,j}(s, t_k) = \mathbf{P}_i(s, t_k)$ for $k \leq j$ and $\mathbf{P}_{i,j}(s, t_{\text{sink}}) = 1 - \Sigma_{k=1}^j \mathbf{P}_i(s, t_k)$. We set $L_{i,j} = L_i$ and again restrict $S_{i,j}$ to sequences reachable from s_0 with positive $\mathbf{P}_{i,j}$ transition probabilities.*

The unfolding $M_{3,3}^{s_0}$ for the labeled Markov chain M of Figure 2(a) is depicted in Figure 2(b). Finite unfoldings are not the usual finite unfoldings since we add a sink state. This addition gives then rise to desired simulations:

Lemma 4. *For all models M with initial state s_0 and $i, j \in \mathbb{N}$, the finite unfolding $M_{i,j}^{s_0}$ simulates M.*

Now we show that Next and Strong Until with $> p$ bounds have finite unfoldings of the model as witnesses.

Lemma 5. *Let M be a model, $\mathsf{q}, \mathsf{r} \in \text{AP}$ be propositions, and $M \vDash^{\mathsf{p}} [\alpha]_{>p}$ for $\alpha \in \{\mathsf{X}\,\mathsf{q}, \mathsf{q}U\mathsf{r}\}$. There are i_0, j_0 with $M_{i,j}^{s_0} \vDash^{\mathsf{p}} [\alpha]_{>p}$ for all $i \geq i_0$ and $j \geq j_0$.*

Proof. Let α be $\mathsf{X}\,\mathsf{q}$. By assumption $M \vDash^{\mathsf{p}} [\mathsf{X}\,\mathsf{q}]_{>p}$. If s_0 has finitely many successors, the claim is obviously true. Otherwise, let $t_1, t_2, \ldots$ be the successors of s_0 ordered so that $\mathbf{P}(s_0, t_l) \geq \mathbf{P}(s_0, t_{l+1})$ for every $l \geq 1$. Let $t_{m_1}, t_{m_2}, \ldots$ be the sub-sequence of those states t_i with $M^{t_i} \vDash^{\mathsf{p}} \mathsf{q}$. Then $M \vDash^{\mathsf{p}} [\mathsf{X}\,\mathsf{q}]_{>p}$ implies $\Sigma_{l=1}^{\infty} \mathbf{P}(s_0, t_{m_l}) > p$. Thus there is some l_0 with $\Sigma_{l=1}^{l_0} \mathbf{P}(s_0, t_{m_l}) > p$. Let $j_0 = m_{l_0}$. For every $i \geq 1$ and $j \geq j_0$ it is then easily seen that $M_{i,j}^{s_0} \vDash^{\mathsf{p}} [\mathsf{X}\,\mathsf{q}]_{>p}$.

Now let α be $\mathsf{q}U\mathsf{r}$. Consider first the case that M is finitely branching. It is simple to see that for all $i \geq 0$ we have $\text{Prob}_{M_i^{s_0}}^{\mathsf{p}}(s_0, \mathsf{q}U\mathsf{r}) \leq \text{Prob}_{M_{i+1}^{s_0}}^{\mathsf{p}}(s_0, \mathsf{q}U\mathsf{r})$ and that $\lim_{i \to \infty} \text{Prob}_{M_i}^{\mathsf{p}}(s_0, \mathsf{q}U\mathsf{r}) = \text{Prob}_M^{\mathsf{p}}(s_0, \mathsf{q}U\mathsf{r})$. Hence, for some i_0 we have that $\text{Prob}_{M_{i_0}^{s_0}}^{\mathsf{p}}(s_0, \mathsf{q}U\mathsf{r}) > p$ and for every $i \geq i_0$ we have $M_i^{s_0} \vDash^{\mathsf{p}} [\mathsf{q}U\mathsf{r}]_{>p}$.

$$\phi_{\text{pos}} ::= q \mid \neg q \mid \phi_{\text{pos}} \wedge \phi_{\text{pos}} \mid \phi_{\text{pos}} \vee \phi_{\text{pos}} \mid \neg\phi_{\text{neg}} \mid [\alpha_{\text{pos}}]_{>p} \mid [\alpha_{\text{neg}}]_{<p}$$
$$\phi_{\text{neg}} ::= q \mid \neg q \mid \phi_{\text{neg}} \wedge \phi_{\text{neg}} \mid \phi_{\text{neg}} \vee \phi_{\text{neg}} \mid \neg\phi_{\text{pos}} \mid [\alpha_{\text{neg}}]_{\geq p} \mid [\alpha_{\text{pos}}]_{\leq p}$$

$$\alpha_{\text{pos}} ::= X\,\phi_{\text{pos}} \mid \phi_{\text{pos}}U^{\leq k}\phi_{\text{pos}} \qquad\qquad \alpha_{\text{neg}} ::= X\,\phi_{\text{neg}} \mid \phi_{\text{neg}}\,W^{\leq k}\,\phi_{\text{neg}}$$

Fig. 3. PCTL$_>$, our complete fragment of PCTL, defined as all ϕ_{pos} above where $q \in AP$, $k \in \mathbb{N} \cup \{\infty\}$ and $p \in [0,1]$

If M has infinite branching the proof is similar. As before, there is some i_0 such that $M_{i_0}^{s_0} \vDash^p [qUr]_{>p}$. For every $j \in \mathbb{N}$ we have $\text{Prob}^p_{M_{i_0,j}^{s_0}}(s_0, qUr) \leq \text{Prob}^p_{M_{i_0,j+1}^{s_0}}(s_0, qUr)$ and that $\lim_{j\to\infty} \text{Prob}^p_{M_{i_0,j}^{s_0}}(s_0, qUr) = \text{Prob}^p_{M_{i_0}^{s_0}}(s_0, qUr)$. Hence, for some j_0 we have $\text{Prob}^p_{M_{i_0,j_0}^{s_0}}(s_0, qUr) > p$ and the lemma follows. □

Weak Until and Next with $\geq p$ bounds have finite counter-examples.

Corollary 2. *Let $M \nvDash^o [\alpha]_{\geq p}$ for $\alpha \in \{X\,q, q\,W\,r\}$ and a model M. Then there exist i_0 and j_0 such that for all $i \geq i_0$ and $j \geq j_0$ we have $M_{i,j}^{s_0} \nvDash^o [\alpha]_{\geq p}$.*

Proof. For α being $X\,q$ this follows from $[X\,\varphi]_{>p} \equiv \neg[X\,\neg\varphi]_{\geq 1-p}$ over two-valued models and from the duality of the optimistic and pessimistic semantics in three-valued models. For α being $q\,W\,r$, we similarly exploit that $[\varphi_1\,W\,\varphi_2]_{\geq p}$ is equivalent to $\neg[\neg\varphi_2 U(\neg\varphi_1 \wedge \neg\varphi_2)]_{>1-p}$ over two-valued models. □

We state and prove our main result, the completeness of PCTL$_>$, which is defined in Figure 3. GTNNF normalforms of PCTL$_>$ allow only $[U]_{>p}$ and $[X]_{>p}$ type operators. That is, they disallow Weak Until and the comparison $\geq p$.

Although any finite-state abstraction would be sufficient for completeness we show a stronger result: the abstraction can be chosen as finite unfolding.

Theorem 1 (Completeness of PCTL$_>$). *Let M be a Markov chain with initial state s_0, ϕ a formula in PCTL$_>$, and $M \vDash \phi$. Then there exist i, j such that the finite unfolding $M_{i,j}^{s_0}$ of M pessimistically satisfies ϕ, i.e. $M_{i,j}^{s_0} \vDash^p \phi$.*

Proof. We strengthen the claim with a dual claim for formulae in the negative part of PCTL$_>$ and for the optimistic semantics: "For ϕ in the negative part ϕ_{neg} of PCTL$_>$, if $M^s \nvDash \phi$ then there exist i, j such that $M_{i,j}^s \nvDash^o \phi$." We show this extended claim by structural induction on ϕ, simultaneously for all states s.

- Let ϕ be q. If $M^s \vDash q$ then for every $i \geq 0$ and $j \geq 0$ we have $M_{i,j}^s \vDash^p q$. Dually, if $M^s \nvDash q$ then for every $i \geq 0$ and $j \geq 0$ we have $M_{i,j}^s \nvDash^o q$.
- For the Boolean connectives $\phi_1 \wedge \phi_2$ and $\phi_1 \vee \phi_2$ and a state s, we take as bounds the maximum of the bounds i_k and j_k for sub-formulae ϕ_k obtained by induction for state s. These bounds work for the dual case as well.
- For a negation $\varphi = \neg\psi_{\text{neg}}$ and a state s, if $M^s \vDash \neg\psi_{\text{neg}}$, then $M^s \nvDash \psi_{\text{neg}}$. By induction, there are i and j with $M_{i,j}^s \nvDash^o \psi_{\text{neg}}$. Thus $M_{i,j}^s \vDash^p \neg\psi_{\text{neg}}$. Dually, for a negation $\varphi = \neg\psi_{\text{pos}}$ and a state s, if $M^s \nvDash \neg\psi_{\text{pos}}$, then $M^s \vDash \psi_{\text{pos}}$. By induction, there are i and j with $M_{i,j}^s \vDash^p \psi_{\text{pos}}$, so $M_{i,j}^s \nvDash^o \neg\psi_{\text{pos}}$.

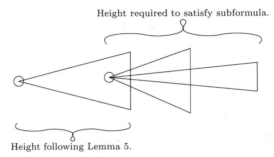

Fig. 4. Intuitively an unfolding for a sub-formula can be attached to every inner state of the unfolding of the formula. The resulting maximal height is still finite.

- We now consider the path modalities X, U, and W.
  - For formula $\varphi = [\mathsf{X}\,\psi_{\mathrm{pos}}]_{>p}$ and a state s such that $M^s \vDash \varphi$, we treat ψ_{pos} as a proposition that labels the states of M. By (the proof of) Lemma 5, there is some j_0' such that for every $i \geq 1$ and $j \geq j_0'$ we have $M_{i,j}^s \vDash^{\mathsf{P}} \varphi$. Let $t_1, \ldots, t_{j_0}$ be the first j_0' successors of s. For t_k there exists i_0^k and j_0^k such that if $M^{t_k} \vDash \psi_{\mathrm{pos}}$ we have $M_{i_0^k,j_0^k}^{t_k} \vDash^{\mathsf{P}} \psi_{\mathrm{pos}}$. Let $i_0 = 1 + \max_k(i_0^k)$ and $j_0 = \max(j_0', \max_k(j_0^k))$. It follows that $M_{i_0,j_0}^s \vDash^{\mathsf{P}} \varphi$.
  - Let $\varphi = [\mathsf{X}\,\psi_{\mathrm{neg}}]_{\geq p}$ with $M^s \nvDash \varphi$. The proof is similar to the one in the previous item and uses Corollary 2.
  - For $\varphi = [\psi_1 U \psi_2]_{>p}$, with ψ_1 and ψ_2 in the positive fragment ϕ_{pos}, and a state s with $M^s \vDash [\psi_1 U \psi_2]_{>p}$, we initially treat ψ_1 and ψ_2 as propositions that label the states of M. By Lemma 5 there are i_0' and j_0' such that for every $i \geq i_0'$ and $j \geq j_0'$ we have $M_{i,j}^s \vDash^{\mathsf{P}} [\psi_1 U \psi_2]_{>p}$. Now we no longer treat the ψ_i as atoms: Let $t_1, \ldots, t_m$ be all the states appearing in $M_{i_0',j_0'}$. For $\alpha \in \{1,2\}$ and every t_k there exists $i_0^{k,\alpha}$ and $j_0^{k,\alpha}$ such that if $M^{t_k} \vDash \psi_\alpha$ we have $M_{i_0^{k,\alpha},j_0^{k,1}}^{t_k} \vDash^{\mathsf{P}} \psi_\alpha$. Let $i_0 = i_0' + \max_{k,\alpha}(i_0^{k,\alpha})$ and $j_0 = \max(j_0', \max_{k,\alpha}(j_0^{k,\alpha}))$ (see Figure 4). It follows that $M_{i_0,j_0}^s \vDash^{\mathsf{P}} \varphi$.
  - The proof for $\varphi = [\psi_1 \,\mathsf{W}\, \psi_2]_{\geq p}$, with ψ_1 and ψ_2 in the fragment ϕ_{neg}, and a state s such that $M^s \nvDash [\psi_1 U \psi_2]_{\geq p}$ is similar to the one in the previous item and uses Corollary 2.
  - Formula $[\alpha_{\mathrm{neg}}]_{<p}$ is equivalent to $\neg[\alpha_{\mathrm{neg}}]_{\geq 1-p}$ of form $\neg\varphi_{\mathrm{pos}}$. Formula $[\alpha_{\mathrm{pos}}]_{\leq p}$ is equivalent to $\neg[\alpha_{\mathrm{pos}}]_{>1-p}$ of form $\neg\varphi_{\mathrm{neg}}$. Thus this case follows by induction. For example, for state s, we have e.g. $M_{i_0,j_0}^s \vDash^{\mathsf{P}} [\alpha_{\mathrm{neg}}]_{<p}$ iff $M_{i_0,j_0}^s \vDash^{\mathsf{P}} \neg[\alpha_{\mathrm{neg}}]_{\geq 1-p}$ iff $M_{i_0,j_0}^s \nvDash^{\circ} [\alpha_{\mathrm{neg}}]_{\geq 1-p}$. $\square$

We now show that the results in Section 3 imply that PCTL fragments that allow combinations of the operators we disallow cannot be complete. To that end, we first prove an additional incompleteness result.

Lemma 6. *Not all formulae of form $[[\phi U \psi]_{>p}\,\mathsf{W}\,\rho]_{>p'}$ are complete.*

Proof. Let φ be $[[q U r]_{>0}\,\mathsf{W}\,\mathsf{ff}]_{>0}$ and M be as in Figure 5. It is simple to see that $M \vDash \varphi$. Suppose there is a finite-state model A such that $A \preceq M$ and $A \vDash^{\mathsf{P}} \varphi$.

Fig. 5. Concrete Markov chain M that satisfies $[[qU r]_{>0} W ff]_{>0}$

Let a be the initial state of A such that $a \preceq s_0$. As $A \models^p \varphi$, there is a bottom strongly connected component (SCC) in A such that every state in this SCC satisfies pessimistically $[qU r]_{>0}$. By a pigeon-hole principle, we can find a state a' in this SCC that is labeled by r and simulates states s_i for infinitely many i. Consider a cycle from a' to itself. This cycle has some fixed length n. As for every $i > 0$ the distance from s_i to s_{i+1} is $i + 1$, this is a contradiction. $\square$

We can now prove that static extensions of $PCTL_>$ are incomplete.

Theorem 2. *Consider a PCTL fragment κ that contains one of the following combinations of PCTL operators: (i) $[\phi W \psi]_{\geq p}$, (ii) $[\phi U \psi]_{\geq p}$, (iii) $[X \phi]_{\geq p}$ and $[\phi U \psi]_{>p}$, or (iv) $[\phi W \psi]_{>p}$ and $[\phi U \psi]_{>p}$. Then κ is incomplete.*

Proof. The first three items follow from Lemmas 2 and 3 in Section 3. The last item follows from Lemma 6 above. $\square$

5   Discussion and Conclusions

From a practical perspective, our completeness results mean that those PCTL formulae whose Strong Untils occur under positive polarity and Weak Untils under negative polarity are complete for our abstraction framework: Given such a formula, we can determine all its occurrences of path modalities whose negation polarity and threshold type do not match. Then we can change all such threshold types and adjust their probability with a small perturbation in situ. For example, a Weak Until under negative polarity with $> .99$ threshold could be made complete by making it a Weak Until with $\geq .99 + 10^{-12}$ threshold without compromising the original intent of that property. But our results offer no algorithm and no bounds for the numbers i and j of Theorem 1. In fact, we do not know whether satisfiability of the logic $PCTL_>$ is decidable.

Let us conclude. We investigated whether the truth of formulae in probabilistic computation tree logic over infinite-state Markov chains can, in principle, be witnessed by finite-state Markov chains that simulate such infinite-state models of formulae and allow for 3-valued interpretations of atomic propositions. Negative results were presented for certain combinations of path modalities and probability threshold type, e.g. for Weak Until with strict threshold type. Positive results were proved for a sizeable fragment of PCTL formulae whose path modalities all occur in a statically determined combination of negation polarity and threshold type. Finally, we showed that static extensions of that complete fragment of PCTL are incomplete.

Acknowledgments. Mark Kattenbelt discussed with us incompleteness of stochastic games for MDPs. This research was supported by UK EPSRC project *Complete and Efficient Checks for Branching-Time Abstractions (EP/E028985/1)* and the Computing Laboratory Oxford University, which hosted the first author's sabbatical leave.

References

1. Hansson, H., Jonsson, B.: A logic for reasoning about time and reliability. Formal Aspects of Computing 6, 512–535 (1994)
2. Kwiatkowska, M.: Model checking for probability and time: From theory to practice. In: Proc. of LICS 2003. IEEE Computer Society Press, Los Alamitos (2003)
3. Larsen, K.G., Skou, A.: Bisimulation through probabilistic testing. Information and Computation 94, 1–28 (1991)
4. Jonsson, B., Larsen, K.: Specification and refinement of probabilistic processes. In: Proc. of LICS 1991. IEEE Computer Society Press, Los Alamitos (1991)
5. Fecher, H., Leucker, M., Wolf, V.: Don't know in probabilistic systems. In: SPIN Workshop on Model Checking of Software (2006)
6. Fecher, H., Huth, M., Piterman, N., Wagner, D.: Hintikka Games for PCTL on Labeled Markov Chains. In: Proc. of QEST 2008. IEEE Computer Society, Los Alamitos (2008)
7. Kattenbelt, M., Huth, M.: Abstraction Framework for Markov Decision Processes and PCTL Via Games. Technical Report RR-09-01, Oxford University Computing Laboratory (2009)
8. Kemeny, J., Snell, J., Knapp, A.: Denumerable Markov Chains. Springer, Heidelberg (1976)
9. Kleene, S.: Introduction to Metamathematics. Van Nostrand (1952)
10. Godefroid, P., Huth, M., Jagadeesan, R.: Abstraction-based model checking using modal transition systems. In: Larsen, K.G., Nielsen, M. (eds.) CONCUR 2001. LNCS, vol. 2154, p. 426. Springer, Heidelberg (2001)
11. Huth, M.: On finite-state approximants for probabilistic computation tree logic. Theoretical Computer Science 346, 113–134 (2005)
12. Dams, D., Namjoshi, K.: The existence of finite abstractions for branching time model checking. In: Proc. of LICS 2004. IEEE Computer Society Press, Los Alamitos (2004)
13. Bianco, A., de Alfaro, L.: Model checking of probabilistic and nondeterministic systems. In: Proceedings of the 15th Conference on Foundations of Software Technology and Theoretical Computer Science, pp. 499–513. Springer, Heidelberg (1995)

Closure Operators for Order Structures[*]

Ryszard Janicki[1], Dai Tri Man Lê[2,**], and Nadezhda Zubkova[1]

[1] Department of Computing and Software, McMaster University,
Hamilton, Canada L8S 4K1
{janicki,zubkovna}@mcmaster.ca
[2] Department of Computer Science, University of Toronto,
Toronto, Canada M5S 3G4
ledt@cs.toronto.edu

Abstract. We argue that closure operators are fundamental tools for the study of relationships between order structures and their sequence representations. We also propose and analyse a closure operator for interval order structures.

1 Introduction

While the two major models of concurrency, interleaving abstraction ([2,22]) and partially ordered causality ([5,15,23]), have been very successful, they have some limitations. Neither of them can model the "not later than" relationship effectively, which causes problems with specifying priorities, error recovery, time testing, inhibitor nets, etc. (see for instance [4,9,12,16,17,18]). A solution, proposed independently (in this order) in [19,8] and [10], suggests modeling concurrent behaviours by a triple $(X, \prec, \sqsubset)$, where X is the set of event occurrences, and $\prec$ and $\sqsubset$ are binary relations on X. The relation $\prec$ is "causality" (i.e. an abstraction of the "earlier than" relationship), and $\sqsubset$ is "weak causality" (an abstraction of the "not later than" relationship). For this model, the following two kinds of relational structures are of special importance: *stratified order structures* (*so-structures*) and *interval order structures* (*io-structures*). The former structures can fully model concurrent behaviours when system executions (operational semantics) are described in terms of stratified orders, while the latter structures can fully model concurrent behaviours when system executions are described in terms of interval orders [9,13]. It was argued in [11] (and also implicitly in 1914 Wiener's paper [26]) that any execution that can be observed by a single observer must be an interval order. Thus, io-structures provide a very general model of concurrency. However, the theory of io-structures is far less developed than the simpler theory of so-structures.

When dealing with partial orders, many constructions use the fundamental notion of *transitive closure* of relations. The analogue of transitive closure for so-structures, called $\Diamond$-*closure*, has been proposed in [12] and successfully used in [12,16,17,18] and others. However, a similar concept for io-structures has not yet been proposed. In this paper we introduce the concept of $\blacklozenge$-*closure* for io-structures and show that it has the same kind of properties as transitive closure and $\Diamond$-closure.

---

[*] Partially supported by NSERC Grant of Canada.
[**] Partially supported by Ontario Graduate Scholarship.

M. Kutyłowski, M. Gębala, and W. Charatonik (Eds.): FCT 2009, LNCS 5699, pp. 217–229, 2009.
© Springer-Verlag Berlin Heidelberg 2009

The paper is structured as follows. Section 2 provides some mathematical preliminaries, while basic properties of Mazurkiewicz traces are discussed in Section 3. In Section 4 old and new properties of so-structures are discussed. Section 5 is devoted to io-structures and their ♦-closure operator. Section 6 contains some final comments.

2   Relations, Partial Orders and Transitive Closure

In this section, we recall some well-known mathematical concepts and results that will be used frequently in this paper.

Let X be a set and $R_1, R_2 \subseteq X \times X$ are two relations on X. We define $R_1 \circ R_2 \overset{df}{=} \{(x,y) \mid \exists z \in Z. \ (x,z) \in R_1 \wedge (y,z) \in R_2\}$, and $id_X \overset{df}{=} \{(x,x) \mid x \in X\}$. For each relation $R \subseteq X \times X$, we define R^+, the *transitive closure* of R, as $R^+ \overset{df}{=} \bigcup_{i=1}^{\infty} R^i$, and the *reflexive and transitive closure* of R, as $R^* = \bigcup_{i=0}^{\infty} R^i$, where $R^0 = id_X$ and $R^{i+1} = R^i \circ R$ for $i > 0$.

A binary relation $R \subseteq X \times X$ is: *irreflexive* iff for all $a \in X. \neg(aRa)$; *transitive* iff for all $a,b,c \in X. \ aRb \wedge bRc \implies aRc$; and *acyclic* iff for all $a \in X. \ \neg(aR^+a)$.

A relation $< \subseteq X \times X$ is a *(strict) partial order* if it is irreflexive and transitive, i.e. for all $a,c,b \in X, a \not< a$ and $a < b < c \implies a < c$. We also define:

$$a \frown_< b \overset{df}{\iff} \neg(a < b) \wedge \neg(b < a) \wedge a \neq b$$
$$a <^\frown b \overset{df}{\iff} a < b \vee a \frown_< b$$

Note that $a \frown_< b$ means a and b are *incomparable* (w.r.t. $<$) elements of X.

Let $<$ be a partial order on a set x. Then

1. $<$ is *total* if $\frown_< = \emptyset$. In other words, for all $a,b \in X, a < b \vee b < a \vee a = b$. For clarity, we will reserve the symbol $\lhd$ to denote total orders;
2. $<$ is *stratified* if $a \frown_< b \frown_< c \implies a \frown_< c \vee a = c$, i.e., the relation $\frown_< \cup \, id_X$ is an equivalence relation on X.
3. $<$ is *interval* if for all $a,b,c,d \in X, a < c \wedge b < d \implies a < d \vee b < c$.

It is clear from these definitions that every total order is stratified and every stratified order is interval.

Given a partial order $< \subseteq X \times X$, a relation $<' \subseteq X \times X$ is an *extension* of $<$ if $< \subseteq <'$. For convenience, we define $\mathsf{Total}(<) \overset{df}{=} \{\lhd \subseteq X \times X \mid \lhd \text{ is a total order and } < \subseteq \lhd\}$. In other words, the set $\mathsf{Total}(<)$ consists of all the *total order extensions* of $<$.

By Szpilrajn's Theorem [25], we know that every partial order $<$ is uniquely represented by the the the set $\mathsf{Total}(<)$. Szpilrajn's Theorem can be stated as following:

Theorem 1 (Szpilrajn [25]). *For every partial order* $<$, $< = \bigcap_{\lhd \in \mathsf{Total}(<)} \lhd$.   □

Stratified orders are often defined in an alternative way, namely, a partial order $<$ on X is stratified if and only if there exists a total order $\lhd$ on some Y and a mapping $\phi : X \to Y$ such that $\forall x,y \in X. \ x < y \iff \phi(x) \lhd \phi(y)$. This definition is illustrated in Figure 1, where $\phi(a) = \{a\}$, $\phi(b) = \phi(c) = \{b,c\}$, $\phi(d) = \{d\}$. Note that for all $x,y \in \{a,b,c,d\}$ we have $x <_2 y \iff \phi(x) \lhd_2 \phi(y)$, where the total order $\lhd_2$ can be concisely represented by a *step sequence* $\{a\}\{b,c\}\{d\}$. As a consequence, stratified orders and step sequences can uniquely represent each other (cf. [12,14,20]).

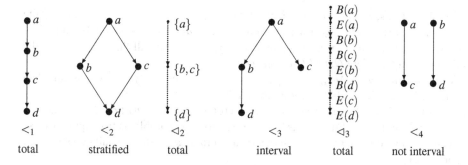

Fig. 1. Various types of partial orders (represented as Hasse diagrams). The partial order $<_1$ is an extension of $<_2$, $<_2$ is an extension of $<_3$, and $<_3$ is and extension of $<_4$. Note that order $<_1$, being total, is uniquely represented by a sequence $abcd$, the stratified order $<_2$ is uniquely represented by a step sequence $\{a\}\{b,c\}\{d\}$, and the interval order $<_3$ is (*not* uniquely) represented by a sequence that represents $\lhd_3$, i.e. $B(a)E(a)B(b)B(c)E(b)B(d)E(c)E(d)$.

For the interval orders, the name and intuition follow from Fishburn's Theorem:

Theorem 2 (Fishburn [6]). *A partial order $<$ on X is interval iff there exists a total order $\lhd$ on some T and two mappings $B, E : X \to T$ such that for all $x, y \in X$,*

1. $B(x) \lhd E(y)$, and   *2. $x < y \iff E(x) \lhd B(y)$.*   □

Usually $B(x)$ is interpreted as the beginning and $E(x)$ as the end of an *interval* x. The intuition of Fishburn's theorem is illustrated in Figure 1 with $<_3$ and $\lhd_3$. For all $x, y \in \{a, b, c, d\}$, we have $B(x) \lhd_3 E(x)$ and $x <_3 y \iff E(x) \lhd_3 B(y)$.

We will next recall the fundamental properties of transitive closure operator.

Proposition 1. *Let $R \subseteq X \times X$.*

1. If R is irreflexive then $R \subseteq R^+ \setminus id_X$,
2. $(R^+)^+ = R^+$,
3. R^+ is a partial order if and only if R^+ is irreflexive,
4. if R is a partial order then $R^+ = R$.
5. if R is a partial order and $R_0 \subseteq R$, then R_0^+ is a partial order and $R_0^+ \subseteq R$.   □

These properties were extended to the $\Diamond$-closure operator for so-structures in [12] and will be extended to the ♦-closure operator for io-structures in Section 5.

3 Partial Orders Generated by Mazurkiewicz Traces

A triple $(X, *, \mathbb{1})$, where X is a set, $*$ is a total binary operation on X, and $\mathbb{1} \in X$, is called a *monoid* [3], if $(a * b) * c = a * (b * c)$ and $a * \mathbb{1} = \mathbb{1} * a = a$, for all $a, b, c \in X$.

A nonempty equivalence relation $\sim \subseteq X \times X$ is a *congruence* in the monoid $(X, *, \mathbb{1})$ if for all $a_1, a_2, b_1, b_2 \in X$, $a_1 \sim b_1 \wedge a_2 \sim b_2 \Rightarrow (a_1 * a_2) \sim (b_1 * b_2)$.

The triple $(X / \sim, \circledast, [\mathbb{1}])$, where $[a] \circledast [b] = [a * b]$, is called the *quotient monoid* of $(X, *, 1)$ under the congruence $\sim$. The symbols $*$ and $\circledast$ are often omitted if this does not lead to any discrepancy.

Let $M = (X, *, \mathbb{1})$ be a *monoid* and let $EQ = \{\ x_i = y_i \mid i = 1, \ldots, n\ \}$ be a finite set of *equations*. Define $\equiv_{EQ}$ (or just $\equiv$) to be the *least congruence* on M satisfying, $x_i = y_i \implies x_i \equiv_{EQ} y_i$, for each equation $x_i = y_i \in EQ$. We call the relation $\equiv_{EQ}$ the *congruence defined by EQ*, or *EQ-congruence*.

The *quotient monoid* $M_{\equiv_{EQ}} = (X/\equiv_{EQ}, \circledast, [\mathbb{1}])$, where $[x] \circledast [y] = [x * y]$, is called an *equational monoid* (see [14,20] for more details).

Monoids of *Mazurkiewicz traces* (or *traces*) (cf. [5,21]) are *equational monoids over sequences*. The theory of traces has been utilised to tackle problems from quite diverse areas including combinatorics, graph theory, algebra, logic and, especially concurrency theory [5,21].

Applications of traces in concurrency theory are originated from the fact that traces are *sequence representation of partial orders*, which gives traces the ability to model "true concurrency" semantics. We will now recall the definition of a *trace monoid*.

Definition 1 ([5,21]). *Let $M = (E^*, *, \lambda)$ be a* free monoid *generated by E, and let the relation $ind \subseteq E \times E$ be an irreflexive and symmetric relation (called* independency*), and $EQ = \{ab = ba \mid (a,b) \in ind\}$. Let $\equiv_{ind}$, called* trace congruence*, be the congruence defined by EQ. Then the equational monoid $M_{\equiv_{ind}} = (E^*/\equiv_{ind}, \circledast, [\lambda])$ is a monoid of* traces*. The pair (E, ind) is called a* trace alphabet*.*

We will omit the subscript *ind* from trace congruence if it causes no ambiguity.

Example 1. Let $E = \{a, b, c\}$, $ind = \{(b,c), (c,b)\}$, i.e., $EQ = \{\ bc = cb\ \}$. Given three sequences $s = abcbca$, $s_1 = abc$ and $s_2 = bca$, we can generate the traces $[s] = \{abcbca, abccba, acbbca, acbcba, abbcca, accbba\}$, $[s_1] = \{abc, acb\}$ and $[s_2] = \{bca, cba\}$. Note that $[s] = [s_1] \circledast [s_2]$ since $[abcbca] = [abc] \circledast [bca] = [abc * bca]$.

Each trace represents a finite partial order in the following sense. For the trace $[s]$ from Example 1, we can define $\Sigma_{[s]} = \{a^{(1)}, b^{(1)}, c^{(1)}, b^{(2)}, c^{(2)}, a^{(2)}\}$ to be the set of all *enumerated events* occurring in $[s]$, where $a^{(1)}$ and $a^{(2)}$ simply denote the first and the second occurrences of a respectively in the sequence s_1. Then the partially ordered set (poset) $(\Sigma_{[s]}, \prec_{[s]})$ represented by $[s]$ is depicted in the diagram on the right (arcs inferred from transitivity are omitted for simplicity).

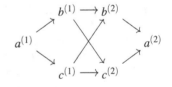

In fact, the total orders induced by the elements of $[s]$ comprise *all* the total extensions of $\prec_{[s]}$ (see [21]), which by Theorem 1 implies that $[s]$ *uniquely determines* the partial order $\prec_{[s]}$.

Remark 1. Given a sequence s, to construct the partial order $\prec_{[s]}$ represented by $[s]$, we *do not* need to build up to exponentially many elements of $[s]$. We can simply construct the direct acyclic graph $(\Sigma_{[s]}, \prec_s)$, where $x^{(i)} \prec_s y^{(j)}$ iff $x^{(i)}$ occurs before $y^{(j)}$ on the sequence s and $(x, y) \notin ind$. The relation $\prec_s$ is usually *not* the same as the partial order $\prec_{[s]}$. However, after applying the *transitive closure* operator, we have $\prec_{[s]} = \prec_s^+$. To extend this simple idea to the more difficult cases of constructing stratified or io-structures from their sequence representations, it is inevitable that we have to generalise the *transitive closure* operator to these order structures.

4   Stratified Order Structures, Comtraces, and $\Diamond$-Closure

A *relational structure* is a triple $S = (X, R_1, R_2)$, where $R_1, R_2 \subseteq X \times X$. We will write $S = (X, R_1, R_2) \subseteq S' = (X, R'_1, R'_2)$ iff $R_1 \subseteq R'_1$ and $R_2 \subseteq R'_2$.

Definition 2 ([11]). *A stratified order structures (so-structure) is a relational structure* $S = (X, \prec, \sqsubset)$, *such that for all* $a, b, c \in X$, *the following hold:*

S1:	$a \not\prec a$	S3:	$a \sqsubset b \sqsubset c \wedge a \neq c \implies a \sqsubset c$
S2:	$a \prec b \implies a \sqsubset b$	S4:	$a \sqsubset b \prec c \vee a \prec b \sqsubset c \implies a \prec c$

So-structures were independently introduced in [8] and [10]. Their comprehensive theory has been presented in [12,13]. They have been successfully applied to model inhibitor and priority systems, asynchronous races, synthesis problems, etc., [17] (see [9] for more references).

The relation $\prec$ is called *causality* and represents the "earlier than" relationship, and the relation $\sqsubset$ is called *weak causality* and represents the "not later than" relationship. The axioms S1–S4 model the mutual relationship between "earlier than" and "not later than" relations, provided that the system runs are defined as stratified orders.

A stratified order $<$ on X is a *stratified extension* of a so-structure $S = (X, \prec, \sqsubset)$ if $\prec \subseteq <$ and $\sqsubset \subseteq <^\frown$. The set of all stratified extensions of S will be denoted by $\mathrm{Strat}(S)$.

Theorem 3 ([13]). *For every so-structure* $S = (X, \prec, \sqsubset)$:

$$S = \left(X, \bigcap_{<\in\mathrm{Strat}(S)} <, \bigcap_{<\in\mathrm{Strat}(S)} <^\frown \right). \qquad \square$$

The above theorem is a generalisation of Szpilrajn's Theorem to so-structures and is interpreted as the proof of the claim that so-structures uniquely represent sets of equivalent system runs provided that the system operational semantics can be fully described in terms of stratified orders (see [9,13] for details).

We will now present the concept of $\Diamond$-closure that plays a substantial role in most of the applications of so-structures for modelling concurrent systems (cf. [13,16,17]).

Definition 3 ([12]). *For every relational structure* $S = (X, R_1, R_2)$ *we define* $S^\Diamond$ *as*

$$S^\Diamond \stackrel{df}{=} \left(X, \prec^\Diamond_{R_1,R_2}, \sqsubset^\Diamond_{R_1,R_2} \right) = \left(X, (R_1 \cup R_2)^* \circ R_1 \circ (R_1 \cup R_2)^*, (R_1 \cup R_2)^* \setminus id_X \right).$$

Intuitively the $\Diamond$-closure is a generalisation of transitive closure for relations to so-structures. The theorem below shows that the $\Diamond$-closure has all the properties formulated for transitive closure in Proposition 1.

Theorem 4 ([12]). *Let* $S = (X, R_1, R_2)$ *be a relational structure.*

1. *If* R_2 *is irreflexive then* $S \subseteq S^\Diamond$.
2. $(S^\Diamond)^\Diamond = S^\Diamond$.
3. $S^\Diamond$ *is a so-structure if and only if the relation* $\prec^\Diamond_{R_1,R_2}$ *is irreflexive.*
4. *If* S *is a so-structure then* $S = S^\Diamond$.
5. *Let* S *be a so-structure and let* $S_0 \subseteq S$. *Then* $S_0^\Diamond \subseteq S$ *and* $S_0^\Diamond$ *is a so-structure.* $\qquad \square$

Among others, Theorem 4 helps us to show a relationship between so-structures and *comtraces*, an extension of Mazurkiewicz traces that allows us to model the "not later than" relationship using quotient monoids of *step sequence* monoids [12,14,20].

Definition 4 ([12]). *Let E be a finite set (of events) and let $ser \subseteq sim \subset E \times E$ be two relations called* serialisability *and* simultaneity *respectively and the relation sim is irreflexive and symmetric. Then the triple (E, sim, ser) is called the* comtrace alphabet.

Intuitively, if $(a,b) \in sim$ then a and b can occur simultaneously, while $(a,b) \in ser$ means that a and b may occur simultaneously or a may occur before b (i.e., both executions are equivalent). We define $\mathbb{S}$, the set of all (potential) *steps*, as the set of all cliques of the graph (E, sim), i.e., $\mathbb{S} \overset{df}{=} \{A \mid A \neq \emptyset \wedge \forall a,b \in A. \ (a = b \vee (a,b) \in sim)\}$. Hence, the triple $(\mathbb{S}^*, *, \lambda)$, where "$*$" denotes the step sequence concatenation operator (usually omitted), is a *monoid of step sequences*.

Definition 5 ([12]). *Let $\theta = (E, sim, ser)$ be a comtrace alphabet and let $\equiv_{ser}$, called* comtrace congruence, *be the EQ-congruence defined by the set of equations:*
$$EQ = \{A = BC \mid A = B \cup C \in \mathbb{S} \wedge B \times C \subseteq ser\}.$$
Then the equational monoid $(\mathbb{S}^*/\equiv_{ser}, \circledast, [\lambda])$ is called a monoid of comtraces *over θ.*

We will omit the subscript *ser* from comtrace congruence if it causes no ambiguity.

Example 2. Let $E = \{a,b,c\}$, $sim = \{(b,c),(c,b)\}$ and $ser = \{(b,c)\}$. Then we have $\mathbb{S} = \{\{a\},\{b\},\{c\},\{b,c\}\}$, $EQ = \{\{b,c\} = \{b\}\{c\}\}$. A step sequence $s = \{a\}\{b,c\}\{a\}$ generates $[s] = \{\{a\}\{b,c\}\{a\}, \{a\}\{b\}\{c\}\{a\}, \{a,b\}\{c\}\{a\}, \{b\}\{a\}\{c\}\{a\}\}$ as its comtrace. Note that $\{a\}\{c\}\{b\}\{a\} \notin [s]$.

Let $u = A_1 \ldots A_k$ be a step sequence. By $\bar{u} = \bar{A}_1 \ldots \bar{A}_k$ be the *event enumerated* representation of u. We will skip a lengthy but intuitively obvious formal definition (cf. [12]), but for instance, from Example 2, $\bar{s} = \{a^{(1)}\}\{b^{(1)}, c^{(1)}\}\{a^{(2)}\}$. Let $\Sigma_u = \bigcup_{i=1}^k \bar{A}_i$ denote the set of all enumerated events occurring in u, for example, $\Sigma_s = \{a^{(1)}, a^{(2)}, b^{(1)}, c^{(1)}\}$. For each $\alpha \in \Sigma_u$, let $pos_u(\alpha)$ denote the consecutive number of a step where α belongs, i.e. if $\alpha \in \bar{A}_j$ then $pos_u(\alpha) = j$. For our example, $pos_s(a^{(2)}) = 3$, $pos_s(b^{(1)}) = 2$, etc. For each enumerated even $\alpha = e^{(i)}$, let $l(\alpha)$ denote the *label* of α, i.e. $l(\alpha) = l(e^{(i)}) = e$. One can easily show that $u \equiv v \implies \Sigma_u = \Sigma_v$, so we can define $\Sigma_{[u]} = \Sigma_u$.

Given a step sequence u, we define the stratified order $\lhd_u \subseteq \Sigma_u \times \Sigma_u$ induced by u by: $\alpha \lhd_u \beta \overset{df}{\iff} pos_u(\alpha) < pos_u(\beta)$. Then it can be easily checked that the stratified orders induced by the step sequences of the comtrace $[s]$ from Example 2 are exactly the stratified extensions of the so-structure $S_{[s]} = (\Sigma_{[s]}, \prec_{[s]}, \sqsubset_{[s]})$ on the right. The dotted edge denotes $\sqsubset_{[s]}$, while the solid edges denote both $\prec_{[s]}$ and $\sqsubset_{[s]}$.

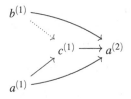

Analogous to Remark 1 for traces, given a comtrace alphabet (E, sim, ser) and a step sequence u, we do *not* need to analyse any other elements of $[u]$ except u itself to construct the so-structure $S_{[u]}$, which the comtrace $[u]$ represents. We will now show how the $\Diamond$-closure operator helps us to build the desired construction.

Definition 6 ([12]). *Let* $u \in \mathbb{S}^*$. *We define the relations* $\prec_u, \sqsubset_u \subseteq \Sigma_{[u]} \times \Sigma_{[u]}$ *as:*

1. $\alpha \prec_u \beta \overset{df}{\Longleftrightarrow} \alpha \lhd_u \beta \wedge (l(\alpha), l(\beta)) \notin ser,$
2. $\alpha \sqsubset_u \beta \overset{df}{\Longleftrightarrow} \alpha \lhd_u^{\frown} \beta \wedge (l(\beta), l(\alpha)) \notin ser.$

Definition 6 describes two basic *"local"* invariants of the elements of $\Sigma_\mathbf{u}$. The relation $\prec_u$ captures the situation when α *always precedes* β, and the relation $\sqsubset_u$ captures the situation when α *never follows* β. However, since $\prec_u$ and $\sqsubset_u$ are "locally" invariant, the relation structure $(\Sigma_{[u]}, \prec_u, \sqsubset_u)$ might not contain "global" invariants that can be inferred from (S3) and (S4) of Definition 2. For instance, the step sequence s from Example 2 generates the following relations $\prec_s = \{(a^{(1)}, c^{(1)}), (a^{(1)}, a^{(2)}), (c^{(1)}, a^{(2)})\}$ and $\sqsubset_s = \prec_s \cup \{(b^{(1)}, c^{(1)})\}$, where the edge $(b^{(1)}, a^{(2)})$ from $\prec_{[s]}$ and $\sqsubset_{[s]}$ is absent from both of these relations. To make sure all invariants are included, we need $\Diamond$-closure.

Definition 7. *Given a step sequence* $u \in \mathbb{S}^*$ *and its respective comtrace* $[u] \in \mathbb{S}^*/\equiv$. *We define the relational structures* $S_{[u]}$ *as:* $\quad S_{[u]} \overset{df}{=} \left(\Sigma_{[u]}, \prec_u, \sqsubset_u \right)^{\Diamond}$.

The relational structure $S_{[u]}$ is the so-structure defined by the comtrace $[u]$. The following theorem justifies the names and summarises the following nontrivial results concerning the so-structures generated by comtraces. The proofs of these results heavily use the properties of $\Diamond$-closure from Theorem 4.

Theorem 5 ([12,13]). *For all* $u, v \in \mathbb{S}^*$, *we have*

1. $S_{[u]}$ *is a so-structure and* $S_{[u]} = \left(\Sigma_{[u]}, \bigcap_{x \in [u]} \lhd_x, \bigcap_{x \in [u]} \lhd_x^{\frown} \right)$,
2. $u \equiv v \Longleftrightarrow S_{[u]} = S_{[v]}$,
3. $ext\left(S_{[u]}\right) = \{\lhd_s \mid s \in [u]\}$. $\hfill \square$

Note that a generalisation of Theorem 5 to *generalised stratified order structures (gso-structures)* [9], an extension of so-structures which can additionally model the "non-simultaneously" relationship, was recently shown in [14,20]. A sequence representation of gso-structures called *generalised comtraces* were proposed and shown to represent precisely finite gso-structures. The intuition of the approach in [20] is similar to what we discussed here and the $\Diamond$-closure operator was applied extensively.

5 Interval Order Structures and $\blacklozenge$-Closure

This section contains the major contribution of this paper. We start with a short presentation of some properties on io-structures, then we define $\blacklozenge$-closure, the main concept of this paper, and prove the equivalence of Theorem 4. Because io-structures are more complex than so-structures, the proofs are more involved than that of Theorem 4.

Definition 8 ([11]). *An interval order structure (io-structure) is a relational structure* $S = (X, \prec, \sqsubset)$, *such that for all* $a, b, c, d \in X$, *the following hold:*

$I1: \ a \not\sqsubset a$	$I4: \ a \prec b \sqsubset c \vee a \sqsubset b \prec c \Longrightarrow a \sqsubset c$
$I2: \ a \prec b \Longrightarrow a \sqsubset b$	$I5: \ a \prec b \sqsubset c \prec d \Longrightarrow a \prec d$
$I3: \ a \prec b \prec c \Longrightarrow a \prec c$	$I6: \ a \sqsubset b \prec c \sqsubset d \Longrightarrow a \sqsubset d \vee a = d$

Here the *causality* relation $\prec$ also represents the "earlier than" relationship, and the *weak causality* relation $\sqsubseteq$ represents the "not later than" relationship but under the assumption that the system runs are interval orders.

Proposition 2 ([11])

1. $\prec$ *is a partial order such that* $a \prec b \Rightarrow b \not\sqsubseteq a$ *and* $a \sqsubseteq b \Rightarrow b \not\prec a$.
2. *If* $<$ *is an interval order on* X, *then* $(X, <, <^\frown)$ *is an io-structure.* $\square$

Interval order structures were independently introduced in [19] and [10]. Some of their properties have been presented in [13], yet their theory is not as well-developed and much less often applied than that of so-structures [9]. The lack of an operator analogous to the $\Diamond$-closure prevented us from building a working relationship between io-structures and sequence models of concurrency such as Mazurkiewicz traces and comtraces.

Theorem 6 ([13]). *Every so-structure is an io-structure.* $\square$

Since every so-structure is an io-structure, many properties of so-structures also hold for io-structures. Furthermore, we also have an analogue of Theorem 3 for interval orders and io-structures.

An interval order $<$ on X is an *interval extension* of an io-structure $S = (X, \prec, \sqsubseteq)$ if $\prec \subseteq <$ and $\sqsubseteq \subseteq <^\frown$. The set of all interval extensions of S will be denoted by $\mathsf{Interv}(S)$.

Theorem 7 ([13]). *For each io-structure* $S = (X, \prec, \sqsubseteq)$, *we have*
$$S = \left(X, \bigcap\nolimits_{<\in\mathsf{Interv}(S)} <, \bigcap\nolimits_{<\in\mathsf{Interv}(S)} <^\frown \right).$$
    $\square$

The above theorem is a generalisation of Szpilrajn's Theorem to io-structures. It is interpreted as the proof of the claim that io-structures uniquely represent sets of equivalent system runs, provided that the system's operational semantics can be fully described in terms of interval orders (see [9,13] for details). An example of a simple interval order structure which illustrates the main ideas behind this concept is shown in Figure 2.

Before defining the concept of $\blacklozenge$-closure and proving its properties, we need to introduce some auxiliary notions and prove some preliminary results.

Definition 9. *Let* $R_1, R_2 \subseteq X \times X$ *be two relations and let* $\langle S_1, \ldots, S_k \rangle$ *be a sequence of relations such that* $S_i \in \{R_1, R_2\}$, $i = 1, \ldots, k$.

1. *A sequence* $\langle S_1, \ldots, S_k \rangle$ *has* $\uplus$-*property w.r.t.* (R_1, R_2), *if for all* i, $1 \le i < k$, *we have* $\neg(S_i = S_{i+1} = R_2)$, *i.e. there are no two consecutive* R_2's.
2. *A sequence* $\langle S_1, \ldots, S_k \rangle$ *has* $\oplus$-*property w.r.t.* (R_1, R_2), *if* $k \ge 1$, $S_1 = S_k = R_1$ *and the sequence* $\langle S_2, \ldots, S_{k-1} \rangle$ *has* $\uplus$-*property w.r.t.* (R_1, R_2);
3. $R_1 \uplus R_2 = \bigcup_{k \ge 0} \{ S_1 \circ \ldots \circ S_k \mid \langle S_1, \ldots, S_k \rangle$ *has* $\uplus$-*property w.r.t.* $(R_1, R_2) \}$.
4. $R_1 \oplus R_2 = \bigcup_{k \ge 1} \{ S_1 \circ \ldots \circ S_k \mid \langle S_1, \ldots, S_k \rangle$ *has* $\oplus$-*property w.r.t.* $(R_1, R_2) \}$.

For example the sequence $\langle R_1, R_2, R_2, R_1 \rangle$ has neither $\uplus$- nor $\oplus$-property, the empty sequence $\langle \rangle$ and the sequence $\langle R_1, R_1, R_2, R_1, R_2 \rangle$ has $\uplus$-property but not $\oplus$-property, and $\langle R_1, R_1, R_2, R_1, R_2, R_1 \rangle$ has $\oplus$-property. We will omit the suffix "w.r.t. (R_1, R_2)" if the relations R_1 and R_2 are clear from the context. The relations $R_1 \oplus R_2$ and $R_1 \uplus R_2$ can easily be defined by appropriate regular expressions built from R_1 and R_2.

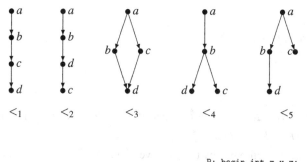

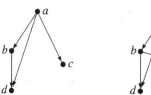 

Fig. 2. An example of a simple interval order structure $S = (X, \prec, \sqsubset)$, with $X = \{a, b, c, d\}$ and its set of all interval extensions $\mathsf{Interv}(S) = \{<_1, <_2, <_3, <_4, <_5\}$. The orders $<_1$ and $<_2$ are total, $<_3$ and $<_4$ are stratified and $<_5$ is interval but not stratified. The elements of $\mathsf{Interv}(S)$ are all equivalent runs (executions) of the program P involving the actions a, b, c and d, so the interval order structure uniquely defines a concurrent behaviour (history) of P (see [9] for details). The elements of $\mathsf{Interv}(S)$ are represented as Hasse diagrams, while $\prec$ and $\sqsubset$ are represented as graphs of their entire relations. In this case $\prec$ equals $<_5$, as there are not so many partial orders over the four elements set, but the interpretations of $<_5$ and $\prec$ are different. The incomparability in $<_5$ is interpreted as *simultaneity* while in $\prec$ as *having no casual relationship*.

Proposition 3. *Let* $R_1, R_2 \subseteq X \times X$ *be two relations. Then*

1. $R_1 \oplus R_2 = (R_1^+ \circ R_2)^* \circ R_1^+$,
2. $R_1 \uplus R_2 = (R_2 \cup id_X) \circ (R_1 \cup R_1 \Diamond R_2)^*$,
3. $R_1 \oplus R_2 \subseteq R_1 \uplus R_2$,
4. $(R_1 \oplus R_2) \uplus (R_1 \uplus R_2) \subseteq (R_1 \uplus R_2)$,
5. $(R_1 \oplus R_2) \oplus (R_1 \uplus R_2) \subseteq (R_1 \oplus R_2)$.

Proof. Follows immediately from Definition 9.   □

We can now define the main concept of this paper, the concept of ♦-*closure*.

Definition 10. *For every relational structure* $S = (X, R_1, R_2)$ *we define* $S^{\blacklozenge}$, *the* ♦-*closure of S, as:*

$$S^{\blacklozenge} \stackrel{df}{=} (X, \prec_{R_1, R_2}^{\blacklozenge}, \sqsubset_{R_1, R_2}^{\blacklozenge}) = (X, R_1 \oplus R_2, (R_1 \uplus R_2) \setminus id_X).$$

The ♦-closure is an extension of ◊-closure of so-structures and transitive closure of relations to io-structures. We will start by proving equivalences of Theorem 4(1,2).

Proposition 4

1. *If R_2 is irreflexive, then $S \subseteq S^{\blacklozenge}$.*
2. *$\left(S^{\blacklozenge}\right)^{\blacklozenge} = S^{\blacklozenge}$.*

Proof

1. By the definition $R_1 \subseteq R_1 \oplus R_2 = \prec^{\blacklozenge}_{R_1,R_2}$ and $R_2 \subseteq R_1 \uplus R_2$. Hence, if R_2 is irreflexive, $R_2 \setminus id_X \subseteq (R_1 \uplus R_2) \setminus id_X = \sqsubset^{\blacklozenge}_{R_1,R_2}$.
2. ($\supseteq$) Since $\sqsubset_{R_1,R_2}$ is irreflexive, by (1) we have $S^{\blacklozenge} \subseteq (S^{\blacklozenge})^{\blacklozenge}$.
   ($\subseteq$) We need to show that $\prec^{\blacklozenge}_{\prec^{\blacklozenge}_{R_1,R_2}, \sqsubset^{\blacklozenge}_{R_1,R_2}} \subseteq \prec^{\blacklozenge}_{R_1,R_2}$ and $\sqsubset^{\blacklozenge}_{\prec^{\blacklozenge}_{R_1,R_2}, \sqsubset^{\blacklozenge}_{R_1,R_2}} \subseteq \sqsubset^{\blacklozenge}_{R_1,R_2}$, which
   means $(R_1 \oplus R_2) \oplus (R_1 \uplus R_2) \subseteq R_1 \oplus R_2$, and $(R_1 \oplus R_2) \uplus (R_1 \uplus R_2) \subseteq R_1 \uplus R_2$. But
   this follows from Proposition 3(4,5). $\square$

Proposition 4(2) states that $\blacklozenge$-closure is *idempotent*, and justifies the name *closure* (cf. [24]).

Note that the exact replica of Theorem 4(3) is false. Consider an example, where $X = \{a,b\}$, $R_1 = \{(a,b)\}$ and $R_2 = \{(b,a)\}$. Thus, $\prec^{\blacklozenge}_{R_1,R_2} = \{(a,b)\}$ and $\sqsubset^{\blacklozenge}_{R_1,R_2} = \{(a,b),(b,a)\}$, so $\prec^{\blacklozenge}_{R_1,R_2}$ is irreflexive, but $(X, \prec^{\blacklozenge}_{R_1,R_2}, \sqsubset^{\blacklozenge}_{R_1,R_2})$ is not an io-structure since $a \prec^{\blacklozenge}_{R_1,R_2} b \sqsubset^{\blacklozenge}_{R_1,R_2} a \implies a \sqsubset a$, which contradicts (I1) from Definition 8. To find the necessary and sufficient condition for the $\blacklozenge$-closure of a relational structure to be an io-structure, we need a new concept.

Definition 11. *A relational structure $S = (X, R_1, R_2)$ is i-directed if*

1. *$R_1 \oplus R_2$ is irreflexive, and*
2. *$\forall a,b \in X. (a,b) \in R_2 \implies (b,a) \notin R_1 \oplus R_2$.*

Proposition 5. *$S^{\blacklozenge}$ is an io-structure if and only if $S = (X, R_1, R_2)$ is i-directed.*

Proof. ($\Rightarrow$) If $S^{\blacklozenge}$ is an io-structure then by (I1) and (I2), $\prec^{\blacklozenge}_{R_1,R_2} = R_1 \oplus R_2$ is irreflexive. Suppose $(a,b) \in R_2$ and $(b,a) \in R_1 \oplus R_2$. Since $R_2 \subseteq \sqsubset^{\blacklozenge}_{R_1,R_2}$, we have $a \prec^{\blacklozenge}_{R_1,R_2} b$ and $b \sqsubset^{\blacklozenge}_{R_1,R_2} a$, which contradicts Proposition 2(1).

($\Leftarrow$) We need to show that the conditions of Definition 8 are satisfied.

(I1) Clearly $(R_1 \uplus R_2) \setminus id_X$ is irreflexive.
(I2) From Corollary 3(3) we have $\prec^{\blacklozenge}_{R_1,R_2} \subseteq R_1 \uplus R_2$. Since $\prec^{\blacklozenge}_{R_1,R_2}$ is irreflexive, $\prec^{\blacklozenge}_{R_1,R_2} \subseteq (R_1 \uplus R_2) \setminus id_X = \sqsubset^{\blacklozenge}_{R_1,R_2}$.
(I3) Let $a \prec^{\blacklozenge}_{R_1,R_2} b$ and let $b \prec^{\blacklozenge}_{R_1,R_2} c$. This means $aS_1 \circ \ldots \circ S_k bQ_1 \circ \ldots \circ Q_r c$, where $\langle S_1, \ldots, S_k \rangle$ and $\langle Q_1, \ldots, Q_r \rangle$ both have $\oplus$-property. Hence $\langle S_1, \ldots, S_k, Q_1, \ldots, Q_r \rangle$ also has $\oplus$-property. Thus, $a \prec_{R_1,R_2} c$.
(I4) Let $a \prec^{\blacklozenge}_{R_1,R_2} b$ and let $b \sqsubset^{\blacklozenge}_{R_1,R_2} c$. This means $aS_1 \circ \ldots \circ S_k bQ_1 \circ \ldots \circ Q_r c$, where $\langle S_1, \ldots, S_k \rangle$ satisfies $\oplus$-property, and $\langle Q_1, \ldots, Q_r \rangle$ satisfies $\uplus$-property. Hence the sequence $\langle S_1, \ldots, S_k, Q_1, \ldots, Q_r \rangle$ has $\uplus$-property and thus $(a,c) \in R_1 \uplus R_2$. Suppose $a = c$. Since $a \prec^{\blacklozenge}_{R_1,R_2} b$ and $b \sqsubset^{\blacklozenge}_{R_1,R_2} c$, this means $aR_1 \circ S_1 \circ \ldots \circ S_k \circ R_1 b$, and

$bQ_1 \circ Q_2 \circ \ldots \circ Q_{s-1} \circ Q_s a$, where $S_i, Q_i \in \{R_1, R_2\}$. Either Q_1 or Q_s are equal to R_2, otherwise $b \prec^\blacklozenge_{R_1,R_2} a$, contradicting that $\prec^\blacklozenge_{R_1,R_2}$ is irreflexive. Suppose $Q_1 = R_2$. This means $Q_2 = R_1$. Thus there is some b_1 such that $bR_2b_1R_1 \circ Q_3 \circ \ldots \circ Q_s \circ R_1 \circ S_1 \circ \ldots \circ S_k \circ R_1 b$, which means $(b_1, b) \in R_1 \oplus R_2$, contradicting Definition 11(2). Hence $Q_1 = R_1$ and $Q_s = R_2$, i.e. $Q_{s-1} = R_1$. Thus, there is some b_s such that $b_s R_2 a$ and $aR_1 \circ S_1 \circ \ldots \circ S_k \circ R_1 \circ Q_1 \circ \ldots \circ R_1 b_s$, which means $(a, b_s) \in R_1 \oplus R_2$, contradicting Definition 11(2). Therefore $a \neq c$, i.e. $(a, c) \in (R_1 \uplus R_2) \setminus idx = \sqsubset^\blacklozenge_{R_1,R_2}$.

For the case when $a \sqsubset^\blacklozenge_{R_1,R_2} b \prec^\blacklozenge_{R_1,R_2} c$, we proceed almost identically.

(I5) Let $a \prec^\blacklozenge_{R_1,R_2} b \sqsubset^\blacklozenge_{R_1,R_2} c \prec^\blacklozenge_{R_1,R_2} d$. Thus, there are sequences $\langle S_1, \ldots, S_k \rangle$, $\langle P_1, \ldots, P_s \rangle$ and $\langle Q_1, \ldots, Q_r \rangle$, such that $aS_1 \circ \ldots \circ S_k bP_1 \circ \ldots \circ P_s cQ_1 \circ \ldots \circ Q_r d$, where $\langle S_1, \ldots, S_k \rangle$ and $\langle Q_1, \ldots, Q_r \rangle$ have $\oplus$-property and $\langle P_1, \ldots, P_s \rangle$ has $\uplus$-property. It follows that $\langle S_1, \ldots, S_k, Q_1, \ldots, Q_r, P_1, \ldots, P_s \rangle$ has $\oplus$-property and thus $a \prec^\blacklozenge_{R_1,R_2} d$.

(I6) Let $a \sqsubset^\blacklozenge_{R_1,R_2} b \prec^\blacklozenge_{R_1,R_2} c \sqsubset^\blacklozenge_{R_1,R_2} d$. Thus, there are sequences $\langle S_1, \ldots, S_k \rangle$, $\langle P_1, \ldots, P_s \rangle$ and $\langle Q_1, \ldots, Q_r \rangle$, such that $aS_1 \circ \ldots \circ S_k bP_1 \circ \ldots \circ P_s cQ_1 \circ \ldots \circ Q_r d$, where $\langle S_1, \ldots, S_k \rangle$ and $\langle Q_1, \ldots, Q_r \rangle$ have $\uplus$-property and $\langle P_1, \ldots, P_s \rangle$ has $\oplus$-property. It follows that $\langle S_1, \ldots, S_k, Q_1, \ldots, Q_r, P_1, \ldots, P_s \rangle$ has $\uplus$-property. So $a \sqsubset^\blacklozenge_{R_1,R_2} b$ or $a = d$. $\square$

The fact that the above result is slightly weaker than Theorem 4(3) does not seem to matter much as in virtually all applications of $\lozenge$-closure in [12] and [17], the relations R_1 and R_2 satisfy the equivalence of the conditions of Definition 11 for so-structures. The below result appears to be quite useful for various potential applications of $\blacklozenge$-closure.

Proposition 6. *Let $S = (X, R_1, R_2)$ be a relational structure and let $< \subseteq X \times X$ be an interval order such that $R_1 \subseteq <$ and $R_2 \subseteq <^\frown$. Then S is i-directed.*

Proof. By Proposition 2(2), $(X, <, <^\frown)$ is an io-structure, so it satisfies I1–I6. We have $R_1^+ \subseteq <^+ = <$, so $R_1 \oplus R_2 = (R_1^+ \circ R_2)^* \circ R_1^+ \subseteq (< \circ R_2)^* \circ < = \bigcup_{i=0}^\infty ((< \circ R_2)^i \circ <)$. For each i, we have $(< \circ R_2)^i \circ < \subseteq (< \circ <^\frown)^i \circ <$ and then by applying (I5) i times, we have $(< \circ <^\frown)^i \circ < \subseteq <$. Hence $R_1 \oplus R_2 \subseteq <$. i.e. $R_1 \oplus R_2$ is irreflexive. If $(a, b) \in R_2$ then $a <^\frown b$, i.e. $\neg(b < a)$ and also $(a, b) \notin R_1 \oplus R_2$ as $R_1 \oplus R_2 \subseteq <$. $\square$

Both $\lozenge$- and $\blacklozenge$-closures are often used for the cases like the one in Definition 7, so we can then use the above results to simplifies the proofs.

We now prove an analogue of Theorem 4(4), which states that io-structures are fixed points of $\blacklozenge$-closure.

Proposition 7. *If $S = (X, \prec, \sqsubset)$ is an io-structure then $S = S^\blacklozenge$.*

Proof. ($\subseteq$) Since S is an io-structure, $\sqsubset$ is irreflexive. Thus, by Proposition 4(1), $S \subseteq S^\blacklozenge$. ($\supseteq$) We will first show that $\prec \oplus \sqsubset \subseteq \prec$. Since $\prec \oplus \sqsubset = (\prec^+ \circ \sqsubset)^* \circ \prec^+$, it suffices to show that for each $i \geq 1$, $j \geq 0$, $k \geq 1$, $(\prec^i \circ \sqsubset)^j \prec^k \subseteq \prec$. From (I3) it follows $\prec^i \subseteq \prec$ and $\prec^k \subseteq \prec$, so $(\prec^i \circ \sqsubset)^j \circ \prec^k \subseteq (\prec \circ \sqsubset)^j \circ \prec$. By apply (I5) from right to left i times, we have $(\prec \circ \sqsubset)^j \prec \subseteq \prec$. Thus, $\prec \oplus \sqsubset \subseteq \prec$.

It remains to show $(\prec \uplus \sqsubset) \setminus idx \subseteq \sqsubset$. By Proposition 3(2), $\prec \uplus \sqsubset = (\sqsubset \cup idx) \circ (\prec \cup \prec \circ \sqsubset)^*$. It suffices to show that for all $i \geq 0$, $(\sqsubset \cup idx) \circ (\prec \cup \prec \circ \sqsubset)^i \subseteq \sqsubset \cup idx$. The case when $i = 0$ is trivial. For $i > 0$, by the induction hypothesis, we have $(\sqsubset \cup idx) \circ (\prec \cup \prec \circ \sqsubset)^{i-1} \subseteq \sqsubset \cup idx$. It suffices to show $(\sqsubset \cup idx) \circ (\prec \cup \prec \circ \sqsubset) \subseteq \sqsubset \cup idx$. But this holds since, by (I4) and (I6), $((\sqsubset \cup idx) \circ \prec) \cup ((\sqsubset \cup idx) \circ \prec \circ \sqsubset) \subseteq \sqsubset \cup idx$. $\square$

Directly from Proposition 7 we obtain the below result which will be used in the proof of the analogue of Theorem 4(5).

Corollary 1. *Every io-structure is i-directed.*   □

Proposition 8. *Let $S = (X, \prec, \sqsubset)$ be an io-structure and let $S_0 \subseteq S$. Then $S_0^\blacklozenge \subseteq S$ and $S_0^\blacklozenge$ is an io-structure.*

Proof. From Proposition 7 it immediately follows $S_0^\blacklozenge \subseteq S^\blacklozenge = S$.

Due to Proposition 5 it suffices to show that S_0 is i-directed. Let $S_0 = (X, R_1, R_2)$. We have $R_1 \oplus R_2 \subseteq \prec \oplus \sqsubset =^{\text{(Proposition 7)}} \prec$. Since $\prec$ is irreflexive, $R_1 \oplus R_2$ is irreflexive as well. Let $(a,b) \in R_2$. Since $R_2 \subseteq \sqsubset$, we have $a \sqsubset b$ which by Corollary 1, implies $(b,a) \notin \prec \oplus \sqsubset$. Since $R_1 \oplus R_2 \subseteq \prec \oplus \sqsubset$, $(b,a) \notin R_1 \oplus R_2$. Therefore S_0 is i-directed.   □

We can also show that $\blacklozenge$-closure is indeed a generalisation of $\lozenge$-closure.

Proposition 9. *If S is so-structure then $S = S^\lozenge = S^\blacklozenge$.*

Proof. A consequence of Theorem 4(4), Theorem 6 and Proposition 7.   □

6 Final Comments

A concept of $\blacklozenge$-closure has been defined for io-structures. It is an equivalence of $\lozenge$-closure of so-structures ([12]) and classical transitive closure of relations. It has also been proven that, in principle, $\blacklozenge$-closure has the same properties as $\lozenge$-closure and transitive closure. Because the definition of $\blacklozenge$-closure was more elaborate, the proofs were substantially more complex than their counterparts for $\lozenge$-closure. Nevertheless, only one property of $\blacklozenge$-closure is slightly weaker than its $\lozenge$-closure counterpart.

The counterpart of comtraces for io-structures has not been fully developed yet, but its foundation has been established. Fishburn's Theorem (Theorem 2) states that each interval order can be represented by an appropriate total order of the interval beginnings and ends. The below fundamental theorem states that each io-structure can be represented by an appropriate partial (not necessarily interval) order of the beginnings and ends.

Theorem 8 (Abraham, Ben-David, Magodor [1]). *A relational structure $S = (X, \prec, \sqsubset)$ is an io-structure iff there exists a partial order $\lhd$ on some Y and two mappings $B, E : X \to Y$ such that $B(X) \cap E(X) = \emptyset$ and for each*

1. $B(x) \lhd E(x)$,   2. $x \prec y \iff E(x) \lhd B(y)$,   3. $x \sqsubset y \iff B(x) \lhd E(y)$.   □

Szpilrajn's Theorem (Theorem 1) allows us to represent each partial order by its total extensions. The combination of these three theorems and Theorem 7 makes it possible to construct "interval traces", a version of Mazurkiewicz traces over an appropriate monoid of sequences of beginnings and ends, and then use "interval traces" to represent io-structures via Theorem 8. This topic is beyond the scope of this paper; however, the properties of $\blacklozenge$-closure are essential tools in this process.

Acknowledgement. The authors thank all three anonymous referees whose comments have helped us improve the final version of this paper significantly.

References

1. Abraham, U., Ben-David, S., Magodor, M.: On global-time and inter-process communication. In: Semantics for Concurrency, Workshops in Computing, pp. 311–323. Springer, Heidelberg (1990)
2. Begstra, J.A., et al. (eds.): The Handbook of Process Algebras. Elsevier Science, Amsterdam (2000)
3. Burris, S., Sankappanavar, H.P.: A Course in Universal Algebra. Springer, New York (1981)
4. Best, E., Koutny, M.: Petri net semantics of priority systems. Theoretical Computer Science 94, 141–158 (1992)
5. Diekert, V., Rozenberg, G. (eds.): The Book of Traces. World Scientific, Singapore (1995)
6. Fishburn, P.C.: Intransitive indifference with unequal indifference intervals. Journal of Mathematical Psychology 7, 144–149 (1970)
7. Fishburn, P.C.: Interval Orders and Interval Graphs. John Wiley, New York (1985)
8. Gaifman, H., Pratt, V.: Partial Order Models of Concurrency and the Computation of Function. In: Proc. LICS 1987, pp. 72–85 (1987)
9. Janicki, R.: Relational Structures Model of Concurrency. Acta Informatica 45(4), 279–320 (2008)
10. Janicki, R., Koutny, M.: Invariants and Paradigms of Concurrency Theory. In: Aarts, E.H.L., van Leeuwen, J., Rem, M. (eds.) PARLE 1991. LNCS, vol. 506, pp. 59–74. Springer, Heidelberg (1991)
11. Janicki, R., Koutny, M.: Structure of Concurrency. Theoretical Computer Science 112(1), 5–52 (1993)
12. Janicki, R., Koutny, M.: Semantics of Inhibitor Nets. Information and Computation 123(1), 1–16 (1995)
13. Janicki, R., Koutny, M.: Fundamentals of Modelling Concurrency Using Discrete Relational Structures. Acta Informatica 34, 367–388 (1997)
14. Janicki, R., Lê, D.T.M.: Modelling Concurrency with Quotient Monoids. In: van Hee, K.M., Valk, R. (eds.) PETRI NETS 2008. LNCS, vol. 5062, pp. 251–269. Springer, Heidelberg (2008)
15. Jensen, K.: Coloured Petri Nets, vol. 1,2,3. Springer, Heidelberg (1997)
16. Juhás, G., Lorenz, R., Mauser, S.: Synchronous + Concurrent + Sequential = Earlier than + Not later than. In: Proc. ACSD 2006, pp. 261–272. IEEE Computer Society Press, Los Alamitos (2006)
17. Kleijn, H.C.M., Koutny, M.: Process Semantics of General Inhibitor Nets. Information and Computation 190, 18–69 (2004)
18. Kleijn, J., Koutny, M.: Formal Languages and Concurrent Behaviour. Studies in Computational Intelligence 113, 125–182 (2008)
19. Lamport, L.: The mutual exclusion problem: Part I - a theory of interprocess communication; Part II - statements and solutions. Journal of ACM 33(2), 313–326 (1986)
20. Lê, D.T.M.: Studies in Comtrace Monoids. Master Thesis, Department of Computing and Software, McMaster University (2008)
21. Mazurkiewicz, A.: Concurrent Program Schemes and Their Interpretation. TR DAIMI PB-78, Comp. Science Depart. Aarhus University (1977)
22. Milner, R.: Operational and Algebraic Semantics of Concurrent Processes. In: van Leuween, J. (ed.) Handbook of Theoretical Computer Science, vol. 2, pp. 1201–1242. Elsevier, Amsterdam (1993)
23. Reisig, W.: Elements of Distributed Algorithms. Springer, Heidelberg (1998)
24. Rosen, K.H.: Discrete Mathematics and Its Applications. McGraw-Hill, New York (1999)
25. Szpilrajn, E.: Sur l'extension de l'ordre partiel. Fundam. Mathematicae 16, 386–389 (1930)
26. Wiener, N.: A contribution to the Theory of Relative Position. Proc. Camb. Philos. Soc. 17, 441–449 (1914)

Correcting Sorted Sequences in a Single Hop Radio Network*

Marcin Kik

Institute of Mathematics and Computer Science,
Wrocław University of Technology
Wybrzeże Wyspiańskiego 27, 50-370 Wrocław, Poland
Marcin.Kik@pwr.wroc.pl

Abstract. By k-*disturbed sequence* we mean a sequence obtained from a
sorted sequence by changing the values of at most k elements. We present
an algorithm for single-hop radio networks that sorts a k-disturbed
sequence of length n (where each station stores single key) in time
$4n + k \cdot (\lceil \lg k \rceil^2 + \lceil \lg(n - k + 1) \rceil + 6\lceil \lg k \rceil) - 2$ with energetic cost
$3 \cdot \lceil \frac{(\lceil \lg k \rceil + 1)(\lceil \lg k \rceil + 2)}{2\lfloor n/k \rfloor} \rceil + 4 \cdot \lceil \frac{\lceil \lg k \rceil}{\lfloor n/k \rfloor} \rceil + 10$. If $\frac{(\lceil \lg k \rceil + 1)(\lceil \lg k \rceil + 2)}{2} + \lceil \lg k \rceil \leq \lfloor n/k \rfloor$ then the energetic cost is bounded by 14.

1 Introduction

By k-*disturbed sequence* we mean a sequence obtained from a sorted sequence by
changing the values of at most k elements. We consider the problem of sorting
k-disturbed sequence of length n, for a relatively small value of k. We call it
k-*correction problem*. Our model of computation is a single hop radio network.
Such network consists of n stations $s_0, \ldots, s_{n-1}$ communicating with each other
by exchanging short radio messages. The stations are synchronized. Time is
divided into *slots*. Within a single time slot a single message can be broadcast.
During each time slot each station is either listening or sending or idle. If it
is sending or listening then it dissipates a unit of energy. We assume that the
stations are powered by batteries. Therefore we want to minimize *energetic cost*
of the algorithm, i.e. the maximum over all stations of non-idle time slots. We
consider *single hop* network: Each station is in the range of any other station.
If two or more stations send messages simultaneously, then a *collision* occurs.
Since our algorithm is avoiding collisions, we do not need to state precisely what
happens during the collisions and whether they are detectable.

Algorithm for k-correction can be applied whenever we want to keep sorted
a sequence of values that can change infrequently. As one example consider the
following scenario: The stations are deployed in some area and equipped with
sensors measuring some relatively stable value (e.g. temperature or air pressure).
We want to keep the measured values sorted. Thus our algorithm can be invoked
periodically, if we expect that the number of values changed within each period
is substantially lower than n.

---

* This work has been supported by MNiSW grant N N206 1842 33.

M. Kutyłowski, M. Gębala, and W. Charatonik (Eds.): FCT 2009, LNCS 5699, pp. 230–241, 2009.

The naive solution of our problem is to sort the input sequence using one of the existing sorting algorithms (e.g. [9], [4]). However, the energetic cost of such algorithms is $\Omega(\log n)$ and the time of energetically efficient algorithms is $\Omega(n \cdot \log n)$. The direct simulation of comparator sorting networks (e.g. [1], [2]), where each comparator between two positions is simulated in two time slots by the corresponding two stations, leads to quite efficient sorting algorithms. The problem of k-correction has also been studied for the comparator networks (e.g [7], [10]). However, they are practically efficient for very small (sub-polynomial) and fixed values of k. On the other hand, the algorithms for radio networks can be adaptive, and we can use the fact that each station can notice the change of its own key. The value of k in our algorithm can be arbitrary (even as large as $n - 1$, although the normal merge-sort (i.e. [4]) is more efficient for k close to n). The costs of the algorithm (time and energetic cost) are adapted to the actual value of k. As long as $\frac{(\lceil \lg k \rceil + 1)(\lceil \lg k \rceil + 2)}{2} + \lceil \lg k \rceil \le \lfloor n/k \rfloor$, the energetic cost of our algorithm is bounded by 14 and for arbitrary k it is bounded by $3 \cdot \lceil \frac{(\lceil \lg k \rceil + 1)(\lceil \lg k \rceil + 2)}{2 \lfloor n/k \rfloor} \rceil + 4 \cdot \lceil \frac{\lceil \lg k \rceil}{\lfloor n/k \rfloor} \rceil + 10$. Moreover, the algorithm uses only a constant number of variables within each station.

2 Preliminaries

Each station s_i initially stores a key in its local variable $oldKey[s_i]$. Variable $oldIdx[s_i]$ is the index of $oldKey[s_i]$ in the sorted sequence of keys. (The indexes are numbered from 0 to $n - 1$.) The station s_i also stores a new value of its key in $newKey[s_i]$ which is either equal to or different from $oldKey[s_i]$. The task of each s_i is to compute $newIdx[s_i]$ which is the index of $newKey[s_i]$ in the sorted sequence of the new keys. (The keys remain in their originating stations. We just compute their positions in the sorted sequence.)

In this paper "lg" denotes "$\log_2$". Whenever we define a permutation π of $\{0, \ldots, n - 1\}$, π^{-1} denotes the permutation reverse to π.

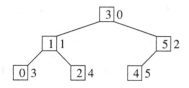

Fig. 1. The tree of T_6

Let T_m be a balanced binary tree consisting of m nodes, such that the last level of T_m is filled from left to right (see Figure 1). We define two ways of indexing of the nodes of T_m:

y-**indexing:** The y-index of the root is zero and, for each node with y-index y, the indexes of its left and the right son are $l(y) = 2(y + 1) - 1$ and

$r(y) = 2(y + 1)$, respectively. For y-index y the level of y in the tree is $lev(y) = \lfloor \log_2(y + 1) \rfloor$ and, if $y > 0$, then the y-index of its parent is $p(y) = \lfloor (y - 1)/2 \rfloor$.

x-**indexing:** The x-indexing is obtained by numbering the nodes in the in-order with the numbers $0, \ldots, m - 1$.

On Figure 1: The x-index is printed inside each node and the y-index – to the right of the node. *Binary search ordering* bso_m is a permutation of $\{0, \ldots, m-1\}$, such that $bso_m(x) = y$ if and only if the node with x-index x has the y-index equal to y. We define some functions and algorithm that can be used for efficient computation of bso. The height of T_m is $h(m) = \lceil \log_2(m + 1) \rceil$. The size of full binary tree of height h is $fs(h) = 2^h - 1$. Thus the number of missing leaves on the last level of T_m is $ml(m) = fs(h(m)) - m$. Let $ls(m)$ be the size of the left subtree of the root of T_m. If $m \leq 1$ then $ls(m) = 0$ else $ls(m) = fs(h(m) - 1) - \max\{0, ml(m) - 2^{h(m)-2}\}$. (The left subtree is full if there are at most $2^{h(m)-2}$ missing leaves in T_m.) Thus the size of the right subtree of the root of T_m is $rs(m) = m - 1 - ls(m)$. The position of y-index y within its level is $inlev(y) = y - fs(lev(y))$. Using these functions we can define efficient algorithm for computing bso (see Algorithm 1). Note that the **while** loop in Algorithm 1 iterates at most $h(m) \approx \lg m$ times and each iteration involves a constant number of computations of elementary functions. Thus the computation of bso is efficient.

```
function bso_m(x)
if x ∉ {0, ..., m - 1} then return x;  (* x outside domain *)
y ← 0;  (* y-index of the current node. We start from the root. *)
x_1 ← ls(m);  (* x-index of the root is the size of its left subtree *)
m_1 ← m;  (* size of the subtree of current node *)
while x_1 ≠ x do
    if x < x_1 then
        y ← l(y);  (* y-index of the left child *)
        m_1 ← ls(m_1);  (* size of the left subtree *)
        x_1 ← x_1 - m_1 + ls(m_1);  (* x-index of the left child *)
    else
        y ← r(y);  (* y-index of the right child *)
        m_1 ← rs(m_1);  (* size of the right subtree *)
        x_1 ← x_1 + ls(m_1) + 1;  (* x-index of the right child *)
return y;
```

Algorithm 1. Permutation bso_m

In the remaining algorithms we also use functions $at(l, i) = fs(l) + i$ (the y-index of the ith node at level l) and $levsize_m(l)$ (the size of the lth level of T_m). Note that, for $0 \leq l < h(m) - 1$, $levsize_m(l) = 2^l$ and, for $l = h(m) - 1$, $levsize_m(l) = 2^l - ml(m)$.

3 Description of the Algorithm

The network performs Algorithm 2. The general idea is to isolate the modified keys, sort them and merge them with the (sorted) sequence of the unmodified keys. We also try to balance the energetic costs among almost **all** the stations by forcing them to act as *virtual workers*.

```
begin
    split-and-count;
    (* all stations have learned k – the number of changed keys *)
    if k ≥ n/3 then
        apply sorting algorithm to compute new ranks of keys (e.g. the simple
        merge-sort from [4] without permuting the keys between the stations as
        is done in [6])
    else if k > 0 then
        assign-workers;
        sort;
        final-merge;
        Each sᵢ does: oldIdx[sᵢ] ← newIdx[sᵢ]; oldKey[sᵢ] ← newKey[sᵢ];
end
```

Algorithm 2. Correction algorithm

Initially each station recognizes whether its key is changed. Then the stations perform the procedure split-and-count (Algorithm 3) that counts the number of changed keys and computes the initial position of each key either in the sequence of not changed keys (called *a-sequence*) or in the sequence of the changed keys (called *b-sequence*). Split-and-count is similar to the first phase of the counting sort algorithm ([3]). The ordering of the keys within a-sequence and within b-sequence is the same as in the original sorted sequence. Thus the a-sequence is already sorted.

Then the procedure assign-workers (Algorithm 4) assigns equal number of stations (*workers*) to each key (*b-key*) from the b-sequence. Each real station s simulates one *virtual station vs* that is used as a worker.

Next the b-sequence is sorted by a simple merge-sort algorithm ([4]), however the energy required by each b-key is balanced among all the workers (virtual stations) assigned to this key. This is done by the procedure sort (Algorithm 5). Sorting is done by merging neighboring blocks of sorted b-keys of length m into sorted blocks of length $2m$. We start with $m = 1$ (sorted singletons) and end-up with $m \geq k$. Procedure merge($[i_1, i_2]$, $[i_3, i_4]$) (Algorithm 6) merges the block of b-keys on positions $i_1, \ldots, i_2$ with the block of b-keys on positions $i_3, \ldots, i_4$.

To merge the blocks each b-key from one block learns its rank in the other block and adds it to its index in the sorted sequence of the b-keys from its own block. In the procedure rank($[i_1, i_2]$, $\langle b_0, \ldots, b_{m-1} \rangle$, d) (Algorithm 8), each b-key

```
procedure split-and-count
Each s_i does (in parallel): begin
    idx[s_i] ← oldIdx[s_i]; idx_a[s_i] ← NIL; idx_b[s_i] ← NIL; sum[s_i] ← 0;
    key[s_i] ← newKey[s_i];
    if newKey[s_i] ≠ oldKey[s_i] then changed[s_i] ← 1 else changed[s_i] ← 0;
end
for time slot t ← 0 to n − 2 do
    Station s_i with idx[s_i] = t does: begin
        if changed[s_i] = 1 then idx_b[s_i] ← sum[s_i]
        else idx_a[s_i] ← idx[s_i] − sum[s_i];
        s_i sends msg, where msg = sum[s_i] + changed[s_i];
    end
    Station s_j with idx[s_j] = t + 1 receives msg and does: sum[s_j] ← msg;
in time slot n − 1: begin
    Station s_i with idx[s_i] = n − 1 does: begin
        if changed[s_i] = 1 then idx_b[s_i] ← sum[s_i]
        else idx_a[s_i] ← idx[s_i] − sum[s_i];
        s_i sends msg, where msg = sum[s_i] + changed[s_i];
    end
    Each station s_j receives msg and does k[s_j] ← msg; (* number of changed
    keys *)
end
```

Algorithm 3. Split and count

```
procedure assign-workers
(* Each s_i has the same value k[s_i] denoted by k. *)
(* The value ⌊n/k⌋ is denoted by gs (group size) *)
for time slot t ← 0 to k − 1 do
    The station s_i with idx_b[s_i] = t sends msg, where msg = newKey[s_i];
    Each s_j with t · gs ≤ j < (t + 1) · gs, does: begin
        s_j creates virtual station vs_{t,t'}, where t' = j mod gs;
        vs_{t,t'} receives msg;
        key[vs_{t,t'}] ← msg; (* vs_{t,t'} will be the t'th worker for tth changed key *)
        rworker[vs_{t,t'}] ← 0; (* initial index of current r-worker *)
        iworker[vs_{t,t'}] ← gs − 1; (* initial index of current i-worker *)
    end
```

Algorithm 4. Assigning workers

from the block $[i_1, i_2]$ learns its rank in the block of keys stored in the stations $b_0, \ldots, b_{m_1}$. Each worker can act as an *i-worker* or as a *r-worker*. The task of an i-worker (respectively, r-worker) is to update the current index (respectively, rank) of its b-key. For *stability* of sorting and avoiding collisions of indexes, the parameter d (either zero or one) is used to decide whether the b-key from the

---

procedure sort
Each virtual station does: $m \leftarrow 1$;
Each $vs_{i,j}$ with $j = iworker[vs_{i,j}]$ does: $idx[vs_{i,j}] \leftarrow 0$;
while $m < k$ **do**
$\quad$ **for** $i \leftarrow 0$ **to** $\lfloor \frac{k}{2m} \rfloor - 1$ **do**
$\quad\quad$ $\lfloor$ merge$([2i \cdot m, (2i+1)m - 1], \ [(2i+1)m, (2i+2)m - 1])$;
$\quad$ **if** $k \bmod (2m) > m$ **then**
$\quad\quad$ $\lfloor$ merge$([i, i+m-1], \ [i+m, k-1])$, where $i = \lfloor \frac{k}{2m} \rfloor \cdot 2m$;
$\quad$ $\lfloor$ Each virtual station does: $m \leftarrow 2 \cdot m$;

Algorithm 5. Sorting

---

procedure merge$([i_1, i_2], [i_3, i_4])$
begin
$\quad$ (* Let b_i denote $vs_{i,j}$ with $iworker[vs_{i,j}] = j$. *)
$\quad$ rank$([i_1, i_2], \langle b_{i_3}, \ldots, b_{i_4} \rangle, 0)$;
$\quad$ rank$([i_3, i_4], \langle b_{i_1}, \ldots, b_{i_2} \rangle, 1)$;
$\quad$ transfer-indexes$([i_1, i_2])$;
$\quad$ transfer-indexes$([i_3, i_4])$;
end

Algorithm 6. Merging

---

procedure transfer-indexes$([i_1, i_2])$
(* For each $i \in [i_1, i_2]$, all $vs_{i,j}$ have the same value of $iworker[vs_{i,j}]$, denoted
here by iw_i. Let $iw'_i = (iw_i - 1) \bmod gs$.*)
for *time slot* $t \leftarrow 0$ **to** $i_2 - i_1$ **do**
$\quad$ Let $r = i_1 + t$; $vs_{r,iw}$ sends $msg = newIdx[vs_{r,iw}]$ to $vs_{r,iw'}$, and $vs_{r,iw'}$
$\quad$ does: $idx[vs_{r,iw'}] \leftarrow msg$.
Each $vs_{i,j}$, for $i_1 \leq i \leq i_2$, does: $iworker[vs_{i,j}] \leftarrow iw'$.

Algorithm 7. Transferring indexes

block $[i_1, i_2]$ should be ranked before or after the equal b-keys from $b_0, \ldots, b_{m_1}$.
Each b-key from $b_0, \ldots, b_{m_1}$ is broadcast only once (by its current i-worker).
Each i-worker knows the index idx of b-key in the sorted sequence of its block.
These indexes are permuted by the bso_m an the keys are transmitted according
to this permutation. Thus, the sorted sequence is transmitted level by level of
the T_m-tree and each b-key (that knows its rank in the previously transmitted
levels) has to listen only once to determine its rank (the *newRank*) on the
currently transmitted level. In the T_m-tree, each level is interleaved with the
sorted sequence consisting of all the elements above this level. The last level of

---

procedure rank($[i_1, i_2]$,$\langle b_0, \ldots, b_{m-1} \rangle$,$d$)
For $i_1 \leq i \leq i_2$, each $vs_{i,j}$ with $j = rworker[vs_{i,j}]$ does: $rank[vs_{i,j}] \leftarrow 0$.
for $l \leftarrow 0$ **to** $h(m) - 2$ **do**
  (* Let a_i be the $vs_{i,j}$ with $rworker[vs_{i,j}] = j$ *)
  lrank(l, $\langle a_{i_1}, \ldots, a_{i_2} \rangle$,$\langle b_0, \ldots, b_{m-1} \rangle$,$d$);
  transfer-ranks($[i_1, i_2]$);
(* Let a_i be the $vs_{i,j}$ with $rworker[vs_{i,j}] = j$ *)
lrank($h(m) - 1$, $\langle a_{i_1}, \ldots, a_{i_2} \rangle$,$\langle b_0, \ldots, b_{m-1} \rangle$,$d$); (* on the last level of T_m *)
send-ranks-to-indexes($[i_1, i_2]$);

Algorithm 8. Ranking

---

procedure lrank(l,$\langle a_0, \ldots, a_{l-1} \rangle$, $\langle b_0, \ldots, b_{m-1} \rangle$,$d$);
for *time slot* $r \leftarrow 0$ **to** $levsize_m(l) - 1$ **do**
  The unique b_j with $bso_m(idx[b_j]) = at(l, r)$ sends $msg = key[b_j]$.
  Each a_i with $rank[a_i] = r$ listens and does: **begin**
    if *(key[a_i]* $\leq$ *msg and $d = 0$)* or *(key[a_i]* $<$ *msg and $d = 1$)* **then**
      $newRank[a_i] \leftarrow 2r$;
    else
      $newRank[a_i] \leftarrow 2r + 1$;
  end
  (* The following may happen if l is the last level of the tree T_m of bso_m. *)
  Each a_i with $rank[a_i] \geq levsize_m(l)$ does:
  $newRank[a_i] \leftarrow rank[a_i] + levsize_m(l)$;

Algorithm 9. Level ranking

---

procedure transfer-ranks($[i_1, i_2]$)
(* For each $i \in [i_1, i_2]$, all $vs_{i,j}$ have the same value of $rworker[vs_{i,j}]$, denoted
here by rw_i. Let $rw_i' = (rw_i + 1) \bmod gs$.*)
for *time slot* $t \leftarrow 0$ **to** $i_2 - i_1$ **do**
  Let $i = i_1 + t$; vs_{i,rw_i} sends $msg = newRank[vs_{i,rw_i}]$ to $vs_{i,rw_i'}$, and $vs_{i,rw_i'}$
  does: $rank[vs_{i,rw_i'}] \leftarrow msg$.
Each $vs_{i,j}$, for $i_1 \leq i \leq i_2$, does: $rworker[vs_{i,j}] \leftarrow rw_i'$.

Algorithm 10. Transferring ranks

T_m may be non-full, therefore in the computation of $newRank$ in the lrank for
the last level we are considering this case by adding the size of the level to the
ranks of the b-keys ranked after it.

To avoid excessive energy loss in a single station, each level of the bso_m-tree is
transmitted in a separate procedure lrank (Algorithm 9) and between the lranks

---

procedure send-ranks-to-indexes($[i_1, i_2]$)
(* For each $i \in [i_1, i_2]$, all $vs_{i,j}$ have the same value of $rworker[vs_{i,j}]$ and of $iworker[vs_{i,j}]$, denoted here by rw_i and iw_i respectively. Let $rw_i' = (rw_i + 1) \bmod gs$.*)
for *time slot* $t \leftarrow 0$ **to** $i_2 - i_1$ **do**
  Let $i = i_1 + t$;
  vs_{i,rw_i} sends $msg = newRank[vs_{i,rw_i}]$ to vs_{i,iw_i}, and vs_{i,iw_i} does:
  $newIdx[vs_{i,iw_i}] \leftarrow idx[vs_{i,iw_i}] + msg$.
Each $vs_{i,j}$, for $i_1 \leq i \leq i_2$, does: $rworker[vs_{i,j}] \leftarrow rw_i'$.

Algorithm 11. Sending and adding ranks to indexes

---

procedure final-merge
(* For $0 \leq i < n - k$, let a_i be the station s_j with $idx_a[s_j] = i$. For $0 \leq i < k$, let b_i be the s_j with $idx_b[s_j] = i$.*)
Each a_i does: $idx[a_i] \leftarrow idx_a[a_i]$;
rank($[0, k - 1], \langle a_0, \ldots, a_{n-k-1} \rangle, 0$);
(* b_t listens to the message msg sent during the t-th time slot of send-ranks-to-indexes in the above rank procedure, and does: $rank[b_t] \leftarrow msg$ *)
(* Let v_i be the $vs_{i,j}$ with $iworker[vs_{i,j}] = j$. *)
A: **for** $t \leftarrow 0$ **to** $k - 1$ **do**
      v_t sends $msg = newIdx[v_t]$ to b_t and b_t does:
      $newIdx[b_t] \leftarrow msg$; $idx[b_t] \leftarrow msg - rank[b_t]$;
    The b_i with $idx[b_i] = k - 1$ does: $last[b_i] \leftarrow TRUE$
B: **for** $t \leftarrow k - 1$ **downto** 1 **do**
      the b_i with $idx[b_i] = t$ sends $msg = rank[b_i]$;
      the b_j with $idx[b_j] = t - 1$ listens and does:
      if $rank[b_j] \neq msg$ **then** $last[b_j] \leftarrow TRUE$ **else** $last[b_i] \leftarrow FALSE$;
    Each a_i does: **if** $i = 0$ **then** $mov[a_i] \leftarrow 0$ **else** $mov[a_i] \leftarrow NIL$;
C: **for** $t \leftarrow 0$ **to** $n - k - 1$ **do**
      the b_i with $rank[b_i] = t$ and $last[b_i] = TRUE$ sends $msg = idx[b_i]$;
      a_t listens and if it received msg then it does: $mov[a_t] \leftarrow msg + 1$;
D: **for** $t \leftarrow 0$ **to** $n - k - 2$ **do**
      a_t sends $msg = mov[a_t]$;
      If $mov[a_{t+1}] = NIL$ then a_{t+1} listens and does: $mov[a_{t+1}] \leftarrow msg$;
    Each a_i does $newIdx[a_i] \leftarrow idx_a[a_i] + mov[a_i]$.

Algorithm 12. Final merging of a-sequence with b-sequence

the task of ranking on the next level is transferred from the current r-worker to the next r-worker by transfer-ranks (Algorithm 10). After the lrank for the last level, the current r-worker knows the rank of its b-key in the whole transmitted sequence and sends it to the corresponding i-worker (in the procedure send-ranks-to-indexes – Algorithm 11). The i-worker can now compute the index of the b-key in the merged sequence.

As soon as each i-worker knows the index of its b-key in the merged sequence, these indexes are transferred to the next i-workers in the procedures transfer-indexes.

After the b-sequence is sorted, the procedure final-merge (Algorithm 12) merges the two sorted sequences: a-sequence with b-sequence. First we use the workers to perform ranking of each b-key in the a-sequence. Each station b_t learns the rank of $newKey[b_t]$ in the a-sequence by overhearing the t-th time slot of the procedure send-ranks-to-indexes concluding this ranking. Then (in the loop **A:**) each b-key learns its index in the sorted b-sequence (variable idx) and in the final output sequence (variable $newIdx$). In the loop **B:** each b-key learns the rank of its successor in the b-sequence. Thus each b-key knows whether it is the last b-key with the same rank. Then (in the loop **C:**) each a-key key_a is informed by the last b-key key_b with the $rank$ equal to to the position of key_a in the a-sequence about its $rank$ in the b-sequence. Next (in the loop **D:**), each informed a-key informs its uninformed successors in the a-sequence about their rank in the b-sequence. Finally, each a-key computes its position in the sorted output sequence as the sum of its position in its own sequence and its rank in the other sequence. Here, each b-key is ranked before the equal or greater a-keys.

4   Analysis of Complexity

Time: Time of split-and-count is $t_1 = n$. Time of assign-workers is $t_2 = k$. Let t_3 be the time of sort. Let $t_M(m_1, m_2)$ denote the time of merging two sequences with lengths m_1 and m_2. $t_M(m_1, m_2) = t_R(m_1, m_2) + t_R(m_2, m_1) + m_1 + m_2$, where $t_R(m', m'')$ is time of ranking m' elements in the sequence of length m'' and $m_1 + m_2$ is the time of transfer-indexes. Note that $t_R(m', m'') = m'' + h(m'') \cdot m'$, where m'' is the total time spent in all Iranks and $h(m'') \cdot m'$ is the remaining time (spent in transfer-ranks and send-ranks-to-indexes). Thus $t_3 \leq \sum_{i=0}^{\lceil \lg k \rceil - 1} \lceil k/2^{i+1} \rceil \cdot t_M(2^i, 2^i) \leq k(\lceil \lg k \rceil^2 + 6\lceil \lg k \rceil)$ (see Appendix A). Let t_4 be the time of final-merge. $t_4 = t_R(k, n-k) + k + (k-1) + (n-k) + (n-k-1) = (n-k) + k \cdot \lceil \lg(n-k+1) \rceil + k + (k-1) + (n-k) + (n-k-1) = k \cdot \lceil \lg(n-k+1) \rceil + 3n - k - 2$. Thus the total time is: $t_1 + t_2 + t_3 + t_4 \leq 4n + k \cdot (\lceil \lg k \rceil^2 + \lceil \lg(n-k+1) \rceil + 6\lceil \lg k \rceil) - 2$.

Energy: In the procedure split-and-count each station broadcasts once and listens at most twice. After that each station acts either as a-station or a b-station. In assign-workers each b-station broadcasts once and each station listens once. In the procedures sort and final-merge, the energy used for each b-key key_t with idx_b equal t is balanced among the $gs = \lfloor n/k \rfloor$ virtual stations $vs_{t,0}, \ldots, vs_{t,gs-1}$. By current r-worker (respectively, i-worker) we mean the virtual station $vs_{t,j}$ with $rworker[vs_{t,j}] = j$ (respectively, $iworker[vs_{t,j}] = j$). The tasks of r-worker and of i-worker are transferred in round-robin fashion in opposite directions. Initially, $vs_{t,0}$ becomes the first r-worker of its group and $v_{t,gs-1}$ becomes the first i-worker of its group. Each time $vs_{t,i}$ becomes r-worker it listens at most twice (once in transfer-ranks and once in Irank) and broadcasts once (either in the next transfer-ranks or in send-ranks-to-indexes). Then the $vs_{t,(i+1) \bmod gs}$ becomes the next r-worker. The key_t requires α r-workers, where $\alpha \leq \sum_{i=0}^{\lceil \lg k \rceil} h(2^i) = \frac{(\lceil \lg k \rceil+1)(\lceil \lg k \rceil+2)}{2}$. (The last component of the sum comes from the rank in final-merge.) Each time $v_{t,i}$ becomes i-worker it listens at most twice (once in transfer-indexes and once in send-ranks-to-indexes) and broadcasts twice (once in rank and once either in the next transfer-indexes or in the loop **A:** of final-merge). Then the $v_{t,(i-1) \bmod gs}$ becomes the next i-worker. The key key_t requires β i-workers, where $\beta \leq \lceil \lg k \rceil$. We split the energy used by the virtual station $vs_{t,i}$ into two components: the energy used as r-worker: e_r and the energy used as i-worker: e_i. Since $vs_{t,i}$ becomes r-worker (respectively, i-worker) once $\lfloor n/k \rfloor$ times, we have $e_r \leq 3 \cdot \lceil \frac{\alpha}{\lfloor n/k \rfloor} \rceil$ and $e_i \leq 4 \cdot \lceil \frac{\beta}{\lfloor n/k \rfloor} \rceil$. If $\beta + \alpha \leq \lfloor n/k \rfloor$ then the energy used by $vs_{t,i}$ is at most 4, otherwise it can be bounded by $e_r + e_i$. In the procedure final-merge, each b-station listens at most three times (once in rank, once in loop **A:**, and once in loop **B:**) and broadcasts at most twice (once in loop **B:** and once in loop **C:**). Each a-station listens at most twice (once in loop **C:** and once in loop **D:**) and broadcasts at most twice (once in rank and once in loop **D:**). Let e_a (respectively, e_b) denote the energy used by a-station (respectively, b-station). Thus, $e_a = 5$ and $e_b = 7$ and the total energy used by each station can be bound by: $3+\max\{e_a, e_b\}+e_i+e_r \leq 10+3\cdot \lceil \frac{(\lceil \lg k \rceil+1)(\lceil \lg k \rceil+2)}{2\lfloor n/k \rfloor} \rceil+4\cdot \lceil \frac{\lceil \lg k \rceil}{\lfloor n/k \rfloor} \rceil$. Additionally, if $\frac{(\lceil \lg k \rceil+1)(\lceil \lg k \rceil+2)}{2} + \lceil \lg k \rceil \leq \lfloor n/k \rfloor$ then the energetic cost is bounded by 14.

5   Conclusions and Final Remarks

The following theorem concludes the discussion of previous sections:

Theorem 1. *There exists an algorithm that sorts a k-disturbed sequence of length n distributed among n stations of single-hop radio network in time at most $4n + k \cdot (\lceil \lg k \rceil^2 + \lceil \lg(n - k + 1) \rceil + 6\lceil \lg k \rceil) - 2$ with energetic cost at most $3 \cdot \lceil \frac{(\lceil \lg k \rceil+1)(\lceil \lg k \rceil+2)}{2\lfloor n/k \rfloor} \rceil + 4 \cdot \lceil \frac{\lceil \lg k \rceil}{\lfloor n/k \rfloor} \rceil + 10$. If $\frac{(\lceil \lg k \rceil+1)(\lceil \lg k \rceil+2)}{2} + \lceil \lg k \rceil \leq \lfloor n/k \rfloor$ then the energetic cost of the algorithm is bounded by 14.* $\square$

Consider a scenario in which the algorithm is invoked periodically. The stations with largest indexes have greater chance of not being used as virtual worker (if $n \bmod \lfloor n/k \rfloor \neq 0$). Since the the indexes of the stations are independent of the indexes of the keys in the sequence, we can try to balance this chance among all stations by re-indexing them between the periods (for example, by adding one modulo n to each index).

Our algorithm is designed for reliable network (i.e. each transmitted message is received by each listening station with probability one). It would be interesting to consider k-correction in unreliable networks. (Sorting algorithm for such networks has been proposed in [6]).

References

1. Ajtai, M., Komlós, J., Szemerédi, E.: Sorting in c log n parallel steps. Combinatorica 3, 1–19 (1983)
2. Batcher, K.E.: Sorting networks and their applications. In: Proceedings of 32nd AFIPS, pp. 307–314 (1968)

3. Gębala, M., Kik, M.: Counting-Sort and Routing in a Single Hop Radio Network. In: Kutyłowski, M., Cichoń, J., Kubiak, P. (eds.) ALGOSENSORS 2007. LNCS, vol. 4837, pp. 138–149. Springer, Heidelberg (2008)
4. Kik, M.: Merging and Merge-sort in a Single Hop Radio Network. In: Wiedermann, J., Tel, G., Pokorný, J., Bieliková, M., Štuller, J. (eds.) SOFSEM 2006. LNCS, vol. 3831, pp. 341–349. Springer, Heidelberg (2006)
5. Kik, M.: Sorting Long Sequences in a Single Hop Radio Network. In: Královič, R., Urzyczyn, P. (eds.) MFCS 2006. LNCS, vol. 4162, pp. 573–583. Springer, Heidelberg (2006)
6. Kik, M.: Ranking and Sorting in Unreliable Single Hop Radio Network. In: Coudert, D., Simplot-Ryl, D., Stojmenovic, I. (eds.) ADHOC-NOW 2008. LNCS, vol. 5198, pp. 333–344. Springer, Heidelberg (2008)
7. Kik, M., Kutyłowski, M., Piotrów, M.: Correction Networks. In: ICPP 1999, pp. 40–47 (1999)
8. Nakano, K.: An Optimal Randomized Ranking Algorithm on the k-channel Broadcast Communication Model. In: ICPP 2002, pp. 493–500 (2002)
9. Singh, M., Prasanna, V.K.: Energy-Optimal and Energy-Balanced Sorting in a Single-Hop Sensor Network. In: PERCOM (March 2003)
10. Stachowiak, G.: Fibonacci Correction Networks. In: Halldórsson, M.M. (ed.) SWAT 2000. LNCS, vol. 1851, pp. 535–548. Springer, Heidelberg (2000)

A   Analysis of Time Complexity of the Procedure Sort

$$t_3 \leq \sum_{i=0}^{\lceil \lg k \rceil - 1} \lceil k/2^{i+1} \rceil \cdot t_M(2^i, 2^i)$$

$$= \sum_{i=0}^{\lceil \lg k \rceil - 1} \lceil k/2^{i+1} \rceil \cdot (2 \cdot t_R(2^i, 2^i) + 2 \cdot 2^i)$$

$$= \sum_{i=0}^{\lceil \lg k \rceil - 1} \lceil k/2^{i+1} \rceil \cdot (2 \cdot (2^i + h(2^i) \cdot 2^i) + 2 \cdot 2^i)$$

$$= \sum_{i=0}^{\lceil \lg k \rceil - 1} \lceil k/2^{i+1} \rceil \cdot 2^{i+1}(2 + h(2^i)).$$

Since $h(2^i) = i + 1$, we have:

$$t_3 = \sum_{i=0}^{\lceil \lg k \rceil - 1} \lceil k/2^{i+1} \rceil \cdot 2^{i+1}(3 + i)$$

$$\leq \sum_{i=0}^{\lceil \lg k \rceil - 1} (k/2^{i+1} + 1) \cdot 2^{i+1}(3 + i)$$

$$= \sum_{i=0}^{\lceil \lg k \rceil - 1} (k + 2^{i+1})(3 + i).$$

For $0 \leq i \leq \lceil \lg k \rceil - 1$, we have $2^{i+1} < k$. Thus

$$
\begin{aligned}
t_3 &\leq \sum_{i=0}^{\lceil \lg k \rceil - 1} 2 \cdot k \cdot (3 + i) \\
&= 6k \lceil \lg k \rceil + 2k \cdot \sum_{i=0}^{\lceil \lg k \rceil - 1} i \\
&= 6k \lceil \lg k \rceil + 2k \cdot \frac{(\lceil \lg k \rceil - 1) \lceil \lg k \rceil}{2} \\
&\leq k(\lceil \lg k \rceil^2 + 6 \lceil \lg k \rceil).
\end{aligned}
$$

A Local Distributed Algorithm to Approximate MST in Unit Disc Graphs*

Krzysztof Krzywdziński

Faculty of Mathematics and Computer Science, Adam Mickiewicz University,
60–769 Poznań, Poland
kkrzywd@amu.edu.pl

Abstract. We present a new distributed algorithm, which finds a good approximation of the Minimum Spanning Tree in the Unit Disc Graphs. Our algorithm, in $O(d^2)$ synchronous rounds, where d is an input parameter, finds a subgraph H of the Unit Disc Graph G which contains a Minimum Spanning Tree of G. Moreover, H is planar, does not contain cycles of weight smaller than $d/3$ and the weight of H is $(1 + O(1/d))$ approximation of the weight of the Minimum Spanning Tree of G.

1 Introduction

Consider a set V - the set of points on the plane. A Unit Disc Graph (UDG) is a graph with vertex set V and the edge set E consisting of those pairs of vertices, which are at distance at most 1 (i.e. $E = \{(u,v)|u,v \in V \text{ and } \|u,v\| \leq 1\}$, where $\|\cdot,\cdot\|$ is an Euclidian norm). Therefore in UDG's, by default, we assign to e(u,v) a weight $w(u,v)$ equal to the distance between their endpoints, i.e., $w(u,v) = \|u,v\|$.

UDG can be used as a model of wireless ad hoc networks such as cell phone networks or sensor networks, in which all communication ranges are identical. Here cell phones, sensors or other devices, which form a network, are represented by the vertices while edges represent possible communication links.

One of the most important characteristics of such graphs (networks) is the weight of its Minimum Spanning Tree (MST), defined as the spanning tree with the minimum weight (minimum sum of weights of its edges). Finding MST is instrumental in the design of data and communication networks, the network all communication ranges are identical. For example, in ad hoc sensor networks MST is the optimal routing tree for data aggregation (see [1]) and the broadcasting based on MST consumes, up to a constant factor, almost optimum. We should point out that, for general graphs, the problem of finding MST in distributed way has been considered before, including [2,3,4,5,6], as well as [7,8,9,10].

In our paper we present a new distributed algorithm, called ALMOSTMST, which finds a good approximation of the Minimum Spanning Tree in Unit Disc Graphs in $O(d^2)$ synchronous rounds, where d is an input parameter. More precisely, it finds a subgraph K of the Unit Disc Graph G such that K contains

---

* This work was supported by grant N206 017 32/2452 for years 2007-2010.

M. Kutyłowski, M. Gębala, and W. Charatonik (Eds.): FCT 2009, LNCS 5699, pp. 242–249, 2009.

a minimum spanning tree of G. Moreover, K is planar, does not have cycles of weight less than $d/3$ and, most importantly, the weight of K is $(1 + O(1/d))$-approximation of the weight of a minimum spanning tree of G. The key idea behind the construction of our algorithm is an application of so-called "three lattices" method, developed in [11]. A similar idea of lattice translation has been introduced independently by Lillis, Pemmaraju and Pirwani in [12].

At *COCOON'2003* Xiang-Yang Li (see [9]) presented a distributed localized algorithm, called here APPROXMST, which finds a low weight subgraph L of a Unit Disc Graph G, such that L contains some MST of G as a subgraph, and L is bounded degree planar graph whose total edge length (weight) is within a *multiplicative constant* factor of the weight of MST of G. The construction of APPROXMST is based on a concept of relative neighborhood graph (RNG).

Our algorithm takes a graph L generated by the algorithm APPROXMST as an input, and produces its subgraph K (and so a subgraph of G) which, in constant number of distributed rounds, approximates the weight of MST of G to within a factor $1 + O(1/d)$. To get such significant improvement over APPROXMST in terms of the approximation factor our algorithm incurs some additional cost in terms of the number of communication rounds. The algorithm runs in $poly(d)$ synchronous rounds. So, if d is chosen to be a constant, our algorithm runs in $O(1)$ rounds. Unfortunately both the locality and communication cost are rising. Namely, instead of only two-hop information gathering, as in APPROXMST, our algorithm uses $O(d^2)$-hops. Also the communication cost of ALMOSTMST, for an n vertex graph, is $O(n^2)$, to compare with $O(n)$ for APPROXMST.

Our paper is organized as follows: in Section 2 we present the main algorithm, basic definitions and the idea of three lattice method. In Section 3 we prove that the graph K contains $MST(G)$, does not have short cycles and that its weight is $(1 + O(1/d))$-approximation of the weight of MST(G). We finish Section 3 with the proof that the algorithm works in $poly(d)$ synchronous rounds.

2   Main Result

The presented algorithm will work in distributed, synchronous, message-passing model of computations. We model the network as a Unit Disc Graph (UDG). Network nodes correspond to vertices in the graph and unit radius discs centered at the points correspond to communication range. Two nodes are said to be able to communicate directly if and only if their euclidean distance is within 1. Here we also assume that every computational unit (vertex) is equipped with the Global Positioning System (GPS), or knows its position on the plane by other sources. Moreover, to simplify arguments, let us assume that local clocks of vertices of UDG can be synchronized i.e., assume that we perform computations in rounds (model LOCAL defined in [13]). In each round a vertex can send, receive messages from its neighbors, and can perform some local computations. While we assume a synchronous model of computation, it is not hard to adapt our algorithm to the asynchronous setting.

Recall that by the weight of an edge ($e = (u, v)$) in UDG we will mean an Euclidean distance between v and u and denote it by $w(e) = \|v, u\|$. If $H \subseteq G$ is a subgraph of G then the weight of H we define as $w(H) = \sum_{e \in E(H)} w(e)$. For a given connected graph G, MST(G) is a spanning tree T of G such that $w(T)$ is minimal possible over all spanning trees of G.

As we have already mentioned, the main idea of our algorithm is to use three square lattices to compute locally optimal solutions inside the appropriate squares formed by those lattices. We call this approach the three lattices method. In this technique we divide the plane into three separate lattices which define three classes of squares. In the first step we compute optimal solutions inside squares of the first class. In the second step we correct those solutions inside squares of the second class and next we perform corrections inside squares of the third class.

Consider a lattice $L_d^{(0,0)}$ (with origin in $(0,0)$ and which consists of parallel horizontal and vertical lines at distance d) and two other lattices $L_d^{(d/3,d/3)}$ and $L_d^{(2d/3,2d/3)}$ (obtained from $L_d^{(0,0)}$ by moving it by vectors $(d/3, d/3)$ and $(2d/3, 2d/3)$, respectively (see Figure 1). The set of interiors of squares determined by lattice $L_d^{(\nu_1, \nu_2)}$ are denoted by $S_d^{(\nu_1, \nu_2)}$. We denote by $G[\mathcal{S}]$ a subgraph of G induced by vertices contained in the square $\mathcal{S}$ (i.e. vertices from the set $\{v \in V(G) : v \in \mathcal{S}\}$)in a square lattice.

Let G be a connected graph and let H be a subgraph of G, such that it has k connected components $H_1, H_2, \ldots H_k$.

Define first a simple procedure SPANSUB in the following way:

SPANSUB(G, H)
Input: A graph G and its subgraph H.
Output: A spanning subgraph S of G, $S = S(G, H)$.

1. $V(S) := V(G)$
2. $E(S) := (E(G) \setminus E(H)) \cup \left(\bigcup_{i=1}^{k} E(\text{MST}(H_i)) \right)$

Our algorithm repeatedly calls the above procedure and consists of the following main steps:

ALMOSTMST
Input: Connected Unit Disc Graph G and input parameter d .
Output: Graph K which contains MST(G) .

(1) Run APPROXMST with graph G as the input and L as the output.
(2) Run SPANSUB$\left(L, \bigcup_{\mathcal{S} \in \mathcal{S}_d^{(0,0)}} L[\mathcal{S}] \right)$, return graph N'.
(3) Run SPANSUB$\left(N', \bigcup_{\mathcal{S} \in \mathcal{S}_d^{(d/3,d/3)}} N'[\mathcal{S}] \right)$, return graph N''.
(4) Run SPANSUB$\left(N'', \bigcup_{\mathcal{S} \in \mathcal{S}_d^{(2d/3,2d/3)}} N''[\mathcal{S}] \right)$, return graph K.

In the theorem below, we summarize properties of the output graph of the algorithm ALMOSTMST.

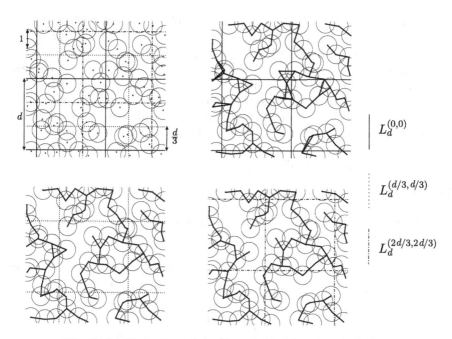

$L_d^{(0,0)}$

$L_d^{(d/3,d/3)}$

$L_d^{(2d/3,2d/3)}$

Fig. 1. An illustration of the idea of algorithm ALMOSTMST

Theorem 1. *Let G be a Unit Disc Graph and let d be a input parameter, $d > 9$. Suppose that K is an output graph of the algorithm ALMOSTMST. Then K is planar graph with bounded degrees, $MST(G) \subseteq K$, $w(K) \leq (1 + \frac{6}{d-6})w(MST(G))$ and weight of each cycle of K is at least $d/3$. Moreover algorithm ALMOSTMST can be implemented in $O(d^2)$ synchronous rounds in LOCAL model of computations.*

3   Correctness of ALMOSTMST Algorithm

We shall prove Theorem 1 via a sequence of lemmas.

Lemma 2. *Let G be a connected Unit Disc Graph. Output graph K of the algorithm ALMOSTMST is planar, has bounded degrees and contains $MST(G)$.*

Proof. Planarity and bounded degree property of K simply follow from the observation that K is a subgraph of the graph L generated by the algorithm APPROXMST.

Recall that L contains $MST(G)$ (see [9]). It remains to prove that K contains $MST(G)$ as well. For simplicity, we assume that all edges of G have different weights and so $MST(G)$ is unique.

If we analyze the main ingredient of the algorithm ALMOSTMST we see that only thing that remains to be shown is that if H is a connected subgraph of the connected graph G then $MST(G) \subseteq \text{SPANSUB}(G, H)$. By the definition of the procedure SPANSUB it is equivalent to showing that $E(MST(G)) \subseteq (E(G) \setminus E(H)) \cup (E(MST(H)))$.

Suppose that $E(\mathrm{MST}(G))$ is not a subset of $(E(G)\backslash E(H))\cup(E(MST(H)))$. So there exists an edge $e = uv$ such that $e \in (E(\mathrm{MST}(G)) \cap E(H)) \backslash E(\mathrm{MST}(H))$. Since H is connected, there exists a path in $\mathrm{MST}(H)$ joining vertices u and v. Denote it by $p_{u,v}$. The edge $e \notin \mathrm{MST}(H)$ thus $\forall_{e' \in p_{u,v}} w(e') < w(e)$ (otherwise we could replace any of the edges from $p_{u,v}$ by e and form a spanning tree with a smaller weight). Now consider a graph $M = \mathrm{MST}(G) \backslash e$ which contains two connected components M_u (with vertex u) and M_v (with vertex v). At least one edge $e' \in p_{u,v}$ connects M_u with M_v. Therefore we can construct the spanning tree $M' = (\mathrm{MST}(G) \cup e') \backslash e$ such that $w(M') < \mathrm{MST}(G)$ (we have assumed that $w(e') < w(e)$), a contradiction.

The following observation will be helpful in the proof of Lemma 4.

Fact 3. *For any three points* $q_0 \in L_d^{(0,0)}$, $q_1 \in L_d^{(d/3,d/3)}$ *and* $q_2 \in L_d^{(2d/3,2d/3)}$ *we have* $\|q_0, q_1\| + \|q_0, q_2\| \geq d/3$.

Proof. Let $\left\|q_0, L_d^{(\nu_1,\nu_2)}\right\| = \min_{q' \in L_d^{(\nu_1,\nu_2)}} \|q_0, q'\|$ and choose an arbitrary point $q_0 = (x, y)$ lying on the segment with ends in $(0,0)$ and $(0, d)$. Then

$$\left\|q_0, L_d^{(d/3,d/3)}\right\| = \begin{cases} d/3 - y & \text{if } y \in [0, d/3] \\ y - d/3 & \text{if } y \in [d/3, 2d/3] \\ d/3 & \text{if } y \in [2d/3, d] \end{cases}$$

$$\left\|q_0, L_d^{(2d/3,2d/3)}\right\| = \begin{cases} d/3 & \text{if } y \in [0, d/3] \\ 2d/3 - y & \text{if } y \in [d/3, 2d/3] \\ y - 2d/3 & \text{if } y \in [2d/3, d]. \end{cases}$$

Therefore

$$\left\|q_0, L_d^{d/3,d/3)}\right\| + \left\|q_0, L_d^{(2d/3,2d/3)}\right\| = \begin{cases} 2d/3 - y & \text{if } y \in [0, d/3] \\ d/3 & \text{if } y \in [d/3, 2d/3] \\ y - d/3 & \text{if } y \in [2d/3, d]. \end{cases}$$

Thus, for such choice of q_0 the sum is always at least $d/3$ and it is easily seen that it also holds for other possible choices of a position of q_0.

Lemma 4. *All cycles in output graph* K *of the algorithm* ALMOSTMST *have weight at least* $d/3$.

Proof. The conclusion follows from the observation that if C is a cycle in the graph K, then it must intersect all three lattices $L_d^{(0,0)}$, $L_d^{(d/3,d/3)}$ and $L_d^{(2d/3,2d/3)}$. Otherwise, assume that C does not cross $L_d^{(0,0)}$ and is entirely contained in the square $\mathcal{S} \in \mathcal{S}_d^{(0,0)}$. It is however impossible since at least one edge of C would then be deleted in the first step of the algorithm ALMOSTMST. Similar argument also works in the case when C avoids intersection with two other lattices. So, let q_0, q_1 and q_2 be points in which C crosses $L_d^{(0,0)}$, $L_d^{(d/3,d/3)}$ and $L_d^{(2d/3,2d/3)}$, respectively. Then, by Fact 3, $w(C) \geq \|q_0, q_1\| + \|q_0, q_2\| \geq d/3$, and the lemma follows.

Lemma 5. *Output graph K of the algorithm* ALMOSTMST *satisfies*

$$w(K) \leq (1 + 6/(d-6))w(MST(G)).$$

Proof. Since the graph K is a subgraph of the graph L generated by the algorithm APPROXMST, therefore K is planar. Denote by $|F(K)|$ the number of bounded faces in the plane embedding of K. Every bounded face corresponds to some cycle C and by Lemma 4 each such C has weight at least $d/3$. Since every edge in C belongs to the frontier of at most two faces, therefore

$$w(K) \geq \frac{|F(K)|}{2} \frac{d}{3}.$$

By Lemma 2, K contains $MST(G)$. By Euler's formula $|V(K)| - |E(K)| + |F(K)| = 1$ (remind that $F(K)$ is the number of bounded faces), so $MST(G)$ can be extracted from K by the removal of exactly $|F(K)|$ edges. Since each edge have weight at most 1 we have

$$\frac{|F(K)| d}{6} \leq w(K) \leq |F(K)| + w(MST(G)).$$

Thus,

$$|F(K)| \leq \frac{6w(MST(G))}{d-6},$$

which implies that

$$w(K) \leq \left(1 + \frac{6}{d-6}\right) w(MST(G)).$$

Finally, let us show that ALMOSTMST algorithm, under the LOCAL model of computation, can be implemented in $poly(d)$ synchronous rounds. The implementation is based on FINDINGMSTINSQUARE procedure described below.

FINDINGMSTINSQUARE
Input: Connected component H' of $H[S]$ where H is a subgraph of the Unit Disc Graph G.
Output: MST(H') .

(1) Select a leader in H'.
(2) Apply BFS procedure on the graph H' in order to deliver to the leader complete information about weights of all the edges in H'.
(3) The leader of H', using Kruskal algorithm, computes MST(H').
(4) The leader of H', using BFS procedure, sends information to all vertices of H' about the edges which belong to MST(H').

Lemma 6. *Let d be a length of a side of a square $\mathcal{S}$. Then the algorithm* FIND-
INGMSTINSQUARE *works in is $O(d^2)$ synchronous rounds in LOCAL model of computations.*

Proof. First observe that steps (1), (2) and (4) of the algorithm FINDINGMSTIN-
SQUARE take $O(diam(H[\mathcal{S}]))$ synchronous rounds, where $diam(H[\mathcal{S}])$ denotes
the diameter of graph $H[\mathcal{S}]$). Under the LOCAL model of computation, step (3)
of the algorithm FINDINGMSTINSQUARE takes a single synchronous round.

It remains to show that if $H' \subseteq H[\mathcal{S}]$ is connected then $diam(H') = O(d^2)$.
Denote by $c(r, v)$ a disc of radius r with the center in a vertex v. If we take
two distinct vertices $w_i, w_j \in \text{MIS}(H')$ (maximal independent set of H') then
$\|w_i, w_j\| > 1$, so discs $c\left(\frac{1}{2}, w_i\right)$ and $c\left(\frac{1}{2}, w_j\right)$ are disjoint. Obviously every
$c\left(\frac{1}{2}, w_i\right)$ lie in a square of side $d+1$. Such a square contains at most $\frac{(d+1)^2}{\pi/4}$ disjoint
discs of radius $\frac{1}{2}$, therefore $\text{MIS}(H')$ is at most $\frac{4(d+1)^2}{\pi}$. Let $v, w \in G[\mathcal{S}]$ be two
vertices such that the shortest path $p_{v,w}$ between v and w has length equal to the
diameter of H'. It is obvious that if we choose every second vertex on that path,
it will form an independent set. Therefore $diam(H') \leq 2|\text{MIS}(H')| \leq \frac{8(d+1)^2}{\pi}$.

References

1. Krishnamachari, B., Estrin, D., Wicker, S.: The impact of data aggregation in
   wireless sensor networks. In: Proceedings of the Int. Workshop on Distributed
   Event-Based Systems. (July 2002)
2. Faloutsos, M., Molle, M.: Creating optimal distributed algorithms for minimum
   spanning trees (1995)
3. Gallager, R.G., Humblet, P.A., Spira, P.M.: A distributed algorithm for minimum-
   weight spanning trees. ACM Trans. Program. Lang. Syst. 5(1), 66–77 (1983)
4. Garay, J.A., Kutten, S., Peleg, D.: A sub-linear time distributed algorithm for
   minimum-weight spanning trees (extended abstract). In: IEEE Symposium on
   Foundations of Computer Science, pp. 659–668 (1993)
5. Peleg, D., Rubinovich, V.: A near-tight lower bound on the time complexity of
   distributed minimum-weight spanning tree construction. SIAM J. Comput. 30(5),
   1427–1442 (2000)
6. Chin, F.Y.L., Ting, H.F.: An almost linear time and o(n log n + e) messages
   distributed algorithm for minimum-weight spanning trees. In: FOCS, pp. 257–266
   (1985)
7. Arya, S., Smid, M.: Efficient construction of a bounded degree spanner with low
   weight. In: van Leeuwen, J. (ed.) ESA 1994. LNCS, vol. 855, pp. 48–59. Springer,
   Heidelberg (1994)
8. Khan, M., Pandurangan, G., Kumar, V.: Distributed algorithms for constructing
   approximate minimum spanning trees in wireless sensor networks. IEEE Transactions on Parallel and Distributed Systems (to appear)
9. Li, X.Y.: Approximate mst for udg locally. In: Warnow, T.J., Zhu, B. (eds.)
   COCOON 2003. LNCS, vol. 2697, pp. 364–373. Springer, Heidelberg (2003)
10. Blin, L., Butelle, F.: A very fast (linear time) distributed algorithm, on general
    graphs, for the minimum-weight spanning tree. In: Cardenas, R.G. (ed.) OPODIS,
    Studia Informatica Universalis, Suger, Saint-Denis, rue Catulienne, France, pp.
    113–124 (2001)

11. Krzywdziński, K.: Efficient construction of (d+1,3d)-Ruling Set in Wireless Ad Hoc Networks. In: Nguyen, N.T., Katarzyniak, R., Janiak, A. (eds.) Challenges in Computational Collective Intelligence. SCI (2009)
12. Lillis, K.M., Pemmaraju, S.V., Pirwani, I.A.: control and geographic routing in realistic wireless networks. In: Kranakis, E., Opatrny, J. (eds.) ADHOC-NOW 2007. LNCS, vol. 4686, pp. 15–31. Springer, Heidelberg (2007)
13. Peleg, D.: Distributed computing: a locality-sensitive approach. Society for Industrial and Applied Mathematics, Philadelphia (2000)

Small-Space Analogues of Valiant's Classes

Meena Mahajan and B.V. Raghavendra Rao

The Institute of Mathematical Sciences, Chennai 600 113, India
{meena,bvrr}@imsc.res.in

Abstract. In the uniform circuit model of computation, the width of a boolean circuit exactly characterises the "space" complexity of the computed function. Looking for a similar relationship in Valiant's algebraic model of computation, we propose width of an arithmetic circuit as a possible measure of space. We introduce the class VL as an algebraic variant of deterministic log-space L. In the uniform setting, we show that our definition coincides with that of VPSPACE at polynomial width.

Further, to define algebraic variants of non-deterministic space-bounded classes, we introduce the notion of "read-once" certificates for arithmetic circuits. We show that polynomial-size algebraic branching programs can be expressed as a read-once exponential sum over polynomials in VL, *i.e.* VBP $\in \Sigma^R \cdot$ VL. We also show that $\Sigma^R \cdot$ VBP = VBP, *i.e.* VBPs are stable under read-once exponential sums. Further, we show that read-once exponential sums over a restricted class of constant-width arithmetic circuits are within VQP, and this is the largest known such subclass of poly-log-width circuits with this property.

1   Introduction

In the arithmetic circuit model of computation, Valiant introduced the classes VP and VNP to capture the complexity of polynomial families ([1], see also [2]). Over Boolean computation these classes correspond roughly to P and NP; over arithmetic computation with Boolean inputs they correspond roughly to #LogCFL and #P. Given the rich structure within P and LogCFL, it is natural to ask for a complexity theory that can describe arithmetic computation at this level. In particular, there are two well-known hierarchies within polynomial-size Boolean circuit families: the NC hierarchy based on depth, modelling parallel time on a parallel computer, and the SC hierarchy based on width, modelling simultaneous time-space complexity of P machines. It is straightforward to adapt Valiant's definition of VP to NC. But an adaptation capturing a space-bound is more tricky, especially when dealing with sub-linear space. The main question is: what would be a "right" measure for space? Two obvious choices are: 1) the number of arithmetic "cells" or registers used during the course of computation (i.e., the unit-space model), and 2) the size of a succinct description of the polynomials computed at each cell. A third choice is the complexity of computing the coefficient function for polynomials in the family. All three of these space measures have been studied in the literature, [3,4,5,6], with varying degrees of success. In particular, the models [3,5,6], when adapted to logarithmic space,

M. Kutyłowski, M. Gębala, and W. Charatonik (Eds.): FCT 2009, LNCS 5699, pp. 250–261, 2009.
© Springer-Verlag Berlin Heidelberg 2009

are too powerful to give meaningful insights into small-space classes, whereas the model of [4] as defined for log-space is too weak.

In this paper, we propose yet another model for describing space-bounded computations of families of polynomials. Our model is based on width of arithmetic circuits, and captures both succinctness of coefficients and ease of evaluating the polynomials. Special cases of this model have been studied in the past: in [7], such circuits over $\mathbb{Z}$ with Boolean inputs and an additional syntactic degree restriction are studied, while in [8,9] such circuits over arbitrary rings but restricted to be syntactic multilinear are studied. We show that our notion of space VSPACE(s) coincides with that of [5,6] at polynomial space with uniformity (Theorem 1), and so far avoids the pitfalls of being too powerful or too weak at logarithmic space.

Continuing along this approach, we propose a way of describing non-deterministic space-bounded computation in this context. The specific motivation for this is to obtain an analogue of the class non-deterministic log-space NL as well as an analogue of the result that VNP $= \varSigma \cdot$ VP. Again, there is a well-known model for NL that easily carries over to the arithmetic setting, namely polynomial-size branching programs BP. But we are unable to compare VBP with our version of VL. Our model here for NL is based on read-once certificates, which also provide the correct description of NL in terms of L in the Boolean world. We show that the arithmetization of this model, $\varSigma^R \cdot$ VL does contain arithmetic branching programs (Theorem 2).

Surprisingly, we are unable to show a good upper bound on the complexity of read-once certified log-space polynomial families. This raises the question: Is the read-once certification procedure inherently too powerful? We show that this is not always the case; for branching programs, read-once-certification adds no power at all (Theorem 3). Similarly, for polylog-width circuits where the syntactic degree is bounded by a polynomial, read-once certification does not take us beyond VQP (Theorem 4). Further, if the circuit is multiplicatively disjoint and of constant width, then read-once certification does not take us beyond VP.

2   Preliminaries

We use standard definitions for complexity classes such as polynomial space PSPACE, NC, L, NL and LogCFL (see *e.g.* [10],[11]).

An arithmetic circuit over a ring $\langle \mathbb{K}, +, \times, 0, 1 \rangle$ is a directed acyclic graph C, where vertices with non-zero in-degree are labelled from $\{+, \times\}$, and vertices of zero-in-degree (called *leaf* nodes) are labelled from $X \cup \mathbb{K}$, where $X = \{x_1 \ldots, x_n\}$ is the set of variable inputs to the circuit. An output node of C is a node of zero out-degree, and it computes a polynomial in $\mathbb{K}[X]$. (A circuit can have more than one output node, thus computing a set of polynomials.)

The following definitions apply to both arithmetic and boolean circuits, hence we simply use the term circuit. *Depth* of a circuit is the length of a longest path from a leaf node to an output node. *Size* of the circuit is the number of nodes and edges in it. *Width* of a layered circuit is the maximum number of nodes at any particular layer. We assume that all output nodes appear at the last layer.

Polynomial size poly-log depth Boolean circuits form the class NC; NC^1 is the subclass of log-depth circuits and is known to be contained in L. Polynomial size poly-log width boolean circuits form the class SC; SC^0 is the subclass of constant-width circuits and SC^1 is the subclass of log-width circuits. It is known that SC^0 equals NC^1 ([12]) and uniform SC^1 equals L.

An arithmetic (resp. Boolean) circuit C is said to be *skew* if for every multiplication gate $f = g \times h$ (resp. $\wedge$ gate $f = g \wedge h$), either h or g is in $X \cup \mathbb{K}$. C is said to be *weakly skew* if for every $f = g \times h$, either the edge (g, f) or (h, f) is a bridge in the circuit, i.e removing the edge disconnects the circuit. Poly-size Boolean skew circuits are known to characterise NL([13]).

An *algebraic branching program* (BP for short) over a ring $\mathbb{K}$ is a layered directed acyclic graph, where edges are labelled from $\{x_1, \ldots, x_n\} \cup \mathbb{K}$. There are two designated nodes, s and t, where s has zero in-degree and t has zero out-degree. Size of a BP is the number of nodes and edges in it and width is the maximum number of nodes at any layer. Length of a BP is the number of layers in it. Depth of a BP B equals $1 + \mathsf{length}(B)$. The polynomial P computed by a BP is the sum of weights of all s-t paths in P, where weight of a path is the product of all edge labels in the path. We will also consider multi output BPs, where the above is generalised in the obvious way to several nodes $t_1, t_2, \ldots, t_m$ existing at the last level. Note that BPs can be simulated by skew circuits and vice versa with a constant blow up in the width.

VP denotes the class of families of polynomials $(f_n)_{n \geq 0}$ such that $\forall n \geq 0$

- $f_n \in \mathbb{K}[x_1, \ldots, x_{u(n)}]$, where $u \leq \mathsf{poly}(n)$
- $\deg(f_n) \leq \mathsf{poly}(n)$
- f_n can be computed by a polynomial size arithmetic circuit.

VP_e is the sub-class of VP corresponding to poly-size arithmetic formula (*i.e.* circuits with out-degree at most 1). If f_n can be computed by arithmetic circuits with resource bounds the same as NC^1 or SC^0 or SC^1, then we say the family is in VNC^1 or VSC^0 or VSC^1 respectively. It is known that VP_e is the same as VNC^1. If the circuits computing f_n have quasipolynomial size $2^{\log^c n}$, we say that $\{f_n\}$ is in the class VQP.

A polynomial family $(f_n)_{n \geq 0}$ is in VNP if there exists a family $(g_\ell)_{n \geq 0}$ in VP such that $f_n(X) = \sum_{e \in \{0,1\}^m} g_n(X, e)$, where m is bounded by $\mathsf{poly}(n)$.

We let VBP and VBWBP stand for classes corresponding to *poly*-size BPs of *poly* and *constant* width, respectively. Without loss of generality, we can treat these classes as skew circuits. ([14])

Let $\mathcal{C}$ be a complexity class defined in terms of Turing machines. A circuit family $(B_n)_{n \geq 0}$ is said to be $\mathcal{C}$-uniform, if the direct connection language for B_n can be decided in $\mathcal{C}$. (see [10])

3   Notion of Space for Arithmetic Computations?

In the case of boolean computations, the notion of "width" of a circuit captures the notion of space in the Turing machine model (under certain uniformity assumptions). In the case of arithmetic computations, defining a notion of "space bounded computation" seems to be a hard task.

3.1 Previously Studied Notions

One possible measure for space is the number of arithmetic "cells" or registers used in the course of computation (i.e., the unit-space model). Michaux [3] showed that with this notion of space, any language that is decided by a machine in the Blum-Shub-Smale model of computation (a general model for algebraic computation capturing the idea of computation over reals, [15]; see also [2]) can also be computed using $O(1)$ registers. Hence there is no space-hierarchy theorem under this space measure.

Another possible measure is the size of a succinct description of the polynomials computed at each cell. In [4], Naurois introduced a notion of weak space in the Blum-Shub-Smale model, and introduced the corresponding log space classes LOGSPACE $_W$ and PSPACE$_W$. This is in fact a way of measuring the complexity of succinctly describing the polynomials computed by or represented at each "real" cell. Though this is a very natural notion of "succinctness" of describing a polynomial, this definition has a few drawbacks:

1. LOGSPACE $_W$ seems to be too weak to contain even NC^1 over $\mathbb{R}$, which is in contrast to the situation in the Boolean world.
2. The polynomials representable at every cell have to be "sparse", i.e., the number of monomials with non-zero coefficients should be bounded by some polynomial in the number of variables.

The second condition above makes the notion of weak space very restrictive if we adapt the definition to the Valiant's algebraic computation model. This is because the corresponding log-space class in this model will be computing only sparse polynomials, but in the non-uniform setting sparse polynomials are known to be contained in a highly restrictive class called skew formula ([8]), which is in fact a proper subclass of constant depth arithmetic circuits (i.e., VAC^0).

Koiran and Perifel ([5,6]) suggested a notion of polynomial space for Valiant's ([1,2]) classes. The main purpose of their definition was to prove a transfer theorem over $\mathbb{R}$ and $\mathbb{C}$. Under their definition Uniform-VPSPACE (the non-uniform counterpart can be defined similarly) is defined as the set of families (f_n) of multivariate polynomials $f_n \in F[x_1, \ldots, x_{u(n)}]$ with integer coefficients such that

- $u(n)$ is bounded by a polynomial in n.
- Size of coefficients of f_n is bounded by $2^{poly(n)}$.
- Degree of f_n is bounded by $2^{poly(n)}$.
- Every bit of the coefficient function of f_n is computable in PSPACE.

In [5], it was observed that the class VPSPACE is equivalent to the class of polynomials computed by arithmetic circuits of polynomial depth and exponential size. Such Boolean circuits compute exactly PSPACE, hence the name VPSPACE. Thus one approach to get reasonable smaller space complexity classes is to generalise this definition. We can consider VSPACE($s(n)$) to consist of families $(f_n)_{n \geq 1}$ of polynomials satisfying the following:

- $f_n \in \mathbb{Z}[x_1, \ldots, x_{u(n)}]$, where $u(n)$, the number of variables in f_n, is bounded by some polynomial in n.
- Degree of f_n is bounded by $2^{s(n)}$.
- The number of bits required to represent each of the coefficients of f_n is bounded by $2^{s(n)}$, *i.e.* the coefficients of f_n are in the range $[-2^{2^{s(n)}}, 2^{2^{s(n)}}]$
- Given n in unary, an index $i \in [1, 2^{s(n)}]$, and a monomial M, the ith bit of the coefficient of M in f_n is computable in DSPACE($s(n)$).

It is easy to see that with this definition, even the permanent function PERM_n is in log-space. Thus VSPACE($\log n$) would be too big a class to be an arithmetic version of log-space. The reason here is that this definition, unlike that of [4], goes to the other extreme of considering only the complexity of coefficient functions and ignores the resource needed to add the monomials with non-zero coefficients. The relationship between the complexity of coefficient functions and the polynomials themselves is explored more thoroughly in [16].

3.2 Defining VSPACE in Terms of Circuit Width

In this section we propose width of a (layered) circuit as a possible measure of space for arithmetic computations.

Definition 1. *Let* VWIDTH(S) *(with $S = S(n)$) be the class of polynomial families $(f_n)_{n \geq 0}$ with the following properties,*

- *The number of variables $u(n)$ in f_n is bounded by* poly(n)
- *$f_n \in \mathbb{Z}[x_1, \ldots, x_{u(n)}]$, i.e f_n has only integer coefficients*
- *$\deg(f) \leq \max\{2^{S(n)}, \mathsf{poly}(n)\}$.*
- *The coefficients of f_n are representable using $\max\{2^{S(n)}, \mathsf{poly}(n)\}$ many bits.*
- *f_n is computable by an arithmetic circuit of width $S(n)$ and size $\leq \max\{2^{S(n)}, \mathsf{poly}(n)\}$.*

Further, if the arithmetic circuits in the last condition are DSPACE(S)-uniform, we call the family Uniform-VWIDTH(S).

Remark 1. In [7], poly size circuits of log width and poly degree were introduced. The above definition generalises this definition to arbitrary width. A notable difference is that in [7] and [8], the degree bound was on the *syntactic degree* of the width-bounded circuits rather than on the degree of output polynomial. This was necessary to bound the degree of the output polynomial as well as the size of its coefficients. Here we do not deal with syntactic degree but independently bound the degree of the polynomial as well as the values of the coefficients.

We show in Theorem 1 below that with this definition, uniform VWIDTH(poly) coincides with uniform VPSPACE as defined in [5]; thus polynomial width indeed corresponds to polynomial space. Motivated by this equivalence, we define the following complexity classes:

Definition 2. VSPACE($S(n)$) = VWIDTH($S(n)$)
*Uniform-*VSPACE($S(n)$)= *Uniform-*VWIDTH($S(n)$)

We denote the log-space class by VL; thus VL = VWIDTH($\log n$) = VSC^1.

The following containments and equalities follow directly from known results about width-constrained arithmetic circuits.

Lemma 1 ([17,7,8,9]). $\mathsf{VBWBP} = \mathsf{VNC}^1 = \mathsf{VP}_e \subseteq \mathsf{VSPACE}(O(1)) = \mathsf{VSC}^0 \subseteq \mathsf{VL} = \mathsf{VSC}^1 \subseteq \mathsf{VP}$

Thus VL according to this definition is in VP and avoids the trivially "too-powerful" trap; also, it contains VNC^1 and thus avoids the "too weak" trap.

The following closure property is easy to see.

Lemma 2. *For every* $S(n) > \log n$, *the classes* $\mathsf{VSPACE}(S(n))$ *are closed under polynomially bounded summations and constant many products.*

3.3 Comparing $\mathsf{VPSPACE}$ and $\mathsf{VWIDTH}(\mathsf{poly})$

This subsection is devoted to proving the following equivalence,

Theorem 1. *The class* $Uniform\text{-}\mathsf{VPSPACE}$ *as defined in [5] coincides with* $Uniform\text{-}\mathsf{VWIDTH}(\mathsf{poly})$.

The equivalence follows from the two lemmas below.

Lemma 3. $Uniform\text{-}\mathsf{VPSPACE} \subseteq Uniform\text{-}\mathsf{VWIDTH}(\mathsf{poly})$.

The converse direction is a little more tedious, but essentially follows from the Lagrange interpolation formula for multivariate polynomials.

Lemma 4. $Uniform\text{-}\mathsf{VWIDTH}(\mathsf{poly}) \subseteq Uniform\text{-}\mathsf{VPSPACE}$.

Lemma 4 requires that the VWIDTH family be uniform (with a direct-connection uniformity condition). If the VWIDTH family is non-uniform, this problem cannot be circumvented with polynomial advice, since the circuit has exp-size.

4 Read-Once Certificates

In general, non-deterministic complexity classes can be defined via existential quantifiers. *e.g.* , $\mathsf{NP} = \exists \cdot P$. In the algebraic setting, Valiant ([1], [2]) introduced the class VNP (algebraic counterpart of NP) obtained as an "exponential" sum of values of a polynomial size arithmetic circuit. *i.e.* , $\mathsf{VNP} = \Sigma \cdot P$. Valiant also showed that $\mathsf{VNP} = \Sigma \cdot \mathsf{VP}_e$, which equals $\Sigma \cdot \mathsf{VNC}^1$.

If we consider smaller classes, NL is the natural non-deterministic version of L. However to capture it via existential quantifiers, we need to restrict the use of the certificate, since otherwise $\exists \cdot \mathsf{L} = \mathsf{NP}$. It is known that with the notion of "read once" certificates (see, *e.g.* , [11], Chapter 4) one can express NL as an existential quantification over L. Analogously, we propose a notion of "read-once" certificates in the context of arithmetic circuits so that we can get meaningful classes by taking exponential sums over classes that are below VP.

Definition 3. *Let C be a layered arithmetic circuit with ℓ layers. Let $X = \{x_1, \ldots, x_n\}$ and $Y = \{y_1, \ldots, y_m\}$ be the input variables of C. C is said to be "read-once certified" in Y if the layers of C can be partitioned into m blocks, such that each block reads exactly one variable from Y. That is, C satisfies the following:*

- *There is a fixed permutation $\pi \in S_m$ such that the variables of Y appear in the order $y_{\pi(1)}, \ldots, y_{\pi(m)}$ along any leaf-to-root path.*
- *There exist indices $0 = i_1 \leq \ldots \leq i_m \leq \ell$ such that the variable $y_{\pi(j)}$ appears only from layers $i_j + 1$ to i_{j+1}.*

We usually assume, without loss of generality, that π is the identity permutation. Now we define the the exponential sum over read-once certified circuits.

Definition 4. *Let $\mathcal{C}$ be any arithmetic circuit complexity class. A polynomial family $(f_n)_{n \geq 0}$ is said to be in the class $\Sigma^R \cdot \mathcal{C}$, if there is a family $(g_n)_{n \geq 0}$ such that $f_n(X) = \sum_{Y \in \{0,1\}^{m(n)}} g_n(X, Y)$ and g_n is computed by a circuit of type $\mathcal{C}$ that is read-once certified in Y and $m(n) \leq \mathsf{poly}(n)$.*

We also use the term "read once exponential sum" over $\mathcal{C}$ to denote $\Sigma^R \cdot \mathcal{C}$.

For circuits of width polynomial or more, the restriction to read-once certification is immaterial: the circuit can read a variable once and carry its value forward to any desired layer via internal gates. This is equivalent to saying that for a P machine, read-once input is the same as two-way-readable input. Thus

Lemma 5. $\Sigma^R \cdot \mathsf{VP} = \Sigma \cdot \mathsf{VP} = \mathsf{VNP}$

Having seen that the read-once certificate definition is general enough for the case of large width circuits, we turn our focus on circuits of smaller width. Once the width of the circuit is substantially smaller than the number of bits in the certificate, the read-once property becomes a real restriction. If this restriction correctly captures non-determinism, we would expect that in analogy to BP = NL = $\Sigma^R \cdot$ L, we should be able to show that VBP equals $\Sigma^R \cdot$ VL. In a partial answer, we show in the following theorem one direction: read-once exponential sums over VL are indeed powerful enough to contain VBP.

Theorem 2. $\mathsf{VBP} \subseteq \Sigma^R \cdot \mathsf{VL}$.

In order to prove the above theorem, we consider a problem that is complete for VBP under projections. (see [2] for definition of a projection). Let $G_n = (V_n, E_n)$ (with $V_n = \{1, \ldots, n\}$) be the complete layered graph with variable $x_{i,j}$ as label on the edge $(i, j) \in E_n$. Let $s = 1$ and $t = n$ denote two special nodes in G_n. Let $X = (x_{i,j})_{i,j \in \{1, \ldots, n\}}$. For any directed $s - t$ path $P = \langle v_0, v_1, \ldots, v_\ell, v_{\ell+1} \rangle$ in G_n, let M_P denote the monomial that is the product of the variables corresponding to edges in P. Let $PATH_G^n = \sum_P M_P$, where P is over all the $s - t$ paths in G_n.

Proposition 1. *(folklore) $(PATH_G^n)_{n \geq 0}$ is complete for VBP under projections.*

We prove theorem 2 by showing that $PATH_G^n \in \Sigma^R \cdot \mathsf{VL}$.

Proof (of theorem 2). Here onwards we drop the index n from G_n.

We define function $h_G(Y, Z)$: $\{0,1\}^{\lceil \log n \rceil} \times \{0,1\}^{n^2} \to \{0,1\}$ as follows. Assume that the variables in $Y = \{y_1, \ldots, y_k\}$ and $Z = \{z_{1,1}, \ldots, z_{n,n}\}$ take only values from $\{0,1\}$. $h_G(Y, Z) = 1$ if and only if $Z = z_{1,1}, \ldots, z_{n,n}$ represents a directed s-t path in G of length exactly ℓ, where ℓ written in binary is $y_1 \ldots y_k$, and Z reads off the entries of X in column-major order. Note that $s - t$ paths P in G are in one-to-one correspondence with assignments to Y, Z such that $h_G(Y, Z) = 1$. Hence

$$PATH_G^n = \sum_P M_P = \sum_{Y,Z} h_G(Y, Z) \, [\text{ weight of path specified by } Y, Z]$$

$$= \sum_{Y,Z} h_G(Y, Z) \prod_{i,j} (x_{i,j} z_{i,j} + (1 - z_{i,j}))$$

There is a deterministic log-space algorithm A which computes $h_G(Y, Z)$ when Y, Z is given on a "read once" input tape (see [11]). Let C be the corresponding $\log n$ width boolean circuit. (w.l.o.g., all negation gates in C are at the leaves.) Call its natural arithmetization D. Since Y and Z are on a read-once input tape, it is easy to see that C, and hence D, are read-once certified in the variables from Y and Z. We can attach, parallel to D, constant-width circuitry that collects factors of the product $\prod_{i,j} (x_{i,j} z_{i,j} + (1 - z_{i,j}))$ as and when the $z_{i,j}$ variables are read, and finally multiplies this with $h_G(Y, Z)$. The resulting circuit remains $O(\log n)$-width, and remains read-once certified on Y, Z. $\square$

While we are unable to show the converse, we are also unable to show a reasonable upper bound on $\Sigma^R \cdot \mathsf{VL}$. It is not even clear if $\Sigma^R \cdot \mathsf{VL}$ is contained in VP. One possible interpretation is that the Σ^R operator is too powerful and can lift up small classes unreasonably. We show that this is not the case in general; in particular, it does not lift up VBP and VBWBP.

Theorem 3

1. $\Sigma^R \cdot \mathsf{VBP} = \mathsf{VBP}$

2. $\Sigma^R \cdot \mathsf{VBWBP} = \mathsf{VBWBP}$

This theorem follows from Lemma 6 below, and from the facts that weakly skew circuits can be transformed into (1) skew circuits ([14]), and (2) skew circuits with a quadratic blowup in width ([9]). First, a definition.

Definition 5. *For $f \in \mathbb{K}[X, Y]$ with $X = \{x_1, \ldots, x_n\}$ and $Y = \{y_1, \ldots, y_m\}$, $E_Y(f)$ denotes the exponential sum of $f(X, Y)$ over all Boolean settings of Y. That is,*

$$E_Y(f)(X) = \sum_{e \subseteq \{0,1\}^m} f(X, e)$$

Lemma 6. *Let C be a layered skew arithmetic circuit on variables $X \cup Y$. Suppose C is read-once certified in Y. Let $w = \mathsf{width}(C)$, $s = \mathsf{size}(C)$ and*

ℓ = *the number of layers in* C. *Let* $f_1, \ldots, f_w$ *denote the output gates (also the polynomials computed by them) of* C. *There exists a weakly skew circuit* C', *of size* $O(mw^4 s)$ *and width* $4w$, *that computes all the exponential sums* $E_Y(f_1), \ldots, E_Y(f_w)$.

Proof. We proceed by induction on $m = |Y|$. In the base case when $m = 1$, $E_Y(f_j)(X) = f_j(X, 0) + f_j(X, 1)$. Putting two copies of C next to each other, one with $y = 0$ and the other with $y = 1$ hardwired, and adding corresponding outputs, gives the desired circuit.

Assume now that the lemma is true for all skew circuits with $m' = |Y| < m$. Let C be a given circuit where $|Y| = m$. Let Y' denote $Y \setminus \{y_m\} = \{y_1, \ldots, y_{m-1}\}$. As per definition 3, the layers of C can be partitioned into m blocks, with the kth block reading only y_k from Y. Let $0 = i_1 \leq i_2 \leq \ldots \leq i_m \leq \ell$ be the layer indices such that y_k is read between layers $i_k + 1$ and i_{k+1}. Let $f_1, \ldots, f_w$ be the output gates of C.

We slice C into two parts: the bottom $m - 1$ blocks of the partition together form the circuit D, and the top block forms the circuit C_m. Let $g_1, \ldots, g_w$ be the output gates of D. These are also the inputs to C_m; we symbolically relabel the non-leaf inputs at level 0 and the outputs of C_m as $Z_1, \ldots Z_w$ and $h_1, \ldots, h_w$. Clearly, C_m and D are both skew circuits of width w. Further, each h_j depends on X, y_m and Z; that is, $h_1, \ldots, h_w \in R[Z_1, \ldots, Z_w]$ where $R = \mathbb{K}[X, y_m]$. Similarly, each g_j depends on X and Y'; $g_1, \ldots, g_w \in \mathbb{K}[X, Y']$. The values computed by C can be expressed as $f_j(X, Y) = h_j(X, y_m, g_1(X, Y'), \ldots, g_w(X, Y'))$.

Since C and C_m are skew circuits, and since the variables Z_j represent non-leaf gates of C, C_m must be linear in these variables. Hence each h_j can be written as $h_j(X, y_m, Z) = c_j + \sum_{k=1}^{w} c_{j,k} Z_k$, where the coefficients $c_j, c_{j,k} \in \mathbb{K}[X, y_m]$. Combining this with the expression for f_j, we have

$$f_j(X, Y) = h_j(X, y_m, g_1(X, Y'), \ldots, g_w(X, Y'))$$
$$= c_j(X, y_m) + \sum_{k=1}^{w} c_{j,k}(X, y_m) g_k(X, Y') \qquad \text{and hence}$$

$$\sum_{e \in \{0,1\}^m} f_j(X, e) = \sum_{e \in \{0,1\}^m} \left[c_j(X, e_m) + \sum_{k=1}^{w} c_{j,k}(X, e_m) g_k(X, e') \right]$$
$$= 2^{m-1} \sum_{e_m = 0}^{1} c_j(X, e_m) + \sum_{k=1}^{w} \sum_{e \in \{0,1\}^m} c_{j,k}(X, e_m) g_k(X, e')$$

$$= 2^{m-1} \sum_{e_m = 0}^{1} c_j(X, e_m) + \sum_{k=1}^{w} \left(\sum_{e_m \in \{0,1\}} c_{j,k}(X, e_m) \right) \left(\sum_{e' \in \{0,1\}^{m-1}} g_k(X, e') \right)$$

Thus $E_Y(f_j)(X) = 2^{m-1} E_{y_m}(c_j)(X) + \sum_{k=1}^{w} E_{y_m}(c_{j,k})(X) E_{Y'}(g_k)(X)$

By induction, we know that there is a weakly skew circuit D' of width $4w$ and size $O((m-1)w^4 s)$ computing $E_{Y'}(g_k)(X)$ for all k simultaneously.

To compute $E_{y_m}(c_j)(X)$, note that a copy of C_m with all leaves labelled Z_k replaced by 0 computes exactly $c_j(X, y_m)$. So the sum can be computed as in the base case, in width $w+1$ and size $2(\text{size}(C_m)+1)$. Multiplying this by 2^{m-1} in the standard way adds nothing to width and 2 to size, so overall width is $w+1$ and size is at most $2s+4$.

To compute $E_{y_m}(c_{j,k})(X)$, we modify C_m as follows: replace leaves labelled Z_k by the constant 1, replace leaves labelled $Z_{k'}$ for $k' \neq k$ by 0, leave the rest of the circuit unchanged, and let h_j be the output gate. This circuit computes $c_j(X, y_m) + c_{j,k}(X, y_m)$. Subtracting $c_j(X, y_m)$ (as computed above) from this gives $c_{j,k}(X, y_m)$. Now, the sum can be computed as in the base case. Again, to compute $E_{y_m}(c_{j,k})(X)$, we use two copies of the difference circuit with $y_m = 0$ and $y_m = 1$ hardwired, and add their outputs. It is easy to see that this circuit has width $w+2$ and size at most $4(w+2)\text{size}(C_m) \leq 4(w+2)s$.

Putting together these circuits naively may increase width too much. So we position D' at the bottom, and carry w wires upwards from it corresponding to its w outputs. Alongside these wires, we position circuitry to accumulate the terms for each f_j and to carry forward already-computed f_k's. The width in this part is w for the wires carrying the outputs of D', w for wires carrying the values $E_Y(f_j)$, $w+2$ for computing the terms in the sum above (they are computed sequentially so the width does not add up), and 2 for computing partial sums in this process, overall at most $3w+4$. Thus the resulting circuit has width at most $\max\{\text{width}(D'), 3w+4\} \leq 4w$.

To bound the size of the circuit, we bound its depth in the part above D' by d; then size is at most $\text{size}(D') + \text{width}^2 \times d$. The circuit has w modules to compute the $E_Y(f_j)$s. The depth of each module can be bounded by the depth to compute $E_{y_m}(c_j)$ plus w times the depth to compute any one $E_{y_m}(c_{j,k})$, that is, at most $(2s+4) + w^2 \times 4(w+2)s$. So $d \leq w^2(2s+4+4sw(w+2)) = \theta(w^4 s)$, and the size bound follows. □

5 Read-Once Exponential Sums of Some Restricted Circuits

In this section, we explore how far the result of Theorem 3 can be pushed to larger classes within VP. In effect, we ask whether the technique of Lemma 6 is applicable to larger classes of circuits. Such a question is relevant because we do not have any bound (better than VNP) even for $\Sigma^R \cdot \text{VSC}^0$ and $\Sigma^R \cdot \text{VL}$.

One generalization we consider is multiplicative disjointness. An arithmetic circuit C is said to be multiplicatively disjoint (md) if every multiplication gate operates on sub-circuits which are not connected to each other. (See [14].) *i.e.* if $g = u \times v$ then the sub-circuits rooted at u and v are disjoint. Multiplicative disjointness generalises skewness and weak-skewness.

A further generalization is polynomial syntactic degree. Let C be an arithmetic circuit computing the polynomial $f \in \mathbb{K}[X]$. The *syntactic degree* of C is the degree of the polynomial $f' \in \mathbb{K}[X, y]$ computed by the circuit C' which is obtained by replacing all the leaves in C labelled by a constant from $\mathbb{K}$ with the variable y. The syntactic degree is an upper bound on the actual degree of the polynomial computed, though the two can differ significantly. All multiplicatively disjoint circuits have syntactic degree bounded by their size.

We add a prefix md- to denote the multiplicative disjoint version of a class. *e.g.* md-VSC^0 denotes class of all polynomials that are computed by constant width arithmetic circuits of polynomial size which are also multiplicatively disjoint. For $i \geq 0$, let VsSC^i denote the sub-class of families of polynomials in VSC^i whose witness circuits also have syntactic degree bounded by $\mathsf{poly}(n)$. Analogous classes sSC^i in the Boolean and counting worlds have been studied in [7].

Examining the proof of Lemma 6, we see that the main barrier in extending it to these larger classes is that when we slice C into D and C_m, C_m is no longer linear in the "slice variables" Z. However, for md-circuits, C_m is multilinear in Z. As far as computing the coefficients $c_{j,\alpha}$ goes, where α describes a multilinear monomial, this is not a problem; in [9], it is shown that for such circuits the coefficient function can be computed efficiently. There is a cost to pay in size because the number of multilinear monomials is much larger. To handle this, we modify the inductive step, slicing C not at the last block but at a level that halves the number of Y variables read above and below it. This works out fine for constant-width, but results in quasipolynomial blow-up in size for larger widths.

Formally, we show the following:

Lemma 7. *Let C be a layered multiplicatively disjoint circuit of width w and size s on variables $X \cup Y$. Let ℓ be the number of layers in C. Suppose C is read-once certified in Y. Let $f_1 \ldots, f_w$ be the output gates of C. Then, there is an arithmetic circuit C' of size $sm^{O(w)}$ which computes $E_Y(f_1), \ldots, E_Y(f_w)$.*

For VsSC circuits, the "upper half" circuit is not even multilinear. So we need to explicitly account for each monomial up to the overall degree, and compute the coefficient of each. We show that this is possible, if a quasipolynomial blow-up in size is allowed. Formally,

Lemma 8. *Let C be a layered arithmetic circuit size of s on the variables $X \cup Y \cup Z$. Let d be the syntactic degree bound on C and w be its width. Let $f \in R[Z]$ be a polynomial computed by C, where $R = \mathbb{K}[X, Y]$. Let $t = \langle t_1, \ldots, t_w \rangle$ be a degree sequence for variables from Z. Then $\mathsf{coeff}_f(Z^t)$ can be computed by a circuit of width $w + 2$ and size $O((d+1)^{2w})$, where $Z^t = \prod_{k=1}^{w} Z^{t_k}$.*

As a consequence of Lemmas 7, 8, we have the following:

Theorem 4

- $\Sigma^R \cdot md\text{-}\mathsf{VSC}^0 \subseteq \mathsf{VP}$.
- $\Sigma^R \cdot md\text{-}\mathsf{VSC} \subseteq \mathsf{VQP}$.
- *For all $i \geq 0$, $\Sigma^R \cdot \mathsf{VsSC}^i \subseteq \mathsf{VQP}$.*

References

1. Valiant, L.G.: Completeness classes in algebra. In: Symposium on Theory of Computing STOC, pp. 249–261 (1979)
2. Bürgisser, P.: Completeness and Reduction in Algebraic Complexity Theory. Algorithms and Computation in Mathematics. Springer, Heidelberg (2000)
3. Michaux, C.: Une remarque à propos des machines sur $\mathbb{R}$ introduites par Blum, Shub et Smale. Comptes Rendus de l'Académie des Sciences de Paris 309(7), 435–437 (1989)
4. de Naurois, P.J.: A Measure of Space for Computing over the Reals. In: Beckmann, A., Berger, U., Löwe, B., Tucker, J.V. (eds.) CiE 2006. LNCS, vol. 3988, pp. 231–240. Springer, Heidelberg (2006)
5. Koiran, P., Perifel, S.: VPSPACE and a Transfer Theorem over the Reals. In: Thomas, W., Weil, P. (eds.) STACS 2007. LNCS, vol. 4393, pp. 417–428. Springer, Heidelberg (2007)
6. Koiran, P., Perifel, S.: VPSPACE and a Transfer Theorem over the Complex Field. In: Kučera, L., Kučera, A. (eds.) MFCS 2007. LNCS, vol. 4708, pp. 359–370. Springer, Heidelberg (2007)
7. Limaye, N., Mahajan, M., Rao, B.V.R.: Arithmetizing classes around NC^1 and L. In: Thomas, W., Weil, P. (eds.) STACS 2007. LNCS, vol. 4393, pp. 477–488. Springer, Heidelberg (2007); full version in ECCC TR07-087
8. Mahajan, M., Rao, B.V.R.: Arithmetic circuits, syntactic multilinearity and skew formulae. In: Ochmański, E., Tyszkiewicz, J. (eds.) MFCS 2008. LNCS, vol. 5162, pp. 455–466. Springer, Heidelberg (2008); full version in ECCC TR08-048
9. Jansen, M., Rao, B.: Simulation of arithmetical circuits by branching programs preserving constant width and syntactic multilinearity. In: Frid, A.E., Morozov, A., Rybalchenko, A., Wagner, K.W. (eds.) CSR 2009. LNCS, vol. 5675, Springer, Heidelberg (2009)
10. Vollmer, H.: Introduction to Circuit Complexity: A Uniform Approach. Springer, New York (1999)
11. Arora, S., Barak, B.: Complexity Theory: A Modern Approach (to be published) (2009)
12. Barrington, D.: Bounded-width polynomial-size branching programs recognize exactly those languages in NC^1. Journal of Computer and System Sciences 38(1), 150–164 (1989)
13. Venkateswaran, H.: Circuit definitions of nondeterministic complexity classes. SIAM Journal on Computing 21, 655–670 (1992)
14. Malod, G., Portier, N.: Characterizing Valiant's algebraic complexity classes. In: Královič, R., Urzyczyn, P. (eds.) MFCS 2006. LNCS, vol. 4162, pp. 704–716. Springer, Heidelberg (2006)
15. Blum, L., Cucker, F., Shub, M., Smale, S.: Complexity and Real Computation. Springer, Heidelberg (1997)
16. Malod, G.: The complexity of polynomials and their coefficient functions. In: IEEE Conference on Computational Complexity, pp. 193–204 (2007)
17. Caussinus, H., McKenzie, P., Thérien, D., Vollmer, H.: Nondeterministic NC^1 computation. Journal of Computer and System Sciences 57, 200–212 (1998)

Small Weakly Universal Turing Machines*

Turlough Neary[1] and Damien Woods[2]

[1] Boole Centre for Research in Informatics,
University College Cork, Ireland
tneary@cs.may.ie
[2] Department of Computer Science and Artificial Intelligence
University of Seville, Spain
dwoods@us.es

Abstract. We give small universal Turing machines with state-symbol pairs of $(6,2)$, $(3,3)$ and $(2,4)$. These machines are weakly universal, which means that they have an infinitely repeated word to the left of their input and another to the right. They simulate Rule 110 and are currently the smallest known weakly universal Turing machines. Despite their small size these machines are efficient polynomial time simulators of Turing machines.

1 Introduction

Shannon [22] was the first to consider the problem of finding the smallest universal Turing machine, where size is the number of states and symbols. Here we say that a Turing machine is standard if it has a single one-dimensional tape, one tape head, and is deterministic [7]. Over the years, small universal programs were given for a number of variants on the standard model. By generalising the standard model we often find smaller universal programs. One such generalisation is to allow the blank portion of the Turing machine's tape to have an infinitely repeated word to the left, and another to the right. We refer to such universal machines as weakly universal Turing machines, and they are the subject of this work.

Beginning in the early sixties Minsky and Watanabe engaged in a vigorous competition to see who could come up with the smallest universal Turing machine [13,14,23,24]. In 1961, Watanabe [23] gave a 6-state, 5-symbol machine that was the first weakly universal machine. In 1962, Minsky [14] found a small 7-state, 4-symbol standard universal Turing machine. Not to be out-done, Watanabe improved on his earlier machine to give 5-state, 4-symbol and 7-state, 3-symbol weakly universal machines [24].

* Turlough Neary is funded by the Irish Research Council for Science, Engineering and Technology and by Science Foundation Ireland Research Frontiers Programme grant number 07/RFP/CSMF641. Damien Woods was supported by a Project of Excellence from the Junta de Andalucía grant TIC-581, and by Science Foundation Ireland grant 04/IN3/1524.

M. Kutyłowski, M. Gębala, and W. Charatonik (Eds.): FCT 2009, LNCS 5699, pp. 262–273, 2009.
© Springer-Verlag Berlin Heidelberg 2009

The 7-state universal Turing machine of Minsky has received much attention. Minsky's machine simulates Turing machines via 2-tag systems, which were proved universal by Cocke and Minsky [3]. The technique of simulating 2-tag systems, pioneered by Minsky, was extended by Rogozhin [21] to give the (then) smallest known universal Turing machines for a number of state-symbol pairs. Many of these 2-tag simulators were subsequently reduced in size by Kudlek and Rogozhin [9], and Baiocchi [2]. Neary and Woods [17] gave small universal machines that simulate Turing machines via a new variant of tag systems called bi-tag systems. All of the smallest known universal Turing machines, that obey the standard definition (deterministic, one tape, one head), simulate either 2-tag or bi-tag systems. They are plotted as circles and triangles in Figure 1. To get the polynomial time overhead for 2-tag simulators in Figure 1 the 2-tag simulation of Turing Machines given in [15,26] is used instead of the exponentially slow technique given in [3].

The small weak machines of Watanabe have received little attention. In particular the 5-state and 7-state machines seem little known and are largely ignored in the literature. It is worth noting that while all other weak machines simulate Turing machine via other simple models, Watanabe's weak machines simulate Turing machines directly. His machines are the most time efficient of the small weak machines. More precisely, let t be the running time of any deterministic single tape Turing machine M, then Watanabe's machines are the smallest weak machines that simulate M with a time overhead of $O(t^2)$.

We often refer to Watanabe's machines as being semi-weak. Semi-weak machines are a restriction of weak machines: they have an infinitely repeated word to one side of their input, and on the other side they have a (standard) infinitely repeated blank symbol. Recently, Woods and Neary [28] have given semi-weakly universal machines that simulate cyclic tag systems with state-symbol pairs of $(3, 7)$, $(4, 5)$ and $(2, 13)$. All of the smallest known semi-weakly universal machines are plotted as diamonds in Figure 1.

Cook [4] and Wolfram [25], recently gave weakly universal Turing machines, smaller than Watanabe's semi-weak machines, that simulate the universal cellular automaton Rule 110. These machines have state-symbol pairs of $(7, 2)$, $(4, 3)$, $(3, 4)$ and $(2, 5)$ and are plotted as hollow squares in Figure 1. (Note that David Eppstein constructed the $(7, 2)$ machine to be found in [4].)

Here we present weakly universal Turing machines with state-symbol pairs of $(6, 2)$, $(3, 3)$ and $(2, 4)$ making them the smallest known weakly universal machines. Our machines efficiently simulate (single tape, deterministic) Turing machines in time $O(t^4 \log^2 t)$, via Rule 110. These machines are plotted as solid squares in Figure 1 and induce a weakly universal curve.

Weakness has not been the only generalisation on the standard model in the search for small universal Turing machines. Priese [20] gave a 2-state, 4-symbol machine with a 2-dimensional tape, and a 2-state, 2-symbol machine with a 2-dimensional tape and 2 tape heads. Margenstern and Pavlotskaya [11] gave a 2-state, 3-symbol Turing machine that is universal when coupled with a finite automaton. The Turing machine part of this couple uses only 5 instructions, and

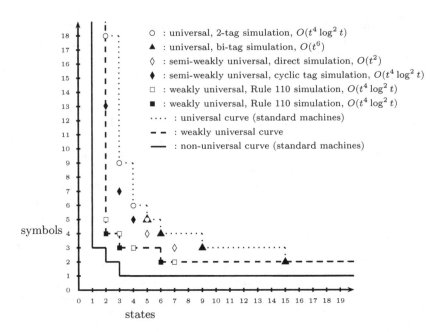

Fig. 1. State-symbol plot of small universal Turing machines. Each of our new weak machines is represented by a solid square. These machines induce a weakly universal curve. Simulation time overheads are specified. The non-universal curve shows standard machines that are known to have a decidable halting problem.

they also show that the halting problem is decidable for couples in which the Turing machine has only 4 instructions. Hence, it is not possible to have a universal couple with a 4-instruction Turing machine that simulates any Turing machine M and halts if and only if M halts. Thus, they have given the smallest possible Turing machine that is universal when coupled with a finite automaton. It is worth noting that the weakly universal machines that we present in this paper have the smallest number of instructions of any known universal machines with polynomial time overhead. This comparison even includes all other generalised Turing machine models such as those mentioned above: all known machines that use fewer instructions but generalise other aspects (multiple tapes, coupling with automata etc.) of the model are exponentially slow.

More on small universal Turing machines, and related notions, can be found in [10,15,27].

1.1   Preliminaries

The Turing machines considered in this paper are deterministic and have a single bi-infinite tape. We let $U_{m,n}$ denote our weakly universal Turing machine with m states and n symbols. We write $c_1 \vdash c_2$ if a configuration c_2 is obtained from c_1 via a single computation step. We let $c_1 \vdash^s c_2$ denote a sequence of s computation steps, and let $c_1 \vdash^* c_2$ denote zero or more computation steps.

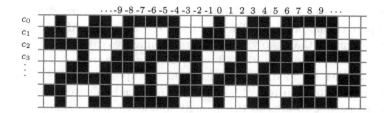

Fig. 2. Seven consecutive timesteps of Rule 110. These seven timesteps show the evolution of the background ether that is used in the proof [4] of universality of Rule 110. Each black or each white square represents, a Rule 110 cell containing, state 1 or 0 respectively. Each cell is identified by the index given above it. To the left of each row of cells there is a configuration label that identifies that row.

2   Rule 110

Rule 110 is a very simple (2 state, nearest neighbour, one dimensional) cellular automaton. It is composed of a sequence of cells $\ldots p_{-1}p_0p_1 \ldots$ where each cell has a binary state $p_i \in \{0,1\}$. At timestep $s+1$, the value $p_{i,s+1} = F(p_{i-1,s}, p_{i,s}, p_{i+1,s})$ of the cell at position i is given by the synchronous local update function F

$$
\begin{aligned}
F(0,0,0) &= 0 & F(1,0,0) &= 0 \\
F(0,0,1) &= 1 & F(1,0,1) &= 1 \\
F(0,1,0) &= 1 & F(1,1,0) &= 1 \\
F(0,1,1) &= 1 & F(1,1,1) &= 0
\end{aligned}
\tag{1}
$$

Rule 110 was proven universal by Cook [4] (Cook's proof is sketched in [25]). Neary and Woods [16] proved that Rule 110 simulates Turing machines efficiently in polynomial time $O(t^3 \log t)$, an exponential improvement. This time overhead was further improved to $O(t^2 \log t)$ [15]. Rule 110 simulates cyclic tag systems in linear time. The weak machines in this paper, and in [4,25], simulate Rule 110 with a quadratic polynomial increase in time and hence simulate Turing machines in time $O(t^4 \log^2 t)$. It is worth noting that the prediction problem [5] for these machines is P-complete, and this is also the case when we consider only bounded initial conditions [16].

3   Three Small Weakly Universal Turing Machines

The following observation is one of the reasons for the improvement in size over previous weak machines, and gives some insight into the simulation algorithm we use. Notice from Equation (1) that the value of the update function F, with the exception of $F(0,1,1)$ and $F(1,1,1)$, may be determined using only the rightmost two states. Each of our universal Turing machines exploit this fact as follows. The machines scan from right to left, and in six of the eight cases they need only remember the cell immediately to the right of the current cell i in order to compute the update for i. Thus for these six cases we need only store a single cell value, rather than two values. The remaining two cases are simulated as follows. If two consecutive encoded states with value 1 are read, it is assumed that there is another encoded 1 to the left and the update $F(1,1,1) = 0$ is simulated. If our assumption proves false (we instead read an encoded 0 to the left), then our machine returns to the wrongly updated cell and simulates the update $F(0,1,1) = 1$.

Before giving our three small Rule 110 simulators, we give some further background explanation. Rule 110 simulates Turing machines via cyclic tag systems. A Rule 110 instance that simulates a cyclic tag system computation is of the following form (for more details see [4]). The input to the cyclic tag system is encoded in a contiguous finite number of Rule 110 cells. On the left of the input a fixed constant word (representing the 'ossifiers') is repeated infinitely many times. On the right, another fixed constant word (representing the cyclic tag system program/appendants, and the 'leaders') is repeated infinitely many times. Both of these repeated words are independent of the input.

As in [4], our weakly universal machines operate by traversing a finite amount of the tape from left to right and then from right to left. This simulates a single timestep of Rule 110 over a finite part of the encoded infinite Rule 110 instance. With each simulated timestep the length of a traversal increases. To ensure that each traversal is of finite length, the left blank word l and the right blank word r of each of our weak machines must have a special form. These words contain special subwords or symbols that terminate each traversal, causing the tape head to turn. When the head is turning it overwrites any symbols that caused a turn. Thus the number of cells that are being updated increases monotonically over time. This technique simulates Rule 110 properly if the initial condition is set up so that within each repeated blank word, the subword between each successive turn point is shifted one timestep forward in time.

In the sequel we describe the computation of our three machines by showing a simulation of the update on the ether in Figure 2. In the next paragraph below, we outline why this example is in fact general enough to prove universality. First, we must define blank words that are suitable for this example. The left blank word l, on the Turing machine tape, encodes the Rule 110 sequence 0001. In the initial configuration as we move left each subsequent sequence 0001 is one timestep further ahead. To see this note from Figure 2 that 0001 occupies, cells -7 to -4 in configuration c_1, cells -11 to -8 in c_2, cells -15 to -12 in c_3, etc. Similarly, the right blank word r encodes the Rule 110 sequence 110011. Looking at the initial configuration, as we move right from cell 0, in the first blank word the first four cells 1100 are shifted two timesteps ahead, and the next two cells 11 are shifted a further one timestep. To see this note from Figure 2 that 1100 occupies cells 1 to 4 in c_2 and 11 occupies cells 5 and 6 in c_3. In each subsequent sequence the first four cells 1100 are shifted only one timestep ahead and the last two cells 11 are shifted one further timestep. In each row the ether in Figure 2 repeats every 14 cells and if the number of timesteps s between two rows is $s \equiv 0$

mod 7 then the two rows are identical. The periodic nature of the ether, in both time and space, allows us to construct such blank words.

It should be noted that the machines we present here, and those in [4,25], require suitable blank words to simulate a Rule 110 instance directly. If no suitable blank words can be found (i.e. if it is not possible to construct subwords that terminate traversals in the encoding) then it may be the case that the particular instance can not be simulated directly. In the sequel our machines simulate the background ether that is used in the universality proof of Rule 110 [4]. The gliders used by Cook [4] that move through this ether are periodic in time and space. Thus, we can construct blank words that include these gliders and place the subwords that terminate traversals in the ether. By this reasoning, our example is sufficiently general to prove that our machines simulate Turing machines via Rule 110 and we do not give a full (and possibly tedious) proof of correctness. For $U_{3,3}$ we explicitly simulate three updates from Figure 2, which is general enough so that an update [Equation (1)] on each of the eight possible three state combinations is simulated. We give shorter examples for the machines $U_{2,4}$ and $U_{6,2}$ as they use the same simulation algorithm as $U_{3,3}$.

As with the machines in [4,25], the machines we present here do not halt. Cook [4] shows how a special glider may be produced during the simulation of a Turing machine by Rule 110. This glider may be used to simulate halting as the encoding can be such that it is generated by Rule 110 if and only if the simulated machine halts. The glider would be encoded on the tape of our machines as a unique, constant word.

3.1 $U_{3,3}$

We begin by describing an *initial* configuration of $U_{3,3}$. To the left of, and including, the tape head position, the Rule 110 state 0 is encoded by 0, and the Rule 110 state 1 is encoded by either 1 or b. The word $1b0$ is used to terminate a left traversal. (Note an exception: the 1 in the subword $1b0$ encodes the Rule 110 state 0.) To the right of the tape head position, the Rule 110 state 0 is encoded by 1, and the Rule 110 state 1 is encoded by 0 or b. The tape symbol 0 is used to terminate a right traversal. The left and right blank words, described in paragraph 4 of Section 3, are encoded as $001b$ and $0b110b$ respectively.

Table 1. Table of behaviour for $U_{3,3}$

	u_1	u_2	u_3
0	$1Lu_1$	$0Ru_1$	bLu_1
1	bLu_2	$1Lu_2$	$0Ru_3$
b	bLu_3		$1Ru_3$

We give an example of $U_{3,3}$ simulating the three successive Rule 110 timesteps $c_0 \vdash c_1 \vdash c_2 \vdash c_3$ given in Figure 2. In the below configurations the current state of $U_{3,3}$ is highlighted in bold, to the left of its tape contents. The tape head position of $U_{3,3}$ is given by an underline and the start state is u_1. The configuration immediately below encodes c_0 from Figure 2 with the tape head over cell index 0.

$$
\begin{array}{llllllll}
& \mathbf{u_1}, & \ldots 001b & 001b & 001b & 000\underline{1} & 0b110b & 0b110b\ldots \\
\vdash & \mathbf{u_2}, & \ldots 001b & 001b & 001b & 000\underline{b} & 0b110b & 0b110b\ldots \\
\vdash & \mathbf{u_1}, & \ldots 001b & 001b & 001b & 000\underline{b} & 0b110b & 0b110b\ldots \\
\vdash & \mathbf{u_3}, & \ldots 001b & 001b & 001b & 00\underline{0}b & 0b110b & 0b110b\ldots \\
\vdash & \mathbf{u_1}, & \ldots 001b & 001b & 001b & 0\underline{0}bb & 0b110b & 0b110b\ldots \\
\vdash^2 & \mathbf{u_1}, & \ldots 001b & 001b & 001\underline{b} & 11bb & 0b110b & 0b110b\ldots \\
\vdash & \mathbf{u_3}, & \ldots 001b & 001b & 00\underline{1}b & 11bb & 0b110b & 0b110b\ldots \\
\end{array}
$$

When the tape head reads the subword $1b0$ the left traversal is complete and the right traversal begins.

$$
\begin{array}{llllllll}
\vdash^6 & \mathbf{u_3}, & \ldots 001b & 001b & 0001 & 0011 & \underline{0}b110b & 0b110b\ldots \\
\vdash & \mathbf{u_1}, & \ldots 001b & 001b & \mathbf{0001} & \mathbf{001\underline{1}} & bb110b & 0b110b\ldots \\
\end{array}
$$

Immediately after the tape head reads a 0, during a right traversal, the simulation of timestep $c_0 \vdash c_1$ is complete. To see this, compare the part of the Turing machine tape in bold with cells -7 to 0 of configuration c_1 in Figure 2. We continue our simulation to give timestep $c_1 \vdash c_2$.

$$
\begin{array}{llllllll}
\vdash & \mathbf{u_2}, & \ldots 001b & 001b & 0001 & 00\underline{1}b & bb110b & 0b110b\ldots \\
\vdash & \mathbf{u_2}, & \ldots 001b & 001b & 0001 & 0\underline{0}1b & bb110b & 0b110b\ldots \\
\vdash & \mathbf{u_1}, & \ldots 001b & 001b & 0001 & 001\underline{b} & bb110b & 0b110b\ldots \\
\vdash & \mathbf{u_2}, & \ldots 001b & 001b & 0001 & 00\underline{0}bb & bb110b & 0b110b\ldots \\
\vdash^3 & \mathbf{u_1}, & \ldots 001b & 001b & 0001 & \underline{0}bbb & bb110b & 0b110b\ldots \\
\vdash^2 & \mathbf{u_2}, & \ldots 001b & 001b & 000\underline{0}b & 1bbb & bb110b & 0b110b\ldots \\
\vdash^3 & \mathbf{u_1}, & \ldots 001b & 001b & 00\underline{0}bb & 1bbb & bb110b & 0b110b\ldots \\
\vdash^3 & \mathbf{u_3}, & \ldots 001b & 00\underline{1}b & 11bb & 1bbb & bb110b & 0b110b\ldots \\
\vdash^{15} & \mathbf{u_1}, & \ldots 001b & \mathbf{0001} & \mathbf{0011} & \mathbf{0111} & \mathbf{110\underline{0}}bb & 0b110b\ldots \\
\end{array}
$$

The simulation of timestep $c_1 \vdash c_2$ is complete. To see this, compare the part of the Turing machine tape in bold with cells -11 to 4 of configuration c_2 in Figure 2. We continue our simulation to give timestep $c_2 \vdash c_3$.

$$
\begin{array}{llllllll}
\vdash^3 & \mathbf{u_2}, & \ldots 001b & 0001 & 0011 & 0111 & \underline{1}b11bb & 0b110b\ldots \\
\vdash^4 & \mathbf{u_2}, & \ldots 001b & 0001 & 0011 & \underline{0}111 & 1b11bb & 0b110b\ldots \\
\end{array}
$$

$\vdash^5$ $\boldsymbol{u_1}$, ... $001b$ 0001 $001\underline{1}$ $bb11$ $1b11bb$ $0b110b$...

$\vdash^2$ $\boldsymbol{u_2}$, ... $001b$ 0001 $0\underline{0}1b$ $bb11$ $1b11bb$ $0b110b$...

$\vdash^5$ $\boldsymbol{u_1}$, ... $001b$ 0001 $\underline{0}bbb$ $bb11$ $1b11bb$ $0b110b$...

$\vdash^2$ $\boldsymbol{u_2}$, ... $001b$ $000\underline{b}$ $1bbb$ $bb11$ $1b11bb$ $0b110b$...

$\vdash^6$ $\boldsymbol{u_3}$, ... $00\underline{1}b$ $11bb$ $1bbb$ $bb11$ $1b11bb$ $0b110b$...

$\vdash^{21}$ $\boldsymbol{u_1}$, ... $\mathbf{0001}$ $\mathbf{0011}$ $\mathbf{0111}$ $\mathbf{1100}$ $\mathbf{01001\underline{1}}$ $bb110b$...

The simulation of timestep $c_2 \vdash c_3$ is complete. To see this, compare the part of the Turing machine tape in bold with cells -15 to 6 of configuration c_3 in Figure 2.

3.2 $U_{2,4}$

We begin by describing an *initial* configuration of $U_{2,4}$. To the left of, and including, the tape head position, the Rule 110 state 0 is encoded by either 0 or $\emptyset$ and the Rule 110 state 1 is encoded by either 1 or $\mathnormal{1}\!\!\!/$. The word $\emptyset 1$ is used to terminate a left traversal. To the right of the tape head position, the Rule 110 state 0 is encoded by $\emptyset$ and the Rule 110 state 1 is encoded by $\mathnormal{1}\!\!\!/$ or 0. The tape symbol 0 is used to terminate a right traversal. The left and right blank words, from paragraph 4 of Section 3, are encoded as $00\emptyset 1$ and $0\mathnormal{1}\!\!\!/\emptyset\emptyset 0\mathnormal{1}\!\!\!/$ respectively.

Table 2. Table of behaviour for $U_{2,4}$

	u_1	u_2
0	$\emptyset\,Lu_1$	$\mathnormal{1}\!\!\!/\,Ru_1$
1	$\mathnormal{1}\!\!\!/\,Lu_2$	$\emptyset\,Lu_2$
$\emptyset$	$\mathnormal{1}\!\!\!/\,Lu_1$	$0Ru_2$
$\mathnormal{1}\!\!\!/$	$\mathnormal{1}\!\!\!/\,Lu_1$	$1Ru_2$

We give an example of $U_{2,4}$ simulating the two successive Rule 110 timesteps $c_0 \vdash c_1 \vdash c_2$ given in Figure 2. The configuration immediately below encodes c_0 from Figure 2 with the tape head over cell index 0.

$\boldsymbol{u_1}$, ... $00\emptyset 1$ $00\emptyset 1$ $00\emptyset 1$ $000\underline{1}$ $0\mathnormal{1}\!\!\!/\emptyset\emptyset 0\mathnormal{1}\!\!\!/$ $0\mathnormal{1}\!\!\!/\emptyset\emptyset 0\mathnormal{1}\!\!\!/$...

$\vdash^6$ $\boldsymbol{u_1}$, ... $00\emptyset 1$ $00\emptyset 1$ $00\emptyset\underline{1}$ $\emptyset\emptyset\mathnormal{1}\!\!\!/\mathnormal{1}\!\!\!/$ $0\mathnormal{1}\!\!\!/\emptyset\emptyset 0\mathnormal{1}\!\!\!/$ $0\mathnormal{1}\!\!\!/\emptyset\emptyset 0\mathnormal{1}\!\!\!/$...

$\vdash$ $\boldsymbol{u_2}$, ... $00\emptyset 1$ $00\emptyset 1$ $00\emptyset\underline{\mathnormal{1}\!\!\!/}$ $\emptyset\emptyset\mathnormal{1}\!\!\!/\mathnormal{1}\!\!\!/$ $0\mathnormal{1}\!\!\!/\emptyset\emptyset 0\mathnormal{1}\!\!\!/$ $0\mathnormal{1}\!\!\!/\emptyset\emptyset 0\mathnormal{1}\!\!\!/$...

When the tape head reads the subword $\emptyset 1$ the left traversal is complete and the right traversal begins.

$\vdash^6$ $\boldsymbol{u_2}$, ... $00\emptyset 1$ $00\emptyset 1$ 0001 0011 $\underline{0}\mathnormal{1}\!\!\!/\emptyset\emptyset 0\mathnormal{1}\!\!\!/$ $0\mathnormal{1}\!\!\!/\emptyset\emptyset 0\mathnormal{1}\!\!\!/$...

$\vdash$ $\boldsymbol{u_1}$, ... $00\emptyset 1$ $00\emptyset 1$ $\mathbf{0001}$ $\mathbf{0011}$ $\mathnormal{1}\!\!\!/\underline{\mathnormal{1}\!\!\!/}\emptyset\emptyset 0\mathnormal{1}\!\!\!/$ $0\mathnormal{1}\!\!\!/\emptyset\emptyset 0\mathnormal{1}\!\!\!/$...

Immediately after the tape head reads a 0, during a right traversal, the simulation of timestep $c_0 \vdash c_1$ is complete. To see this, compare the part of the Turing machine tape in bold with cells -7 to 0 of configuration c_1 in Figure 2. We continue our simulation to give timestep $c_1 \vdash c_2$.

$\vdash^2$ $\boldsymbol{u_1},\ \ldots 00\emptyset 1 \quad 00\emptyset 1 \quad 0001 \quad 001\underline{1} \quad \not1\not1\emptyset\emptyset0\not1 \quad 0\not1\emptyset\emptyset0\not1\ldots$

$\vdash^2$ $\boldsymbol{u_2},\ \ldots 00\emptyset 1 \quad 00\emptyset 1 \quad 0001 \quad 00\underline{\emptyset}\not1 \quad \not1\not1\emptyset\emptyset0\not1 \quad 0\not1\emptyset\emptyset0\not1\ldots$

$\vdash$ $\boldsymbol{u_1},\ \ldots 00\emptyset 1 \quad 00\emptyset 1 \quad 0001 \quad 0\not1\underline{\emptyset}\not1 \quad \not1\not1\emptyset\emptyset0\not1 \quad 0\not1\emptyset\emptyset0\not1\ldots$

$\vdash^4$ $\boldsymbol{u_2},\ \ldots 00\emptyset 1 \quad 00\emptyset 1 \quad 00\underline{0}\not1 \quad \emptyset\not1\not1\not1 \quad \not1\not1\emptyset\emptyset0\not1 \quad 0\not1\emptyset\emptyset0\not1\ldots$

$\vdash^5$ $\boldsymbol{u_1},\ \ldots 00\emptyset 1 \quad 00\emptyset\underline{1} \quad \emptyset\emptyset\not1\not1 \quad \emptyset\not1\not1\not1 \quad \not1\not1\emptyset\emptyset0\not1 \quad 0\not1\emptyset\emptyset0\not1\ldots$

$\vdash$ $\boldsymbol{u_2},\ \ldots 00\emptyset 1 \quad 00\emptyset\underline{\not1} \quad \emptyset\emptyset\not1\not1 \quad \emptyset\not1\not1\not1 \quad \not1\not1\emptyset\emptyset0\not1 \quad 0\not1\emptyset\emptyset0\not1\ldots$

$\vdash^{15}$ $\boldsymbol{u_1},\ \ldots 00\emptyset 1 \quad \mathbf{0001} \quad \mathbf{0011} \quad \mathbf{0111} \quad \mathbf{1100}\underline{\not1\not1} \quad 0\not1\emptyset\emptyset0\not1\ldots$

The simulation of timestep $c_1 \vdash c_2$ is complete. To see this, compare the part of the Turing machine tape in bold with cells -11 to 4 of configuration c_2 in Figure 2.

3.3 $U_{6,2}$

We begin by describing an *initial* configuration of $U_{6,2}$. To the left of, and including, the tape head position, the Rule 110 state 0 is encoded by the word 00 and the Rule 110 state 1 is encoded by the word 11. The word 010100 is used to terminate a left traversal and encodes the sequence of Rule 110 states 010. To the right of the tape head position the Rule 110 state 0 is encoded by the word 00 and the Rule 110 state 1 is encoded by either of the words 01 or 10. The word 10 is used to terminate a right traversal. The left and right blank words, from paragraph 4 of Section 3, are encoded as 00000101 and 100100001001 respectively.

Table 3. Table of behaviour for $U_{6,2}$

	u_1	u_2	u_3	u_4	u_5	u_6
0	$0Lu_1$	$0Lu_6$	$0Ru_2$	$1Ru_5$	$1Lu_4$	$1Lu_1$
1	$1Lu_2$	$0Lu_3$	$1Lu_3$	$0Ru_6$	$1Ru_4$	$0Ru_4$

To illustrate the operation of $U_{6,2}$ we simulate the Rule 110 timestep $c_0 \vdash c_1$ given in Figure 2. The configuration immediately below encodes c_0 from Figure 2 with the tape head over cell index 0.

$\boldsymbol{u_1},\ \ldots 00000101 \quad 00000101 \quad 0000001\underline{1} \quad 100100001001\ldots$

$\vdash$ $\boldsymbol{u_2},\ \ldots 00000101 \quad 00000101 \quad 000000\underline{1}1 \quad 100100001001\ldots$

$\vdash$ $\boldsymbol{u_3},\ \ldots 00000101 \quad 00000101 \quad 00000\underline{0}01 \quad 100100001001\ldots$

$\vdash$ $\boldsymbol{u_2},\ \ldots 00000101 \quad 00000101 \quad 0000000\underline{1} \quad 100100001001\ldots$

$\vdash u_6, \ldots 00000101 \quad 00000101 \quad 0000\underline{0}001 \quad 100100001001\ldots$

$\vdash u_1, \ldots 00000101 \quad 00000101 \quad 0000\underline{0}101 \quad 100100001001\ldots$

$\vdash^5 u_1, \ldots 00000101 \quad 0000010\underline{1} \quad 00000101 \quad 100100001001\ldots$

$\vdash u_2, \ldots 00000101 \quad 000001\underline{0}1 \quad 00000101 \quad 100100001001\ldots$

$\vdash u_6, \ldots 00000101 \quad 00000\underline{1}01 \quad 00000101 \quad 100100001001\ldots$

$\vdash u_4, \ldots 00000101 \quad 0000000\underline{0}1 \quad 00000101 \quad 100100001001\ldots$

When the tape head reads the subword 10100 the left traversal is complete and the right traversal begins.

$\vdash u_5, \ldots 00000101 \quad 0000001\underline{1} \quad 00000101 \quad 100100001001\ldots$

$\vdash u_4, \ldots 00000101 \quad 00000011 \quad \underline{0}0000101 \quad 100100001001\ldots$

$\vdash u_5, \ldots 00000101 \quad 00000011 \quad 1\underline{0}000101 \quad 100100001001\ldots$

$\vdash u_4, \ldots 00000101 \quad 00000011 \quad \underline{1}1000101 \quad 100100001001\ldots$

$\vdash u_6, \ldots 00000101 \quad 00000011 \quad 0\underline{1}000101 \quad 100100001001\ldots$

$\vdash u_4, \ldots 00000101 \quad 00000011 \quad 00\underline{0}00101 \quad 100100001001\ldots$

$\vdash^4 u_4, \ldots 00000101 \quad 00000011 \quad 0000\underline{0}101 \quad 100100001001\ldots$

$\vdash u_5, \ldots 00000101 \quad 00000011 \quad 0000\underline{1}101 \quad 100100001001\ldots$

$\vdash u_4, \ldots 00000101 \quad 00000011 \quad 00001\underline{1}01 \quad 100100001001\ldots$

$\vdash^2 u_4, \ldots 00000101 \quad 00000011 \quad 00001111 \quad \underline{1}00100001001\ldots$

$\vdash u_6, \ldots 00000101 \quad 00000011 \quad 00001111 \quad 0\underline{0}0100001001\ldots$

$\vdash u_1, \ldots 00000101 \quad \mathbf{00000011} \quad \mathbf{00001111} \quad \underline{0}10100001001\ldots$

Immediately after the tape head reads a 10, during a right traversal, the simulation of timestep $c_0 \vdash c_1$ is complete. To see this, compare the part of the Turing machine tape in bold (recall 0 and 1 are encoded as 00 and 11 respectively) with cells -7 to 0 of configuration c_1 in Figure 2.

4   Discussion on Lower Bounds

The pursuit to find the smallest possible universal Turing machine must also involve the search for lower bounds, finding the largest Turing machines that are in some sense non-universal. One approach is to settle the decidability of the halting problem, but this approach is not suitable for the machines we have presented.

It is known that the halting problem is decidable for (standard) Turing machines with the following state-symbol pairs $(2, 2)$ [8,18], $(3, 2)$ [19], $(2, 3)$ (claimed by Pavlotskaya [18]), $(1, n)$ [6] and $(n, 1)$ (trivial), where $n \geqslant 1$. Then, these decidability results imply that a universal Turing machine, that simulates any Turing machine M and halts if and only if M halts, is not possible for these state-symbol pairs. Hence these results give lower bounds on the size of universal machines of this type. While it is trivial to prove that the halting problem is decidable for (possibly halting) weak machines with state-symbol pairs of the form $(n, 1)$, it is not known whether the other decidability results above generalise to (possibly halting) weak Turing machines.

The weakly universal machines presented in this paper, and those in [4,25], do not halt. Hence the non-universality results discussed in the previous paragraph would have to be generalised to *non-halting weak* machines to give lower bounds that are relevant for our machines. This may prove difficult for two reasons. The first issue is that, intuitively speaking, weakness gives quite an advantage. For instance, the program of a universal machine may be encoded in one of the infinitely repeated blank words of the weak machine. The second issue is related to the problem of defining a computation. Informally, a computation could be defined as a sequence of configurations that ends in a special terminal configuration. For non-halting machines, there are many ways to define a terminal configuration. Given a definition of terminal configuration we may prove that the terminal configuration problem (will a machine ever enter a terminal configuration) is decidable for a machine or set of machines. However this result may not hold as a proof of non-universality if we subsequently alter our definition of terminal configuration. In fact, it may be easily shown that the Turing machine $U_{2,4}$ from Table 2, which we prove weakly universal, is provably non-universal when it is restricted to the standard blank background.

It is trivial that no weakly universal Turing machines exist for the state-symbol pair $(n, 1)$ even when we consider machines with no halting condition. We also believe that relevant decidability results for the state-symbol pair $(2, 2)$ may be given. If this is true, then the problem of whether or not there are 2-state and 3-state weakly universal machines remains open for only $(2, 3)$ and $(3, 2)$ respectively.

Margenstern [10], Baiocchi [1], and Michel [12] have found small machines that simulate iterations of the $3x + 1$ problem and other Collatz-like functions. The smallest known weakly universal machines are almost at the minimum possible size, thus implementing the Collatz problem on weak machines could be an interesting way of exploring the little space remaining between these machines and the state-symbol pairs where weak universality is not possible.

References

1. Baiocchi, C.: 3N+1, UTM e tag-system. Technical Report Pubblicazione 98/38, Dipartimento di Matematico, Università di Roma (1998) (in Italian)
2. Baiocchi, C.: Three small universal Turing machines. In: Margenstern, M., Rogozhin, Y. (eds.) MCU 2001. LNCS, vol. 2055, pp. 1–10. Springer, Heidelberg (2001)
3. Cocke, J., Minsky, M.: Universality of tag systems with $P = 2$. Journal of the ACM 11(1), 15–20 (1964)
4. Cook, M.: Universality in elementary cellular automata. Complex Systems 15(1), 1–40 (2004)
5. Greenlaw, R., Hoover, H.J., Ruzzo, W.L.: Limits to parallel computation: P-completeness theory. Oxford University Press, Oxford (1995)

6. Hermann, G.: The uniform halting problem for generalized one state Turing machines. In: Proceedings, Ninth Annual Symposium on Switching and Automata Theory (FOCS), pp. 368–372. IEEE, New York (1968)
7. Hopcroft, J.E., Ullman, J.D.: Introduction to automata theory, languages, and computation. Addison-Wesley, Reading (1979)
8. Kudlek, M.: Small deterministic Turing machines. Theoretical Computer Science 168(2), 241–255 (1996)
9. Kudlek, M., Rogozhin, Y.: A universal Turing machine with 3 states and 9 symbols. In: Kuich, W., Rozenberg, G., Salomaa, A. (eds.) DLT 2001. LNCS, vol. 2295, pp. 311–318. Springer, Heidelberg (2002)
10. Margenstern, M.: Frontier between decidability and undecidability: A survey. Theoretical Computer Science 231(2), 217–251 (2000)
11. Margenstern, M., Pavlotskaya, L.: On the optimal number of instructions for universality of Turing machines connected with a finite automaton. International Journal of Algebra and Computation 13(2), 133–202 (2003)
12. Michel, P.: Small Turing machines and the generalized busy beaver competition. Theoretical Computer Science 326(1-3), 45–56 (2004)
13. Minsky, M.: A 6-symbol 7-state universal Turing machines. Technical Report 54-G-027, MIT (1960)
14. Minsky, M.: Size and structure of universal Turing machines using tag systems. In: Recursive Function Theory, Proceedings, Symposium in Pure Mathematics, vol. 5, pp. 229–238. AMS, Provelence (1962)
15. Neary, T.: Small universal Turing machines. PhD thesis, Department of Computer Science, National University of Ireland, Maynooth (2008)
16. Neary, T., Woods, D.: P-completeness of cellular automaton Rule 110. In: Bugliesi, M., Preneel, B., Sassone, V., Wegener, I. (eds.) ICALP 2006. LNCS, vol. 4051, pp. 132–143. Springer, Heidelberg (2006)
17. Neary, T., Woods, D.: Four small universal Turing machines. Fundamenta Informaticae 91(1), 123–144 (2009)
18. Pavlotskaya, L.: Solvability of the halting problem for certain classes of Turing machines. Mathematical Notes (Springer) 13(6), 537–541 (1973)
19. Pavlotskaya, L.: Dostatochnye uslovija razreshimosti problemy ostanovki dlja mashin T'juring. Problemi kibernetiki, 91–118 (1978) (in Russian)
20. Priese, L.: Towards a precise characterization of the complexity of universal and non-universal Turing machines. Siam journal of Computing 8(4), 508–523 (1979)
21. Rogozhin, Y.: Small universal Turing machines. Theoretical Computer Science 168(2), 215–240 (1996)
22. Shannon, C.E.: A universal Turing machine with two internal states. Automata Studies, Annals of Mathematics Studies 34, 157–165 (1956)
23. Watanabe, S.: 5-symbol 8-state and 5-symbol 6-state universal Turing machines. Journal of ACM 8(4), 476–483 (1961)
24. Watanabe, S.: 4-symbol 5-state universal Turing machine. Information Processing Society of Japan Magazine 13(9), 588–592 (1972)
25. Wolfram, S.: A new kind of science. Wolfram Media, Champaign (2002)
26. Woods, D., Neary, T.: On the time complexity of 2-tag systems and small universal Turing machines. In: 47th Annual IEEE Symposium on Foundations of Computer Science (FOCS), pp. 439–448. IEEE, New York (2006)
27. Woods, D., Neary, T.: The complexity of small universal Turing machines: A survey. Theoretical Computer Science 410(4–5), 443–450 (2009)
28. Woods, D., Neary, T.: Small semi-weakly universal Turing machines. Fundamenta Informaticae 91(1), 179–195 (2009)

Open Maps Bisimulations for Higher Dimensional Automata Models*

Elena S. Oshevskaya

Sobolev Institute of Mathematics
Siberian Branch of the Russian Academy of Sciences
4 Acad. Koptyug avenue, 630090, Novosibirsk, Russia
eso@iis.nsk.su

Abstract. The intention of the paper is to show the applicability of the general categorical framework of open maps to the setting of two models – higher dimensional automata (HDA) and timed higher dimensional automata (THDA) – in order to transfer general concepts of equivalences to the models. First, we define categories of the models under consideration, whose morphisms are to be thought of as simulations. Then, accompanying (sub)categories of observations are chosen relative to which the corresponding notions of open maps are developed. Finally, we use the open maps framework to obtain two abstract bisimulations which are established to coincide with hereditary history preserving bisimulations on HDA and THDA, respectively.

1 Introduction

Geometrical methods in concurrency theory have appeared recently for modelling, analysis and verification of the behaviour of concurrent systems. The most popular geometric model for concurrency is higher dimensional automata (HDA) which have been proposed by V. Pratt [22]. Actually at about the same time a bisimulation semantics has been given for HDA in [6]. Based on the concepts of HDA, numerous papers have emerged in the literature. Basic strands of research are concerned with giving true concurrent semantics to concurrent languages [11,8,2], with analyzing correctness of distributed databases [3], with formalizing the fault-tolerant implementation of distributed programs [12,10,13]. The relationships between higher dimensional automata and other true concurrent models have been thoroughly studied in the paper [7]. Real-time extensions of HDA (THDA) have been investigated by Goubault [9].

In an attempt to explain and unify apparent differences between the extensive amount of research within the field of bisimulation equivalences, several category theoretic approaches to the matter have appeared. One of them was initiated by Joyal, Nielsen, and Winskel in [15] where they proposed an abstract way of capturing the notion of bisimulation through the so-called spans of open maps:

---

* This work is supported in part by the DFG-RFBR (grant No 436 RUS 113/1002/01, 09-01-91334).

first, a category of models of computations is chosen, then a subcategory of observation is chosen relative to which open maps are defined; two models are bisimilar if there exists a span of open maps between the models. The abstract definition of bisimilarity makes possible a uniform definition of bisimulation over different models ranging from interleaving models like transition systems [18] to true concurrency models like event structures [15], Petri nets [19], transition systems with independence [15], higher dimensional transition systems [24], higher dimensional automata [4]. The papers [14] and [26] transfer the concepts of abstract bisimularity to timed models — timed transition systems and timed event structures, respectively.

The contribution of the paper is to show the applicability of the general categorical framework of open maps to provide abstract characterizations of hereditary history preserving bisimulations in the setting of two models – HDA and THDA. In addition to the possibility of a uniform definition of bisimulation over different models presented as categories, the open maps based bisimilarity allows one to apply general results from the categorical setting (e.g. the existence of canonical models and characteristic games and logics) to concrete behavioural equivalences. In contrast to [4], we treat the notion of hereditary history preserving bisimulation [1] but not bisimulation [17]. Unlike [20], we exploit a slightly different definition of a model run, which allows us to uniformly apply the open maps approach to the the setting of both HDA and THDA.

The rest of the paper is organized as follows. The following two sections concentrate on HDA and THDA, respectively. First, the basic notions and notations concerning the structure and behaviour of the models under consideration are introduced. Then, it is defined categories of the models and accompanying (sub)categories of observations, to which the corresponding notions of open maps are developed. Also, behavioural characterizations of the open maps are provided. Finally, the abstract equivalences based on spans of the open maps are shown to coincide with hereditary history preserving bisimulations on HDA and on THDA, respectively. Section 4 contains conclusion and some remarks on future work. In Appendix, we give a short introduction to open maps as presented in [15]. For lack of the space, the proofs are relegated to the paper [21].

2   (Untimed) HDA

2.1   Basic Definitions

In this section, we present the model of higher dimensional automata (HDA) – a geometric model for true concurrency based on the ideas of the works by V. Pratt [22] and R. van Glabbeek [6]. HDA are generalizations of the usual models of automata, also known as process graphs, state transition diagrams or labelled transition systems. The basic idea of HDA is to use the higher dimensions to represent the concurrent execution of processes. In contrast to interleaving models, HDA are built as sets of 0-cubes (points) and 1-cubes (edges) between 0-cubes but also as sets of 2-cubes (squares) between 1-cubes, 3-cubes (cubes) between 2-cubes and more generally n-cubes (hypercubes) between $(n-1)$-cubes.

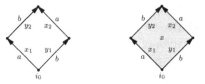

Fig. 1.

In this way, n-cubes represent concurrent executions of n actions. For example, for two actions a and b, we model the mutually exclusive execution of a and b by the HDA consisting of the 1-cubes x_1, y_1 and x_2, y_2 (in some sense, x_2 and y_2 are copies of x_1 and y_1, respectively), as shown at the left-hand side of Figure 1, whereas the concurrent execution of a and b is modelled by 2-dimensional surface x labelled by $\{a, b\}$ and delineated by the 1-cubes x_1, y_1 and x_2, y_2, as shown at the right-hand side of Figure 1. Thus, in HDA non-determinism arises as holes but concurrency is modelled by hypercubes with the interior filled. It is natural to graphically represent n-cubes as n-dimensional objects whose boundaries are the $(n-1)$-cubes from which they can start and to which they end up. The 2-cube x shown at the right-hand side of Figure 1 can start from x_1 or y_1. Similarly, x ends up to x_2 and y_2. Thus, the boundary of the square can be divided into two source boundary functions d_1^0, d_2^0 with $d_1^0(x) = x_1$, $d_2^0(x) = y_1$ and two target boundary functions d_1^1, d_2^1 with $d_1^1(x) = x_2$, $d_2^1(x) = y_2$. In addition, we fix a distinguished basepoint called the *initial point* and denoted as i_0.

The following is the (well known but presented in a slightly different manner) definition of HDA from [7].

Definition 1. *A precubical set M is a collection of sets $(M_n)_{n \in \mathbb{N}}$, such that $M_n \cap M_k = \emptyset$ for all $n \neq k$, together with boundary functions $M_n \overset{d_i^0}{\underset{d_j^1}{\rightrightarrows}} M_{n-1}$ for all $n \in \mathbb{N}$ and $i, j = 1 \ldots n$, such that $d_i^k \circ d_j^m = d_{j-1}^m \circ d_i^k$ ($i < j$, $k, m = 0, 1$).*

Definition 2. *A (labelled) HDA is a tuple $\mathrm{M} = (M, i_{0_M}, L, l)$, where M is a precubical set, $i_{0_M} \in M_0$ is a distinguished basepoint of M, called the* initial *point, L is an alphabet of actions, $l : M_1 \to L$ is a labelling function such that $l(d_i^0(x)) = l(d_i^1(x))$ ($i = 1, 2$), for all $x \in M_2$.*[1]

We shall henceforth assume any HDA to satisfy the following: for $x \in M_n$, $|\{d_1^m \circ \ldots d_{i-1}^m \circ d_{i+1}^m \circ \ldots \circ d_n^m(x) | i = 1 \ldots n\}| = n$, for all $m = 0, 1$. This means that any n-cube starts from n distinct edges and ends up to n distinct edges.

In order to reason about the behaviour of HDA, we introduce the following notions and notations. A *cubical path* in an HDA is a sequence $P = p_0 p_1 \ldots p_k$ of cubes such that $p_{s-1} = d_i^0(p_s)$ or $p_s = d_j^1(p_{s-1})$ ($s = 1 \ldots k$). A cubical path $P = p_0 p_1 \ldots p_k$ is *acyclic* if there are no other relations between the p_s than the

---

[1] To extend l to all $x \in M_n$ define $l(x) = \emptyset$, for $n = 0$, and $l(x) := \biguplus \{l(y) \mid y = d_1^0 \circ \ldots d_{i-1}^0 \circ d_{i+1}^0 \circ \ldots \circ d_n^0(x), i = 1, \ldots, n\}$ ($\biguplus$ is the union of multisets), for $n > 1$.

ones above. For cubical paths P and Q, we write $P \to Q$ if Q is an extension of P. A *cubical run* is a cubical path P with $p_0 = i_{0_M}$.

Two cubical paths $P = p_0 \ldots p_s \ldots p_k$ and $P' = p_0 \ldots p_{s-1}p'_s p_{s+1} \ldots p_k$ $(s = 1 \ldots k - 1)$ in M are *s-adjacent* (denoted $\overset{s}{\leftrightarrow}$) if one can be obtained from the other by replacing (for $i < j$ and $m = 0, 1$) either a segment $\overset{d_i^0}{\longrightarrow}$ $p_s \overset{d_j^m}{\longrightarrow}$ with a segment $\overset{d_{j-1}^m}{\longrightarrow} p'_s \overset{d_i^0}{\longrightarrow}$; or a segment $\overset{d_j^m}{\longrightarrow} p_s \overset{d_i^1}{\longrightarrow}$ with a segment $\overset{d_i^1}{\longrightarrow} p'_s \overset{d_{j-1}^m}{\longrightarrow}$. The *homotopy* relation on the cubical paths in M is the reflexive transitive closure of the adjacency relation $\leftrightarrow = \cup_s \overset{s}{\leftrightarrow}$. Moreover, P and P' are *(s, u, v)-adjacent* (denoted $P \overset{(s,u,v)}{\longleftrightarrow} P'$) if P' can be obtained from P by an s-adjacency replacement of the segment $\overset{d_u^n}{\longrightarrow} p_s \overset{d_v^l}{\longrightarrow}$.

Further, we define a behavioural equivalence on HDA, called hereditary history preserving bisimulation (hhp-bisimulation), which is in close similarity with the corresponding definition from [1,7].

Definition 3. *Let* M *and* N *be HDA.*

Cubical runs $P = p_0 \ldots p_k$ in M *and $Q = q_0 \ldots q_k$ in* N *are called l-related iff $l_M(p_j) = l_N(q_j)$ for all $j = 0 \ldots k$.*

A binary relation $\mathcal{R}$ on cubical runs in M *and* N *is called a hereditary history preserving bisimulation (hhp-bisimulation) between* M *and* N *if for any $(P, Q) \in \mathcal{R}$, P and Q are l-related and the following conditions are satisfied:*

1. *if $P \to P'$ then there exists Q' such that $Q \to Q'$ and $(P', Q') \in \mathcal{R}$,*
2. *if $Q \to Q'$ then there exists P' such that $P \to P'$ and $(P', Q') \in \mathcal{R}$,*
3. *if $P' \to P$ then there exists Q' such that $Q' \to Q$ and $(P', Q') \in \mathcal{R}$,*
4. *if $Q' \to Q$ then there exists P' such that $P' \to P$ and $(P', Q') \in \mathcal{R}$,*
5. *if $P \overset{(s,u,v)}{\longleftrightarrow} P'$ then there exists Q' such that $Q \overset{(s,u,v)}{\longleftrightarrow} Q'$ and $(P', Q') \in \mathcal{R}$,*
6. *if $Q \overset{(s,u,v)}{\longleftrightarrow} Q'$ then there exists P' such that $P \overset{(s,u,v)}{\longleftrightarrow} P'$ and $(P', Q') \in \mathcal{R}$.*

HDA M *and* N *are hhp-bisimilar if there exists an hhp-bisimulation between them which relates their initial points (regarded as cubical runs).*

Note, hhp-bisimulation is indeed an equivalence relation.

Example 1. To get more intuition about the above concept, we consider examples of HDA shown in Figures 2 and 3. For the HDA in Figure 2, the boundary functions are given as follows: $d_1^0(x_1) = p_1$, $d_2^0(x_1) = p_2$, $d_1^0(x_2) = p_3$, $d_2^0(x_2) = p_2$ for the left-hand HDA, and $d_1^0(y) = q_1$, $d_2^0(y) = q_2$ for the right-hand HDA. It is easy to see that the HDA are hhp-bisimilar. For the HDA in Figure 3, the boundary functions are given as follows: $d_1^0(x_1) = p_1$, $d_2^1(x_1) = p_5$, $d_1^0(x_2) = p_1$, $d_2^1(x_2) = p_2$, $d_2^0(x_3) = p_4$, $d_1^1(x_3) = p_3$, $d_1^0(x_4) = p_5$, $d_2^0(x_4) = p_6$, for the left-hand HDA, and $d_1^0(y_1) = q_1$, $d_2^1(y_1) = q_6$, $d_1^0(y_2) = q_1$, $d_2^1(y_2) = q_2$, $d_2^0(y_3) = q_4$, $d_1^1(y_3) = q_5$, $d_1^0(y_4) = q_6$, $d_2^1(y_4) = q_7$, $d_2^0(y_5) = q_2$, $d_1^1(y_5) = q_3$, for the right-hand HDA. We then have that the run $(sp_1 s_1 p_2 s_2 p_3 s_3)$ in the left-hand HDA can be related only to the run $(tq_1 t_1 q_2 t_2 q_3 t_3)$ in the right-hand HDA. Moreover, we

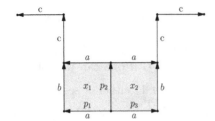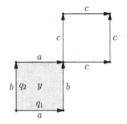

Fig. 2.

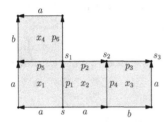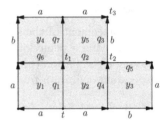

Fig. 3.

can see that $(tq_1t_1q_2t_2q_3t_3) \overset{(5,1,1)}{\longleftrightarrow} (tq_1t_1q_2y_5q_3t_3)$ in the right-hand HDA. Then, there should exist a run P in the left-hand HDA such that $(sp_1s_1p_2s_2p_3s_3) \overset{(5,1,1)}{\longleftrightarrow} P$ but it is not the case.

2.2   Open Maps Characterization

In this subsection, we first define a category of HDA, **HDA**, whose morphisms will be simulation morphisms following the approach of [15]. We then specify an accompanying (sub)category **Obs** of observations, to which the corresponding notion of open maps is developed. We finally use the open maps framework to obtain abstract bisimulation which is established to coincide with hhp-bisimulation on HDA.

Define a morphism between two HDA, which is a pair of functions, mapping labels and cubes of the simulated system to simulating labels and cubes of the other, satisfying some requirements.

Definition 4. *Let* $\mathrm{M} = (M, m_{0_M}, L_M, l_M)$ *and* $\mathrm{N} = (N, i_{0_N}, L_N, l_N)$ *be HDA. A mapping* $\mathrm{f} = \langle f, \alpha \rangle$ *(where* $f = \cup f_n$, $f_n : M_n \to N_n$, $\alpha : L_M \to L_N$*) is called a morphism from* M *to* N *iff it holds: 1.* $f_0(i_{0_M}) = i_{0_N}$, *2.* $l_N \circ f = \alpha \circ l_M$, *3.* $f_n \circ d_i^m = d_i^m \circ f_{n+1}$.

The first condition guarantees that morphisms preserve initial points; the second and third conditions ensure the consistency of labels and boundaries of cubes, respectively.

Consider a simulation property of a morphism defined prior to that.

Proposition 1. *If* $f = \langle f, \alpha \rangle$ *is a morphism from* M *to* N *then for all cubical runs* P *in* M *it holds:*

1. *whenever* $P \longrightarrow P'$ *in* M, *then* $f(P) \longrightarrow f(P')$ *in* N,
2. *whenever* $P \overset{(s,u,v)}{\longleftrightarrow} P'$ *in* M, *then* $f(P) \overset{(s,u,v)}{\longleftrightarrow} f(P')$ *in* N.

HDA with morphisms between them form a category HDA, **HDA**, in which the composition of two morphisms $f = \langle f, \alpha \rangle : M \to M'$ and $g = \langle g, \beta \rangle : M' \to M''$ is $g \circ f = \langle g \circ f, \beta \circ \alpha \rangle : M \to M''$, and the identity morphism is a pair of the identity functions.

For our purposes we need to endow **HDA** with a fibred structure. Denote **HDA**$_L$ the subcategory of **HDA** whose objects are HDA labelled over L and morphisms have the identity label component. We shall follow similar conventions for the other categories defined in the paper.

Relying on the standards of HDA and the paper [15] (also, see Appendix), we would like to choose 'observation objects' with morphisms between them so as to form a subcategory of observations of the category of HDA. An *observation* is a HDA having the form of an acyclic cubical run. We use **Obs** to denote the full subcategory of observations of the category **HDA**.

Our next aim is to characterize **Obs**$_L$-open morphisms relative to the subcategory of observations defined prior to that. In the below characterization, the first condition is usually referred to as the "higher-dimensional" zig-zag property and the second one ensures that **Obs**$_L$-open morphisms reflect concurrency.

Theorem 1. *A morphism* $f = \langle f, 1_L \rangle : M \to N$ *of* **HDA**$_L$ *is* **Obs**$_L$*-open iff for all cubical runs* P *in* M *it holds:*

1. *whenever* $f(P) \longrightarrow Q'$ *in* N, *then* $P \longrightarrow P'$ *and* $f(P') = Q'$, *for some cubical run* P' *in* M,
2. *whenever* $f(P) \overset{(s,u,v)}{\longleftrightarrow} Q'$ *in* N, *then* $P \overset{(s,u,v)}{\longleftrightarrow} P'$ *and* $f(P') = Q'$, *for some cubical run* P' *in* M.

At last, the coincidence of **Obs**$_L$-bisimulation and hhp-bisimulation is established.

Theorem 2. *Two HDA (with the same set* L *of labels) are* **Obs**$_L$*-bisimilar iff they are hhp-bisimilar.*

3   Timed HDA

3.1   Basic Definitions

We begin with presenting the concept of a timed HDA (THDA) [9] – a timed extension of HDA. THDA are defined as a geometric shape together with an structure given by cubes realized on this shape, and a family of norms defining the infinitesimal duration of a computation in all directions. Time is measured as the length of paths in cubes.

Introduce some auxiliary notions and notations. Consider a unit cube of dimension n in $\mathbb{R}^n$: $\square_n := \{(t_1, \ldots, t_n) \in \mathbb{R}^n \mid 0 \le t_i \le 1,\ i = 1, \ldots, n\}$, for $n > 0$, and $\square_0 := \{0\}$, for $n = 0$. Let $\overset{\circ}{\square}_n$ denote the topological interior of $\square_n$, i.e. $\overset{\circ}{\square}_n := \{(t_1, \ldots, t_n) \in \mathbb{R}^n \mid 0 < t_i < 1,\ i = 1, \ldots, n\}$, for $n > 0$, and $\overset{\circ}{\square}_0 := \{0\}$, for $n = 0$.

In order to define a THDA we first need a geometric shape (topological space) X. We are especially interested in compactly generated Hausdorff topological spaces[2] [16]. Then we should give a differential structure on X to be able to measure time. In our case the differential structure on X is given by cubes. Intuitively, cubes should be a sort of deformed cubes, so we define them as continuous functions $x : \square_n \to X$ which induce homeomorphisms from $\overset{\circ}{\square}_n$ to their images. Thus, $x : \square_n \to X$ gives the trivial structure of manifold[3] to $x(\overset{\circ}{\square}_n)$. For a cube $x(\overset{\circ}{\square}_n)$, we can define its coordinates as follows: $(x(t_1, \ldots, t_n))_i = t_i$ $(i = 1, \ldots, n,\ n > 0)$. We consider functions $x : \square_n \to X$ to be continuously deformed cubes only in their interior since we may want to identify some of their boundaries to get cyclic shapes. To do this we need functions characterizing the boundaries of cubes. Assume $\delta_i^m : \square_{n-1} \to \square_n$ $(i \in \{1, \ldots, n\},\ m \in \{0,1\})$ to be continuous functions defined as follows: $\delta_i^m(t_1, \ldots, t_{n-1}) = (t_1, \ldots, t_{i-1}, m, t_i, \ldots, t_{n-1})$, for $n > 1$, and $\delta_1^m(0) = (m)$, for $n = 1$. We then have $\delta_i^k \delta_j^m = \delta_{j+1}^m \delta_i^k$ for $i \le j$. To be able to take boundaries we should require the collection of cubes to be stable by composition with boundary functions. To illustrate the concepts, consider Figure 4. We have the edge $\square_1$, the square $\square_2$ and the torus T. Moreover, x_1 continuously maps the edge $\square_1$ into small circle of T so that $x_1(\overset{\circ}{\square}_1)$ is small circle without a point, and x_2 continuously maps the square $\square_2$ into T so that $x_2(\overset{\circ}{\square}_2)$ is a torus without small and big circles. Then, we get $x_1 = x_2 \circ \delta_1^0$.

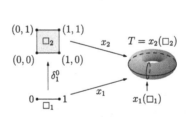

Fig. 4.

We can now split our cubes into sets X_n containing only cubes with the domain $\square_n$. Also, we require X to be covered by all its cubes, i.e. X is the disjoint union $\bigsqcup_{x \in X_n,\ n \in \mathbb{N}} (x(\overset{\circ}{\square}_n))$.

---

[2] In topology, a compactly generated space is a topological space X satisfying the following condition: each subspace $U \subset X$ which intersects every compact subset K of X in a closed set is itself closed.

[3] The definition of the notion of manifold can be found in [25].

Finally, to measure the time (length) of cubes from X, we are to have a norm $\| \cdot \|_u$ on the tangent space $T_u X =_{def} T_u x(\overset{\circ}{\square}_n)$ $(u \in x(\overset{\circ}{\square}_n))$ at every $u \in X$ (for further details see [25]). A tangent space $T_u x(\overset{\circ}{\square}_n)$ is an n-dimensional space consisting of the tangent vectors $\dot{u}$ of the curves through a point u, which can be measured by the norm. Intuitively, a tangent space contains the possible "directions" in which one can pass through u and the norm can be seen as an infinitesimal duration of the computation at u. In order to be consistent with the space, the norm should be continuous on X, i.e. $F(u, \dot{u}) = \| \dot{u} \|_u$ is a continuous function w.r.t. u. Note the fact that the norm $\| \cdot \|_u$ is continuious w.r.t. $\dot{u}$ on a tangent space follows from the properties of the norm [9].

We are now ready to define (labelled) THDA. For full details and explanations on the definitions related to THDA, we refer the reader to [9], where the concept has been first introduced.

Definition 5. *A (labelled) THDA is a tuple* $X = (X, i_{0_X}, L, l, \| \cdot \|_X)$, *where*

- *X is a compactly generated Hausdorff topological space together with a presentation of X by singular cubes, i.e. X is the disjoint union* $\bigsqcup\limits_{x \in X_n,\, n \in \mathbb{N}} (x(\overset{\circ}{\square}_n))$, *where X_n consists of continuous functions $x^n : \square_n \to X$ which induce homeomorphisms from $\overset{\circ}{\square}_n$ to its image and are such that $x^n \circ \delta_i^m \in X_{n-1}$ for all $i = 1, \ldots, n$ and $m = 0, 1$ (note, $x^0 \circ \delta_i^m = x^0$),*
- *i_{0_X} is a distinguished basepoint of X called the* initial point *and represented in the form of $i_{0_X} = x(0)$ for some function $x \in X_0$,*
- *L is a set of labels,*
- *$l : X_1 \to L$ is a labelling function[4] such that $l(x \circ \delta_i^0) = l(x \circ \delta_i^1)$ $(i = 1, 2)$, for all $x \in X_2$,*
- *X is given a family of norms $\| \cdot \|_u$ on every tangent space $T_u X =_{def} T_u x(\overset{\circ}{\square}_n)$ $(u \in x(\overset{\circ}{\square}_n))$ such that $F(u, \dot{u}) = \| \dot{u} \|_u$ is a continuous function $(u \in X)$.*

We shall henceforth assume any THDA to satisfy the following: for $x \in X_n$ $|\{x \circ \delta_n^m \circ \ldots \circ \delta_{i+1}^m \circ \delta_{i-1}^m \circ \ldots \circ \delta_1^m | i = 1 \ldots n\}| = n$ for all $m = 0, 1$.

In order to know how much time cubes of a THDA may take, we introduce the following definition of paths as being particular curves between two points in X. A continuous function $\gamma : [0, 1] \to X$ is called a *path* in a THDA X if γ is differentiable in each cube (of non-zero dimension) having nonempty intersection with $\gamma([0, 1])$ and is increasing w.r.t. each coordinate in such the cubes. The *length* of a path γ is calculated as follows: $length(\gamma) = \int\limits_0^1 \| \frac{d\gamma}{dt}(t) \|_{\gamma(t)} dt$[5]. A *run* is a path γ with $\gamma(0) = i_0$. A point $u \in X$ is called *reachable* if there exists a run γ such that $\gamma(1) = u$.

---

[4] To extend l to all $x \in X_n$ define $l(x) = \emptyset$, for $n = 0$, and $l(x) := \biguplus \{l(y) \mid y = x \circ \delta_n^0 \circ \ldots \delta_{i+1}^0 \circ \delta_{i-1}^0 \circ \ldots \circ \delta_1^0,\ i \in \{1, \ldots, n\}\}$ ($\biguplus$ is the union of multisets), for $n > 1$.

[5] The integral is actually the sum of the integrals over intervals in which γ is a differentiable function.

Let γ_1 and γ_2 be paths from $\gamma_1(0) = \gamma_2(0)$ to $\gamma_1(1) = \gamma_2(1)$ in X. A continous function $h : [0,1] \times [0,1] \to X$ is a homotopy between γ_1 and γ_2 iff 1. $h(0,t) = \gamma_1(t)$, for all $t \in [0,1]$, 2. $h(1,t) = \gamma_2(t)$, for all $t \in [0,1]$, 3. $t \mapsto h(s,t)$ is a path from $\gamma_1(0)$ to $\gamma_1(1)$ in X, for all $s \in [0,1]$. This defines an equivalence relation on paths starting and ending at the same points in X. The equivalent class of a path γ is denoted by $[\gamma]$.

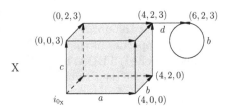

Fig. 5.

Example 2. Figure 5 shows a trivial example of a THDA. The THDA $X = (X = x(\square_3) \cup x_1(\square_1) \cup x_0(\square_1)$, $i_{0_X} = (0,0,0)$, $L_X = \{a,b,c,d\}$, l_X, $\| \cdot \|_X)$ is generated by the 3-cube $x(t_1,t_2,t_3) = (4t_1, 2t_2, 3t_3)$ $((t_1,t_2,t_3) \in \square_3)$, the 1-cube $x_1(t) = (4 + 2t, 2, 3)$ $(t \in \square_1)$ and the unit circle $x_0(t) = (6 - \sin(2\pi t), 2, 2 + \cos(2\pi t))$ $(t \in \square_1)$ which is depicted by the filled-in cube, the segment and the circle, respectively. The labelling function is given by $l_X(x \circ \delta_3^0 \circ \delta_2^0) = a$, $l_X(x \circ \delta_3^0 \circ \delta_1^0) = b$, $l_X(x \circ \delta_2^0 \circ \delta_1^0) = c$, $l_X(x_1) = d$ and $l_X(x_0) = b$. The norm $\| \cdot \|_X$ is induced by the Euclidean one in $\mathbb{R}^3$. Notice that geometrically, the interior of the filled-in cube consists of the union of all paths where occurrences of a, b and c overlap in time. The lengths of the runs travelled along the 1-cube labelled by a (b or c) are equal to 4 (2 or 3, respectively). Then the lengths of all runs in the filled-in cube are varied between $\sqrt{4^2 + 2^2 + 3^2}$ and $4 + 2 + 3$.

Note, when $X = (X, i_0, L, l, \| \cdot \|_X)$ is a THDA, it is easy to see that $M = (\cup_n X_n, i_0, L, l)$ is an HDA, where for any $x \in X_n$ $d_i^m(x) = x \circ \delta_i^m$ ($m = 0, 1$ and $i = 1 \ldots n$), and n-cubes are considered as discrete values but not as continuous functions. The definitions of a cubical path (run), s- and (s, u, v)-adjacency, homotopy on HDA can be used for THDA. Further, we extend the notion of hhp-bisimulation to THDA as follows.

Definition 6. *Let* X *and* Y *be THDA.*

Cubical runs $P = p_0 \ldots p_k$ *in* X *and* $Q = q_0 \ldots q_k$ *in* Y *are called d-related iff for all* $0 \le j \le k$ *it holds:* $\|d_t p_j(\mathring{t})\|_{p_j(t)} = \|d_t q_j(\mathring{t})\|_{q_j(t)}$ *for all* $\mathring{t} \in T_t \mathring{\square}_{\dim p_j}$ *and* $t \in \mathring{\square}_{\dim p_j}$.

A binary relation $\mathcal{R}$ *on cubical runs in* X *and* Y *is called a timed hhp-bisimulation between* X *and* Y *iff* $\mathcal{R}$ *is an hhp-bisimulation and for any* $(P, Q) \in \mathcal{R}$, *P and Q are d-related.*

THDA X *and* Y *are timed hhp-bisimilar if there exists a timed hhp-bisimulation between them which relates their initial points (regarded as cubical runs).*

Clearly, timed hhp-bisimulation is indeed an equivalence relation.

Example 3. Consider the representations shown in Figure 2 as THDA whose spaces included in $\mathbb{R}^2$. At the left-hand side, we have THDA X $= (X = x_1(\square_2) \cup x_2(\square_2) \cup p_4(\square_1) \cup p_5(\square_1) \cup p_6(\square_1) \cup p_7(\square_1), i_{0_X} = (0,0), L_X = \{a,b,c\}, l_X, \|\cdot\|_X)$. It is generated by the 2-cubes: $x_1(t_1, t_2) = (t_1, t_2), x_2(t_1, t_2) = (-t_1, t_2) ((t_1, t_2) \in \square_2)$ and the 1-cubs: $p_4(t) = (1, 1 + t), p_5(t) = (1, 2 + t), p_6(t) = (-1, 1 + t)$ and $p_7(t) = (-1, 2 + t) (t \in \square_1)$. The labelling function is depicted in Figure 2. The norm $\|\cdot\|_X$ is induced by the Euclidean one in $\mathbb{R}^2$. Next, at the right-hand side we have THDA Y $= (Y = y(\square_2) \cup q_3(\square_1) \cup q_4(\square_1) \cup q_5(\square_1) \cup q_6(\square_1), i_{0_Y} = (0,0), L_Y = \{a,b,c\}, l_Y, \|\cdot\|_Y)$. It is generated by the 2-cube $y(t \in \square_1)(t_1, t_2) = (t_1, \lambda t_2) ((t_1, t_2) \in \square_2)$ and the 1-cubs: $q_3(t) = (1 + t, \lambda), q_4(t) = (2, \lambda + t), q_5(t) = (1, \lambda + t)$ and $q_6(t) = (1 + t, 1 + \lambda) (t \in \square_1)$. The labelling function is depicted in Figure 2. The norm $\|\cdot\|_Y$ is induced by the Euclidean one in $\mathbb{R}^2$. If $\lambda = 1$, then THDA X and Y are timed hhp-bisimilar, otherwise they are not.

3.2   Open Maps Characterization

In this subsection, we proceed to show that timed hhp-bisimulation can be characterized using the open maps framework (see Appendix).

Consider the definition of a morphism that is a pair of functions, mapping points and labels of the simulated system to simulating points and labels of the other, satisfying some requirements. Note, we want morphisms to contract time.

Definition 7. *Let* X $= (X, i_{0_X}, L_X, l_X, \|\cdot\|_X)$ *and* Y $= (Y, i_{0_Y}, L_Y, l_Y, \|\cdot\|_Y)$ *be THDA. A mapping* f $= \langle f, \alpha \rangle$ *(where* $f : X \to Y$ *is a continuous function,* $\alpha : L_X \to L_Y$ *is a function) is called a* morphism *from* X *to* Y *iff it holds:*

1. $f(i_{0_X}) = i_{0_Y}$,
2. *for all functions* $x \in X_n$ *(*$n \in \mathbb{N}$*), there exists a function* $y \in Y_n$ *such that* $l_Y(y) = \alpha(l_X(x))$ *and the diagram:* $\square_n \xrightarrow{x} X, \square_n \xrightarrow{y} Y$ *and* $X \xrightarrow{f} Y$, *commutes*[6].
3. $\|d_u f(\dot{u})\|_{f(u)} \leq \|\dot{u}\|_u$ *for all* $\dot{u} \in T_u X$ *and* $u \in X$.

The first condition guarantees that morphisms preserve initial points. The second ensures that an n-cube maps to a n-cube and labels of the n-cubes coincide (α is matched to f). The third condition guarantees that the length of each path in X is not less than the length of its image. If in the third condition we have $\|d_u f(\dot{u})\|_{f(u)} = \|\dot{u}\|_u$ for all $\dot{u} \in T_u X$ and $u \in X$, then f preserves the length of every path (i.e. f is an isometry).

We next establish that the morphisms defined prior to that represent some notions of simulation of the behaviour of one system by the other.

Proposition 2. *If* f $= \langle f, \alpha \rangle$ *is a morphism from* X *to* Y, *then for all cubical runs* $P = p_0, \ldots, p_k$ *in* X *it holds:*

---

[6] The commutativity of the diagram guarantees $y^{-1} \circ f \circ x = id$ on $\overset{\circ}{\square}_n$. Hence, we have $f \in C^\infty$.

1. *whenever $P \longrightarrow P'$ in X, then $f(P) \longrightarrow f(P')$ in Y,*
2. *whenever $P \overset{(s,u,v)}{\longleftrightarrow} P'$ in X, then $f(P) \overset{(s,u,v)}{\longleftrightarrow} f(P')$ in Y,*
3. $\|d_u f(\dot{u})\|_{f(u)} \leq \|\dot{u}\|_u$ *for all $\dot{u} \in T_u p_j(\overset{\circ}{\square}_{\dim p_j})$, $u \in p_j(\overset{\circ}{\square}_{\dim p_j})$, $j = 1 \ldots k$.*

THDA with morphisms between them form a category of THDA, **THDA**, in which the composition of two morphisms $f = \langle f, \alpha \rangle : X \to Y$ and $g = \langle g, \beta \rangle : Y \to Z$ is $g \circ f = \langle g \circ f, \beta \circ \alpha \rangle : X \to Z$, and the identity morphism is a pair of the identity functions.

An *observation* is a THDA having the form of an acyclic cubical run. We use **TObs**$_L$ to denote the full subcategory of observations of the category **THDA**$_L$.

Further, we provide a behavioural criterion of **TObs**$_L$-open morphisms which is crucial to formulate an open maps characterization of timed hhp-bisimulation (see Appendix).

Theorem 3. *A morphism* $f = \langle f, 1_L \rangle : X \to Y$ *of* **THDA**$_L$ *is* **TObs**$_L$*-open iff for all cubical runs P in X it holds:*

1. *whenever $f(P) \longrightarrow Q'$ in Y, then $P \longrightarrow P'$ and $f(P') = Q'$, for some cubical run P' in X,*
2. *whenever $f(P) \overset{(s,u,v)}{\longleftrightarrow} Q'$ in Y, then $P \overset{(s,u,v)}{\longleftrightarrow} P'$ and $f(P') = Q'$, for some cubical run P' in X,*
3. $d_u f$ *is an isometry for all reachable points $u \in X$.*

Finally, the coincidence of **TObs**$_L$-bisimulation and timed hhp-bisimulation is established.

Theorem 4. *Two THDA (with the same set L of labels) are* **TObs**$_L$*-bisimilar iff they are timed hhp-bisimilar.*

4   Conclusion

The paper focuses on open maps characterizations of hhp-bisimulation on HDA and timed hhp-bisimulation on THDA. We remark that the equivalences have been attacked using homotopy techniques, following the papers [7,24]. In particular, guided by our intuitive understanding of what it means for a higher dimensional automata model to be simulated by another one, we have defined categories of HDA and THDA and accompanying (sub)categories of observations, to which the corresponding notions of open maps have been developed. We have used the open maps framework [15] to obtain abstract bisimulations which have been established to coincide with the mentioned above bisimulations on HDA and THDA. The open maps based bisimilarity makes possible a uniform definition of bisimulation over different models presented as categories and allows one to apply general results from the categorical setting (e.g. the existence of canonical models and characteristic games and logics) to concrete behavioural equivalences.

As a matter of future work, it would be interesting to extend the results obtained in the paper [5] to weak variant of bisimulation on HDA and THDA, combining open maps and presheaf approaches. Also, we plan some investigation on coalgebraic characterizations [23] of bisimulation in the setting of HDA and THDA.

References

1. Bednarczyk, M.A.: Hereditory history preserving bisimulation or what is the power of the future perfect in program logics. Technical Report, Polish Academy of Science (1991)
2. Cridlig, R.: Implementing a static analyzer of concurrent programs: Problems and perspectives. In: Dam, M. (ed.) LOMAPS-WS 1996. LNCS, vol. 1192, pp. 244–259. Springer, Heidelberg (1997)
3. Fajstrup, L., Goubault, E., Raussen, M.: Detecting deadlocks in concurrent systems. In: Sangiorgi, D., de Simone, R. (eds.) CONCUR 1998. LNCS, vol. 1466, pp. 332–347. Springer, Heidelberg (1998)
4. Fahrenberg, U.: A Category of Higher-Dimensional Automata. In: Sassone, V. (ed.) FOSSACS 2005. LNCS, vol. 3441, pp. 187–201. Springer, Heidelberg (2005)
5. Fiore, M., Cattani, G.L., Winskel, G.: Weak bisimulation and open maps. In: 14th Annual IEEE Symposium on Logic in Computer Science, pp. 214–225. IEEE Computer Society Press, Washington (1999)
6. van Glabbeek, R.J.: Bisimulation semantics for higher dimensional automata, http://theory.stanford.edu/~rvg/hda
7. van Glabbeek, R.J.: On the Expressiveness of higher dimensional automata. Theor. Comput. Sci. 356(3), 265–290 (2006)
8. Goubault, E.: Domains of higher-dimensional automata. In: Best, E. (ed.) CONCUR 1993. LNCS, vol. 715, pp. 293–307. Springer, Heidelberg (1993)
9. Goubault, E.: The Geometry of Concurrency. Ph.D. thesis. Ecole Normale Superieure, Paris (1995)
10. Goubault, E.: A semantic view on distributed computability and complexity. In: 3rd Theory and Formal Methods Section Workshop. Imperial College Press, London (1996)
11. Goubault, E., Jensen, T.P.: Homology of higher-dimensional automata. In: Cleaveland, W.R. (ed.) CONCUR 1992. LNCS, vol. 630, pp. 254–268. Springer, Heidelberg (1992)
12. Herlihy, M., Shavit, N.: A simple constructive computability theorem for wait-free computation. In: 26th Annual ACM Symposium on Theory of Computing, pp. 243–252. ACM Press, New York (1994)
13. Herlihy, M., Rajsbaum, S.: New perspectives in distributed computing. In: Kutyłowski, M., Wierzbicki, T., Pacholski, L. (eds.) MFCS 1999. LNCS, vol. 1672, pp. 170–186. Springer, Heidelberg (1999)
14. Hune, T., Nielsen, M.: Timed bisimulation and open maps. In: Brim, L., Gruska, J., Zlatuška, J. (eds.) MFCS 1998. LNCS, vol. 1450, pp. 378–387. Springer, Heidelberg (1998)
15. Joyal, A., Nielsen, M., Winskel, G.: Bisimulation from open maps. Inform. Comput. 127(2), 164–185 (1996)
16. MacLane, S.: Categories for the working mathematician. Springer, New York (1998)

17. Milner, R.: Communication and concurrency. Prentice-Hall, Upper Saddle River (1989)
18. Nielsen, M., Cheng, A.: Observing behaviour categorically. In: Thiagarajan, P.S. (ed.) FST&TCS 1995. LNCS, vol. 1026, pp. 263–278. Springer, Heidelberg (1995)
19. Nielsen, M., Winskel, G.: Petri nets and bisimulation. Theor. Comput. Sci. 153(1-2), 211–244 (1996)
20. Oshevskaya, E.S.: A categorical account of bisimulation for timed higher dimensional automata. In: 15th International Workshop on Concurrency, Specification and Programming, pp. 174–185. Humboldt-Universitaet zu Berlin, Berlin (2006)
21. Oshevskaya, E.S.: Open Maps Bisimulations for Higher Dimensional Automata Models, http://www.iis.nsk.su/virb/osh09.zip
22. Pratt, V.R.: Modeling concurrency with geometry. In: 18th Annual ACM Symposium on Principles of Programming Languages, pp. 311–322. ACM Press, New York (1991)
23. Rutten, J.J.M.M.: Universal coalgebra: a theory of systems. Theor. Comput. Sci. 249, 3–80 (2000)
24. Sassone, V., Cattani, G.L.: Higher-dimensional transition systems. In: 11th Annual IEEE Symposium on Logic in Computer Science, pp. 55–62. IEEE Computer Society Press, Los Alamitos (1996)
25. Sharpe, R.W.: Differential Geometry. Springer, New York (1997)
26. Virbitskaite, I.B., Gribovskaya, N.S.: Open maps and observational equivalences for timed partial order models. Fundam. Inform. 60(1-4), 383–399 (2004)
27. Winskel, G., Nielsen, M.: Models for concurrency. In: Handbook of Logic in Computer Science, vol. 4, pp. 1–148. Oxford University Press, London (1995)

Appendix: Introduction to Open Maps

We briefly recall the basic definitions from [15].

First, a category which represents a model of computation has to be identified. Let us denote this category by $\mathcal{M}$. A morphism $f : X \longrightarrow Y$ in $\mathcal{M}$ should intuitively be thought of as a simulation of X in Y. Then, inside the category $\mathcal{M}$, one chooses a subcategory of 'observation objects' and 'observation extension' morphisms between these objects. The *category of observations* is denoted by $\mathcal{P}$. Given an observation (object) O in $\mathcal{P}$ and a model X in $\mathcal{M}$, then O is said to be an *observable behaviour* of X if there exists a morphism $p : O \longrightarrow X$ in $\mathcal{M}$. In this case, p can be thought of as representing a particular way of realizing O in X.

Next, one identifies morphisms $f : X \longrightarrow Y$ which have the property that whenever an observable behaviour of X can be extended via f in Y then that extension can be matched by an extension of the observable behaviour in X. A morphism $f : X \to Y$ in $\mathcal{M}$ is called $\mathcal{P}$-open if whenever $m : O_1 \to O_2$ in $\mathcal{P}$, $p : O_1 \to X$, $q : O_2 \to Y$ in $\mathcal{M}$ such that $f \circ p = q \circ m$, there exists a morphism $r : O_2 \to X$ in $\mathcal{M}$ such that $p = r \circ m$ and $q = f \circ r$.

Finally, an abstract notion of bisimilarity is introduced. As reported in [15], the open map approach provides general concepts of bisimilarity for any categorical model of computation. The definition is given in terms of spans of open maps. Two models X and Y in $\mathcal{M}$ are said to be $\mathcal{P}$-bisimilar if there exists a span $X \xleftarrow{f} Z \xrightarrow{f'} Y$ with vertex Z and $\mathcal{P}$-open morphisms.

Decision Version of the Road Coloring Problem Is NP-Complete

Adam Roman

Institute of Computer Science
Jagiellonian University, Cracow, Poland
roman@ii.uj.edu.pl

Abstract. After Trahtman in his brilliant paper [10] solved the Road Coloring Problem, a couple of new problems have arisen in the field of synchronizing automata. Some of them naturally extends questions related to the 'classical' version of synchronization. Particulary, it is known that the problem of finding the synchronizing word of a given length for a given automaton is NP-complete. Volkov [11] asked, what is the complexity of the following problem: given a constant out-degree digraph G (possibly with multiple edges) and a natural number m, does there exist a synchronizing word of length m for some synchronizing labeling of G. In this paper we show that this decision version of the Road Coloring Problem is NP-complete.

1 Introduction

The Road Coloring Problem (RCP) originates in [1] and it was stated explicitly in the paper of Adler et al. [2]. It can be stated as follows: let G be a strongly connected, constant out-degree finite digraph, such that the greatest common divisor of the lengths of all cycles in G equals 1. Is there an edge labeling, turning G into a deterministic finite synchronizing automaton? The problem is of great importance in automata theory, because the synchronizing property makes the automaton behavior resistant to errors that could occur in an input word: after the error is detected, the synchronizing word can reset the automaton to its initial state, as if there was no error. In this way we are getting back the control over automaton action. In his paper, Trahtman [10] says:

> The problem appeared first in the context of symbolic dynamics and is important also in this area. Together with the Černý conjecture [6,8], the road coloring problem belongs to the most fascinating problems in the theory of finite automata. However, at the same time it was considered as a "notorious open problem" [5].

Trahtman [10] solved the RCP by showing that the synchronizing labeling exists for any strongly connected, constant out-degree finite digraph G if and only if the gcd of the lengths of all cycles in G equal to 1. RCP uses a notion of synchronization, which, in fact, was introduced few years before the work of Adler

M. Kutyłowski, M. Gębala, and W. Charatonik (Eds.): FCT 2009, LNCS 5699, pp. 287–297, 2009.

et al. The 'classical' version of synchronizing problem (SP) is as follows: given a *labeled* graph G with constant out-degree, find the (minimal) synchronizing word for G. In RCP it is *our* task to find some synchronizing coloring, in SP the labeling is already given. There are several questions about the complexity of different variants of SP, important from the practical point of view. These are:

(P1) given a labeled constant out-degree graph G, check if there exists a synchronizing word for G,

(P2) given a labeled constant out-degree graph G and natural number m, check if G can be synchronized by some word of length m,

(P3) given a labeled constant out-degree graph G and natural number m, check if the minimal synchronizing word for G has length m.

It is a well-known fact, that (P1) can be solved in polynomial time and that (P2) is NP-complete [4]. Recently, Volkov [12] has given (referring to the unpublished result of Samotij [7]), that finding the synchronizing word of minimal length for a given synchronizing coloring is hard. More precisely, (P3) is coNP-hard. Under the $P \neq NP$ assumption we see that (P2) is harder than (P1). Notice that (P2) is polynomially reducible to (P3), because of NP-hardness of the last one. But coNP-hardness of (P3) implies that (P3) is not polynomially reducible to (P2), unless NP=coNP, which is strongly believed to be false. Therefore, under assumptions $P \neq NP$ and $NP \neq coNP$, we can say that (P3) is harder than (P2) and (P2) is harder than (P1).

The solution of the RCP opened a new, broad field of research. For example, [3,9] deal with the algorithms for finding the synchronizing coloring, given a graph G. We can reformulate (P1)-(P3) in the 'RCP fasion':

(P1') given a constant out-degree graph G, check if there exists a synchronizing word for some labeling of G,

(P2') given a constant out-degree graph G and natural number m, check if G can be synchronized by some word of length m for some synchronizing coloring,

(P3') given a constant out-degree graph G and natural number m, check if the minimal synchronizing word for G has length m for some synchronizing coloring.

During the Wroclaw Conference on Černý Conjecture, Volkov [11] presented some new open problems related to the RCP. Among others he asked about the complexity of (P2') and (P3'). Similar to (P1)-(P3), the answers for (P1')-(P3') are also of practical nature. In [13], Volkov gives a good example of application of the RCP-type problems to the real life: let a transportation network be given. We can model it as a digraph G with vertices representing network nodes and arrows representing one-way roads. Each road has a unique labeling (a color). Suppose we want to help people to orientate in this network in case they get lost. A good solution would be to provide them a sequence of road labels, such that no matter where they start, after walking the roads according to this sequence they will reach some common node. So, we want to find the shortest possible synchronizing sequence for some labeling of G. If G is strongly connected and with constant out-degree, this is exactly the (P2') or (P3') problem. Therefore it is important to know what are the complexities of problems like (P1')-(P3').

Polynomial algorithms that find the synchronizing coloring for G, described in [3,9], prove that (P1') can be solved in a polynomial time. It is a natural question, if the 'hardness hierarchy' of (P1')-(P3') is similar to (P1)-(P3). Namely, we ask if (P2') is essentially harder than (P1') and if (P3') is harder than (P2'). In this paper we show that the slightly weaker assumption in (P2') in comparison to (P2) (an unlabeled graph instead of an automaton) does not change the problem difficulty: (P2') is NP-complete.

The rest of this paper is organized as follows: in the next section we give the formal definitions. They will be used in Section 3, where the main result is presented.

2   Preliminaries

An *automaton* is a triple $\mathcal{A} = (Q, A, \delta)$, where Q is a nonempty, finite set of states, A is a finite alphabet and $\delta : Q \times A \to Q$ is the transition function, called also the automaton action. By A^* we denote the free monoid over A, consisting of all finite words over A. The empty word of length 0 is denoted by ε. Sometimes, for the sake of simplicity, we will write $p.a = q$ instead of $\delta(p, a) = q$. It is convenient to extend the δ function to subsets in the usual way: for $P \subset Q$ we define $P.\varepsilon = P$, $P.a = \bigcup_{p \in P} \{p.a\}$. We say that $w \in A^*$ *synchronizes* $\mathcal{A} = (Q, A, \delta)$ if $|Q.w| = 1$. If such a word exists, $\mathcal{A}$ is called a *synchronizing automaton*.

Let G be a constant out-degree, strongly connected, finite digraph $G = (V, E)$, where V is a finite set of vertices and E is a (multi)set of edges. Let k be the out-degree of each vertex and let A be a k-element alphabet. A *path* in G is a sequence of vertices $(v_1, v_2, ..., v_n)$ such that $(v_i, v_{i+1}) \in E$ for each $1 \leq i \leq n-1$. The *length* of the path is the number of its vertices minus one. A *labeling* of G is a function $L : E \to A$, which assigns letters from A to the edges in such a way that for each vertex $v \in V$ all of its k outgoing edges have pairwise different labels (colors). By $reach_n(v)$ we define the set of all vertices that can be reached from v by some path of length n: $reach_n(v) = \{v.w : w \in A^n\}$. We also define $reach(v) = \bigcup_{n=0}^{\infty} reach_n(v) = \{v.w : w \in A^*\}$.

In RCP one assumes G to be a strongly connected graph. In our solution we use a connected digraph (denoted later by $G(\varphi)$) with one strongly connected component C. This does not violate the reasoning, because for each labeling there exists a finite word which transforms all states into C and then we deal only with C. The assumptions about gcd for cycles are important only with reference to the strongly connected component C. It is also possible to modify our $G(\varphi)$ to be a strongly connected graph, but this would complicate the solution by introducing some "technical" tricks. Therefore we stay with $G(\varphi)$ as a connected digraph with one strongly connected component.

3   Main Theorem

We consider the following ROAD-COLORING-SYNCHR-WORD problem:

- INPUT: a constant out-degree digraph G and a natural number m (assume $m \geq 8$);
- OUTPUT: "YES", if there exists a synchronizing word of length m for some synchronizing labeling of G. "NO" otherwise.

It is clear that the ROAD-COLORING-SYNCHR-WORD is in NP: given the labeling and the word W one can check if W synchronizes G and it can be done in $O(|W| \cdot |G|)$ time. The only difficulty appears when W is exponential in $|G|$. But it is easy to show (by combining Trahtman's algorithm [9] with Eppstein's one [4]) that the minimal synchronizing word for any synchronizing coloring of G is polynomial in $|G|$. So if W is large, it suffices to find a shorter word W' of polynomial length. To obtain the long solution W it suffices to concatenate some arbitrarily chosen word U of length $|W| - |W'|$ with W'. Clearly, $W = UW'$ is a synchronizng word of length $|W|$ for a labeling of G found by Trahtman's algorithm.

We will prove that ROAD-COLORING-SYNCHR-WORD is NP-complete by reducing 3-SAT to the problem. Let φ be a 3-SAT formula in a standard, conjunctive normal form with n clauses and N variables $x_1, \neg x_1, ..., x_N, \neg x_N$. By a "standard" form we mean that:

- if literal $l_j \in c_i$, then $\neg l_j \notin c_i$,
- for each $j = 1, ..., N$ there exist two clauses c_i and c_k, $i \neq k$, such that $l_j \in c_i$ and $\neg l_j \in c_k$
- Γ_φ is connected, where $\Gamma_\varphi = (X, E)$, $X = \{x_1, ..., x_N, \neg x_1, ..., \neg x_N\}$ and for $i \neq j$ $\{l_i, l_j\} \in E$ iff there is a clause c_k, such that $l_i, l_j \in c_k$.

Notice that if Γ_φ is not connected and has k components, the formula can be split into k formulas and for each of them we can assign variables values independently.

We will construct a digraph $G = G(\varphi) = (V, E)$, such that there exists a synchronizing word of length m for some synchronizing labeling of G if and only if φ is satisfiable. The main construction of G is presented in Fig. 2. G has a constant out-degree 3, so we will consider automata over 3-letter alphabet $\{a, b, c\}$. Graph G_i, together with its neighborhood, is depicted in Fig. 3. Graph G consists of $(n + 2N) + 2N(m - 5) + 4N(m - 4) + 4N + 5(m - 4) + 5 = n + 6Nm - 20N + 5m - 15$ nodes. For the sake of simplicity, some edges are not shown in Fig. 2. For each $1 \leq i \leq N$ the missing edges from nodes x_i^{m-4} and y_i^{m-4} (two for each node) go to nodes x_i and $\neg x_i$ resp. Missing edges from t, u, w (two for each node) go to t^1, u^1, w^1 resp. One missing edge from v goes to v^1. Finally, for each $1 \leq i \leq m$, one missing node from r_i goes to r_i^1. The lack of these edges should cause no confusion to the reader, because they will not play any role in our considerations.

Before we pass to the proof of the main theorem, let us shortly describe the main steps of the proof:

1. show that satisfiability of φ implies the existence of labeling, for which we can obtain a specific set of states after the transformation with the first letter of some word (Lemma 1),
2. show that any $m - 4$-letter word transforms the whole set Q of states to the set containing some fixed set S, and if φ is satisfiable, then for some labeling δ we can transform Q exactly to S; but if φ is not satisfiable, then δ will transform Q to S plus at least some one additional state q (Lemma 2),
3. show that S can be synchronized by the word of length 4 and cannot be synchronized by any shorter word (Lemma 3 and 4),
4. show that $S \cup \{q\}$ cannot be synchronized by any word of length at most 4 (Lemma 5).

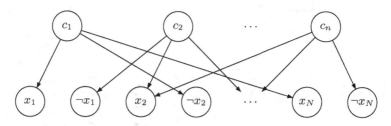

Fig. 1. Part of the main graph construction. Edges in this part depend on the φ formula. φ is satisfiable if and only if we can label this graph with $\{a, b, c\}$, such that $\{c_1, ..., c_n\}.a$ does not contain simultaneously a literal and it's negation.

Top part of the graph, shown in Fig. 1 and denoted by G_φ, depends on the φ formula. It is constructed as follows: if clause c_j contains literal $l_i \in \{x_i, \neg x_i\}$, we put $(c_j, l_i) \in E$.

Lemma 1. *Let* $C = \{c_1, c_2, ..., c_n\} \subset V$. *The following statements are equivalent:*

(a) φ *is satisfiable,*
(b) *there exists a labeling* δ *for* G_φ, *such that*

$$\forall 1 \leq i \leq N\ x_i \notin C.a \vee \neg x_i \notin C.a.$$

Proof. $(a \Rightarrow b)$ Let φ be satisfiable. Then there exists an assignment such that in each clause there exists at least one literal l_j with true value. We put

$$\delta(c_j, a) = l_j. \tag{1}$$

If there are two or more true values, we can take the one with the smallest index. It is clear that, if $c_j.a = l_i$ for some i, j, then for each $k \neq j$ we have $c_k.a \neq \neg l_i$.
$(b \Rightarrow a)$ Let δ be the labeling fulfilling condition (b). We assign the logic values to literals as follows: if $\delta(c_j, a) = l_j$, then we assign true to l_j. This assignment is correct and there is at least one literal with true value in each clause.

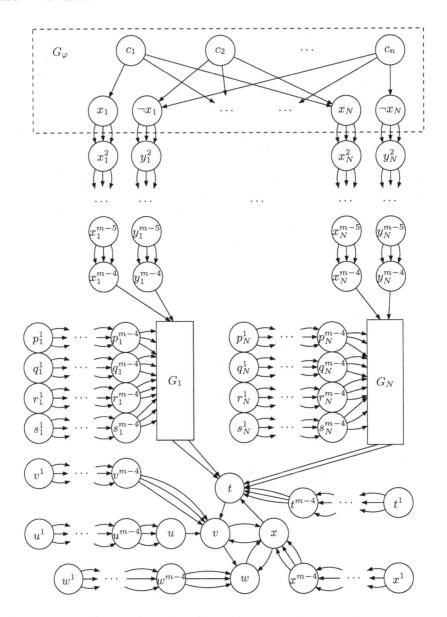

Fig. 2. Graph G - the main construction

Let $A = \{a, b, c\}$, $Q = V$ and let $\mathcal{A} = (Q, A, \delta)$ be an automaton with underlying graph G from Fig. 2. Let us define the sets: $D_i = \{p_i, q_i, r_i, s_i\}$ ($1 \leq i \leq N$), $E = \{t, u, v, w, x\}$ and put $D = \bigcup_{i=1}^{N} D_i$. The following Proposition is straightforward.

Proposition 1. $\forall W \in A^{m-4}$ $Q.W \supseteq D \cup E$.

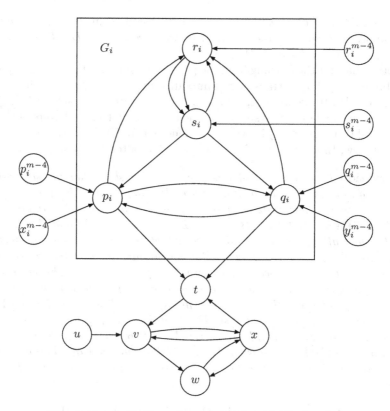

Fig. 3. Graph G_i (in rectangle) and its neighborhood

Lemma 2. *Let φ be satisfiable, $W \in A^{m-4}$ and for $C = \{c_1, \ldots, c_n\}$ let δ be defined according to (1). Then $|Q.W| \geq 5m+5$ and there exist $z_i \in \{x_i^{m-4}, y_i^{m-4}\}$, $i = 1, 2, \ldots, N$, such that*

$$D \cup E \cup \{z_1, \ldots, z_N\} \subseteq \delta(Q, W). \tag{2}$$

Moreover, there exists a labeling δ and unique $W_0 \in A^{m-4}$, for which relation (2) is an equality.

Proof. The first part of the thesis flows directly from Lemma 1, Proposition 1 and direct analysis of G. For the second part of the thesis, consider any labeling δ for which the following conditions hold:

- edges going from $\{c_1, \ldots, c_n\}$ are labeled according to (1),
- $\forall 1 \leq i \leq N$ $x_i^{m-4}.a = p_i, y_i^{m-4}.a = q_i$,
- $t.a = v$, $u.a = v$, $v.a \in \{w, x\}$, $w.a = x$, $x.a \in \{v, w\}$,
- $\forall 1 \leq i \leq m$ $r_i.a = s_i$.

We have $Q.a^{m-4} = D \cup E \cup \{z_1, \ldots, z_N\}$ and $|Q.a^{m-4}| = 5m + 5$. Notice that each x_i^{m-4} and y_i^{m-4} has only one edge going to G_i. For any word W of length

$k < m - 4$ the set $\{x_1^{m-4}, y_1^{m-4}, ..., x_N^{m-4}, y_N^{m-4}\}$ is contained in $Q.W$. These two facts imply that for $m - 4$-letter word W we have $Q.W = D \cup E \cup \{z_1, ..., z_N\}$ if and only if $W = W_0 = a^{m-4}$.

Notice that, for the labeling from the proof of Lemma 2, $Q.a^{m-4}$ is the smallest possible set, which Q is transformed into after $m - 4$ first letters of the synchronizing word W. It always contains $D \cup E$ and one state from each $\{x_i^{m-4}, y_i^{m-4}\}$. Therefore, in the later analysis we assume that the first $m - 4$ letters of the analyzed word W transform Q into this set (denote it by B). From the synchronizing point of view, this is the 'best' case we can be in after $m - 4$ steps.

Observation 1. *In the rest of this paper we will show that the shortest synchronizing word for any automaton with underlying graph G is of length at least m. So B can be synchronized by some 4-letter word $a_1 a_2 a_3 a_4$. If there exists $k \in \{1, 2, 3\}$ such that $B.a_1, B.a_1 a_2, ..., B.a_1...a_k \subset D \cup E$ and $B.a_1...a_{k+1} \not\subset D \cup E$, then after $m - 4 + k$ steps we are at least in one state g, such that $g \in \{p_i^1, q_i^1, r_i^1, s_i^1, t^1, u^1, v^1, w^1, x^1\}$. But synchronization can take place only in a state from $reach(t)$, so we have to transform g at least to t. The shortest such path is of length $m - 3$, so together with the beginning of the synchronizing word, a^{m-4}, this word has length $l \geq (m-4)+(m-3) = 2m-7 \geq m+8-7 = m+1 > m$. This shows, that if we are in the set $D \cup E$ it does not pay to us to use a transformation α, for which $(D \cup E).\alpha \not\subset (D \cup E)$. Therefore it is convenient to treat the automaton $(D \cup E)$ as a partial (or carefully synchronizing) automaton, that is, we can use only edges that does not transform any state from $D \cup E$ outside this set.*

Automata with underlying graphs D_i are 'independent' in the sense, that in order to find the minimal synchronizing word for automaton with underlying graph $D \cup E$ it is enough to find such a word for an automaton with underlying graph $D_i \cup E$ for some $i \in \{1, ..., N\}$ and define labelings in all $D_j, j \neq i$ to be the same as in D_i. In the following considerations we will investigate this problem for the automata $\mathcal{A} = (Q_G, A, \delta_G)$, $\mathcal{A}_x = (Q_x, A, \delta_x)$ and $\mathcal{A}_y = (Q_y, A, \delta_y)$, where the corresponding underlying graphs are: $Q_G = D_i \cup E \cup \{x_i^{m-4}, y_i^{m-4}\}$, $Q_x = Q_G \setminus \{y_i^{m-4}\}$, $Q_y = Q_G \setminus \{x_i^{m-4}\}$ and the transition functions are just δ restricted to the corresponding induced graphs. The i value is arbitrary, but fixed.

Lemma 3. *There exists no synchronizing word of length less then 4 for any of automata $\mathcal{A}_x$, $\mathcal{A}_y$ and $\mathcal{A}$.*

Proof. We will show that $Q_G \setminus \{x_i^{m-4}, y_i^{m-4}\}$ cannot be synchronized by any word of length less than 4. It is clear that there is no synchronizing word of length 1. We have $reach_2(u) \cap reach_2(r_i) = \emptyset$, so there is no synchronizing word of length 2. We have $reach_3(x) \cap reach_3(r_i) = \{v, w, x\} \cap \{p_i, q_i, r_i, s_i, t\} = \emptyset$, so there is also no synchronizing word of length 3.

Lemma 4. *There exists a synchronizing word of length 4 for $\mathcal{A}_x$ and for $\mathcal{A}_y$.*

Proof. We will show this for $\mathcal{A}_y$, for $\mathcal{A}_x$ the proof is similar. Consider the following labeling:

$$u.a = v \quad v.a = x \quad v.b = w$$
$$w.a = x \quad x.a = v \quad x.b = w$$
$$x.c = t \quad t.a = v \quad p_i.a = q_i$$
$$p_i.b = r_i \quad p_i.c = t \quad q_i.a = r_i$$
$$q_i.b = p_i \quad q_i.c = t \quad r_i.a = s_i$$
$$r_i.b = s_i \quad s_i.a = q_i \quad s_i.b = p_i \quad y_i^{m-4}.a = q_i.$$

One can easily check that $Q_x.abac = \{t\}$.

Lemma 5. *There exists no synchronizing word of length 4 for $\mathcal{A}$.*

Proof. From the G_φ construction it is necessary that (a) $r_i.a = s_i$, (b) $u.a = v$, (c) $w.a = x$ and (d) $t.a = v$. We have $\bigcap_{\alpha \in Q_G} reach_4(\alpha) = \{t, v\}$, so these are the only possible synchronizing states.

Case 1. Suppose first that, there exists $W = a_1 a_2 a_3 a_4$, such that $Q_G.W = \{t\}$. From Observation 1 we have $a_1 = a$. The only two opportunities for r_i to reach t in 4 steps are $P_1 = r_i \to s_i \to p_i \to q_i \to t$ and $P'_1 = r_i \to s_i \to q_i \to p_i \to t$. Because of the 'symmetry' between p_i and q_i we can consider only the first path, P_1. For the second one the reasoning is similar. The only way for u to reach t in 4 steps is the path $P_2 = u \to v \to w \to x \to t$. Comparing P_1 and P_2 and taking into account (a)-(d) we have that $p_i.a = q_i$. Let $s_i.Y = p_i$. Then $v.Y = w$ and because $v.a = x \neq w$ (v can reach t only if transformed into x in the first step), necessarily $Y \neq a$. So we have $a_1 = a$, $a_2 = Y \neq a$. Now consider the state x_i^{m-4}. We have $x_i^{m-4}.aY = p.Y \in \{r_i, t\}$, but neither $reach_2(r_i)$ nor $reach_2(t)$ contains t, so there is no path of length 4 leading from x_i^{m-4} to t.

Case 2. Suppose now that there exists $W' = a_1 a_2 a_3 a_4$ such that $Q_G.W = \{v\}$. Again, there must hold $r_i.a = s_i$, $u.a = v$, $t.a = v$, $w.a = x$. There are only two ways for r_i to reach v: $P_1 = r_i \to s_i \to p_i \to t \to v$ and $P_2 = r_i \to s_i \to q_i \to t \to v$. As in Case 1., because of the 'symmetry' between p_i and q_i we can choose, without loss of generality, one of them, say P_1. Let $s.Y = p$ and $p.Z = t$, where $Y, Z \in \{a, b, c\}$. There is only one possible path of length 4 from x_i^{m-4} to v: $P_2 = x_i^{m-4} \to p_i \to q_i \to t \to v$ and only one such path from y_i^{m-4} to v: $P_4 = y_i^{m-4} \to q_i \to p_i \to t \to v$. Comparing P_1, P_2 and P_3 we have that $p.Y = q$ (which, in view of $p.Z = t$, implies $Y \neq Z$), $q.Z = t$ and $q.Y = p$. The last one implies $q.a = r$. The synchronizing word of length 4, if exists, has form $aYZa$, where $Y, Z \neq a$. But $q.a = r$ and $v \notin reach_3(r)$, so we cannot construct a synchronizing word of length 4 with v as a synchronizing state.

Now we are ready to state the main theorem:

Theorem 1. ROAD-COLORING-SYNCHR-WORD *is NP-complete.*

Proof. From Lemmata 2, 3, 4, 5 we have that there exists a minimal synchronizing word of length m for some automaton with underlying graph G if and only if we can construct a labeling, such that $\forall 1 \leq i \leq N$ $(x_i^{m-4} \notin C.a^{m-4} \vee \neg x_i^{m-4} \notin C.a^{m-4})$. This is equivalent to $\forall 1 \leq i \leq N$ $(x_i \notin C.a \vee \neg x_i \notin C.a)$, and by Lemma 1 this can be done if and only if the corresponding formula φ is satisfiable.

We can easily obtain the following

Remark 1. (P3') is NP-hard.

To prove this, it is enough to verify that the minimal synchronizing word for any labeling of G has length $\geq m$ and the lower bound m is achieved if and only if the corresponding formula φ is satisfiable. This comes from Lemmata 1-5.

4   Conclusions and Future Work

We presented three complexity problems (P1)-(P3) for synchronizing automata, which are important not only from the theoretical, but also from the practical point of view. In the light of Trahtman's Road Coloring Theorem, these problems can be reformulated, in the 'RCP-fashion', as (P1')-(P3'). It is a natural question to ask about their complexities. The main theorem states that (P2') is NP-complete. The present state of knowledge about these problems is given in the following table.

Table 1. Complexities of decision version of problems related to the synchronizing automata

synchronizing automata	Road Coloring version
(P1) **P**	(P1') **P**
(P2) **NP-complete** [4]	(P2') **NP-complete** (this paper)
(P3) **coNP-hard** [7]	(P3') **NP-hard** (this paper)

Although complexities of (P2), (P2') are the same, it is not an obvious fact: in (P2) we ask about some synchronizing word w of a given length, but the graph labeling δ is given and it may happen that δ is 'difficult' to synchronize. In (P2') version we ask about the same word, but here it is our decision to choose δ. This may suggest that (P2') is easier than (P2), because we have much more room of manoeuvre in the first one. Unfortunately, this does not help us much: both (P2) and (P2') are NP-complete. It is an open question if the complexity of (P3') is the same as for (P3). In the light of results from Table 1. we conjecture that (P3') is coNP-hard.

Acknowledgements

I would like to thank to the anonymous referees for valuable comments and remarks, which allowed me to increase the readability and quality of this paper.

References

1. Adler, R.L., Weiss, B.: Similarity of automorphisms of the torus. Memoirs of the Amer. Math. Soc. 98 (1970)
2. Adler, R.L., Goodwyn, L.W., Weiss, B.: Equivalence of topological Markov shifts. Israel J. of Math. 27, 49–63 (1977)
3. Béal, M.-P., Perrin, D.: A quadratic algorithm for road coloring. arXiv:0803.0726v6 (2008)
4. Eppstein, D.: Reset sequences for monotonic automata. SIAM Journal of Computing 19, 500–510 (1990)
5. Lind, D., Marcus, B.: An Introduction to Symbolic Dynamics and Coding. Cambridge University Press, Cambridge (1995)
6. Pin, J.E.: On two combinatorial problems arising from automata theory. Annals of Discrete Math. 17, 535–548 (1983)
7. Samotij, W.: A note on the complexity of the problem of finding shortest synchronizing words. In: Proc. AutoMathA 2007, Automata: from Mathematics to Applications, Univ. Palermo (CD) (2007)
8. Trahtman, A.N.: Notable trends concerning the synchronization of graphs and automata. In: CTW 2006. El. Notes in Discrete Math., vol. 25, pp. 173–175 (2006)
9. Trahtman, A.N.: A Subquadratic Algorithm for Road Coloring. arXiv:0801.2838v1 (2008)
10. Trahtman, A.N.: Road Coloring Problem. Israel J. of Mathematics (to appear)
11. Volkov, M.: Open Problems on Synchronizing Automata. In: Conference 'Around the Černý Conjecture', Wroclaw (2008)
12. Volkov, M.: Synchronizing Automata and Černý Conjecture. In: Martín-Vide, C., Otto, F., Fernau, H. (eds.) LATA 2008. LNCS, vol. 5196, pp. 11–27. Springer, Heidelberg (2008)
13. Volkov, M.: Synchronizing Automata and the Road Coloring Theorem. In: Tutorial on Workshop on Algebra, Combinatorics and Complexity, WACC 2008, Moscow, Russia (2008)

NP-Completeness of *st*-Orientations for Plane Graphs

Sadish Sadasivam and Huaming Zhang*

Computer Science Department
University of Alabama in Huntsville
Huntsville, AL, 35899, USA
{ssadasiv,hzhang}@cs.uah.edu

Abstract. An *st-orientation* or *bipolar orientation* of a 2-connected graph G is an orientation of its edges to generate a directed acyclic graph with a single source s and a single sink t. Given a plane graph G and two vertices s and t on the exterior face of G, the problem of finding an optimum *st*-orientation, i.e., an *st*-orientation in which the length of the longest *st-path* is minimized, was first proposed indirectly by Rosenstiehl and Tarjan in [14] and then later directly by He and Kao in [6]. In this paper, we prove that, given a 2-connected plane graph G, two vertices s, t, on the exterior face of G and a positive integer K, the decision problem of whether G has an *st*-orientation, where the maximum length of an *st*-path is $\leq K$, is NP-Complete. This solves a long standing open problem on the complexity of optimum *st*-orientations for plane graphs.

1 Introduction

Given a 2-connected graph $G = (V, E)$ and two vertices s, $t \in V(G)$, an *st-orientation* (also known as *bipolar orientation* or *st-numbering* [3]) is an orientation of the edges of G, such that a directed acyclic graph with s as the single source and t as the single sink is produced. The properties of *st*-orientations have been extensively studied [7,8,14] and *st*-orientations have wide applications in graph drawing [12], network routing [1,9] and graph partitioning [10]. Starting with an undirected 2-connected graph G, many graph drawing algorithms use an *st*-orientation of G in order to compute drawings of G, such as hierarchical drawings [2], visibility representations [15] and orthogonal drawings [11]. Additionally, the length of the longest *st-path* (an *st-path* is a directed path from s to t) determines certain characteristics of the drawing. The complexity of the problem of finding an optimum *st*-orientation for general graphs has been shown to be NP-Hard by Gallai in 1968 [4]. In contrast, the complexity of the problem of finding an optimum *st*-orientation for a plane graph, i.e., one that minimizes the length of its longest *st*-path remained open for over two decades, as the question was first proposed in 1986 [14] for planar layouts of planar graphs. Later, the same question was proposed in [6] for planar graph drawings in 1995. In this paper, we investigate the complexity of finding optimum *st*-orientations for plane

* Corresponding author. His research is supported in part by NSF grant CCF-0728830.

M. Kutyłowski, M. Gębala, and W. Charatonik (Eds.): FCT 2009, LNCS 5699, pp. 298–309, 2009.
© Springer-Verlag Berlin Heidelberg 2009

graphs. By a reduction from the 3-PARTITION [5] problem, we show that, given a 2-connected plane graph G, two vertices s, t, on the exterior face of G and a positive integer K, the decision problem of whether G has an *st*-orientation where the length of the longest *st*-path $\leq K$, is NP-Complete. This proves that the long standing open problem of finding an optimum *st*-orientation for a plane graph is NP-Hard.

The rest of the paper is organized as follows. Section 2 introduces the 3-PARTITION problem. Section 3 introduces the *st*-ORIENTATION problem and presents the reduction from the 3-PARTITION problem and proves the NP-Completeness of the *st*-ORIENTATION problem.

2   3-PARTITION

3-PARTITION is shown to be NP-Complete in the strong sense in [5], i.e., it cannot be solved by a pseudo-polynomial time algorithm unless P = NP.

Instance: A finite multiset $S = \{x_1, x_2, x_3, ..., x_n\}$ of $n = 3 \times m$ positive integers that satisfy $\frac{B}{4} < x_i < \frac{B}{2}, 1 \leq i \leq n$, where the sum of the numbers in S is $m \times B$.

Question: Can S be partitioned into m subsets $S_1, S_2, ..., S_m$, such that the sum of the numbers in each subset is B. The subsets $S_1, S_2, ..., S_m$, must form a partition of S in the sense that they are disjoint and they cover S.

Lemma 1. *3-PARTITION remains strongly NP-Complete even if we limit the number of partitions to be an odd number.*

Proof. Let P be an instance of 3-PARTITION with variables n, m, B and the multiset $S = \{x_i, 1 \leq i \leq n\}$, where m is an *even* number. Construct an instance P' of 3-PARTITION from P with variables $n' = n + 3$, $m' = m + 1$, $B' = 9 \times B$ and the multiset $S' = \{9 \times x_i, 1 \leq i \leq n\} \cup \{3B - 2, 3B + 1, 3B + 1\}$, where m' is an *odd* number. Since $B \geq 3$, it is easy to verify that both $(3B - 2)$ and $(3B + 1)$ are greater than $\frac{B'}{4}$ and less than $\frac{B'}{2}$. Therefore, P' is indeed an instance of 3-PARTITION, in which its elements should be partitioned into an odd number $(m + 1)$ of subsets.

Note that, in a solution to P', the three elements $(3B - 2)$, $(3B + 1)$ and $(3B + 1)$ must be in a single partition, since all the other elements in S' are divisible by 3. Thus, if P is an *yes* instance, then P' is an *yes* instance and vice versa, i.e., the instances P and P' are equivalent. Thus, 3-PARTITION remains strongly NP-Complete even if we limit the number of partitions to be an *odd* number. □

3   *st*-ORIENTATION Is NP-Complete

Now we formally introduce the *st*-ORIENTATION decision problem:

Instance: An undirected 2-connected plane graph $G = (V, E)$, two vertices s, t on the exterior face of G and a positive integer K.

Question: Is there an st-orientation of G with s as the single source and t as the single sink, such that the length of the longest st-path is $\leq K$.

Given an st-orientation of G, we can easily verify in linear time whether the length of the longest st-path is $\leq K$ [7,14,8]. Thus, st-ORIENTATION is in NP.

3.1   Construction of the Graph G for st-ORIENTATION

We intend to establish a polynomial reduction from 3-PARTITION to st-ORIENTATION to show that st-ORIENTATION is indeed NP-Complete. In this subsection, we introduce the quite sophisticated reduction.

According to Lemma 1, without loss of generality, we can assume that m is *odd* and $m > 1$. Given an instance of 3-PARTITION as defined in Section 2, and in which m is odd, the construction of the graph G for the equivalent instance of st-ORIENTATION is shown in Fig. 1, Fig. 2 and Fig. 3. In Fig. 1, Fig. 2 and Fig. 3, ignore the direction of the edges and the red and green colors on the edges for now, as these will be used later in the reduction. In Fig. 1 and Fig. 2, a brown text near an "edge" denotes that it is actually a path of that length, i.e., a brown text of D near an "edge" denotes that it is actually a path of length D. Edges without brown text around them are regular edges. It is worth mentioning that, in this reduction from an instance of 3-PARTITION to an equivalent instance of st-ORIENTATION, we do not necessarily need to require the condition $\frac{B}{4} < x_i < \frac{B}{2}$, where $1 \leq i \leq n$, i.e., the number of elements in a partition need not be *three*. The reason we choose this more restricted version of 3-PARTITION problem for reduction is purely for presentation purposes.

We define the following variables: $f = \lfloor m/2 \rfloor$, $e = 8f \times n$, $D = 4e + 8m + B + 3$ and the value of K for the corresponding instance of st-ORIENTATION as $K = 8fD + (2D + 2) + 4e + 8m + B < 8fD + 3D$, where m, n and B are values from the instance of 3-PARTITION.

For each x_i in 3-PARTITION, a subgraph G_i is constructed as shown in Fig. 1 and this subgraph G_i is the *corresponding subgraph* of x_i. As shown in Fig. 1, the triangular shaped face formed by a path of length D and two other edges is a *dividing triangle*. The path of length D in a dividing triangle is a *ditch*. The three vertices of degree *three* on the boundary of a dividing triangle are *corner vertices*. For each corner vertex, there is exactly one edge adjacent to it that is not on the boundary of the dividing triangle and this edge is a *corner edge*. As shown in Fig. 1, within each G_i, the value of x_i itself is represented by exactly one horizontal path of length $(x_i + 1)$, that connects two dividing triangles. This path is the *corresponding path* of x_i and is denoted by P_i. G_x denotes the subgraph for which $V(G_x) = \cup_{i=1}^{n} V(G_i)$ and $E(G_x) = \cup_{i=1}^{n} E(G_i)$.

A subgraph G_{st} that contains the vertices s and t is constructed as shown in Fig. 2. The overall graph G for st-ORIENTATION is such that, $V(G) = V(G_{st}) \cup V(G_x)$ and $E(G) = E(G_{st}) \cup E(G_x)$. An example construction of G with $m = 5$ is shown in Fig. 3. We use the following notation to represent the vertices in G:

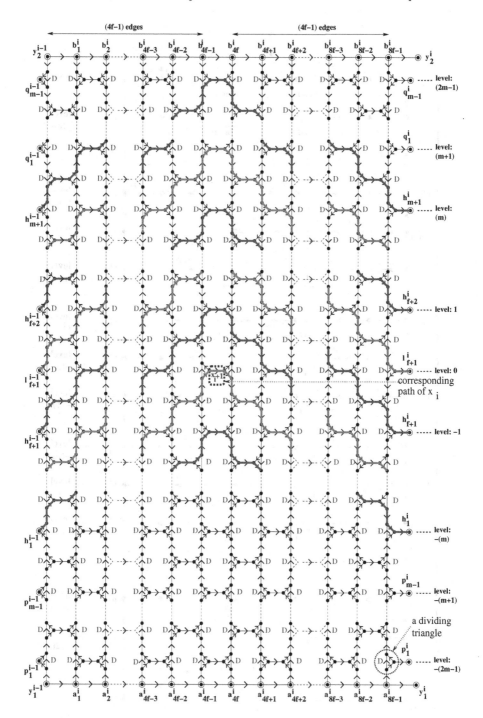

Fig. 1. The subgraph G_i that is constructed for each x_i in 3-PARTITION. Thus, there will be n such subgraphs.

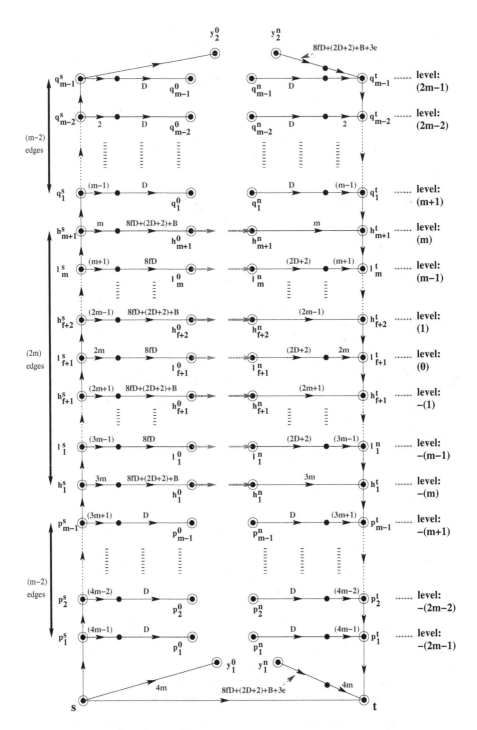

Fig. 2. The subgraph G_{st} that contains the vertices s and t

n * (8f) edges

(8f) edges   (8f) edges   (8f) edges

m−2
edges

2m
edges

m−2
edges

s   t

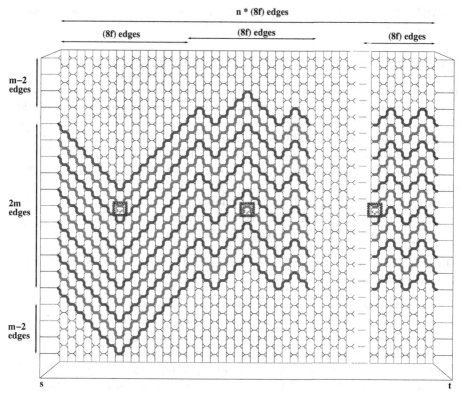

Fig. 3. An example st-orientation that is generated with $m = 5$

- Y_i, P_i, Q_i, L_i and H_i denote the set of vertices $\{y_1^i, y_2^i\}$, $\{p_1^i, p_2^i, ..., p_{m-1}^i\}$, $\{q_1^i, q_2^i, ..., q_{m-1}^i\}$, $\{l_1^i, l_2^i, ..., l_m^i\}$ and $\{h_1^i, h_2^i, ..., h_{m+1}^i\}$ respectively, where $0 \leq i \leq n$.
- V_i denotes the set of vertices $P_i \cup Q_i \cup L_i \cup H_i \cup Y_i$, where $0 \leq i \leq n$.
- P_s, P_t, Q_s, Q_t, L_s, L_t, H_s and H_t denote the set of vertices $\{p_1^s, p_2^s, ..., p_{m-1}^s\}$, $\{p_1^t, p_2^t, ..., p_{m-1}^t\}$, $\{q_1^s, q_2^s, ..., q_{m-1}^s\}$, $\{q_1^t, q_2^t, ..., q_{m-1}^t\}$, $\{l_1^s, l_2^s, ..., l_m^s\}$, $\{l_1^t, l_2^t, ..., l_m^t\}$, $\{h_1^s, h_2^s, ..., h_{m+1}^s\}$ and $\{h_1^t, h_2^t, ..., h_{m+1}^t\}$ respectively.
- V_s and V_t denote the set of vertices $P_s \cup Q_s \cup L_s \cup H_s$ and $P_t \cup Q_t \cup L_t \cup H_t$ respectively.

Observe that $V(G_i) \cap V(G_{i+1}) = V_i$, where $1 \leq i \leq (n-1)$, $V(G_1) \cap V(G_{st}) = V_0$ and $V(G_n) \cap V(G_{st}) = V_n$. In the graph G, the horizontal paths adjacent to the vertices in $V_i - Y_i$, $0 \leq i \leq n$, and the horizontal paths connecting two dividing triangles between the vertical paths a_{2j-1}^i to b_{2j-1}^i and a_{2j}^i to b_{2j}^i, $1 \leq j \leq 4f - 1$, are assigned a *level* from $-(2m - 1)$ to $(2m - 1)$ in increasing order from bottom to top, for a total of $(4m - 1)$ levels, as shown in Fig. 1 and 2. Thus, the corresponding path P_i of x_i is at level 0.

It is straight-forward to prove that G is a 2-connected plane graph and $|V(G)|$ is of polynomial size in the variables n, m and B of 3-PARTITION. (Since

3-PARTITION is NP-Complete in the strong sense, we can measure the size of the constructed graph by n, m and B directly.)

3.2 st-Orientations of G with Length of Longest st-Path $\leq K$

Let $\mathcal{O}$ denote an st-orientation of G and $length_{\mathcal{O}}(u, v)$ denote the length of the longest directed path from u to v in an st-orientation $\mathcal{O}$ of G. An st-orientation $\mathcal{O}$ of G is a *satisfying st-orientation* of G if $length_{\mathcal{O}}(s, t) \leq K$. Note that the maximum degree of a vertex in G is *three*. Thus, in any st-orientation $\mathcal{O}$ of G, a *blend vertex* is a vertex that has two incoming edges and a *fork vertex* is a vertex that has two outgoing edges. Also, for each dividing triangle, its three corner edges cannot be all incoming (directed towards the dividing triangle) or all outgoing (directed away from the dividing triangle). Thus, a *blend triangle* is a dividing triangle that has two incoming corner edges and a *fork triangle* is a dividing triangle that has two outgoing corner edges.

Lemma 2. *In any satisfying st-orientation $\mathcal{O}$ of G, the directions of the following edges must be as follows:*

1. *The two faces having the edge (s, t) on its boundary must have their edges directed such that they form two directed paths from s to t.*
2. *In subgraph G_{st}, the horizontal path between a vertex $u \in V_s$ and $v \in V_0 - Y_0$, where both u and v are at the same level, must be directed from u to v.*
3. *In subgraph G_{st}, the horizontal path between a vertex $u \in V_t$ and $v \in V_n - Y_n$, where both u and v are at the same level, must be directed from v to u.*

Proof. (1) This is straight-forward, as the boundary of each face in an st-orientation must be made up of two lateral paths [7,8,14]. Thus, $length_{\mathcal{O}}(y_1^n, t) > 8fD + 2D$ and $length_{\mathcal{O}}(y_2^n, t) > 8fD + 2D$. (2) If the direction of the edges on the horizontal path between u and v is from v to u, then $length_{\mathcal{O}}(s, t) \geq length_{\mathcal{O}}(s, v) + length_{\mathcal{O}}(v, u) + length_{\mathcal{O}}(u, y_2^n) + length_{\mathcal{O}}(y_2^n, t) > length_{\mathcal{O}}(v, u) + length_{\mathcal{O}}(y_2^n, t) > D + (8fD + 2D) > K$. Thus, the edges must be directed from u to v. (3) Note that $length_{\mathcal{O}}(q_{m-1}^t, t)$ must be $< 4m$. If there is a directed path from u to v, then there is a directed path from q_{m-1}^t to v. The path from v to t must still go through a vertex in $V_n - \{v\}$, however, for all $w \in V_n$, $length_{\mathcal{O}}(w, t) \geq 4m$. Thus, it follows that there cannot be a path from q_{m-1}^t to v and hence the edges between u and v must be directed from v to u. $\square$

In any satisfying st-orientation $\mathcal{O}$ of G, we identify some edges as red or green based on the following criteria:

- A directed edge $(u, v) \in E(G_x)$, is denoted as a *red edge* (marked in red color in the figures in this paper) if it satisfies at least one of the following: (1) $u \in H_0$, (2) u has a directed path from a vertex in H_0.
- A directed edge $(u, v) \in E(G_x)$ is denoted as a *green edge* (marked in green color in the figures in this paper) if it satisfies at least one of the following: (1) $v \in L_n$, (2) v has a directed path to a vertex in L_n.

We prove that every satisfying *st*-orientation $\mathcal{O}$ of G must have these red and green edges. From Lemma 2, it follows that, for a red edge (u, v), $length_{\mathcal{O}}(s, u) > 8fD + 2D$ and for a green edge (u, v), $length_{\mathcal{O}}(s, v) < 8fD + D$. Thus, an edge cannot be both a red edge and a green edge. A set of red edges (green edges, respectively) that form a simple directed path is defined as a *red path* (*green path*, respectively). An edge that is neither a red edge nor a green edge is a *black edge*.

Lemma 3. *In any satisfying st-orientation $\mathcal{O}$ of G, a directed path from a vertex $u \in H_0$ to t can only go through a vertex $v \in H_n$ and cannot go through any vertex $w \in V_n - H_n$.*

Proof. Any directed path from the vertex u to t must go through a vertex in V_n. Since $length_{\mathcal{O}}(s, u) > 8fD + 2D$ and $length_{\mathcal{O}}(w, t) > D$, the path from u to t cannot go through any vertex $w \in V_n - H_n$ and the only possibility is to go through a vertex $v \in H_n$. $\qquad\square$

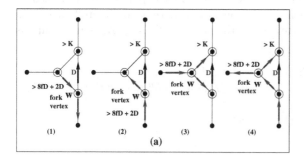 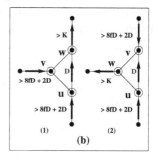

Fig. 4. (a) Proof of Lemma 4: A red path cannot have a fork vertex in it. (b) Proof of Lemma 5.

Lemma 4. *In any satisfying st-orientation $\mathcal{O}$ of G, a directed red path from a vertex $u \in H_0$ to a vertex $v \in H_n$ cannot have a fork vertex in it.*

Proof. Since any directed path from u to t cannot go through a vertex in Y_n, this path does not have any vertex from the boundary of the two faces that have the edge (s, t) on its boundary. Thus, if this path has a fork vertex, it has to be one of the corner vertices of a dividing triangle. As illustrated in Fig. 4 (a), since a dividing triangle has the ditch of length D as one of its sides, a red path cannot fork at one of its corner vertices, otherwise $length_{\mathcal{O}}(s, t) > K$. Hence, it follows that a path of red edges does not contain a fork vertex in it and all the edges adjacent to a red path are directed towards the path. This implies that the directed path from u to t is unique and goes through exactly one vertex in H_n. $\qquad\square$

Lemma 5. *In any satisfying st-orientation $\mathcal{O}$ of G, for any blend triangle, at least one of its corner vertices with incoming corner edge, say v, must satisfy $length_{\mathcal{O}}(s, v) < 8fD + 2D$.*

Proof. The proof is by contradiction. For a blend triangle, let u and v be the corner vertices with an incoming corner edge and w be the corner vertex with an outgoing corner edge. Let $length_{\mathcal{O}}(s, u) \geq 8fD + 2D$ and $length_{\mathcal{O}}(s, v) \geq 8fD + 2D$. Then, as shown in Fig. 4 (b), $length_{\mathcal{O}}(s, w) > K$. □

From Lemma 5, it follows that in any satisfying st-orientation $\mathcal{O}$ of G, a blend triangle cannot have two incoming red corner edges, since any vertex v on a red path has $length_{\mathcal{O}}(s, v) > 8fD + 2D$. Thus, the red paths from $u, v \in H_0$, with $u \neq v$, to some vertices in H_n cannot have a common vertex, i.e., the two paths do not meet at a common vertex. Also, from Lemmas 3, 4 and 5, it follows that in any satisfying st-orientation $\mathcal{O}$ of G, there is exactly one directed path from h_j^0 to t and this path must go through the vertex h_j^n, where $1 \leq j \leq (m + 1)$. Also, within the subgraph G_x, all the edges on this path are red edges. Since all the edges adjacent to a red path from h_j^0 to h_j^n are directed towards the path, there is no directed path from a vertex on one side of the path to a vertex on the other side of the path. Thus, if these $(m + 1)$ red paths are visualized as boundaries dividing G_x into $(m+2)$ regions, then there is no directed path from a vertex in one region to a vertex in another region. These regions in G_x are as follows:

- R_0 is the region below the red path from h_1^0 to h_1^n.
- R_j is the region between the red paths from h_j^0 to h_j^n and from h_{j+1}^0 to h_{j+1}^n, where $1 \leq j \leq m$.
- R_{m+1} is the region above the red path from h_{m+1}^0 to h_{m+1}^n.

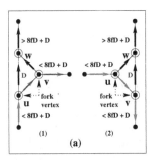 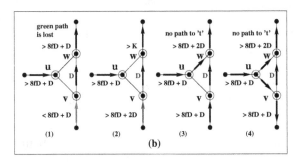

Fig. 5. (a) Proof of Lemma 6: A green edge cannot fork into two green edges. (b) Proof of Lemma 7: The corresponding path P_i consists of only green edges.

Lemma 6. *In any satisfying st-orientation $\mathcal{O}$ of G, there is no directed path from $V_0 - \{l_j^0\}$ to l_j^n and there is exactly one directed path from l_j^0 to l_j^n, where $1 \leq j \leq m$.*

Proof. None of the vertices in $V_0 - \{l_j^0\}$ are in region R_j and hence there is no directed path from a vertex in $V_0 - \{l_j^0\}$ to l_j^n. Since the vertex l_j^n has a directed path from s, this path must come through l_j^0. The directed path from l_j^0 to l_j^n consists of all green edges. In order to have more than one directed path from l_j^0 to l_j^n, a green edge must fork at some corner vertex that has two outgoing green edges. As shown in Fig. 5 (a), this scenario is impossible due to the presence of the ditch of length D. Whenever a green edge forks at the corner vertices of a dividing triangle, one of the other corner vertices w, will have $length_{\mathcal{O}}(s, w) > 8fD + D$ and hence cannot have a directed path to l_j^n.   □

Lemma 7. *In any satisfying st-orientation $\mathcal{O}$ of G, the corresponding path P_i of x_i, $1 \le i \le n$, must consist of only green edges, i.e., all edges on a corresponding path must also be on a green path from some l_j^0 to l_j^n, $1 \le j \le m$.*

Proof. Note that the red path from h_1^0 to h_1^n is always below level 0 and the red path from h_{m+1}^0 to h_{m+1}^n is always above level 0 (since, there are a total of $(2m + 1)$ red and green paths). Thus, the corresponding path P_i of x_i must be in one of the regions $R_j, 1 \le j \le m$, i.e., it cannot be in the region R_0 or R_{m+1}. It is obvious that a red path cannot go through the corresponding path P_i of x_i. Also, from Fig. 5 (a) and Lemma 6, it is obvious that within the region $R_j, 1 \le j \le m$, every corner vertex v of a dividing triangle that is not on a green path has $length_{\mathcal{O}}(s, v) > 8fD + D$. Hence, if the corresponding path P_i of some x_i consists of non-green edges, then, consider the corner vertex u of the dividing triangle, to which the corresponding path is directed towards in the st-orientation. This corner vertex has $length_{\mathcal{O}}(s, u) > 8fD + D$. We have the following cases to consider as shown in Fig. 5 (b):

Case 1: If the dividing triangle is a blend triangle and has an incoming green edge at vertex v, then that green path cannot continue forward towards a vertex in L_n.

Case 2: If the dividing triangle is a blend triangle and has an incoming red edge at vertex v, then the other corner vertex w will have $length_{\mathcal{O}}(s, w) > K$.

Case 3: If the dividing triangle is a blend triangle and has an incoming edge that is neither red nor green at vertex v, then the other corner vertex w will have $length_{\mathcal{O}}(s, w) > 8fD + 2D$. In this case, the path from w to t can only go through one of the vertices in H_n, which means it has a common vertex with one of the red paths, but this is impossible as shown in Lemma 5.

Case 4: If the dividing triangle is a fork triangle, then the other corner vertex w will have $length_{\mathcal{O}}(s, w) > 8fD + 2D$. The proof is same as Case 3.

Thus, the corresponding path P_i of any x_i, $1 \le i \le n$, must consist of only green edges, i.e., all edges on a corresponding path must also be on a green path from some l_j^0 to l_j^n, where $1 \le j \le m$.   □

3.3   Correctness of the Reduction from 3-PARTITION to st-ORIENTATION

Lemma 8. *For an instance of st-ORIENTATION, a satisfying st-orientation $\mathcal{O}$ of G can be constructed in polynomial time, given a solution to the corresponding instance of 3-PARTITION.*

Proof. Assign directions to the edges in G as shown in Fig. 1 and 2. The red edges form $(m+1)$ directed red paths and each red path originates from h_j^0, goes through h_j^i in each G_i and ends in h_j^n, where $1 \leq j \leq (m+1)$. The green edges form m directed green paths representing the m partitions in 3-PARTITION and each green path originates from l_j^0, goes through l_j^i in each G_i and ends in l_j^n, where $1 \leq j \leq m$. In a solution to 3-PARTITION, if x_i belongs to a set S_j, $1 \leq j \leq m$, then orient the red and green paths up and down as needed such that the green path from l_j^0 goes through the matching path P_i of x_i in G_i, as shown in Fig. 1 and 3. The edges in G_{st} are assigned directions as shown in Fig. 2. The edges in G_x are assigned directions as shown in Fig. 1 as follows:

1. All the horizontal edges are directed from left to right.
2. All edges incident to a red-path are directed towards it and all edges incident to a green-path are directed away from it.
3. In the region R_0, the direction of the non-horizontal edges is upwards and in the region R_{m+1} the direction of the non-horizontal edges is downwards.
4. In the region R_j, $1 \leq j \leq m$, the edges are oriented such that they are directed from the green path to the red path.

Observe that except for the green path that goes through the matching path P_i of x_i, each green or red path has a length of $4 \times 8f$ within G_i. The green path that goes through the matching path P_i of x_i, has a length of $4 \times 8f + x_i$ within G_i. Since each green path goes only through the corresponding paths of the elements in a partition, it has a length of $4 \times 8f \times n + B$ within G_x. Thus, each st-path that goes through a vertex in L_n has length $= 4m + 8fD + 4 \times 8f \times n + B + (2D+2) + 4m = K$. Similarly, each st-path that goes through a vertex in H_n has length $= 4m + 8fD + (2D+2) + B + 4 \times 8f \times n + 4m = K$. The maximum length of an st-path through any vertex in $P_n \cup Q_n$ is $4m + e + 8fD + 8f + D + 4m \leq K$. Also, it can be readily seen that the length of an st-path through any vertex in Y_n is also $\leq K$. Thus, a satisfying st-orientation $\mathcal{O}$ of G with $length_{\mathcal{O}}(s,t) \leq K$ can be constructed from a solution to 3-PARTITION and it is trivial to prove that this construction can be done in polynomial time.   □

Lemma 9. *A solution to an instance of 3-PARTITION can be obtained in polynomial time, given a satisfying st-orientation $\mathcal{O}$ of G to the corresponding instance of st-ORIENTATION.*

Proof. From Lemma 7, each corresponding path P_i of x_i, $1 \leq i \leq n$, lies on a green path. Note that the length of a green path within each G_i is at least $4 \times 8f$. Since the length of any green path within G_x must be $\leq 4 \times 8f \times n + B$, the corresponding paths must be distributed among the m green paths, such that the length of each green path within G_x is exactly $4 \times 8f \times n + B$. This distribution gives us the required solution for 3-PARTITION and it is trivial to prove that this solution can be obtained in polynomial time from $\mathcal{O}$ of G.   □

We now have our main theorem as follows:

Theorem 1. *Given a 2-connected plane graph $G = (V, E)$, two vertices s, t, on the exterior face of G and a positive integer K, the decision problem of whether G has an st-orientation $\mathcal{O}$, such that the length of the longest st-path is $\leq K$, is NP-Complete.*

Proof. The proof of Theorem 1 follows from Lemmas 8 and 9.   □

References

1. Annexstein, F., Berman, K.: Directional routing via generalized st-numberings. Discrete Mathematics 13, 268–279 (2000)
2. Battista, G.D., Eades, P., Tamassia, R., Tollis, I.G.: Graph Drawing: Algorithms for the Visualization of Graphs. Prentice Hall, Englewood Cliffs (1999)
3. Even, S., Tarjan, R.E.: Computing an st-Numbering. Theoretical Computer Science 2, 339–344 (1976)
4. Gallai, T.: On directed paths and circuits. In: Theory of Graphs: International Symposium, pp. 215–232 (1968)
5. Garey, M.R., Johnson, D.S.: Computers and Intractability; A Guide to the Theory of NP-Completeness. W. H. Freeman & Co., New York (1990)
6. He, X., Kao, M.: Regular edge labelings and drawings of planar graphs. In: Tamassia, R., Tollis, I.G. (eds.) GD 1994. LNCS, vol. 894, pp. 96–103. Springer, Heidelberg (1995)
7. Lempel, A., Even, S., Cederbaum, I.: An algorithm for planarity testing of graphs. In: Theory of Graphs. Proc. of an International Symposium, Rome, July 1966, pp. 215–232 (1967)
8. Mendez, P.O.: Orientations bipolaires, PhD thesis, Ecole des Hautes Etudes en Sciences Sociales, Paris (1994)
9. Mursalin, A., Asaduzzaman, S., Saidur, R., Matsumoto, M.: Proposal for st-routing. Telecommunication Systems 25, 287–298 (2004)
10. Nakano, S., Saidur, M.R., Nishizeki, T.: A linear-time algorithm for four-partitioning four-connected planar graphs. Information Processing Letters 62, 315–322 (1997)
11. Papakostas, A., Tollis, I.G.: Algorithms for area-efficient orthogonal drawings. Computational Geometry: Theory and Applications 9, 83–110 (1998)
12. Papamanthou, C., Tollis, I.G.: Applications of Parameterized st-Orientations in Graph Drawing Algorithms. In: Healy, P., Nikolov, N.S. (eds.) GD 2005. LNCS, vol. 3843, pp. 355–367. Springer, Heidelberg (2006)
13. Papamanthou, C., Tollis, I.G.: Algorithms for computing a parameterized st-orientation. Theoretical Computer Science 408, 224–240 (2008)
14. Rosenstiehl, P., Tarjan, R.E.: Rectilinear Planar Layouts and Bipolar Orientations of Planar Graphs. Discrete & Computational Geometry 1, 343–353 (1986)
15. Tamassia, R., Tollis, I.G.: A unified approach to visibility representations of planar graphs. Discrete and Computational Geometry 1, 321–341 (1986)

Equivalence of Deterministic Nested Word to Word Transducers

Sławomir Staworko[1,3], Grégoire Laurence[2,3], Aurélien Lemay[2,3], and Joachim Niehren[1,3]

[1] INRIA, Lille
[2] University of Lille
[3] Mostrare project, INRIA & LIFL (CNRS UMR8022)

Abstract. We study the equivalence problem of deterministic nested word to word transducers and show it to be surprisingly robust. Modulo polynomial time reductions, it can be identified with 4 equivalence problems for diverse classes of deterministic non-copying order-preserving transducers. In particular, we present polynomial time back and fourth reductions to the morphism equivalence problem on context free languages, which is known to be solvable in polynomial time.

Keywords: Trees, transducers, automata, context-free grammars, XML.

1 Introduction

Nested word automata (NAs) [1] are tree automata, that operate on linearizations of unranked trees in streaming manner. All nodes of the tree are visited twice, as usual in preorder traversals. At the first visit (opening event), a symbol is to be pushed onto a stack that is popped at the second visit (closing event). NAs were introduced as a reformulation of visibly pushdown automata [2] and proved equivalent to pushdown forest automata [11] and streaming tree automata [6].

More formally, a nested word over Σ is a word of parenthesis in $\hat{\Sigma} = \{\text{op}, \text{cl}\} \times \Sigma$, such that all opening parenthesis are properly closed. We consider nested words as linearizations of unranked trees. For instance, the linearization of $a(b(c), d)$ is the nested word $(\text{op}, a) \cdot (\text{op}, b) \cdot (\text{op}, c) \cdot (\text{cl}, c) \cdot (\text{cl}, b) \cdot (\text{op}, d) \cdot (\text{cl}, d) \cdot (\text{cl}, a)$, or in XML notation `<a><b><c></c></b><d></d></a>`. NAs process nested words from left to right, while passing finite state information from opening to matching closing parenthesis.

In this paper, we study nested word to word transducers (N2Ws). These process input nested words such as NAs, while producing output letters in parallel, both from left to right. N2Ws are pushdown transducers that must push at opening and pop at closing parenthesis (see Fig. 2 for an example of a N2W-transduction). N2Ws were first introduced in [15], where they were called *visibly pushdown transducers*. Our notion is slightly more general in that we do not impose any well-nesting conditions on output words. Furthermore, we do not assume *synchronization*, i.e., that deletion and renaming operations on matching

M. Kutyłowski, M. Gębala, and W. Charatonik (Eds.): FCT 2009, LNCS 5699, pp. 310–322, 2009.

opening and closing parenthesis are in sync (see Fig. 3). Synchronization is a sufficient restriction to make type checking decidable.

N2Ws T with input alphabet Σ and output alphabet Δ define relations $[\![T]\!]$: $\mathcal{T}_\Sigma \times \Delta^*$ mapping unranked trees with labels in Σ to words with letters in Δ. They have rules of the following two forms:

$$q \xrightarrow{\text{op } a/w:\gamma} q' \quad \text{or} \quad q \xrightarrow{\text{cl } a/w:\gamma} q'$$

where q, q' are states, γ a stack symbol, $a \in \Sigma$ an input label, and $w \in \Delta^*$ a word of output letters. An opening rule applies in state q, consumes an opening parenthesis (op, a) from the input, pushes a symbol γ onto the stack, concatenates w to the output word, and goes into state q'. Closing rules are applied similarly, except that they pop symbol γ from the stack. Note that we do not permit rules with ϵ input (blind insertion) as they are incompatible with determinism.

We call an N2W *deterministic* or a dN2W, if 1. it has a unique initial state, 2. opening rules are determined by the current state q and input label a, and 3. closing rules are determined by q, a, and the current stack symbol γ. Every dN2W T with input alphabet Σ and output alphabet Δ defines a partial function $[\![T]\!] : \mathcal{T}_\Sigma \to \Delta^*$. Since dN2Ws can be identified with deterministic pushdown transducer, it follows from the very general result of Szenergues [16] that equivalence of dN2Ws is decidable.

We call an N2W *top-down*, if it is top-down as an NA, i.e., if all its closing rules have the form $q \xrightarrow{\text{cl } a/w:q'} q'$, so that the closing state is already determined by the stack symbol pushed at opening time. A *top-down deterministic* N2W or a dN2W$^\downarrow$ is a deterministic N2W that is top-down. Similarly to top-down deterministic tree automata, dN2W$^\downarrow$ are less expressive than dN2Ws.

We consider two kinds of standard transducers on *ranked* trees [8,4], ranked tree to word transducers (R2Ws) which may either be top-down deterministic (dR2W$^\downarrow$s) or bottom-up deterministic (dR2W$^\uparrow$s). Our main results are polynomial time reductions between all of the following problems:

1. equivalence of dN2Ws,
2. equivalence of dN2Ws$^\downarrow$,
3. equivalence of dR2W$^\downarrow$s that are non-copying and order-preserving,
4. equivalence of dR2W$^\uparrow$s that are non-copying and order-preserving,
5. equivalence of morphisms on context free languages.

Plandowski [13,14] has shown that the last problem is decidable in polynomial time. Since all of our reductions are in polynomial time, all of the above problems are decidable in polynomial time too. This result has not been stated before for any of the first 4 problems. It should be noticed, that equivalence of tree-to-tree transducers can be reduced to equivalence of tree-to-word transducers that linearize output trees. As a consequence, we obtain polynomial time algorithms for deciding equivalence of top-down and bottom-up deterministic tree-to-tree transducers that are non-copying and order-preserving.

Our main motivation is to define XML document transformation in a deterministic manner, as for instance by the W3C standard XSLT. Various classes of tree transducers have been proposed to this end before [10,9]. Also the class of dN2Ws[↓] does neither allow tree copying nor tree permutation operations. However, we believe this is a good compromise between complexity results and expressive power. For instance, it can express more than non-copying and order-preserving transducers from [10]. In particular, it ·can express most usual "stylesheet-like" XML to HTML transformations (e.g. Fig. 2). Also, it is suitable to model streamed-like processing.

Related Work. As shown by [5], the equivalence of top-down deterministic tree-to-tree transducers (dR2Rs[↓]) can be decided in polynomial time. This result is orthogonal to ours. It is more general in that copying and permutations are permitted, but cannot capture word output of dR2W[↓]s, since lacking the word concatenation operation. Every tree-to-tree transducer can be transformed into a tree-to-word transducer by composition with the yield function. This has been done for instance in order to measure the generating capacities of tree transducers [8]. However, since different trees may have the same yield, one cannot reduce the equivalence problem of tree-to-tree transducers to that of tree-to-word transducers this way (if not adding concatenation operations or macros).

The methods used in this paper are reminiscent of those used by Culik and Karhumäki to show decidability of equivalence of synchronized deterministic pushdown automata and transducers, e.g. see [7]. Intuitively, two deterministic pushdown automata are synchronized if their stacks have *almost* the same height throughout every computation. Then, their execution can be simulated with a single pushdown automaton, very much in the spirit of Lemma 3. In this setting the complexity of this approach is exponential. We take advantage of the observation that two N2Ws can be viewed as synchronized pushdown transducers, and moreover, the stacks always have *exactly* the same height.

2   Nested Word to Word Transducers

Let Σ be a finite set of labels. We define the set of unranked trees $\mathcal{T}_\Sigma$ to be the least set that contains all pairs $a(t_1, \ldots, t_n)$ consisting of a label $a \in \Sigma$ and a tuple of unranked trees $(t_1, \ldots, t_n) \in (\mathcal{T}_\Sigma)^n$ for some $n \geq 0$, i.e. $\mathcal{T}_\Sigma = \Sigma \times \cup_{n \geq 0}(\mathcal{T}_\Sigma)^n$. When writing XML documents into files, unranked trees are usually linearized in a preorder traversal to words $lin(t) \in \hat{\Sigma}^*$ where $\hat{\Sigma} = \{\mathrm{op}, \mathrm{cl}\} \times \Sigma$.

$$lin(a(t_1, \ldots, t_n)) = (\mathrm{op}, a) \cdot lin(t_1) \cdot \ldots \cdot lin(t_n) \cdot (\mathrm{cl}, a)$$

Linearizations of unranked trees are words in $\hat{\Sigma}^*$ that are well-nested in that all opening parenthesis are properly closed. See Fig. 1 for an example. We define the set of all *nested words* over Σ by $N_\Sigma = \{lin(t) \mid t \in \mathcal{T}_\Sigma\}$. More general definitions can be found in the literature. We impose 4 restrictions, of which only the first matters technically, while the others simplify presentation: (1) No dangling opening or closing parenthesis. As a consequence, segments of nested words between two positions do not need to be nested words. (2) No internal letters, which are neither opening nor closing. (3) No corresponding parenthesis

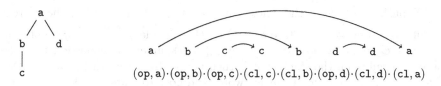

Fig. 1. Example of a tree and its linearization into a nested word

with different labels (for instance, $(\text{op}\,a)(\text{cl}\,b)$ is not well nested). (4) No hedges, i.e. sequences of unranked trees: these can be represented by unranked trees by adding artificial roots.

A *nested word to word transducer* (N2W) T is a tuple of finite sets $T = (\Sigma, \Delta, Q, \Gamma, rul, init, fin)$ such that $init, fin \subseteq Q$ and $rul \subseteq Q^2 \times \hat{\Sigma} \times \Delta^* \times \Gamma$. There are labels $a \in \Sigma$ of input trees, an alphabet for output words $u \in \Delta^*$, states $q \in Q$, and stack symbols $\gamma \in \Gamma$. We denote rules r equal to $((q, q'), (\alpha, a), u, \gamma)$ as $q \xrightarrow{\alpha\, a/u:\gamma} q'$. We denote $lhs(r) = q$ (for left hand side), $rhs(r) = q'$ (for right hand side), $act(r) = (\alpha, a)$ (for action), $output(r) = u$ and $ssy(r) = \gamma$ (for stack symbol). Note that our definition of N2Ws excludes rules with ϵ-input. A *nested word automaton* (NA) is a N2W which always outputs the empty word, so that all rules are of the form $q \xrightarrow{\alpha\, a/\epsilon:\gamma} q'$. The main interest of NAs compared to tree automata [1] is that they combine top-down and bottom-up processing by operating on preorder linearizations of unranked trees (nested words). N2W is a suitable choice to model transformations that do not require copying or reordering, for instance simple XML to HTML transformations (Fig. 2).

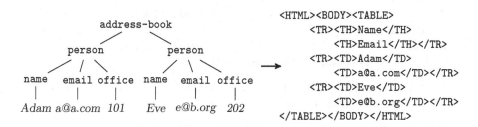

Fig. 2. An example of XML to HTML transformation

An N2W defines a relation $[\![T]\!] \subseteq T_\Sigma \times \Delta^*$. We will present two equivalent definitions of $[\![T]\!]$. The first interprets T as a pushdown transducer, which inputs nested words in N_Σ and outputs words in Δ^*. The pushdown is "visible" in that it pushes (resp. pops) when reading opening (resp. closing) parenthesis. We define the set of configurations of an N2W by $\hat{\Sigma}^* \times Q \times \Gamma^* \times \Delta^*$. Every configuration $C = (w, q, S, u)$ has an input word w, a state q, a stack S and an output word u. We call C initial for $t \in T_\Sigma$ if $w = lin(t)$, $q \in init$, $S = \epsilon$, and $u = \epsilon$. We call C a final configuration for u if $w = \epsilon$, $q \in fin$, and $S = \epsilon$. An opening rule $q \xrightarrow{\text{op}\,a/u':\gamma} q'$ applies in state $q \in Q$, reads an opening parenthesis (op, a) where

$a \in \Sigma$ pushes $\gamma \in \Gamma$ to the stack, concatenates u' to the end of the current output word, and goes to state $q' \in Q$. A closing rule $q \xrightarrow{\text{cl}\, a/u':\gamma} q'$ applies in state $q \in Q$, reads a closing parenthesis (cl, a) under the condition that the top-most symbol on the stack is γ. It then pops γ from the stack, concatenates u' to the end of the current output word, and goes to state q'. The transitions between configurations is defined as follow:

$$\frac{q \xrightarrow{\text{op}\, a/u':\gamma} q' \in rul}{((\text{op}, a) \cdot w, q, S, u) \to (w, q', \gamma \cdot S, u \cdot u')} \qquad \frac{q \xrightarrow{\text{cl}\, a/u':\gamma} q' \in rul}{((\text{cl}, a) \cdot w, q, \gamma \cdot S, u) \to (w, q', S, u \cdot u')}$$

We say that a N2W T transforms unranked tree t to word u if T licences a transition sequence $C \to^* C'$ where C is initial for t and C' final for u, and define the relation $[\![T]\!] = \{(t, u) \in \mathcal{T}_\Sigma \times \Delta^* \mid T \text{ transforms } t \text{ to } u\}$. Also, an NA A recognizes the tree language $L(A) = \{t \in \mathcal{T}_\Sigma \mid (t, \epsilon) \in [\![A]\!]\}$.

The second characterization of $[\![T]\!]$ is based on runs, which annotate opening and closing events of nodes of unranked trees by rules. As usual, a single run of an automata on a tree is supposed to capture all information of all intermediate configurations leading to acceptance. We define the set of nodes of an unranked trees by $nod(a(t_1, \ldots, t_n)) = \{\epsilon\} \cup \{i \cdot \pi \mid \pi \in nod(t_i)\}$. An event is a member of the set $\widehat{nod}(t)$, i.e. an element of a preorder traversal of t. The set $\widehat{nod}(t)$ is totally ordered: the first event is the opening of the root (op, ϵ), the last event is the closing of the root (cl, ϵ), etc. We write $(\alpha, \pi) < (\alpha', \pi')$ if (α, π) is properly before (α', π') in this order and define $pr(\alpha, \pi) \in \widehat{nod}(t)$ to be the immediate predecessor of $(\alpha, \pi) \in \widehat{nod}(t)$ in that order.

A *run* of an N2W on a tree $t \in \mathcal{T}_\Sigma$ is a function $R : \widehat{nod}(t) \to rul$ such that $lhs(R(\text{op}, \epsilon)) \in init$, and for any $(\alpha, \pi) \in \widehat{nod}(t)$, $ssy(R(\text{op}, \pi)) = ssy(R(\text{cl}, \pi))$, $rhs(R(pr(\alpha, \pi))) = lhs(R(\alpha, \pi))$, and $act(R(\alpha, \pi)) = (\alpha, a)$, where a is the label of the node π in t. We call R *successful* if $rhs(R(\text{cl}, \epsilon)) \in fin$.

See Fig. 3 for an example of a successful run.

Lemma 1. $[\![T]\!] = \{(t, output(R(e_1)) \cdot \ldots \cdot output(R(e_n))) \mid t \in \mathcal{T}_\Sigma, R$ *successful run of T on t, the events of t are $e_1 < \ldots < e_n\}$.*

An N2W T is *deterministic* or an dN2W if it satisfies (1) for all $q \in Q$ and $a \in \Sigma$ there exists at most one $\gamma \in \Gamma$, $u \in \Delta^*$, and $q' \in Q$ such that $q \xrightarrow{\text{op}\, a/u:\gamma} q'$ belongs to rul; (2) for all $q \in Q$, $a \in \Sigma$, and $\gamma \in \Gamma$ there is at most one $u \in \Delta^*$ and $q' \in Q$ such that $q \xrightarrow{\text{cl}\, a/u:\gamma} q'$ belongs to rul; (3) there exists at most one state in *init*.

An N2W is *top-down* if $Q = \Gamma$ and all closing rules have the form $q \xrightarrow{\text{cl}\, a/u:q'} q'$. An N2W is *top-down deterministic* (dN2W$^\downarrow$) if it is top-down and deterministic. A dNA is a dN2W and an NA, and a dNA$^\downarrow$ is a dN2W$^\downarrow$ and an NA.

It is known that dNAs can recognize all regular languages of unranked trees, while dNA$^\downarrow$s are properly less expressive. This is similar to the case of ranked trees, where bottom-up deterministic tree automata can recognize all regular languages, while top-down deterministic tree automata capture only path closed

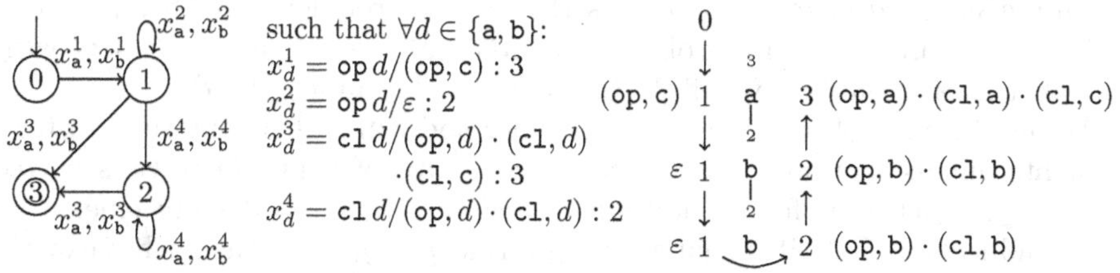

Fig. 3. An example dN2w$^{\downarrow}$ with a successful run on a(b(b)). For a node α of the input tree, we put $output(R(\mathtt{op},\alpha))$ and $rhs(R(\mathtt{op},\alpha))$ on its left, $rhs(R(\mathtt{cl},\alpha))$ and $output(R(\mathtt{cl},\alpha))$ on its right, and $ssy(R(\_,\alpha))$ above it.

languages. Emptiness of NAs can be checked in quadratic time. Intersection and complementation for dNAs can be performed in polynomial time. We can thus check inclusion and equivalence of dNAs in polynomial time too. We also remark that the set of all possible outputs of a N2W can be defined by a context-free grammar of size polynomial in the size of the N2W. Using the results of [17] we show that verifying that a N2W outputs only well-balanced words is in PTIME.

As an example, we consider a transformation $\tau : \mathcal{T}_\Sigma \to \hat{\Delta}$ where $\Sigma = \{\mathtt{a}, \mathtt{b}\}$ and $\Delta = \Sigma \cup \{\mathtt{c}\}$. τ "turns 90 degree clockwise" the input tree: a(b(b(a(b)))) is mapped to (the linearization of) c(b, a, b, b, a)). More generally, transformation τ maps tree $a_1(a_2(...(a_n)...))$ to $lin(\mathtt{c}(a_n, ..., a_1))$ where $a_1, ..., a_n \in \Sigma$ and $n \geq 0$. We define τ with a dN2w$^{\downarrow}$ in Fig. 3 with $Q = \Gamma = \{0, 1, 2, 3\}$, $init = \{0\}$ and $fin = \{3\}$. Except for the opening c parenthesis, all output is produced at closing time. A run of T on the input tree a(b(b)) is shown in Fig. 3 too. The inverse transformation modulo linearization $\tau' : \mathcal{T}_\Delta \to \hat{\Sigma}$ cannot be expressed by any N2W since we would have to read a horizontal word from the right to the left. This is impossible, similarly to word inversion by one-way string transducers.

For every class $\mathcal{C}$ of transducers, we define the $\mathcal{C}$-equivalence problem. Its input are two transducers $T_1, T_2 \in \mathcal{C}$ with the same alphabets, and its output is yes if $[\![T_1]\!] = [\![T_2]\!]$ and no otherwise.

3   Morphism Equivalence on CFGs

We relate dN2ws and dN2ws$^{\downarrow}$-equivalence to word morphism equivalence on CFGs [14,13]. A (word) morphism is a total function $M : \Sigma^* \to \Delta^*$ such that $M(v \cdot u) = M(v) \cdot M(u)$. It is uniquely specified by the values taken on letters of Σ. We use the set $\{(a, M(a)) \mid a \in \Sigma\}$ as the representation of M with size $|M| = \sum_{a \in \Sigma} |M(a)|$.

A context-free grammar (CFG) over Σ is a tuple $G = (\Sigma, Q, init, rul)$, where Σ is the set of terminals, Q is the set of nonterminals or states, $init \subseteq Q$ the set of start states, $rul \subseteq Q \times (\Sigma \cup Q^*)$ a set of rules. We denote rules r as $q \to \omega$ where $q \in Q$ is its left-hand side ($lhs(r)$) and $\omega \in \Sigma \cup Q^*$ its right-hand side ($rhs(r)$). The size of a rule $|r|$ is the length of its rhs. The size of a grammar G is $|G| = |\Sigma| + |Q| + \Sigma_{r \in rul}|r|$. The set $L(G)$ of words recognized by G is defined in the standard way.

Morphism equivalence on CFGs is the decision problem, which inputs two finite sets Σ and Δ, two morphisms $M_1, M_2 : \Sigma^* \to \Delta^*$, and a CFG G with alphabet Σ, and outputs yes iff $M_1(w) = M_2(w)$ for all $w \in L(G)$.

We need extended parse trees, whose inner nodes are labeled by rules instead of nonterminals. Formally, an *extended parse tree* of a grammar G is a tree $t \in \mathcal{T}_{rul \cup \Sigma}$, such that for all nodes $\pi \in nod(t)$: 1. inner nodes are labeled by rules and leafs in Σ, 2. if the label of π is a rule $q \to q_1 \cdots q_n$ then π has exactly n children, and for all $1 \le i \le n$ child $\pi \cdot i$ is labeled by a rule with *lhs* q_i, and 3. if the label of π is a rule $q \to a$ then π has exactly one child which is a leaf labeled a. Extended parse trees are ranked trees, when using the size of a rule as its arity. As usually, given a tree t we define $yield(t)$ to be the concatenation of the labels of all leaves in left-to-right order. Clearly, $w \in L(G)$ if and only if there exists an extended parse tree t of G with $w = yield(t)$.

Lemma 2. *For every morphism $M : \Sigma^* \to \Delta^*$ and CFG G with alphabet Σ, we can construct in time $O(|M| + |G|^2)$ a dN2W$^\downarrow$ T with alphabet Σ and Δ such that $[\![T]\!] = \{(t, M(yield(t))) \mid t$ extended parse tree of $G\}$.*

Proof (sketch). We take the grammar $G = (\Sigma, Q_G, init_G, rul_G)$ and construct an dN2W$^\downarrow$ $T = (\Sigma', \Delta, Q_T, \Gamma_T, init_T, rul_T, fin_T)$ that takes as an input extended parse tree of G t and outputs $M(yield(t))$. This can be done top-down deterministically since extended parse trees contain all necessary information. Let $\Sigma' = Q_G \cup \Sigma$, $Q_T = \Gamma_T = \{(r,j) \mid r \in rul_G, 0 \le j \le |r|\} \cup \{\mathsf{o}, \mathsf{d}, \mathsf{f}\}$, $init_T = \{\mathsf{o}\}$, $fin_T = \{\mathsf{f}\}$, and rul_T consists of the following transitions:

$$\frac{r \in rul_G \quad lhs(r) \in init_G}{\mathsf{o} \xrightarrow{\mathrm{op}\ r/\varepsilon:\mathsf{f}} (r,0)} \qquad \frac{r \in rul_G \quad rhs(r) = a}{(r,0) \xrightarrow{\mathrm{op}\ a/M(a):(r,1)} \mathsf{d}}$$

$$(r,|r|) \xrightarrow{\mathrm{cl}\ r/\varepsilon:\mathsf{f}} \mathsf{f} \qquad\qquad \mathsf{d} \xrightarrow{\mathrm{cl}\ a/\varepsilon:(r,1)} (r,1)$$

$$\frac{r, r' \in rul_G \quad rhs(r) = q_1 \cdots q_k \quad 1 \le j \le |r| \quad lhs(r') = q_j}{(r,j-1) \xrightarrow{\mathrm{op}\ r'/\varepsilon:(r,j)} (r',0)}$$

$$(r',|r'|) \xrightarrow{\mathrm{cl}\ r'/\varepsilon:(r,j)} (r,j) \qquad\qquad\qquad \square$$

Proposition 1. *Morphism equivalence on CFGs can be reduced in quadratic time to dN2W$^\downarrow$-equivalence.*

Proof. Take two morphisms $M_1, M_2 : \Sigma^* \to \Delta^*$ and a CFG G, and let T_1 and T_2 be obtained with the construction described in Lemma 2 for M_1 with G and M_2 with G respectively, in $O(|G|^2 + |M_1| + |M_2|)$. Since T_1 and T_2 have the same domain, it should be clear that T_1 and T_2 are equivalent if and only if M_1 and M_2 are equivalent on G. $\square$

We next reduce dN2W-equivalence to morphism equivalence on CFGs. Let T_1 and T_2 be two N2Ws with input alphabet Σ and output alphabet Δ. Let $t \in \mathcal{T}_\Sigma$ be a tree whose events are $e_1 < \ldots < e_n$. A *successful parallel run* of T_1 and T_2 on tree t is a word s with alphabet $\mathcal{R} = rul_{T_1} \times rul_{T_2}$ such that there exist two successful runs R_1 of T_1 and R_2 of T_2 on t with $s = (R_1(e_1), R_2(e_1)) \cdot \ldots \cdot (R_1(e_n), R_2(e_n))$.

We use two morphisms M_1 and M_2 from $\mathcal{R}$ to Δ such that:

$$M_i((r_1, r_2)) = u \quad \text{if } r_i = q \xrightarrow{\alpha\, a/u:\gamma} q'$$

If s is a successful parallel run of T_1 and T_2 on t, then $(t, M_i(s)) \in [\![T_i]\!]$.

Lemma 3. *For any two* N2W*s T_1 and T_2 with the same alphabets there exists a* CFG *G such that $L(G)$ is the set of all successful parallel runs of T_1 and T_2.*

Proof (sketch). We construct the grammar $G = (\mathcal{R}, Q_G, init_G, rul_G)$ as follows. The set of nonterminals is $Q_G = \{\circ\} \cup Q_{T_1}^2 \times Q_{T_2}^2$. A nonterminal $((p_1, q_1), (p_2, q_2))$ is supposed to produce a parallel run of T_1 from p_1 to q_1 and T_2 from p_2 to q_2 (on the same input). There is only one start symbol $init_G = \{\circ\}$ and the rules in rul_G are defined follows:

$$\frac{r_1, r_1' \in rul_{T_1} \quad r_1 = p_1 \xrightarrow{op\, a/u_1:\gamma_1} q_1 \quad r_1' = p_1' \xrightarrow{cl\, a/u_1':\gamma_1} q_1' \quad p_1 \in init_{T_1} \quad q_1' \in fin_{T_1}}{}$$

$$\frac{r_2, r_2' \in rul_{T_2} \quad r_2 = p_2 \xrightarrow{op\, a/u_2:\gamma_2} q_2 \quad r_2' = p_2' \xrightarrow{cl\, a/u_2':\gamma_2} q_2' \quad p_2 \in init_{T_2} \quad q_2' \in fin_{T_2}}{\circ \rightarrow (r_1, r_2) \cdot ((q_1, p_1), (q_2, p_2)) \cdot (r_1', r_2')}$$

$$\frac{\begin{array}{c} r_1, r_1' \in rul_{T_1} \quad r_1 = p_1 \xrightarrow{op\, a/u_1:\gamma_1} q_1 \quad r_1' = p_1' \xrightarrow{cl\, a/u_1':\gamma_1} q_1', \\ r_2, r_2' \in rul_{T_2} \quad r_2 = p_2 \xrightarrow{op\, a/u_2:\gamma_2} q_2 \quad r_2' = p_2' \xrightarrow{cl\, a/u_2':\gamma_2} q_2' \end{array}}{((p_1, q_1'), (p_2, q_2')) \rightarrow (r_1, r_2) \cdot ((q_1, p_1), (q_2, p_2)) \cdot (r_1', r_2')}$$

$$\frac{p_1, p_1', q_1 \in Q_{T_1} \quad p_2, p_2', q_2 \in Q_{T_2}}{((p_1, q_1), (p_2, q_2)) \rightarrow ((p_1, p_1'), (p_2, p_2')) \cdot ((p_1', q_1), (p_2', q_2))} \qquad \frac{q_1 \in Q_{T_1}, \; q_2 \in Q_{T_2}}{((q_1, q_1), (q_2, q_2)) \rightarrow \varepsilon} \qquad \square$$

Proposition 2. *dN2W-equivalence can be reduced in polynomial time to morphism equivalence on* CFG*s.*

Proof. Let T_1 and T_2 be two dN2Ws with the input alphabet Σ and the output alphabet Δ. First, we need to verify that the domains of T_1 and T_2 coincide. To do that, we test equivalence of the dNAs that define the domains of T_1 and T_2 (obtained by removing the output components from transitions). We recall that this can be done in polynomial time due to determinism.

If the domains of T_1 and T_2 are equal, let G be the grammar constructed in Lemma 3, and M_1 and M_2 the two morphisms defined above. Clearly, T_1 is equivalent to T_2 if and only if M_1 is equivalent to M_2 on G. $\qquad \square$

Interestingly, composing Proposition 2 with Proposition 1 allows us to reduce dN2W-equivalence to dN2W$^\downarrow$-equivalence, the latter dealing with a weaker model than the former. The converse reduction is trivial.

Corollary 1. *dN2W-equivalence can be reduced in polynomial time to dN2W$^\downarrow$-equivalence, and vice versa.*

4 Top-Down Ranked Tree to Word Transducers

We now relate dN2Ws$^\downarrow$ to standard top-down deterministic transducers on ranked trees, based on binary encoding of unranked trees.

$$fcns(a(t_1, \ldots, t_n)) = a(fcns'(t_1, \ldots, t_n), \#)$$
$$fcns'(a(t_1^1, \ldots, t_1^m), t_2, \ldots, t_n) =$$
$$\qquad a(fcns'(t_1^1, \ldots, t_1^m), fcns'(t_2, \ldots, t_n))$$
$$fcns'(()) = \#$$

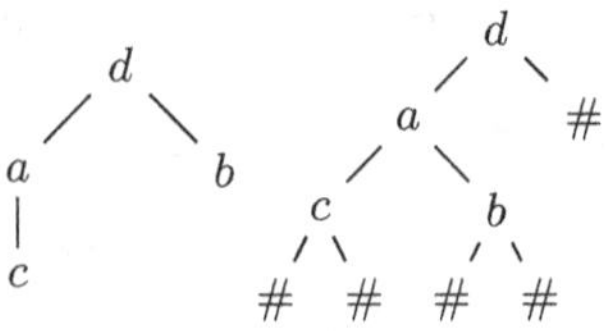

Fig. 4. First-child next-sibling encoding

A ranked alphabet consists of a set Σ and a arity function $ar : \Sigma \rightarrow \mathbb{N}$. The set $\mathcal{T}_\Sigma^r$ of ranked trees over Σ is the least subset of $\mathcal{T}_\Sigma$ that contains all trees $a(t_1, \ldots, t_{ar(a)})$ with $t_i \in \mathcal{T}_\Sigma^r$.

We fix an infinite sequence of pairwise distinct tree variables $(\mathbf{x}_i)_{i \in \mathbb{N}}$. A *top-down ranked-tree to word transducer* (R2W$^\downarrow$) is a tuple $S = (\Sigma, \Delta, Q, init, rul)$, where Σ is a ranked alphabet, Δ a finite set, $init \subseteq Q$, and rul a finite set of rules of the form $q(a(\mathbf{x}_1, \ldots, \mathbf{x}_{ar(a)})) \rightarrow w$ where $q \in Q$ and w is a word over alphabet $\Delta \uplus \{p(\mathbf{x}_i) \mid p \in Q, 1 \leq i \leq ar(a)\}$. An R2W$^\downarrow$ S is *top-down deterministic* or a dR2W$^\downarrow$s if for every $a \in \Sigma$ there exists at most one state $q \in init$ such that $q(a(\mathbf{x}_1, \ldots, \mathbf{x}_{ar(a)})) \rightarrow w \in rul$ for some w, and if there exist no two rules in rul with the same left hand side.

The semantics of S is defined in terms of the relations $[\![S]\!]_q \subseteq \mathcal{T}_\Sigma^r \times \Delta^*$, where $q \in Q$, intuitively representing the transformation performed by S in state q. Formally, $(a(t_1, \ldots, t_k), u) \in [\![S]\!]_q$ if and only if there exists $q(a(\mathbf{x}_1, \ldots, \mathbf{x}_k)) \rightarrow w$ in rul such that u is obtained by replacing in w every occurrence of $p(\mathbf{x}_i)$ by u_i for some $(t_i, u_i) \in [\![S]\!]_p$ (if some $p(\mathbf{x}_i)$ occurs more than once in w, then different pairs $(t_i, u_i), (t_i, u_i') \in [\![S]\!]_p$ can be used for replacement). Finally, the transformation defined by S is $[\![S]\!] = \bigcup_{q \in init} [\![S]\!]_q$.

From now, we will restrict ourselves to noncopying and order-preserving dR2W$^\downarrow$s. These are dR2W$^\downarrow$s with rules of the form:

$$q(a(\mathbf{x}_1, \ldots, \mathbf{x}_k)) \rightarrow u_0 \cdot q_1(\mathbf{x}_1) \cdot u_1 \cdot \ldots \cdot u_{k-1} \cdot q_k(\mathbf{x}_k) \cdot u_k,$$

where $u_i \in \Delta^*$ for all $i \in \{1, \ldots, k\}$. Given this restriction, we can drop variables from the rules, and simply denote them as $q(a) \rightarrow u_0 \cdot q_1 \cdot \ldots \cdot q_k \cdot u_k$.

Our first result, shows that any transformation definable with a dN2W$^\downarrow$ can be expressed by a noncopying order-preserving dR2W$^\downarrow$s, modulo a binary encoding of input trees. Here we use Rabin's encoding of unranked trees as usual, often called *first-child next-sibling* encoding. An unranked tree over Σ is represented using a binary tree whose inner nodes are labeled with Σ (binary symbol) and leaves with $\#$ (constant symbol not belonging to Σ). Formally, the encoding is defined and illustrated by an example in Fig. 4.

Proposition 3. *For any* dN2W$^\downarrow$ *T we can construct in time $O(|\Sigma|^2 * |Q_T|^2)$ a noncopying order-preserving* dR2W$^\downarrow$s *S with $[\![S]\!] = \{(fcns(t), u) \mid (t, u) \in [\![T]\!]\}$.*

Proof (sketch). Let $T = (\Sigma, \Delta, Q_T, \Gamma_T, init_T, rul_T, fin_T)$ and recall that $\Gamma_T = Q_T$ because T is a dN2W$^\downarrow$. We defined $S = (\Sigma \cup \{\#\}, \Delta, Q_S, init_S, rul_S)$ such that $Q_S = init_T \cup \{q_\#\} \cup Q_T \times \Sigma \times \Gamma_T$, $init_S = init_T$, and rul_S consists of the following rules:

$$\frac{q_0 \in init_T \quad q_2 \in fin_T \quad q_0 \xrightarrow{\text{op } a/u:q_2} q_1 \in rul_T}{q_0(a) \to u \cdot (q_1, a, q_2) \cdot q_\#} \qquad \frac{q \xrightarrow{\text{cl } a/u:q'} q' \in rul_T}{(q, a, q')(\#) \to u}$$

$$\frac{b \in \Sigma \quad p \in Q_T \quad q \xrightarrow{\text{op } a/u:q_2} q_1 \in rul_T}{(q, b, p)(a) \to u \cdot (q_1, a, q_2) \cdot (q_2, b, p)} \qquad \frac{true}{q_\#(\#) \to \varepsilon}$$

Intuitively, the state (q, a, γ) corresponds to T being in state q, having γ on the top of the stack, and a being the label of the parent of the current node. The introduction of the state $q_\#$ makes sure that S accepts on the input only trees that are result of the first-child next-sibling encoding of some unranked tree. One can then prove inductively that $[\![S]\!] = \{(fcns(t), u) \mid (t, u) \in [\![T]\!]\}$. $\qquad \square$

Next, we show the converse, i.e. that every transformation defined with a dR2w$^\downarrow$s can be expressed by dN2w$^\downarrow$. This time no encoding is necessary since unranked trees comprise a subset of ranked trees.

Proposition 4. *noncopying order-preserving* dR2w$^\downarrow$s S *can be converted to* dN2ws$^\downarrow$ T *with* $[\![S]\!] = [\![T]\!]$ *in time* $O(|S| * n)$ *where* $n = max(\{ar(x) \mid x \in \Sigma\})$.

Proof (sketch). Let $S = (\Sigma, \Delta, states_S, init_S, rul_S)$. We extend the arity function ar to rul_S in the following way: $ar(q(a) \to w) = ar(a)$.

The constructed dN2w$^\downarrow$ is $T = (\Sigma, \Delta, Q_T, \Gamma_T, init_T, rul_T, fin_T)$, where $Q_T = \Gamma_T = \{(r, j) \mid r \in rul_S, 0 \leq j \leq ar(r)\} \cup \{\mathsf{o}, \mathsf{f}\}$, $init_T = \{\mathsf{o}\}$, $fin_T = \{\mathsf{f}\}$, and rul_S consists of the following rules

$$\frac{q_0 \in init_S}{r = q_0(a) \to u_0 \cdot q_1 \ldots q_k \cdot u_k \in rul_S}$$
$$\mathsf{o} \xrightarrow{\text{op } a/u_o:\mathsf{f}} (r, 0)$$
$$(r, k) \xrightarrow{\text{cl } a/\varepsilon:\mathsf{f}} \mathsf{f}$$

$$\frac{r = q(a) \to u_0 \cdot q_1 \ldots q_j \cdot u_j \ldots q_k \cdot u_k \in rul_S}{r' = q_j(b) \to v_0 \cdot p_1 \ldots p_m \cdot v_m \quad 1 \leq j \leq k}$$
$$(r, j-1) \xrightarrow{\text{op } b/v_o:(r,j)} (r', 0)$$
$$(r', m) \xrightarrow{\text{cl } b/u_j:(r,j)} (r, j)$$

Intuitively, when the transducer is in the state (r, j), it processes the rule $r = q_0(a) \to u_0 \cdot q_1 \ldots q_k \cdot u_k$, has just written out u_j, and is about to handle the state q_{j+1} (or to close the parenthesis a if $j = k$). $[\![S]\!] = [\![T]\!]$ is proved with an inductive proof. $\qquad \square$

Corollary 2. *Equivalence of noncopying order-preserving* dR2w$^\downarrow$s *can be reduced in polynomial time to* dN2w$^\downarrow$-*equivalence, and vice versa.*

5 Bottom-Up Ranked Tree to Word Transducers

Even though the expressive power of bottom-up and top-down deterministic tree transducers are uncomparable, we can show their equivalence problems are the same. Here we use direct reductions, that are inspired from the reduction of dN2w-equivalence to dN2w$^\downarrow$-equivalence.

We fix an infinite sequence of pairwise distinct variables $(X_i)_{i \in \mathbb{N}}$ for output words. A *bottom-up ranked-tree to word transducer* (R2W$^\uparrow$) is a tuple $S = (\Sigma, \Delta, Q, fin, rul)$ with rules in rul of the form: $a(q_1(X_1), \ldots, q_k(X_k)) \to q(w)$ where $k = ar(a)$ $q, q_i \in Q$, and w is a word with alphabet $\Delta \uplus \{X_1, \ldots, X_k\}$. The semantics $[\![S]\!] \subseteq T_\Sigma^r \times \Delta^*$ can be defined as follows:

$$\frac{a(q_1(X_1), \ldots, q_k(X_k)) \to q(w) \in rul \quad (t_1, u_1) \in [\![S]\!]_{q_1} \quad \ldots \quad (t_k, u_k) \in [\![S]\!]_{q_k}}{(a(t_1, \ldots, t_k), w[u_1/X_1, \ldots, u_n/X_n]) \in [\![S]\!]_q} \qquad \frac{true}{[\![S]\!] = \cup_{q \in fin} [\![S]\!]_q}$$

An R2W$^\uparrow$ S is *bottom-up deterministic* (or a dR2W$^\uparrow$) if no two rules of S have the same left-hand side. In this case, $[\![S]\!]$ defines a partial function.

From now on, we will only consider noncopying and order-preserving R2W$^\uparrow$s, i.e., R2W$^\uparrow$s with rules restricted to the form $a(q_1(X_1), \ldots, q_k(X_k)) \to q(u_0 \cdot X_1 \cdot u_1 \cdots X_k \cdot u_k)$. Since noncopying, such R2W$^\uparrow$s can be translated to R2W$^\downarrow$s defining the same relation, and vice versa. A rule as above is transformed to $q(a) \to u_0 \cdot q_1 \cdot u_1 \cdots q_k \cdot u_k$, while final states of the bottom-up transducer become initial states of its top-down version. We can thus talk of R2Ws in the noncopying case, rather than distinguishing R2W$^\uparrow$s and R2W$^\downarrow$s artificially.

Given two noncopying order-preserving R2Ws S_1 and S_2 with the same alphabets Σ and Δ, a *successful parallel run* of S_1 and S_2 is a tree s over alphabet $\mathcal{R} = rul_{S_1} \times rul_{S_2}$ with nodes $\pi \in nod(s)$ labeled by some pair of rules (r_1^π, r_2^π) such that (1) the label of the root of s satisfies $r_i^\epsilon = q_i(\_) \to \_$ for some $q_i \in fin_{S_i}$, and (2) for all nodes $\pi \in nod(s)$ with $r_i^\pi = q_i(a_i) \to u_i^0 \cdot q_i^1 \ldots q_i^{k_i} \cdot u_i^{k_i}$, it holds that $a_1 = a_2$ and thus $k_1 = k_2 = ar(a_1) = ar(a_2)$ and that π has exactly $k = k_1 = k_2$ children $\pi \cdot j$ labeled by rules $r_i^{\pi \cdot j} = q_i^j(\_) \to \_$ where $1 \le j \le k$ and $1 \le i \le 2$. For every successful parallel run s we define $input(s) \in T_\Sigma^r$ and the $output_i(s) \in \Delta^*$ as follows, where $r_i = q_i(a) \to u_i^0 \cdot q_i^1 \ldots q_i^k \cdot u_i^k$:

$$input((r_1, r_2)(s_1, \ldots, s_k)) = a(input(s_1), \ldots, input(s_k))$$
$$output_i((r_1, r_2)(s_1, \ldots, s_k)) = u_i^0 \cdot output_i(s_1) \ldots output_i(s_k) \cdot u_i^k$$

Lemma 4. *Let S_1 and S_2 be noncopying and order-preserving R2Ws over the alphabets Σ and Δ. Then, for all $t \in T_\Sigma^r$ and $u_1, u_2 \in \Delta^*$ we have that $(t, u_1) \in [\![S_1]\!]$ and $(t, u_2) \in [\![S_2]\!]$ if and only if there exists a successful parallel run s of S_1 and S_2 such that $input(s) = t$, $output_1(s) = u_1$, and $output_2(s) = u_2$.*

Proposition 5. *Equivalence of noncopying and order-preserving dR2W$^\uparrow$s S_1 and S_2 can be reduced in $O(|S_1| \times |S_2|)$ to equivalence of noncopying and order-preserving dR2W$^\downarrow$s, and vice versa.*

Indeed, taking for example two noncopying and order-preserving dR2W$^\uparrow$s S_1 and S_2 over the same domain (otherwise, it just a problem of equivalence over tree automata that can be dealt in $O(|S_1| \times |S_2|)$, see [3]), one can build two dR2W$^\downarrow$s S_1' and S_2' with $[\![S_i']\!]$ containing $(s, output_i(s))$ where s is a parallel run of S_1 and S_2. Lemma 4 then finishes the reduction.

6   Conclusion and Future Work

We have shown that various classes of tree-to-word transducers have the same equivalence problem modulo polynomial time reductions. Our results are based on a new relationship to the morphism equivalence problem on CFGs that we established. Our equivalences do not carry over to tree-to-tree transducers without macros or concatenation operations, since these cannot express word morphisms on CFGs in any obvious manner (Lemma 3). The classes of deterministic nested word transducers that we have proposed here, open up quite a number of questions of interest for the XML, formal language, tree automata and grammatical inference communities. For instance, grammatical inference algorithm algorithms often relies on Myhill-Nerode theorem, which is closely linked with equivalence problem (for example, see [12] for a learning algorithm for a class of word transducers). So far, there lack results on type checking, minimization, and learnability.

References

1. Alur, R.: Marrying words and trees. ACM SIGMOD-SIGACT-SIGART SPDS 26, 233–242 (2007)
2. Alur, R., Madhusudan, P.: Visibly pushdown languages. ACM STC 36, 202–211 (2004)
3. Champavère, J., Gilleron, R., Lemay, A., Niehren, J.: Efficient Inclusion Checking for Deterministic Tree Automata and DTDs. In: Martín-Vide, C., Otto, F., Fernau, H. (eds.) LATA 2008. LNCS, vol. 5196, pp. 184–195. Springer, Heidelberg (2008)
4. Comon, H., Dauchet, M., Gilleron, R., Löding, C., Jacquemard, F., Lugiez, D., Tison, S., Tommas, M.: Tree Auto. Tech. and App. online (revised 2007)
5. Engelfriet, J., Maneth, S., Seidl, H.: Deciding Equiv. of Top-Down XML Transformations in Poly. Time. Journal of Comp. and Syst. Sci. (to appear, 2009)
6. Gauwin, O., Niehren, J., Roos, Y.: Streaming tree automata. IPL 109(1), 13–17 (2008)
7. Culik II, K., Karhumäki, J.: Synchronizable deterministic pushdown automata and the decidability of their equivalence. Acta Inf. 23(5), 597–605 (1986)
8. Maneth. S.: Models of Tree Translation. PhD Thesis
9. Maneth, S., Berlea, A., Perst, T., Seidl, H.: Type checking with macro tree transducers. ACM SPDS 24, 283–294 (2005)
10. Martens, W., Neven, F.: Typechecking top-down uniform unranked tree transducers. In: Calvanese, D., Lenzerini, M., Motwani, R. (eds.) ICDT 2003. LNCS, vol. 2572, pp. 64–78. Springer, Heidelberg (2002)
11. Neumann, A., Seidl, H.: Locating matches of tree patterns in forests. Found. of Soft. Tech. and Theor. Comp. Sci., 134–145 (1998)
12. Oncina, J., Garcia, P., Vidal, E.: Learn. Subseq. Transd. for Patt. Recogn. and Interpretation Tasks. Trans. on Patt. Anal. and Mach. Intel. 15, 448–458 (1993)
13. Plandowski, W.: Testing Equivalence of Morphisms on Context-Free Languages. In: van Leeuwen, J. (ed.) ESA 1994. LNCS, vol. 855, pp. 460–470. Springer, Heidelberg (1994)
14. Karhumäki, J., Plandowski, W., Rytter, W.: Polynomial Size Test Sets for Context-Free Languages. J. Comput. Syst. Sci. 50(1), 11–19 (1995)

15. Raskin, J.-F., Servais, F.: Visibly pushdown transducers. In: Aceto, L., Damgård, I., Goldberg, L.A., Halldórsson, M.M., Ingólfsdóttir, A., Walukiewicz, I. (eds.) ICALP 2008, Part II. LNCS, vol. 5126, pp. 386–397. Springer, Heidelberg (2008)
16. Sénizergues, G.: The equivalence problem for deterministic pushdown automata is decidable. In: Degano, P., Gorrieri, R., Marchetti-Spaccamela, A. (eds.) ICALP 1997. LNCS, vol. 1256, pp. 671–681. Springer, Heidelberg (1997)
17. Tozawa, A., Minamide, Y.: Complexity results on balanced context-free languages. In: Seidl, H. (ed.) FOSSACS 2007. LNCS, vol. 4423, pp. 346–360. Springer, Heidelberg (2007)

Reachability in $K_{3,3}$-Free Graphs and K_5-Free Graphs Is in Unambiguous Log-Space

Thomas Thierauf[1] and Fabian Wagner[2],[*]

[1] Fak. Elektronik und Informatik, HTW Aalen, 73430 Aalen, Germany
[2] Inst. für Theoretische Informatik, Universität Ulm, 89069 Ulm, Germany
{thomas.thierauf,fabian.wagner}@uni-ulm.de

Abstract. We show that the reachability problem for directed graphs that are either $K_{3,3}$-free or K_5-free is in unambiguous log-space, UL ∩ coUL. This significantly extends the result of Bourke, Tewari, and Vinodchandran that the reachability problem for directed planar graphs is in UL ∩ coUL.

1 Introduction

For undirected graphs, the reachability problem is L-complete [8] and for general graphs it is NL-complete. The reachability problem on planar graphs is in UL ∩ coUL and is hard for L [3]. These results are built on work of [9] and [1].

We study reachability on extensions of planar graphs. Our main result is that reachability for directed $K_{3,3}$-free graphs and directed K_5-free graphs log-space-reduces to planar reachability. Thus, both problems are in UL ∩ coUL. One motivation for our results clearly is to improve the complexity upper bounds of certain reachability problems, from NL to UL in this case. Another aspect is that thereby we also consider the relationship of complexity classes, namely of UL vs. NL. The major open question is whether one can extend our results further such that we finally get a collapse of NL to UL.

In the case of a $K_{3,3}$-free graph G, our technique is to decompose G into biconnected components which are further decomposed into planar triconnected components and K_5-components. We construct a tree where the nodes are associated with these components (cf. [12]), the PlaK₅-*component tree*.

For reachability from vertices s to t in graph G we consider the simple path P in the PlaK₅-component tree from component nodes S to T, where s and t are contained. We split the graph into components along the separating pairs we have on path P. A s-t-path must contain vertices of all these separating pairs and we have to test reachability on all these components. The crucial step is to replace all the K_5-components in the tree by planar components such that the reachability is not changed. Then we recombine the planar components into a planar graph H such that there is a path from s to t in G if and only if this holds too in H. The construction can be carried out in log-space.

[*] Supported by DFG grant TO 200/2-2.

M. Kutyłowski, M. Gębala, and W. Charatonik (Eds.): FCT 2009, LNCS 5699, pp. 323–334, 2009.

There also exists a decomposition of K_5-free graphs (cf. Khuller [6]). This is obtained by decomposing the graph into triconnected components. Each triconnected component is either planar, the four-rung Mobius ladder, also called V_8, or it is constructed by taking 3-clique sums of planar 4-connected components [13]. We replace the V_8-components by planar components such that the reachability is not changed. Then we recombine the planar components into a planar graph. A difficulty that arises here is that we cannot use the 3-clique sum operation to recombine the components, because this would result again in a non-planar graph. Instead, we carefully add copies of the components that can be arranged in a planar way such that the reachability is not altered. All the steps can be accomplished in log-space.

Our transformations from $K_{3,3}$-free or K_5-free graphs to planar graphs also maintain the distances of the vertices. Hence, distances in $K_{3,3}$- or K_5-free graphs can be computed in $\mathsf{UL} \cap \mathsf{coUL}$. The same is true for longest paths when considering directed acyclic graphs (DAG's), but this requires some extra arguments.

In Section 3 we prove that reachability on $K_{3,3}$-free graphs reduces to planar reachability. In Section 4 we prove that reachability on K_5-free graphs reduces to planar reachability. We omit proofs of lemmas for space reasons, which are provided in the full version of the paper.

2   Definitions and Notations

Let $G = (V, E)$ be a graph. For $U \subseteq V$ let $G \setminus U$ be the *induced subgraph* of G on $V \setminus U$. Let $S \subseteq V$ with $|S| = k$. S is a *k-separating set* if $G \setminus S$ is not connected. The vertices of a k-separating set are called *articulation point (or cut vertex)* for $k = 1$, *separating pair* for $k = 2$, and *separating triple* for $k = 3$. G is *k-connected* if it contains no $(k-1)$-separating set. A 1-connected graph is simply called *connected*. The connected components of $G \setminus S$ are called the *split components of S*. We also say that S *separates* u from v if $u \in S$, $v \in S$, or u and v are in different components of $G \setminus S$. A $K_{3,3}$-free graph (K_5-free graph) is an undirected graph which does not contain a $K_{3,3}$ (or K_5) as a minor.

Tree Decomposition of Connected Planar Graphs. We decompose the connected graph G into biconnected components, and define the *biconnected component tree* based on these components (see [5]). There is a node in the tree for each maximal biconnected component of G and for each articulation point. An *articulation point node* is connected to a *biconnected component node* if the articulation point is contained as vertex in the biconnected component. In the special case that two articulation points u, v are adjacent, there is a component node which consists of one edge $\{u, v\}$. This node is connected to the articulation point nodes for u and v. The biconnected component tree of an undirected graph can be computed in log-space.

Tree Decomposition of Biconnected Planar Graphs. For biconnected graphs, Hopcroft and Tarjan [5] introduced the decomposition into separating pairs and *triconnected components*. The latter are essentially maximal 3-connected components and, for technical reasons, *cycles* and *3-bonds*.

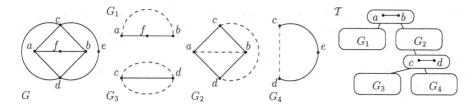

Fig. 1. [4] The decomposition of G into triconnected components $G_1, \ldots, G_4$ and the triconnected component tree $\mathcal{T}$. The dashed lines are virtual edges. The separating pairs are $\{a, b\}$ and $\{c, d\}$. Since $\{c, d\}$ is connected by an edge in G, we also get $\{c, d\}$ as triple-bond G_3. The virtual edges corresponding to the 3-connected separating pairs are drawn with dashed lines.

Hopcroft and Tarjan proved that this decomposition has a tree structure. We define the *triconnected component tree* that has these components as nodes similar to that of [4]. There is an edge between the *separating pair node* for $\{a, b\}$ and the *triconnected component node* for C, if $\{a, b\}$ is contained in C (connected by a *virtual edge*). The resulting graph on these nodes is a tree $\mathcal{T}$ which is rooted at an arbitrary separating pair. For an example see Figure 1. Datta et. al. [4] showed that when the graph is in addition *planar*, then the triconnected component tree can be computed in log-space. In the full version, we extend this to non-planar graphs.

Let $\mathcal{T}$ be a biconnected or a triconnected component tree. We define the size of such a tree. The *size of an individual component node* of $\mathcal{T}$ is the number of nodes in the component. The *size of the tree* $\mathcal{T}$, denoted by $|\mathcal{T}|$, is the sum of the sizes of its component nodes. Let $\mathcal{T}_C$ be a component tree rooted at an arbitrary node C and let $\mathcal{T}_{C'}$ be a subtree of $\mathcal{T}$ rooted at a child C' of C. We call C' a *large child* of C, if $|\mathcal{T}_{C'}| > |\mathcal{T}_C|/2$.

Complexity. L (log-space) is the class of languages accepted by *deterministic* and NL (respectively UL) by (*unambiguous*) *nondeterministic* log-space Turing-machines. Unambiguous means, there exists at most one accepting computation path. coUL is the class of complements of languages in UL. We also use the fact that $\mathsf{L}^{\mathsf{UL} \cap \mathsf{coUL}} = \mathsf{UL} \cap \mathsf{coUL}$ (c.f. Thierauf and Wagner [10]). We denote *log-space many-one reductions* by $\leq_m^L$ and *log-space Turing reductions* by $\leq_T^L$.

3   Reachability in $K_{3,3}$-Free Graphs

We give a log-space reduction from the reachability problem for directed $K_{3,3}$-free graphs to the reachability problem for directed planar graphs which is known to be in $\mathsf{UL} \cap \mathsf{coUL}$ [3].

For the reduction, we decompose the given graph G into triconnected components. For the decomposition, we consider G as *undirected*. That is, each directed edge of G is considered as an undirected edge. After the decomposition we consider the components again as directed graphs.

Tree Decomposition. We consider the decomposition of biconnected $K_{3,3}$-free graphs into triconnected components. Tutte [11] proved that the decomposition is unique. Moreover, Asano [2] proved that it has the following form.

Lemma 1. [2] *Each triconnected component of a $K_{3,3}$-free graph is planar or exactly the graph K_5.*

The triconnected components are the nodes of the triconnected component tree. For our purpose it suffices to distinguish between planar and non-planar components. Vazirani [12] recombines the *planar* triconnected components that are neighbors in the tree into one planar component. This defines a new tree with alternating planar and K_5-component nodes which we call the PlaK$_5$-*component tree*. Vazirani [12] showed that the PlaK$_5$-component tree is unique and can be computed in NC$_2$. Here we give a simpler and more direct construction that works in log-space.

Lemma 2. *Let $G = (V, E)$ be a $K_{3,3}$-free biconnected undirected graph. A set $K \subseteq V$ of 5 vertices is a K_5-minor in G if and only if for every pair $u, v \in K$ either $\{u, v\} \in E$ or $\{u, v\}$ is a separating pair in G such that the three remaining vertices of K are all in one split component of $G \setminus \{u, v\}$.*

As a consequence, we can compute all the K_5-components of a biconnected undirected graph in log-space: cycle through all the $\binom{n}{5}$ sets of 5 vertices and check the condition of Lemma 2 for each set. With the K_5-components in hand, we show that we can compute the PlaK$_5$-component tree in log-space. For proof details we refer to the full version of the paper.

Theorem 1. *The decomposition of a $K_{3,3}$-free biconnected graph into a PlaK$_5$-component tree can be computed in log-space.*[1]

Reduction to the Planar Case. We construct a reduction from the reachability problem for directed $K_{3,3}$-free graphs to the reachability problem for directed planar graphs.

Theorem 2. $K_{3,3}$-*free reachability $\leq_T^L$ planar reachability.*

It suffices to consider *biconnected* directed $K_{3,3}$-free graphs, because a path from s to t visits all articulation points which separate s from t.

Lemma 3. *Reachability $\leq_T^L$ biconnected reachability.*

Let $G = (V, E)$ be a biconnected directed $K_{3,3}$-free graph and s, t be two vertices in G. Let $\mathcal{T}_G$ be the PlaK$_5$-component tree of G. Let S be the biconnected component that contains s and T the one that contains t.

We partition the tree into subtrees and consider the reachability problem for these subtrees. Then we replace *non-planar* components of $\mathcal{T}_G$ by *planar* components such that the reachability condition remains unchanged.

---

[1] The result came up in discussion with Samir Datta, Nutan Limaye, and Prajakta Nimbhorkar. The proof presented here was developed in this paper.

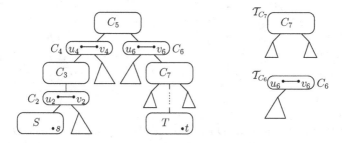

Fig. 2. Partitioning of the PlaK$_5$-component tree $\mathcal{T}_G$ into pieces $\mathcal{T}_{C_i}$. The boxes indicate component nodes and the triangles indicate subtrees.

Partitioning of G into Subgraphs. Consider the simple path from S to T in $\mathcal{T}_G$, say $S = C_1, C_2, \ldots, C_l = T$. A path from s to t always contains vertices of separating pairs, say $\{u_i, v_i\}$, which are shared by the component nodes C_{i-1} and C_{i+1}. For an example see Figure 2. A path p from s to t must visit at least one vertex of each of these separating pairs. Once we have reached C_i, then p will not go back to C_{i-1}, because otherwise p would not be simple. On the other hand, p can pass through one sibling of C_{i-1} before it goes to the parent C_{i+1}.

We partition the reachability problem into subproblems. For a component node C_i define the tree $\mathcal{T}_{C_i}$ as the subtree of $\mathcal{T}_G$ rooted at C_i, where the branches to C_{i-1} and C_{i+1} are cut off. Let G_i be the graph corresponding to $\mathcal{T}_{C_i}$.

Lemma 4. *Any simple path p from s to t in G can be written as a concatenation of paths, $p = p_1, \ldots, p_l$, such that*

- *path p_1 goes from s to u_2 or v_2 in G_1,*
- *path p_i is a path from u_{i-1} or v_{i-1} to u_{i+1} or v_{i+1} in G_i, $i \in \{3, 5, \ldots, l-2\}$*
- *path p_i is a path from u_i or v_i to u_i or v_i in G_i, for all $i \in \{2, 4, \ldots, l-1\}$*
- *path p_l is a path from u_{l-1} or v_{l-1} to t in G_l.*

In the reachability problems for G_i, we search for a path from u_{i-1} (or v_{i-1}) to u_{i+1} (or v_{i+1}). Each separating pair is connected by a virtual edge. If C_i is a separating pair node $\{u_i, v_i\}$, then we have to check whether there is a path from u_i to v_i or vice versa in G_i.

Lemma 5. *There is a path from u_{i-1} or v_{i-1} to u_{i+1} or v_{i+1} in G_i if and only if there exists a path in C_i such that for virtual edges $\{a, b\}$ on this path there exists a path from a to b in the child component of C_i.*

Because we have K_5-component nodes, it is not clear yet, how we can test reachability in UL∩coUL. We transform the $K_{3,3}$-free graph into a planar graph.

Transforming a K$_5$-Component into a Planar Component. Let $\mathcal{T}_{C_i}$ be a PlaK$_5$-component tree rooted at C_i as described above. We start with the root C_i and traverse the tree in depth first manner. When we reach a K_5-component node D, then we replace it by a planar component D' as described next such that the reachability problem does not change. This results in a new component tree of a planar graph G'.

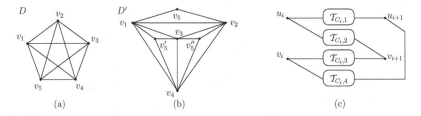

Fig. 3. (a) A K_5-component node D and (b) the planar component node D' where v_5' and v_5'' are copies of v_5. For example, an edge (v_1, v_5) in D occurs twice in D', as (v_1, v_5) and (v_1, v_5'). The edges of D and D' are drawn undirected to not overload the picture. Note that only the virtual edges are undirected. (c) The construction if D is the root of $\mathcal{T}_{C_i}$. Because there are four reachability problems, we have four versions of D, say $D_1, \ldots, D_4$ which replace the root in $\mathcal{T}_{C_i}$. This leads to four trees $\mathcal{T}_{C_i,1}, \ldots, \mathcal{T}_{C_i,4}$. The resulting graph is planar.

Lemma 6. *There is a log-space algorithm that transforms G into a planar graph G' such that there is a path from s to t in G if and only if there is such a path in G'.*

Let D be a K_5-component node with vertices $v_1, \ldots, v_5$. Let $\mathcal{T}_{C_i}$ be the subtree that contains D. Let N be the size of the subtree rooted at D in $\mathcal{T}_{C_i}$. Since our algorithm works recursively and in order to have a log-space bound, we would like to have recursive calls only on subtrees of small size, i.e. a fraction of N. Recall, that there can be at most one large child. In the following, we consider the situation that we search a path from v_1 to v_2 in D and we have a large child at v_3, v_4. The same construction works if there is no large child, and it can be easily adapted to the case that the large child is at another pair. The graph D' is defined as shown in Figure 3 and has the following properties:

1. D' is planar.
2. Every path from v_1 to v_2 in D exists as well in D', possibly going through one of the copies v_5' or v_5'' instead of v_5.
3. D' contains the edge $\{v_3, v_4\}$ once. Thus we visit a large child only once.
4. Vertices v_1 and v_2 are on the outer face of D'.

The last property is important for the special case when D is the root of the subtree, i.e. $D = C_i$. Then we have two vertices u_i, v_i and ask whether we can reach two other vertices u_{i+1} and v_{i+1} and all these vertices belong to D. For a planar arrangement, we make the construction as shown in Figure 3 (c). For example, D_1 is a copy of D where v_1 is identified with u_i and v_2 with u_{i+1}. In total, this gives four combinations of reachability questions. Hence, we make four copies of the whole planar graph corresponding to $\mathcal{T}_{C_i}$, one for each path from a vertex of the incoming separating pair to a vertex of the outgoing separating pair. Note, that this case can occur only at the root, and not in the recursion in the tree $\mathcal{T}_{C_i}$. Therefore, we can afford to make the four copies. The replacement of the K_5-components is done recursively in depth-first manner with all the copies of children (i.e. the subtrees rooted at separating pairs) which we have in the new components D'. Consequently, we give new names to vertices in the copies of the subtrees.

We do this for all edges on all paths in D'. The order of the edges is given by the order in which they appear on the input tape. We can always recompute the new planar component D', because we can recompute the sizes of the subtrees of D. We can always refer to which copy of a separating pair we went into recursion by storing $O(1)$ bits on the work-tape when we go into recursion. Hence, whenever we have to change vertex names, we can recompute the new vertex names of the copy of a separating pair. We need such bits at each level of recursion. Since the sizes of the copied subtrees are at most $1/2$ the size of the tree, there are at most logarithmically many levels of recursion. Hence, the algorithm runs in log-space. Let N be the size of the $\mathsf{PlaK_5}$-component tree of G.

Lemma 7. *The resulting graph G' after the transformation of the K_5 components is planar, has size $\mathcal{S}(N)$ polynomial in N and there are simple paths from u_i or v_i to u_{i+1} or v_{i+1} in G_i if and only if there are corresponding simple paths in G'.*

For some constant k we get the following space bound for G':

$$\mathcal{S}(N) = k \cdot \mathcal{S}(N/2) + O(N)$$

Hence, $\mathcal{S}(N)$ is polynomial in N. This finishes the proof of Theorem 2.

Corollary 1. $K_{3,3}$*-free reachability is in* $\mathsf{UL} \cap \mathsf{coUL}$.

4   Reachability in K_5-Free Graphs

We give a log-space reduction from the reachability problem for directed K_5-free graphs to the reachability problem for directed planar graphs. For the reduction, we decompose the given graph G into 3-connected and 4-connected components. For the decomposition we consider G as undirected. It follows from a theorem of Wagner [13] that besides planar components we also obtain non-planar components this way: The four-rung Mobius ladder, also called V_8 (see Figure 4), a 3-connected graph on 8 vertices, which is non-planar because it contains a $K_{3,3}$. The remaining 3-connected non-planar components are further decomposed into 4-connected components which are all planar.

The key step in the reduction is to replace the V_8-components by planar components similar as for the K_5. For the remaining non-planar components we define trees for a decomposition into 4-connected components. We will show, that this can be done in log-space.

4.1   The Tree Decomposition

Khuller [6] described a decomposition of K_5-free graphs with a clique-sum operation. If two graphs G_1 and G_2 each contain cliques of equal size, the *clique-sum* of G_1 and G_2 is a graph G formed from their disjoint union by identifying pairs of vertices in these two cliques to form a single shared clique, and then possibly deleting some of the clique edges. A $(\leq k)$-*clique-sum* is a clique-sum in which both cliques have *at most* k vertices. If G can be constructed by repeatedly taking $(\leq k)$-clique-sums starting from graphs isomorphic to members of some graph class $\mathcal{G}$ then we say $G \in \langle \mathcal{G} \rangle_k$.

Theorem 3. [13] *Let $\mathcal{C}$ be the class of all planar graphs together with the four-rung Mobius ladder V_8. Then $\langle \mathcal{C} \rangle_3$ is the class of all graphs with no K_5-minor.*

Note, some of the clique sum operations, e.g. those in which both cliques have one or two vertices, lead to planar graphs which are not 3-connected. Therefore, we decompose planar graphs into 3-connected components in beforehand. We make two easy observations with respect to the above clique-sum operation. If we built the (≤ 3)-clique-sum of two 3-connected planar graphs, then the three vertices of the joint clique are a separating triple in the resulting graph. Hence, the 4-connected components of a graph which is built as the 3-clique-sum of planar graphs must all be planar. The V_8 is non-planar and 3-connected, but not 4-connected. Furthermore, the V_8 cannot be part of a 3-clique sum operation where all the tree vertices are chosen from the V_8. By Theorem 3 and the two observations we have the following situation.

Corollary 2. (cf. [6]) *A 3-connected non-planar component of a K_5-free undirected graph is either the V_8 or its 4-connected components are all planar.*

In the following we argue that the 3-connected and 4-connected components can be computed in log-space. Similar to the decomposition algorithm of Vazirani [12], we decompose the K_5-free graph into triconnected components. That is, we first decompose it into biconnected components and then these components further into triconnected components. This can be done in log-space.

The Triconnected Component Tree for Biconnected K_5-Free Graphs. Datta et.al. [4] show how to construct the triconnected component tree for a planar biconnected graph in log-space. We give a different construction which is suitable for K_5-free biconnected graphs. The difference is, that the 3-connected components must not be planar. Equivalently, we define the *triconnected component tree $\mathcal{T}$* for a K_5-free biconnected graph G which also contains nodes for non-planar triconnected components.

Lemma 8. *The triconnected component tree for a K_5-free biconnected graph can be computed in log-space.*

Decomposition into 4-Connected Components. It remains to further decompose the 3-connected components which are non-planar and not the V_8. We decompose such a component C into 4-connected components. Intuitively, we start with a root separating triple and recursively decompose a split component at those separating triples which split off subgraphs of maximum size. The resulting components are 4-connected.

We define a tree T with nodes for separating triples and the 4-connected components. A *separating triple node* is connected to a *4-connected component node* if the separating triple is contained in the 4-connected component. Choose one separating triple τ_{root} in C as the root node of T. The resulting graph is a tree, the *4-connected component tree of C*.

Lemma 9. *The 4-connected component tree of a 3-connected K_5-free graph can be computed in log-space.*

4.2 Reachability on K_5-Free Graphs

Theorem 4. K_5-*free reachability* $\leq_m^L$ *planar reachability.*

Let G be a connected graph and s and t be two vertices in G. By Lemma 3 and Lemma 5, we can partition the reachability problem for G into reachability problems on the triconnected components of G. If it is non-planar, then we distinguish the two cases whether the triconnected component is the V_8 or not.

In a triconnected component tree, a triconnected component has an incoming separating pair $\{u_i, v_i\}$ and an outgoing separating pair $\{u_{i+1}, v_{i+1}\}$. We consider four reachability tests, from u_i to u_{i+1}, from u_i to v_{i+1}, from v_i to u_{i+1} and from v_i to v_{i+1}. For each of these reachability tests, we construct a planar copy of the triconnected non-planar component and connect them as shown in Figure 3 (c) on page 328.

Transforming a V_8-Component into a Planar Component. Let $\mathcal{T}_C$ be a triconnected component tree rooted at some node C. Let D be a V_8-component node in $\mathcal{T}_C$ and $v_1, \ldots, v_8$ the vertices in D. We transform D into a planar component D' such that the reachability question remains unchanged. The transformation is shown in Figure 4. For this, let $v_1, \ldots, v_4$ be four vertices in D such that v_1, v_2 are pairwise different. Assume, that we search for a path from v_1 to v_2 in D and that $\{v_3, v_4\}$ is a virtual edge in D which corresponds to a large child of D. By construction, D' has the following properties.

- For each path from v_1 to v_2 that does *not* contain $\{v_3, v_4\}$, D' contains a copy of this path, i.e. a copy of all vertices and edges on this path.
- For all paths from v_1 to v_2 containing $\{v_3, v_4\}$, D' contains a copy of the sub-path from v_1 to v_3 and v_4 to v_2 or vice versa from v_1 to v_4 and v_3 to v_2.
- D' contains the virtual edge $\{v_3, v_4\}$ exactly once.
- v_1 and v_2 are both on the outer-face of D'. This property is important in the case, that D is the root of $\mathcal{T}_C$ (i.e. $D = C$).
- D' with all copies of paths is planar and contains $O(1)$ copies of each edge.

The replacement of the V_8-components is done recursively in depth-first manner with all the copies of children (i.e. the subtrees rooted at separating pairs) which we have in the new components D'. Consequently, we give new names to vertices in the copies of the subtrees. We do this for all edges on all paths in D'. The order of the edges is given by the order in which they appear on the input

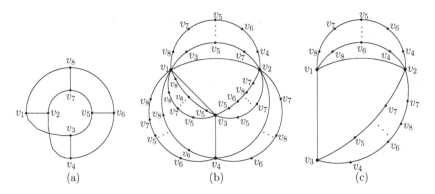

Fig. 4. To simplify matters, we do not identify copies of vertices which share the same label. (a) The V_8 component D with edges drawn undirected. (b) The planar component D' is shown schematically. We consider $\{v_1, v_2\} \cap \{v_3, v_4\} = \emptyset$ where paths from v_1 to v_2 are copied. Paths containing $\{v_3, v_4\}$ are indicated in the part below $\{v_1, v_2\}$. (c) D' in the case that (v_1, v_3) is the large child.

tape. We can always recompute the new planar component D', because we can recompute the sizes of subtrees of D. We can always recompute from which copy of a separating pair we went into recursion by storing $O(1)$ bits on the work-tape when we go into recursion. So, when we have to change vertex names, then we can recompute the new vertex names of the copied separating pair. We need such bits at each level of recursion. Since the sizes of the copied subtrees are at most $1/2$ the size of the tree, there are at most logarithmically many levels of recursion. Hence, the algorithm runs in log-space and the resulting planar graph is of size polynomial in the size of the given graph.

Planar Arrangement of Split Components in a 4-Connected Component Tree. After the replacement of V_8-components by planar components, we have to consider the other non-planar 3-connected components. We have decomposed them into planar 4-connected components. We have to recombine all the components into one planar graph. However, we cannot simply reverse the decomposition process because the 3-clique sum of the 4-connected (planar) components could result in a non-planar 3-connected component. To get around this problem we make copies of some of the components and arrange the copies in a planar way. This has to be done carefully such that the size of the graph constructed that way stays polynomial in the size of the input graph.

Consider a 4-connected component tree $\mathcal{T}$. Let S and T be the component nodes in $\mathcal{T}$ where vertices s and t are contained in, respectively. Consider S as the root of $\mathcal{T}$ i.e., let $\mathcal{T}_S = \mathcal{T}$ and let P be a simple path from S to T in $\mathcal{T}_S$. We describe how to find a planar arrangement of the components of $\mathcal{T}_S$. We start by putting the component S in the new planar arrangement. Inductively assume that we have put some component C and let τ be a child node of C in $\mathcal{T}_S$. Let furthermore the children of τ be the nodes $C_1, \ldots, C_k$. Precisely one of the children is put once in the planar arrangement, the other children are put

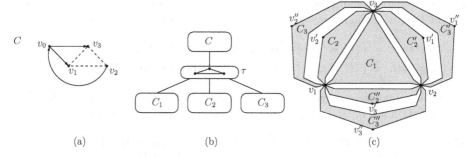

Fig. 5. (a) A planar 4-connected component C with separating triple $\tau = \{v_1, v_2, v_3\}$. The edges of τ are virtual edges, indicated with dashed lines. (b) The 4-connected component tree with nodes C, τ and its children, C_1, C_2 and C_3. (c) The planar arrangement of C_1, C_2 and C_3 at τ is obtained by making copies of C_2 and C_3 (i.e. C_2', C_2'' and C_3', C_3'') and vertices v_i (i.e. v_i', v_i'') for $1 \leq i \leq 3$.

three times, i.e. there are two additional copies which are connected to copies of the vertices of τ. Figure 5 shows the construction. By G' we denote the resulting planar arranged graph which we obtain for G.

The construction does not change the reachability properties. For example, if there is a path from v_1 to v_2 in G which goes through the component C_2 and also passes v_3, then there will be a path from v_1 to v_2 in G' which goes through the copy C_2'' of C_2 and passes the copy v_3'' instead of v_3. If there is no path from v_1 to v_2 in G then there is no path from v_1 to v_2 in the constructed planar graph either. The child which is put only once is selected as follows:

1. If a child C_i of τ is a node on path P then we select C_i.
2. If no child of τ is a node on P but there is a large child C_j then we select C_j.
3. Otherwise, we select an arbitrary component, say C_1.

Let N be the size of the triconnected component tree rooted at node C. We emphasize that in case 1, if a large child is copied three times because another child of τ is on path P then this situation does not occur recursively, because the ancestors of the copied large child do not belong to P. Hence, the planar arranged graph G' is of polynomial size $\mathcal{S}(N)$, because we just copy recursively subgraphs of size smaller than $N/2$ even if we consider the exception of case 1. The recursion equation is again $\mathcal{S}(N) = k \cdot \mathcal{S}(N/2) + O(N)$ for some constant k. Also, with similar arguments this construction gives a log-space algorithm, (i.e. in each of the $O(\log n)$ levels of recursion we store $O(1)$ bits on the work-tape). This finishes the proof of Theorem 4. Since reachability for planar graphs is in UL $\cap$ coUL [3], we get the following corollary.

Corollary 3. K_5-free reachability is in UL $\cap$ coUL.

Further Results. The graph transformations increase the number of simple paths between incoming and outgoing vertices of a component, but the *distances* between vertices remain the same. Although it is not as obvious, the same is true for the length of the *longest simple paths* between vertices in DAG's. Let

$$\text{Distance} = \{\, (G, s, t, k) \mid G \text{ contains a } s\text{-}t\text{-path of length } \leq k \,\},$$
$$\text{Long-Path} = \{\, (G, s, t, k) \mid G \text{ contains a simple } s\text{-}t\text{-path of length } \geq k \,\}.$$

Since the distance problem for planar graphs and the longest path problem for planar DAGs are in UL ∩ coUL [7,10], we get the following corollary.

Corollary 4. Distance *for $K_{3,3}$-free and K_5-free graphs is in* UL ∩ coUL. Long-Path *for $K_{3,3}$-free and K_5-free DAGs is in* UL ∩ coUL.

Acknowledgment. We thank S. Datta, N. Limaye, P. Nimbhorkar, M. Szegedy, R. Tewari, J. Torán and the referees for comments and helpful discussions.

References

1. Allender, E., Datta, S., Roy, S.: The directed planar reachability problem. In: Sarukkai, S., Sen, S. (eds.) FSTTCS 2005. LNCS, vol. 3821, pp. 238–249. Springer, Heidelberg (2005)
2. Asano, T.: An approach to the subgraph homeomorphism problem. Theoretical Computer Science 38 (1985)
3. Bourke, C., Tewari, R., Vinodchandran, N.: Directed planar reachability is in unambiguous log-space. In: Annual IEEE Conference on Computational Complexity (CCC), pp. 217–221 (2007)
4. Datta, S., Limaye, N., Nimbhorkar, P., Thierauf, T., Wagner, F.: Planar graph isomorphism is in log-space. Technical report, arXiv:0809.2319v2 (2009)
5. Hopcroft, J.E., Tarjan, R.E.: Dividing a graph into triconnected components. SIAM Journal on Computing 2(3), 135–158 (1973)
6. Khuller, S.: Parallel algorithms for K_5-minor free graphs. Technical Report TR88-909, Cornell University, Computer Science Department (1988)
7. Limaye, N., Mahajan, M., Nimbhorkar, P.: Longest paths in planar dags in unambiguous logspace. In: Computing: The Australian Theory Symposium (CATS), vol. 94 (2009)
8. Reingold, O.: Undirected st-connectivity in log-space. In: Proceedings of the 37th annual ACM Symposium on Theory of Computing (STOC), pp. 376–385 (2005)
9. Reinhardt, K., Allender, E.: Making nondeterminism unambiguous. SIAM Journal of Computing 29(4), 1118–1131 (2000)
10. Thierauf, T., Wagner, F.: The isomorphism problem for planar 3-connected graphs is in unambiguous logspace. In: Proceedings of the 25th Annual Symposium on Theoretical Aspects of Computer Science (STACS), pp. 633–644 (2008)
11. Tutte, W.T.: Connectivity in graphs. University of Toronto Press (1966)
12. Vazirani, V.V.: NC algorithms for computing the number of perfect matchings in $K_{3,3}$-free graphs and related problems. Information and Computation 80 (1989)
13. Wagner, K.: Über eine Eigenschaft der ebenen Komplexe. In: Mathematical Annalen, vol. 114 (1937)

Energy Complexity and Depth of Threshold Circuits

Kei Uchizawa[1,*], Takao Nishizeki[1], and Eiji Takimoto[2,**]

[1] Graduate School of Information Sciences, Tohoku University, Aramaki Aoba-aza
6-6-05, Aoba-ku, Sendai, 980-8579, Japan
[2] Department of Informatics, Graduate School of Information Science and Electrical
Engineering, Kyushu University, 744 Motooka, Nishi-ku, Fukuoka 819-0395, Japan
{uchizawa,nishi}@ecei.tohoku.ac.jp, eiji@i.kyushu-u.ac.jp

Abstract. In the paper we show that there is a close relationship between the energy complexity and the depth of threshold circuits computing any Boolean function although they have completely different
physical meanings. Suppose that a Boolean function f can be computed
by a threshold circuit C of energy complexity e and hence at most e
threshold gates in C output "1" for any input to C. We then prove that
the function f can be computed also by a threshold circuit C' of depth
$2e + 1$ and hence the parallel computation time of C' is $2e + 1$. If the size
of C is s, that is, there are s threshold gates in C, then the size s' of C'
is $s' = 2es + 1$. Thus, if the size s of C is polynomial in the number n of
input variables, then the size s' of C' is polynomial in n, too.

1 Introduction

A threshold (logic) gate is a theoretical model of a neuron, and a threshold
(logic) circuit, which is a combinatorial circuit consisting of threshold gates, is a
theoretical model of a neural circuit in the brain. A threshold circuit is intensively
studied for a few decades [1,2,3,4,5]. Information processing in a neural circuit
results from "firing" of neurons. Recent studies in biology report that a neuron
consumes a large amount of energy for firing, and consequently the firing rate
of neurons is quiet low[6,7]. Based on the fact above, the *energy complexity* e
of a threshold circuit C is defined as the maximum number of threshold gates
outputting "1" over all inputs to C[8]. There have been known several results
on the energy complexity of threshold circuits [8,9,10], and it turns out that the
energy complexity e of C has a close relationship with other major complexity
measures such as the size s and the depth d; the *size* s of C is the number of
threshold gates in C; and the *depth* d of C is the length of the longest directed
path going from an input node to the output gate in C, and corresponds to the
parallel computation time. In particular, there is a tradeoff $n \leq s^e$ between the
size s and the energy complexity e of threshold circuits computing the PARITY

* Supported by MEXT Grant-in-Aid for Young Scientists (B) No.21700003.
** Supported by MEXT Grant-in-Aid for Scientific Research (C) No.20500001.

M. Kutyłowski, M. Gębala, and W. Charatonik (Eds.): FCT 2009, LNCS 5699, pp. 335–345, 2009.
© Springer-Verlag Berlin Heidelberg 2009

function of n variables [10]. On the other hand, there is a tradeoff $n \leq 2s^{d-1}$ between the size s and the depth d of threshold circuits computing the PARITY function [11], and a tradeoff $n \leq (s/d)^{d-\epsilon}$ also holds for any $\epsilon > 0$ [12]. In all these tradeoffs, the left hand side is the number n of input variables, while either the energy complexity e or the depth d appears in the exponent of s in the right hand side. Thus the two measures, energy e and depth d, play the similar role in the tradeoffs at least for circuits computing the PARITY function, although the two measures have completely different physical meanings. Thus, the energy complexity e seems to have a close relationship with the depth d not only for the circuits computing the PARITY function but also for circuits computing any Boolean function.

In the paper, we investigate a relationship between the energy complexity and the depth of threshold circuits computing any Boolean function, and obtain the following result as the main theorem: if a Boolean function f can be computed by a threshold circuit C of energy complexity e, then f can be computed also by a threshold circuit C' of depth $d' = 2e + 1$. If C has size s, then C' has size $s' = 2es + 1$. Thus, if a Boolean function of n variables can be computed by a threshold circuit C of constant energy complexity and polynomial size in n, then f can be computed also by a threshold circuit C' of constant depth and polynomial size. Since the proof of the main theorem is constructive, a threshold circuit C' of shallow depth can be immediately obtained from a circuit C of small energy complexity.

The rest of the paper is organized as follows. In Section 2, we first define some terms on threshold circuits, and then present the main theorem. In Section 3, we prove the main theorem. In Section 4, we conclude with some remarks.

2   Definitions and Main Theorem

In the section, we first define some terms on threshold circuits, and then present the main theorem and a corollary.

A *threshold gate* in the paper is the so-called linear threshold logic gate, and can have an arbitrary number k of inputs. For every input $\boldsymbol{z} = (z_1, z_2, \cdots, z_k) \in \{0,1\}^k$ to a threshold gate g with weights $w_1, w_2, \cdots, w_k$ and a threshold t, the output $g(\boldsymbol{z})$ of the gate g for $\boldsymbol{z}$ is defined as follows:

$$g(\boldsymbol{z}) = \begin{cases} 1 & \text{if } \sum_{i=1}^{k} w_i z_i \geq t; \\ 0 & \text{otherwise.} \end{cases}$$

We assume that the weights $w_1, w_2, \cdots, w_k$ and the threshold t are arbitrary real numbers.

A *threshold (logic) circuit* C is a combinatorial circuit consisting of threshold gates, and is represented by a directed acyclic graph, as illustrated in Figs. 1 and 2. We denote by n the number of inputs to C, and by $\boldsymbol{x} = (x_1, x_2, \cdots, x_n)$ the input variables to C. The underlying directed acyclic graph of C has n nodes of in-degree 0, each of which corresponds to one of the n input variables and is called an *input node*. The *size* s of a threshold circuit C is the number of threshold gates in C.

Let C be a threshold circuit of size s, and let $g_1, g_2, \cdots, g_s$ be the s gates in C. Then the input z_i to a gate g_i, $1 \leq i \leq s$, either consists of the inputs $x_1, x_2, \cdots, x_n$ to C and the outputs of the gates other than g_i or consists of some of them. However, we denote by $g_i[x]$ the output $g_i(z_i)$ of g_i for z_i, because x decides $g_i(z_i)$. Thus $g_i[x] = g_i(z_i)$.

Let $f : \{0,1\}^n \to \{0,1\}$ be a Boolean function of n variables. (Our main theorem can be immediately generalized to an m-output Boolean function $f : \{0,1\}^n \to \{0,1\}^m$ for any positive integer m, as stated in Section 4.) Let g_s be a gate of out-degree 0 in C, and let the output $g_s[x]$ of g_s be the *output* $C(x)$ *of* C. Thus, $C(x) = g_s[x]$ for every input $x \in \{0,1\}^n$. The gate g_s is called the *output gate* of C. A threshold circuit C *computes* a Boolean function $f : \{0,1\}^n \to \{0,1\}$ if $C(x) = f(x)$ for every input $x \in \{0,1\}^n$.

We say that a gate g_i, $1 \leq i \leq s$, is *in the l-th layer* of a circuit C if there are l gates (including g_i) on the longest path from an input node to g_i in the underlying graph of a circuit C. The *depth* d of C is the number of gates on the longest path to the output gate g_s.

For each input $x \in \{0,1\}^n$ to a circuit C, we denote by $e_C(x)$ the number of gates fired by x, that is,

$$e_C(x) = \sum_{i=1}^{s} g_i[x].$$

We then define the *energy complexity* e_C of C as

$$e_C = \max_{x \in \{0,1\}^n} e_C(x).$$

Thus, the energy complexity e_C is the maximum number of gates outputting "1" over all inputs $x \in \{0,1\}^n$. Obviously $0 \leq e_C \leq s$. We often denote $e_C(x)$ and e_C simply by $e(x)$ and e, respectively.

We are now ready to present our main result as the following theorem, whose proof will be given in the next section.

Theorem 1. *If a Boolean function f can be computed by a threshold circuit C of energy complexity e and size s, then f can be computed also by a threshold circuit C' of depth $d' = 2e + 1$ and size $s' = 2es + 1$.*

Since $s' = 2es + 1 \leq 2s^2 + 1$, s' is polynomial in n if s is polynomial in n. We thus have the following corollary.

Corollary 1. *If a Boolean function f can be computed by a polynomial-size threshold circuit C of energy complexity e, then f can be computed also by a polynomial-size threshold circuit C' of depth $d' = 2e + 1$.*

A Boolean function f is *non-trivial* if $f(x) = 1$ for some $x \in \{0,1\}^n$ and $f(x') = 0$ for some $x' \in \{0,1\}^n$. If f is non-trivial, then the upper bound $d' \leq 2e + 1$ on the depth d' of C' in Theorem 1 can be improved to $d' \leq 2e$, as

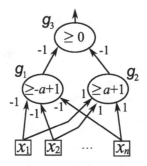

Fig. 1. Threshold circuit computing f in Eq. (1)

stated in Section 4. The bound $d' \leq 2e$ cannot be improved to $d' \leq (2 - \epsilon)e$ for any number $\epsilon > 0$, as follows. Let n be the number of input variables, and let $n \geq 2$. Let a be an integer such that $0 < a < n$, and let f be

$$f(x) = \begin{cases} 1 \text{ if } \sum_{i=1}^{n} x_i = a; \\ 0 \text{ otherwise.} \end{cases} \qquad (1)$$

Then f is non-trivial, and can be computed by the threshold circuit C in Fig. 1, which has the energy complexity $e = 1$. However, f cannot be computed by any threshold circuit C' of depth $d' = 1 \leq (2 - \epsilon)e$.

3   Proof of Theorem 1

We prove Theorem 1 in this section.

Suppose that a Boolean function f can be computed by a threshold circuit C of energy complexity e and size s. In Section 3.1, we construct a threshold circuit C' computing f, and show that C' has depth $d' = 2e + 1$ and size $s' = 2es + 1$. In Section 3.2, we prove that C' computes f.

3.1   Construction of C'

Suppose that a threshold circuit C computing f consists of s threshold gates $g_1, g_2, \cdots, g_s$, and that g_s is the output gate of C. One may assume that $g_1, g_2, \cdots, g_s$ are topologically ordered with respect to the underlying acyclic graph of C. Thus, for each i, $1 \leq i \leq s$, the input z_i to a gate g_i either consists of all the n inputs $x_1, x_2, \cdots, x_n$ to C and the outputs of all the $i - 1$ gates $g_1, g_2, \cdots, g_{i-1}$ preceding g_i or consists of some of them. We denote the weights of g_i for inputs $x_1, x_2, \cdots, x_n$ by $w_{i,1}, w_{i,2}, \cdots, w_{i,n}$, respectively, and denote the weights of g_i for the outputs of $g_1, g_2, \cdots, g_{i-1}$ by $\hat{w}_{i,1}, \hat{w}_{i,2}, \cdots, \hat{w}_{i,i-1}$, respectively. Some of the weights may be zero. Let t_i be the threshold of g_i. Then the output $g_i[x]$ of g_i is

$$g_i[x] = \text{sign} \left(\sum_{j=1}^{n} w_{i,j} x_j + \sum_{k=1}^{i-1} \hat{w}_{i,k} g_k[x] - t_i \right). \qquad (2)$$

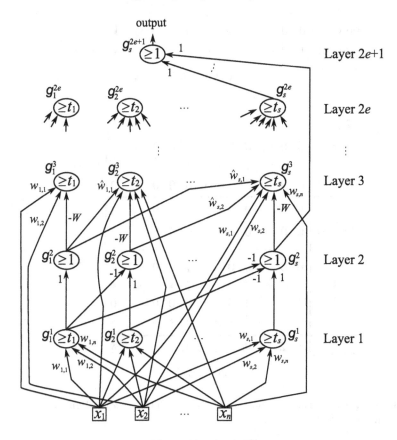

Fig. 2. Sketch of C'

Figure 2 illustrates the circuit C' which we are going to construct. The circuit C' has depth $d' = 2e+1$. There are exactly s gates $g_1^l, g_2^l, \cdots, g_s^l$ in the l-th layer of C' for each integer l, $1 \le l \le 2e$, and there is only the output gate g_s^{2e+1} of C' in the top $(2e+1)$-st layer of C'. Thus C' has size $s' = 2es + 1$.

Intuitively speaking, each pair of consecutive layers of C' "finds" the next gate with output 1 in C. More precisely, the circuit C' satisfies the following lemma, whose proof is omitted in this extended abstract due to the page limitation.

Lemma 1. *Let $x \in \{0,1\}^n$ be an arbitrary input to C. Let $g_{a_1}, g_{a_2}, \cdots, g_{a_{e(x)}}$ be the $e(x)$ gates outputting "1" for x, and let $1 \le a_1 < a_2 < \cdots < a_{e(x)} \le s$. Thus g_{a_1} fires first, g_{a_2} fires second, and subsequently $g_{a_{e(x)}}$ fires last for x in C, as illustrated in Fig. 3(a) for x such that $f(x) = g_s(x) = 1$. Then the following (a) and (b) hold. (See Fig. 3(b).)*

(a) For every integer l, $1 \le l \le e(x)$, the gate $g_{a_l}^{2l-1}$ first fires among the s gates in the $(2l-1)$-st layer of C', and only the gate $g_{a_l}^{2l}$ fires among the s gates in the $2l$-th layer of C'. That is, for every integer l, $1 \le l \le e(x)$, and every index i, $1 \le i \le s$,

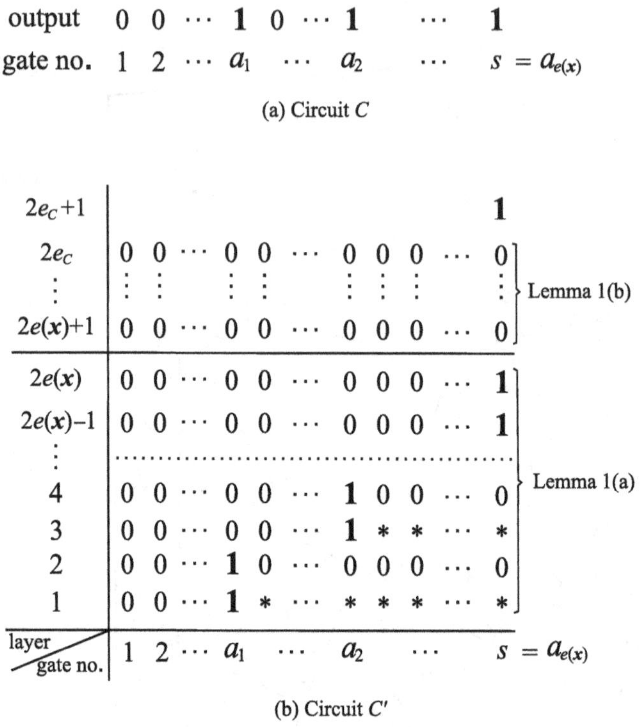
output 0 0 ··· 1 0 ··· 1 ··· 1
gate no. 1 2 ··· a1 ··· a2 ··· s = ae(x)
(a) Circuit C
2eC+1
2eC
2e(x)+1
2e(x)
2e(x)−1
4
3
2
1
Lemma 1(b)
Lemma 1(a)
layer
gate no.
1 2 ··· a1 ··· a2 ··· s = ae(x)
(b) Circuit C′

Fig. 3. Firing patterns of (a) C and (b) C' for $\boldsymbol{x}$ such that $f(\boldsymbol{x}) = 1$ and $1 \leq e(\boldsymbol{x}) < e_C$, where $*$ means 0 or 1

$$g_i^{2l-1}[\boldsymbol{x}] = \begin{cases} 0 \text{ if } 1 \leq i \leq a_l - 1; \\ 1 \text{ if } i = a_l \end{cases} \tag{3}$$

and

$$g_i^{2l}[\boldsymbol{x}] = \begin{cases} 1 \text{ if } i = a_l; \\ 0 \text{ otherwise.} \end{cases} \tag{4}$$

(b) None of the gates in the l-th layer, $2e(\boldsymbol{x}) + 1 \leq l \leq 2e_C$, fires. That is, for every integer l, $e(\boldsymbol{x}) + 1 \leq l \leq e_C$, and every index i, $1 \leq i \leq s$,

$$g_i^{2l-1}[\boldsymbol{x}] = 0 \tag{5}$$

and

$$g_i^{2l}[\boldsymbol{x}] = 0. \tag{6}$$

We now show how to construct C' by separating the $2e + 1$ layers into the following four sets of layers.

⟨1⟩ *First layer*

Each gate g_i^1, $1 \leq i \leq s$, in the first layer of C' has the same threshold t_i as g_i in C, and receives inputs only from the input nodes $x_1, x_2, \cdots, x_n$ with the same weights as g_i. Thus, the output $g_i^1[\boldsymbol{x}]$ of g_i^1 is

$$g_i^1[\boldsymbol{x}] = \mathrm{sign}\left(\sum_{j=1}^n w_{i,j} x_j - t_i\right) \tag{7}$$

for every input $\boldsymbol{x} \in \{0,1\}^n$. From Eq. (2) and Eq. (7), we have

$$g_i^1[\boldsymbol{x}] = g_i[\boldsymbol{x}] \text{ if } g_1[\boldsymbol{x}] = g_2[\boldsymbol{x}] = \cdots = g_{i-1}[\boldsymbol{x}] = 0. \tag{8}$$

If $e(\boldsymbol{x}) \geq 1$, then the gate g_{a_1} fires first for $\boldsymbol{x}$ in C and hence we have from (8)

$$g_i^1(\boldsymbol{x}) = \begin{cases} 0 \text{ if } 1 \leq i \leq a_1 - 1; \\ 1 \text{ if } i = a_1. \end{cases} \tag{9}$$

Thus Eq. (3) holds for $l = 1$. If $e(\boldsymbol{x}) = 0$, then $g_i[\boldsymbol{x}] = 0$ for every i, $1 \leq i \leq s$, and hence by (8)

$$g_i^1[\boldsymbol{x}] = 0 \tag{10}$$

for every i, $1 \leq i \leq s$. Thus Eq. (5) holds for $l = 1$.

⟨2⟩ *Even-numbered layers*

We design gates g_i^{2l}, $1 \leq i \leq s$, in the $2l$-th layer, $1 \leq l \leq e$, as follows. The gate g_i^{2l} receives, as inputs, only the outputs of i gates $g_1^{2l-1}, g_2^{2l-1}, \cdots, g_i^{2l-1}$ in the $(2l-1)$-st layer. The weights for the outputs of $g_1^{2l-1}, g_2^{2l-1}, \cdots, g_{i-1}^{2l-1}$ are -1's, and the weight for the output of g_i^{2l-1} is 1. The gate g_i^{2l} has a threshold 1. Thus, the output $g_i^{2l}[\boldsymbol{x}]$ of g_i^{2l} is

$$g_i^{2l}[\boldsymbol{x}] = \mathrm{sign}\left(-\sum_{k=1}^{i-1} g_k^{2l-1}[\boldsymbol{x}] + g_i^{2l-1}[\boldsymbol{x}] - 1\right) \tag{11}$$

for every input $\boldsymbol{x} \in \{0,1\}^n$. Therefore,

$$g_i^{2l}[\boldsymbol{x}] = 1 \text{ if and only if}$$
$$g_1^{2l-1}[\boldsymbol{x}] = g_2^{2l-1}[\boldsymbol{x}] = \cdots = g_{i-1}^{2l-1}[\boldsymbol{x}] = 0 \text{ and } g_i^{2l-1}[\boldsymbol{x}] = 1. \tag{12}$$

Hence, if g_i^{2l-1} fires first among the s gates in the $(2l-1)$-st layer, then only g_i^{2l} fires among the s gates in the $2l$-th layer.

Let $l = 1$, and consider gates g_i^2, $1 \leq i \leq s$, in the second layer. If $e(\boldsymbol{x}) \geq 1$, then Eqs. (9) and (12) imply

$$g_i^2[\boldsymbol{x}] = \begin{cases} 1 \text{ if } i = a_1; \\ 0 \text{ otherwise.} \end{cases} \tag{13}$$

Thus Eq. (4) holds for $l = 1$. If $e(\boldsymbol{x}) = 0$, then Eqs. (10) and (12) imply that $g_i^2[\boldsymbol{x}] = 0$ for every i, $1 \le i \le s$. Thus Eq. (6) holds for $l = 1$.

⟨3⟩ *Odd-numbered layers*
We now design gate g_i^{2l-1}, $1 \le i \le s$, in the $(2l-1)$-st layer, $2 \le l \le e$. The gate g_i^{2l-1} has the same threshold t_i as g_i in C, and receives inputs $x_1, x_2, \cdots, x_n$ with the same weights as g_i in C. Thus the weights of g_i^{2l-1} for $x_1, x_2, \cdots, x_n$ are $w_{i,1}, w_{i,2}, \cdots, w_{i,n}$, respectively. The gate g_i^{2l-1} receives, as inputs, also the outputs of gates $g_1^{2m}, g_2^{2m}, \cdots, g_{i-1}^{2m}$ in the $2m$-th layer for each m, $1 \le m \le l-1$, with weights $\hat{w}_{i,1}, \hat{w}_{i,2}, \cdots, \hat{w}_{i,i-1}$, respectively. In addition, g_i^{2l-1} receives the output of g_i^{2m} with weight $-W$ for each m, $1 \le m \le l-1$, where W is a sufficiently large positive integer. For example, we choose W so that

$$W > \max_{1 \le i \le s} \max_{\boldsymbol{x} \in \{0,1\}^n} \left(\sum_{j=1}^{n} w_{i,j} x_j + \sum_{k=1}^{i-1} \hat{w}_{i,k} g_k[\boldsymbol{x}] - t_i \right). \tag{14}$$

We thus have

$$g_i^{2l-1}[\boldsymbol{x}] = \text{sign} \left(\sum_{j=1}^{n} w_{i,j} x_j + \sum_{m=1}^{l-1} \sum_{k=1}^{i-1} \hat{w}_{i,k} g_k^{2m}[\boldsymbol{x}] - \sum_{m=1}^{l-1} W g_i^{2m}[\boldsymbol{x}] - t_i \right). \tag{15}$$

Hence, g_i^{2l-1} does not fire if at least one of the $l-1$ gates $g_i^2, g_i^4, \cdots, g_i^{2(l-1)}$ fires.

⟨4⟩ *Top layer*
There is only the output gate g_s^{2e+1} in the top $(2e+1)$-st layer of C'. The threshold of the gate g_s^{2e+1} is 1, and g_s^{2e+1} receives the outputs of e gates $g_s^2, g_s^4, \cdots, g_s^{2e}$ with weights 1. Thus

$$g_s^{2e+1}[\boldsymbol{x}] = \text{sign} \left(\sum_{l=1}^{e} g_s^{2l}[\boldsymbol{x}] - 1 \right). \tag{16}$$

Hence, g_s^{2e+1} computes the OR of outputs of $g_s^2, g_s^4, \cdots, g_s^{2e}$.

We have thus completed the construction of C'.

3.2 C' Computes f

In the section, we prove that the circuit C' constructed in Section 3.1 computes f, that is, $C'(\boldsymbol{x}) = f(\boldsymbol{x})$ for every input $\boldsymbol{x} \in \{0,1\}^n$. We separate the proof into two cases, $f(\boldsymbol{x}) = 1$ and $f(\boldsymbol{x}) = 0$, as follows.

Case 1: $f(x) = 1$.
In the case, $f(x) = C(x) = g_s[x] = 1$, and hence $e(x) \geq 1$ and $a_{e(x)} = s$ as illustrated in Fig. 3(a). Substituting $i = s$ and $l = 1, 2, \cdots, e(x)$ in Eq. (4), we obtain

$$g_s^2[x] = g_s^4[x] = \cdots = g_s^{2(e(x)-1)}[x] = 0 \tag{17}$$

and

$$g_s^{2e(x)}[x] = 1. \tag{18}$$

Substituting $i = s$ and $l = e(x) + 1, e(x) + 2, \cdots, e$ in Eq. (6), we have

$$g_s^{2(e(x)+1)}[x] = g_s^{2(e(x)+2)}[x] = \cdots = g_s^{2e}[x] = 0. \tag{19}$$

By Eqs. (17)–(19), we have

$$\sum_{l=1}^{e} g_s^{2l}[x] = 1. \tag{20}$$

Equations (16) and (20) imply that

$$C'(x) = g_s^{2e+1}[x] = \text{sign}(0) = 1 = f(x).$$

Case 2: $f(x) = 0$.
In the case, $f(x) = C(x) = g_s[x] = 0$ and hence $a_1, a_2, \cdots, a_{e(x)} < s$. Therefore, by Eq. (4) and Eq. (6), we have

$$\sum_{l=1}^{e} g_s^{2l}[x] = 0. \tag{21}$$

Equations (16) and (21) imply that

$$C'(x) = g_s^{2e+1}[x] = \text{sign}(-1) = 0 = f(x).$$

4   Conclusions

In the paper, we prove that if a Boolean function f can be computed by a threshold circuit C of energy complexity e and size s then the function f can be computed also by a threshold circuit C' of depth $d' = 2e + 1$ and $s' = 2es + 1$. Lemma 1 implies that the energy complexity e' of C' satisfies $e' \leq e(s + 1) + 1$. Thus, the energy complexity e' of C' is not necessarily small even if the energy complexity e of C is small. Let n_{wire} be the number of wires in C, that is, n_{wire} is the number of all the non-zero weights $w_{i,j}$ and $\hat{w}_{i,k}$, $1 \leq i \leq s$, $1 \leq j \leq n$, $1 \leq k \leq i-1$, in C. Then the number n'_{wire} of wires in C' is $n'_{\text{wire}} \leq es^2 + e^2 n_{\text{wire}}$. Let n_{in} be the maximum fan-in of gates in C, then the maximum fan-in n'_{in} of gates in C' is $n'_{\text{in}} \leq \max\{s, e(n_{\text{in}} + 1)\}$. If all the weights and thresholds in C are integers, then all of them in C' are integers, too.

One can indeed decrease the depth d' of the circuit C' in Theorem 1 by 1 if f is non-trivial and hence $e \geq 1$, as follows. Since the $s - 1$ gates $g_1^{2e}, g_2^{2e}, \cdots, g_{s-1}^{2e}$ in the $2e$-th layer have out-degree 0 as illustrated in Fig. 2, these $s - 1$ gates can be removed from C'. The two gates g_s^{2e} and g_s^{2e+1} can be merged into a single output gate of C'. One can thus construct a circuit C' of depth $d' = 2e$ and size $s' = s(2e - 1) + 1$.

One can easily generalize Theorem 1 for an m-output Boolean function f : $\{0, 1\}^n \to \{0, 1\}^m$, where m is any positive integer, as follows. If such a function f can be computed by a threshold circuit C of energy complexity e and size s, then f can be computed also by a threshold circuit C' of depth $d' = 2e + 1$ and size $s' = 2es + m$. The construction of C' is similar to that in Section 3.1 except for the top layer, in which there are m output gates of C', each corresponds to one of the m output gates in C and is designed similarly as g_s^{2e+1}.

One would expect that the following proposition, which is a converse proposition of Corollary 1, holds: if f can be computed by a polynomial-size threshold circuit C of depth d, then f can be computed also by a polynomial-size threshold circuit C' of energy $e' = O(d)$. However, the proposition does not hold, as follows. The addition of two n-bit numbers can be computed by a polynomial-size threshold circuit C of depth $d = 2$ [5], while every circuit C' computing the addition has energy complexity $e \geq n$.

A polynomial-size threshold circuit of constant depth has big computational power; for example, not only the addition but also the multiplication and division of two n-bit numbers can be computed by such a circuit [13,14,15]. On the other hand, some functions cannot be computed by any polynomial-size threshold circuit of depth 2 or 3 under some restrictions on weights, thresholds, fan-ins, etc. [16,17,18,19]. It is interesting to know whether there is a function $f : \{0, 1\}^n \to \{0, 1\}$ which cannot be computed by any polynomial-size threshold circuit of constant energy complexity.

References

1. Minsky, M., Papert, S.: Perceptrons: An Introduction to Computational Geometry. MIT Press, Cambridge (1988)
2. Parberry, I.: Circuit Complexity and Neural Networks. MIT Press, Cambridge (1994)
3. Shao-Chin, S., Nishino, T.: The complexity of threshold circuits for parity functions. IEICE Transactions on Information and Systems 80(1), 91–93 (1997)
4. Sima, J., Orponen, P.: General-purpose computation with neural networks: A survey of complexity theoretic result. Neural Computation 15, 2727–2778 (2003)
5. Siu, K.Y., Roychowdhury, V., Kailath, T.: Discrete Neural Computation; A Theoretical Foundation. Prentice-Hall, Inc., Upper Saddle River (1995)
6. Lennie, P.: The cost of cortical computation. Current Biology 13, 493–497 (2003)
7. Margrie, T.W., Brecht, M., Sakmann, B.: In vivo, low-resistance, whole-cell recordings from neurons in the anaesthetized and awake mammalian brain. Pflugers Arch 444(4), 491–498 (2002)

8. Uchizawa, K., Douglas, R., Maass, W.: On the computational power of threshold circuits with sparse activity. Neural Computation 18(12), 2994–3008 (2006)
9. Uchizawa, K., Takimoto, E.: Exponential lower bounds on the size of threshold circuits with small energy complexity. Theoretical Computer Science 407, 474–487 (2008)
10. Uchizawa, K., Takimoto, E., Nishizeki, T.: Size and energy of threshold circuits computing mod functions. In: 34th International Symposium on Mathematical Foundations of Computer Science (to appear, 2009)
11. Impagliazzo, R., Paturi, R., Saks, M.E.: Size-depth trade-offs for threshold circuits. SIAM Journal on Computing 26(3), 693–707 (1997)
12. Siu, K.Y., Roychowdhury, V.P., Kailath, T.: Rational approximation techniques for analysis of neural networks. IEEE Transactions on Information Theory 40(2), 455–466 (1994)
13. Siu, K.Y., Bruck, J., Kailath, T., Hofmeister, T.: Depth efficient neural networks for division and related problems. IEEE Transaction on Infromation theory 39, 946–956 (1992)
14. Siu, K.Y., Roychowdhury, V.: On optimal depth threshold circuits for multiplication and related problems. SIAM Journal on Discrete Mathematics 7(2), 284–292 (1994)
15. Yeh, C.H., Varvarigos, E.A.: Depth-efficient threshold circuits for multiplication and symmetric function computation. In: Cai, J.-Y., Wong, C.K. (eds.) COCOON 1996. LNCS, vol. 1090, pp. 231–240. Springer, Heidelberg (1996)
16. Amano, K., Maruoka, A.: On the complexity of depth-2 circuits with threshold gates. In: Jedrzejowicz, J., Szepietowski, A. (eds.) MFCS 2005. LNCS, vol. 3618, pp. 107–118. Springer, Heidelberg (2005)
17. Forster, J.: A linear lower bound on the unbounded error probabilistic communication complexity. Journal of Computer and System Sciences 65, 612–625 (2002)
18. Hajnal, A., Maass, W., Pudlák, P., Szegedy, M., Turá, G.: Threshold circuits of bounded depth. Journal of Computer and System Sciences 46, 129–154 (1993)
19. Håstad, J., Goldmann, M.: On the power of small-depth threshold circuits. Computational Complexity 1, 113–129 (1993)

1-Local 17/12-Competitive Algorithm for Multicoloring Hexagonal Graphs

Rafał Witkowski

Adam Mickiewicz University,
Faculty of Mathematics and Computer Science,
Poznań, Poland
rmiw@amu.edu.pl

Abstract. In the frequency allocation problem we are given a cellular telephone network whose geographical coverage area is divided into cells where phone calls are serviced by frequencies assigned to them, so that none of the pairs of calls emanating from the same or neighboring cells is assigned the same frequency. The problem is to use the frequencies efficiently, i.e. minimize the span of used frequencies. The frequency allocation problem can be regarded as a multicoloring problem on a weighted hexagonal graph. In this paper we present a 1-local 17/12-competitive distributed algorithm for a multicoloring of hexagonal graph, thereby improving the competitiveness ratio of previously known best 1-local 13/9-competitive algorithm (see [1]).

1 Introduction

The basic problem concerning cellular networks concentrates on assigning sets of frequencies (colors) to transmitters (vertices) in order to avoid unacceptable interference (see [7]). In an ordinary cellular model the transmitters are centers of hexagonal cells and the corresponding adjacency graph is a subgraph of the infinite triangular lattice. In our model to each vertex v of a the triangular lattice T we assign a non-negative integer $d(v)$, called the *demand* (or *weight*) of the vertex v. A *proper multicoloring* of G is a mapping φ from $V(G)$ to subsets of integers (colors) $[n] = \{1, 2, \ldots, n\}$, such that $|\varphi(v)| = d(v)$ for any vertex $v \in G$ and $\varphi(v) \cap \varphi(u) = \emptyset$ for any pair of adjacent vertices u and v in the graph G. The minimal n for which there exists a proper multicoloring of G, denoted by $\chi_m(G)$, is called the *multichromatic number* of G. A *hexagonal graph* $G = (V, E, d)$ is the vertex weighted subgraph of T, induced by the set of its vertices with positive demands (the idea of hexagonal graphs arise naturally in studies concerning cellular networks). The multichromatic number is closely related to the *weighted clique number* $\omega(G)$, which is defined as the maximum over all cliques of G of their weights, where the weight of a clique is the sum of demands on its vertices. Obviously, for any graph, $\chi_m(G) \geq \omega(G)$, while for hexagonal graphs (see, for example, [2], [3], [6]), $\chi_m(G) \leq \left\lceil \frac{4\omega(G)}{3} \right\rceil + O(1)$. Since all proofs of the upper bound are constructive, therefore it implies the existence of a *4/3-competitive*

M. Kutyłowski, M. Gębala, and W. Charatonik (Eds.): FCT 2009, LNCS 5699, pp. 346–356, 2009.

algorithm, i.e. algorithms which can online serve calls with the approximation ratio equal to 4/3 respectively to the weighted clique number (see [5], [8]). It should be also mentioned that McDiarmid and Reed showed in [3] that to decide whether $\chi_m(G) = \omega(G)$ is NP-complete.

In distributed graph algorithms a special role plays their "locality" property. An algorithm is *k-local* if the computation at any vertex v uses only the information about the demands of the vertices at distance at most k from v. For hexagonal graphs the best previously known 1-local algorithm for multicoloring is 13/9-competitive, and it has been presented in [1]. In this paper we develop a new 1-local algorithm which uses no more than $\lceil \frac{17}{12}\omega(G) \rceil + O(1)$ colors, thus improving the result from [1]. Our algorithm substantially differs from previous ones. Those algorithms (e.g. [1], [2]) are composed of two stages. At the first stage, a triangle-free hexagonal graph with weighted clique number no larger than $\lceil \omega(G)/3 \rceil$ is constructed from G, while at the second stage an algorithm for multicoloring a triangle-free hexagonal graph is used (see [1], [10], [11]). Our algorithm skips the second stage entirely.

Theorem 1. *There is a 1-local distributed approximation algorithm for multi-coloring hexagonal graphs which uses at most $\lceil \frac{17}{12}\omega(G) \rceil + O(1)$ colors. Time complexity of the algorithm at each vertex is constant.*

In [8] it was proved that a k-local c-approximate offline algorithm can be easily converted to a k-local c-competitive online algorithm. Hence,

Corollary 1. *There is a 1-local 17/12-competitive algorithm for multicoloring hexagonal graphs.*

In the next Section we formally define some basic terminology, while in Section 3 we present the algorithm and prove Theorem 1.

2   Basic Definition and Useful Facts

Following the notation from [3], the vertices of the triangular lattice T can be described as follows: the position of each vertex is an integer linear combination $x\boldsymbol{p}+y\boldsymbol{q}$ of two vectors $\boldsymbol{p} = (1,0)$ and $\boldsymbol{q} = (\frac{1}{2}, \frac{\sqrt{3}}{2})$. Thus vertices of the triangular lattice may be identified with pairs (x,y) of integers. Two vertices are adjacent when the Euclidean distance between them is one. Therefore each vertex (x,y) has six neighbors: $(x-1,y), (x-1,y+1), (x,y+1), (x+1,y), (x+1,y-1), (x,y-1)$. For simplicity we refer to the neighbors as: *left, up-left, up-right, right, down-right* and *down-left*. We define a *hexagonal graph* $G = (V,E)$ as an induced subgraph of the triangular lattice (see Figure 1).

There exists an obvious 3-coloring of the infinite triangular lattice which gives partition of the vertex set of any hexagonal graph into three independent sets. Let us denote a color of any vertex v in this 3-coloring by $bc(v)$ and call it a *base color* (for simplicity we will use *red, green* and *blue* as base colors and their arrangement is given in Figure 1), i.e. $bc(v) \in \{R, G, B\}$.

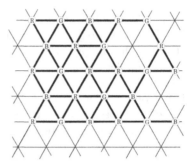

Fig. 1. An example of a hexagonal graph

We call a *triangle-free hexagonal graph* an induced subgraph of the triangular lattice without 3-clique. We define a *corner* in a triangle-free hexagonal graph as a vertex which has at least two neighbors and none of them are at angle π. A vertex is a *right corner* if it has an up-right or a down-right neighbor, and otherwise it is a *left corner* (see Figure 2). A vertex which is not a corner is called a *non-corner*.

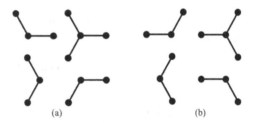

Fig. 2. All possibilities for: (a) - left corners, (b) - right corners

In graph $G = (V, E)$, we call a coloring $f : V \to \{1, \ldots, k\}$ *k-good* if for every odd cycle in G and for every i, $1 \le i \le k$, there is a vertex $v \in V$ in the cycle such that $f(v) = i$. A *graph is k-good* if such coloring exists.

Lemma 1. [4] *Consider a 3-coloring of the triangular lattice (R, G, B). Every odd cycle of the triangle-free hexagonal graph G contains at least one non-corner vertex of every color.*

Proof. Assume without loss of generality that there exists an odd cycle in the graph which does not have a non-corner vertex colored red. Notice that in the 3-coloring of the triangular lattice, a corner has all its neighbors colored by the same color (they are at the angle $2\pi/3$ since the graph is triangle-free). Hence, if all neighbors of a red colored corner are blue, we can recolor this corner by green color and vice-versa. That gives a valid 2-coloring of an odd cycle, a contradiction.   □

Note that two successive corners in any cycle cannot be both left (right). By Lemma 1 and since every cycle has at least one left and one right corner, we get the following observation:

Proposition 1. *Any triangle-free hexagonal graph G is 5-good.*

One can also give an explicit 5-good coloring of every triangle-free hexagonal graph by assigning colors in the following way:

- PINK – to non-corner vertices with base color equal to red,
- LIME – to non-corner vertices with base color equal to green,
- AQUA – to non-corner vertices with base color equal to blue,
- WHITE – to left corner vertices,
- YELLOW – to right corner vertices.

We denote color of a vertex v in this 5-good coloring by $ec(v)$ and call it an *extra color* of v (for simplicity we will use *pink, lime, aqua, white* and *yellow* as extra colors, see Figure 3) , i.e. $ec(v) \in \{P, L, A, W, Y\}$.

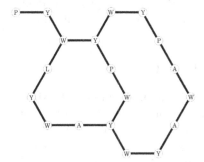

Fig. 3. An example of a triangle-free hexagonal graph with 5-good coloring

Notice that if a graph G is 5-good then after removing vertices colored by any of those five colors, the resulting graph is bipartite. For any weighted bipartite graph H, $\chi_m(H) = \omega(H)$ (see [6]), and it can be optimally multicolored by the following procedure.

Procedure 2. *Let $H = (V', V'', E, d)$ be a weighted bipartite graph. We get an optimal multicoloring of H if to each vertex $v \in V'$ we assign a set of colors $\{1, 2, \ldots, d(v)\}$, while with each vertex $v \in V''$ we associate a set of colors $\{m(v) + 1, m(v) + 2, \ldots, m(v) + d(v)\}$, where $m(v) = \max\{d(u) : \{u, v\} \in E\}$.*

Notice that in any weighted hexagonal graph G, a subgraph of the triangular lattice T induced by vertices with positive demands $d(v)$, the only cliques are triangles, edges and isolated vertices. Note also that we assume that all vertices of T which are not in G have to have demand $d(v) = 0$. Therefore, the weighted clique number of G can be computed as follows:

$$\omega(G) = \max\{d(u) + d(v) + d(t) : \{u, v, t\} \in \tau(T)\},$$

where $\tau(T)$ is the set of all triangles of T.

For each vertex $v \in G$, define *base function* κ as

$$\kappa(v) = \max\{a(v, u, t) : \{v, u, t\} \in \tau(T)\},$$

where $a(u, v, t) = \lceil (d(u) + d(v) + d(t))/3 \rceil$, is an average weight of the triangle $\{u, v, t\} \in \tau(T)$. It is easy to observe that the following fact holds.

Proposition 2. *For each $v \in G$,*

$$\kappa(v) \leq \left\lceil \frac{\omega(G)}{3} \right\rceil$$

We call vertex v *heavy* if $d(v) > \kappa(v)$, otherwise we call it *light*. If $d(v) > 2\kappa(v)$ we call vertex *very heavy*.

To color vertices of G we use colors from appropriate *palette*. For a given color c, its palette is defined as a set of pairs $\{(c, i)\}_{i \in \mathbb{N}}$. A palette is called *base color palette* if $c \in \{R, G, B\}$, while it is called *extra color palette* if $c \in \{P, L, A, W, Y\}$.

In our model of computations we assume that each vertex knows its coordinates as well as its own demand (weight) and demands of all it neighbors. With this knowledge, each vertex has to color itself properly in constant time in a distributed way.

3   Algorithm and Its Correctness

Our algorithm consists of two main phases. In the first phase vertices take $\kappa(v)$ colors from its base color palette, so use no more than $\omega(G)$ colors. After this phase all light vertices are fully colored while the remaining vertices create a triangle-free hexagonal graph with weighted clique number not exceeding $\lceil \omega(G)/3 \rceil$ (after technical removing very heavy vertices). In the second phase we construct 5-good coloring of the remaining graph. Recall that in 5-good coloring, a graph is bipartite after removing vertices of any of these five colors. If we use Procedure 2 and color such graphs optimally with weight function equal in each vertex to $1/4$ of its demands, then we would fully color the remaining graph and use no more than $5/4$ colors than it is needed. Due to the proof of Lemma 1, bipartition is easy to find after removing any class of non-corners (pink, aqua or lime vertices). Unfortunately we cannot obtain this bipartition in our 1-local model of computation when we remove any class of corners (white or yellow vertices). We can do it only for non-corners, while corners have to be satisfied in a separate way – by using free colors from base color palettes.

More precisely, our algorithm consists of the following steps:

Algorithm

Step 0: For each vertex $v = (x, y) \in V$ compute its base color $bc(v)$

$$bc(v) = \begin{cases} R & \text{if} \quad x + 2y \bmod 3 = 0 \\ G & \text{if} \quad x + 2y \bmod 3 = 1 \\ B & \text{if} \quad x + 2y \bmod 3 = 2 \end{cases},$$

and its base function value

$$\kappa(v) = \max\left\{ \left\lceil \frac{d(u) + d(v) + d(t)}{3} \right\rceil : \{v, u, t\} \in \tau(T) \right\}.$$

Step 1: For each vertex $v \in V$ assign to v $\min\{\kappa(v), d(v)\}$ colors from its base color palette. Construct a new weighted triangle-free hexagonal graph $G_1 = (V_1, E_1, d_1)$ where $d_1(v) = \max\{d(v) - \kappa(v), 0\}$, $V_1 \subseteq V$ is the set of vertices with $d_1(v) > 0$ (heavy vertices) and $E_1 \subseteq E$ is the set of all edges in G with both endpoints from V_1 (E_1 is induced by V_1).

Step 2: For each vertex $v \in V_1$ with $d_1(v) > \kappa(v)$ (very heavy vertices) assign free colors from the first $\kappa(v)$ of base color palettes of its neighbors in T. Construct a new graph $G_2 = (V_2, E_2, d_2)$ where d_2 is the difference between $d_1(v)$ and the number of assigned colors in this Step, $V_2 \subseteq V_1$ is the set of vertices with $d_2(v) > 0$ and $E_2 \subseteq E_1$ is the set of all edges in G_1 with both endpoints from V_2 (E_2 is induced by V_2).

Step 3: Determine 5-good coloring of G_2: for each vertex $v \in V_2$ compute its extra color $ec(v)$

$$ec(v) = \begin{cases} P & \text{if } v \text{ is non-corner in } G_2 \text{ and } bc(v) = R \\ L & \text{if } v \text{ is non-corner in } G_2 \text{ and } bc(v) = G \\ A & \text{if } v \text{ is non-corner in } G_2 \text{ and } bc(v) = B \\ W & \text{if } v \text{ is left corner in } G_2 \\ Y & \text{if } v \text{ is right corner in } G_2 \end{cases}$$

Step 4: For each class of non-corners (pink, lime, aqua) do as follows: remove from G_2 all pink (lime, aqua) vertices and based on the proof of Lemma 1 find a bipartition of the remaining graph. Apply Procedure 2 to satisfy 1/4 demands in G_2 by colors from pink (lime, aqua) extra color palette.

Step 5: For each class of corners (white, yellow) do as follows: remove from G_2 all white (yellow) vertices and:

  5a find a bipartition of non-corners using their positions in the triangular lattice T and apply Procedure 2 to satisfy 1/4 demands in G_2 by colors from white (yellow) extra color palette.

  5b for each corner satisfy 1/4 its demands in G_2 by the free colors of first $\kappa(v)$ from base color palettes of its light neighbors in T.

Correctness proof

At the very beginning of the algorithm there is a 1-local communication when each vertex finds out about the demands of all its neighbors. From now on, no more communication will be needed. Recall that each vertex knows its position (x, y) on the triangular lattice T.

In Step 0 there is nothing to prove.

In Step 1 each heavy vertex v assigns $\kappa(v)$ colors from its base color palette, while each light vertex u assigns $d(u)$ colors from its base color palette. Note that G_1 consists only of heavy vertices, therefore G_1 is a triangle-free hexagonal graph.

For any $\{v, u, t\} \in \tau(G)$, since $3 \min \{\kappa(v), \kappa(u), \kappa(t)\} \geq d(v) + d(u) + d(t)$ and $\min \{\kappa(v), \kappa(u), \kappa(t)\} \geq \min \{d(v), d(u), d(t)\}$, at most two of $d_1(v), d_1(u), d_1(t)$ are strictly positive and at least one of the vertices u, v and t has all its required colors totally assigned in Step 1. Therefore, the graph G_1 does not contain 3-clique, i.e. it is a triangle-free hexagonal graph. The remaining weight of each vertex $v \in G_1$ is

$$d_1(v) = d(v) - \kappa(v).$$

In Step 2 only vertices with $d_1(v) > \kappa(v)$ (very heavy vertices) are colored. If vertex v is very heavy in G then it is isolated in G_1 (all its neighbors are light in G). Otherwise, for some $\{v, u, t\} \in \tau(T)$ we would have

$$d(v) + d(u) > 2\kappa(v) + \kappa(u) \geq 3a(v, u, t) \geq d(v) + d(u),$$

a contradiction. Without loss of generality we may assume that $bc(v) = R$. Denote by

$$D_G(v) = \min\{\kappa(v) - d(u) : \{u, v\} \in T, bc(u) = G\},$$

$$D_B(v) = \min\{\kappa(v) - d(u) : \{u, v\} \in T, bc(u) = B\}.$$

Obviously, $D_G(v), D_B(v) > 0$ for very heavy vertices $v \in G_1$. Since in Step 1 each light vertex t uses exactly $d(t)$ colors from its base color palette, we have at least $D_G(v)$ free colors from the green base color palette and at least $D_B(v)$ free colors from the blue base color palette, so that vertex v can assign those colors to itself. Then, we would have G_2 with $w(G_2) \leq \lceil w(G)/3 \rceil$. To prove it, we will need the following lemma:

Lemma 2. *In G_1 for every edge $\{v, u\} \in E_1$ holds:*

$$d_1(v) + d_1(u) \leq \kappa(v), \quad d_1(u) + d_1(v) \leq \kappa(u).$$

Proof. Assume that v and u are heavy vertices in G and $d_1(v) + d_1(u) > \kappa(v)$. Then for some $\{v, u, t\} \in \tau(T)$ we have:

$$d(v) + d(u) = d_1(v) + \kappa(v) + d_1(u) + \kappa(u) > 2\kappa(v) + \kappa(u) \geq 3a(u, v, t) \geq d(u) + d(v),$$

again a contradiction.   □

Proposition 3

$$w(G_2) \leq \lceil w(G)/3 \rceil.$$

Proof. Recall that in a hexagonal graph the only cliques are triangles, edges and isolated vertices. Since G_1 is a triangle-free hexagonal graph, G_2 also does not contain any triangle, so we have only edges and isolated vertices to check.

For each edge $\{v, u\} \in E_2$ from Lemma 2 and Proposition 2 we have:

$$d_2(v) + d_2(u) \leq d_1(v) + d_1(u) \leq \kappa(v) \leq \lceil w(G)/3 \rceil.$$

For each isolated vertex $v \in G_2$ we should have $d_2(v) \leq \lceil w(G)/3 \rceil$. Indeed, if $d_2(v) \leq \kappa(v)$, then it holds by Proposition 2. If $d_2(v) > \kappa(v)$, then $d_1(v) > \kappa(v)$, so v has to borrow colors from its neighbors' base color palettes in Step 2. Then, for $bc(v) = R$,

$$d_2(v) = d_1(v) - D_G(v) - D_B(v) \leq d(v) - \kappa(v) - \kappa(v) + d(u) - \kappa(v) + d(t) \leq$$

$$\leq 3a(v, u, t) - 3\kappa(v) \leq 0$$

for some $\{v, u, t\} \in \tau(T)$. Hence, $d_2(v) \leq \lceil \omega(G)/3 \rceil$, and so $\omega(G_2) \leq \lceil \omega(G)/3 \rceil$.   □

In Step 3 each vertex v has to decide whether it is a corner in G_2 or not. Only heavy neighbors of v can still exist in G_2. Unfortunately, in 1-local model v does not know which of his neighbors are heavy (and still exist in G_2) and which are light. Vertex v knows only where its neighbors with $d(u) \leq \max\{a(v, u, t) : \{v, u, t\} \in \tau(T)\}$ are located. We call those vertices *slight neighbors* of v. They must be light and, so, they are fully colored in Step 1. Thus, v knows where it cannot have neighbors in G_2 and presumes that all its neighbors which are not slight, still exist in G_2. Based on that knowledge, it can decide whether it is a corner or not. In each triangle in $\tau(T)$ containing v at least one neighbor of v is slight, so v has at least three such neighbors. If vertex v has more than four slight neighbors, then it is a non-corner. If vertex v has four slight neighbors, then the remaining two are not slight. In this case if an angle between those two are π, then v is non-corner, otherwise it is a corner – a right corner if its down-left, up-left and right neighbors are slight, and a left corner if its down-right, up-right and left neighbors are slight. If vertex v has three slight neighbors, then it is a corner and distinction between left and right is determined in the same way as above.

Step 4 strictly depends on a 5-good coloring of graph G_2 (function ec). For simplicity, consider only graph $G_P = (V_P, E_P, \lceil d_2/4 \rceil)$ where V_P is obtained from V_2 by removing pink vertices, $E_P \subseteq E_2$ is the set of edges of G_2 with both endpoints in V_P and weight function is $1/4$ of weight function in G_2. (Similarly we can define G_L for lime vertices and G_A for aqua vertices and the analysis is identical.) Since for G_P we remove pink vertices from G_2, therefore by Lemma 1, graph G_P is bipartite. We can easily find bipartition of this graph using base colors (function bc): we put to the first set of the bipartition all non-corners with base color equal to blue and red corners for which all neighbors in G_2 are green; while to the second set we put all non-corners with base color equal to green and red corners for which all neighbors in G_2 are blue. Next, we can apply Procedure 2 to G_P with bipartition defined above and weight function on each vertex v equal to $\lceil d_2(v)/4 \rceil$, assigning colors from the pink extra color palette. The problem is that, under 1-locality assumption, vertices cannot calculate value of d_2 of the neighbors, which is needed in Procedure 2 to calculate value $m(v) = \max\{\lceil d_2(u)/4 \rceil : \{u, v\} \in E_2\}$. However, we can replace $d_2(u)$ by $d_2^v(u)$, which is the number of expected demands on vertex u in vertex v after Step 2, and take $m'(v) = \max\{\lceil d_2^v(u)/4 \rceil : \{u, v\} \in E_2\}$. More precisely,

$$d_2^v(u) = d(u) - \max\{a(u, v, t) : \{u, v, t\} \in \tau(T)\}$$

Note that $d_2^v(u) \geq d_2(u)$ for any $\{u, v\} \in E_2$. However, for every $\{v, u\} \in E_2$ we have

$$d_2(v) + d_2^v(u) \leq \kappa(v).$$

Assume that this inequality does not hold. Denote by

$$b(u, v) = \max\{a(u, v, t) : \{u, v, t\} \in \tau(T)\}.$$

Then for some $\{t, v, u\} \in \tau(T)$ we have:

$$d(v) + d(u) = d_2(v) + \kappa(v) + d_2^v(u) + b(u, v) > 2\kappa(v) + b(u, v) \geq$$

$$\geq 3a(u, v, t) \geq d(u) + d(v),$$

a contradiction. Hence, if we use d_2^v instead of d_2 in each vertex from the second set of our bipartition, we have new $\omega(G_2)$ and inequality from Proposition 3 still holds. Thus, Procedure 2 works and uses at most $\lceil \omega(G_2)/4 \rceil$ colors in G_P.

In Steps 5 and 5a we proceed almost in the same way. For simplicity, consider only graph $G_W = (V_W, E_W, \lceil d_2/4 \rceil)$ where V_W is obtained from V_2 by removing white vertices, $E_W \subseteq E_2$ is the set of edges from G_2 with both endpoints in V_W and the weight function is $1/4$ of the weight function in G_2. (Similarly we can define G_Y for yellow vertices and the analysis is identical.) Since we take G_2 without white vertices, in G_W there are not any left corners and we have only right corners and non-corners. In 5a we apply Procedure 2 to non-corners and assign colors from the white extra color palette. We find a bipartition using *parity function* p on each vertex. Parity is a function which calculates whether $v = (x, y)$ is "even" or "odd" vertex on the line to which it belongs. Formally:

- if v has up-left, up-right, down-left, down-right slight neighbors then

$$p(v) = x \bmod 2$$

- if v has left, up-left, right, down-right slight neighbors then

$$p(v) = y \bmod 2$$

- if v has left, down-left, right, up-right slight neighbors then

$$p(v) = y \bmod 2$$

In Step 5b for G_W we take right corners and go back for a while to the base color palettes. If vertex $v \in G_2$ is a corner, it means that it has three slight neighbors with the same base color. Without loss of generality, assume that $bc(v) = R$ and its slight neighbors' base color is blue. Recall function D_B from Step 2 – we have $D_B(v)$ free colors from blue base color palette. We should have $d_2(v) \leq D_B(v)$. Let $\Delta = \{u, v, t\} \in \tau(T)$ be a triangle such that t is the green vertex which is not slight neighbor of v, and u is the blue vertex which is a slight neighbor of v. Denote by $s_\Delta(t) = d(t) - a(u, v, t)$. Then we have

$$0 \geq d(v) - a(u,v,t) + d(t) - a(u,v,t) + d(u) - a(u,v,t) \geq$$
$$\geq d(v) - \kappa(v) + s_\Delta(t) + d(u) - \kappa(v) \geq d_1(v) + s_\Delta(t) - D_B(v) \geq$$
$$\geq d_2(v) + s_\Delta(t) - D_B(v)$$

Since t is not a slight neighbor of v, $d_2(v) < D_B(v)$. Therefore, vertex v has as much as $d_2(v)$ free colors from the blue base color palette at his disposal, while it needs just $\lceil d_2(v)/4 \rceil$.

In both rounds of Step 5b (white and yellow vertices) we do the same for every right and left corners. We have to be careful not to cause a conflict when some right and left corners are adjacent in G_2. Then we cannot use the same color from the base colors palette from common slight neighbors. To ensure that, for left corners we can take only "even colors" and for right corners only "odd colors" from the base color palettes (recall that we think of colors in a palette as integers). We can do this because we have four times more free colors than we need in each corner, and two times more than may be needed for any two adjacent corners.

During Steps 4 and 5 each vertex v participates in exactly four from five rounds (in each round one extra color is removed from G_2) and $\lceil d_2(v)/4 \rceil$ colors are assigned in each. Therefore, at the end, all demands are satisfied.

Ratio

We claim that during the first phase (Steps 1 and 2) our algorithm uses at most $\omega(G) + 3$ colors. To see this notice that in Step 1 each vertex v uses at most $\kappa(v)$ colors from its base color palette and, by Proposition 2 and the fact that there are three base colors, we know that no more than $3 \lceil \omega(G)/3 \rceil \leq \omega(G) + 3$ colors are used. Note also that in Step 2 we use only those colors from base color palettes which have not been used in Step 1, so overall no more than $\omega(G) + 3$ colors are used in total in the first phase.

To count the number of colors used in the second phase (Steps 4 and 5) notice that we divide the demands of each vertex in G_2 into four equal parts. Each vertex v participates in four from five rounds and assigns $\lceil d_2(v)/4 \rceil$ colors in each round. Since in each round of Step 4 and 5a we use $\omega(G_2)/4 + 2$ colors from extra color palettes, we use only $5(\omega(G_2)/4 + 2)$ colors in total, while in 5b, when vertex cannot use an extra color palette, it borrows some colors from the base color palettes of its neighbors that have not been used by them in the previous steps, in order to avoid an introduction of any new colors.

Let $A(G)$ denote the number of colors used by our algorithm for the graph G. Thus, since $\omega(G_2) \leq \lceil \omega(G)/3 \rceil \leq \omega(G)/3 + 1$, the total number of colors used by our algorithm is at most

$$A(G) \leq \omega(G) + 3 + 5 \left(\frac{\omega(G_2)}{4} + 2 \right) \leq \omega(G) + 3 + \frac{5\omega(G)}{12} + \frac{5}{4} + 10 \leq \frac{17}{12}\omega(G) + 15.$$

So, the performance ratio for our strategy is $17/12$ and we arrived at the thesis of Theorem 1.

4 Conclusion

We have given a 17/12-approximation algorithm for multicoloring hexagonal graphs. This implies a 17/12-competitive solution for the online frequency allocation problem, which involves servicing calls in each cell in a cellular network. The distributed algorithm is practical in the sense that frequency allocation for each base station is done locally, based on the information about itself and its neighbors only, and the time complexity is constant.

References

1. Chin, F.Y.L., Zhang, Y., Zhu, H.: A 1-local 13/9-competitive Algorithm for Multicoloring Hexagonal Graphs. In: Lin, G. (ed.) COCOON 2007. LNCS, vol. 4598, pp. 526–536. Springer, Heidelberg (2007)
2. Sparl, P., Zerovnik, J.: 2-local 4/3-competitive Algorithm for Multicoloring Hexagonal Graphs. Journal of Algorithms 55(1), 29–41 (2005)
3. McDiarmid, C., Reed, B.: Channel assignment and weighted coloring. Networks 36(2), 114–117 (2000)
4. Sudeep, K.S., Vishwanathan, S.: A technique for multicoloring triangle-free hexagonal graphs. Discrete Mathematics 300, 256–259 (2005)
5. Narayanan, L.: Channel assignment and graph multicoloring. In: Handbook of wireless networks and mobile computing, pp. 71–94. Wiley, New York (2002)
6. Narayanan, L., Shende, S.M.: Static frequency assignment in cellular networks. Algorithmica 29(3), 396–409 (2001)
7. Hale, W.K.: Frequency assignment: theory and applications. Proceedings of the IEEE 68(12), 1497–1514 (1980)
8. Janssen, J., Krizanc, D., Narayanan, L., Shende, S.: Distributed Online Frequency Assignment in Cellular Network. Journal of Algorithms 36(2), 119–151 (2000)
9. Havet, F.: Channel assignment and multicoloring of the induced subgraphs of the triangular lattice. Discrete Mathematics 233, 219–231 (2001)
10. Sparl, P., Zerovnik, J.: 2-local 5/4-competitive algorithm for multicoloring triangle-free hexagonal graphs. Information Processing Letters 90(5), 239–246 (2004)
11. Zerownik, J.: A distributed 6/5-competitive algorithm for multicoloring triangle-free hexagonal graphs. International Journal of Pure and Applied Mathematics 23(2), 141–156 (2005)

Author Index